# CICERO
# PHILIPPICS

# CICERO
# PHILIPPICS

EDITED AND TRANSLATED BY

## D. R. SHACKLETON BAILEY

THE UNIVERSITY OF NORTH CAROLINA PRESS

CHAPEL HILL AND LONDON

The publication of this work was made possible in part through
a grant from the National Endowment for the Humanities,
a federal agency whose mission is to award grants
to support education, scholarship, media programming,
libraries, and museums, in order to bring the results
of cultural activities to a broad, general public.

Library of Congress Cataloging in Publication Data

Cicero, Marcus Tullius.
Philippics.

Bibliography: p.
Includes index.
1. Cicero, Marcus Tullius—Translations, English.
I. Bailey, D. R. Shackleton (David Roy Shackleton),
1917–    .  II. Title.
PA6280.A1   1985      875'.01      85-1029

ISBN 0-8078-1657-4

Designed by Naomi P. Slifkin

# CONTENTS

# PREFACE

For all their importance as a historical source and their considerable merit as literature Cicero's *Philippics* remain a comparatively neglected area. P. Fedeli in his Teubner edition of 1982 has provided a comprehensive apparatus criticus and bibliography, but not, in my opinion, a really critical text. There exists no satisfactory English translation and no adequate commentary. The latter desideratum should one day be met by a historian and expert on Roman political institutions, and one of the two principal purposes I have had in mind was to provide such a commentator with a textual and interpretative foundation on which to build. The other is to make the speeches more accessible to students and others interested. The introductions and explanatory notes aim only at providing a necessary minimum. For detailed historical background there are plenty of places to go: standard histories of Rome, R. Syme's *The Roman Revolution* (Oxford, 1939), and recent Ciceronian biographies such as D. Stockton's *Cicero: A Political Biography* (Oxford, 1971) and E. Rawson's *Cicero* (London, 1975).

The textual appendix and references to my earlier textual articles are naturally for specialists and provide explanations or justifications of readings adopted or advanced, particularly conjectures of my own. But I have practiced brevity and deliberately refrained from comment where I feel that none ought to be needed.

I desire to thank the University of North Carolina Press and especially Laura Oaks, who has spared no pains.

Cambridge, Massachusetts
January 1985

# INTRODUCTION

The victory of C. Julius Caesar over Pompey and his republican allies at Pharsalia in August 48 B.C. put Rome and her empire, apart from some pockets of resistance, under the control of one man. That had happened once before, nearly forty years previously, when Sulla defeated the opposition in Italy. Sulla's object was to restore a republican constitution of the kind he approved of; having done that, he retired and Rome lived with his constitution, more or less, until civil war broke out again in 49. Whether Caesar began that war with any definite political intentions is open to conjecture. What seems certain is that during his few years of supreme power, much of them spent fighting resurgent republicans overseas, he arrived at no political solution except his personal autocracy. Hence in the main the conspiracy which struck him down on the Ides of March 44, as he was on the point of setting out for one more war, against distant Parthia.

The leading conspirators, M. Brutus (more formally Q. Servilius Caepio Brutus) and C. Cassius Longinus, both former Pompeians who had been pardoned and advanced by Caesar, and D. Brutus Albinus, Caesar's former lieutenant and close friend, had apparently looked no further than the act. With Caesar gone they seem to have expected the wheels of the Republic to begin turning again automatically. Caesar's foremost adherent and colleague in the consulship of the year, M. Antonius (Mark Antony), had not been harmed. He fled into hiding, but presently reemerged to negotiate with the assassins, or liberators, on the Capitol. At a meeting of the Senate two days after the killing (17 March) a compromise took shape. On Cicero's motion the Senate decreed an amnesty and at the same time confirmed all Caesar's measures and appointments (*acta*).

The story of the following months has often been told. In summary, Antony and his new colleague as consul, P. Cornelius Dolabella (formerly Cicero's son-in-law), at first took a conciliatory line with the Senate, which seems for the most part to have been eager for a restored republic, especially in the lower echelons and despite the fact that most of the members were of Caesar's creation. But M. Brutus and Cassius, both praetors for the year whose official duties lay in Rome, were soon driven out by hostile mobs, leaving Antony in control of the situation. Caesar's widow had given him her husband's papers, and with the assistance of Caesar's secretary he forged orders as convenient and passed them off as Caesar's memoranda, valid with the rest of Caesar's *acta*. In June, not without intimidation exercised through Caesar's old soldiers, he provided for his future with a law which gave him Cisalpine Gaul for a term of five years in place of the existing governor, D. Brutus, who had gone there under Caesar's appointment. With the province went command of four legions which had been assembled in Macedonia by Caesar for the Parthian war. There was one complication. Caesar's eighteen-year-old great-nephew, C. Octavius, was with these legions. Under Caesar's will he became Caesar's heir and adopted son. Arriving in Italy in April, he became Antony's rival for the loyalty of the pro-Caesarian Roman populace and, more important, the veteran soldiers who had been settled in large numbers on the land in Campania.

Cicero, now in his sixty-third year, had no advance knowledge of Caesar's assassination but wholeheartedly applauded it. The results, however, disappointed him, and on 5 April he left Rome for his villas in Campania. Later he decided to visit his son, who was studying in Athens, and actually got as far as Syracuse, on 1 August. That same day in Rome the Senate heard an attack upon Antony's political conduct from a senior consular, none other than Caesar's father-in-law and Cicero's old enemy, L. Calpurnius Piso Caesoninus, not normally hostile to Antony and later on almost his partisan. Nobody backed him up.

As Cicero explained to his friend Atticus in a contemporary letter (*Att.* 16.7) and subsequently to the Senate, hopeful news from Rome reached him on 7 August, while he was waiting for a fair wind to continue his journey. It looked as though Antony and the "liberators" were about to settle their differences. That prospect was to prove delusive, but Cicero promptly reversed course and set out on the way back to Rome. He reentered the city on the last day of the month, and on 2 September delivered in the Senate, Antony not present, the challenge which in its published form became the First Philippic.

> We shall never know after what private hesitations Cicero set foot on the fatal ladder. Perhaps this time he did not hesitate at all. The mortifications and disappointments of his later career and the calamities of his private life had only sharpened his urge for primacy—not power such as Caesar had had and Pompey had been suspected of wanting, but in the words of his speech, "equality in freedom, primacy in esteem." Much in his record that looked like timidity was really an incapacity or reluctance to seize the essential in a complex moral problem. But the case of the Republic against Antony in 44 held no complexities for Cicero. Conscience chimed with ambition, striking his hour.[1]

1. D. R. Shackleton Bailey, *Cicero* (London, 1971) 246–47.

# INTRODUCTION

The fourteen Philippics were delivered between 2 September 44 and 21 April 43, except for the second, which was not delivered at all. The name, taken from Demosthenes' orations against Philip of Macedon, was Cicero's own coinage, originally a sort of joke.[2] Brutus wrote from Dyrrachium on 1 April of having read the fifth and tenth, spoken on 1 January and in mid-February.[3] Hence it appears that the speeches were edited by Cicero and circulated soon after delivery. Quotations show that at least three more Philippics existed in antiquity.

## SUGGESTED READING

I have confined this list to books published in English during the twentieth century.

Cicero. *Letters to Atticus* and *Letters to His Friends*. 3 vols. Translated by D. R. Shackleton Bailey. Penguin Classics. London, 1978.

Badian, E. *Publicans and Sinners*. Ithaca, N.Y., 1982.

Bailey, D. R. Shackleton. *Cicero*. London, 1971.

Brunt, P. A. *Italian Manpower*. Oxford, 1971.

*The Cambridge Ancient History*. Vol. 9. Cambridge, 1932.

Frisch, H. *Cicero's Fight for the Republic*. Copenhagen, 1946.

Gruen, E. S. *The Last Generation of the Roman Republic*. Berkeley, Los Angeles, and London, 1974.

Heitland, W. E. *The Roman Republic*. Vol. 3. Cambridge, 1923.

Holmes, T. Rice. *The Roman Republic*. Vol. 2. Oxford, 1923.

Mitchell, T. N. *Cicero: The Ascending Years*. New Haven and London, 1979.

Rawson, B. *The Politics of Friendship: Pompey and Cicero*. Sydney, 1978.

Rawson, E. *Cicero*. London, 1975.

Scullard, H. H. *From the Gracchi to Nero*. 3rd ed. London, 1970.

Smith, R. E. *Cicero the Statesman*. Cambridge, 1966.

———. *The Failure of the Roman Republic*. Cambridge, 1955.

Stockton, D. *Cicero: A Political Biography*. Oxford, 1971.

Syme, R. *The Roman Revolution*. Oxford, 1939.

Wooten, C. W. *Cicero's Philippics and Their Demosthenic Model*. Chapel Hill and London, 1983.

---

2. Cic. *Ad M. Brutum* 3 (2.3).4.
3. Ibid.

# INTRODUCTION

## *Note on Primary Historical Sources*

Apart from the *Philippics* themselves, Cicero's contemporary correspondence is of capital importance. Later come Greek narratives: certain of the *Parallel Lives* of Plutarch (fl. A.D. 90), the *History of the Civil Wars* of Appian (fl. 130), and the *Roman History* of Cassius Dio (fl. 200). These writers drew on works (now lost) by contemporaries or near-contemporaries, especially the Latin historians Asinius Pollio and Livy, and in Plutarch's case (life of Cicero) the biography of Cicero by his freedman and secretary, Tiro. Extensive fragments also survive of a courtier-like life of Augustus (Caesar Octavianus) in Greek by Nicolaus of Damascus.

# MANUSCRIPTS AND EDITIONS

The oldest manuscript of the *Philippics* is $V$ = tabularii Basilicae Vaticanae H 25 of the ninth century. Other manuscripts used by editors since A. C. Clark are as follows.[1]

$b$ = Bernensis 104 of the late thirteenth or early fourteenth century.

$c$ = consensus of three manuscripts called by Clark "familia Colotiana" from their affinity to a lost manuscript belonging to Angelius Colotius: Paris. Lat. 5802 (thirteenth century); Paris. Lat. 6602 (thirteenth century); Berolin. Philipp. 1794 (twelfth century). They contain only the first four speeches.

$n$ = Vossianus Lat. O 2 of the tenth or eleventh century.

$s$ = Vaticanus Lat. 3228 of the tenth century.

$t$ = Monacensis 18787 (formerly Tegernseensis 787) of the eleventh century.

$v$ = Vaticanus Lat. 3227 of the early twelfth century.

All these manuscripts have been shown to descend from a single archetype. It has further been demonstrated that the manuscripts other than $V$, known collectively as $D$, represent a common tradition separate from $V$. Within $D$, $c$ is closer than any to $V$, while $b$ and $t$ have affinities with $c$ as opposed to the group $nsv$.[2] Fedeli cites Clark in *CR* 14 (1900) 42: "the result then is that $c$ are nearer to $V$ than any other members of $D$, and often serve to bridge over the gulf between $D$ and $V$. This is of particular importance as showing that the good readings found in $b$ are not due to conjecture, but represent an ancient tradition. As $b$ contains all the *Philippics* while $c$ contain only I–IV, this conclusion is distinctly comforting."

$V$ has been extensively corrected by later hands ($V^2$); most of these corrections are also found in $D$.

Cited by recent editors but of little practical value is a twelfth-century florilegium known as *Cus.* from its one-time owner Cardinal Cusanus. It usually agrees with $V$ against $D$, but is full of clumsy interpolations and omissions (ignored in my apparatus).

"Inter Philippicorum codices $V$ iure principem obtinet locum."[3] True, for $V$ is an "honest" manuscript, clear of interpolation, to which $D$ has been heavily

---

1. For detail see the preface to P. Fedeli's Teubner edition of 1982.
2. On $t$ see Fedeli, xi.
3. Fedeli, xiii.

subjected. But it is the work of an ignorant scribe,[4] full of trivial errors and some not trivial, whereas *D* offers much that is not only right but unquestionably authentic, as when it fills in *V*'s lacunae, major and minor. Sometimes, moreover, *D* is vindicated against *V* by superior rhythm:

1.5    urbis minarentur *D*: urbis minitarentur *V*.

1.15   fecistis adhuc, audiatis *D*: adhuc fecistis, audiatis *V*

1.27   audio factum *D*: audio esse factum *V*.

1.29   de utriusque vestrum errore reticere *D*: utriusque vestrum errorem reticere *V*.

1.29   in rem publicam fama meritorum *c, Isidore*: fama *om. cett.*

2.63   splendida *D*: splendidiora *V*.

3.3    in salute rei publicae collocavit *D*: in rei publicae salute collocavit *V*.

3.21   ducibus iudicari *D*: iudicari ducibus *V*.

3.23   tam fuisset ferus *D*: tam ferus fuisset *V*

3.34   urbem opprimere potuisset *D*: opprimere urbem potuisset *V*

5.7    interpretatione augurum *D*: interpretatione *V*

8.18   nostri triumpharunt *bnst*: nostri triumphaverunt *Vv*

10.15   causā reponatur *DV²*: causā ponatur *V*

In these instances *V*'s reading offers a clausula normally avoided by Cicero.[5] Since the good clausulae in *D* cannot reasonably be set down to coincidence or deliberate improvement, they are to be accepted and regarded as a warning to editors against too heavy a commitment to the superiority of *V*. "L'éclecticisme s'impose."[6]

Inferior manuscripts are usually cited by the compendious symbol ς.

The *Philippics* were first printed in 1471 in Rome and Venice. P. Fedeli's Teubner (Leipzig) text of 1982 lists twenty-nine editions, including A. C.

---

4. See Clark, *CR* 14 (1900) 403: "The writer of *V* knew no Latin."

5. See W. H. Shewring in the *Oxford Classical Dictionary²* (Oxford, 1970) 889.

6. Boulanger and Wuilleumier (Budé), 1:35. In all these instances Fedeli follows *V*, relying on E. Fraenkel's *Leseproben aus Reden Ciceros und Catos* (Rome, 1968). But this product of Fraenkel's closing years is no safe guide. In Appendix 6 (198–200) it sets out to disprove the "widespread error" ("ein verbreiteter Irrtum") that Cicero avoided the "heroic clausula," - ⌣ ⌣ - ×. The examples quoted are far too few to do that even if they were all valid. But Fraenkel failed to distinguish between abrupt, brief questions or exclamations like *Mil.* 79 *quid vultu extimuistis?* and *Deiot.* 21 *di te perduint, fugitive*, to which rhythmical rules do not apply, and full-blown periods. His list includes two syncopations (*Arch.* 22 *eiciamus* and *Mil.* 101 *proicietur*: see T. Zielinski, *Das Clauselgesetz in Ciceros Reden*, Leipzig, 1904, 184ff.), two of *V*'s misreadings (*Phil.* 1.29 *errorem reticere* and 3.3: see above), and an extract from Mark Antony's letter in *Phil.* 13.25 (*obsidione*)! Zielinski's contention that the first syllable of *flagravit* in *Marc.* 27 is to be scanned long is called "undenkbar." Is it? Fraenkel could never have so run amok in his prime.

Clark's Oxford Classical Text (1918), F. Schoell's Teubner (1918), and A. Boulanger and P. Wuilleumier's Budé (1959–60). His apparatus (on which mine is mainly based) is far more detailed than any previous one, with numerous references to his extensive bibliography. This work needed doing, and will not need to be done again.

No general commentary has appeared since that of J. R. King (Oxford, 1878), a mediocre work. J. D. Denniston's commentary on the first and second speeches (Oxford, 1926) is notably alert and well-informed as to historical content.

At least three English translations exist, the most recent being that of W. C. A. Ker in the Loeb series (1926). It not seldom misrepresents the original.

# ABBREVIATIONS

*AJP*   *American Journal of Philology*

*CP*   *Classical Philology*

*CR*   *Classical Review*

Crawford   M. H. Crawford, *Roman Republican Coinage*, 2 vols. (Cambridge. 1974)

Denniston   J. D. Denniston, *M. Tulli Ciceronis in M. Antonium Orationes Philippicae Prima et Secunda* (Oxford, 1926)

Fe(deli)   P. Fedeli, *In M. Antonium Orationes Philippicae XIV* (Leipzig, 1982)

Keil   H. Keil, *Grammatici Latini*, 8 vols. (reprinted Hildesheim, 1961)

*JRS*   *Journal of Roman Studies*

SB[1]   D. R. Shackleton Bailey, "On Cicero's Speeches," *Harvard Studies in Classical Philology* 83 (1979) 238–85 (*Philippics*, 280–85)

SB[2]   D. R. Shackleton Bailey, "Notes on Cicero's *Philippics*," *Philologus* 126 (1982) 217–26

*TLL*   *Thesaurus Linguae Latinae*

Two Studies   D. R. Shackleton Bailey, *Two Studies in Roman Nomenclature*, American Classical Studies 3 (University Park, Pa., 1976)

# SIGLA

$V$ = cod. tabularii Basilicae Vaticanae H 25 saec. IX

$b$ = cod. Bernensis 104, saec. XIII–XIV

$c$ = familia Colotiana, i.e. codicum Paris. Lat. 5802 (saec. XIII), Paris. Lat. 6602 (saec. XIII), Berolin. Philipp. 1794 (olim 201, saec. XII) consensus

$n$ = cod. Vossianus Lat. O 2, saec. X–XI

$s$ = cod. Vaticanus Lat. 3228, saec. X

$t$ = cod. Monacensis 18787 (olim Tegernseensis 787), saec. XI

$v$ = cod. Vaticanus Lat. 3227, saec. XII

$D$ = codicum *bcnstv* consensus

*Cus.* = cod. Nicolai Cusani, saec. XII, excerpta continens

$\varsigma$ = codd. deteriores

Numeri 1 et 2 lectionibus in apparatu critico additi ad ea quae scripsi in *Harvard Studies in Classical Philology* 83 (1979) 280–85 et *Philologus* 126 (1982) 217–26, numerus 3 ad appendicem criticam referendi sunt.

# CICERO
# PHILIPPICS

# I

## INTRODUCTION

On the last day of August 44 Cicero entered the city with a large crowd to welcome him. The Senate met the following day, but Cicero sent excuses, not liking the agenda (1.13). Antony broke into threats. On the next day, 2 September, in Antony's absence the First Philippic was delivered.

Cicero's decision to return to Rome is explained in detail in the First Philippic: he had never felt entirely comfortable about leaving Italy at a time of crisis. The speech is a comprehensive attack on Antony's political record in recent months. Nominal relations of friendship still in being precluded the personalities so prominent in the rest of the series. But the innuendo of financial corruption in 1.33 is enough to show that Cicero's forbearance was only tactical. The speech was a defiance, an assertion of the speaker's readiness to lead resistance to Antony's abuse of magisterial authority. Antony could not overlook it. In view of the apparent strength of Antony's position in military terms, with Caesar's veterans close by and Caesar's legions, of which as consul he was commander in chief, on their way from Macedonia, Cicero's courage was undeniable. He was acting in full awareness of risk and by his own choice. There would be no turning back.

**1** Ante quam de re publica, patres conscripti, dicam ea quae dicenda hoc tempore arbitror, exponam vobis breviter consilium et profectionis et reversionis meae.

Ego cum sperarem aliquando ad vestrum consilium auctoritatemque rem publicam esse revocatam, manendum mihi statuebam quasi in vigilia   5 quadam consulari ac senatoria. nec vero usquam discedebam nec a re publica deiciebam oculos ex eo die quo in aedem Telluris convocati sumus. in quo templo, quantum in me fuit, ieci fundamenta pacis Atheniensium-que renovavi vetus exemplum; Graecum etiam verbum usurpavi quo tum in sedandis discordiis usa erat civitas illa, atque omnem memoriam dis-   10 cordiarum oblivione sempiterna delendam censui.

**2** Praeclara tum oratio M. Antoni, egregia etiam voluntas; pax denique per eum et per liberos eius cum praestantissimis civibus confirmata est. atque his principiis reliqua consentiebant. ad deliberationes eas quas habebat domi de re publica principes civitatis adhibebat; ad hunc ordi-   15 nem res optimas deferebat; nihil tum nisi quod erat notum omnibus in C. Caesaris commentariis reperiebatur; summa constantia ad ea quae quaesita erant respondebat. **3** num qui exsules restituti? unum aiebat, praeterea neminem. num immunitates datae? "nullae" respondebat. ad-sentiri etiam nos Ser. Sulpicio, clarissimo viro, voluit, ne qua tabula post   20 Idus† Martias† ullius decreti Caesaris aut benefici figeretur.

Multa praetereo eaque praeclara; ad singulare enim M. Antoni factum festinat oratio. dictaturam, quae iam vim regiae potestatis obsederat, funditus ex re publica sustulit; de qua ne sententias quidem diximus.

---

**1** 9 renouaui *V Cus. bnsv*: reuocaui *ct*    10 discordiis usa erat] discordauerat *c*: -cors erat *n*: -cordiis erat *tv*    **2** 16 referebat *Ernesti*    17 reperiebat *Kraffert*    summa cum dignitate constantia (*ex subst-* $t^2$) *D*    **3** 19 nullae respondebat *om. bnstv*: nullas r- *Wesenberg*    21 Martias *cruce signavi: anne* Nov(embris)$^2$?    22 ea quae (eaque quod *v*) clara sunt *D*    23 uim iam *bcnsv*    24 de qua re (*melius* qua de re) ⟨: de quo *Stangl*

**1** Members of the Senate: Before I say what I think it right to say at this time on public affairs, let me briefly explain to you my reasons for leaving Rome and for returning.

Hoping as I did that the Commonwealth had at last been restored to your guidance and authority, I took the view that as a consular and a senator I ought to stay on guard, so to speak. In fact, from the day we were summoned to the temple of Tellus I never left Rome or took my eyes off the political scene.[1] In that temple, so far as was in my power, I laid the foundations of peace. I revived the ancient Athenian precedent, even adopting the Greek term which was used by that community at the time in laying their quarrels to rest.[2] I proposed that all recollection of disputes should be obliterated and forgotten for the rest of time.

**2** Marcus Antonius made a fine speech on that occasion and showed signal goodwill. Finally, through him and his son,[3] peace with our most distinguished fellow countrymen was established. And the sequel was of a piece with these beginnings. Antonius regularly brought the leaders of our community into the deliberations on state affairs which he was in the habit of holding at his home. He laid some admirable proposals before this House. Nothing at that time was discovered in Gaius Caesar's memoranda except what was common knowledge. His replies to questions were perfectly assured. **3** Had any exiles been restored? Yes, one,[4] he said, nobody else. Had any exemptions been granted? None, was his answer. He even asked us to vote for a motion by our distinguished fellow member Servius Sulpicius providing that no placard[5] of any order or grant of Caesar's should be posted after the Ides of *.[6]

I pass over many items, notable items, as my tongue hastens on to Marcus Antonius' most remarkable gesture, the total abolition of the office of dictator; an office which had usurped the power of absolute monarchy. We did not so

---

1. A noteworthy misstatement. Cicero's letters show that he was not in Rome between 5 April and 31 August.

2. Doubtless ἀμνηστία (contra Denniston), though that word does not occur in Xenophon's account of the occasion (*Hell.* 2.4.38–43), the restoration of Athenian democracy in 403. Cf. Nep. *Thras.* 3.2 *legem tulit ne quis ante actarum rerum accusaretur . . . eamque illi oblivionis appellarunt*; Val. Max. 4.1 Ext. 4 *haec oblivio, quam Athenienses ἀμνηστίαν vocant*; Hist. Aug. *Aurel.* 39.4, Plut. *Brut.* 19.

3. An infant. Antony used him as a hostage. The plural *liberi* is sometimes used of a single child.

4. Sex. Cloelius (formerly miscalled Clodius, once a henchman of P. Clodius Pulcher); cf. 2.7–10.

5. Bronze plate inscribed with the order and posted up on the Capitol.

6. March, according to the manuscripts. But no such ruling was observed by Antony. On this difficult problem see SB².

scriptum senatus consultum quod fieri vellet attulit, quo recitato auctoritatem eius summo studio secuti sumus eique amplissimis verbis per senatus consultum gratias egimus.

**4** Lux quaedam videbatur oblata non modo regno, quod pertuleramus,
sed etiam regni timore sublato, magnumque pignus ab eo rei publicae     5
datum, se liberam civitatem esse velle, cum dictatoris nomen, quod
saepe iustum fuisset, propter perpetuae dictaturae recentem memoriam
funditus ex re publica sustulisset. **5** liberatus periculo caedis paucis post
diebus senatus; uncus impactus est fugitivo illi qui in Mari nomen inva-
serat. atque haec omnia communiter cum collega; alia porro propria     10
Dolabellae quae, nisi collega afuisset, credo eis futura fuisse communia.
nam cum serperet in urbe infinitum malum idque manaret in dies latius,
idemque bustum in foro facerent qui illam insepultam sepulturam effe-
cerant, et cotidie magis magisque perditi homines cum sui[s] similibus
servis tectis ac templis urbis minarentur, talis animadversio fuit Dolabellae     15
cum in audacis sceleratosque servos, tum in impuros et nefarios liberos,
talisque eversio illius exsecratae columnae ut mihi mirum videatur tam
valde reliquum tempus ab illo uno die dissensisse.

**6** Ecce enim Kalendis Iuniis, quibus ut adessemus edixerant, mutata
omnia: nihil per senatum, multa et magna per populum et absente populo     20
et invito. consules designati negabant se audere in senatum venire; patriae
liberatores urbe carebant ea cuius a cervicibus iugum servile deiecerant,
quos tamen ipsi consules in contionibus et in omni sermone laudabant.
veterani qui appellabantur, quibus hic ordo diligentissime caverat, non
ad conservationem earum rerum quas habebant, sed ad spem novarum     25
praedarum incitabantur. quae cum audire mallem quam videre habe-

**5** 8 c(a)edis periculo *D*     9 c. mari *bcnst, schol. Hor. Carm. 1.35.19*     12 urbe *bct*:
-em *Vnsv*     14 suis *codd., corr. Angelius*     15 minarentur *D*: minita- *V, clausula minus
bona*     16 in *om. Vn¹v*     et] et in *V*     **6** 19 edixerat *t*     23 et in contionibus
*D*     24 qui appellabantur *om. Arusianus* (*Keil 7:488*), *del. Ernesti*: qui appellantur *ct,
fort. recte*: appellabantur (*del.* qui) *post* habebant *transt. Hirschfelder*

much as debate the subject. Antonius brought the draft of a decree which he said he wished the Senate to pass. As soon as it had been read aloud, we enthusiastically followed his lead and voted him our unstinted thanks.

**4** It seemed as though a light had shone before us, with the removal not only of the monarchy which we had endured, but even the fear of its recurrence. Yes, it seemed as though Antonius had given the Commonwealth a mighty pledge of his desire for a free community by totally removing from our constitution the name of dictator, legitimate as that had often been, because of the recollection of Dictatorship in Perpetuity fresh on our minds. **5** A few days later the Senate was relieved from the threat of a massacre. The hook[7] was planted in the body of the runaway who had usurped the name of Marius. In all of this Antonius acted jointly with his colleague. There were other acts for which Dolabella was solely responsible, acts which I imagine would have been their joint responsibility but for the absence of his colleague. An uncontrolled infection was spreading in Rome, wider and wider day by day. The authors of Caesar's abortive[8] burial were raising a tomb in the Forum. More and more as each day went by desperados with slaves like themselves were threatening the houses and temples of our city. Dolabella took drastic action, punishing the foul ruffians of freemen as well as their bold and criminal slaves and demolishing that accursed pillar.[9] I find it strange that his subsequent record stands in such sharp contrast to that one day's work.

**6** For all at once, on the Kalends of June, on which day they had summoned us for a meeting, everything was changed.[10] Many important measures were put through, but none through the Senate; they were put through the popular assembly—in the absence of the people and against their will. The consuls-elect[11] said they did not dare attend the Senate. The liberators of their country were banished from the city whose neck they had released from slavery; and yet the consuls themselves lauded them in public speeches and in all their conversation. The veterans, as they were called,[12] of whose interests this House had taken the greatest care, were stirred up, not to preserve what they already had but to hope for fresh plunder. All this I preferred to hear of than to

7. The body of an executed criminal was dragged by a hook and thrown into the Tiber.

8. Lit. "unburied."

9. Raised to Caesar in the Forum.

10. This rhetorical contrast between the Kalends of June and the period preceding is shown to be false by Cicero's contemporary letters. As far back as 22 April he had written to Atticus in high indignation about Antony's unscrupulous proceedings (*Att.* 14.12.1).

11. See p. 107.

12. This has puzzled commentators. I think it refers to the fact that the term *veterani*, which properly included all ex-soldiers, was at this time generally used for those of Caesar. The present, *appellantur*, may be right.

remque ius legationis liberum, ea mente discessi ut adessem Kalendis
Ianuariis, quod initium senatus cogendi fore videbatur.

**7** Exposui, patres conscripti, profectionis consilium: nunc reversionis,
quae plus admirationis habet, breviter exponam. cum Brundisium iterque
illud quod tritum in Graeciam est non sine causa vitavissem, Kalendis    5
Sextilibus veni Syracusas, quod ab ea urbe transmissio in Graeciam
laudabatur: quae tamen urbs mihi coniunctissima plus una me nocte
cupiens retinere non potuit. veritus sum ne meus repentinus ad meos
necessarios adventus suspicionis aliquid adferret, si essem commoratus.
cum autem me ex Sicilia ad Leucopetram, quod est promunturium agri    10
Regini, venti detulissent, ab eo loco conscendi ut transmitterem; nec
ita multum provectus reiectus Austro sum in eum ipsum locum unde
conscenderam. **8** cumque intempesta nox esset mansissemque in villa
P. Valeri, comitis et familiaris mei, postridieque apud eundem ventum
exspectans manerem, municipes Regini complures ad me venerunt, ex eis    15
quidam Roma recentes: a quibus primum accipio Antoni contionem, quae
mihi ita placuit ut ea lecta de reversione primum coeperim cogitare. nec
ita multo post edictum Bruti adfertur et Cassi, quod quidem mihi, fortasse quod eos plus etiam rei publicae quam familiaritatis gratia diligo,
plenum aequitatis videbatur. addebant praeterea—fit enim plerumque    20
ut ei qui boni quid volunt adferre adfingant aliquid quo faciant id quod
nuntiant laetius—rem conventuram: Kalendis Sextilibus senatum frequentem fore; Antonium, repudiatis malis suasoribus, remissis provinciis
Galliis, ad auctoritatem senatus esse rediturum.

**9** Tum vero tanta sum cupiditate incensus ad reditum ut mihi nulli ne-    25
que remi neque venti satis facerent, non quo me ad tempus occursurum

---

1 liberae *Beroaldus*     **7** 11–12 transmitteremus austro $V^1$, *medd. omissis*: nec ita multum
si coniunctus proiectus *add. in mg.* $V^2$     **8** 16 m. antoni *D*     22 Sextilibus *del. Madvig*:
Sept. *Halm* (*vide Fe.*)     senatum frequentem *om.* $V^1$

see. Having the grant of an honorary commission,[13] I left Rome with the intention of returning by the Kalends of January, the earliest date, as appeared likely, for a convocation of the Senate.[14]

**7** So much, Members of the Senate, for my reason for leaving. Now I shall briefly explain the reason for my return, which is likely to occasion more surprise. Avoiding for good cause[15] the beaten track to Greece via Brundisium, I arrived at Syracuse on the Kalends of Sextilis,[16] since the crossing from there to Greece had a good reputation. I have very close ties with that city, but they could not keep me more than a single night, much as they wished it. I was nervous lest if I made a stay my sudden arrival among my old connections might give rise to some suspicion. From Sicily the wind carried me to Leucopetra, a promontory in the district of Regium, and from there I embarked for the crossing; but I had not got far when the south wind carried me back right to my point of embarkation. **8** It was in the middle of the night, and I put up in a country house belonging to my friend and traveling companion Publius Valerius. As I stayed there the following day waiting for a wind, a number of residents of Regium came over to see me, among them some recently returned from the capital. From them I got for the first time a copy of Marcus Antonius' speech,[17] which pleased me so much that after reading it I first began to think of turning back. Not very long afterwards I was brought a copy of Brutus' and Cassius' manifesto, which struck me—perhaps because I regard them even more highly on public grounds than I do for friendship's sake—as eminently fair. My visitors added that there would be a settlement— we know how often would-be bearers of good news add a little of their own invention to make their report the more agreeable. There was to be a full meeting of the Senate on the Kalends of Sextilis, Antonius would turn his back on his bad advisors, give up the Gallic provinces, and be once again the Senate's to command.

**9** That fired me with such eagerness to get home that neither oar nor wind made speed enough; not that I was afraid of missing the great moment, but I

13. In point of fact Dolabella, as prospective governor of Syria, had given Cicero an honorary position as his legate, enabling him to leave Italy (for which senators needed official authorization) and go wherever he pleased. The Latin, which I have felt obliged to paraphrase, seems to be deliberately ambiguous, suggesting that the *legatio* was of the kind called "free" (granted by the Senate) and concealing the obligation to Dolabella.

14. Seemingly an allusion, perhaps ironic, to the fact that Antony's legislation at the beginning of June was put through a popular assembly, not the Senate which he had summoned, indicating that he was not likely to summon it again during his consulship.

15. Fear of falling in with Antony's troops (*Att.* 16.5.3).

16. August.

17. Nothing further is known of this.

non putarem, sed ne tardius quam cuperem rei publicae gratularer. atque
ego celeriter Veliam devectus Brutum vidi, quanto meo dolore non dico.
turpe mihi ipsi videbatur in eam urbem me audere reverti ex qua Brutus
cederet, et ibi velle tuto esse ubi ille non posset. neque vero illum simili-
ter atque ipse eram commotum esse vidi. erectus enim maximi et pulcher-   5
rimi facti sui conscientia nihil de suo casu, multa de vestro querebatur.
**10** exque eo primum cognovi quae Kalendis Sextilibus in senatu fuisset
L. Pisonis oratio: qui quamquam parum erat—id enim ipsum a Bruto au-
dieram—a quibus debuerat adiutus, tamen et Bruti testimonio—quo quid
potest esse gravius?—et omnium praedicatione quos postea vidi magnam   10
mihi videbatur gloriam consecutus. hunc igitur ut sequerer properavi
quem praesentes non sunt secuti, non ut proficerem aliquid—nec enim
sperabam id nec praestare poteram—sed ut, si quid mihi humanitus
accidisset—multa autem impendere videntur praeter naturam etiam
praeterque fatum—huius tamen diei vocem testem rei publicae relin-   15
querem meae perpetuae erga se voluntatis.

    **11** Quoniam utriusque consili causam, patres conscripti, probatam
vobis esse confido, prius quam de re publica dicere incipio, pauca querar
de hesterna M. Antoni iniuria: cui sum amicus, idque me non nullo eius
officio debere esse prae me semper tuli.   20

    Quid tandem erat causae cur die hesterno in senatum tam acerbe
cogerer? solusne aberam, an non saepe minus frequentes fuistis, an ea res
agebatur ut etiam aegrotos deferri oporteret? Hannibal, credo, erat ad
portas aut de Pyrrhi pace agebatur, ad quam causam etiam Appium illum
et caecum et senem delatum esse memoriae proditum est. **12** de supplica-   25
tionibus referebatur, quo in genere senatores deesse non solent. coguntur
enim non pignoribus, sed eorum de quorum honore agitur gratia; quod
idem fit, cum de triumpho refertur. ita sine cura consules sunt, ut paene
liberum sit senatori non adesse. qui cum mihi mos notus esset cumque e
via languerem et mihimet displicerem, misi pro amicitia qui hoc ei di-   30
ceret. at ille vobis audientibus cum fabris se domum meam venturum esse

**9** 1 non *om. D*     4 non posset *om. V*[1]: non esset *coni. Halm*     5 et] atque *nsv*: ac *edd.*
*ante Fe. de V errantes*     **10** 7 exque eo] ex quo *D, fort. recte*     12 quem *om. V*[1]     neque enim *D, Gell. 13.1.1*     14 uidentur *V, Gell., Lact. Plac. ad Stat. Theb. 3.205*: -ebantur
*D, Serv. ad Aen. 4.653*     etiam *V, Gell., Lact. Plac.*: *om. D, Serv.*     15 tamen *om. D,
Gell.*     **11** 18 confido] -do etiam *V*[1]     18–19 quaerar hs (= *hic supple*) de hesterna in
senatum *V*[1], *medd. omissis*     19 die hesterno in senatum *Halm ex vestigiis cod.* V: in
senatum (-u *s*) hesterno (ext- *bt*) die *D*     22 minus *codd.*] *num* magis?[3]     23 deferre
*V*     **12** 27 quorum de *D*     30 hoc ediceret *D*     31 audientibus . . . se *om. V*[1]

could not wait to congratulate the Commonwealth. So I made good time to
Velia, where I saw Brutus, I will not say with what distress. I felt ashamed.
There was I, daring to return to a city from which Brutus was withdrawing,
wishing to live in safety in a place where there was none for him. However, I
found no such agitation on his part as I felt myself. Exalted by the consciousness of his great and noble act, he said no word of complaint about his own
predicament, but many about yours, gentlemen. **10** It was from him that I first
learned of Lucius Piso's speech in the Senate on the Kalends of Sextilis. He
did not get the support he should have got (that too I heard from Brutus), but
on Brutus' testimony, the weightiest in the world, and on the laudatory report
of all whom I saw later, it seemed to me that Piso had covered himself with
glory. So I made haste in order to follow his lead, as those present failed to do.
I was not trying to achieve anything; that was not in my hopes or power to
guarantee. But should anything befall me such as may happen to any of us
(many dangers, moreover, appear to loom even beyond the course of nature
and destiny),[18] I wished to leave the words I speak today as witnesses to the
Commonwealth of my abiding loyalty.

**11** Members of the Senate, I am confident that my reasons for both decisions have met with your approval. Now before I begin to speak on public
affairs, let me say a few words in protest against Marcus Antonius' offensive
behavior yesterday—I am his friend and I have always acknowledged that I
ought to be such on account of a service he once rendered me.[19]

Now what cause was there yesterday for me to be summoned to attend the
Senate in such harsh terms? Was I the only absentee? Has the House not often
been less well attended? Was the business in hand such as to demand the
attendance even of invalids? Hannibal was at the gates, I suppose; or peace
with Pyrrhus was at issue—the business for which history tells us that the great
Appius[20] was brought in, blind and aged as he was. **12** In fact, the business
before the House concerned Thanksgivings, and senators are not usually
lacking on such occasions. They are brought together not by pledges[21] but by
their willingness to oblige the persons whose honors are under consideration.
The same applies when a Triumph is in question. The consuls do not have to
worry, so that a member is pretty much at liberty to stay away. Knowing the
custom and feeling weak and out of sorts from my journey, I sent a message to
that effect to Antonius as a friend: and Antonius in your presence declared that
he would come to my house with a squad of workmen! That was really letting

18. I.e. natural causes of death. Nature and destiny here amount to the same thing. So in 12.30.
19. See 2.5–6.
20. Appius Claudius Caecus, on 28 October 279.
21. Liable to forfeit if a senator was absent without good cause.

dixit. nimis iracunde hoc quidem et valde intemperanter. cuius enim malefici tanta ista poena est ut dicere in hoc ordine auderet se publicis operis
disturbaturum publice ex senatus sententia aedificatam domum? quis autem umquam tanto damno senatorem coegit? aut quid est ultra pignus aut
multam?                                                                                          5

Quod si scisset quam sententiam dicturus essem, remisisset aliquid
profecto de severitate cogendi. **13** an me censetis, patres conscripti, quod
vos inviti secuti estis, decreturum fuisse, ut parentalia cum supplica-
tionibus miscerentur, ut inexpiabiles religiones in rem publicam indu-
cerentur, ut decernerentur supplicationes mortuo? nihil dico cui. fuerit        10
ille L. Brutus qui et ipse dominatu regio rem publicam liberavit et ad similem virtutem et simile factum stirpem iam prope in quingentesimum
annum propagavit: adduci tamen non possem ut quemquam mortuum
coniungerem cum deorum immortalium religione; ut, cuius sepulcrum
nusquam exstet ubi parentetur, ei publice supplicetur. ego vero eam         15
sententiam dixissem ut me adversus populum Romanum, si qui accidisset
gravior rei publicae casus, si bellum, si morbus, si fames, facile possem
defendere; quae partim iam sunt, partim timeo ne impendeant. sed hoc
ignoscant di immortales velim et populo Romano, qui id non probat, et
huic ordini, qui decrevit invitus.                                                               20

**14** Quid? de reliquis rei publicae malis licetne dicere? mihi vero licet
et semper licebit dignitatem tueri, mortem contemnere. potestas modo
veniendi in hunc locum sit: dicendi periculum non recuso. atque utinam,
patres conscripti, Kalendis Sextilibus adesse potuissem! non quo profici
potuerit aliquid, sed ne unus modo consularis, quod tum accidit, dignus    25
illo honore, dignus re publica inveniretur. qua quidem ex re magnum
accipio dolorem, homines amplissimis populi Romani beneficiis usos
L. Pisonem ducem optimae sententiae non secutos. idcircone nos populus
Romanus consules fecit ut in altissimo gradu dignitatis locati rem publicam pro nihilo haberemus? non modo voce nemo L. Pisoni consularis      30
sed ne voltu quidem adsensus est. **15** quae, malum, est ista voluntaria

---

2 tanta] ita *t: om. bcnsv*      esset *Weber*      **13** 10 mortuorum (monstru- *v*) *D*      cui] cui'
*n:* qui *Vb¹st*      11 L. *om. V:* licet *schol. Luc. 5.207*      12 iam prope in *V:* prope in *cb²:*
in prope in *sv:* in prope *b¹n:* in *t:* prope *schol. Luc.*      14 deorum *om. V*      15 usquam *b,*
*vulg.; sed cf.* 2.107      16 dixissem P.C. *cnstv*      19 id *om. nstv*      **14** 21 uero *V Cus.:*
uerum *D*      30 pisonis *bntv*      consulari³ *Vcn²s²*

his temper run away with him! What is the misdemeanor which carries so grave a penalty that he dared to say in this House that he would use public employees to demolish a house built at public expense by order of the Senate?[22] Who ever compelled a senator's attendance by so heavy a forfeit? What is there beyond a pledge or a fine?

Now if Antonius had known what I would have said in the House, I fancy he might have somewhat toned down the sternness of his summons. **13** For you will scarcely suppose, Members of the Senate, that I should have voted for the proposal to which you agreed against your will, namely that offerings to the dead be mixed up with Thanksgivings,[23] the Commonwealth involved in an inexpiable sacrilege, Thanksgivings decreed to a dead man. Never mind *which* dead man. Let us say it was Lucius Brutus, who freed the Commonwealth from regal despotism and now, almost five hundred years later, has inspired his descendants to a courage and a deed like to his own: even so I could not assent to the conjunction of any dead man with the worship of the Immortal Gods, to prayers of thanksgiving addressed to one whose tomb, where offerings can be made to the departed spirit, is nowhere to be found. No, I should have spoken in such a vein that in the event of some national disaster—war, pestilence, famine—I could easily defend myself before the Roman People. Some of these disasters are already upon us, others, I fear, hang over our heads. But I hope the Immortal Gods will pardon the Roman People, who do not approve of what was done, and this House, which passed the decree against its will.

**14** What of our other public ills? Is it permitted to speak of them? Permitted it is to me, and ever shall be, to maintain honor and despise death. Let me but have the power to enter this place and I do not decline the risk of speaking. And I only wish, Members of the Senate, that I could have been present on the Kalends of Sextilis; not that anything could have been accomplished, but to prevent what actually occurred, namely that only one consular should have been found worthy of his office and of the Commonwealth. It grieves me to the heart that gentlemen who have enjoyed the highest gifts the Roman People can bestow did not follow the lead given by Piso in his admirable motion. Surely the Roman People did not make us consuls in order that we in so exalted a station, the highest in the land, should set the Commonwealth at naught. No consular supported Lucius Piso by word or even by look. **15** For pity's sake,

---

22. After Cicero's return from exile in 57 his house on the Palatine, which had been demolished, was rebuilt with a grant from the Senate (which he considered insufficient).

23. The Parentalia was a festival (13–21 February) at which offerings were made to the dead. Antony seems to have proposed that at all Thanksgivings (*supplicationes*) a day should be added in honor of Caesar. "Mixed up" is probably only a manner of speaking, as we might talk of bringing the funeral service to a wedding.

servitus? fuerit quaedam necessaria; ⟨nunc non est ita⟩. neque ego hoc ab omnibus eis desidero qui sententiam consulari loco dicunt. alia causa est eorum quorum silentio ignosco, alia eorum quorum vocem requiro. quos quidem doleo in suspicionem populo Romano venire non metu, quod ipsum esset turpe, sed alium alia de causa deesse dignitati suae. qua re 5 primum maximas gratias et ago et habeo Pisoni, qui non quid efficere posset in re publica cogitavit, sed quid facere ipse deberet. deinde a vobis, patres conscripti, peto ut, etiam si sequi minus audebitis orationem atque auctoritatem meam, benigne me tamen, ut fecistis adhuc, audiatis.                                                                        10

**16** Primum igitur acta Caesaris servanda censeo, non quo probem— quis enim id quidem potest?—sed quia rationem habendam maxime arbitror pacis atque oti. vellem adesset M. Antonius, modo sine advocatis—sed, ut opinor, licet ei minus valere, quod mihi heri per illum non licebat; doceret me vel potius vos, patres conscripti, quem ad modum 15 ipse Caesaris acta defenderet. an in commentariolis et chirographis et libellis se uno auctore prolatis, ne prolatis quidem sed tantum modo dictis, acta Caesaris firma erunt: quae ille in aes incidit, in quo populi iussa perpetuasque leges esse voluit, pro nihilo habebuntur? **17** equidem existimo nihil tam esse in actis Caesaris quam leges Caesaris. an, si cui 20 quid ille promisit, id erit fixum, quod idem non facere potuit? ut multis multa promissa non fecit: quae tamen multo plura illo mortuo reperta sunt quam a vivo beneficia per omnis annos tributa et data. sed ea non muto, non moveo: summo etiam studio illius praeclara acta defendo. pecunia utinam ad Opis maneret! cruenta illa quidem, sed his temporibus, quoniam 25 eis quorum est non redditur, necessaria. quamquam ea quoque sit effusa, si ita in actis fuit. **18** ecquid est quod tam proprie dici possit actum eius qui togatus in re publica cum potestate imperioque versatus sit quam

**15** 1 *anne* quondam*?*        *lacunam, quam ita supplevi,*[1] *ante agnoverat Kayser*        nec *D*        4 populo Romano venire] peruenire *V*[1]        metu] modo metus *V*        6 et habeo et ago *D* (*v. Fe.*)        l. pisoni *D*        6 quid quisquam *Reid*        8 rationem *Gomperz* (*vide quae scripsi ad Fam. 3.13.1* auctoritate, oratione, sententia)        9 adhuc fecistis[3] *V*        **16** 12 enim eam *V*[1]        13 adesset M. *Halm*: adessem *V*[1]: -sset *D*        15 licebat *D*: *om. V*[1]: licuit *V*[2] (*numero minus bono; et cf.* 1.36 cum adesse . . . non licebat)        doceret *om. V*[1]        17 se *del. C. F. W. Müller*        ac ne *D* (*v. Fe.*)        **17** 21 non facere *Muretus*: facere non *codd., sententia certe refragante*        24 etiam *om. V*        praeclara illius *D*

what is this voluntary slavery? Granted that slavery in some sort was unavoidable in time past: it is not so now. At the same time I do not expect this from everyone who speaks as a consular.[24] It is not the same with those whose silence I pardon[25] as with those whose voice I demand. I am sorry that the latter are suspected by the Roman People of failing in what is due to their rank, not out of fear, which would be dishonorable enough, but for their several particular reasons. And so in the first place I thank Piso most warmly and sincerely; he did not think about how much he could achieve politically but about his own duty. In the second place, Members of the Senate, let me request of you to give me a courteous hearing, as you have thus far, even if you do not venture to follow what I say and advise.

**16** First, then, I declare myself in favor of maintaining Caesar's acts; not that I approve of them (who can?) but because I think peace and quiet should be our first consideration. I wish Marcus Antonius were here present—without his consultants;[26] but I suppose he has a right to be indisposed, a right he did not allow *me* yesterday. If he were here, he would show me, or rather you, Members of the Senate, how *he* goes about defending Caesar's acts. It seems that those contained in scraps of memoranda and holographs and papers produced on Antonius' sole authority, or not so much as produced but merely alleged, are to stand; whereas measures which Caesar inscribed on bronze, as legislative acts of the people and permanently valid statutes, are to be treated as of no account. **17** Now *I* consider that nothing is so decidedly an act of Caesar's as Caesar's laws. If he made a promise to somebody, is that to be hard and fast?—a promise which Caesar might or might not have carried out, just as he made many promises to many people which he did not fulfil; though those found after his death far outnumber the favors granted and given by him in all the years of his life. However, I am not tampering with them, not at all; I am an enthusiastic defender of Caesar's splendid acts. One *could* wish the money[27] in the temple of Ops were still there. Stained as it was with blood, it would come in handy these days, since it is not being returned to its owners. Well, it has been dissipated; let that too pass, if it was so ordered in the acts. **18** Is there anything which can so properly be called an act of one who in a civilian capacity has wielded power and authority in the Commonwealth as a law? Ask

---

24. Lit. "in the consular position." The consulars spoke first (after the consuls-elect, if any) in an order determined each year by whichever consul presided during January.

25. Apparently a reference to Antony's uncle, L. Julius Caesar.

26. *Advocati* were persons accompanying a party to a trial or suit in order to render legal advice or simply moral support. Here used ironically of Antony's armed guards.

27. Partly deriving from the sales of confiscated property. Its embezzlement by Antony and Dolabella started in March (cf. 2.93, *Att.* 14.14.5).

lex? quaere acta Gracchi: leges Semproniae proferentur. quaere Sullae:
Corneliae. quid? Pompei tertius consulatus in quibus actis constitit?
nempe in legibus. de Caesare ipso si quaereres quidnam egisset in urbe et
in toga, leges multas responderet se et praeclaras tulisse, chirographa
vero aut mutaret aut non daret aut, si dedisset, non istas res in actis suis   5
duceret. sed haec ipsa concedo; quibusdam etiam in rebus coniveo; in
maximis vero rebus, id est in legibus, acta Caesaris dissolvi ferendum
non puto.

**19** Quae lex melior, utilior, optima etiam re publica saepius flagitata
quam ne praetoriae provinciae plus quam annum neve plus quam bien-   10
nium consulares obtinerentur? hac lege sublata videturne vobis posse
Caesaris acta servari? quid? lege quae promulgata est de tertia decuria
nonne omnes iudiciariae leges Caesaris dissolvuntur? et vos acta Caesaris
defenditis qui leges eius evertitis? nisi forte, si quid memoriae causa
ret⟨t⟩ulit in libellum, id numerabitur in actis et, quamvis iniquum et   15
inutile sit, defendetur: quod ad populum centuriatis comitiis tulit, id in
actis Caesaris non habebitur. **20** at quae est ista tertia decuria? "centurionum" inquit. quid? isti ordini iudicatus lege Iulia, etiam ante Pompeia,
Aurelia non patebat? "census praefiniebatur," inquit. non centurioni
quidem solum sed equiti etiam Romano; itaque viri fortissimi atque   20
honestissimi qui ordines duxerunt res et iudicant et iudicaverunt. "non
quaero" inquit "istos: quicumque ordinem duxit, iudicet." at si ferretis
quicumque equo meruisset, quod est lautius, nemini probaretis; in iudice
enim spectari et fortuna debet et dignitas. "non quaero" inquit "ista: addo
etiam iudices manipularis ex legione Alaudarum. aliter enim nostri negant   25

**18** 2 cn. pompei(i) *D*     3 nempe *DV*², *Mar. Victorinus De defin. 31 ed. Stangl*: *om.*
*V*¹     a caesare *D* (de C- *om. Vict.*)     6 haec *V*: ea *D*, *Vict.*     7 in *c*, *Vict.*: *om.*
*Vbnstv*     id . . . legibus *del. Jordan*     **19** 10 neu *nstv*     11 posse *om. D*     12 ea
lege *D*     decuria iudicum *D*     15 retulit *V*¹*D*, *ut solent*     **20** 17 est *om. V*     18
etiam ante] -amne *D*     20–21 honestissimi atque fortissimi *D*     23 laudatius *D*

for the acts of Gracchus and you will be shown the Sempronian laws. Ask for Sulla's and you will be shown the Cornelian laws. What were the acts which made up Pompey's third consulship? Why, his legislation. If you could ask Caesar himself what he had done in Rome in civilian dress, he would answer that he had put through many fine laws. As for holographs, he would either change them or not issue them or, if he had issued them, he would not consider them among his acts. However, this also I concede, in certain matters I am even ready to turn a blind eye; but in the most important matters of all, that is to say laws, I do not think it tolerable that Caesar's acts should be set aside.

**19** The law providing that praetorian provinces be held for not more than one year and consular for not more than two is an outstandingly good and useful law, often demanded even in the best days of the Commonwealth. When this law is abolished, do you think it possible for Caesar's acts to be maintained? What about the law which has been promulgated concerning the third panel?[28] Does it not set aside the whole of Caesar's judiciary legislation? And are you subverters of Caesar's legislation defending his acts? Or perhaps we should say that if Caesar jotted something in a notebook as an aid to memory, we must count that among his acts and defend it, no matter how unjust and inadvisable it may be, whereas a law which he submitted to the people at an assembly of the Centuries is not to be regarded as an act of Caesar's? **20** However, what is this third panel? "It is of centurions," says he. Indeed? Were not juries open to that class under the Julian law, and even earlier under the Pompeian and Aurelian?[29] "That was with a property qualification," he says. Well, but this applied not merely to a centurion but to a Roman knight. And so brave and respectable persons who have served as centurions are sitting on juries and have done so in the past. "I am not interested in them," he says. "Every man who has served as centurion must sit on juries." But if you and your colleague were making the same proposal with respect to every man who has seen service with the cavalry, which carries more of a cachet, nobody would be persuaded. In a juror both means and status ought to be considered. "I am not interested in all that," he says. "In addition, I am giving the right to private soldiers of the Larks Legion.[30] Our people[31] say that otherwise they

28. Of persons eligible for jury service. Of the three panels, chosen from senators, knights, and *tribuni aerarii* (whatever exactly they were), Caesar had abolished the third. This new third panel was added by Antony.

29. The Aurelian law of 70 provided that juries should be composed equally from the three classes (see n. 28 above). Pompey's law, passed in his third consulship (52), introduced certain modifications.

30. Raised by Caesar from Transalpine Gaul and granted Roman citizenship.

31. Caesar's followers.

posse se salvos esse." o contumeliosum honorem eis quos ad iudicandum
nec opinantis vocatis! hic enim est ⟨prope dicam⟩ legis index ut ei res in
tertia decuria iudicent qui libere iudicare non audeant. in quo quantus
error est, di immortales, eorum qui istam legem excogitaverunt! ut enim
quisque sordidissimus videbitur, ita libentissime severitate iudicandi sor-      5
dis suas eluet laborabitque ut honestis decuriis potius dignus videatur
quam in turpem iure coniectus.

   **21** Altera promulgata lex est ut de vi et maiestatis damnati ad populum
provocent, si velint. haec utrum tandem lex est an legum omnium disso-
lutio? quis est autem hodie cuius intersit istam legem†manere†? nemo    10
reus est legibus illis, nemo quem futurum putemus. armis enim gesta
numquam profecto in iudicium vocabuntur. "at res popularis." utinam
quidem aliquid velletis esse populare! omnes enim iam cives de rei
publicae salute una et mente et voce consentiunt. quae est igitur ista
cupiditas legis eius ferendae quae turpitudinem summam habeat, gratiam    15
nullam? quid enim turpius quam qui maiestatem populi Romani minuerit
per vim, eum damnatum iudicio ad eam ipsam vim reverti propter quam
sit iure damnatus? **22** Sed quid plura de lege disputo? quasi vero id agatur
ut quisquam provocet: id agitur, id fertur ne quis omnino umquam istis
legibus reus fiat. Quis enim aut accusator tam amens reperietur qui reo    20
condemnato obici se multitudini conductae velit, aut iudex qui reum dam-
nare audeat, ut ipse ad operas mercennarias statim protrahatur? non igitur
provocatio ista lege datur, sed duae maxime salutares leges quaestiones-
que tolluntur. quid est aliud hortari adulescentis ut turbulenti, ut seditiosi,
ut perniciosi cives velint esse? quam autem ad pestem furor tribunicius    25
impelli non poterit his duabus quaestionibus de vi et maiestate sublatis?
**23** quid quod obrogatur legibus Caesaris, quae iubent ei qui de vi itemque
ei qui maiestatis damnatus sit aqua et igni interdici? quibus cum provocatio datur, nonne acta Caesaris rescinduntur? quae quidem ego, patres
conscripti, qui illa numquam probavi, tamen ita conservanda concordiae    30
causa arbitratus sum ut non modo, quas vivus leges Caesar tulisset, infir-

---

2 prope dicam *addidi*[3]     res *om. bcntv*     **21** 8 ut et *Vb*     maiestatis *Halm*: -ates *V*: de
(*om. v*) maiestate *D*     9 haec *V Cus.*: haecum *cn¹s¹v*: haec cum *btn²s²*     10 autem
*scripsi*: enim *codd.*     manere *V*: uenire *D*: sanciri *Halm, peiora alii*: *fort.* rogari[2]     11
istis (-ius *b*) legibus *D*     12 ad res populares (-ris *V²*) *V¹D, corr. Naugerius*     13 esse
*del. Eberhard, clausula refragante*     **22** 21 obici se] -cere *V¹*: -cere se *V²*     24 hortari
*V²*: -aria *V¹*: adhortari *D*     25 ad rei p. pestem *D*     26 de ui et de maiestate *D*: de ui et
maiestatis *Halm*: *del. Cobet*     **23** 27 ei qui *om. V*     30 tamen *om. D*     31 caesar
leges *cnsv*

cannot keep their footing." To those whom you and your colleague are summoning out of the blue to sit as jurors the honor is an insult. The rubric to the
law all but states that the third panel shall consist of jurors who dare not render
an independent verdict. Ah, but what a monumental error the contrivers of this
law are making! Why, the spottier a man's reputation, the more eager he will
be to wash away his spots by strictness in the jury box, the harder he will try to
look as though he ought to be on a respectable panel, instead of being rightly
thrust into a disreputable one.

**21** Another law has been promulgated giving persons convicted of violence
and lèse-majesté a right of appeal to the people. Is this a law or the cancellation
of all laws? Besides, who is there today who has any interest in the enactment
of such a law? Nobody stands accused under those laws, nobody is expected to
be accused, for obviously acts of warfare will never be brought before a court
of law. "A popular gesture." I only wish you gentlemen wanted anything you
do to be popular,[32] for all Romans are now of one mind and voice concerning
the welfare of the Commonwealth. So why are you so anxious to pass a law
which disgraces its authors and wins them no friends? For a disgrace it is, that
a person who has lowered the majesty of the Roman People by violence and
been found guilty in court should return to the self-same violence on account
of which he has been justly condemned. **22** But I need not go on talking about
the law, as though its purpose were to allow appeals; its purpose, its meaning,
is that nobody should ever be charged under the said laws.[33] No prosecutor
will be found crazy enough to court exposure to a hired crowd after the accused
is found guilty, and no juror is going to dare convict a defendant with the
prospect of being dragged up immediately before a mercenary gang. Therefore
this law does not grant a right of appeal; it does away with two very salutary
laws and courts. Does not this constitute an invitation to our young men to
become turbulent agitators, a menace to the community? There will be no
desperate step to which the subversive tendencies of tribunes cannot be in-
cited, once these two courts, of violence and of lèse-majesté, are abolished.
**23** Again, is not this to cancel the laws of Caesar, which declare that any man
found guilty of violence, and likewise any man found guilty of lèse-majesté, is
to be outlawed? When the right of appeal is granted to such, are not Caesar's
acts rescinded? I, who never approved these acts, Members of the Senate,
judged that they should be retained for concord's sake, and am so firmly of that
opinion that I am against invalidating at this time not only the laws which

32. Cicero likes to make play with *popularis* in its general meaning, "pleasing to the people,"
and its use as a political term for "democratic"—i.e. antisenatorial—politicians and measures.

33. Cicero's arguments are not always formally consistent with one another. He has just said
that nobody would have been prosecuted under these laws anyway.

mandas hoc tempore non putarem, sed ne illas quidem quas post mortem Caesaris prolatas esse et fixas videtis.

**24** De exsilio reducti a mortuo; civitas data non solum singulis sed nationibus et provinciis universis a mortuo; immunitatibus infinitis sublata vectigalia a mortuo. ergo haec uno verum optimo auctore domo prolata 5 defendimus: eas leges quas ipse nobis inspectantibus recitavit, pronuntiavit, tulit, quibus latis gloriabatur eisque legibus rem publicam contineri putabat, de provinciis, de iudiciis, eas, inquam, Caesaris leges nos qui defendimus acta Caesaris evertendas putamus? **25** ac de his tamen legibus quae promulgatae sunt saltem queri possumus: de eis quae iam latae di- 10 cuntur ne illud quidem licuit. illae enim sine ulla promulgatione latae sunt ante quam scriptae.

Quaero autem quid sit cur aut ego aut quisquam vestrum, patres conscripti, bonis tribunis plebi leges malas metuat. paratos habemus qui intercedant, paratos qui rem publicam religione defendant: vacui metu 15 esse debemus. "quas tu mihi" inquit "intercessiones, quas religiones?" eas scilicet quibus rei publicae salus continetur. "neglegimus ista et nimis antiqua ac stulta ducimus: forum saepietur; omnes claudentur aditus; armati in praesidiis multis locis collocabuntur." **26** quid tum? quod ita erit gestum, id lex erit? et in aes incidi iubebitis, credo, illa legitima: 20 "Consules populum iure rogaverunt"—hocine a maioribus accepimus ius rogandi?—"populusque iure scivit." qui populus? isne qui exclusus est? quo iure? an eo quod vi et armis omne sublatum est? atque haec dico de futuris, quod est amicorum ante dicere ea quae vitari possint: quae si facta non erunt, refelletur oratio mea. loquor de legibus promulgatis, de 25 quibus est integrum vobis, demonstro vitia: tollite! denuntio vim, arma: removete!

**27** Irasci quidem vos mihi, Dolabella, pro re publica dicenti non oportebit. quamquam te quidem id facturum non arbitror—novi facilitatem tuam; collegam tuum aiunt in hac sua fortuna, quae bona ipsi 30 videtur—mihi, ne gravius quippiam dicam, avorum et avunculi sui con-

---

**24** 4 a mortuo *om. nsv*　　5 verum] uiro *D*　　6 nobis] nouos *V*[1]　　promulgauit *ante* recitavit *add. O. Müller*　　7 continere *D*　　9 uertendas *D*　　putabimus *b*[1]*n*: -auimus *stv*　　**25** 11 illud *om. V*[1]: id *coni. Halm*　　sine ulla] nulla *D*　　14 plebi] -is *V*[2]: pl. *D*　　**26** 21 hoc enim a *DV*[2]　　23 ego haec (hoc *b*) *D*　　26–27 uim: arma remouete *dist. c*: uim arma, r- *Poggius*　　**27** 28 uos quidem *D*　　29 oportebat *V*[1]　　noui enim *bcnsv*

Caesar passed while yet alive but even those which you see produced and posted after Caesar's death.

**24** Exiles have been restored by a dead man; citizenship has been conferred, not only upon individuals but on tribes and whole provinces,[34] by a dead man; revenues have been abolished through countless exemptions by a dead man. Well, we defend these ordinances, produced from a private house on the authority (admittedly excellent) of one individual. What of the laws which Caesar in person read out and published and carried before our eyes, the laws in which he gloried as their sponsor, on which he believed the existence of the Commonwealth to depend, the laws on the provinces and the courts? Yes, those laws of Caesar: do we, who defend Caesar's acts, think them expendable? **25** Laws which have been promulgated are at least open to protest on our part; but even that was not permitted in the case of laws alleged to have already been passed. They were passed without any promulgation before they were drafted.[35]

And now I put a question: why should I or any of you, Members of the Senate, fear bad laws when we have good tribunes of the plebs? There they are, ready to use their veto, ready to defend the Commonwealth by the sanctity of their office. Our minds should be at ease. "Vetoes?" says he. "Sanctions? What are you talking about?" Why, naturally, those which are bound up with the survival of the Commonwealth. "Oh, we take no notice of that sort of thing. Antiquated nonsense, that's what we think of it. The Forum will be fenced off, all entries barred. Armed men will be posted on guard at many points." **26** And then what? Will something so transacted be a law? I suppose you will have the legal formula engraved on bronze: "The Consuls lawfully proposed to the People"—is *this* the traditional right of proposal?—"and the People lawfully enacted." What people? The people which was shut out? Lawfully? Are you referring to a legality which has been abolished by armed violence? Now understand, I am speaking of the future—it is the part of friends to speak of evils which can be avoided. If they do not come to pass, my words will be refuted. I am talking about promulgated laws, as to which your hands are still free, and pointing out flaws: remove them. I warn of violence, of armed force: take it away.

**27** You and your colleague, Dolabella, must not be angry with me for speaking out on behalf of the Commonwealth. To be sure, I do not suppose that *you* will be; I know your easy temper. They say that your colleague in the fortune that is now his, good fortune as he thinks—for my own part, I think (to

---

34. An exaggeration. The only province granted Roman citizenship was Sicily, which already possessed it in large measure. Crete was given "free" status (see 2.97).

35. I.e. they were never passed at all; cf. 5.7.

sulatum si imitaretur, fortunatior videretur—sed eum iracundum audio
factum. video autem quam sit odiosum habere eundem iratum et armatum, cum tanta praesertim gladiorum sit impunitas: sed proponam ius, ut
opinor, aequum, quod M. Antonium non arbitror repudiaturum. ego, si
quid in vitam eius aut in mores cum contumelia dixero, quo minus mihi      5
inimicissimus sit non recusabo; sin consuetudinem meam quam in re publica semper habui tenuero, id est si libere quae sentiam de re publica
dixero, primum deprecor ne irascatur; deinde, si hoc non impetro, peto ut
sic irascatur ut civi. armis utatur, si ita necesse est, ut dicit, sui de-
fendendi causa: eis qui pro re publica quae ipsis visa erunt dixerint ista      10
arma ne noceant. quid hac postulatione dici potest aequius? **28** quod
si, ut mihi a quibusdam eius familiaribus dictum est, omnis eum quae
habetur contra voluntatem eius oratio graviter offendit, etiam si nulla
inest contumelia, feremus amici naturam. sed idem illi ita mecum loquuntur: "non idem tibi adversario Caesaris licebit quod Pisoni socero,"      15
et simul admonent quiddam quod cavebimus; nec erit iustior in senatum
non veniendi morbi causa quam mortis.

    **29** Sed per deos immortalis!—te enim intuens, Dolabella, qui es mihi
carissimus, non possum de utriusque vestrum errore reticere. credo enim
vos nobilis homines magna quaedam spectantis non pecuniam, ut quidam      20
nimis creduli suspicantur, quae semper ab amplissimo quoque clarissimo-
que contempta est, non opes violentas et populo Romano minime ferendam potentiam, sed caritatem civium et gloriam concupivisse. est autem gloria laus recte factorum magnorumque in rem publicam fama
meritorum, quae cum optimi cuiusque, tum etiam multitudinis testi-      25
monio comprobatur. **30** dicerem, Dolabella, qui recte factorum fructus
esset, nisi te praeter ceteros paulisper esse expertum viderem. quem
potes recordari in vita illuxisse tibi diem laetiorem quam cum expiato
foro, dissipato concursu impiorum, principibus sceleris poena adfectis,
te domum recepisti? cuius ordinis, cuius generis, cuius denique fortunae      30
studia tum laudi et gratulationi tuae se non obtulerunt? quin mihi etiam,

2 esse factum *V*    iratum eundem *D*    6 sin] si *D*    meam] eam *Kornitzer*    6–7
quam . . . habui *om. V*¹    **28** 14 locuntur *V*: *om. D*    16–17 nec erit . . . mortis *An-*
*tonii familiaribus dant plerique*    **29** 18–19 qui . . . carissimus *om. V*¹    19 de . . .
errore] utriusque uestrum errorem *V*    23–24 est . . . laus] gloria est laus *Cus.*: ea est
autem (a- est *nsv*) g- et l- *DV*²: est au- g- ea l- *coni. Clark*    24 in rem publica *V*: in re
publica *Cus.*    fama *c, Isid. Orig. 2.30.2*: *om. V Cus. bnstv* (*v. Fe.*)    **30** 27 praeter
ceteros *om. D*    29 urbe incendio et tedis [*i.e. caedis*] metu liberata³ *post* adfectis *add.*
*V*²    31 obtulerunt] tulerunt *V*: optarent *nsv*

put it thus mildly) he would be more fortunate if he took the consulships of his grandparents and his maternal uncle[36] as his models—anyhow, I hear that he has become choleric. And I am well aware how tiresome it is to have a man angry when he carries a weapon, especially in times when swords are used with so much impunity. But I shall make what seems to me a fair proposition, one which I do not think Marcus Antonius will reject. If I say anything offensive concerning his career and character, I shall not object to his becoming my mortal enemy. On the other hand, if I hold to my invariable practice in public life, that is, if I speak my mind freely on public affairs, in the first place I beg him not to be angry; and if that plea fails, then I ask him to be angry with me as a fellow citizen. Let him use arms, if that is necessary (as he says it is), for his own defense, but let those arms do no injury to people who speak their own minds on behalf of the Commonwealth. Well, what can be fairer than what I am asking? **28** Certain of his intimates, however, tell me that any language held contrary to his wishes gravely offends him, even if no insult is involved. If that be so, I shall put up with a friend's humor. But I am told by these same persons: "You were an adversary of Caesar; you cannot expect to be allowed the same latitude as Piso, Caesar's father-in-law"; and they go on to give me a hint which I shall bear in mind. As an excuse for not attending the Senate, death will be as good as illness.

**29** Now in the Immortal Gods' name, when I look at you, Dolabella, very dear to me as you are, I cannot keep silent about the mistake which both of you gentlemen are making. As men of noble birth I believe you aim high. I do not suppose you have set your minds on money, as certain overcredulous folk suspect, for money has ever been despised by great and famous men; nor yet on might backed by violence and power such as the Roman People can nowise tolerate—not on these then, but on glory and a place in the hearts of your countrymen. What is glory? It is the credit for laudable actions and the reputation earned by notable public services, approved by the testimony of the best among us and also by that of the multitude. **30** I should be telling you, Dolabella, how laudable actions are rewarded, if I did not know that for a short while you had more experience of it than any other man. Surely you can remember no happier or brighter day in your life than the day you returned home after purging the Forum, dispersing the concourse of traitors, and punishing the ringleaders. People of all classes, sorts, and conditions came up to you on your way with enthusiastic praise and congratulation. Honest men[37]

---

36. M. Antonius (99), L. Julius Caesar (90), and L. Julius Caesar (64).

37. As in previous translations I use this expression for Cicero's *boni*: solid, substantial citizens and supporters of the existing order (*les honnêtes hommes, les gens de bien*).

quo auctore te in his rebus uti arbitrabantur, et gratias boni viri agebant
et tuo nomine gratulabantur. recordare, quaeso, Dolabella, consensum
illum theatri, cum omnes earum rerum obliti propter quas fuerant tibi
offensi significarent se beneficio novo memoriam veteris doloris abiecisse.
**31** hanc tu, P. Dolabella—magno loquor cum dolore—hanc tu, inquam,    5
potuisti aequo animo tantam dignitatem deponere?
   Tu autem, M. Antoni—absentem enim appello—unum illum diem
quo in aede Telluris senatus fuit non omnibus his mensibus quibus te
quidam multum a me dissentientes beatum putant anteponis? quae fuit
oratio de concordia! quanto metu senatus, quanta sollicitudine civitas   10
tum a te liberata est cum collegam tuum, depositis inimicitiis, oblitus
auspiciorum a te ipso augure populi Romani nuntiato⟨rum⟩, illo primum
die collegam tibi esse voluisti; cum tuus parvus filius in Capitolium a te
missus pacis obses fuit! **32** quo senatus die laetior, quo populus Romanus? qui quidem nulla in contione umquam frequentior fuit. tum denique  15
liberati per viros fortissimos videbamur, quia, ut illi voluerant, libertatem
pax consequebatur.
   Proximo, altero, tertio, denique reliquis consecutis diebus non inter-
mittebas quasi donum aliquod cotidie adferre rei publicae; maximum autem illud quod dictaturae nomen sustulisti. haec inusta est a te, a te,     20
inquam, mortuo Caesari nota ad ignominiam sempiternam. ut enim propter unius M. Manli scelus decreto gentis Manliae neminem patricium
Manlium ⟨Marcum⟩ vocari licet, sic tu propter unius dictatoris odium
nomen dictatoris funditus sustulisti. **33** num te, cum haec pro salute rei
publicae tanta gessisses, fortunae tuae, num amplitudinis, num claritatis,   25
num gloriae paenitebat? unde igitur subito tanta ista mutatio? non possum
adduci ut suspicer te pecunia captum. licet quod cuique libet loquatur,
credere non est necesse. nihil enim umquam in te sordidum, nihil humile
cognovi. quamquam solent domestici depravare non numquam; sed novi
firmitatem tuam. atque utinam ut culpam, sic etiam suspicionem vitare    30

4 significa(ue)runt *bcnsv*    se *om. V*    **31** 7 te *D*    enim *om. D*    10 oratio tua
*Muretus*    senatus *Ernesti*: ueteranis *V*[1]: -rani *bctV*[2]: -ri *s*: -ris *v*: cetera *n*: *del. Manutius,
alia alii* (*v. Fe.*)    11 cum collegam tuum] tu c- *bct*: tuum c- (collega *v*) *nsv*    12
auspiciorum . . . nuntiatorum *Faërnus*: auspiciorum a te ipso augure pronuntiate (-ante *V*[2])
*V*: auspicia te ipso augure nuntiante *D*: auspici a te ipso augure p. R. nuntiati *Madvig*    primo *bcstv*    13 cum tuus *Halm*: K. t- *ctv*: R. t- *ns*: licet t- *b*: tunc *V*    **32** 14
p(opulus) R(omanus) *om. V*[1]    16 per *om. V*    18 proximo *del. Eberhard*, altero *del.
Cobet* (*cf. Plat. Crit.* 44a οὐ τοίνυν τῆς ἐπιούσης ἡμέρας . . . ἀλλὰ τῆς ἑτέρας)    23
Marcum *add. Gulielmius*    **33** 24 te cum haec *V Cus.*: haec te cum *D*    25 claritatis]
civium caritatis *Busche coll.* 1.29    26 num gloriae *D Cus. V*[2]: *om. V*[1]    28–29 in te
. . . quamquam *om. D* (*nisi quod* tam sanctum est non *b*)

were actually thanking *me* and congratulating me on your account under the impression that I had been your mentor in these proceedings. My friend, pray remember the unanimous applause in the theater, when all present, forgetting their past grievances against you, made it plain that after this recent benefaction they had cast aside the recollection of old bitterness.[38] **31** This honor— with much pain I say it—this signal honor, Publius Dolabella, could you calmly lay it down?

And you, Marcus Antonius—I address you though you are not here—surely you prize that one day when the Senate met in Tellus' temple beyond all these latter months in which some folk with whom I profoundly disagree admire your felicity? What a speech you made about concord! You delivered the Senate from fear, the community from anxiety, when you dropped your quarrel with your colleague and, forgetting the auspices previously announced by yourself as augur of the Roman People,[39] that day for the first time you desired him to *be* your colleague; and you sent your little son up to the Capitol as a hostage for peace. **32** Never was a happier day for the Senate and for the Roman People, who never attended any public assembly in greater numbers. Only then did we feel liberated by that brave company,[40] for peace was following in the wake of freedom, as they had hoped it would.

The next day and the next and the next and onwards, one day after another you brought the Commonwealth a daily gift, so to speak; the greatest of all, when you abolished the name of dictatorship. Thereby you—yes, *you*— branded Caesar in his grave with everlasting infamy. Because of a crime committed by one of its members, Marcus Manlius, no patrician belonging to the Manlian clan may be called Marcus; so the clan decreed.[41] Just so you totally abolished the name of dictator because of the hatred felt for one particular dictator. **33** After these magnificent contributions to the welfare of the Commonwealth were you not satisfied with your success? Were you not great enough, famous enough, glorious enough? If you were, why this sudden reversal? I cannot bring myself to suspect that you yielded to a pecuniary temptation. People may say what they please; one does not have to believe them. I have never seen anything mean or sordid in your character. True, men are sometimes corrupted by those close to them.[42] But I know what stout stuff you are made of. It is a pity you could not avoid the suspicion as you avoided

---

38. Allusion to Dolabella's tribunate in 47, when he proposed a cancellation of debts.
. 39. Cf. 2.79–84.
40. Caesar's assassins.
41. Suspected of aiming at despotic power, he was killed in 384. On the action of the *gens* Manlia see Liv. 6.20.14.
42. Antony's wife Fulvia is meant; cf. SB[2] on 2.93.

potuisses! illud magis vereor ne ignorans verum iter gloriae gloriosum
putes plus te unum posse quam omnis et metui a civibus tuis quam diligi
malis. quod si ita putas, totam ignoras viam gloriae. carum esse civem,
bene de re publica mereri, laudari, coli, diligi gloriosum est; metui vero
et in odio esse invidiosum, detestabile, imbecillum, caducum. **34** quod 5
videmus etiam in fabula illi ipsi qui "oderint, dum metuant" dixerit
perniciosum fuisse. utinam, M. Antoni, avum tuum meminisses! de quo
tamen audisti multa ex me eaque saepissime. putasne illum immortalitatem mereri voluisse, ut propter armorum habendorum licentiam me-
tueretur? illa erat vita, illa secunda fortuna, libertate esse parem ceteris, 10
principem dignitate. itaque, ut omittam res avi tui prosperas, acerbissimum eius supremum diem malim quam L. Cinnae dominatum, a quo ille
crudelissime est interfectus. **35** sed quid oratione te flectam? si enim
exitus C. Caesaris efficere non potest ut malis carus esse quam metui, nihil cuiusquam proficiet nec valebit oratio. quem qui beatum fuisse putant, 15
miseri ipsi sunt. beatus est nemo qui ea lege vivit ut non modo impune
sed etiam cum summa interfectoris gloria interfici possit.

Qua re flecte te, quaeso, et maiores tuos respice atque ita guberna rem
publicam ut natum esse te cives tui gaudeant: sine quo nec beatus nec
clarus nec tutus quisquam esse omni⟨no⟩ potest. **36** populi quidem Ro- 20
mani iudicia multa ambo habetis, quibus vos non satis moveri permoleste
fero. quid enim gladiatoribus clamores innumerabilium civium? quid
populi versus? quid Pompei statuae plausus infiniti, quid duobus tribunis
plebis qui vobis adversantur? parumne haec significant incredibiliter con-
sentientem populi Romani universi voluntatem? quid? Apollinarium 25
ludorum plausus vel testimonia potius et iudicia populi Romani parum
magna vobis videbantur? o beatos illos qui, cum adesse ipsis propter vim
armorum non licebat, aderant tamen et in medullis populi Romani ac

2–3 quam diligi malis *om.* V (*cf. Off. 2.29*)    4 p(ublica) *om.* V[1]    5 et detestabile
V    **34** 6 in fabulis ipsi illi D    dixerint *bstvn*[2]: -rant *n*[1]    7 M. *om. nstv*    8 multa
ex me audisti *t*: m- audiui ex me *bcnsv*    eaque *Faërnus*: aquae V: *om.* D    10 *anne*
erant vota?[1]    cum ceteris D    12 mallem *bcnsv*    **35** 14 hoc *ante* non *bnst*    19 te
*om.* V[1]    20 carus *Clark*[3]    nec tutus[3] *coni. Muretus*: nec unctus V: *om.* D: nec iucun-
dus *Weber: alii alia*    esse quisquam D    omnino potest *Muretus*: omni potestate V:
potest D    **36** 21 vos non *Poggius*: uobis non V: non *bv*[2]: *om. cnstv*[1]    22 gladiatorii
*bcnt*: -ris *s*: -ri *v*    23 duobus *Faërnus*: ii V*c*: u *t*: hi *vn*[2]: his *n*[1]*s*    26–27 parum
magna] praua (parua *t*) D

the guilt. What I am more afraid of is that in ignorance of the true path of glory you think it glorious to have more power than the rest of us put together and prefer the fear of your countrymen to their esteem. If you think on those lines, you are utterly ignorant of the way to glory. It is glorious to be a citizen dear to the community,[43] to deserve well of the Commonwealth, to be praised and courted and esteemed. But to be feared and hated carries ill-will, execration, weakness, insecurity. **34** Even in the play we see how it ruined the very character[44] who said "Let them hate me, so they fear me." Ah, Marcus Antonius, would that you remembered your grandfather! But you have heard me talk of him much and often! Do you think *he* would have wished to live for ever, if that involved license to keep an armed following and thus be feared by his fellows? No, the life and success he wanted meant parity in freedom, primacy in prestige. And so, to say nothing of your grandfather's time of prosperity, I would prefer that bitterest last day of his life to the autocracy of Lucius Cinna, who cruelly murdered him. **35** But why try to turn you from your course with words? If Gaius Caesar's end cannot convince you that it is better to be loved than feared, nobody's words will do any good or make any impression. Those who think Caesar was happy are themselves miserable. No man is happy who lives on such terms that he can be killed not only with impunity but to the supreme glory of his killer.

So turn, I beg you. Think of your ancestors and so guide the Commonwealth that your fellow countrymen will be glad that you were born. Without that no man can be happy or famous or safe. **36** The Roman People have expressed their sentiments to both of you by many signs. I am very sorry that these have not had as much effect upon you as they should. The shouts of countless voices at the gladiators, the verses passed from hand to hand, the endless applause for Pompeius' statue and for two tribunes of the plebs[45] who oppose you and your colleague—is not all this enough to signify a truly extraordinary consensus of the entire Roman People? And then there was the applause at the Apollinarian games, or rather the people's testimony and expression of their feelings.[46] Did you find that insufficient? Happy were they who were kept away by force of arms but present none the less, deep down in the people's hearts. Or did you

43. *Carum.* This might be added in support of the manuscript reading *care Maecenas* in Hor. *Carm.* 1.20.5; see D. R. Shackleton Bailey, *Profile of Horace* (London and Cambridge, Mass., 1982) 90.

44. Atreus, in Accius' play of that name.

45. Ti. Cannutius and L. Cassius Longinus, brother of the tyrannicide (or possibly D. Carfulenus; cf. 3.23).

46. As city praetor M. Brutus was responsible for producing these games, which began on 6 July, but in his absence Antony's brother Gaius took his place. The performance of Accius' play *Tereus* produced a popular demonstration in favor of Brutus. Cf. 10.8.

visceribus haerebant! nisi forte Accio tum plaudi et sexagesimo post anno palmam dari, non Bruto putabatis; qui ludis suis ita caruit ut in illo apparatissimo spectaculo studium populus Romanus tribueret absenti, desiderium liberatoris sui perpetuo plausu et clamore leniret. **37** equidem is sum qui istos plausus, cum popularibus civibus tribuerentur, semper contempserim; idemque cum a summis, mediis, infimis, cum denique ab universis hoc idem fit, cumque ei qui ante sequi populi consensum solebant fugiunt, non plausum illum, sed iudicium puto. sin haec leviora vobis videntur, quae sunt gravissima, num etiam hoc contemnitis quod sensistis tam caram populo Romano vitam A. Hirti fuisse? satis erat enim probatum illum esse populo Romano, ut est; iucundum amicis, in quo vincit omnis; carum suis, quibus est ille carissimus: tantam tamen sollicitudinem bonorum, tantum timorem in quo meminimus? certe in nullo. **38** quid igitur? hoc vos, per deos immortalis, quale sit non interpretamini? quid? eos de vestra vita cogitare non censetis quibus eorum quos sperant rei publicae consulturos vita tam cara sit?

Cepi fructum, patres conscripti, reversionis meae, quoniam et ea dixi ut, quicumque casus consecutus esset, exstaret constantiae meae testimonium, et sum a vobis benigne ac diligenter auditus. quae potestas si mihi saepius sine meo vestroque periculo fiet, utar: si minus, quantum potero, non tam mihi me quam rei publicae reservabo. mihi fere satis est quod vixi vel ad aetatem vel ad gloriam: huc si quid accesserit, non tam mihi quam vobis reique publicae accesserit.

2 putabitis (-batis *b*) bruto *D*     3 studium suum *V*$^2$     tribuerit *V*$^1$*D*     ut (*del. V*$^2$) absenti *V*$^1$: absenti, ut *Faërnus*: et abs- *Mittermayer*     **37** 7 assensum *Eberhard*     10 A.
*om. V*$^1$     10–11 enim (*om. t*) erat probatum *cntv*: enim p- erat *b*     11 est] esset *bcnt*:
esse *v*     12 ille$^2$ *scripsi*: ipse *V*: *om. D*     13 timorem omnium in *D*     **38** 14 non *om.*
*D*     17 et ea] ea *bcst*: mea *nv*     18 conscienti(a)e *cnsv*     21 mihi (*alt.*)] qui m- *V*

think it was Accius who won the applause and the prize sixty years later,[47] and not Brutus? Brutus could not watch his own games, but at that magnificent spectacle the people paid him in his absence the tribute of their affection, assuaging their longing for their deliverer with sustained clapping and shouting. **37** For my part, I have always despised such applause when bestowed on "popular" politicians. But when it comes from all ranks from the highest to the lowest, from everybody present in fact, and when those who used to follow the popular consensus take off in the opposite direction, why, I no longer regard it as applause but as a verdict. However, if you take a light view of these demonstrations, which are in fact highly impressive, you have noticed the deep concern of the Roman People for Aulus Hirtius' life:[48] does that too seem a trifle to you? It was enough to be well thought of by the Roman People, as he is, a delight to his friends (no man is more so), loved by his family, who love him very dearly; but the anxiety among honest folk, the alarm—do we remember the like of it in any other such case? Assuredly not. **38** Well then, in Heaven's name, do you not understand what it means? People who set so high a value on the lives of those whom they expect to act for the good of the Commonwealth—do you suppose that they entertain no thoughts about *your* lives?[49]

Members of the Senate, I am well rewarded for my return. Whatever chance may now befall, my words will stand as a witness to my steadfast purpose; and you have given me a courteous and attentive hearing. If I have the opportunity to address you again from time to time without danger to you or myself, I shall take advantage of it. If not, to the best of my ability I shall preserve my life, not so much for myself as for the Commonwealth. For myself, I have lived pretty well long enough, whether in years or in glory.[50] If more is to come, it will come not so much for me as for you and for the Commonwealth.

---

47. I.e. after the first performance.
48. Hirtius had been seriously ill and was still in poor health.
49. A threat expressed with deliberate ambiguity; see SB[2].
50. Almost the same words are attributed to Caesar in *Marc.* 25; see SB[1].

# II

## INTRODUCTION

After Cicero's launching of the First Philippic Antony retired to his villa at Tibur (formerly the property of Pompey's father-in-law Metellus Scipio) to prepare his reply. Delivered at a meeting of the Senate on 19 September 44, this was a violent attack on Cicero's whole career. On 9 October Antony left for Brundisium to take command of the four Caesarian legions recently arrived from Macedonia. Cicero had remained in or near Rome but left again for Campania later in the month. On 25 October his rejoinder to Antony, the Second Philippic, was sent to Atticus (*Att.* 15.13.1): "to be kept back and put out at your discretion. But when shall we see the day when you will think it proper to publish it?" On 5 November Cicero replied to certain amendments suggested by Atticus (*Att.* 16.11.1). That is the last we hear, but after Antony's departure for Cisalpine Gaul at the end of November there would be no reason for further delay.

The speech therefore is a pamphlet in oratorical form supposed to have been delivered in Antony's presence on 19 September. Juvenal singles it out in his Tenth Satire as Cicero's masterpiece (*divina Philippica*). But the point he was making, that eloquence cost Cicero his life, imposed the selection, since this is not only much the longest of the series but is par excellence a political and personal attack on Antony. Some readers may rather agree with Kingsley Amis's schoolmaster: "For a man so long and so thoroughly dead it was remarkable how much boredom, and also how precise an image of nasty silliness Cicero could generate." But the piece should be read at a stretch; otherwise the cumulative impact is lost, leaving only intemperance and pettiness.

**1** Quonam meo fato, patres conscripti, fieri dicam ut nemo his annis viginti rei publicae fuerit hostis qui non bellum eodem tempore mihi quoque indixerit? nec vero necesse est quemquam a me nominari: vobiscum ipsi recordamini. mihi poenarum illi plus quam optarem dederunt: te miror, Antoni, quorum facta imitere, eorum exitus non perhorrescere. atque 5 hoc in aliis minus mirabar. nemo enim illorum inimicus mihi fuit voluntarius, omnes a me rei publicae causa lacessiti. tu ne verbo quidem violatus, ut audacior quam Catilina, furiosior quam Clodius viderere, ultro me maledictis lacessisti, tuamque a me alienationem commendationem tibi ad impios civis fore putavisti. **2** quid ⟨enim⟩ putem? contemptumne 10 me? non video nec in vita nec in gratia nec in rebus gestis nec in hac mea mediocritate ingeni quid despicere possit Antonius. an in senatu facillime de me detrahi posse credidit? qui ordo clarissimis civibus bene gestae rei publicae testimonium multis, mihi uni conservatae dedit. an decertare mecum voluit contentione dicendi? hoc quidem est beneficium. quid 15 enim plenius, quid uberius mihi quam et pro me et contra Antonium dicere? illud profecto est: non existimavit sui similibus probari posse se esse hostem patriae, nisi mihi esset inimicus.

**3** Cui prius quam de ceteris rebus respondeo, de amicitia quam a me violatam esse criminatus est, quod ego gravissimum crimen iudico, 20 pauca dicam. contra rem suam me nescio quando venisse questus est. an ego non venirem contra alienum pro familiari et necessario, non venirem contra gratiam non virtutis spe, sed aetatis flore collectam, non venirem contra iniuriam quam iste intercessoris iniquissimi beneficio obtinuit, non iure praetorio? sed hoc idcirco commemoratum a te puto ut te infimo 25 ordini commendares, ⟨cum omnes te⟩ recordarentur libertini generum et liberos tuos nepotes Q. Fadi, libertini hominis, fuisse.

At enim te in disciplinam meam tradideras—nam ita dixisti—domum meam ventitaras. ne tu, si id fecisses, melius famae, melius pudicitiae

**1** 3 a me quemquam *D*　　5 pertimescere *t, Isid. Orig. 2.9.12, Cassiod. Rhet. Lat. ed. Halm 499.26*　　8 l. catilina *DV*²　　p. clodius *DV*²　　8–9 ultro me maledictis *Faёrnus:* ut romae ma- *V*¹: ultro ma- me *DV*²　　**2** 10 enim³ (*vel* enim aliud) *addidi* (*deest etiam ap. Quint. 11.1.25*)　　16 mihi quam *Campe:* q- m- *codd.*　　17 est *om. V*　　suis *D*　　se *om. V*　　**3** 22 necessario meo *D*　　25–27 sed hoc . . . fuisse *om. D*　　25 ut *Poggius:* uit *V:* uti *Halm*　　26 cum omnes te *Halm: om. V*¹: cum omnes *V*²: cum te o- *ed. Aldina*　　libertini ς: -num *V*

1 Members of the Senate: to what fatality of mine should I ascribe the fact that in these twenty years there was never an enemy of the Commonwealth who did not at the same time declare war on me? There is no need for me to mention any names. Consult your own memories. These persons have paid me penalties greater than I should have desired. It surprises me, Antonius, that you do not dread the fate of those whose actions you imitate. In other cases I was less surprised by this phenomenon, for none of those people became my enemy by choice; they were all challenged by me for the Commonwealth's sake. Whereas you, against whom I never said a word, have assailed me with unprovoked abuse, as though you wished to look more reckless than Catiline and madder than Clodius, reckoning that your alienation from me would recommend you to disloyal citizens. 2 What else am I to think? That I am held in contempt? I really fail to see anything in my life, my connections, my public record, or such modest talent as I possess, for Antonius to despise. Perhaps he thought that the Senate was the place where I could most easily be disparaged. Well, this House has given many famous Romans its testimonials of good service to the Commonwealth rendered in positions of responsibility: only I have received one for saving it. Perhaps he wished to meet me in an oratorical duel. That is kind of him. Could I find any richer or more rewarding theme than in defending myself and attacking Antonius? No, it must be as I said: he did not think people like himself would accept him as an enemy of his country unless he were an enemy of mine.

3 Before I reply on other matters, let me say a few words about the friendship which he says I violated—a charge which I take extremely seriously. He complained that at some time or other I appeared against his interests in a civil case. Of course I did. I appeared against a stranger on behalf of a friend and connection,[1] in opposition to influence gathered not by the promise of manly excellence but by youthful good looks, in opposition to an unfair advantage which he had gained by favor of a grossly biased veto, not by due process of law. But I imagine you brought up this incident to recommend yourself to the groundlings, in reminding them all that you were a freedman's son-in-law and that your children were the grandchildren of a freedman, Quintus Fadius.[2]

You say that you had put yourself under my direction (your words), had been a frequent visitor in my house. If indeed you had done so, it would have been

---

1. The friend's name was Sicca (*Att.* 16.11.1), often mentioned in Cicero's letters, but nothing is known of the case.

2. "Son-in-law" (*gener*) seems to be a sarcasm, not to be taken literally. The wording here and in 13.23 indicates that Antony was not actually married to Fadia, though he acknowledged paternity of her children. So C. L. Babcock, *AJP* 86 (1965) 13 n. 25.

tuae consuluisses. sed neque fecisti nec, si cuperes, tibi id per C. Curionem facere licuisset.

**4** Auguratus petitionem mihi te concessisse dixisti. o incredibilem audaciam, o impudentiam praedicandam! quo enim tempore me augurem a toto collegio expetitum Cn. Pompeius et Q. Hortensius nominaverunt— 5 nec enim licebat a pluribus nominari—tu nec solvendo eras nec te ullo modo nisi eversa re publica fore incolumem putabas. poteras autem eo tempore auguratum petere cum in Italia Curio non esset, aut tum cum es factus unam tribum sine Curione ferre potuisses? cuius etiam familiares de vi condemnati sunt quod tui nimis studiosi fuissent. 10

**5** At beneficio sum tuo usus. quo? quamquam illud ipsum quod commemoras semper prae me tuli: malui me tibi debere confiteri quam cuiquam minus prudenti non satis gratus videri. sed quo beneficio? quod me Brundisi non occideris? quem ipse victor, qui tibi, ut tute gloriari solebas, detulerat ex latronibus suis principatum, salvum esse voluisset, in Italiam 15 ire iussisset, eum tu occideres? fac potuisse. quod est aliud, patres conscripti, beneficium latronum nisi ut commemorare possint eis se dedisse vitam quibus non ademerint? quod si esset beneficium, numquam ei qui illum interfecerunt a quo erant conservati, quos tu ipse clarissimos viros soles appellare, tantam essent gloriam consecuti. quale autem beneficium 20 est quod te abstinueris nefario scelere? qua in re non tam iucundum mihi videri debuit non interfectum ⟨me⟩ a te quam miserum te id impune facere potuisse.

**6** Sed sit beneficium, quando quidem maius accipi a latrone nullum potuit: in quo potes me dicere ingratum? an de interitu rei publicae queri 25 non debui, ne in te ingratus viderer? at in illa querela misera quidem et luctuosa, sed mihi pro hoc gradu in quo me senatus populusque Romanus collocavit necessaria, quid est dictum a me cum contumelia, quid non moderate, quid non amice? quod quidem cuius temperantiae fuit, de M. Antonio querentem abstinere maledicto, praesertim cum tu reliquias 30

1 C. *om. V*    **4** 6 nec (*pr.*)] neque *D*    nec solvendo eras] nec s- era aderas *b*: nec solus deeras *nv*: nec solus eras *s*: nec eras *t*    7 p(ublica) *om. V*[1]    incolumem fore *cv*    8 italiae *V*: -ia *C. Halm*    **5** 11 usus tuo *D*    13 quod] quo *b*[1]*nstv*[1]    14 occiderit *V*[1]    16 tu] ut *V*    18 ii (*vel* hi) *D*: *om. V*    19 conseruati ⟨: -tio *V*: seruati *D*    20 appellare soles *D*    21–22 uideri mihi *D*    me *add. Madvig*    quam *om. V*    id te *D*    **6** 26 at in] an in (in *om. t*) *D*    30 maledicti *V*[1] (-tu *V*[2]): -tis *Faërnus*

the better for your reputation and your morals. But you did not; and even if you had so wished, Gaius Curio would not have let you.[3]

**4** You have asserted that you left me a free field as candidate for the augurate.[4] Scandalous impudence! How dare you? When Gnaeus Pompeius and Quintus Hortensius put my name forward at the instance of the entire College, no more than two nominators being permitted, you were a bankrupt who saw your only salvation in the overthrow of the Commonwealth. Besides, you could not stand for the augurate with Curio out of Italy, and when you were elected you would not have carried a single tribe without Curio. Friends of his were actually convicted of violence because of their excessive zeal on your behalf.

**5** You say I took a kindness from you. What kindness? To be sure, what you are talking about is something which I have always been the first to acknowledge. I have preferred to confess myself in your debt rather than let some foolish person think me wanting in gratitude. But what was the kindness? That you did not kill me at Brundisium? Were you to kill one whom the conqueror himself, who, as you used to boast, had made you chief of his robber band, had wished to spare and ordered to return to Italy?[5] Suppose you had the power. That is the sort of kindness one gets from bandits, Members of the Senate: they can say they granted their lives to those whose lives they did not take. If that was a kindness, those who killed the man who had spared them, whom you yourself often call "illustrious gentlemen," would never have won so much glory. But where is the kindness in abstaining from an atrocious crime? How was I to feel? Not, surely, so much pleased at not having been killed by you as indignant that you should have had the power to do it with impunity.

**6** But grant it was a kindness, since none greater could be accepted from a bandit: where can you say I have been ungrateful? Should I have refrained from protesting at the destruction of the Commonwealth for fear of seeming ungrateful to you? And yet, in making that protest, a melancholy, mournful business but one to which I was constrained by the rank in which the Senate and People of Rome have placed me, did I say an offensive word, was not my tone throughout moderate and friendly? That required a good deal of self-restraint—to complain of Marcus Antonius while refraining from personal-

---

3. This does not imply hostility to Cicero on Curio's part; it "is merely a hit at Antony's subservience to a possessive lover" (SB[2]).

4. Cicero was elected in 53, as generally supposed (but see SB[2], 219). Antony was elected through Caesar's influence in 50.

5. After Pharsalia. Cicero's letters confirm this statement and show that his life was never in the slightest danger. But it suited him to exaggerate the risks he had run in the republican cause.

rei publicae dissipavisses, cum domi tuae turpissimo mercatu omnia essent venalia, cum leges eas quae numquam promulgatae essent et de te et a te latas confiterere, cum auspicia augur, intercessionem consul sustulisses, cum esses foedissime stipatus armatis, cum omnis impuritates pudica in domo cotidie susciperes vino lustrisque confectus. 7 at ego, tamquam mihi cum M. Crasso contentio esset, quocum multae et magnae fuerunt, non cum uno gladiatore nequissimo, de re publica graviter querens de homine nihil dixi. itaque hodie perficiam ut intellegat quantum a me beneficium tum acceperit.

At etiam litteras, quas me sibi misisse diceret, recitavit homo et humanitatis expers et vitae communis ignarus. quis enim umquam, qui paulum modo bonorum consuetudinem nosset, litteras ad se ab amico missas offensione aliqua interposita in medium protulit palamque recitavit? quid est aliud tollere ex vita vitae societatem, tollere amicorum colloquia absentium? quam multa ioca solent esse in epistulis quae, prolata si sint, inepta videantur, quam multa seria neque tamen ullo modo divulganda! 8 sit hoc inhumanitatis: stultitiam incredibilem videte. quid habes quod mihi opponas, homo diserte, ut Mustelae tamen Seio et Tironi Numisio videris—qui cum hoc ipso tempore stent cum gladiis in conspectu senatus, ego quoque te disertum putabo, si ostenderis quo modo sis eos inter sicarios defensurus—sed quid opponas tandem, si negem me umquam ad te istas litteras misisse? quo me teste convincas? an chirographo, in quo habes scientiam quaestuosam? qui possis? sunt enim librari manu. iam invideo magistro tuo, qui te tanta mercede quantam iam proferam nihil sapere doceat. 9 quid enim est minus non dico oratoris, sed hominis quam id obicere adversario quod ille si verbo negarit longius progredi non

5 pudica] imp- $V^1$, *Nonius 333 (v. Fe.)*    **7** 6 quamquam *t*: tam *V*    et] etiam *V*    **8** intellegas *V*    11–12 paulum modo] paulo *V*    14 ex *Halm*: et *V*: e *D*    15 ioca *n*, *Servius ad Aen. 1.806*: loca *Vbcstv*    esse *om. V*    **8** 17 inhumanitatis tuae *D*    18 ut mustelae tamen seio (tamen scio *nsv*: tam inscio *c*)] mus et laetam esse *V*    et Tironi Numisio *om. V*    19 ipso] ipsum o *V in ras.*: isto *cnstv*    20 te quoque *V*    22 conuinces *bcnst*    23 libera *D*    25 docuit *D*

ities! And that too after you had scattered the last remnants of the Common-wealth to the winds, when everything was up for sale at your house in a shameful market, when you were acknowledging laws which had never been promulgated as passed concerning yourself[6] and by yourself, when as augur you had abolished the auspices and as consul the right of veto, when you were surrounded by your abominable armed bodyguard, when every day you were wallowing in every kind of vice in a virtuous house,[7] exhausted by drink and debauchery? **7** And yet: as though I were in a controversy with Marcus Crassus, with whom I had many notable affrays, and not with a worthless gladiator, I complained in grave terms on public grounds but said nothing about the man. Very well, today I shall make him realize just how considerable a kindness he had from *me* on that occasion.

Then there is the letter he said I wrote him.[8] In his hopeless ignorance of civilized conduct and the usages of society, he read it aloud. Has anyone possessing the least acquaintance with the behavior of gentlemen ever produced a letter written to him by a friend with whom he had subsequently had a difference and read it aloud in public? That amounts to robbing life of its social foundations, abolishing intercourse between absent friends. How many jokes find their way into letters which would seem silly if produced in public, along with much that is serious but on no account to be divulged! **8** So much for ill-breeding. But look at the crass stupidity of the thing. What would you have to say to me in reply, clever orator that you are or at least appear to be in the eyes of Mustela Seius and Tiro Numisius—why, there they are, standing sword in hand in full view of the Senate! I too shall call you a clever speaker if you will show me how you intend to defend them in the appropriate court of law[9]—but I ask you, how would you reply if I were to deny ever having sent you that letter? Where is your witness to contradict me? Would you prove it by the handwriting? You have a lucrative knowledge of that subject,[10] but how could you when the letter is in the hand of a secretary? I really envy that coach of yours;[11] I shall shortly be revealing how much you pay him to teach you to be a fool. **9** To charge an opponent with something the bringer of the charge cannot follow up if his opponent simply denies it—that is not the act of a rational

6. It was illegal to propose a law conferring any office or function on the proposer or his family or colleagues (*Leg. agr.* 2.21).

7. The house that had formerly been Pompey's; cf. 2.69.

8. In reply to Antony's request for Cicero's permission to recall Sex. Cloelius from exile (cf. 1.3). Both letters are extant (*Att.* 14.13A, 14.13B). Cicero's is fulsome.

9. The *queastio inter sicarios* dealt with charges of murder and carrying weapons in public.

10. Allusion to the forging of Caesarian memoranda.

11. The Sicilian rhetorician Sex. Clodius.

possit qui obiecerit? at ego non nego, teque in isto ipso convinco non inhumanitatis solum sed etiam amentiae. quod enim verbum in istis litteris est non plenum humanitatis, offici, benevolentiae? omne autem crimen tuum est quod de te in his litteris non male existimem, quod scribam tamquam ad civem, tamquam ad bonum virum, non tamquam ad     5
sceleratum et latronem. at ego tuas litteras, etsi iure poteram a te lacessitus, tamen non proferam: quibus petis ut tibi per me liceat quendam de exsilio reducere, adiurasque id te invito me non esse facturum; idque a me impetras⟨ti⟩. quid enim me interponerem audaciae tuae, quam neque auctoritas huius ordinis neque existimatio populi Romani neque leges ul-     10
lae possent coercere? **10** verum tamen quid erat quod me rogares, si erat is de quo rogabas Caesaris lege reductus? sed videlicet meam gratiam voluit esse, in quo ne ipsius quidem ulla esse poterat lege lata.

Sed cum mihi, patres conscripti, et pro me aliquid et in M. Antonium multa dicenda sint, alterum peto a vobis ut me pro me dicentem benigne,     15
alterum ipse efficiam ut, contra illum cum dicam, attente audiatis. simul illud oro: si meam cum in omni vita tum in dicendo moderationem modestiamque cognostis, ne me hodie, cum isti, ut provocavit, respondero, oblitum esse putetis mei. non tractabo ut consulem: ne ille quidem me ut consularem. etsi ille nullo modo consul, vel quod ita vivit vel quod ita     20
rem publicam gerit vel quod ita factus est, ego sine ulla controversia consularis.

**11** Ut igitur intellegeretis qualem ipse se consulem profiteretur, obiecit mihi consulatum meum. qui consulatus verbo meus, patres conscripti, re vester fuit. quid enim ego constitui, quid gessi, quid egi nisi ex huius     25
ordinis consilio, auctoritate, sententia? haec tu homo sapiens, non solum eloquens, apud eos quorum consilio sapientiaque gesta sunt ausus es vituperare? quis autem meum consulatum praeter te et P. Clodium qui vituperaret inventus est? cuius quidem tibi fatum, sicuti C. Curioni, manet, quoniam id domi tuae est quod fuit illorum utrique fatale.     30

**12** Non placet M. Antonio consulatus meus. At placuit P. Servilio, ut eum primum nominem ex illius temporis consularibus qui proxime est mortuus; placuit Q. Catulo, cuius semper in hac re publica vivet auctoritas; placuit duobus Lucullis, M. Crasso, Q. Hortensio, C. Curioni,

---

**9** 2–3 solum . . . humanitatis *om. D*     5 scribebam *V*     9 impetrasti *Bake*: -ras *codd.*     quam] quem *bcnst*     **10** 12 lege Caesaris reductus *Watt*: *fort.* l- r- C-     18 respondero] -deo *t*: -debo *bcnsv*     20 est consul *D*     **11** 23 se *om. sv*     consulem] -sul *cn¹stv*: -em se *n²*     26 sententiae *V, unde* -tia? *et coni. C. F. W. Müller*     28 te et P. Clodium *Muretus*: te p. aut clod. *V*: p. clod. *D*: te Publiumque Cl- *P. R. Müller*: te ac P. Cl- *Schöll*     29 sicut *bcstv*     curioni *V¹* (c. *add. V²*): c. curionem (centur- *v*) *D*     30 domi *st, Arusian. 7:491 Keil*: domui *c*: domu *n*: domus *Vbv*     **12** 32 primo *D*     33 placuit Q. *ς*: -it quae *V*: -itque l. (-it p. *v*) *D*     uiuit *D*

human being, to say nothing of an orator. But I am not denying it. On this very point I prove you not only a cad but an imbecile. There is not a word in that letter which does not breathe courtesy, helpfulness, goodwill. All you can say against it is that in this letter I don't think badly of you, I write as though I were writing to a fellow citizen and a gentleman, not to a criminal and a brigand. On my side I shall not produce *your* letter, though after such provocation I have the right to do so. In it you ask my permission to bring a certain person back from exile and swear that you will not do so against my will. I gave it. Why should I stand in the way of your audacity, which neither the authority of this House nor public opinion nor any laws could check? **10** And yet, why ask me, if the man concerned was brought home by a law of Caesar's? I suppose Antonius wanted it to come as a favor from me—whereas if a law had been passed, it could not even count as a favor from himself!

Members of the Senate, I have something to say on my own behalf and a good deal to say against Marcus Antonius. As to the former, I crave your indulgence; of your attention when I denounce *him* I shall myself make sure. And I have another request. I think you give me credit for moderation and modesty as a man and as a speaker: do not suppose that I am forgetting myself today when I give this man the answer he has provoked. I shall not treat him as a consul any more than he has treated me as a consular—though he, after all, is nothing of a consul, neither in his mode of life nor in his official conduct nor in the manner of his election; whereas I without any question am a consular.

**11** Well then, in order to let you see what kind of consul he professes himself to be, he reproached me with *my* consulship. Members of the Senate, that consulship was mine only in name; in reality it was yours. Every decision, every official act, everything I did was done by the advice and authority and vote of this House. And now you, as a man of sense and not merely of eloquence, have dared to abuse these proceedings in front of those whose advice and wisdom determined them! Who was ever heard abusing my consulship except yourself and Publius Clodius, whose fate awaits you, as it awaited Gaius Curio, since you have that in your house which proved fatal to them both?[12]

**12** Marcus Antonius disapproves of my consulship. But Publius Servilius approved of it—I name him first among the consulars of that time because he is the latest to die. So did Quintus Catulus, a name that will ever live respected in this Commonwealth. So likewise the two Luculli, Marcus Crassus, Quintus

12. Clodius and Curio, the two previous husbands of Antony's wife Fulvia, had both died violent deaths.

C. Pisoni, M'. Glabrioni, M'. Lepido, L. Vulcatio, C. Figulo, ⟨placuit⟩
D. Silano, L. Murenae, qui tum erant consules designati; placuit idem
quod consularibus M. Catoni, qui cum multa vita excedens providit, tum
quod te consulem non vidit. maxime vero consulatum meum Cn. Pompeius probavit qui, ut me primum decedens ex Syria vidit, complexus et      5
gratulans meo beneficio patriam se visurum esse dixit. sed quid singulos
commemoro? frequentissimo senatui sic placuit ut esset nemo qui mihi
non ut parenti gratias ageret, qui mihi non vitam suam, fortunas, liberos,
rem publicam referret acceptam.

**13** Sed quoniam illis quos nominavi tot et talibus viris res publica  10
orbata est, veniamus ad vivos, qui duo de consularium numero reliqui
sunt. L. Cotta, vir summo ingenio summaque prudentia, rebus eis gestis
quas tu reprehendis supplicationem decrevit verbis amplissimis, eique illi
ipsi quos modo nominavi consulares senatusque cunctus adsensus est; qui
honos post conditam hanc urbem habitus est togato ante me nemini.  15
**14** L. Caesar, avunculus tuus, qua oratione, qua constantia, qua gravitate
sententiam dixit in sororis suae virum, vitricum tuum! hunc tu cum
auctorem et praeceptorem omnium consiliorum totiusque vitae debuisses
habere, vitrici te similem quam avunculi maluisti. huius ego alienus
consiliis consul usus sum: tu, sororis filius, ecquid ad eum umquam de re  20
publica rettulisti? at ad quos refert, di immortales? ad eos scilicet quorum
nobis etiam dies natales audiendi sunt. **15** "hodie non descendit Antonius." "cur?" "dat nataliciam in hortis." "cui?" neminem nominabo:
putate tum Phormioni alicui, tum Gnathoni, tum etiam Ballioni. o foedi-
tatem hominis flagitiosam, o impudentiam, nequitiam, libidinem non  25
ferendam! tu cum principem senatorem, civem singularem tam pro-
pinquum habeas, ad eum de re publica nihil referas, referas ad eos qui
suam rem nullam habent, tuam exhauriunt?

Tuus videlicet salutaris consulatus, perniciosus meus. Adeone pudorem
cum pudicitia perdidisti ut hoc in eo templo dicere ausus sis in quo ego  30
senatum illum qui quondam florens orbi terrarum praesidebat consu-

---

1 M'. Glabrioni, M'. Lepido *Muretus*: m. gl- m. le- *V*: m. le- m. gl- *D*      *post* Vulcatio
*fort. addendum* L. Torquato[1]      placuit *addidi*      2 D. *om. V*      3 quod] qui *Koch*
5 ut primum (-um me *b*[2]) *b*[1]: ut te p- *n*[1]*sv*: ut p- te *t*      8 non mihi *D*      **13** 11 e (ex *sn*[2]: et
*cn*[1]) consulari *D*      **14** 19 esse maluisti *D*      20 consul usus sum] consultus ussum (sum
*V*[2]) *V*[1]: consul tum u- sum *coni. Halm*      21 p(ublica) *om. V*[1]      at ad *Faërnus*: ad ad *V*[1]:
ad *DV*[2]      **15** 23 natalicia *D*      24 putate tum] -at eum *V*[2]: putato te (*vel* -tote) eum *bcnst*:
-abo eum te *v*      etiam *om. D*      27 refers ad eos refers *D*      28 suam rem] domum
suam *D*

Hortensius, Gaius Curio, Gaius Piso, Manius Glabrio, Manius Lepidus, Lucius Vulcatius, Gaius Figulus.[13] So too the two consuls-elect, Decimus Silanus and Lucius Murena. The consulars' approval was shared by Marcus Cato, who in taking leave of life spared himself many sorry sights but none sorrier than you as consul. Above all, Gnaeus Pompeius approved my consulship. At our first meeting on his return from Syria he embraced me and congratulated me, saying that he owed it to me that he would see Rome again. But I need not mention individuals. A crowded meeting of the Senate approved so heartily that every member present thanked me as a son might thank a father, acknowledging himself indebted to me for life, goods, children, and Commonwealth.

**13** Since, however, all the distinguished personages whom I have named are now lost to the Commonwealth, let me come to the living. Out of the roll of consulars two are still with us. There is the wise and gifted Lucius Cotta. *He* proposed a Thanksgiving in the most flattering terms for the actions which you reprobate, and the entire Senate, including these same consulars whose names I have just rehearsed, agreed to the motion. Never before since the foundation of Rome had that honor been granted to a civilian. **14** There is also Lucius Caesar, your uncle, who made a most eloquent, resolute, and impressive speech against his own brother-in-law, your stepfather.[14] You should have made him your guide and mentor in all decisions, in your whole life; but you chose to resemble your stepfather rather than your uncle. As consul I availed myself of his counsels, though I had no connection with him: you are his sister's son, but have you ever once consulted him on public affairs? Whom then does Antonius consult? We may well ask! Those gentry, I suppose, whose very birthdays have to be brought to our notice. **15** "Antonius is not appearing in public today." "Oh, why is that?" "He is giving a birthday party in his house outside town."[15] "For whom?" Well, gentlemen, I won't name names. One day it will be for some Phormio, let us suppose, another for Gnatho, and another for Ballio even.[16] Foul! Infamous! How to tolerate such shamelessness, worthlessness, licentiousness? You have so close a relative, a leading senator, an outstanding member of the community, and you never consult him; those you do consult have nothing of their own and drain what is yours.

So your consulship is a blessing and mine was a disaster! Your tongue must have become as loose as your life if you dare to say such a thing in the very temple where I used to consult the Senate in its greatest days, when it ruled the

---

13. The list is in official order of seniority, except that on that basis Curio (the elder) should come before the Luculli. On the consulars omitted see SB[1].

14. The Catilinarian conspirator P. Cornelius Lentulus Sura.

15. *Horti*, usually but misleadingly rendered "gardens," means a house and grounds in or near a city but outside the city boundary. Rome had long outgrown its ancient boundary, the *pomerium*.

16. Characters from Plautus and Terence. The first two are parasites, the third a pimp.

lebam, tu homines perditissimos cum gladiis collocavisti? **16** at etiam
ausus es—quid autem est quod tu non audeas?—clivum Capitolinum dicere me consule plenum servorum armatorum fuisse. ut illa, credo,
nefaria senatus consulta fierent, vim adferebam senatui! o miser, sive illa
tibi nota non sunt—nihil enim boni nosti—sive sunt, qui apud talis viros　5
tam impudenter loquare! quis enim eques Romanus, quis praeter te adulescens nobilis, quis ullius ordinis qui se civem esse meminisset, cum senatus in hoc templo esset, in clivo Capitolino non fuit, quis nomen non
dedit? quamquam nec scribae sufficere nec tabulae nomina illorum capere potuerunt. **17** etenim cum homines nefarii de patriae parricidio con-　10
fiterentur, consciorum indiciis, sua manu, voce paene litterarum coacti se
urbem inflammare, civis trucidare, vastare Italiam, delere rem publicam
consensisse, quis esset qui ad salutem communem defendendam non
excitaretur, praesertim cum senatus populusque Romanus haberet ducem,
qualis si qui nunc esset, tibi idem quod illis accidit contigisset?　15

　Ad sepulturam corpus vitrici sui negat a me datum. hoc vero ne P. quidem Clodius dixit umquam: quem, quia iure ei inimicus fui, doleo a te
omnibus vitiis iam esse superatum. **18** qui autem tibi venit in mentem re-
digere in memoriam nostram te domi P. Lentuli esse educatum? an verebare ne non putaremus natura te potuisse tam improbum evadere, nisi　20
accessisset etiam disciplina? tam autem eras excors ut tota in oratione tua
tecum ipse pugnares, non modo non cohaerentia inter se diceres sed
maxime diiuncta atque contraria, ut non tanta mecum quanta tibi tecum
esset contentio. vitricum tuum fuisse in tanto scelere fatebare, poena
adfectum querebare. ita quod proprie meum est laudasti; quod totum est　25
senatus reprehendisti. nam comprehensio sontium mea, animadversio
senatus fuit. homo disertus non intellegit eum quem contra dicit laudari a
se, eos apud quos dicit vituperari.

　**19** Iam illud cuius est, non dico audaciae—cupit enim se audacem—
sed, quod minime vult, stultitiae, qua vincit omnis, clivi Capitolini　30
mentionem facere, cum inter subsellia nostra versentur armati, cum
in hac cella Concordiae, di immortales, in qua me consule salutares
sententiae dictae sunt, quibus ad hanc diem viximus, cum gladiis homines collocati stent! accusa senatum; accusa equestrem ordinem, qui

---

**16** 2 autem] enim *Arusian. 7:458 Keil*　　4 consulta tum (-ltum *v*) *D*　　o miserum
*D*　　7 esse *om. D*　　**17** 11 cum consciorum *V*　　17 fui inimicus *D*　　18 iam] eum
*V*: *del. Halm* (cui quia iure in- fui, doleo . . . eum esse *Stürenburg*)　　**18** 20 te] *num* te
non*?*[3]　　tam] non *Nonius 293*　　21 tua *V Cus.*: *om. D*　　22 non modo *V Cus.*: ut non
m- *D*　　23 diiuncta *A. Klotz*: disiu- *codd. Cus.*　　25 totum est] totum *D*　　**19** 29
audacem dici *D*

world, and where you have posted desperados carrying weapons. **16** You have even dared to say (but what don't you dare?) that when I was consul Capitol Rise[17] was full of armed slaves. I forced the Senate to pass those nefarious decrees under threat of violence, is that it? Miserable wretch, whether you don't know what happened (wholesome knowledge does not come your way) or whether you do! Such shameless talk before such an audience! When the Senate met in this temple, not one Roman knight, not one young nobleman except you, nobody of any class who remembered he was a Roman, but stood on Capitol Rise and volunteered his services. There were not clerks enough or tablets enough to take the names. **17** For wicked men were confessing to treason against the fatherland, forced by the evidence of their accomplices and their own handwriting, writing which almost cried aloud, they admitted their plot to set Rome on fire, slaughter her citizens, lay Italy waste, and destroy the Commonwealth. Who but would be stirred to defend the common weal? Remember, the Senate and People of Rome had a leader then; had they such a leader now, what happened to the plotters would have happened to you.

He says I refused to give up his stepfather's body for burial. Even Publius Clodius never said that, Clodius, who to my regret (for I had good reason to be his enemy) has now been outdone by you in all his vices. **18** How, I wonder, did it occur to you to remind us that you were brought up in Publius Lentulus' house? Were you perhaps afraid that we might fail to believe that you could have turned out such a rogue by mere nature without the assistance of training? But in your witlessness you were fighting yourself all through your speech. Not only did what you say lack coherence, it was downright out of joint and self-contradictory. You were more in conflict with yourself than with me. You admitted that your stepfather was involved in that monstrous crime but complained of his punishment, thus praising what is properly mine and blaming what is entirely the Senate's. For the arrest of the guilty men was my doing, their punishment was the Senate's. Indeed a clever pleader! He does not understand that he is praising his opponent and abusing his audience.

**19** Now look at another point. In his audacity, or rather (since he likes to be thought audacious) his unrivaled stupidity (which is the last thing he wants to hear), he makes mention of Capitol Rise, when armed men are moving among our benches and stand posted sword in hand in this very sanctuary of Concord (I call the Immortal Gods to witness) where salutary measures were proposed when I was consul, measures by which we have lived down to this day. Accuse the Senate by all means, accuse the order of knights, which on that occasion

---

17. Clivus Capitolinus, part of the via Sacra, a road leading from the Forum up to the Capitol, passing the temple of Concord.

tum cum senatu copulatus fuit; accusa omnis ordines, omnis civis, dum
confiteare hunc ordinem hoc ipso tempore ab Ituraeis circumsederi. haec
tu non propter audaciam dicis tam impudenter, sed quia tantam rerum re-
pugnantiam non vide[a]s. nihil profecto sapis. quid est enim dementius
quam, cum rei publicae perniciosa arma ipse ceperis, obicere alteri      5
salutaria?

**20** At etiam quodam loco facetus esse voluisti. quam id te, di boni, non
decebat! in quo est tua culpa non nulla; aliquid enim salis a mima uxore
trahere potuisti. "cedant arma togae." quid? tum nonne cesserunt? at
postea tuis armis cessit toga. quaeramus igitur utrum melius fuerit li-    10
bertati populi Romani sceleratorum arma an libertatem nostram armis
tuis cedere. nec vero tibi de versibus plura respondebo: tantum dicam breviter, te neque illos neque ullas omnino litteras nosse; me nec rei publicae
nec amicis umquam defuisse, et tamen omni genere monumentorum
meorum perfecisse operis subsicivis ut meae vigiliae meaeque litterae et    15
iuventuti utilitatis et nomini Romano laudis aliquid adferrent. sed haec
non huius temporis: maiora videamus.

**21** P. Clodium meo consilio interfectum esse dixisti. quidnam homines
putarent, si tum occisus esset cum tu illum in foro inspectante populo Romano gladio insecutus es negotiumque transegisses, nisi se ille in scalas    20
tabernae librariae coniecisset eisque oppilatis impetum tuum compres-
sisset? quod quidem ego favisse me tibi fateor, suasisse ne tu quidem
dicis. at Miloni ne favere quidem potui; prius enim rem transegit quam
quisquam eum facturum id suspicaretur. at ego suasi. scilicet is animus
erat Milonis ut prodesse rei publicae sine suasore non posset. at laetatus    25
sum. quid ergo? in tanta laetitia cunctae civitatis me unum tristem esse
opportebat? **22** quamquam de morte Clodi fuit quaestio, non satis pru-
denter illa quidem constituta—quid enim attinebat nova lege quaeri de
eo qui hominem occidisset, cum esset legibus quaestio constituta?—

3 quia] qui *nstv*   4 vides *Ernesti*: -eas *codd.*   *anne* sed, qui . . . videas, nihil (*alii
alia: v. Fe.*)?   5 ipse *post* cum *D*   **20** 7 te *V, Arusian. 7:465 Keil*: *om. D*   8 non
*om. cnstv*   12 plura] tuis *t*: *om. bcnsv*   13 te *ante* omnino *nsv*: *om. bct*   14 et] at
*c*: ut *stv*   15 perfecissem subsiciuis *t*: operis sub- *om. V*   17 ad maiora ueniamus
*D*   **21** 19 inspectante *bct, schol. Bob. ad Mil. 40*: sp- *Vnsv* (*v. Fe.*)   20 gladio *V,
schol.*: gl- stricto *D*   20–21 se *ante* coniecisset *schol.*: *om. nsv*   22 quod quidem]
sed quid *bcst*: sed *nv*   23 potui suadere *V¹*   24 facturum id suspicaretur *V*: susp- eum
(*del. n²*) facturum esse *bn¹sv*: sciscitaretur rem (*om. c*) f- e- *ct*   **22** 27 p. clodii *D*

was united with the Senate, accuse all classes, all citizens—so long as you confess that this House at this very moment is surrounded by Ituraeans![18] It is not audacity that makes you say these shameless things, but your failure to perceive glaring inconsistencies. Obviously you are a fool, for nothing could be more senseless than to reproach another man for using armed force in the public interest when you have resorted to it yourself to the public injury.

**20** At one point you even tried to be funny, and, Heavens, what a poor hand you made of it! That is partly your own fault—you might have picked up a little humor from your comedy-star spouse.[19] "Let arms yield to the gown."[20] Well, and didn't they at that time? Later on, it is true, the gown yielded to *your* arms. So let us ask a question, which was better: that the arms of criminals yield to the freedom of the Roman People or that our freedom yield to your arms? But I will not make you any further answer about the verses. I merely remark that you know nothing about them or about any kind of literature. I, on the other hand, while never failing in my obligations to the Commonwealth and to my friends, have employed my spare hours in producing works in a variety of genres that will preserve my name, in order that what I have written in the watches of the night may be of some profit to my juniors and bring some credit to the Roman name. But this is no time to speak of such things; let us move to greater matters.

**21** You say that I instigated the killing of Publius Clodius. Now what would people have thought if he had lost his life on the memorable occasion[21] when you chased him with a sword in the Forum before the eyes of the public and would have finished the job if he had not flung himself under the stairs[22] of a bookshop and barricaded them, thus stopping your rush? I admit that my sympathies were on your side on that occasion, but even you don't say that I put you up to it. On the other hand, I could not even go that far in Milo's case, since he finished the business before anybody suspected that he was going to set about it. You say I put him up to it—as though Milo lacked spirit to do the Commonwealth a service unless somebody egged him on! Ah, but I rejoiced. Of course. Was mine to be the only gloomy face when the whole community was making merry? **22** Remember, however, that there was an inquiry into Clodius' death—not very wisely constituted, it is true; what was the point of a new law to try a homicide when a legally constituted court already existed for

18. Archers from Transjordan.

19. Antony's mistress, Volumnia Cytheris, an actress in mime.

20. Part of a line from Cicero's poem on his consulship. It was seized upon by his detractors (*Off.* 1.77).

21. Probably in 52; cf. 2.49.

22. A favorite hiding place; see *Mil.* 40 and Denniston's note on this passage.

quaesitum est tamen: quod igitur, cum res agebatur, nemo in me dixit, id tot annis post tu es inventus qui diceres.

**23** Quod vero dicere ausus es idque multis verbis, opera mea Pompeium a Caesaris amicitia esse diiunctum ob eamque causam culpa mea bellum civile esse natum, in eo non tu quidem tota re sed, quod maximum est,   5 temporibus errasti. ego M. Bibulo, praestantissimo cive, consule nihil praetermisi, quantum facere enitique potui, quin Pompeium a Caesaris coniunctione avocarem. in quo Caesar felicior fuit; ipse enim Pompeium a mea familiaritate diiunxit. postea vero quam se totum Pompeius Caesari tradidit, quid ego illum ab eo distrahere conarer? stulti erat sperare,  10 suadere impudentis. **24** duo tamen tempora inciderunt quibus aliquid contra Caesarem Pompeio suaserim; ea velim reprehendas, si potes: unum ne quinquenni imperium Caesari prorogaret, alterum ne pateretur ferri ut absentis eius ratio haberetur. quorum si utrumvis persuasissem, in has miserias numquam incidissemus. atque idem ego, cum iam opes  15 omnis et suas et populi Romani Pompeius ad Caesarem detulisset, sero-que ea sentire coepisset quae ego multo ante provideram, inferrique patriae bellum viderem nefarium, pacis, concordiae, compositionis auctor esse non destiti, meaque illa vox est nota multis: "utinam, Cn. Pompei, cum C. Caesare societatem aut numquam coisses aut numquam diremis-  20 ses! fuit alterum gravitatis, alterum prudentiae tuae." haec mea, M. Antoni, semper et de Pompeio et de re publica consilia fuerunt; quae si va-luissent, res publica staret, tu tuis flagitiis, egestate, infamia concidisses.

**25** Sed haec vetera, illud vero recens, Caesarem meo consilio interfec-tum. iam vereor, patres conscripti, ne, quod turpissimum est, praevarica-  25 torem mihi apposuisse videar, qui me non solum meis laudibus ornaret sed etiam oneraret alienis. quis enim meum in ista societate gloriosissimi facti nomen audivit? cuius autem qui in eo numero fuisset nomen est occultatum? occultatum dico? cuius non statim divulgatum? citius dixerim

1 id] at *n¹t*: et *s*: ut *v*      **23** 4 disiunctum *D*      6 ciue (*cf.* 13.2, 14.6)] ciui *cnsv*: cui *t*      7 innitique *nstv¹*: nit- *b*      8 fuit felicior *cnstv*      9 disiunxit *D*      **24** 14 fieri *D*      15–16 omnes opes *D*      17 ego *om. bt*      18 nefarium uiderem *D*      19 non] *om. cns¹tv*      19–20 Cn. *et* C. *D, Prisc. 2:395, 407 Keil: om. V*      21 gravitatis alterum *om. V¹*      **25** 27 oneraret *om. V*      27–28 in istius conscientia (-scia *b*) gloriosissimi facti *bc*: in istius facti c- gloriosissimi (-ma *s*) *nsv*: in i- facti c- gl- facti *t*

that purpose?[23] Be that as it may, there was an inquiry. So do you turn up all these years afterwards to make an accusation against me which nobody made during the actual proceedings?[24]

**23** You further dared to say at no small length that detaching Pompeius from Caesar's friendship was my work and that therefore I am originally to blame for the Civil War. In this you were not entirely wrong, but you were wrong about the timing, which is all-important. In the consulship of that outstanding citizen Marcus Bibulus I did everything I could, no effort spared, to wean Pompeius from his alliance with Caesar. But Caesar had the better luck: he detached Pompeius from his intimacy with *me*. But after Pompeius had put himself entirely in Caesar's hands, why should I try to draw him away? It would have been folly to hope for that, impertinence to advise it. **24** However, there were two occasions when I advised Pompeius against Caesar's interests, and you may blame me if you can: one when I advised him not to prorogue Caesar's five-year command, the other when I cautioned him against letting through the proposal that Caesar should be permitted to stand for office in absentia.[25] If he had listened to me on either point, we should never have fallen on these evil times. But after Pompeius had already put all his own resources and those of the Roman People at Caesar's disposal and begun too late to feel the truth of what I had long ago foreseen, when I saw that a wicked war was threatening the fatherland, I never ceased advocating peace, concord, composition. There is a widely known saying of mine: "Gnaeus Pompeius, I would that either you had never gone into partnership with Gaius Caesar or that you had never dissolved it. The first course would have befitted you as a man of principle, the second as a man of prudence." Such, Marcus Antonius, was the advice I gave over the years concerning Pompeius and concerning the Commonwealth. Had it prevailed, the Commonwealth would still stand and you would have been brought low by your scandalous behavior, your penury and infamy.

**25** All this is ancient history. Here is something recent: he says I instigated Caesar's killing. Members of the Senate, I am really afraid you may fancy I have committed the disgraceful offense of putting up a sham prosecutor against myself, somebody to load me with credit belonging to other people as well as rendering what is rightfully mine. Who ever heard my name among the company which carried out that glorious deed? And of those who did belong to it, whose name has been suppressed, or rather whose was not broadcast immediately? I would sooner say that some who were not in the secret talked at

23. A special court to try Milo for Clodius' murder was set up under a law proposed by Pompey.
24. In fact the charge *was* made; see *Mil.* 47.
25. Cicero probably gave no such advice; see Denniston.

iactasse se aliquos ut fuisse in ea societate viderentur, cum conscii non fuissent, quam ut quisquam celari vellet qui fuisset. **26** quam veri simile porro est in tot hominibus partim obscuris, partim adulescentibus, ne-minem occultantibus meum nomen latere potuisse? etenim si auctores ad liberandam patriam desiderarentur illis a[u]ctoribus, Brutos ego impel- 5 lerem, quorum uterque L. Bruti imaginem cotidie videret, alter etiam Ahalae? hi igitur his maioribus ab alienis potius consilium peterent quam a suis et foris potius quam domo? quid C. Cassius? in ea familia natus quae non modo dominatum sed ne potentiam quidem cuiusquam ferre potuit me auctorem, credo, desideravit! qui etiam sine his clarissimis 10 viris hanc rem in Cilicia ad ostium fluminis Cydni confecisset, si ille ad eam ripam quam constituerat, non ad contrariam navis appulisset. **27** Cn. Domitium non patris interitus, clarissimi viri, non avunculi mors, non spoliatio dignitatis ad recuperandam libertatem, sed mea auctoritas excitavit? an C. Trebonio ego persuasi? cui ne suadere quidem ausus 15 essem. quo etiam maiorem ei res publica gratiam debet, qui libertatem populi Romani unius amicitiae praeposuit depulsorque dominatus quam particeps esse maluit. an L. Tillius Cimber me est auctorem secutus? quem ego magis fecisse illam rem sum admiratus quam facturum putavi, admiratus autem ob eam causam quod immemor beneficiorum, memor 20 patriae fuisset. quid duo Servilii—Cascas dicam an Ahalas? et hos auctoritate mea censes excitatos potius quam caritate rei publicae? longum est persequi ceteros, idque rei publicae praeclarum, fuisse tam multos, ipsis gloriosum.

**28** At quem ad modum me coarguerit homo acutus recordamini. "Cae- 25 sare interfecto" inquit "statim cruentum alte extollens Brutus pugionem Ciceronem nominatim exclamavit atque ei recuperatam libertatem est gratulatus." cur mihi potissimum? qui⟨a⟩ sciebam? vide ne illa causa fuerit appellandi mei quod, cum rem gessisset consimilem rebus eis quas

1 ea] ista *D*    socii cum conscii *b*: s- cum s- *ct*: s- *n¹v*: cum s- *s*: qui s- *n²*    2 celare *D*    fuisset *om. D*    **26** 3–4 neminem occultantibus *del. Koch*    5 actoribus *Madvig*: auc- *codd.*    7 hi igitur his] his ig- *D*    7 ab] orti ab *D*    8 quid? C. Cassius *dist. vulgo*    C. *om.* V¹*nstv*    10 quid V¹    **27** 14 recuperandam (*cf. ad* 4.7 *fin.*)] liberandam ad recipiendam *cn¹stv*: lib- patriam ad recip- *bn²*    15–16 an C. . . . debet *ante* Cn. Domitium (*l.* 13) V    15 ego *om. D*    16 quo] quae V: quare *Halm*    18 L. Tillius *Barbadorius*: l. t. V: l. tullius *D*    cimber me] -brem V    20 sum autem (a- sum *t*) ob *D*    21 duo Servilii²·³ *scripsi*: duos seruilios *Vbc*: d- s- nomina propria (-ne -io *n²*) *n¹stv*    cascam . . . ahalam V    23 tam] tamen *btv*: tum *ns*    23–24 multo ipsis gloriosius est *D*    **28** 26 m. brutus *D, fort. recte* (*vide* 2.30 *init.*)    28 quia *Graevius*: qui *codd.*: quod *Ferrarius*    29 mei] me (a me *c*) *D*

large so as to suggest that they belonged to that association than that any man who did belong would wish to be concealed. **26** Is it likely that my name could have remained hidden among so many, some of them persons unknown to fame, others quite young, persons who concealed nobody? And if those who acted for the liberation of the fatherland needed urging, is it likely that I should instigate the two Bruti, both of whom saw Lucius Brutus' portrait every day, and one of them Ahala's?[26] Sprung from such ancestors, would they seek inspiration from outsiders rather than from their own blood, abroad rather than at home? What of Gaius Cassius? Born in a family which could brook no man's prepotency, to say nothing of despotism,[27] did he need me to prompt him? Even without his illustrious companions he would have taken care of this business in Cilicia at the mouth of the river Cydnus, if Caesar had moored his ships to the bank originally determined instead of the one opposite.[28] **27** Was Gnaeus Domitius[29] spurred to recover freedom by my influence and not by the slaying of his illustrious father, the death of his uncle, the deprivation of his status? Or did I persuade Gaius Trebonius? I should not have ventured even to offer him advice. The Commonwealth owes him gratitude all the greater for placing the freedom of the Roman People above the friendship of an individual and choosing to be an overthrower of despotism rather than a partner in it. Or did Lucius Tillius Cimber follow me as his prompter? I rather admired him for doing that deed than expected it of him—admired because he forgot favors and remembered his country. And then the two Servilii—Cascas shall I call them, or Ahalas? Do you suppose they too were spurred by advice from me rather than by patriotism? It would take me too long to go through the rest of the list; happy for the Commonwealth that there were so many, and glorious for themselves!

**28** However, be good enough to remember how the clever fellow proved his point against me. "The moment Caesar was killed," says he, "Brutus raised his bloodstained dagger high, called on Cicero by name, and congratulated him on the recovery of freedom." Now why me in particular? Because I knew? May I suggest that the reason he called my name was just this: after an achievement

26. M. Brutus was descended through his mother from C. Servilius Ahala, who killed a supposed aspirant to despotism, Sp. Maelius, in 439.

27. According to one tradition Sp. Cassius Vicellinus was put to death by his father in 485 for the same reason. In *Rep.* 2.60, however, Cicero only says that Vicellinus' father bore witness against him at his trial. Here he will rather be thinking of L. Cassius Longinus Ravilla, consul in 127, a strong-minded, not to say crusty, personage, famous for his severity as a judge.

28. This is the only authority for an attempt by Cassius to assassinate Caesar in 47, but Cicero may have had it from Cassius himself.

29. Son of L. Domitius Ahenobarbus, who was killed at Pharsalia, and nephew of Cato.

ipse gesseram, me potissimum testatus est se aemulum mearum laudum exstitisse.

**29** Tu autem, omnium stultissime, non intellegis, si, id quod me arguis, voluisse interfici Caesarem crimen sit, etiam laetatum esse morte Caesaris crimen esse? quid enim interest inter suasorem facti et probatorem? aut quid refert utrum voluerim fieri an gaudeam factum? ecquis est igitur exceptis eis qui illum regnare gaudebant qui illud aut fieri noluerit aut factum improbarit? omnes ergo in culpa. etenim omnes boni, quantum in ipsis fuit, Caesarem occiderunt: aliis consilium, aliis animus, aliis occasio defuit; voluntas nemini.

**30** Sed stuporem hominis vel dicam pecudis attendite. sic enim dixit: "M. Brutus, quem ego honoris causa nomino, cruentum pugionem tenens Ciceronem exclamavit: ex quo intellegi debet eum conscium fuisse." ergo ego sceleratus appellor a te quem tu suspicatum aliquid suspicaris; ille qui stillantem prae se pugionem tulit, is a te honoris causa nominatur. esto; sit in verbis tuis hic stupor: quanto in rebus sententiisque maior! constitue hoc, consul, aliquando, Brutorum, C. Cassi, Cn. Domiti, C. Treboni, reliquorum quam velis esse causam; edormi crapulam, inquam, et exhala. an faces admovendae sunt quae excitent tantae causae indormientem? numquamne intelleges statuendum tibi esse utrum illi qui istam rem gesserunt homicidaene sint an vindices libertatis? **31** attende enim paulisper cogitationemque sobrii hominis punctum temporis suscipe. ego, qui sum illorum, ut ipse fateor, familiaris, ut a te arguor, socius, nego quicquam esse medium: confiteor eos, nisi liberatores populi Romani conservatoresque rei publicae sint, plus quam sicarios, plus quam homicidas, plus etiam quam parricidas esse, si quidem est atrocius patriae parentem quam suum occidere. tu, homo sapiens et considerate, quid dicis? si parricidas, cur honoris causa a te sunt et in hoc ordine et apud populum Romanum semper appellati? cur M. Brutus referente te legibus est solutus, si ab urbe plus quam decem dies afuisset? cur ludi Apollinares incredibili M. Bruti honore celebrati? cur provinciae Bruto, Cassio datae, cur quaestores additi, cur legatorum numerus auctus? atqui

1 laudium *V*    **29** 3 illud non *Cus.*    7 te excepto is (et ii *b*, et iis *Gruter*) qui *D*    gaudebat *D*    8 improbauit *V*    ergo] enim *D*    **30** 12 M. om. *V*    14–15 ille *vel* is *del. voluit Gruter*    15 a te honoris] antenoris *V*: abs te hon- *coni. Halm*    19 quae te *DV²*    21 homicidaene] -dae rei *nsv*: -dae *Vbt*    **31** enim *om. Cus.* (*v. Fe.*)    22 punctum] -to *bcns*: per punctum *Cus.* (*v. Fe.*)    23 ut a] aut ut a *bct*    26 parricidae *D*    29 semper appellati cur *om. V*    te referente *D*    31–32 bruto casso (*corr.* ς) *V*: cassio et br- *D*    32 atqui *Jahn*: -ue *codd.*

similar to my own he called on me rather than another to witness that he was now my rival in glory.

**29** You utter fool! Don't you see that if it were a crime to have wished Caesar killed, which is the charge he brings against me, it would also be a crime to have been glad of Caesar's death? What difference is there between one who advises an action and one who approves of it? What does it matter whether I wanted it done or rejoice at the doing? Well then, is there a man, apart from those who were happy to see Caesar king of Rome, who did not want this to happen or disapproved of the act? So we are all guilty. And, to tell the truth, all honest men killed Caesar so far as in them lay. Some lacked design, some courage, some opportunity: none lacked the will.

**30** Observe the blockishness of the man—brute, I should rather call him. This is what he said: "Marcus Brutus, whose name I mention with respect, called on Cicero as he held his bloodstained dagger: hence it must be inferred that Cicero was in the plot." So then: you call *me* a criminal because you suspect that I suspected something, whereas Brutus, who brandished his dripping weapon, is named by you with respect! Very good, so much for the stupidity in your words. How much greater the stupidity in your actions and opinions! Consul, pray decide at long last how you wish it to stand with the Bruti, Gaius Cassius, Gnaeus Domitius, Gaius Trebonius, and the rest. Sleep off your wine, I say, blow it all out. Asleep on an issue like this? Will it take lighted firebrands to rouse you? Will you never understand that you have to make up your mind whether the authors of that deed are murderers or champions of freedom? **31** Pay attention for a little while. Just for a moment try to think like a sober man. Here am I, their friend, as I myself acknowledge, their partner, as you accuse me of being: and I say that there is no halfway house. If they are not liberators of the Roman People and preservers of the Commonwealth, I confess them to be worse than assassins, worse than murderers, worse even than parricides, if it is a more atrocious crime to kill the father of the fatherland[30] than one's own parent. Well, what say you in your considering wisdom? If you regard them as parricides, why have you always named them with respect both in this House and before the Roman People? Why was Marcus Brutus on your motion granted exemption under the law if he were absent from Rome more than ten days?[31] Why were the Apollinarian games celebrated with exceptional honor to Marcus Brutus?[32] Why were provinces given to Brutus and Cassius, why quaestors assigned, why was the number of

---

30. The title *parens patriae* was one of the honors given to Caesar.
31. For a city praetor this was illegal.
32. See Philippic 1 n. 46 above.

haec acta per te. non igitur homicidas. sequitur ut liberatores tuo iudicio,
quando quidem tertium nihil potest esse. **32** quid est? num conturbo te?
non enim fortasse satis quae diiunctius dicuntur intellegis. sed tamen
haec summa est conclusionis meae: quoniam scelere a te liberati sunt, ab
eodem amplissimis praemiis dignissimos iudicatos.                                5

Itaque iam retexo orationem meam. scribam ad illos ut, si qui forte,
quod a te mihi obiectum est, quaerent sitne verum, ne cui negent. etenim
vereor ne aut celatum me illis ipsis non honestum aut invitatum refugisse
mihi sit turpissimum. quae enim res umquam, pro sancte Iuppiter, non
modo in hac urbe sed in omnibus terris est gesta maior, quae gloriosior,   10
quae commendatior hominum memoriae sempiternae? in huius me tu
consili societatem tamquam in equum Troianum cum principibus inclu-
dis? **33** non recuso; ago etiam gratias, quoquo animo facis. tanta enim res
est ut invidiam istam quam tu in me vis concitare cum laude non com-
parem. quid enim beatius illis quos tu expulsos a te praedicas et rele-    15
gatos? qui locus est aut tam desertus aut tam inhumanus qui illos, cum
accesserint, non adfari atque appetere videatur? qui homines tam agrestes
qui se, cum eos aspexerint, non maximum cepisse vitae fructum putent?
quae vero tam immemor posteritas, quae tam ingratae litterae reperientur
quae eorum gloriam non immortalitatis memoria prosequantur? tu vero    20
ascribe me talem in numerum.

**34** Sed unam rem vereor ne non probes: si enim ⟨in eo⟩ fuissem, non
solum regem sed etiam regnum de re publica sustulissem; et, si meus
stilus ille fuisset, ut dicitur, mihi crede, non solum unum actum sed totam
fabulam confecissem.                                                        25

Quamquam si interfici Caesarem voluisse crimen est, vide, quaeso,
Antoni, quid tibi futurum sit, quem et Narbone hoc consilium cum
C. Trebonio cepisse notissimum est et ob eius consili societatem, cum
interficeretur Caesar, tum te a Trebonio vidimus sevocari. ego autem—
vide quam tecum agam non inimice—quod bene cogitasti aliquando,       30
laudo; quod non indicasti, gratias ago; quod non fecisti, ignosco. virum
res illa quaerebat. **35** quod si te in iudicium quis adducat usurpetque illud
Cassianum, "cui bono fuerit," vide, quaeso, ne haereas. quamquam illud

1 homicidas] -dae *bcnst*      iudicio sint *D*      **32** 3 distinctius *D* (*om. c*)      4 summa est
*V²*: -as *V¹*: est summa (est *om. b*) *D*      5 eodem te *D*      dignissimos iudicatos] -simi -ati
sunt *nsv*: -simi -antur *t*      7 quaerent] -renti *bnstv*: -rant *Ernesti*      8 ab illis ipsis *v*: ab
ip- il- *bcnst*      11 erit hominum *D*      **33** 14 *Fort.* cum omni laude²      16 cum *ed. Cratandrina*: quo *codd.*      19 reperiuntur *bcstv*      **34** 22 in eo fuissem *coni.* C. F. W. *Müller*
(*idem* interf-): f- *codd.*: in iis f- *Eberhard*: fecissem *Schöll*      23 regnum etiam *D*      28
C. *om. V¹*      30 uideo *D*      31 non (*pr.*) *om. V*      uerum *n¹stv*

legates increased?[33] And yet all of this was done through you. Therefore you do not take them for murderers. It follows that in your judgment they are liberators, since there is no third possibility. **32** Ah, I fear I am confusing you. Perhaps you don't quite understand a logical dilemma. However, this in sum is my conclusion: since you have absolved them of crime, by the same token you have judged them deserving of the highest rewards.

So I now take back what I just said. I shall write to them and tell them, if anyone should inquire whether your charge against me is true, not to deny it. Frankly I am afraid that they may be criticized themselves for keeping me in the dark, or else that the refusal of an invitation to join may be highly discreditable to me. For never, holy Jupiter, was a greater deed done in Rome or anywhere else in the world; none more glorious, none more sure to live forever in the memory of mankind. Do you make me a partner in that enterprise, shutting me inside with the leaders as in a Trojan Horse? **33** I do not demur, I even thank you, no matter what your motive. It is so great a matter that I prefer this odium which you seek to stir up against me to any glory. These men whom you boast of having driven out and banished, are they not the happiest of mortals? Is there a region so lonely and uncivilized that it will not seem to speak words of welcome when they approach? Are there any human beings so ignorant as not to rate the sight of them the greatest experience of their lives? No future age will be found so unmindful, no literature so ungrateful as not to preserve their glory in everlasting remembrance. Yes, indeed, add my name to such a roll.

**34** However, there is one item which I fear may not meet with your approval. If I had had a hand in the matter, I should have removed monarchy from the Commonwealth, and not merely the monarch; and if the pen[34] had been mine, as the saying goes, believe me, I should have finished the whole play, not just one act.

But after all, Antonius, if it is a crime to have wished Caesar to be killed, consider, I beg, what is to become of *you*, since it is common knowledge that you planned his death at Narbo with Gaius Trebonius; and it was because of your association with him in that plan that when Caesar was being killed we saw Trebonius take you aside. For my own part (and please note how far I am from treating you as an enemy), I applaud the salutary thought you once entertained. I thank you for not turning informer. I forgive you for not taking action; that enterprise needed a *man*. **35** But if someone takes you to court and quotes that watchword of Cassius,[35] "Who stood to gain?" I really fear you

33. See SB².
34. Caesar's assassins carried their daggers in pen cases (Dio 44.16.1).
35. Ravilla (see n. 27 above).

fuit, ut tu dicebas quidem, omnibus bono qui servire nolebant, tibi tamen
praecipue, qui non modo non servis sed etiam regnas; qui maximo te aere
alieno ad aedem Opis liberavisti; qui per easdem tabulas innumerabilem
pecuniam dissipavisti; ad quem e domo Caesaris tam multa delata sunt;
cuius domi quaestuosissima est falsorum commentariorum et chirographo- 5
rum officina, agrorum, oppidorum, immunitatium, vectigalium flagitio-
sissimae nundinae. **36** etenim quae res egestati et aeri alieno tuo praeter
mortem Caesaris subvenire potuisset? nescio quid conturbatus esse videris: num quid subtimes ne ad te hoc crimen pertinere videatur? libero te
metu: nemo credet umquam. non est tuum de re publica bene mereri. 10
habet istius pulcherrimi facti clarissimos viros res publica auctores. ego
te tantum gaudere dico, fecisse non arguo.

Respondi maximis criminibus: nunc etiam reliquis respondendum est.
**37** castra mihi Pompei atque illud omne tempus obiecisti. quo quidem
tempore si, ut dixi, meum consilium auctoritasque valuisset, tu hodie 15
egeres, nos liberi essemus, res publica non tot duces et exercitus amisisset.
fateor enim me, cum ea quae acciderunt providerem futura, tanta in
maestitia fuisse quanta ceteri optimi cives, si idem providissent, fuissent.
dolebam, dolebam, patres conscripti, rem publicam vestris quondam
meisque consiliis conservatam brevi tempore esse perituram. nec vero 20
eram tam indoctus ignarusque rerum ut frangerer animo propter vitae
cupiditatem, quae me manens conficeret angoribus, dimissa molestiis
omnibus liberaret. illos ego praestantissimos viros, lumina rei publicae,
vivere volebam, tot consularis, tot praetorios, tot honestissimos senatores, omnem praeterea florem nobilitatis ac iuventutis, tum optimorum 25
civium exercitus; qui si viverent, quamvis iniqua condicione pacis—mihi
enim omnis pax cum civibus bello civili utilior videbatur—rem publicam
hodie teneremus. **38** quae sententia si valuisset ac non ei maxime mihi
quorum ego vitae consulebam spe victoriae elati obstitissent, ut alia
omittam, tu certe numquam in hoc ordine vel potius numquam in hac 30
urbe mansisses. at vero Cn. Pompei voluntatem a me alienabat oratio
mea. an ille quemquam plus dilexit, cum ullo aut sermones aut consilia
contulit saepius? quod quidem erat magnum, de summa re publica dis-
sentientis in eadem consuetudine amicitiae permanere. sed et ego quid

**35** 33–1 illud . . . quidem *ita V* (*sed* tu ut): illud quidem (q- i- *n*[1]*sv*) fuit ut tu dicebas *D*
(*varia coniecta*: *equidem verba* ut tu dicebas quidem[3] *libenter extruserim*)     3 aedem *del.*
*Cobet* (*v. Fe.*)     liberasti *nv*: -abis *V*     5 domi] domus *bcnsv*     6 officina agrorum
oppidorum *om. V*     immunitatis (-itas *c*) *D*     **36** 8 mihi esse (e- m- *v*) *D*     13 nunc
*ed. Romana*: num (tunc *t*) *codd.*     **37** 14 obiecistis *V*     15 dixi meum] diximus *V*[1]: -um
*V*[2]     17 prouidem futuram *V*     19 p(ublicam) *om. V*     23 liberauisset *bct*: -asset
*nsv*     **38** 31 abalienabat *D*     33 p(ublica) *om. D*     34 sed et *bcntv*: sed *s*: *om. V*

may find yourself at a loss. True, as you yourself used to say, everybody who did not want to be a slave gained thereby, but particularly you; for not only are you no slave, you are a monarch. You took a vast load of debt off your shoulders at the temple of Ops. You used the same records to squander more money than you could count. Much that was in Caesar's house has been transferred to yours; and there a most lucrative factory of false memoranda and holographs is in operation, and a scandalous market in lands, towns, exemptions, revenues. **36** After all, what but Caesar's death could have relieved your penury and debt? You seem a trifle agitated. Do I perceive a lurking apprehension lest this charge may appear to have something to do with you? Make your mind easy. Nobody will ever believe it. Service to the Commonwealth is not your style. The Commonwealth knows the illustrious authors of that magnificent exploit. I say only that you are glad of it; I don't charge you with having done it.

I have answered the most serious charges. Now I must answer the rest. **37** You brought up Pompeius' camp against me, that whole period. As I have said, if my advice and influence had prevailed at that time, you would be a pauper today, we should be free men, and the Commonwealth would not have lost so many leaders and armies. I admit that, foreseeing what was to come, I was as sad as other good patriots would have been if they had seen as far. Yes, indeed, Members of the Senate, I grieved at the approaching dissolution of the Commonwealth which your counsels and mine had once preserved. I was not so unschooled, however, or so ignorant of the world as to be plunged in dismay because of any clinging to life—a life which while it lasted would plague me with sufferings but once let go would free me from all my troubles. But I wanted my distinguished companions to live, luminaries of the Commonwealth, all those consulars and praetorians, so many highly respected senators, and, besides these, all the flower of our younger nobility, as well as the armies of patriotic citizens. If they were alive, however hard the terms of peace (and I thought any peace with fellow countrymen more advantageous than civil war), we should have a Commonwealth today. **38** If my opinion had prevailed and if those whose lives I was anxious to preserve had not in their confidence of victory been foremost to oppose me, well, to mention only one thing, *you* would assuredly not have remained in this House, or rather in this city. You say that the way I talked lost me Pompeius' friendship. Was there a man for whom he had more regard, with whom he talked and conferred more often? That was no small thing, that we two, who held divergent views on the great question of the hour, should remain on our old friendly footing. But each of us saw what

ille et contra ille quid ego sentirem et spectarem videbat. ego incolumitati civium primum, ut postea dignitati possemus, ille praesenti dignitati potius consulebat. quod autem habebat uterque quid sequeretur, idcirco tolerabilior erat nostra dissensio. **39** quid vero ille singularis vir ac paene divinus de me senserit sciunt qui eum de Pharsalia fuga Paphum persecuti   5
sunt. numquam ab eo mentio de me nisi honorifica, nisi plena amicissimi desideri, cum me vidisse plus fateretur, se speravisse meliora. et eius viri nomine me insectari audes cuius me amicum, te sectorem esse fateare? sed omittatur bellum illud in quo tu nimium felix fuisti. ne ⟨de⟩ iocis quidem respondebo quibus me in castris usum esse dixisti: erant quidem   10
illa castra plena curae; verum tamen homines, quamvis in turbidis rebus sint, tamen, si modo homines sunt, interdum animis relaxantur. **40** quod autem idem maestitiam meam reprehendit, idem iocum, magno argumento est me in utroque fuisse moderatum.

Hereditates mihi negasti venire. utinam hoc tuum verum crimen esset!   15
plures amici mei et necessarii viverent. sed qui istuc tibi venit in mentem? ego enim amplius sestertium ducentiens acceptum hereditatibus rettuli. quamquam in hoc genere fateor feliciorem esse te. me nemo nisi amicus fecit heredem, ut cum illo commodo, si quod erat, animi quidam dolor iungeretur; te is quem tu vidisti numquam, L. Rubrius Casinas [fecit   20
heredem]. **41** et quidem vide quam te amarit is qui albus aterne fuerit ignoras. fratris filium praeterit; Q. Fufi, honestissimi equitis Romani suique amicissimi, quem palam heredem semper factitarat, ne nomen quidem: te, quem numquam viderat ⟨a⟩ut cer⟨t⟩e numquam salutaverat, fecit heredem. velim mihi dicas, nisi molestum est, L. Turselius qua facie   25
fuerit, qua statura, quo municipio, qua tribu. "nihil scio" inquies "nisi quae praedia habuerit." igitur fratrem exheredans te faciebat heredem. in multas praeterea pecunias alienissimorum hominum vi eiectis veris heredibus, tamquam heres esset, invasit. **42** quamquam hoc maxime admiratus sum, mentionem te hereditatum ausum esse facere, cum ipse here-   30
ditatem patris non adisses.

2 civium *melius, puto, abesset*     ut] et *cnsv*: ac *bt*     possemus *et* dignitati (*alt.*) *om.*
*D*     3 quid] quod *Lambinus* (*vide quae scripsi ad Att. 1.12.4*)     **39**ʼ4 singularis] consul-
*D*     5 de pharsalia] pharsalica *D* (*v. Fe.*)     8 me amicum] am- *V*[1]: am- me *coni.*
*Halm*     9 de iocis *Wesenberg*: io- *D*: totis *V*     10–11 illa quidem *bct*     **40** 15 hereditates *Naugerius*: -tate *V*: -tatem *D*     20–21 fecit heredem *del. Madvig* (*clausula, quae
est* —∪∪–∪––, *a Clarkio improbari non debuit; ceterum eadem verba in l.* 19 *removere
possis, ut hic retineas*)     **41** 22–23 *aliter dist. Watt* (*CP 78 [1983] 227*)     23–24
nomen quidem *scripsi*: n- q- perscripsit *D*: nominat q- *V*     24 te *om. D*     aut certe
numquam *Faërnus*: ut (aut *V*[2]) cere n- *V*[1]: ac n- *c*: ac ne umquam *bnstv*     25 turseius *b*:
-secius *cnsv*: -setius *t*     26 inques *V*: -uis *A. Klotz*     27 is igitur *V*[2]     28 vi eiectis] rei-
*bc*: ei- *nsv*     29 esses invasisti *Heumann*: *num* esses invasti?

the other felt and why. My concern was for the survival of our countrymen first and foremost; dignity could be considered later. He cared rather for dignity in the present. The fact that each of us had a reasonable point of view made our disagreement easier to bear. **39** What that eminent man, superman we might almost call him, thought of me is known to those who followed him in his flight from Pharsalia to Paphos. He never mentioned me except in terms of honor, full of affection and the wish that I were by his side, acknowledging that mine had been the surer vision, his the larger hope. Do you dare to attack me in the name of that great man, while you acknowledge that I was his friend whereas you bought up his property? But let us say no more about that war, in which you were all too fortunate. Nor shall I make any reply about the jokes which you say I cracked in camp. It was full of anxiety, that camp; but human beings sometimes relax, even in the most troubled of times, if human they be. **40** But observe how one minute he censures my gloom, the next my jesting—a pretty good indication that I did not overdo either.

You said that bequests do not come my way. I only wish this taunt of yours were true, for more of my friends and connections would still be alive. But what put that into your head? Actually my books show that I have received more than twenty million sesterces in bequests. I must admit, though, that you have better luck than I in this area. Nobody ever made me his heir unless he was a friend, so that any benefit there was came along with a certain amount of grief; whereas Lucius Rubrius of Casinum made you his heir, a man you never saw in your life. **41** How fond he was of you, this person who may have been white or black for aught you know! He passed over his nephew and did not even mention Quintus Fufius, a much respected Roman knight and his close friend, whom he had always made his heir in open declaration; whereas you, whom he had never seen or at any rate never met, he made his heir. Tell me please, if you don't mind, what Lucius Turselius looked like, what was his height, his home town, his tribe. "I know nothing about him," you will say, "except what lands he owned." And so, disinheriting his brother, he went on making you his heir. Besides these, Antonius has seized many sums of money belonging to total strangers, claiming to be their heir and forcibly ejecting the real heirs. **42** But what surprised me most was his daring to mention bequests when he himself had refused to accept his father's estate.[36]

---

36. Because it was encumbered with debts.

Haec ut colligeres, homo amentissime, tot dies in aliena villa decla-
masti? quamquam tu quidem, ut tui familiarissimi dictitant, vini exha-
landi, non ingeni acuendi causa declamitas. at vero adhibes ioci causa
magistrum suffragio tuo et compotorum tuorum rhetorem, cui concessisti
ut in te quae vellet diceret, salsum omnino hominem, sed materia facilis 5
in te et in tuos dicta dicere. vide autem quid intersit inter te et avum tuum.
ille sensim dicebat quod causae prodesset; tu cursim dicis aliena. **43** at
quanta merces rhetori data est! audite, audite, patres conscripti, et cognoscite rei publicae volnera. duo milia iugerum campi Leontini Sex.
Clodio rhetori adsignasti et quidem immunia, ut populi Romani tanta 10
mercede nihil sapere disceres. num etiam hoc, homo audacissime, ex
Caesaris commentariis? sed dicam alio loco et de Leontino agro et de
Campano, quos iste agros ereptos rei publicae turpissimis possessoribus
inquinavit. iam enim, quoniam criminibus eius satis respondi, de ipso
emendatore et correctore nostro quaedam dicenda sunt. nec enim omnia 15
effundam, ut, si saepius decertandum sit, ut erit, semper novus veniam:
quam facultatem mihi multitudo istius vitiorum peccatorumque largitur.

**44** Visne igitur te inspiciamus a puero? sic opinor; a principio ordi-
amur. tenesne memoria praetextatum te decoxisse? "patris" inquies "ista
culpa est." concedo. Etenim est pietatis plena defensio. illud tamen au- 20
daciae tuae quod sedisti in quattuordecim ordinibus, cum esset lege
Roscia decoctoribus certus locus constitutus, quamvis quis fortunae
vitio, non suo decoxisset. sumpsisti virilem, quam statim muliebrem
togam reddidisti. primo vulgare scortum; certa flagiti merces nec ea
parva; sed cito Curio intervenit, qui te a meretricio quaestu abduxit 25
et, tamquam stolam dedisset, in matrimonio stabili et certo collocavit.
**45** nemo umquam puer emptus libidinis causa tam fuit in domini potestate quam tu in Curionis. quotiens te pater eius domu sua eiecit,
quotiens custodes posuit ne limen intrares! cum tu tamen nocte socia,
hortante libidine, cogente mercede, per tegulas demitterere. quae flagitia 30

**42** 3 ingeni acuendi (*v. Fe.*)] ingeniendi *V*     declamas *V*     at] et *c*: tu *nsv*: *om. b*     5
facilis *D, Suet. Gramm. 29.2* (*loco sane mendose perscripto*): f- est *V*     6 vide autem
*om. bc*: v- a- quid *om. nstv*     intersit (quid i- *c*) *post* tuum *D*     tum tuum *V*     7
sensim *om. V*     tu cursim dicis *D*: turi (tuti *V²*) indictis *V*     **44** 19 tenes *V¹*     22
constitutus *om. V¹*     23 uirilem togam *D*     24 togam] stolam *D*     26 et certo et
*V¹*     locauit *D*     **45** 28 domo *D*     30 demitterere *Faërnus*: dimit(t)- *Vbns*: dimittere
*ctv*

58

Was it to rake this stuff together, you addle-brain, that you spent all these days declaiming in a country house that does not belong to you?[37]—though, to be sure, you do that to blow off your wine, not to sharpen your wits, so your intimates say. Ah, but then for a joke you called in a coach, a professional rhetorician voted to be such by you and your boozing partners, and you gave him leave to say what he liked against you—a witty fellow, no doubt, but you and your friends make easy targets for satire. Observe, however, the contrast between you and your grandfather:[38] he took his time and his words advanced his case; you gabble irrelevancies. **43** But what a fee our rhetorician received! Hear me well, Members of the Senate, and learn how the Commonwealth is bleeding. You allocated two thousand jugers[39] in the plain of Leontini to Sextus Clodius, professor of rhetoric, and tax-free at that; so much the Roman People had to pay for you to learn to be a fool! Did this too come from Caesar's memoranda, you unscrupulous scoundrel? But I shall be speaking elsewhere both of the Leontine and the Campanian lands, the lands Antonius snatched from the Commonwealth and befouled with disgraceful tenants. For now, having sufficiently answered his charges, there are certain things I have to say about this censorious corrector of mine. Not that I shall let everything out; I want to come always fresh to the fray if there are to be further bouts, as there will. The multitude of his vices and misdeeds affords me that scope.

**44** Would you like us to examine your record from a boy? Yes, I think that is best. Let us begin from the beginning. Do you recollect that you went bankrupt before you came of age? You will blame your father for that. I allow your defense—so filial! But it was your own insolence that made you sit in the fourteen rows, although bankrupts had their place assigned to them under the Roscian law,[40] even those whose plight was due to bad luck and no fault of their own. You donned the gown of manhood—and promptly it became the uniform of a harlot.[41] You started out as a common whore. Your shame had a fixed price, and no mean one. But presently along came Curio. He took you out of the prostitute's trade, gave you a married lady's robe as it were, and settled you down in steady wedlock. **45** No slave boy bought to satisfy lust was ever so completely in his master's power as you were in Curio's. Time and time again his father threw you out of his house, posting guards to stop you crossing the threshold. But with night to befriend you, lust to encourage you, gain to drive you—they let you down through the roof. Such infamies that house could

---

37. The villa at Tibur which had formerly belonged to Pompey's father-in-law Metellus Scipio.

38. M. Antonius, consul in 99 and a famous advocate.

39. A *iugerum* was a little less than two-thirds of an acre.

40. Passed in 67, it reserved the first fourteen rows of the *cavea* in the theater for knights.

41. The toga was worn by female prostitutes (as well as by men generally). Married women wore a robe (*stola*).

domus illa diutius ferre non potuit. scisne me de rebus mihi notissimis
dicere? recordare tempus illud cum pater Curio maerens iacebat in lecto;
filius se ad pedes meos prosternens, lacrimans, te mihi commendabat;
orabat ut te contra suum patrem, si sestertium sexagiens peteret, de-
fenderem; tantum enim se pro te intercessisse dicebat. ipse autem amore　　5
ardens confirmabat, quod desiderium tui discidi ferre non posset, se in
exsilium iturum. **46** quo tempore ego quanta mala florentissimae familiae
sedavi vel potius sustuli! patri persuasi ut aes alienum fili dissolveret;
redimeret adulescentem, summa spe et animi et ingeni praeditum, rei
familiaris facultatibus eumque non modo tua familiaritate sed etiam　　10
congressione patrio iure et potestate prohiberet. haec tu cum per me acta
meminisses, nisi illis quos videmus gladiis confideres, maledictis me
provocare ausus esses?

　　**47** Sed iam stupra et flagitia omittamus: sunt quaedam quae honeste
non possum dicere; tu autem eo liberior quod ea in te admisisti quae a　　15
verecundo inimico audire non posses. sed reliquum vitae cursum videte,
quem quidem celeriter perstringam. ad haec enim quae in civili bello, in
maximis rei publicae miseriis fecit, et ad ea quae cotidie facit, festinat
animus. quae peto ut, quamquam multo notiora vobis quam mihi sunt,
tamen, ut facitis, attente audiatis. debet enim talibus in rebus excitare　　20
animos non cognitio solum rerum sed etiam recordatio; etsi incidamus,
opinor, media ne nimis sero ad extrema veniamus.

　　**48** Intimus erat in tribunatu Clodio qui sua erga me beneficia commemorat; eius omnium incendiorum fax, cuius etiam domi iam tum quiddam molitus est. quid dicam ipse optime intellegit. inde iter Alexandriam　　25
contra senatus auctoritatem, contra rem publicam et religiones; sed habebat ducem Gabinium, quicum quidvis rectissime facere posset. qui tum
inde reditus aut qualis? prius in ultimam Galliam ex Aegypto quam
domum. quae autem domus? suam enim quisque domum tum obtinebat

4 te³] se *Vvn*²: tu *n*¹　　6 confirmaui at quo *V*: -uit quod *Halm*　　7 esse iturum *D*　　**46**
tanta *D*　　10 a tua non modo *D*　　**47** 21 etsi] tame- *nsv*: iam e- *ct*: sed iam *b*　　22
opinor] oportet *D*　　**48** 24 quiddam (quidam *v*) iam tum *D*　　26 rem p(ublicam) et *om.*
*D*　　29 domus *cnstvV*²　　obtinebant *V*

bear no longer. You know, do you not, that I speak of matters with which I am fully familiar? Please to remember that time when the elder Curio lay in bed eating his heart out. The son fell at my feet in tears, asked me to take care of you, begged me to defend you[42] against his own father if the latter sued for six million sesterces—that being the sum for which he said he had gone surety for you. For himself, in his lover's fever the young man assured me that he could not bear the pain of separation from you, that he would leave the country. **46** It was I who at this point eased the grave troubles of a flourishing family, or rather removed them. I persuaded the old gentleman to settle his son's debt, and so out of the family property to save the credit of a young man whose disposition and talents promised so well; and further, using his right and authority as a father, to forbid him to associate with you or even meet you. Remembering what happened then through my intervention, would you have dared to challenge me with insults if you had not put your trust in those weapons which we see before our eyes?

**47** But let us say no more of shame and debauchery. There are some things of which I cannot decently speak. Your tongue is the freer because you have committed offenses which you could not hear from the lips of a modest enemy. Let me pass on to the rest of the career. I shall only touch upon it rapidly, for I am impatient to get on to what he did in the Civil War, that time of greatest national misery, and to what he is doing every day. You gentlemen know all that much better than I, but still I beg you to listen closely, as you are doing. In matters such as these we should be stirred not only by learning of them but even by remembering them. However, I think I had best cut short the middle of the story lest it take me too long to reach the final stages.

**48** This gentleman who reminds me of the favors he has done me was intimate with Clodius during his tribunate. He was the torch that set light to all Clodius' conflagrations. Also even at this period he was up to something in Clodius' house—he best knows what I mean.[43] Then to Alexandria,[44] in defiance of the Senate's authority, of the Commonwealth, of religious bars— but he served under Gabinius, and anything he did in Gabinius' company could not but be right and proper. So what was the manner of his return? First, he traveled from Egypt to Outer Gaul[45] instead of coming home. And what home? In those days everybody's home was his own, and yours did not exist.

---

42. See Textual Appendix, p. 384.

43. No doubt a hint at an intrigue with Fulvia, then married to Clodius.

44. In 55, when A. Gabinius, then governor of Syria, restored the deposed king of Egypt, Ptolemy Auletes. His action was illegal and on his return to Rome it formed the basis for a charge of *maiestas* (lèse-majesté), on which he was condemned.

45. Lit. "furthest Gaul," i.e. Gaul beyond the old Roman province of Narbonensis, conquered by Caesar in 58–51.

nec erat usquam tua. domum dico? quid erat in terris ubi in tuo pedem
poneres praeter unum Misenum, quod cum sociis tamquam Sisaponem
tenebas? **49** venis e Gallia ad quaesturam petendam. aude dicere te prius
ad parentem tuam venisse quam ad me. acceperam iam ante Caesaris
litteras ut mihi satis fieri paterer a te: itaque ne loqui quidem sum te pas-          5
sus de gratia. postea sum cultus a te, tu a me observatus in petitione
quaesturae; quo quidem tempore P. Clodium approbante populo Romano
in foro es conatus occidere, cumque eam rem tua sponte conarere, non
impulsu meo, tamen ita praedicabas, te non existimare, nisi illum interfe-
cisses, umquam mihi pro tuis in me iniuriis satis esse facturum. in quo          10
demiror cur Milonem impulsu meo rem illam egisse dicas, cum te ultro
mihi idem illud deferentem numquam sim adhortatus. quamquam, si in
eo perseverares, ad tuam gloriam rem illam referri malebam quam ad
meam gratiam. **50** quaestor es factus: deinde continuo sine senatus consulto, sine sorte, sine lege ad Caesarem cucurristi. id enim unum in terris          15
egestatis, aeris alieni, nequitiae perditis vitae rationibus perfugium esse
ducebas. ibi te cum et illius largitionibus et tuis rapinis explevisses, si hoc
est explere, ⟨haurire⟩ quod statim effundas, advolasti egens ad tribunatum, ut in eo magistratu, si posses, viri tui similis esses.

Accipite nunc, quaeso, non ea quae ipse in se atque in domesti-          20
cum [de]decus impure et intemperanter, sed quae in nos fortunasque nostras, id est in universam rem publicam, impie ac nefarie fecerit. ab huius
enim scelere omnium malorum principium natum reperietis. **51** nam cum
L. Lentulo C. Marcello consulibus Kalendis Ianuariis labentem et prope
cadentem rem publicam fulcire cuperetis ipsique C. Caesari, si sana          25
mente esset, consulere velletis, tum iste venditum atque emancipatum tribunatum consiliis vestris opposuit cervicesque suas ei subiecit securi qua
multi minoribus in peccatis occiderunt. in te, M. Antoni, id decrevit

1 neque *D*     **49** 3 venis e *Halm*: -isse *Vct*: -isti *bn*[1]*sv*: -isti in *n*[2]     galliam *D*     4 tuam
*Manutius*: tuum *codd.*     6 postea] potense *V*     sum cultus] c- sum *bc*: custoditus sum
*ntv*: ego sum cultus *coni. Halm, fort. recte*     observatus[3] *D*: ouatus *V*: adiutus[1] *veterum
nescio quis*: *alii alia coni.*     12 quamquam] quoniam *Manutius*: quod *mallem*     13 rem
. . . malebam *om. V*     **50** 18 haurire[2] *add. Faërnus, alii alia*     aduolas *D*     21 decus
*Madvig*: dedecus *codd.* (*nisi quod* deditus *t*)     et] atque *D*     23 principium natum reperietis *om. V*[1]     **51** 24 labantem *bcs*     28 in te] in te autem *nsv*: in mente *t*

Home? Nowhere on earth could you set foot on your own ground, excepting only your place at Misenum,[46] and that you held with partners like a Sisapo.[47] **49** You come back from Gaul to stand for the quaestorship. I challenge you to say that you went to your mother before coming to see me. I had previously received a letter from Caesar asking me to accept your apologies, and so I did not so much as let you speak about making your peace. Afterwards you paid me some attentions and I showed you civility when you were a candidate for the quaestorship. It was at that time you tried to kill Publius Clodius in the Forum with the approval of the Roman People. The attempt was made on your own initiative without any prompting on my part, but you gave out that you felt you would never make amends for the injuries you had done me unless you killed Clodius. I find it surprising that you say I prompted Milo to do that, seeing that when you offered me the same service of your own accord I never encouraged you. To be sure, I preferred that the exploit (if you persevered) should stand to your credit rather than be regarded as a favor to me. **50** Well, you were elected quaestor; on which immediately, without a decree of the Senate or drawing of lots or any legal justification, you hurried off to Caesar.[48] You reckoned that there lay the one refuge on earth for penury, debt, worthlessness in a ruined career. When you had glutted yourself there with Caesar's largesses and your own plunderings—if glut is the word for gobbling down one minute to throw up the next—you rushed up hungrily for the tribunate, with the intention, if possible, of performing in that office like your—husband.[49]

And now let me tell you, gentlemen, not of impurities and excesses committed against himself and his private good name, but of his impious crimes against ourselves and our fortunes, that is to say against the entire Commonwealth. You will find that all our calamities have their origin in a wicked act of his. **51** On the Kalends of January in the consulship of Lucius Lentulus and Gaius Marcellus the Commonwealth was tottering, almost falling, and you gentlemen were anxious to shore it up. You were ready to consider the interests of Gaius Caesar himself, if he kept his sanity. At that point Antonius placed in opposition to your decisions the office which he had sold lock, stock, and barrel and put his own neck under the axe by which many have lost their lives for lesser offenses. The Senate, a Senate still intact before so many of its lights

---

46. *Misenum* = *villam Misenensem*, as in 2.73. If Misenum had been a town in its own right, an adjectival form would have been used. See my note on *Laterio* in *Att.* 4.7.3. Other examples are *Baiae* (*Att.* 12.40.3, Tac. *Ann.* 13.21.6), *Petrinum* (*Fam.* 6.19.1), and *Bauli* (Tac. *Ann.* 14.4.3). *Unicis Sabinis* in Hor. *Carm.* 2.18.14 has caused much perplexity. No doubt it stands for *fundo Sabino*, "the Sabine country" in Latin being *Sabini*, not *Sabinum*.

47. Location of mines in southern Spain, exploited by a Roman company.

48. Probably in 51; see my note on *Fam.* 2.18.2.

49. Curio, who as tribune in 50 was active on Caesar's behalf.

senatus et quidem incolumis, nondum tot luminibus exstinctis, quod in
hostem togatum decerni est solitum more maiorum. et tu apud patres
conscriptos contra me dicere ausus es, cum ab hoc ordine ego conservator essem, tu hostis rei publicae iudicatus? commemoratio illius tui
sceleris intermissa est, non memoria deleta. dum genus hominum, dum          5
populi Romani nomen exstabit—quod quidem erit, si per te licebit,
sempiternum—tua illa pestifera intercessio nominabitur. **52** quid cupide
a senatu, quid temere fiebat, cum tu unus adulescens universum ordinem
decernere de salute rei publicae prohibuisti, neque id semel sed saepius,
neque tu tecum de senatus auctoritate agi passus es? quid autem agebatur    10
nisi ne delere et evertere rem publicam funditus velles? cum te neque
principes civitatis rogando neque maiores natu monendo neque frequens
senatus agendo de vendita atque addicta sententia movere potui⟨sse⟩t,
tum illud multis rebus ante temptatis necessario tibi vulnus inflictum est
quod paucis ante te, quorum incolumis fuit nemo: **53** tum contra te dedit  15
arma hic ordo consulibus reliquisque imperiis et potestatibus: quae non
effugisses, nisi te ad arma Caesaris contulisses.

Tu, tu, inquam, M. Antoni, princeps C. Caesari omnia perturbare cupienti causam belli contra patriam inferendi dedisti. quid enim aliud ille
dicebat, quam causam sui dementissimi consili et facti adferebat, nisi      20
quod intercessio neglecta, ius tribunicium sublatum, circumscriptus a
senatu esset Antonius? omitto quam haec falsa, quam levia, praesertim
cum omnino nulla causa iusta cuiquam esse possit contra patriam arma
capiendi. sed nihil de Caesare: tibi certe confitendum est causam perni-
ciosissimi belli in persona tua constitisse. **54** o miserum te, si haec intel-  25
legis, miseriorem, si non intellegis hoc litteris mandari, hoc memoriae
prodi, huius rei ne posteritatem quidem omnium saeculorum umquam
immemorem fore, ⟨propter unum te⟩ consules ex Italia expulsos, cumque
eis Cn. Pompeium, quod imperi populi Romani decus ac lumen fuit,
omnis consularis qui per valetudinem exsequi cladem illam fugamque        30
potuissent, praetores, praetorios, tribunos plebis, magnam partem sena-

---

1 luminibus] luminaribus *stv* (lim- *n*)     2–3 patres conscriptos aput *V*     6 per] pro
*V*     licuerit *D*     **52** 9 id *om. V* (*v. Fe.*)     11 ne *om. D*     deleri *bcsv*     evertere
rem p(ublicam) *om. V*¹     euerti *bV*²     velles? cum *ita dist. ns et Madvig*     11–12
neque . . . monendo *om. V*     13 potuisset *Madvig*: -it *codd.*     14 est *om. D*     **53**
18–19 omnia . . . cupienti] ruenti atque omnia permiscere cup- *Aquila, Rhet. Lat. ed. Halm
31*     19 ferendi *Hirschfelder* (*v. Fe.*)     21 sublatum circumscriptus *om. V*¹     24 de]
*om. bcnst*     caesare] -ris *nsv*: -ri *t*     est] sit *nsv*: si *bct*     causa *D*     25 in *om.*
*V*¹     **54** haec] *om. bcstv*     27 prodi *om. V*¹     28 immemorem] meorum *V*     propter
unum te *supplevi*     cumque] que *V*¹     30 sequi *Kübler*

were put out, passed against you, Marcus Antonius, that decree which by ancient usage is passed against a public enemy in our midst[50]—and have you dared to attack me before the assembled Senate, knowing that this House had judged me the savior and you the enemy of the Commonwealth? For a time that crime of yours has not been mentioned, but the memory of it has not been erased. So long as the human race and the name of the Roman People survive (a name which will last for ever if you do not prevent it), that fatal veto of yours will be on the lips of men. **52** Was the Senate acting unfairly or rashly, when you, one young man,[51] forbade the whole House to pass decrees involving the safety of the Commonwealth? Not once, but again and again you did this, refusing to listen to representations made to you on the authority of the Senate. Their one and only purpose was to dissuade you from totally overthrowing the Commonwealth from its foundations. But neither the requests of Rome's leading men nor the warnings of your seniors nor the representations of a full Senate could move you from your corrupt, bought decision. Then it was, after much unsuccessful effort, when no alternative remained, that the stroke fell upon you which few before you have felt and none survived unscathed. **53** Then it was that this House put weapons in the hands of the consuls and other holders of official authority and power, for use against you; weapons which you would not have escaped if you had not betaken yourself to Caesar's army.

Gaius Caesar aimed to overthrow our society. You, yes, you, Marcus Antonius, first gave him a pretext for making war upon his country. What else did Caesar say, what pretext did he allege for his mad design and deed except that the veto had been ignored, the tribunician prerogative annulled, Antonius curtailed of his rights by the Senate? It was false, of course, and frivolous; apart from anything else, no excuse whatsoever can justify any man in taking up arms against the fatherland. But leave that aside, leave Caesar out of it: *you* at least must admit that your person constituted the occasion of that terrible war. **54** What a miserable creature you are if you realize this! More miserable still, if you do not realize what is being recorded by historians, handed down to memory so that in all ages to come it will never pass out of men's minds: namely, that on your sole account the consuls were driven from Italy, and with them Gnaeus Pompeius, the pride and ornament of the Roman empire, as well as all consulars whose health allowed them to follow that disastrous exodus, the praetors, the praetorians, the tribunes of the plebs, a large part of the

---

50. The so-called Ultimate Decree (*senatus consultum ultimum*), tantamount to declaration of martial law, empowering the consuls and other magistrates "to see that no harm befall the Commonwealth."

51. Cicero chooses to ignore Antony's fellow tribune and associate, Q. Cassius Longinus.

tus, omnem subolem iuventutis, uno[que] verbo rem publicam expulsam atque exterminatam suis sedibus! **55** ut igitur in seminibus est causa arborum et stirpium, sic huius luctuosissimi belli semen tu fuisti. doletis tris exercitus populi Romani interfectos: interfecit Antonius. desideratis clarissimos civis: eos quoque vobis eripuit Antonius. auctoritas huius   5 ordinis adflicta est: adflixit Antonius. omnia denique, quae postea vidimus—quid autem mali non vidimus?—si recte ratiocinabimur, uni accepta referemus Antonio. ut Helena Troianis, sic iste huic rei publicae causa belli, causa pestis atque exiti fuit.

    Reliquae partes tribunatus principi similes. omnia perfecit quae sena-   10 tus salva re publica ne fieri possent perfecerat. cuius tamen scelus in scelere cognoscite. **56** restituebat multos calamitosos: in eis patrui nulla mentio. si severus, cur non in omnis? si misericors, cur non in suos? sed omitto ceteros: Licinium Lenticulam de alea condemnatum, collusorem suum, restituit, quasi vero ludere cum condemnato non liceret; sed ⟨id   15 egit⟩ ut quod in alea perdiderat beneficio legis dissolveret. quam attulisti rationem populo Romano cur eum restitui oporteret? absentem, credo, in reos relatum; rem indicta causa iudicatam; nullum fuisse de alea lege iudicium; vi oppressum et armis; postremo, quod de patruo tuo dicebatur, pecunia iudicium esse corruptum! nihil horum. at vir bonus et re   20 publica dignus. nihil id quidem ad rem; ego tamen, quoniam condemnatum esse pro nihilo est, si ita esset, ignoscerem. hominem omnium nequissimum, qui non dubitaret vel in foro alea ludere, lege quae est de alea condemnatum qui in integrum restituit, is non apertissime studium suum ipse profitetur?   25

    **57** In eodem vero tribunatu, cum Caesar in Hispaniam proficiscens huic conculcandam Italiam tradidisset, quae fuit eius peragratio itinerum, lustratio municipiorum! scio me in rebus celebratissimis omnium sermone versari, eaque quae dico dicturusque sum notiora esse omnibus qui in Italia tum fuerunt quam mihi qui non fui: notabo tamen singulas res, etsi   30

---

1 uno *Ferrarius*: unoque *codd.* (*cf. Fin. 2.73*)     **55** 4–6 *post* interfectos *et* civis *et* adflicta est *interrogationis notam ponit Fedeli auctore Watt*     5 vobis] bonis *V*: nobis *Halm*     eripuit *ante* vobis *D*     9 causa (cā? *v. Fe.*) *ante* belli *om. V*     10 principi *cod. Wolfenbüttelensis 278*: -piis *Vbt*: -pibus *c*: -pio *ns*: *om. v*     11 effecerat *Cobet* (*coll.* 10.4), *alii alia, sed v. Fe.*     **56** 12 restituerat *V*     14 denticulam *Vbct*: Denticulum *Heusinger* (*v. Two Studies, 47*)     15–16 sed id egit[3] *scripsi*: sed *codd.*: scilicet *Koch*     21 et ego *D*     22 est si ita esset] si ita *V*     hominem] nem- *nsv*: nemo inest *t*: in eodem uero hominem *V*     23 uel lege *D*     25 profiteretur *V*

Senate, all our rising youth—that in a word the Commonwealth was driven out, banished from its home. **55** Thus, as the cause of trees and shrubs is in their seeds, so you were the seed of this most lamentable war. Gentlemen, you grieve for three Roman armies slaughtered:[52] Antonius slaughtered them. You mourn the loss of our most illustrious fellow countrymen: Antonius robbed you of them too. The authority of this House was shattered: Antonius shattered it. Everything we have seen since that time—and what calamity have we *not* seen?—if we reckon aright, we shall put it down to one man, Antonius. As Helen to Troy, so was he to this Commonwealth, the cause of war, the cause of disaster and destruction.

The remaining episodes of his tribunate were of a piece with the beginning. He accomplished all that the Senate had made impossible so long as the Commonwealth survived. But I will tell you of a crime within a crime. **56** He brought many banished men back home, but among them there was no mention of his uncle.[53] If he is severe, why not to all? If compassionate, why not to his own kith and kin? To say nothing of others, he rehabilitated Licinius Lenticula,[54] his gaming partner who had been condemned for gambling—as though it was not allowable to play with a man under sentence. Ah, but his object was to pay his gambling losses by favor of the law. What reason did you give to the Roman People why it was proper to rehabilitate him? Perhaps he was charged in his absence? Or the case was decided without a hearing? Or gambling was not an indictable offense? Or he was a victim of armed force? Or, finally, as used to be said about your uncle, the jury was bribed? None of these. Well then, he is a good man, worthy of the Commonwealth. That is beside the point; but still, since a conviction counts for nothing, if it were indeed so, I should let the matter rest. In fact he is an arrant scoundrel, who did not hesitate to gamble in the very Forum and was condemned under the gaming law. The author of his rehabilitation has made his own proclivities pretty plain.

**57** In Antonius' year of office as tribune Caesar handed over Italy to be trodden under his boots while himself leaving for Spain. Just think of his progress along the highways, his passages through the towns! I know I am dealing with matters universally talked about and that what I say and am about to say is better known to all who were in Italy at that time than to me, who was elsewhere.[55] I will, however, mention some particulars, although my words

---

52. At the battles of Pharsalia, Thapsus, and Munda.

53. C. Antonius, called Hybrida, Cicero's colleague in the consulship of 63, subsequently exiled for misgovernment in his province of Macedonia.

54. On the cognomen, see *Two Studies*, 47.

55. In fact, Caesar left Rome for Spain on 6 April 49. Cicero remained in Italy another two months, and Antony's extravagances are mentioned in his letters. But he wished it forgotten that he had taken so long to make up his mind to join Pompey.

nullo modo poterit oratio mea satis facere vestrae scientiae. etenim quod
umquam in terris tantum flagitium exstitisse auditum est, tantam turpitudinem, tantum dedecus? **58** vehebatur in essedo tribunus plebis; lictores
laureati antecedebant, inter quos aperta lectica mima portabatur, quam ex
oppidis municipales homines honesti, obviam necessario prodeuntes, non　　5
noto illo et mimico nomine, sed Volumniam consalutabant. sequebatur
raeda cum lenonibus, comites nequissimi; reiecta mater amicam impuri
fili tamquam nurum sequebatur. o miserae mulieris fecunditatem calami-
tosam! horum flagitiorum iste vestigiis omnia municipia, praefecturas,
colonias, totam denique Italiam impressit.　　　　　　　　　　　　　10

　　**59** Reliquorum factorum eius, patres conscripti, difficilis est sane
reprehensio et lubrica. versatus in bello est; saturavit se sanguine dis-
simillimorum sui civium: felix fuit, si potest ulla in scelere esse felicitas.
sed quoniam veteranis cautum esse volumus, quamquam dissimilis est
militum causa et tua—illi secuti sunt, tu quaesisti ducem—tamen, ne apud　　15
illos me in invidiam voces, nihil de genere belli dicam. victor e Thessalia
Brundisium cum legionibus revertisti. ibi me non occidisti. magnum
beneficium! potuisse enim fateor. quamquam nemo erat eorum qui tum
tecum fuerunt qui mihi non censeret parci oportere. **60** tanta est enim
caritas patriae ut vestris etiam legionibus sanctus essem, quod eam a me　　20
servatam esse meminissent. sed fac id te dedisse mihi quod non ademisti,
meque a te habere vitam, quia non a te sit erepta: licuitne mihi per tuas
contumelias hoc tuum beneficium sic tueri ut tuebar, praesertim cum te
haec auditurum videres? **61** venisti Brundisium, in sinum quidem et in
complexum tuae mimulae. quid est? num mentior? quam miserum est id　　25
negare non posse quod sit turpissimum confiteri! si te municipiorum non
pudebat, ne veterani quidem exercitus? quis enim miles fuit qui Brundisi
illam non viderit? quis qui nescierit venisse eam tibi tot dierum viam gra-
tulatum? quis qui non indoluerit tam sero se quam nequam hominem secutus esset cognoscere? **62** Italiae rursus percursatio eadem comite mima;　　30
in oppida militum crudelis et misera deductio; in urbe auri, argenti maximeque vini foeda direptio. accessit ut Caesare ignaro, cum esset ille

**58** 7 leonibus[3] *cod. Harleianus 2682*　　　comites nequissimi *del. Koch*　　*post* nequissimi
*lac. stat. Lutz, fort. recte*　　　recta *V*　　**59** 12 lubirca *V* (*corr.* ç): lubrice *D*　　13 fuit
felix *D*　　16 belli genere *D*　　**60** 21 fac id te dedisse] facit te ded- *nv*: fac te ded- *t*:
fas sit te ded- *s*[2]: faci ut edid- *V*: fac illud te ded- *coni. Halm*　　22 quia] qua *V*: quae
*Graevius*　　　non a te sit] a te non sit *nsv*: non sit a te *t*　　　liceatne *D*　　23 tuum]
*om. cnsv*　　　tuebar] debebam *Watt*　　**61** 26 *anne* municipum (*cf.* 13.18)?　　　non *om.*
*V*　　28 uia *V*　　29 quam nequam ç: q- nec quam *V*: quem (que *b*) *D*

cannot possibly match your knowledge. Nowhere in the world has anything so shocking, scandalous, disgraceful, ever been heard of. **58** A tribune of the plebs riding in a two-wheeler; lictors with laurels preceding,[56] and in their midst a comedienne[57] carried in an open litter; and respectable folk from the country towns, who were obliged to come out and meet the cortège, greeted her not by her well-known stage name but as "Volumnia." Then followed a carriage full of pimps, Antonius' worthless entourage. His mother, relegated to the rear, followed her rake of a son's mistress like a daughter-in-law. Poor unfortunate woman, to be mother of that brood! He left the traces of these infamies in every town, prefecture, and colony, in fact throughout Italy.

**59** To censure his other activities, Members of the Senate, is a matter of some difficulty and delicacy. He took part in the war. He saturated himself with the blood of fellow countrymen who resembled him not at all. He was successful, if there can be success in any crime. But since we do not wish to upset the veterans (not that the soldiers' case and yours is the same; they followed their general, you sought him out), I shall say nothing about the kind of war it was in case you might bring me into their disfavor. You returned victorious from Thessaly to Brundisium with the legions. There you did not kill me.[58] Mighty kind of you! I admit you had the power, even though not one of those who were with you at that time but was in favor of sparing me. **60** Love of country is a potent force: it made my person sacred even to Caesar's legions because they remembered that I had been Rome's preserver. But granted that you gave me what you did not take from me and that I owe you my life because you did not deprive me of it, how could I show proper appreciation of this kindness, as I used to do, after your insults, especially as you were well aware what you would hear in return? **61** Anyway, you arrived in Brundisium, in the lap and arms, that is to say, of your little actress— What's the matter? Am I not telling the truth? A sorry predicament to be unable to deny what it is so disgraceful to admit! If you cared nothing for the opinion of the country towns, what of the veteran army? Was there a soldier who did not see her at Brundisium? Which of them did not know that she had traveled so many days' journey to congratulate you? Which of them was not mortified to learn so late what a worthless wretch he had been following? **62** Then once again a romp through Italy in the same actress's company. Soldiers were settled on the towns, a cruel, distressful operation. In Rome there was an ugly pillaging of gold, silver, and, most of all, wine. On top of all

56. Caesar had made Antony propraetor; hence the lictors. The laurels on their rods (*fasces*) were for Caesar's victories in Gaul.

57. The mime Cytheris; see n. 19 above.

58. See 2.5–6.

Alexandriae, beneficio amicorum eius magister equitum constitueretur. tum existimavit se suo iure cum Hippia vivere et equos vectigalis Sergio mimo tradere; tum sibi non hanc quam nunc male tuetur, sed M. Pisonis domum ubi habitaret legerat. quid ego istius decreta, quid rapinas, quid hereditatum possessiones datas, quid ereptas proferam? cogebat eges- 5 tas; quo se verteret non habebat: nondum ei tanta a L. Rubrio, non a L. Turselio hereditas venerat; nondum in Cn. Pompei locum multorum- que aliorum qui aberant repentinus heres successerat. erat vivendum latronum ritu, ut tantum haberet quantum rapere potuisset.

**63** Sed haec quae robustioris improbitatis sunt, omittamus: loquamur 10 potius de nequissimo genere levitatis. tu istis faucibus, istis lateribus, ista gladiatoria totius corporis firmitate tantum vini in Hippiae nuptiis exhau- seras ut tibi necesse esset in populi Romani conspectu vomere postridie. o rem non modo visu foedam sed etiam auditu! si inter cenam in ipsis tuis immanibus illis poculis hoc tibi accidisset, quis non turpe duceret? in 15 coetu vero populi Romani negotium publicum gerens, magister equitum, cui ructare turpe esset, is vomens frustis esculentis vinum redolentibus gremium suum et totum tribunal implevit. sed haec ipse fatetur esse in suis sordibus: veniamus ad splendida.

**64** Caesar Alexandria se recepit, felix, ut sibi quidem videbatur, mea 20 autem sententia, qui rei publicae sit infelix, felix esse nemo potest. hasta posita pro aede Iovis Statoris bona subiecta Cn. Pompei—miserum me! consumptis enim lacrimis tamen infixus animo haeret dolor—bona, in- quam, Cn. Pompei Magni voci acerbissimae subiecta praeconis. una in illa re servitutis oblita civitas ingemuit servientibusque †animis† cum 25 omnia metu tenerentur, gemitus tamen populi Romani liber fuit. exspec- tantibus omnibus quisnam esset tam impius, tam demens, tam dis homi- nibusque hostis qui ad illud scelus sectionis auderet accedere, inventus

**62** 3 tradere *om. V*[1]     3–4 tum . . . legerat *om. D*     5 hereditatium *Quint. 9.2.47*     7 Cn. *om. V*     **63** 13 in conspectu populi Romani *Quint. 9.4.29, 107*     14–15 in ipsis . . . poculis *codd.* (ipsis *om. nsv*): et in illis immanibus poculis tuis *Quint. 5.10.99* (*om.* et), *8.4.10*: et illis inm- poc- tuis *Iul. Vict. p. 43 ed. Giomini*: atque in ipsis tuis imm- poc- *Arusian. 7:482 Keil*     15 hoc tibi *ante* inter *Quint. et Iul. Vict.*     duceret *b*[1], *Quint. 8.4.10, 9.4.107:* dic- *Vcnstvb*[2]     16 Romani *om. D*     gerens *n*[2], *Quint. 8.4.8, 11.3.39, 167, Arusian.:* gens *V:* reg- *D*     magister equitum *ante* negotium *Arusian. 7:475 Keil*     19 splendidiora *V*     **64** 20–21 ut . . . infelix *om. nsv*     20 uideatur *V*     21 si qui *bct*     infelix[3]] hostis *V:* infensus *A. Klotz*     22 subiecta (-ti *b*) Cn. Pompei *om. Quint. 9.3.29,* subiecta *del. Faërnus, fort. recte*     23 animo haeret *D, Quint. 9.3.29* (*sed 9.2.26* infixus tamen pectori haeret): haberet a- *V*     24 Magni *om. Quint.*     acerbis- simae uoci *Quint.*     25 animis *suspectum:* cunctis *Hirschfelder:* manibus *Koch: fort.* om- nibus (o- cum animi *iam Campe*)     25–26 cum . . . tenerentur *om. D, habet Sen. Contr. 7.2.5* (*sed* quamvis *pro* cum, *om.* Romani)     27 omnibusque *V*

he was appointed master of horse by favor of Caesar's friends without Caesar's knowledge, since Caesar was in Alexandria. After that he felt fully entitled to live with Hippia[59] and hand over hired horses[60] to Sergius the comedian. At that time he had chosen Marcus Piso's house as his residence, not the house which he is now precariously occupying.[61] Need I bring up the orders, the plunderings, the estates of deceased persons bestowed or taken away? Penury drove; he did not know where to turn. Not yet had he come into those fat bequests from Lucius Rubrius and Lucius Turselius, not yet as an improvised heir had he moved into the place of Gnaeus Pompeius and many other absentees. He had to live as highwaymen do, possessing as much as he had been able to rob.

**63** But let us leave aside such acts of sturdy wickedness, and speak rather of arrant worthlessness and frivolity. With that gullet of yours, those lungs, that robust physique which a gladiator might envy, you engulfed such a quantity of wine at Hippia's wedding that the following day you found it necessary to vomit in full view of the Roman People. Disgusting to witness, disgusting even to hear tell of! Had this happened to you at dinner in those same monstrous cups of yours, no one but would have thought it a shameful exhibition: but in an assembly of the Roman People, a master of horse, conducting public business! Where a belch would have been a disgrace, he vomited, filling his lap and his whole platform with morsels of food stinking of wine! Ah well, he admits himself that this was one of his less creditable performances. Let us look at him when he shines.

**64** Caesar returned from Alexandria, a fortunate man, as he considered himself; but in my opinion no man can be fortunate who brings misfortune upon the Commonwealth. A lance[62] was planted in front of the temple of Jupiter Stator, and the property of Gnaeus Pompeius—I can hardly go on; tears may have run dry, but deep in the heart the pain stays—the property, I say, of Gnaeus Pompeius Magnus was subjected to the harsh voice of an auctioneer. Then and only then did the community forget its bondage and groan aloud. * * * were enslaved, for terror ruled all, but the groaning of the Roman People was free. All waited in suspense: what impious madman, what enemy to God and man would dare to commit the heinous crime of a bid? Nobody did—

59. The name means "horsey." It may be male (Greek Hippias) or female. Plutarch (*Ant.* 9) says that this Hippia(s) was a male actor (*mimus*), but that might be only a false deduction from this passage.

60. The facts are otherwise unknown and the meaning of *vectigalis* is doubtful.

61. Pompey's house. Piso is probably the son of M. Pupius Piso, consul in 61 (cf. 3.25). He may have been a Pompeian, though Caesar made him praetor in 44.

62. Symbol of public ownership, used at auctions of confiscated property.

est nemo praeter Antonium, praesertim cum tot essent circum hastam illam qui alia omnia auderent: unus inventus est qui id auderet quod omnium fugisset et reformidasset audacia. **65** tantus igitur te stupor oppressit vel, ut verius dicam, tantus furor ut primum, cum sector sis isto loco natus, deinde cum Pompei sector, non te exsecratum populo Romano, 5 non detestabilem, non omnis tibi deos, non omnis homines et esse inimicos et futuros scias? at quam insolenter statim helluo invasit in eius viri fortunas cuius virtute terribilior erat populus Romanus exteris gentibus, iustitia carior! in eius igitur viri copias cum se subito ingurgitasset, exsultabat gaudio, persona de mimo, "modo egens, repente dives." sed, 10 ut est apud poetam nescio quem, "male parta male dilabuntur." **66** incredibile ac simile portenti est quonam modo illa tam multa quam paucis non dico mensibus sed diebus effuderit. maximus vini numerus fuit, permagnum optimi pondus argenti, pretiosa vestis, multa et lauta supellex et magnifica multis locis, non illa quidem luxuriosi hominis, sed tamen 15 abundantis. horum paucis diebus nihil erat. **67** quae Charybdis tam vorax? Charybdim dico? quae si fuit, animal unum fuit: Oceanus, me dius fidius, vix videtur tot res tam dissipatas, tam distantibus in locis positas tam cito absorbere potuisse. nihil erat clausum, nihil obsignatum, nihil scriptum. apothecae totae nequissimis hominibus condonabantur; 20 alia mimi rapiebant, alia mimae; domus erat aleatoribus referta, plena ebriorum; totos dies potabatur atque id locis pluribus; suggerebantur etiam saepe—non enim semper iste felix—damna aleatoria; conchyliatis Cn. Pompei peristromatis servorum in cellis lectos stratos videres. quam ob rem desinite mirari haec tam celeriter esse consumpta. non modo 25 unius patrimonium quamvis amplum, ut illud fuit, sed urbis et regna celeriter tanta nequitia devorare potuisset. at idem aedis etiam et hortos— **68** o audaciam immanem! tu etiam ingredi illam domum ausus es, tu illud sanctissimum limen intrare, tu illarum aedium dis penatibus os impurissimum ostendere? quam domum aliquamdiu nemo aspicere poterat, 30 nemo sine lacrimis praeterire, hac te in domo tam diu deversari non

---

**65** 5 exsecrandum (-us *b*) *D*    6 non *post* deos *om. D*    et esse] esse *V*    7 viri *om. D*    9 ingurgitauisset *D*    **66** 12 est] sit *c*: si *sv*: *om. bt* (*cf.* 2.53, 113)    **67** 16 tam *codd., Quint. 8.6.70, 12.10.62*: est tam *Sen. Suas. 6.5*    17 charybdim *V, Sen.*: -in *D* (carib-), *Quint. 8.6.70*    animal unum fuit *V, Sen.*: f- a- u- *D, Quint.*: a- f- u- *Serv. ad Aen. 3.420*    17–18 Oceanus me dius fidius ipse *Quint. 12.10.62*: vix me d- f- Oc- *Sen.* (videtur *om.*)    18–19 tot res tamque diuersas uno tempore absoluere potuisset *codd. Sen.*    23 ipse *D*    24 stratos lectos *c, Quint. 8.4.25*    27 *post* hortos *sic dist. Watt, qui* occupauit *simul intellegit*    **68** 28 etiam *om. D*    29–30 os impurissimum osten inportunissimum dere *V*: os import- ostendere *D* (*v. Fe.*)    30 sine lacrimis *ante* adspicere *add.* Cobet, *quod tamen intellegendum est ex succedentibus*    31 diuersari *bct*: diuersa *n¹sv*: uersare *n²*

except Antonius; even though so many stood around that lance who would have stopped at nothing else. Yes, he alone was found to dare an act from which the audacity of all the rest recoiled in consternation. **65** Have you suddenly become so insensate, so insane, to use a better word, as to purchase confiscated goods (a man of your birth!), and those goods Pompeius' goods, without knowing that you are on that account abominable and accursed in the sight of the Roman People and that all Gods and all men are your enemies, now and for ever more? But how insolently the wastrel laid hasty hands on the possessions of the man whose valor made Rome more feared by foreign nations, whose justice made her more loved! Thus, plunging of a sudden into the wealth of such a man, he jubilated like a character in a farce, "beggar one day, rich the next."[63] But, as some playwright[64] has it, "ill gotten is ill spent." **66** It is unbelievable, like a prodigy, how he dissipated so much in a few—not months, but days. There was a great quantity of wine, a very large weight of the finest silver plate, costly draperies, much elegant and magnificent furniture, variously located, the appointments not indeed of a luxurious man, but of an affluent one. A few days later nothing of this remained. **67** Was ever a Charybdis[65] so ravenous? But forget Charybdis, a single creature if it ever existed: upon my soul, I can hardly believe the Ocean could have swallowed up so many objects so rapidly, scattered as they were in places wide apart. Nothing was closed, nothing sealed, nothing written down. Whole cellars were given away to wastrels. Actors snatched this, actresses that. The house was crammed full with gamesters and topers. Tippling went on all day long and in a variety of places too. Often gambling losses would add to the wastage, for Antonius' luck is not invariable. You might see couches in slaves' quarters spread with Gnaeus Pompeius' purple coverlets. So you may cease to wonder at the speed of the consumption. Such prodigality could quickly have devoured cities and kingdoms, let alone one individual's patrimony, however ample—and ample it was. And the house itself, the suburban estates— **68** monstrous audacity! Did you actually dare to enter that house, to cross that hallowed threshold, to show your debauched visage to those household gods? This long while past no man could look at that house or pass it by without tears; are you not ashamed to be lodging in it all this time? Dull though

---

63. Perhaps the title of a mime.
64. Naevius.
65. A whirlpool in the Straits of Messina, mythologically personified as female—exactly what sort of female is nowhere clear.

pudet? in qua, quamvis nihil sapias, tamen nihil tibi potest esse iucundum. an tu illa in vestibulo rostra [spolia] cum aspexisti, domum tuam te introire putas? fieri non potest. quamvis enim sine mente, sine sensu sis, ut es, tamen et te et tua et tuos nosti. nec vero te umquam neque vigilantem neque in somnis credo posse mente consistere. necesse est,　　5
quamvis sis, ut es, violentus et furens, cum tibi obiecta sit species singularis viri, perterritum te de somno excitari, furere etiam saepe vigilantem. **69** me quidem miseret parietum ipsorum atque tectorum. quid enim umquam domus illa viderat nisi pudicum, quid nisi ex optimo more et sanctissima disciplina? fuit enim ille vir, patres conscripti, sicuti scitis,　10
cum foris clarus tum domi admirandus, neque rebus externis magis laudandus quam institutis domesticis. huius in sedibus pro cubiculis stabula, pro conclavibus popinae [tricliniis] sunt. etsi iam negat. nolite quaerere; frugi factus est: illam suam suas res sibi habere iussit, ex duodecim tabulis clavis ademit, exegit. quam porro spectatus civis, quam probatus!　15
cuius ex omni vita nihil est honestius quam quod cum mima fecit divortium. **70** at quam crebro usurpat: "et consul et Antonius!" hoc est dicere, et consul et impudicissimus, et consul et homo nequissimus. quid est enim aliud Antonius? nam si dignitas significaretur in nomine, dixisset, credo, aliquando avus tuus se et consulem et Antonium. numquam dixit.　20
dixisset etiam collega meus, patruus tuus, nisi si tu es solus Antonius.

Sed omitto ea peccata quae non sunt earum partium propria quibus tu rem publicam vexavisti: ad ipsas tuas partis redeo, id est ad civile bellum, quod natum, conflatum, susceptum opera tua est. **71** cui bello ⟨iam⟩ cum propter timiditatem tuam tum propter libidines defuisti. gustaras civilem　25
sanguinem vel potius exsorbueras; fueras in acie Pharsalica antesignanus; L. Domitium, clarissimum et nobilissimum virum, occideras multosque prae⟨te⟩rea qui e proelio effugerant, quos Caesar, ut non nullos, fortasse servasset, crudelissime persecutus trucidaras. quibus rebus tantis ⟨et⟩ talibus gestis quid fuit causae cur in Africam Caesarem non sequerere, cum　30

---

2 in vestibulo *Muretus*: in -loa *V*: uestibula *D*　　rostra *Orelli*: rostra (-an *V*) spolia *codd.*　3 putas introire *coni. Clark numeri gratia*　4 et te et tua et tuos] et (te *V²*) ei tua et uos *V*　6 uinolentus *tn²* (*v. Fe.*)　tibi] ibi *cnsv*　7 furere *propter* furens (*l. 6*) *suspectum, sed v. Fe.*　**69** 9 quid *om. D*　12 aedibus *Ursinus, sed cf.* 2.104　13 conclavibus popinae *Halm*: c- p- triclinis *V*: tricliniis p- *D*　14 illam *codd.* (minimam *supra lin. add. cod. Harleianus 2682; cf. tamen Scaur. 9, Fam. 9.19.1* ad suam): mimulam (mimam *iam Halm*) *Cornelissen*　15 clauis] clausa *nstv*　forasque ex- *Nonius 291* 16 cum] *om. nstv*　**70** 18 homi *V*: omnium *Nohl*　18‒19 est enim] est *b¹t*: enim *v*: enim est *nsb²*　20 et (*pr.*) *om. bcntv*　numquam dixit] numquid *V*　21 tuus *om. V*　23 *anne* istas?　**71** 24 cui bello cum] cur ei bello tum *D*　iam³ *addidi*　25 tum] tuam et *v*: et *bnst*　28 praeterea ç: praerea *V*: *om. D*　e] eo *t*: de *nsv*　29 et *add. Eberhard³*: ac *Schütz*　talibusque *n*　30 quid . . . Africam *om. V*

you are, nothing can be pleasant to you there. Or when you see those ships' beaks in the forecourt, do you imagine it is *your* house you are entering? That is impossible. You may be, indeed you are, mindless and insensate, but you know yourself and what is yours and who. I do not believe you can have a tranquil moment awake or asleep. You may be, indeed you are, a man of violence and fury, but when the likeness of that matchless man is set before you, you must needs start in terror from your slumbers, and even in your waking hours you must often rave. **69** For my part, I pity the very walls and ceilings. That house had seen nothing but what was decorous and in accord with the highest and strictest moral code. For as you know, Members of the Senate, the great man of whom I speak was as admirable at home as he was renowned abroad, and his achievements in foreign lands were no more praiseworthy than his domestic life. Now in his dwelling the bedrooms are brothels, the dining rooms cookshops. Oh, but he now denies it! Don't ask why, he has reformed. He has dismissed that spouse[66] of his, taken away the keys according to the Twelve Tables, put her out of doors. What respectability, what character! The most creditable action of his life is to have divorced an actress! **70** He is so fond of the phrase "Consul and Antonius," which is to say "Consul and Rake," "Consul and Wastrel." What else is Antonius? If the name were a symbol of worth, I imagine your grandfather would now and then have called himself "Consul and Antonius"; but he never did. So would my former colleague, your uncle—unless you are the one and only Antonius.

However, I leave aside misdemeanors which do not especially concern the partisan activity with which you plagued the Commonwealth, and return to that activity, I mean to the Civil War, which was engendered, blown up, undertaken by your doing. **71** Your cowardice and your lusts now kept you out of it. You had tasted the blood of your fellow countrymen, or drained it rather. You had been in the battle of Pharsalia. As an elite fighter,[67] you had slain the illustrious and highborn Lucius Domitius; and many besides, who had escaped from the battlefield and whose lives Caesar might perhaps have spared as he spared some others, you had cruelly pursued and butchered. After such distinguished exploits, how was it that you did not follow Caesar to Africa, where so

---

66. Cytheris.

67. The term *antesignanus* may be a reference to Antony's pursuit of the fugitives; see SB[1]. In fact, Antony commanded Caesar's left wing.

praesertim belli pars tanta restaret? itaque quem locum apud ipsum Caesarem post eius ex Africa reditum obtinuisti? quo numero fuisti? cuius tu
imperatoris quaestor fueras, dictatoris magister equitum, belli princeps,
crudelitatis auctor, praedae socius, testamento, ut dicebas ipse, filius, appellatus es de pecunia quam pro domo, pro hortis, pro sectione debebas. 5
**72** primo respondisti plane ferociter et, ne omnia videar contra te, prope
modum aequa et iusta dicebas: "a me C. Caesar pecuniam? cur potius
quam ego ab illo? an sine me ille vicit? at ne potuit quidem. ego ad illum
belli civilis causam attuli; ego leges perniciosas rogavi; ego arma contra
consules imperatoresque populi Romani, contra senatum populumque 10
Romanum, contra deos patrios arasque et focos, contra patriam tuli. num
sibi soli vicit? quorum facinus est commune, cur non sit eorum praeda
communis?" ius postulabas, sed quid ad rem? plus ille poterat. **73** itaque
excussis tuis vocibus et ad te et ad praedes tuos milites misit, cum repente
a te praeclara illa tabula prolata est. qui risus hominum, tantam esse tabu- 15
lam, tam varias, tam multas possessiones, ex quibus praeter partem Miseni
nihil erat quod is qui auctionaretur posset suum dicere. auctionis vero
miserabilis aspectus: vestis Pompei non multa eaque maculosa; eiusdem
quaedam argentea vasa collisa, sordidata mancipia, ut doleremus quicquam esse ex illis reliqui[s] quod videre possemus. **74** hanc tamen auc- 20
tionem heredes L. Rubri decreto Caesaris prohibuerunt. haerebat nebulo:
quo se verteret non habebat. quin his ipsis temporibus domi Caesaris
percussor ab isto missus deprehensus dicebatur esse cum sica: de quo
Caesar in senatu aperte in te invehens questus est.

Proficiscitur in Hispaniam Caesar paucis tibi ad solvendum propter 25
inopiam tuam prorogatis diebus. ne tum quidem sequeris. tam bonus
gladiator rudem tam cito? hunc igitur quisquam qui in suis partibus, id est
in suis fortunis, tam timidus fuerit pertimescat? **75** profectus est aliquando tandem in Hispaniam; sed tuto, ut ait, pervenire non potuit.
quonam modo igitur Dolabella pervenit? aut non suscipienda fuit ista 30
causa, Antoni, aut, cum suscepisses, defendenda usque ad extremum. ter
depugnavit Caesar cum civibus, in Thessalia, Africa, Hispania. omnibus
adfuit his pugnis Dolabella; in Hispaniensi etiam vulnus accepit. si de
meo iudicio quaeris, nollem; sed tamen consilium a primo reprehenden-

1 restaret (*cf. Gell. 1.22.17*)] praes- *V*      4 testamenti *D*      dicebat *D*      **72** 7 C. *om.*
*D*      8 at ne] anne *bcns*: ac ne *t*: an me *v*      ad eum *Nonius 383*      9 ego leges . . . rogavi
*om. V* (*habet Nonius*)      11 et *om. V*      12 est *om. D*      **73** 14 excussis] *v. Fe.*      15
prolata est *Halm*: -latas *V*: -lata *D*      hominum de te erat *D*      17 is *om. V*      20 reliqui
*Pluygers*: -uis *Vn¹t*: -uiis *Dbcn²sv*      **74** 22 quin] quippe in *D*      iis *Halm*      23 cum
sica de quo] cum in te inuehens sic ad quo *V*      27 cito accepisti *D*      28 fuerat *V*      **75**
29 tandem aliquando *D*      33 in] *om. Vbct*

large a part of the war had still to be fought? So how did you stand with Caesar himself after his return from Africa? How did he rate you? You had been quaestor to him as commander-in-chief, master of horse to him as dictator, you were the prime mover of his war, instigator of his cruelty, partner in his plunder, and under his will, so you used to say yourself, his son: and he came down on you for the money you owed on the house, the suburban residences, the whole purchase. **72** At first you retorted with proper spirit—and, not to appear to be always against you, what you said was almost fair and reasonable: "Caesar demand money from *me*? Why not I from him? Did he win without me? He couldn't. I gave him his pretext for civil war, I proposed pernicious laws, I bore arms against consuls and commanders of the Roman People, against the Senate and the People of Rome, against our ancestral Gods and altars and hearths, against our country. Did he win only for himself? Why shouldn't those who share the guilt share the loot?" You were asking for your right, but what of that? He was the stronger. **73** And so, shrugging aside your protests, he sent soldiers to you and your sureties; at which point you suddenly issued that famous sale catalogue. Loud was the laughter to see so long a list of properties so many and various, of which (except for a share in the Misenum estate) there was not one that the person putting them up could call his own. Ah, but the auction itself was a sorry spectacle. Some draperies of Pompeius', not much and stained at that; certain dented articles of silver, also his, some squalid slaves. It made us sad that anything remained for us to see. **74** However, the heirs of Lucius Rubrius, acting under an order of Caesar's,[68] forbade the auction. Our prodigal was now in a cleft stick, did not know where to turn. At that very time the story went about that an assassin sent by Antonius was arrested in Caesar's house carrying a dagger; Caesar complained and attacked you about it in open Senate.

Having given you a few days' grace in which to pay in consideration of your lack of means, Caesar left for Spain. You did not follow him on this occasion either. Should so good a gladiator have taken his discharge so soon? Not much to fear from one so cowardly in supporting his own side, that is, his own fortunes! **75** At long last he did leave for Spain; but he could not get there safely, so he says. Then how did Dolabella get there? You should either not have enlisted under that banner, Antonius, or having done so you should have fought for it to the end. Three times Caesar met his countrymen in decisive battle, in Thessaly, Africa, and Spain. Dolabella took part in all these engagements, in the Spanish one he was actually wounded. If you ask my opinion, I wish he had not. All the same, if his original choice is censurable, his

68. Details unknown; cf. 2.40.

dum, laudanda constantia. tu vero quid ais? Cn. Pompei liberi tum primum patriam repetebant. esto, fuerit haec partium causa communis. repetebant praeterea deos patrios, aras, focos, larem suum familiarem, in quae tu invaseras. haec cum peterent armis ei quorum erant legibus—etsi in rebus iniquissimis quid potest esse aequi?—tamen quem erat aequissi- 5 mum contra Cn. Pompei liberos pugnare? quem? te sectorem. an ut tu Narbone mensas hospitum convomeres Dolabella pro te in Hispania dimicaret?

**76** Qui vero Narbone reditus! etiam quaerebat cur ego ex ipso cursu tam subito revertissem. exposui nuper, patres conscripti, causam reditus 10 mei. volui, si possem, etiam ante Kalendas Ianuarias prodesse rei publicae. nam quod quaerebas quo modo redissem, primum luce, non tenebris; deinde cum calceis et toga, nullis nec gallicis nec lacerna. at etiam aspicis me et quidem, ut videris, iratus. ne tu iam mecum in gratiam redeas, si scias quam me pudeat nequitiae tuae, cuius te ipsum non pudet. 15 ex omnium omnibus flagitiis nullum turpius vidi, nullum audivi. qui magister equitum fuisse tibi viderere, in proximum annum consulatum peteres vel potius rogares, per municipia coloniasque Galliae, a qua nos tum cum consulatus petebatur, non rogabatur, petere consulatum solebamus, cum gallicis et lacerna cucurristi. 20

**77** At videte levitatem hominis. cum hora diei decima fere ad Saxa Rubra venisset, delituit in quadam cauponula atque ibi se occultans perpotavit ad vesperam; inde cisio celeriter ad urbem advectus domum venit capite obvoluto. ianitor: "quis tu?" "a Marco tabellarius." confestim ad eam cuius causa venerat, eique epistulam tradidit. quam cum illa 25 legeret flens—erat enim scripta amatorie; caput autem litterarum sibi cum illa mima posthac nihil futurum; omnem se amorem abiecisse illim

1 ais *Halm*: es *codd.*      liberi (-er $V^1$) tum]: liberi (-ram *c*) *D*     3 patrios *Faërnus*: partios *V*: penates patrios (propr- *t*) *D*     4 quae tu *D*: quencumque *V*: quae cuncta tu *Orelli*: q- tu impie *coni. Schöll, haud male*     peterent] rep- *bct*     5–6 tamen erat aequissimum contra cn. p. (cn. p. *om. t*) liberos (non *add. s*) cn. p. pugnare (te *add. bc*) sectorem *D*     6 ut tu *Clark*: tutu *V*: tu *D*: ut $n^2$: cum tu *Servius 4:416, 511 Keil, Cledonius 5:22 Keil*     7 cum uomeres (cum conu- *t*) *D*     **76** 9 etiam (*v. Fe.*)]: et tamen *bnsv*: est iam *t*: eius iam *c*: eius tamen *Ferrarius*     13 gallicis $\varsigma$ (*v. infra*): caligis *codd.*, *Iul. Rufinianus Rhet. Lat. ed. Halm* 40 (nec *ante om.*): Gallicis *vulg.* (*cf. e.g. Mart.* 4.4.5 vardaicus)     16 nullum turpius vidi *om.* V     18 per] is per *bct*: is qui per *nsv*     a *om.* V: e *coni. Halm*     18–19 nos tum] nostrum *bct*: *om. nsv*     20 gallicis *Gell.* 13.22.6: calligis (cali- *D*) *codd.*     **77** 21 aut *V*     hominis *V, Gell.* 6.11.6: *om. D*     decima *om.* V     23 vesperam] -rum *D, Gell.*     24 capite] ore *Gell.*     obuoluto] inuo- *D, Gell.*     ianitor rogat *Gell.*     25 deducitur (addu- *b*) *post* eam *D, post* venerat *Gell.*     tradit *Gell.*     illa cum *Gell.*     26 scripta amatorie *Vv, Gell.*: a- s- *bcns*: a- causa s- *t*     litterarum] l- hoc erat *Gell.*     27 illim *Lambinus*: illi non *V*: illinc *bnsv*: illic *ct*: illi *Gell.*

constancy is praiseworthy. But what do *you* have to say? The sons of Gnaeus Pompeius for the first time were reclaiming their fatherland. Very well, let us say that concerned your whole party. Furthermore, they were reclaiming their ancestral Gods, altars, hearths, their family home, which you had invaded. When the legal owners claimed their property in arms, who—I know there can be no justice in such iniquity, but still, *who* could most justly be expected to fight against Gnaeus Pompeius' sons? Who but you, who bought him up? Or was it right that Dolabella should fight for you in Spain while you vomited over your hosts' dinner tables at Narbo?

**76** And now, the manner of his return from Narbo—and he was asking why *I* turned back so suddenly, abandoning my journey! Members of the Senate, I explained the reason for my return not long ago. I wanted, if possible, to be of some use to the Commonwealth even before the Kalends of January.[69] As for your question, *how* did I return, to begin with, it was by daylight, not darkness; secondly, it was in gown[70] and boots, not in cloak and Gaulish slippers. Ah, you are looking at me, you seem annoyed. I assure you, if you knew the shame I feel at your wastrel behavior, which *you* are not ashamed of, you would be friends with me again. No infamy I have ever seen or heard of was more outrageous. You looked upon yourself as a former master of horse, you were standing for the consulship, or rather asking for it, the following year: and you rushed through the townships and colonies of Gaul, the region where we used to canvass for the consulship when that office was stood for and not asked for, in Gaulish slippers and a cloak!

**77** The frivolity of the fellow! Arriving at Red Rocks[71] about four o'clock in the afternoon, he went to ground in a little tavern and stayed in hiding there until sunset, tippling steadily. From that tavern a groom galloped into Rome and through to Antonius' house with his face muffled. Doorman: "Who's there?" "Courier from Marcus." Straightaway he is conducted to the lady[72] on whose account he had come and hands her the letter. She wept as she read—it was a love letter. The main point of it was that he would have nothing to do with the actress in the future; he had jettisoned all love in that quarter and

---

69. In 1.10 Cicero says otherwise.
70. Toga.
71. Saxa Rubra, on the via Flaminia about nine miles north of Rome.
72. Fulvia.

atque in hanc transfudisse—cum mulier fleret uberius, homo misericors
ferre non potuit, caput aperuit, in collum invasit. o hominem nequam!
quid enim aliud dicam? magis proprie nihil possum dicere. ergo, ut te
catamitum, nec opinato cum te ostendisses, praeter spem mulier aspi-
ceret, idcirco urbem terrore nocturno, Italiam multorum dierum metu      5
perturbasti? **78** et domi quidem causam amoris habui⟨s⟩t⟨i⟩, foris etiam
turpiorem, ne L. Plancus praedes tuos venderet. productus autem in
contionem a tribuno plebis cum respondisses te rei tuae causa venisse,
populum etiam dicacem in te reddidisti. sed nimis multa de nugis: ad
maiora veniamus.                                                          10

   C. Caesari ex Hispania redeunti obviam longissime processisti. celeriter isti redisti, ut cognosceret te, si minus fortem, at tamen strenuum.
factus es ei rursus nescio quo modo familiaris. habebat hoc omnino
Caesar: quem plane perditum aere alieno egentemque, si eundem nequam
hominem audacemque cognorat, hunc in familiaritatem libentissime        15
recipiebat. **79** his igitur rebus praeclare commendatus iussus es renuntiari
consul et quidem cum ipso. nihil queror de Dolabella qui tum est impulsus,
inductus, elusus. qua in re quanta fuerit uterque vestrum perfidia in
Dolabellam quis ignorat? ille induxit ut peteret, promissum et receptum
intervertit ad seque transtulit; tu eius perfidiae voluntatem tuam ascrip-   20
sisti. veniunt Kalendae Ianuariae; cogimur in senatum: invectus est copiosius multo in istum et paratius Dolabella quam nunc ego. **80** hic autem
iratus quae dixit, di boni! primum cum Caesar ostendisset se, prius quam
proficisceretur, Dolabellam consulem esse iussurum—quem negant regem, qui et faceret semper eius modi aliquid et diceret—sed cum Caesar   25
ita dixisset, tum hic bonus augur eo se sacerdotio praeditum esse dixit ut
comitia auspiciis vel impedire vel vitiare posset, idque se facturum esse
adseveravit. in quo primum incredibilem stupiditatem hominis cognoscite. **81** quid enim? istud quod te sacerdoti iure facere posse dixisti, si
augur non esses et consul esses, minus facere potuisses? vide ne etiam   30
facilius. nos enim nuntiationem solum habemus, consules et reliqui magistratus etiam spectionem. esto: hoc imperite; nec enim est ab homine
numquam sobrio postulanda prudentia. sed videte impudentiam. multis

---

3 quid . . . dicam *om. Gell. 6.11.5 et 6*      nihil enim magis proprie *Gell.*      4 neque
*D*    cum te] cum *D, Gell.*: cum os *Cobet*    **78** 6 habuisti *Ferrarius*: habuit (habeat *t*[1])
*codd.*    7 suos *cod. Harleianus 2682*    11 C. *om. D*    12 isti] isti et *D*    15 cognorat *ς*: -oram *V*: -ouerat *D*    **79** 16 est *D*    17 de *om. V*[1]    17–19 qui . . . Dolabellam *om. V*[1]    18 utriusque *D*    19 induxit ut peteret *om. V*    **80** 23 iratus] irtus
*V*: mihi iratus *bnt*: m- i- est *s*: miratus *v*    24 negat *V*    **81** 29 enim est *V*    32 spec-
tionem] spectati- *V*[1]: ispectati- *V*[2]: inspecti- *bnsv*

transferred it to this lady. So she wept all the more until her softhearted lord could bear it no longer and, throwing off his muffler, fell into her arms. What a good-for-nothing!— What else shall I call him? I can find no term more appropriate. Night alarm in Rome, Italy in fear and turmoil for days on end, all in order that this Ganymede should show up unexpectedly and give a lady a surprise! **78** Well, indoors you had a lover's reason; out of doors your reason was still more discreditable: you were afraid Lucius Plancus[73] would sell up your sureties. Your reply to a question when brought before a public meeting by a tribune of the plebs made even the common folk witty at your expense: you said you had come to Rome on private business. But there's more than enough about trifles. Let us get to matters of greater moment.

You traveled a great distance to meet Gaius Caesar on his way home from Spain—a rapid out and back again: he should see that if your courage left something to be desired, you were at least a man of energy. Somehow or other you again became one of his cronies. It was a way that Caesar had: let him see a man head over heels in debt, without a penny to his name, then, provided he knew that man for a bold rascal, he would be delighted to welcome him into his familiarity. **79** Since you were admirably commended by these qualities, Caesar gave orders for you to be declared elected consul, and with himself as your colleague. I make no complaint about Dolabella, who was prompted to stand, led on, and then made a fool of. Everybody knows how perfidiously you both behaved toward Dolabella. Caesar led him on to stand for the office, and then, after it had been promised and guaranteed, moved in and transferred it to himself. You became a willing party to his treachery. The Kalends of January came around. We were summoned to the Senate, where Dolabella delivered a much more copious and studied invective against Antonius than I am delivering now. **80** Ye Gods, what a speech angry Antonius made! To begin with, Caesar had made it clear that before leaving Rome he would order that Dolabella be consul (he was always doing and saying that sort of thing, and yet they deny that he was a monarch!)—anyway, Caesar having so pronounced, this adept augur of ours stated that he was invested with a priestly office which enabled him to hold up or invalidate the elections by means of auspices, and he declared that this was his intention. First, just let me point out the egregious stupidity of the man. **81** Think: what you said you could do by your priestly prerogative, would you have been any the less able to do it as consul if you had *not* been an augur? Surely you could have done it even more easily. We augurs only possess the right to report, whereas the consuls and other magistrates also have the right to take observations. Very good, he was ignorant—after all, we cannot demand expertise from a man who is never sober. But consider his

73. One of eight (or six) prefects of Rome (*praefecti urbi*) left in charge by Caesar. He may also have been city praetor.

ante mensibus in senatu dixit se Dolabellae comitia aut prohibiturum auspiciis aut id facturum esse quod fecit. quisquamne divinare potest quid
viti in auspiciis futurum sit, nisi qui de caelo servare constituit? quod neque licet comitiis per leges et si qui servavit, non comitiis habitis sed
prius quam habeantur, debet nuntiare. verum implicata inscientia impu- 5
dentia est: nec scit quod augurem nec facit quod pudentem decet.

**82** Itaque ex illo die recordamini eius usque ad Idus Martias consulatum. quis umquam apparitor tam humilis, tam abiectus? nihil ipse
poterat; omnia rogabat; caput in aversam lecticam inserens, beneficia
quae venderet a collega petebat. ecce Dolabellae comitiorum dies. sorti- 10
tio praerogativae; quiescit. renuntiatur: tacet. prima classis vocatur [re-
nuntiatur], deinde, ita ut adsolet, suffragia, tum secunda classis, quae
omnia sunt citius facta quam dixi. **83** confecto negotio bonus augur—
C. Laelium diceres—"alio die" inquit. o impudentiam singularem! quid
videras, quid senseras, quid audieras? neque enim te de caelo servasse 15
dixisti nec hodie dicis. id igitur obvenit vitium quod tu iam Kalendis
Ianuariis futurum esse provideras et tanto ante praedixeras. ergo hercule
magna, ut spero, tua potius quam rei publicae calamitate ementitus es
auspicia; obstrinxisti religione populum Romanum; augur auguri, consul
consuli obnuntiasti. nolo plura, ne acta Dolabellae videar convellere, quae 20
necesse est aliquando ad nostrum collegium deferantur. **84** sed adrogantiam hominis insolentiamque cognoscite. quam diu tu voles, vitiosus consul Dolabella; rursus, cum voles, salvis auspiciis creatus. si nihil est cum
augur eis verbis nuntiat quibus tu nuntiasti, confitere te, cum "alio die"
dixeris, sobrium non fuisse; sin est aliqua vis in istis verbis, ea quae sit 25
augur a collega requiro.

Sed ne forte ex multis rebus gestis M. Antoni rem unam pulcherrimam
transiliat oratio, ad Lupercalia veniamus. non dissimulat, patres conscripti: apparet esse commotum; sudat, pallet. quidlibet, modo ne [nau-
siet] faciat quod in porticu Minucia fecit. quae potest esse turpitudinis 30

---

1 dixit se dolabellae *n*²: dixisse dolab- *D*: dixit sed lab- *V*    2 posset *V*    4 habitis
(habetis *t*) comitiis *D*    5 inscientia] -citia *bcst*    6 est nec scit *V*: si nec s- *b*: sed nec
s- *c*: si nes- *nstv*    **82** 7 itaque *V*: atque *D*    9 aursam *V*: aduer- *bnstv*    inserens]
infer- *bnstv*    10 uideret *V*    11 renuntiatur *del. Garatoni*    12 ita *om. D*    sex
*ante* suffragia *duce Hirschfelder add. Niebuhr,* equitum *post* suff- *Mommsen*    classis
uocatur *V*    **83** 14 C. *om. D*    15–16 neque . . . nec] nec . . . neque *D*    19 p. r.
religione *D*    20 nuntiauisti (-asti *c*) *D*    **84** 23 si] sed *nstv*    24 tu *om. D*    26
augur] -ris *nstv*    27 M. *om. V*    28 forte transiliat *V*    29 nausiet *del. Cobet, praeeunte Pluygers*

impudence: many months before the event he stated in the Senate that he
would either forbid Dolabella's election by means of auspices or do what in
fact he did. Can anyone foretell a flaw in the auspices unless he has decided to
watch the heavens? But that is illegal at elections; and if anyone has watched,
he should make his announcement not after but before the elections are held.
Ignorance compounded by impudence! He neither knows what an augur ought
to know nor acts as a man of discretion ought to act.

**82** Well, then, pray recall his behavior as consul from that day down to the
Ides of March. Was there ever an orderly so abjectly subservient? He had no
power of his own. He asked for everything. Putting his head into the back of
his colleague's litter, he would beg favors in order to sell them. So the day of
Dolabella's elections comes round. Lots are drawn for the right of first vote.[74]
Antonius makes no move. The result is declared: Antonius keeps mum. The
first class is called up. Then in the usual way the *suffragia*,[75] then the second
class—all sooner done than said. **83** After the business is finished, our adept
augur (a real Gaius Laelius!)[76] says: "Meeting adjourned." Matchless impudence! What had you seen, what had you perceived, what had you heard? You
did not say that you had watched the heavens, nor are you saying so today. So
the flaw which you had already foreseen on the Kalends of January and
predicted so long beforehand duly appeared. Thus you lied about the auspices,
to your own great mischief, I truly hope, and not to that of the Commonwealth.
You involved the Roman People in a breach of religion. Augur to augur,[77]
consul to consul, you announced adverse auspices. I will say no more, lest I
seem to be invalidating Dolabella's official acts, which one day must needs be
referred to our College. **84** But look at the arrogance, the insolence of him! So
long as *you* wish, Dolabella's consulship is flawed; the moment your wishes
change, the auspices were in order. If it means nothing when an augur makes
an announcement in the terms in which you made yours, admit that when you
said "Meeting adjourned" you were not sober. On the other hand, if those
terms have any force, as one augur to another I ask you to tell me what it is.

My review must not pass over the most brilliant of all Marcus Antonius'
exploits. Let us come to the Feast of Lupercal. He doesn't disguise it, Members of the Senate, his agitation is evident, he sweats, turns pale. Anything, as
long as he doesn't do what he did[78] in the Gallery of Minucius! What possible

---

74. On the voting procedure in the Centuriate Assembly (*comitia centuriata*) see L. R. Taylor,
*Roman Voting Assemblies* (Ann Arbor, 1966) 84.

75. The *(sex) suffragia* were the six ancient centuries of Tities, Ramnes, and Luceres. See
Taylor (n. 74 above) 84.

76. C. Laelius Sapiens, friend of the younger Scipio Africanus and a famous augur.

77. Caesar had been made a member of all four of the chief priestly colleges.

78. Vomit; cf. 2.63.

tantae defensio? cupio audire, ut videam [ubi rhetoris sit tanta merces, id est] ubi campus Leontinus appareat. **85** sedebat in rostris collega tuus amictus toga purpurea, in sella aurea, coronatus. escendis, accedis ad sellam ⟨Lupercus⟩—ita eras Lupercus ut te consulem esse meminisse deberes— diadema ostendis. gemitus toto foro. unde diadema? non enim abiectum 5 sustuleras, sed attuleras domo, meditatum et cogitatum scelus. tu diadema imponebas cum plangore populi; ille cum plausu reiciebat. tu ergo unus, scelerate, inventus es qui, cum auctor regni esses eumque quem collegam habebas dominum habere velles, idem temptares quid populus Romanus ferre et pati posset. **86** at etiam misericordiam captabas: supplex te ad 10 pedes abiciebas. quid petens? ut servires? tibi uni peteres, qui ita a puero vixeras ut omnia paterere, ut facile servires; a nobis populoque Romano mandatum id certe non habebas. o praeclaram illam eloquentiam tuam cum es nudus contionatus! quid hoc turpius, quid foedius, quid suppliciis omnibus dignius? num exspectas dum te stimulis fodiamus? haec te, si 15 ullam partem habes sensus, lacerat, haec cruentat oratio. vereor ne imminuam summorum virorum gloriam; dicam tamen dolore commotus: quid indignius quam vivere eum qui imposuerit diadema, cum omnes fateantur iure interfectum esse qui abiecerit? **87** at etiam ascribi iussit in fastis ad Lupercalia C. Caesari, dictatori perpetuo, M. Antonium consulem populi 20 iussu regnum detulisse, Caesarem uti noluisse. iam iam minime miror te otium perturbare; non modo urbem odisse sed etiam lucem; cum perditissimis latronibus non solum de die sed etiam in diem bibere. ubi enim tu in pace consistes? qui locus tibi in legibus et in iudiciis esse potest, quae tu, quantum in te fuit, dominatu regio sustulisti? ideone L. Tarquinius ex- 25 actus, Sp. Cassius, ⟨Sp.⟩ Maelius, M. Manlius necati ut multis post saeculis a M. Antonio, quod fas non est, rex Romae constitueretur?

**88** Sed ad auspicia redeamus; de quibus rebus Idibus Martiis fuit in senatu Caesar acturus. quaero: tum tu quid egisses? audiebam equidem te

1 ubi . . . merces³ *seclusi*    1–2 id est ubi . . . appareat] ubi . . . appareat *D: del. Campe*    **85** 3 ascendis *D*    4 Lupercus² *addidi*    7 reiciebat]: recipie- *bcn¹s¹v*: ac-cipie- *t*    8 regi *V*    eumque quem] eum quem *Vnst:* eumque *v*    collegam] -am regni *nstv*    9 idem] et i- *nstv:* eundem *b*    **86** 11 abiciebas] obic- *n¹sv:* eici- *V*    struires *V:* serviremus *Roell, fort. recte*    15 fodiamus] -am *nstv*    17–18 quid . . . vivere (*cf. Att. 16.11.12*)] nonne indignus tu tueri (-re *t*) *D*    **87** 20 M. *om. V*    23 de *om. V*    ad diem *Arusian. 7:468 Keil*    bibere *Badham:* uiuere *codd., Arusian.*    26 Sp. *n²: om. VD*    **88** 28 rebus Idibus *om. V:* rebus *del. Halm*    29 quidem *D*

excuse can there be for such outrageous conduct? I am anxious to hear it, to see where the plain of Leontini comes into view. **85** Your colleague sat on the rostra, wearing his purple gown, on his golden chair, his garland on his head. Up you come, you approach the chair, as a Lupercus (you *were* a Lupercus, but you should have remembered that you were a consul); you display a diadem. Groans all over the Forum! Where did the diadem come from? You had not picked it out of the gutter. No, you had brought it with you, a planned, premeditated crime. You made to place the diadem on Caesar's head amid the lamentations of the people: he kept refusing it, and the people applauded. You had been urging Caesar to make himself king, you wanted him as a master instead of a colleague, so you and only you were found to make this criminal experiment to determine what the Roman People could bear and suffer. **86** Why, you even tried pathos, throwing yourself as a suppliant at his feet. What was your petition? To be a slave? You should have spoken for yourself; from a boy your life had been such as to make everything tolerable and slavery easy. Assuredly you had no such commission from us and from the Roman People. What a marvelously eloquent speech you made—in the nude![79] Disgraceful, loathsome! No punishment could be too bad! Are you waiting for us to dig your flesh with goads? If you have a trace of feeling, these words of mine tear you, make you bleed. I fear that what I am about to say may derogate from the glory of our greatest, but indignation moves me to say it none the less: how unseemly[80] that he who put on the diadem should be alive when all admit that he who thrust it aside was rightly done to death! **87** Antonius even gave orders that the public records under the appropriate date should show as follows: "Marcus Antonius, Consul, by order of the people offered the title of King to Gaius Caesar, Dictator in Perpetuity: Caesar declined." No wonder quiet times unnerve you, no wonder you hate the city, even the light of day. No wonder you not only drink in the daytime with your crew of desperate characters but drink all day long. What security will you have in peacetime? What place for you can there be among laws and lawcourts, which you, so far as in you lay, abolished under monarchical rule? Was Lucius Tarquinius driven out, were Spurius Cassius, Spurius Maelius, Marcus Manlius put to death, in order that centuries later a king (blasphemous thought!) should be set up by Marcus Antonius in Rome?

**88** Let us, however, get back to the auspices. Caesar intended to raise these matters in the Senate on the Ides of March. I ask you: what would you have

---

79. A Lupercus at the festival wore nothing but an apron or girdle made from the skin of a sacrificial goat.

80. Instead of *quid indignius quam vivere eum*, lit. "what is more unseemly than that he should live?" Atticus suggested *indignissimum est hunc vivere*, "it is most unseemly . . . ." One wonders why. Cicero approved, but apparently did not make the change (*Att.* 16.11.2).

paratum venisse, quod me de ementitis auspiciis, quibus tamen parere necesse erat, putares esse dicturum. sustulit illum diem Fortuna rei publicae. num etiam tuum de auspiciis iudicium interitus Caesaris sustulit? sed incidi in id tempus quod eis rebus in quas ingress⟨ur⟩a erat oratio praevertendum est. quae tua fuga, quae formido praeclaro illo die, quae 5 propter conscientiam scelerum desperatio vitae, cum ex illa fuga beneficio eorum qui te, si sanus esses, salvum esse voluerunt, clam te domum recepisti! **89** o mea frustra semper verissima auguria rerum futurarum! dicebam illis in Capitolio liberatoribus nostris, cum me ad te ire vellent ut ad defendendam rem publicam te adhortarer, quoad metueres, omnia te 10 promissurum; simul ac timere desisses, similem te futurum tui. itaque cum ceteri consulares irent redirent, in sententia mansi: neque te illo die neque postero vidi neque ullam societatem optimis civibus cum importunissimo hoste foedere ullo confirmari posse credidi.

Post diem tertium veni in aedem Telluris et quidem invitus, cum omnis 15 aditus armati obsiderent. **90** qui tibi dies ille, Antoni, fuit! quamquam mihi inimicus subito exstitisti, tamen me tui miseret quod tibi invideris. qui tu vir, di immortales, et quantus fuisses, si illius diei mentem servare potuisses! pacem haberemus, quae erat facta per obsidem puerum nobilem, M. Bambalionis nepotem. quamquam bonum te timor faciebat, non 20 diuturnus magister offici; improbum fecit ea quae, dum timor abest, a te non discedit, audacia. etsi tum, cum optimum te ⟨multi⟩ putabant me quidem dissentiente, funeri tyranni, si illud funus fuit, sceleratissime praefuisti. **91** tua illa pulchra laudatio, tua miseratio, tua cohortatio; tu, tu, inquam, illas faces incendisti, et eas quibus semustilatus ille est et eas 25 quibus incensa L. Bellieni domus deflagravit. tu illos impetus perditorum et ex maxima parte servorum quos nos vi manuque reppulimus in nostras domos immisisti. idem tamen quasi fuligine abstersa reliquis diebus in Capitolio praeclara senatus consulta fecisti, ne qua post Idus †Martias†

1 mentitis *V*    2 diem *del. Kraffert*    rei publicae]: populi r. *nstv*    3 tuum] tum *V*    4 ingressura³ *scripsi*: -essa *codd.*    5 praetereundum *D*    est] si *t*: non est *v*: non sit *bcn*: est non sit *s*    praeclaro *om. D*    **90** 16 dies ille ϛ: dis i- *V*: i- dies m. *D*    18 et] sed *V*    19 nobilem m. antoni filium *D*    20 te bonum *D*    22 multi *addidi*: (*anne* alii¹? *Cf.* 2.92)    23–24 tyranni illius sceleratissimi praefuisti *D*    **91** 25 inquam] *om. cnst*    26 perditorum hominum *D*    29 Martias] *Cf. ad* 1.3

done then? I was told that you had come prepared, because you thought that I would speak about the falsified auspices—which nonetheless had to be obeyed. The Fortune of the Commonwealth struck that day out of time. Did Caesar's death also strike out your judgment concerning the auspices? But I now find myself at a situation which must take precedence over the topics I was about to embark upon. You fled in panic on that glorious day, and in the consciousness of guilt you despaired of your life; but by favor of those who wished you to survive if you were of sound mind, you turned back from your flight and secretly retreated to your house. **89** Ah, my prophecies of things to come! Always true to the letter, always in vain! I told our liberators there in the Capitol, when they wanted me to go to you and urge you to defend the Commonwealth, that you would promise anything as long as you were afraid, but as soon as you had lost your fear you would be like yourself. So when other consulars went to and fro, I held to my opinion. I did not see you that day or the next, neither did I believe that any pact could cement an alliance between loyal citizens and a barbarous public enemy.

Two days later I came into the temple of Tellus, against my own inclination since armed men stood guarding every entrance. **90** What a day that was for you, Marcus Antonius! Though you have suddenly become my enemy, I pity you for the harm you have done to yourself. Heavens, what a great man you would have been if you could have stayed in the frame of mind you were in that day! We would have peace, the peace made through a hostage, a boy of high descent, Marcus Bambalio's grandson.[81] But fear made you honest, and fear as the counselor of duty is short-lived; audacity, which never deserts you so long as fear is absent,[82] made you disloyal. And yet even at that time, when many thought well of you (I did not agree), you presided at the tyrant's funeral, if funeral it was, in a most criminal manner. **91** That beautiful tribute to the deceased, the pathos, the incitement—they were yours.[83] It was you, yes, you, who set light to the firebrands with which Caesar was half-cremated, and to those others which set fire to Lucius Bellienus' house and burned it down. It was you who directed the onslaughts of desperate characters, mostly slaves, against our houses, which we repelled by main force. And yet in the days following, wiping off the soot as it were, you carried some admirable decrees of the Senate in the Capitol, providing that after the Ides of * no record of

---

81. M. Fulvius Bambalio was Fulvia's father. Antony's son was *nobilis* through his father, but *nobilem* followed by *M. Bambalionis nepotem* has to be ironical. Contrary to the general belief, *Phil.* 3.16, where Bambalio is contrasted with the *nobilis* Tuditanus, seems to show that in Cicero's opinion at least he was *not* descended from the consular Fulvii.

82. *Audacia* connotes lack of *moral* scruple.

83. According to Suetonius (*Iul.* 84), Antony said only a very few words of his own, but Cicero's statement is supported by *Att.* 14.10.1 and later historians.

immunitatis tabula neve cuius benefici figeretur. meministi ipse de exsulibus, scis de immunitate quid dixeris. optimum vero quod dictaturae
nomen in perpetuum de re publica sustulisti: quo quidem facto tantum te
cepisse odium regni videbatur ut eius omnem [propter proximum dicta-
torem] metum tolleres. **92** constituta res publica videbatur aliis, mihi vero    5
nullo modo, qui omnia te gubernante naufragia metuebam. num igitur me
fefellit, aut num diutius sui potuit esse dissimilis? inspectantibus vobis
toto Capitolio tabulae figebantur, neque solum singulis veni[e]bant immunitates sed etiam populis universis: civitas non iam singillatim, sed
provinciis totis dabatur. itaque si haec manent, quae stante re publica    10
manere non possunt, provincias universas, patres conscripti, perdidistis,
neque vectigalia solum sed etiam imperium populi Romani huius domesticis nundinis deminutum est. **93** [ubi est septiens miliens quod est in
tabulis quae sunt ad Opis? funestae illius quidem pecuniae, sed tamen
quae nos, si eis quorum erat non redderetur, a tributis posset vindicare. tu    15
autem quadringentiens sestertium quod Idibus Martiis debuisti quonam
modo ante Kalendas Aprilis debere desisti?] sunt ea quidem innumerabilia quae a tuis emebantur non insciente te, sed unum egregium de rege
Deiotaro, populi Romani amicissimo, decretum in Capitolio fixum: quo
proposito nemo erat qui in ipso dolore risum posse⟨t⟩ continere. **94** quis    20
enim cuiquam inimicior quam Deiotaro Caesar? aeque atque huic ordini,
ut equestri, ut Massiliensibus, ut omnibus quibus rem publicam populi
Romani caram esse sentiebat. igitur a quo vivo nec praesens nec absens
rex Deiotarus quicquam aequi boni impe⟨t⟩ravit, apud mortuum factus
est grat⟨ios⟩us. compellarat hospitem praesens, computarat pecuniam    25
[impetrarat], in eius tetrarchia unum ex Graecis comitibus suis collo-
carat, Armeniam abstulerat a se⟨na⟩tu datam. haec vivus eripuit, reddit

1 cuius] cui *c*: cuiusquam *nt*: -sque *sv*    4 omnem] omen nomen *V*    propter proximum
(-mi *Muretus*) dictatoris (-rem *D*)³ *seclusi*    5 metum tolleres] t- m- *nstv*    **92** 7 dissimilis esse *V, numero minus usitato*    8 venibant *Heusinger*: uenieb- *codd.*    9 populis suis
*V*    **93** 13–17 ubi est . . . desisti *post* 2.96 acta defendimus *transp. Nägelsbach, nimirum
recte. Hic reliqui, ne capitum numeri conturbarentur*    13 est in] in *D*    14 opis patebat
(-atur *v*) *D*    15 quae nos *post* redderetur *D*    17 dedisti *V*    sunt ea . . . defendimus
(*p. 90 l. 16*) *om. D*    *ante* sunt ea *verba habet V ex* 2.97 *initio* quid ego . . . loquar
*erroribus parvulis deformata*    18 a tuis *Faërnus*: ad uis *V*    insciente *Poggius*: inis-
cientes *V*    20 posset *Poggius*: posse *V*    **94** 22 et . . . et . . . et *Pluygers* (*v. Fe.*)    23
is igitur *V*²    24 impetravit *Poggius*: imper- *V*    eum mortuum *Ernesti*    25 gratiosus
*Ubaldinus*: -tus *V*    26 impetrarat *del. Clark* (*v. Fe.*)    tetrarchia unum *Faërnus*:
tetrechianum *V*    27 reddidit *Poggius*

exemption or of any grant be posted.[84] You yourself remember what you said about exiles, you know what you said about exemption. Best of all, you removed the name of dictator from the Commonwealth for all time. Thus it appeared that you had developed such a hatred of monarchy that you removed all fear of it. **92** Others thought the Commonwealth was established. I thought nothing of the kind, for I feared all manner of shipwreck with you at helm. Well, was I wrong? Could he be unlike himself for any length of time? Before your eyes, gentlemen, placards were put up all over the Capitol. Exemptions were sold not only to individuals but to whole peoples. Citizenship was given no longer individually but to whole provinces.[85] If these measures stand, as stand they cannot unless the Commonwealth falls, you, Members of the Senate, have lost entire provinces; not revenues only but the very empire of the Roman People has been whittled down in Antonius' private market. **93** Where[86] is the seven hundred million which is on the records kept at the temple of Ops? The money[87] has an evil history to be sure, but if it was not going to be returned to its owners it could save us from special levies. As for you, how was it that before the Kalends of April you had ceased to owe the forty million sesterces which you owed on the Ides of March? There is no counting the items bought from persons close to you[88] not without your knowledge, but one stands out: the order posted on the Capitol concerning King Deiotarus, that faithful friend of the Roman People. When it was put up, nobody could help laughing in the midst of his indignation. **94** For who ever had a worse enemy than Caesar was to Deiotarus? He hated the king as much as he hated this House, or the order of knights, or the people of Massilia,[89] or all those to whom he felt the Commonwealth of the Roman People was precious. And so Deiotarus came into favor with a dead man from whom, when that man was alive, he could get no justice or fair treatment either present or absent. When Deiotarus was his host, Caesar took him to task in person, reckoned a sum, planted one of his Greek companions in his tetrarchy,[90] deprived him of Armenia,[91] which had been given by the Senate. All

---

84. Cf. 1.3.

85. Cf. 1.24.

86. The following passage down to "Ides of March" should probably be transferred to the beginning of the next paragraph ("shall I speak . . ."), as proposed by Nägelsbach.

87. The genitive *pecuniae* seems to depend on *tabulis*.

88. The euphemistic *tuis* refers to Fulvia; see SB[2].

89. The Greek colony of Massilia (Marseilles) wished to remain neutral in the Civil War, but was taken by Caesar's forces in October 49.

90. Mithridates of Pergamum, an adventurer to whom Caesar granted a tetrarchy in Deiotarus' kingdom of Galatia. The phrase *in eius tetrarchia* is misleading; see Denniston's note.

91. I.e. Armenia minor.

mortuus. **95** at quibus verbis! modo aequum sibi videri, modo non iniquum. mira verborum comple⟨xio⟩! at ille ⟨n⟩umquam—semper enim
absenti adfui Deiotaro—quicquam sibi quod nos pro illo postularemus
aequum dixit videri. syngrapha sesterti centiens per legatos, viros bonos
sed timidos et imperitos, sine ⟨no⟩stra, sine reliquorum hospitum regis    5
⟨sententia⟩ facta in gynaecio est, quo in loco plurimae res venierunt et
veneunt. qua ex syngrapha quid sis acturus meditere censeo: rex enim
ipse sua sponte, nullis commentariis Caesaris, simul atque audivit eius
interitum, suo Marte res suas recuperavit. **96** sciebat homo sapiens ius
semper hoc fuisse ut, quae tyranni eripuissent, ea tyrannis interfectis    10
ei quibus erepta essent recuperarent. nemo igitur iure[is] consultus, ne
iste quidem, qui tibi uni est iure consultus, per quem haec agis, ex ista
syngrapha deberi dicet pro eis rebus quae erant ante syngrapham re-
cuperatae. non enim a te emit, sed prius quam tu suum sibi vendere⟨s⟩
ipse possedit. ille vir fuit; nos quidem contemnendi, qui a[u]ctorem    15
odimus, acta defendimus.

**97** Quid ego de commentariis infinitis, quid de innumerabilibus chirographis loquar? quorum etiam institores sunt qui ea tamquam gladiatorum libellos palam venditent. itaque tanti acervi nummorum apud istum
construuntur ut iam expendantur, non numerentur pecuniae. at quam    20
caeca avaritia est! nuper fixa tabula est qua civitates locupletissimae
Cretensium vectigalibus liberantur, statuiturque ne post M. Brutum pro
consule sit Creta provincia. tu mentis compos, tu non constringendus? an
Caesaris decreto Creta post M. Bruti decessum potuit liberari, cum Creta
nihil ad Brutum Caesare vivo pertineret? at huius venditione decreti, ne    25
nihil actum putetis, provinciam Cretam perdidistis. omnino nemo ullius
rei fuit emptor cui defuerit hic venditor.

**98** Et de exsulibus legem quam fixisti Caesar tulit? nullius insector calamitatem: tantum queror, primum eorum reditus inquinatos quorum
causam Caesar dissimilem iudicarit; deinde nescio cur non reliquis idem    30
tribuas: neque enim plus quam tres aut quattuor reliqui sunt. qui simili in
calamitate sunt, cur tua misericordia non simili fruuntur, cur eos habes in

**95** 1 verbis *idem*: ursibus *V*      2 complexio at *idem*: compleat *V*      numquam *idem*: u-
*V*      4 viros *idem*: urtos *V*      5 sine nostra *Muretus*: sines- *V*      6 sententia *om.*
*V*[1]      est *Halm*: et *V*: *del. Poggius*      **96** 10 quae *V*[2]: qui *V*[1]      11 iure *Poggius*: -eis
*V*      13 dicet *Halm*: dicit *V*      14 venderes *Poggius*: -re *V*      15 actorem *Koch*: auct- *V*,
*errore vulgato* (*cf.* 13.2)      **97** 18 institores *Pantagathus*: imitat- (mittat- *t*) *codd.*      21
et nuper *V*      22 vectigalibus *om. D*      23 mentis] -is es *bcstV*[2]      an *Manutius*: in
*codd.*: num *coni. Clark*      27 defuit *V*      **98** 30 dissimilem Caesar *D*      iudicauerit
*nstv*: -auit *c*      reliquis non idem *bcst*: r- i- non *nv*      32 calamitate sunt *Faërnus*: -ates at
*V*: -ate fuerint *D*      simili non (non *om. t*) *D*

this he took away in his lifetime and returns after his death! **95** And in what terms! Sometimes "it seems fair" to him, sometimes "it seems not unfair." A remarkable form of words! But Caesar never said that anything *we* asked of him on Deiotarus' behalf "seemed fair"—I know, for I always appeared for Deiotarus in his absence. A bond for ten million sesterces was signed by envoys, worthy men but timid and inexperienced, without my approval or that of the king's other friends here, in the women's apartments, where a great many things have been sold and are being sold. I advise you to consider well what action you are going to take on that bond. For the king himself, of his own volition and without any memoranda of Caesar's, recovered his possessions with his own strong hand as soon as he heard the news of Caesar's death. **96** He knew in his wisdom that it has ever been lawful for those whose possessions have been seized by tyrants to recover them after the tyrants have been killed. No jurist, not even that gentleman[92] whom only you believe to be a jurist, through whom you are acting in these matters, will say that payment is due on that bond for items which had been recovered before the bond was signed. Deiotarus did not buy from you, he took possession himself before you could sell him his own property. He behaved like a man; but we deserve contempt, who hate the doer but defend his acts.

**97** Shall I speak of the endless memoranda, the innumerable holographs? There are actually peddlers who sell them openly like programmes for the gladiators. Such mountains of coin are built up at Antonius' house that the money is no longer counted but weighed. Avarice is blind. A placard was lately posted exempting the richest communities in Crete from taxation and decreeing that after Marcus Brutus, Proconsul, Crete shall cease to be a province. Are you in your right mind? Should you not be in a straitjacket? Could Crete be freed at the end of Marcus Brutus' term as governor by an order of Caesar's, when Crete had nothing to do with Brutus in Caesar's lifetime? By the sale of this order, in case you gentlemen imagine that nothing has happened, you have lost the province of Crete. In round terms, Antonius has been ready to sell anything anybody was ready to buy.

**98** Again, did Caesar pass the law which you posted up concerning exiles? I do not harry any man's misfortune. I merely complain, first, that a smear has been put upon the returns of those whose cases Caesar judged to be dissimilar; second, I don't know why you are not doing as much for the rest—there are only three or four left over. Why should persons in like misfortune not benefit alike from your compassion? Why do you treat them as you treated your uncle?

---

92. Possibly Sex. Cloelius, who had drafted laws for Clodius.

loco patrui? de quo ferre, cum de reliquis ferres, noluisti: quem etiam ad
censuram petendam impulisti, eamque petitionem comparasti quae et
risus hominum et querelas moveret. **99** cur autem ea comitia non habuisti?
an quia tribunus plebis sinistrum fulmen nuntiabat? cum tua quid interest, nulla auspicia sunt; cum tuorum, tum fis religiosus. quid? eundem in    5
septemviratu nonne destituisti? intervenit enim cui metuisti, credo, ne
salvo capite negare non posses! omnibus eum contumeliis onerasti quem
patris loco, si ulla in te pietas esset, colere debebas. filiam eius, sororem
tuam, eiecisti, alia condicione quaesita et ante perspecta. non est satis:
probri insimulasti pudicissimam feminam. quid est quod addi possit?    10
contentus eo non fuisti: frequentissimo senatu Kalendis Ianuariis sedente
patruo hanc tibi esse cum Dolabella causam odi dicere ausus es quod ab
eo sorori et uxori tuae stuprum esse oblatum comperisses. quis interpretari
potest, impudentiorne qui in senatu, an improbior qui in Dolabellam, an
impurior qui patre audiente, an crudelior qui in illam miseram tam spurce,    15
tam impie dixeris?

   **100** Sed ad chirographa redeamus. quae tua fuit cognitio? acta enim
Caesaris pacis causa confirmata sunt a senatu: quae quidem Caesar egisset,
non ea quae egisse Caesarem dixisset Antonius. unde ista erumpunt, quo
auctore proferuntur? si sunt falsa, cur probantur? si vera, cur veneunt?    20
at sic placuerat ut ex Kalendis Iuniis de Caesaris actis cum consilio
cognosceretis. quod fuit consilium, quem umquam advocasti, quas Kalendas Iunias exspectasti? an eas ad quas te peragratis veteranorum coloniis stipatum armis rettulisti?

   O praeclaram illam percursationem tuam mense Aprili atque Maio,    25
tum cum etiam Capuam coloniam deducere conatus es! quem ad modum
illim abieris vel potius paene non abieris scimus. **101** cui tu urbi mini-
taris. utinam conere, ut aliquando illud "paene" tollatur! at quam nobilis
est tua illa peregrinatio! quid prandiorum apparatus, quid furiosam vino-

**99** 4 an quia] aut qua *V*     fulmen sinistrum *D*     cum] *om. bcnsv*     5 cum *om.*
*D*     sis *D*     6 cui *Madvig*: cum *V*: quem *D*     8 nulla *V*     12 ausus dicere es (es
d- *s*) *D*     15 patre *D*, *Prisc. 2:93 Keil*: -ruo *V Cus.*     **100** 17 fuit tua *D*     18 quae
egisse] cesarem eg- *ntv*: quaeque gessisse *V*     21 ut ex *om. V*     ex *del. Muretus*     22
convocasti *V*     26 coloniam *om. bcnst*     27 illim abieris *constantiae causa scripsi* (*cf.*
2.77, 4.12): illim (illam *V²*) cauieris *V*: illam adieris (aud- *t*) *D*: illinc abi- *Faërnus*     non
abieris *idem*: non habue- *V*: non adie- (aud- *t*) *bcnst*: non *v*     **101** 28–29 nobilis est]
-litata (-tati *b*, -tas *v*) sit *D*

You chose to leave him out when you put through your law about the others. You also prompted him to stand for the censorship, getting up a candidature which evoked general mirth and general protest.[93] **99** And why did you not hold the elections? Was it because a tribune of the plebs announced thunder on the left? When it is you whose interests are concerned, the auspices mean nothing, but when it is your relations, then you develop religious scruples. And did you not let him down in the matter of the Board of Seven?[94] Somebody came in between; I suppose it was more than your life was worth to say no to that somebody? You have heaped all manner of insults on your uncle, whom you should have respected as standing in your father's place if you had any family feeling. You turned his daughter, your cousin,[95] out of your house after you had looked for and previously inspected[96] another match. That was not enough: you accused her, a lady of the utmost propriety, of immoral conduct. How much further could you go? Still not satisfied, at a full meeting of the Senate, on the Kalends of January, in your uncle's presence, you dared to allege as the reason for your hatred of Dolabella that you had discovered his adultery with your cousin and wife. Which was the more extraordinary, your impudence in saying such a thing in the Senate, your rascality in accusing Dolabella, your caddishness in doing so in your uncle's hearing, or your cruelty in making such a filthy, outrageous charge against the unfortunate woman? Who can decide?

**100** But to get back to the holographs: what inquiry did you make? Caesar's acts were confirmed by the Senate for the sake of peace—that is, what Caesar did, not what Antonius might say Caesar had done. Where do these holographs spring from, on whose authority are they produced? If they are forgeries, why are they approved? If genuine, why are they for sale? It was decided that you and your colleague with a board of assessors should hold an inquiry as to Caesar's acts, commencing the Kalends of June. What was the board, whom did you ever call in, which Kalends of June did you wait for? Those same, perhaps, by which you returned surrounded by armed men after your tour of the veterans' colonies?

What a marvelous trip you made in April and May, at which time you attempted to establish a colony at Capua! We know how you got away from that city, or rather almost failed to get away.[97] **101** Now you launch threats against it. I wish you would try. Perhaps we should get rid of the "almost" at last! But what a celebrated progress! No need for me to bring up your elaborate

---

93. C. Antonius (Hybrida) actually became censor in 42.

94. Set up by Antony and Dolabella to distribute land among Caesar's veterans and needy citizens. The circumstances here alluded to are unknown.

95. Antony's first wife Antonia, whom he divorced to marry Fulvia.

96. Adultery is implied.

97. Cf. 12.7.

lentiam tuam proferam? tua ista detrimenta sunt, illa nostra: agrum
Campanum, qui cum de vectigalibus eximebatur ut militibus daretur,
tamen infligi magnum rei publicae vulnus putabamus, hunc tu compranso-
ribus tuis et collusoribus dividebas. mimos dico et mimas, patres conscripti, in agro Campano collocatos. quid iam querar de agro Leontino?　5
quoniam quidem hae quondam arationes Campana et Leontina in populi
Romani patrimonio grandiferae et fructuosae ferebantur. medico tria
milia iugerum: quid si te sanasset? rhetori duo: quid si te disertum facere
potuisset? sed ad iter Italiamque redeamus. **102** deduxisti coloniam Casilinum, quo Caesar ante deduxerat. consuluisti me per litteras de Capua tu　10
quidem, sed idem de Casilino respondissem: possesne, ubi colonia esset,
eo coloniam novam iure deducere. negavi in eam coloniam quae esset
auspicato deducta, dum esset incolumis, coloniam novam iure deduci:
colonos novos ascribi posse rescripsi. tu autem insolentia elatus omni
auspiciorum iure turbato Casilinum coloniam deduxisti, quo erat paucis　15
annis ante deducta, ut vexillum tolleres, ut aratrum circumduceres; cuius
quidem vomere portam Capuae paene perstrinxisti, ut florentis coloniae
territorium minueretur.

**103** Ab hac perturbatione religionum advolas in M. Varronis, sanctissimi atque integerrimi viri, fundum Casinatem. quo iure, quo ore?　20
"eodem," inquies "quo in heredum L. Rubri, quo in heredum L. Turseli
praedia, quo in reliquas innumerabilis possessiones." et si ab hasta,
valeat hasta, valeant tabulae, modo Caesaris, non tuae, quibus debuisti,
non quibus tu te liberavisti. Varronis quidem Casinatem fundum quis
venisse dicit, quis hastam istius venditionis vidit, quis vocem praeconis　25
audivit? misisse te dicis Alexandriam qui emeret a Caesare; ipsum enim
exspectare magnum fuit. **104** quis vero audivit umquam—nullius autem
salus curae pluribus fuit—de fortunis Varronis rem ullam esse detractam?
quid? si etiam scripsit ad te Caesar ut redderes, quid satis potest dici de
tanta impudentia? remove gladios parumper illos quos videmus: iam　30
intelleges aliam causam esse hastae Caesaris, aliam confidentiae et temeritatis tuae. non enim te dominus modo illis sedibus sed quivis amicus,
vicinus, hospes, procurator arcebit. at quam multos dies in ea villa

---

5 Campano] p. c. *D*　　queror *V*　　6 campani et leontini *D*: *tria verba spuria esse susp.*
*Clark*　　7 grandifacere (-di faceret *cv*, -di fenore *b*) *D* (*cf. Mart. Cap. 511*)　　7–8 tria
milia *om. V¹*　　8 quid si] quasi *DV²*　　sanum fecisset *D*　　quid si te] q- (quasi *V²*)
iste *V*: q- si *c*: quasi *nstv*　　**102** 11 respondisset *Vt¹*　　esset] est *D*　　16 tolleres *V*: -ret
*Ps.-Acro ad Hor. Carm. 1.16.21*: uideres *D*　　ut aratrum] et a- *nstv*　　17 praestrinxti
(*vel* -nxi *vel* -nxisti) *Nonius 374*　　**103** 20 quore *V*　　21 quo . . . Rubri *Cf. Att.
16.11.2*　　23 valeat hasta *om. D*　　24 tu te] tute *c*: tu tete *bt*: te *n*: tuae te *v*　　24–25
qui . . . dicet *V*　　26 te *om. V*　　**104** 29 si *om. V*　　scripsit (isc- *V²*) ad] sit a
*V¹*　　32 aedibus *Pluygers*　　sed quiuis] se quibus *V*

luncheons, your frenzied tippling. All that was your loss, but it was ours when you went about dividing the Campanian land between your lunch companions and gaming partners. Why, when that land was taken out of the revenues in order to give it to the soldiers,[98] even that we thought a serious wound inflicted on the Commonwealth. I tell you, Members of the Senate, that comedians and comediennes have been settled on Campanian land. How shall I protest about the land of Leontini? These arable lands of Campania and Leontini were once considered part of the patrimony of the Roman People, heavy-yielding, highly profitable. Three thousand jugers for the doctor: what if he had made you sane? Two for the professor of rhetoric: what if he had been able to make you an orator? But to get back to your journey, to Italy: **102** you founded a colony at Casilinum, where Caesar had founded one previously. You wrote asking my opinion—about Capua, to be sure, but I should have given the same answer about Casilinum: could you legally found a new colony where there was one already? I told you that a new colony could not legally be founded where there was a previous foundation, duly auspicated, still in being; but new colonists could be enrolled. However, in your insolent euphoria you turned all auspical law upside down and founded a colony at Casilinum, where one had been founded a few years previously, erecting the standard and marking out the boundaries with the plough. Indeed you almost grazed the town gate of Capua with that ploughshare so as to diminish the territory of that thriving colony.

**103** After thus disorganizing our religion, you dart into a property near Casinum belonging to Marcus Varro, a gentleman of unblemished life and character. By what right? With what face? "Why, the same," you will say, "as when I invaded the lands of Lucius Rubrius'[99] heirs, and of Lucius Turselius' heirs, and countless other properties." If you got it at a public auction, let that stand, let the records stand: but let them be Caesar's, not yours, records of what you owed, not those by which you got out of debt. Who says that Varro's property near Casinum was ever for sale? Who saw the lance at such a sale or heard the voice of the auctioneer? You say you sent an agent to Alexandria to buy it from Caesar—it would have been too inconvenient, no doubt, to wait for Caesar in person. **104** But who ever heard (and no man has a larger number of concerned well-wishers) that any of Varro's possessions was taken away from him? What if Caesar actually wrote to you directing you to return the place? What can be said to match such colossal impudence? Remove those weapons there for a few minutes and you will soon realize that Caesar's auctions are one thing, your careless assurance another. Not only the proprietor but any friend or neighbor or guest or agent will keep you out of that residence. How many

98. By Caesar in 59 and again in 45.
99. "Scipio's lands" in Cicero's original version. Atticus advised the change (*Att.* 16.11.2).

turpissime es perbacchatus! ab hora tertia bibebatur, ludebatur, vome-
batur. o tecta ipsa misera, "quam dispari domino"—quamquam quo
modo iste dominus?—sed tamen quam ab dispari tenebantur! studiorum
enim suorum ⟨receptaculum⟩ M. Varro voluit illud, non libidinum deversorium. **105** quae in illa villa antea dicebantur, quae cogitabantur,　5
quae litteris mandabantur! iura populi Romani, monumenta maiorum,
omnis sapientiae ratio omnisque doctrinae. at vero te inquilino—non
enim domino—personabant omnia vocibus ebriorum, natabant pavi-
menta vino, madebant parietes, ingenui pueri cum meritoriis, scorta inter
matres familias versabantur. Casino salutatum veniebant, Aquino, In-　10
teramna: admissus est nemo. iure id quidem; in homine enim turpissimo
obsolefiebant dignitatis insignia.

**106** Cum inde Romam proficiscens ad Aquinum accederet, obviam ei
processit, ut est frequens municipium, magna sane multitudo. at iste
operta lectica latus per oppidum est ut mortuus. stulte Aquinates: sed　15
tamen in via habitabant. quid Anagnini? qui, cum essent devii, descende-
runt ut istum, tamquam si esset consul, salutarent. incredibile dictu, sed
†cum vinus† inter omnis constabat neminem esse resalutatum, praesertim cum duos secum Anagninos haberet, Mustelam et Laconem, quorum
alter gladiorum est princeps, alter poculorum. **107** quid ego illas istius　20
minas contumeliasque commemorem quibus invectus est in Sidicinos,
vexavit Puteolanos, quod C. Cassium et Brutos patronos adoptassent?
magno quidem studio, iudicio, benevolentia, caritate, non, ut te et Basi-
lum, vi et armis, et alios vestri similis quos clientis nemo habere velit,
non modo illorum cliens esse.　25

Interea dum tu abes, qui dies ille collegae tuo fuit, cum illud quod
venerari solebas bustum in foro evertit! qua re tibi nuntiata, ut constabat
inter eos qui una fuerunt, concidisti. quid evenerit postea nescio—metum
credo valuisse et arma; collegam quidem de caelo detraxisti effecistique
non tu quidem etiam nunc ut similis tui, sed certe ut dissimilis esset sui.　30

**108** Qui vero inde reditus Romam, quae perturbatio totius urbis! me-
mineramus Cinnam nimis potentem, Sullam postea dominantem, modo

---

1 es] est (*om. s*) *D*　　3 a *D*　　4 receptaculum³ *addidi*　　M. *om. V*¹　　esse illud (i-
*om. s*) *D*　　**105** 5 ante (a te *s*) *D*　　quae cogitabantur *om. D*　　7 doctrina *D*　　10
cas(s)ilino *D*　　12 obsolefaciebant *bc*: -olebant *nstv*　　**106** 15 est per oppidum *D*　　16
deuii *V*: deuia ei *b*: -ia *c*: deuii (-ia *t*) obuiam ei *nsv*　　17 consul] colem *V*¹: consulem
*Faërnus*　　dictum *Vc*　　18 cum vinus] et simul unum cinus *c*: et sermulcinus *t*: et simul
*b*: simul *nsv*: sum uicinus *Madvig, alii alia* (*v. Fe.*)　　19 Mustelam et Laconem] *Cf.*
*Att. 16.11.3*　　20 gladiorum] -iatorum *nstv*　　**107** 22 et] quod *D*　　25 esse (-et *c*)
illorum cliens *D*　　26 tuo *Watt, dubitanter* (*CP 78* [*1983*] *229*): tu *V*: tui *D*　　fuit *om.*
*D*　　quod tu *D*　　30 similis] sit sim- *bcntv*　　**108** 31 reditus inde *D*　　32 l. ci- *V*

days did you spend disgracefully carousing in that villa? From nine o'clock in the morning there was drinking, gambling, vomiting. I pity the very building. "How different a master"[100]—not that Antonius *was* the master—but still, how different! Marcus Varro designed it as a retreat for his studies, not a den of vice. **105** Think of what once used to be said and thought and written down in that villa: the laws of the Roman People, the records of former days, all philosophy, all learning. But when *you* were its tenant, not its proprietor, every room echoed with the shouts of drunkards, the pavements swam with wine, the walls were wet, boys of free birth consorted with child prostitutes, harlots moved among mothers of families. From Casinum and Aquinum and Interamna people came to pay their respects, but nobody was admitted—properly enough, for the symbols of rank were degraded in so infamous an individual.

**106** When he left there for Rome and approached Aquinum, a pretty large crowd came out to meet him, as might be expected from a populous town. He was carried through the streets in a closed litter like a dead man. It was foolish of the people of Aquinum, but they did live on the highway, whereas Anagnia lies at a distance from it. Nonetheless, its folk came down to pay their respects as though he had been a consul. It is unbelievable, but all agreed that nobody's greeting was returned—even though he had two sons of Anagnia with him, Mustela and Laco,[101] one a champion with a sword, the other with a winecup. **107** I need not relate the threats and insults with which he belabored the people of Sidicinum and persecuted the people of Puteoli because they had chosen Gaius Cassius and the Bruti as their patrons. This they had done out of their great liking, approval, goodwill, and affection, not under pressure of armed force, as with you and Basilus[102] and others like you, whom nobody would want to have as clients, let alone be clients of theirs.

Meanwhile in your absence what a glorious day that was for your colleague when he demolished the tomb in the Forum, which you used to revere! When that was reported to you, according to those who were with you at the time, you collapsed. What happened later I do not know; I imagine fear and weapons prevailed. At any rate you dragged your colleague down from the heights and made him—not indeed like yourself even now, but certainly unlike himself.

**108** Then there was your return to Rome: the whole city turned upside down! We remembered the excessive power of Cinna, and the despotism of

---

100. From an unknown play, also cited in *Off.* 1.139 *o domus antiqua / heu quam dispari dominare domino!* "O ancient house, alas how different a master owns you now!"

101. Cicero put in the names after Atticus had asked him who was meant (*Att.* 16.11.3).

102. Cf. *Off.* 3.74. This L. Minucius Basilus (born Satrius) has to be distinguished from Caesar's assassin of the same name; see *Two Studies*, 53–54.

Caesarem regnantem videramus. erant fortasse gladii, sed absconditi nec ita multi. ista vero quae et quanta barbaria est! agmine quadrato cum gladiis sequuntur; scutorum lecticas portari videmus. atque his quidem iam inveteratis, patres conscripti, consuetudine obduruimus. Kalendis Iuniis cum in senatum, ut erat constitutum, venire vellemus, metu perter- 5 riti repente diffugimus. **109** at iste, qui senatu non egeret, neque desideravit quemquam et potius discessu nostro laetatus est statimque illa mirabilia facinora effecit. qui chirographa Caesaris defendisset lucri sui causa, is leges Caesaris easque praeclaras, ut rem publicam concutere posset, evertit. numerum annorum provinciis prorogavit; idemque, cum 10 actorum Caesaris defensor esse deberet, et in publicis et in privatis rebus acta Caesaris rescidit. in publicis nihil est lege gravius; in privatis firmissimum est testamentum. leges alias sine promulgatione sustulit, alias ut tolleret promulgavit. testamentum irritum fecit, quod etiam infimis civibus semper obtentum est. signa, tabulas, quas populo Caesar una cum 15 hortis legavit, eas hic partim in hortos Pompei deportavit, partim in villam Scipionis. **110** et tu in Caesaris memoria diligens, tu illum amas mortuum?

Quem is honorem maiorem consecutus erat quam ut haberet pulvinar, simulacrum, fastigium, flaminem? est ergo flamen, ut Iovi, ut Marti, ut 20 Quirino, sic divo Iulio M. Antonius. quid igitur cessas? cur non inauguraris? sume diem, vide qui te inauguret: collegae sumus; nemo negabit. o detestabilem hominem, sive quod tyranni sacerdos es sive quod mortui! quaero deinceps num hodiernus dies qui sit ignores. nescis heri quartum in circo diem ludorum Romanorum fuisse, te autem ipsum ad populum 25 tulisse ut quintus praeterea dies Caesari tribueretur? cur non sumus praetextati? cur honorem Caesaris tua lege datum deseri patimur? an supplicationes addendo diem contaminari passus es, pulvinaria contaminari noluisti? aut undique religionem tolle aut usque quaque conserva. **111** quaeris placeatne mihi pulvinar esse, fastigium, flaminem. mihi vero 30 nihil istorum placet: sed tu, qui acta Caesaris defendis, quid potes dicere

---

1 sed] sed tamen *bnstv*: sed ita *c*  **109** 7 et] est *V*: *del. n²*: sed *Halm*  11 publicis actis *D*  **110** 21 inauguraris *Halm*: -aras *V*: -are (-aret *n*) *D*  23 quod tyranni] eo quod Caesaris *V*  es *ς*: est *DV² in ras.*  28 die *coni. C. F. W. Müller*  contaminari *om. D*  **111** 30 quaeris] quae res *stv*: queres *n*

Sulla which followed, latterly we had seen Caesar's monarchy. There were weapons perhaps, but hidden and not very numerous. But this uncivilized display of yours—they follow you with drawn swords in battle order. We see litters carried full of shields. All this has become a thing of habit, Members of the Senate. Custom has made us callous. On the Kalends of June, when we wished to enter the Senate as appointed, we took sudden flight in terror. **109** Antonius, who had no need of the Senate, regretted nobody's absence; rather he was pleased to see us disperse and immediately carried out those remarkable coups of his. Having defended Caesar's holographs for his own gain, he proceeded to upset Caesar's laws, excellent laws, in order to shake the Commonwealth. He extended the tenure of provincial office; and the defender of Caesar's acts, as he ought to be, rescinded those acts in matters both public and private. In public affairs nothing has greater weight than a law. In private life the hardest thing to break is a will. As for laws, he annulled some without notice and gave notice of the annulment of others; and he nullified the will, a thing which has always kept its validity even for the humblest. The statues and paintings which Caesar bequeathed to the people along with his suburban villa—Antonius removed them, partly to Pompeius' estates, partly to Scipio's villa. **110** And are *you* concerned for Caesar's memory, do you love him in his grave?

What greater honor had Caesar attained than to have a sacred couch,[103] an image, a gable,[104] a special priest? Just as Jupiter and Mars and Quirinus have their priests, so the divine Julius has Marcus Antonius. Why the delay then? Why are you not inaugurated? Choose a date, choose someone[105] to inaugurate you. We are your colleagues, nobody will refuse. Abominable creature— priest of a tyrant, priest of a dead man! Next let me ask whether you are unaware what day it is. Don't you know that yesterday was the fourth day of the Roman games in the circus?[106] And don't you know that you yourself put a law through an assembly of the people providing that a fifth day be added for Caesar? Why are we not in our holiday clothes? Why do we let the honor granted Caesar by your law be omitted? Perhaps you allowed Thanksgivings to be polluted by adding a day,[107] but did not want the same to happen to the sacred couches? Either abolish religion altogether or preserve it at every point. **111** You ask whether I approve of the sacred couch, the gable, the special priest. Certainly not, none of it has my approval. But you are the defender of

103. At the ceremony of the *lectisternium* images of the gods were borne on couches (*pulvinaria*). Caesar had one as part of his official deification.
104. On his house, his official residence as Pontifex Maximus, as regularly on temples.
105. I.e. an augur.
106. The final stage of the Ludi Romani, lasting from 15 to 18 September.
107. Cf. 1.12–13.

cur alia defendas, alia non cures? nisi forte vis fateri te omnia quaestu
tuo, non illius dignitate metiri. quid ad haec tandem? exspecto enim eloquentiam. disertissimum cognovi avum tuum, at te etiam apertiorem in
dicendo. ille numquam nudus est contionatus: tuum hominis simplicis pectus vidimus. respondebisne ad haec, aut omnino hiscere audebis? ecquid    5
reperies ex tam longa oratione mea cui te respondere posse confidas?

**112** Sed praeterita omittamus: hunc unum diem, unum, inquam, hodiernum diem, hoc punctum temporis, quo loquor, defende, si potes. cur
armatorum corona senatus saeptus est, cur me tui satellites cum gladiis
audiunt, cur valvae Concordiae non patent, cur homines omnium gentium    10
maxime barbaros, Ituraeos, cum sagittis deducis in forum? praesidi sui
causa se facere dicit. non igitur miliens perire est melius quam in sua
civitate sine armatorum praesidio non posse vivere? sed nullum est istuc,
mihi crede, praesidium: caritate te et benevolentia civium saeptum oportet
esse, non armis. **113** eripiet et extorquebit tibi ista populus Romanus,    15
utinam salvis nobis! sed quoquo modo nobiscum egeris, dum istis consiliis
uteris, non potes, mihi crede, esse diuturnus. etenim ista tua minime avara
coniunx, quam ego sine contumelia describo, nimium diu debet populo
Romano tertiam pensionem. habet populus Romanus ad quos guberna-
cula rei publicae deferat: qui ubicumque terrarum sunt, ibi omne est rei    20
publicae praesidium vel potius ipsa res publica, quae se adhuc tantum
modo ulta est, nondum recuperavit. habet quidem certe res publica adulescentis nobilissimos paratos defensores. quam volent illi cedant otio
consulentes; tamen a re publica revocabuntur.

Et nomen pacis dulce est et ipsa res salutaris; sed inter pacem et    25
servitutem plurimum interest. pax est tranquilla libertas, servitus postremum malorum omnium, non modo bello sed morte etiam repellendum.
**114** quod si se ipsos illi nostri liberatores e conspectu nostro abstulerunt,
at exemplum facti reliquerunt. illi quod nemo fecerat fecerunt. Tarqui-
nium Brutus bello est persecutus, qui tum rex fuit cum esse Romae regem    30
licebat; Sp. Cassius, Sp. Maelius, M. Manlius propter suspicionem regni

---

**112** 7 diem hunc unum *D*     12 nonne *D*     14 te *om. D*     **113** 15 et] *om. bnstv*     18–
19 rei p. *D*     21 p(ublica) *om. V*     22 ulta] uita *Vt*: uicta *cnsv*     26 servitus est *Isid.*
*Orig. 2.29.13; Mar. Victorin. De defin. 27 (43) ed. Stangl*     **114** 30 romae regem (rege *b*)
*D*: roma te *V*[1]: romae *V*[2]     31 licebat] liceret *nstv*

Caesar's acts; how can you reconcile defense of some with indifference to others? Unless you choose to admit that you measure everything by your own profit, not Caesar's honor. Well, what have you to say to all this? I await a display of eloquence. I knew your grandfather for a great speaker, but I know you for an even more *open* one. He never addressed a public meeting in the nude, whereas you, plain honest fellow that you are, have let us see your torso.[108] Will you reply to all this, will you dare so much as to open your mouth? Will you find any point in this long speech of mine which you can answer with confidence?

**112** But let us leave aside what is past. This one day, this day that is now passing, this point of time in which I speak: defend it if you can. Why is the Senate surrounded by a circle of armed men, why do your henchmen hear me sword in hand, why are the doors of the temple of Concord not open, why do you bring into the Forum the most barbarous of all races, Ituraeans, with arrows? He says he does it for his protection. Is it not better to die a thousand deaths than to be unable to live in one's own community without an armed guard? But believe me, that is no protection. You should be fenced around by the love and goodwill of your countrymen, not by weapons. **113** The Roman People will take them from you, wrench them out of your hands; I pray that we do not perish in the process. But however you deal with us, believe me, if you continue in your present course, you cannot last long. And indeed, that least acquisitive of ladies, your wife, whom I delineate without disrespect, has owed her third installment to the Roman People over long.[109] The Roman People has men to whom it can commit the helm of state. Wherever in the world they are, there is the entire defense of the Commonwealth, or rather, there *is* the Commonwealth, which so far has only avenged itself, not regained itself. Yes, assuredly the Commonwealth has champions ready to hand, young men of the highest birth. Let them withdraw as they please in their concern for public tranquility: the Commonwealth will recall them.

The name of peace is sweet, the reality brings welfare; but there is a world of difference between peace and servitude. Peace is tranquil liberty, servitude is the worst of all evils, one to be averted not only at the price of war but even of death. **114** If these liberators of ours have removed themselves from our sight, they have left the example of their deed behind them. They did what no man had done before. Brutus waged war against Tarquin, who was king when kings were permitted in Rome. Spurius Cassius, Spurius Maelius, Marcus Manlius were put to death because they were suspected of aiming at monarchy. But

108. Reference to Antony's speech at the Lupercalia (2.86). *Apertum pectus* was a proverbial term for candor.
109. Allusion to the violent deaths of Fulvia's two previous husbands; cf. 2.11.

appetendi sunt necati: hi primum cum gladiis non in regnum appetentem,
sed in regnantem impetum fecerunt. quod cum ipsum factum per se
praeclarum est atque divinum, tum expositum ad imitandum est, praesertim cum illi eam gloriam consecuti sint quae vix caelo capi posse
videatur. etsi enim satis in ipsa conscientia pulcherrimi facti fructus erat,　5
tamen mortali immortalitatem non arbitror esse contemnendam.

**115** Recordare igitur illum, M. Antoni, diem quo dictaturam sustulisti;
pone ante oculos laetitiam senatus populique Romani, confer cum hac
nundinatione tua tuorumque: tum intelleges quantum inter lucrum et
laudem intersit. sed nimirum, ut quidam morbo aliquo et sensus stupore　10
suavitatem cibi non sentiunt, sic libidinosi, avari, facinerosi verae laudis
gustatum non habent. sed si te laus adlicere ad recte faciendum non
potest, ne metus quidem a foedissimis factis potest avocare? iudicia non
metuis: si propter innocentiam, laudo; sin propter vim, non intellegis, qui
isto modo iudicia non timeat, ei quid timendum sit? **116** quod si non　15
metuis viros fortis egregiosque civis, quod a corpore tuo prohibentur
armis, tui te, mihi crede, diutius non ferent. quae est autem vita dies et
noctes timere a suis? nisi vero aut maioribus habes beneficiis obligatos
quam ille quosdam habuit ex eis a quibus est interfectus, aut tu es ulla re
cum eo comparandus. fuit in illo ingenium, ratio, memoria, litterae,　20
cura, cogitatio, diligentia; res bello gesserat, quamvis rei publicae cala-
mitosas, at tamen magnas; multos annos regnare meditatus, magno labore, magnis periculis quod cogitarat effecerat; muneribus, monumentis,
congiariis, epulis multitudinem imperitam delenierat; suos praemiis, ad-
versarios clementiae specie devinxerat. quid multa? attulerat iam liberae　25
civitati partim metu partim patientia consuetudinem serviendi. **117** cum
illo ego te dominandi cupiditate conferre possum, ceteris vero rebus nullo
modo comparandus es. sed ex plurimis malis quae ab illo rei publicae
sunt inusta hoc tamen boni est quod didicit iam populus Romanus quantum cuique crederet, quibus se committeret, a quibus caveret. haec non　30
cogitas, neque intellegis satis esse viris fortibus didicisse quam sit re

---

1 primi *D*　　3 atque diuinum est *D*　　est (*alt.*)] sit *c*: si *bn*¹*sv*: sic *n*²: *om. t*　　6 mor-
tali] m- immortali *V*: *om. D*　　esse *om. D*　　**115** 7 igitur *om. D*　　9 nundinatione
*Lambinus* (immani n- *iam A. Augustinus*): in manum latione *V*: nummatione *D*　　9–10
laudem et lucrum *D*　　12 gustatum] gustum *bnstv*　　14 sin] si *bcnst*: sed *v*　　14–15
intellegis qui . . . ei quid *Muretus*: -egeris qui . . . et quid *V*¹: -gis ei qui . . . quid (quod *t*,
qui *v*) *DV*²　　**116** 17 vita] multas *nstv*　　18 timere] -er *V*¹: -eri *bnsvV*²　　20 eo] illo
*D*　　20–21 litterae cura] -eratura *nstv*　　22 non multos *nstv*　　est meditatus
*D*　　23 magnis] magmultis *V*¹: mul- *V*²　　cogitabat *V*　　24 delenierat *Garatoni*:
-ebat *V*: lenierat *D*　　25 quid multa? attulerat *om. V*¹　　**117** 28 es comparandus] -dus
est *V*¹: -dus es *V*²　　29 boni est] bonis et *V*¹: boni exstitit *Koch*　　30 haec igitur
*D*　　31 neque] nec *bcnsv*: sed *t*

these were the first to come sword in hand, not against an aspirant to monarchy, but a reigning monarch. A splendid, a godlike deed; also one open to imitation, especially as the doers have won glory for which Heaven itself seems scarcely wide enough. The consciousness of so noble an act was reward enough, and yet I do not think a mortal can make no account of immortality.

**115** Therefore remember that day, Marcus Antonius, when you abolished the dictatorship. Put before your mind's eye the joy of the Senate and People of Rome, compare it with this trafficking of yours and of those near to you:[110] then you will understand how wide is the gap between gain and glory. But I suppose it is as with certain invalids who lose the power of sensation and cannot relish their food: the libidinous, the greedy, the criminal are incapable of tasting true glory. But if praise cannot entice you into doing right, cannot fear deter you from the foulest offenses? You do not fear the law. Fine, if innocence is the reason; but if you rely on violence, don't you realize that a person who is not afraid of the law after that fashion has something else to be afraid of? **116** If you do not fear brave men and loyal citizens because they are kept away from your person by weapons, your own people, believe me, will not put up with you for long. And what sort of a life is that, day and night to be afraid of one's own? Or do you have men under greater obligations to you than certain of those who killed him were to Caesar? Are you to be compared to him in any way? Caesar had intellect, calculation, memory, culture, concentration, reflection, industry. His military achievements, even though disastrous to the Commonwealth, had been great. Aiming at monarchy for many years, he worked hard and ran great risks; and so he had accomplished his dream. He had cajoled the ignorant populace with shows and buildings and largesses and feasts. He had bound his own followers by rewards, his adversaries by a show of clemency. In short, he had succeeded in habituating a free community to servitude, partly through its fears, partly through its long-suffering. **117** In your lust for despotic power I can compare you with him, but in all other respects there is no comparison. But out of the many evils which Caesar inflicted on the Commonwealth this much good has come, that the Roman People has learned how much reliance to place on each one of us, whom to trust, whom to beware of.[111] Do you not reflect on this and understand that for brave men it is enough to have learned what a beautiful thing it is to slay a

110. Cf. n. 88 above.

111. It is not easy to see Cicero's point here. Note also the clausula *ā quĭbūs căvēret*, usually avoided.

pulchrum, beneficio gratum, fama gloriosum tyrannum occidere? an,
cum illum homines non tulerint, te ferent? **118** certatim posthac, mihi
crede, ad hoc opus curretur neque occasionis tarditas exspectabitur.

　　Respice, quaeso, aliquando †rem publicam†, M. Antoni; quibus ortus
sis, non quibuscum vivas considera. mecum, ut voles: redi cum re publica　　5
in gratiam. sed de te tu videris; ego de me ipse profitebor. defendi rem
publicam adulescens, non deseram senex: contempsi Catilinae gladios,
non pertimescam tuos. quin etiam corpus libenter obtulerim, si reprae-
sentari morte mea libertas civitatis potest, ut aliquando dolor populi Romani pariat quod iam diu parturit! **119** etenim si abhinc annos prope　　10
viginti hoc ipso in templo negavi posse mortem immaturam esse consulari, quanto verius nunc negabo seni! mihi vero, patres conscripti, iam
etiam optanda mors est, perfuncto rebus eis quas adeptus sum quasque
gessi. duo modo haec opto, unum ut moriens populum Romanum liberum
relinquam—hoc mihi maius ab dis immortalibus dari nihil potest—　　15
alterum ut ita cuique eveniat ut de re publica quisque mereatur.

---

**118** 4 respice . . . quibus] respice quaeso aliquibus *V*: r-, quaeso, aliquando; quibus *Halm*:
resipisce, q-, a-; quibus *Seidler*: anne respice, q-, a-, M. Antoni, respice; quibus*?*　　5 ut
uoles] utiles *V*[1]: uti voles *Halm*　　cum re p. redi *D*　　6 tu ipse *D*　　ipse] ipso *cnsv*:
ipse ipso *t*　　7–8 deseram . . . tuos] -ram sextimescam tuos *V, unde* extimescam *coni.*
*Nohl*　　**119** 12 nunc] non *bnv*: *om. s*　　13–14 adeptus . . . ut *om. V*[1]

tyrant, what gratitude such a benefaction inspires, what fame and glory it brings? Will men put up with you, when they did not put up with Caesar? **118** Believe me, from now on it will be a race to get to the job; there will be no waiting for an opportunity which might be slow in coming.

Look back, Marcus Antonius, even at this late hour, look back. Think of the men from whom you sprang, not of those with whom you associate. Make your peace with me or not, as you please; but make your peace with the Commonwealth. However, as for you, it is for you to determine. As for me, out of my own mouth I will make this declaration: I defended the Commonwealth when I was young; I shall not desert it now that I am old. I despised Catiline's blades; I shall not fear yours. Yes, and I should be happy to offer my body if my death can purchase immediate liberty for the Commonwealth, and the suffering of the Roman People thus at length bring to birth what has so long been in the womb. **119** In this very temple almost twenty years ago I said that death could not be untimely for a consular; with how much greater truth can I now say, "for an old man"! For me, Members of the Senate, death is now something even to be wished for after the honors I have won and the services I have rendered. I make only these two prayers: the first, let me die leaving the Roman People free—the Immortal Gods can grant me no greater boon; the second, let it so befall each man as he deserves of the Commonwealth.

# III

## INTRODUCTION

After leaving for Brundisium on 9 October 44, Antony was given a foretaste of things to come at Suessa Aurunca near the Campanian border, where he executed some refractory troops (3.10, 4.4, 13.18). At Brundisium the legions from Macedonia had been tampered with by Octavian's agents. Dissatisfied with the donative offered by their commander, they mutinied, only temporarily quelled by the slaughter of picked centurions and soldiers (three hundred, Cicero's probably inflated estimate) in the presence of Antony and his wife (3.4, 5.22, 13.18). Meanwhile Octavian was busy in Campania. His name and lavish promises of money raised an army from Caesar's veterans settled on the land, with which he marched on Rome. There he delivered a strong attack on Antony on 9 November, then left to recruit more troops.

Antony had returned to Rome with a legion (the Larks) behind him by the middle of November. He summoned a meeting of the Senate for 24 November, but canceled it on the news of further trouble with the Martian Legion. Along with the rest they had been ordered to march to Cisalpine (Hither) Gaul, there to await Antony's arrival, but on the way they deserted to Octavian and occupied the town of Alba Fucens, a strategic point in central Italy. The meeting of the Senate was deferred to 28 November, but that day brought the report of another defection; the Fourth Legion had followed the example of the Martians. Antony hurriedly changed his plan to have Octavian denounced by the Senate, put through an allocation of provincial governorships, and left for Gaul early next morning. When he got there, D. Brutus refused to vacate the province and fell back to stand siege at Mutina (Modena).

In Rome everything stood suspended in expectation of 1 January, when Hirtius and Pansa, the new consuls appointed by Caesar, were to take office. Both had been leading men in Caesar's party, but neither wanted another dictatorship. Both also were old friends of Cicero; he neither respected nor trusted them but had to admit, in the sequel, that they stood loyally by the Republic. Cicero himself returned to Rome on 9 December. On 20 December the new board of tribunes convened the Senate to discuss security measures for the coming meeting on 1 January. Cicero used the occasion to produce the third of his Philippics, thereby, as he liked to claim afterwards, laying the foundations of a restored Commonwealth (5.30, 6.2; cf. *Fam.* 10.28).

The speech is mainly a review of recent events, abusing Antony and his brother Lucius and praising D. Brutus, Octavian, the deserting legions, and the province of Cisalpine Gaul, all of which are thanked in the decree proposed at the end. The Senate passed it.

**1** Serius omnino, patres conscripti, quam tempus rei publicae postulabat, aliquando tamen convocati sumus; quod flagitabam equidem cotidie, quippe cum bellum nefarium contra aras et focos, contra vitam fortunasque nostras ab homine profligato ac perdito non comparari, sed geri iam viderem. exspectantur Kalendae Ianuariae; quas non exspectat 5 Antonius, qui in provinciam D. Bruti, summi et singularis viri, cum exercitu impetum facere conatur; ex qua se instructum et paratum ad urbem venturum esse minitatur. **2** quae est igitur exspectatio aut quae vel minimi dilatio temporis? quamquam enim adsunt Kalendae Ianuariae, tamen breve tempus longum est imparatis. dies enim adfert vel hora potius, nisi 10 provisum est, magnas saepe clades; certus autem dies non ut sacrifici, sic consili exspectari solet. quod si aut Kalendae Ianuariae fuissent eo die quo primum ex urbe fugit Antonius, aut eae non essent exspectatae, bellum iam nullum haberemus. auctoritate enim senatus consensuque populi Romani facile hominis amentis fregissemus audaciam. quod con- 15 fido equidem consules designatos, simul ut magistratum inierint, esse facturos; sunt enim optimo animo, summo consilio, singulari concordia. mea autem festinatio non victoriae solum avida est sed etiam celeritatis. **3** quo enim usque tantum bellum, tam crudele, tam nefarium privatis consiliis propulsabitur? cur non quam primum publica accedit auctoritas? 20

C. Caesar adulescens, paene potius puer, incredibili ac divina quadam mente atque virtute, cum maxime furor arderet Antoni cumque eius a Brundisio crudelis et pestifer reditus timeretur, nec postulantibus nec cogitantibus, ne[c] optantibus quidem nobis, quia non posse fieri videbatur, firmissimum exercitum ex invicto genere veteranorum militum 25 comparavit patrimoniumque suum effudit: quamquam non sum usus eo verbo quo debui; non enim effudit: in salute rei publicae collocavit. **4** cui quamquam gratia referri tanta non potest quanta debetur, habenda tamen est tanta quantam maximam animi nostri capere possunt. quis enim est tam ignarus rerum, tam nihil de re publica cogitans qui hoc non intel- 30 legat, si M. Antonius a Brundisio cum eis copiis quas se habiturum putabat, Romam, ut minabatur, venire potuisset, nullum genus eum crudelitatis praeteriturum fuisse? quippe qui in hospitis tectis Brundisi for-

**1** 1 tempus *om. V¹* postulabat *Manutius*: -abatuit *V¹*: -auit *DV²* 4 non cogitari *Arusian. 7:458 Keil (cf. quae scripsi ad Att. 6.6.2* cum iam Appius de Eleusine non cogitet) 6 D.] *om. V¹cv* **2** 8 minima *D* 10 vel] et *D* nisi] nihil *V*: si n-*Halm* 11 sacrificiis *Halm* 12 consiliis *V* 13 eae *Halm*: ae *V*: hae *D* 16 ut *V*] ac (simul designatos ac *c*) *D* 18 mea] ea *V* sed *om. V* **3** 21 paene] vel *Cobet coll.* 4.3: *fort.* vel paene 22 tum cum *cV²*: tunc cum *bnstv* 24 ne *Lambinus*: nec *codd.* opinantibus *D* fieri posse non *D* 25 ex *om. D* 26 sumus (simus *b*) usi *D* 27 debui] decuit *D* effudit sed *D* rei p. salute *V* **4** 29 est tanta] t- est *bcntv* 32 putauerat *D*: -arat *Garatoni*

**1** Members of the Senate, we have been called together later than the crisis of the Commonwealth demanded; but we meet at last. I have been pressing every day for a meeting, as I see a wicked war not in preparation but in actual conduct by a profligate and desperate man against our altars and hearths, against our lives and property. We are waiting for the Kalends of January: but Antonius does not wait for them. He is attempting to invade the province of our noble and distinguished fellow countryman Decimus Brutus with an army, and from that province he threatens, when equipped and ready, to march on Rome. **2** Why then the waiting, why a moment's delay? The Kalends of January are nearly come, but even a short time is long for the unready; for a day, or rather an hour, often brings great disasters if precautions have not been taken. A decision is not like a sacrifice,[1] not to be made before a particular day. If the day when Antonius first fled from Rome had been the Kalends of January, or if we had not waited for them, we should not be at war now; for we should easily have quelled the madman's insolence by the authority of the Senate and the consensus of the Roman People. I am confident that the consuls-elect will do that as soon as they take office; for they are thoroughly loyal, of excellent judgment, and agree remarkably well with one another. But I am in a hurry. I am eager, not merely for victory, but for quick victory. **3** How long is a war of such magnitude, a cruel and wicked war, to be beaten back by private initiatives? Why does not public authority come to their support without delay?

When Antonius' fury was at its height and we dreaded his return from Brundisium, cruel and baneful as it would have been, without our asking or thinking or even praying for such a thing because it seemed impossible, a young man, or rather hardly more than a boy, Gaius Caesar, showed a superhuman spirit and energy. Incredibly, he raised a very strong army of veteran soldiers who had never known defeat and lavished his patrimony—no, I have used the wrong word; he did not lavish it, he invested it in the salvation of the Commonwealth. **4** We cannot repay all we owe him, but all the gratitude of which our souls are capable is his due. Ignorant indeed must he be of the world around him, totally careless of the public good, who does not realize that if Marcus Antonius could have returned to Rome, as he threatened to do, with the forces which he expected to have under his command, he would have left no form of cruelty unemployed. Under his host's roof at Brundisium he

---

1. Probably with reference to the sacrifice to Jupiter offered on the Capitol on 1 January each year by the incoming consuls.

tissimos viros optimosque civis iugulari iusserit; quorum ante pedes eius
morientium sanguine os uxoris respersum esse constabat. hac ille crudelitate imbutus, cum multo bonis omnibus veniret iratior quam illis fuerat
quos trucidarat, cui tandem nostrum aut cui omnino bono pepercisset?
**5** qua peste rem publicam privato consilio—neque enim fieri potuit aliter—Caesar liberavit: qui nisi in hac re publica natus esset, rem publicam
scelere Antoni nullam haberemus. sic enim perspicio, sic iudico, nisi
unus adulescens illius furentis impetus crudelissimosque conatus co-
hibuisset, rem publicam funditus interituram fuisse. cui quidem hodierno
die, patres conscripti—nunc enim primum ita convenimus ut illius beneficio possemus ea quae sentiremus libere dicere—tribuenda est auctoritas, ut rem publicam non modo a se susceptam sed etiam a nobis com-
mendatam possit defendere.

**6** Nec vero de legione Martia, quoniam longo intervallo loqui nobis de
re publica licet, sileri potest. quis enim unus fortior, quis amicior umquam rei publicae fuit quam legio Martia universa? quae cum hostem
populi Romani Antonium iudicasset, comes esse eius amentiae noluit: reliquit consulem; quod profecto non fecisset, si eum consulem iudicasset
quem nihil aliud agere, nihil moliri nisi caedem civium atque interitum
civitatis videret. atque ea legio consedit Albae. quam potuit urbem eli-
gere aut opportuniorem ad res gerendas aut fideliorem aut fortiorum virorum aut amic⟨i⟩orum rei publicae civium?

**7** Huius legionis virtutem imitata quarta legio duce L. Egnatuleio
quaestore, civi optimo et fortissimo, C. Caesaris auctoritatem atque exercitum persecuta est. faciendum est igitur nobis, patres conscripti, ut ea
quae sua sponte clarissimus adulescens atque omnium praestantissimus
gessit et gerit, haec auctoritate nostra comprobentur, veteranorumque,
fortissimorum virorum, tum legionis Martiae quartaeque mirabilis consensus ad rem publicam recuperandam laude et testimonio nostro confir-
metur, eorumque commoda, honores, praemia, cum consules designati
magistratum inierint, curae nobis fore hodierno die spondeamus.

**8** Atque ea quidem quae dixi de Caesare deque eius exercitu iam diu
nota sunt nobis. virtute enim admirabili Caesaris constantiaque militum
veteranorum legionumque earum quae optimo iudicio auctoritatem nos-

1 ciues optimos *bnstv*: -esque -mus *c*    iussit *D*    3 bonis] nobis *Christ*    omnibus *Vn²*: homin- *D*    4 uestrum *D*    **5** 5 priuato consilio rem p. *V*    nec *D*    10
illius] de i- *bnstv*    11 ea *om. D*    **6** 15 unus] umquam *nstv*    17 m. Antonium
*D*    iudicauisset *D* (*item in l.* 18)    20 ea *om. V*    21–22 fortiorum . . . amiciorum
*ed. Iuntina*: -tium (-tiorem *D*) . . . -corum *codd.*    **7** 23 huiusce *D*    24 ciue *D*    C.
*om. D*    25 est igitur nobis] i- est n- *cnv*: i- n- est *st*    27 haec] hac *s*: *del. Ernesti (v.*
*Fe.*)    29 laude] -etur *nstv*    **8** 34 optimo iudicio quae *D*

ordered brave soldiers and loyal citizens to be murdered; it was commonly reported that as they lay dying at his feet their blood splashed into his wife's face. Stained by such cruelty, and far more angry with all honest men than he had been with his slaughtered victims, which of us senators, which single honest man would he have spared? **5** From that scourge Caesar by his private initiative—there was no other way—delivered the Commonwealth. Had he not been born in this Commonwealth, through the crime of Antonius we should no longer have a Commonwealth. Yes, it is my perception and judgment, that if this one young man had not checked that hurtling madman's savage purpose, the Commonwealth would have perished utterly. Today, Members of the Senate, since for the first time thanks to him we have met under conditions which make it possible for us to give free expression to our sentiments, we must grant him authority to defend the Commonwealth. He has made himself its champion and we must put it in his hands.

**6** And since after so long an interval we can speak on public affairs, something must needs be said about the Martian Legion. No individual has ever proved a braver and better friend to the Commonwealth than the entire Martian Legion. Judging Antonius to be an enemy of the Roman People, this legion refused to be party to his madness. They deserted the consul, which they would surely not have done if they had judged him to be a consul; but they saw that his only purpose and plan was to massacre citizens and destroy the community. The legion has stationed itself at Alba. It could have chosen no city more strategically suitable or more faithful; none with a braver or more patriotic population.

**7** Modeling itself upon the gallant spirit of this legion, the Fourth Legion, under the command of Quaestor Lucius Egnatuleius, a loyal and courageous citizen, has followed the authority and army of Gaius Caesar. So it is for us, Members of the Senate, to see that what this illustrious and most eminent young man has done and is doing is sanctioned by our authority. We must further confirm by our approval and witness the wonderful unanimity displayed by the gallant veterans and also by the Martian and Fourth legions for the restoration of the Commonwealth. We must this day make our pledge that their interests, honors, and rewards shall be our care when the consuls-elect have come into office.

**8** What I have just said about Caesar and his army has been known to us for some time past. By Caesar's admirable initiative and by the resolution of the veteran soldiers and those legions which with excellent judgment have placed

tram, libertatem populi Romani, virtutem Caesaris secutae sunt a cervicibus nostris est depulsus Antonius. sed haec, ut dixi, superiora: hoc vero recens edictum D. Bruti quod paulo ante propositum est certe silentio non potest praeteriri. pollicetur enim se provinciam Galliam retenturum in senatus populique Romani potestate. o civem natum rei publicae, 5 memorem sui nominis imitatoremque maiorum! neque enim Tarquinio expulso maioribus nostris tam fuit optata libertas quam est depulso Antonio retinenda nobis. **9** illi regibus parere iam a condita urbe didicerant: nos post reges exactos servitutis oblivio ceperat. atque ille Tarquinius quem maiores nostri non tulerunt non crudelis, non impius, sed superbus 10 est habitus et dictus: quod nos vitium in privatis saepe tulimus, id maiores nostri ne in rege quidem ferre potuerunt. L. Brutus regem superbum non tulit: D. Brutus sceleratum atque impium regnare patietur? quid Tarquinius tale qualia innumerabilia et facit et fecit Antonius? senatum etiam reges habebant: nec tamen, ut Antonio senatum habente, in consilio regis 15 versabantur barbari armati. servabant auspicia reges; quae hic consul augurque neglexit, neque solum legibus contra auspicia ferendis sed etiam collega una ferente eo quem ipse ementitis auspiciis vitiosum fecerat. **10** quis autem rex umquam fuit tam insignite impudens ut haberet omnia commoda, beneficia, iura regni venalia? quam hic immunitatem, quam 20 civitatem, quod praemium non vel singulis hominibus vel civitatibus vel universis provinciis vendidit? nihil humile de Tarquinio, nihil sordidum accepimus: at vero huius domi inter quasilla pendebatur aurum, numerabatur pecunia; una in domo omnes quorum intererat totum imperium populi Romani nundinabantur. supplicia vero in civis Romanos nulla Tar- 25 quini accepimus: at hic et Suessae iugulavit eos quos in custodiam dederat et Brundisi ad trecentos fortissimos viros civisque optimos trucidavit. **11** postremo Tarquinius pro populo Romano bellum gerebat tum cum est expulsus: Antonius contra populum Romanum exercitum adducebat tum cum a legionibus relictus nomen Caesaris exercitumque per- 30 timuit neglectisque sacrificiis sollemnibus ante lucem vota ea quae numquam solveret nuncupavit, et hoc tempore in provinciam populi Romani conatur invadere. maius igitur a D. Bruto beneficium populus Romanus et habet et exspectat quam maiores nostri acceperunt a L. Bruto, principe

1 c. caesaris *D*  a *om. V*[1]  2 ut dixi haec *D*  5 potestatem *D*  7 depulso *Faërnus*: depluso *V*: repulso *D*  Antonio] maioribus nostris tam antonio *V*  **9** 8 a *om. D*  didicerunt *coni. Clark, numeri causa*  9 nos post reges] nostrae gens *V*[1]  10 non *ante* impius *om. D*  11 est habitus] h- est *bnsv*  13 patietur] -iatur *bn*[1]*stv*  antonium *post* patietur *habet V*  14 et fecit et facit *cnstv*  18 referente *D*  **10** 23 numerabantur *V*[1]  25 nundinabantur *Vn*[2]: -atur (-us *b*) *D*  **11** 29 expulsus est *D*  30 legionibus omnibus *V*  timuit *V*[1]  31 ea uota *bcns*  34 spectat *V*

themselves behind our authority, the liberty of the Roman People, and the
courage of Caesar, Antonius has been dislodged from our necks. But all this
came earlier, as I have said. Decimus Brutus' manifesto is recent, it has just
been published. Assuredly it must not be passed over in silence. He promises
to keep the province of Gaul in the control of the Senate and People of Rome.
A citizen born for the Commonwealth, mindful of his name, following in the
footsteps of his ancestors! When Tarquin was driven out, our ancestors wel-
comed freedom; no less must we retain it, now that Antonius has been dislodged. **9** *They* had learned obedience to kings right from the foundation of
Rome, but after the expulsion of the kings *we* had forgotten what slavery was.
The Tarquin that our ancestors did not endure was reckoned and called "the
Proud," not "the Cruel" or "the Impious"; our ancestors could not bear in a
king a fault which we have often put up with in private persons. Lucius Brutus
did not brook a proud king: shall Decimus Brutus suffer a felon and traitor to
reign? What did Tarquin ever do to compare with countless deeds and doings
of Antonius? The kings too had a Senate, but armed barbarians did not figure
in the royal council chamber as they do when Antonius holds a Senate. The
kings observed the auspices, which this consul and augur has neglected, not
only by putting through legislation in defiance of the auspices but by doing so
in conjunction with a colleague whose election he himself had flawed by
announcing false auspices. **10** And what king ever had the unmitigated impudence to put up all benefits, grants, and rights in his realm for sale? Exemptions, citizen rights, rewards—are there any which *he* has not sold to individuals or communities or whole provinces? Nothing base or sordid is told of
Tarquin: but in Antonius' house the gold was weighed and the money counted
among the women's wool baskets. In a single dwelling all persons interested
trafficked in the entire empire of the Roman People. We are not told that
Tarquin ever executed Roman citizens: whereas Antonius murdered those
whom he had thrown into custody at Suessa, and at Brundisium he slaughtered
some three hundred brave soldiers and loyal citizens. **11** Finally, at the time
when Tarquin was driven out, he was waging war on behalf of the Roman
People: Antonius was leading an army against the Roman People when he was
deserted by the legions and, in terror of Caesar's name and army, neglecting
the customary sacrifices, he took vows[2] before daybreak which he will never
discharge; and at this moment he is attempting to invade a province of the
Roman People. So the Roman People has and expects a greater boon from
Decimus Brutus than our ancestors received from Lucius Brutus, who founded

2. At 5.24 Antony is said to have left Rome without making the customary sacrifices and
vows.

huius maxime conservandi generis et nominis. **12** cum autem est omnis servitus misera, tum vero intolerabile est servire impuro, impudico, effeminato, numquam ne in metu quidem sobrio. hunc igitur qui Gallia prohibet, privato praesertim consilio, iudicat verissimeque iudicat non esse consulem. faciendum est igitur nobis, patres conscripti, ut D. Bruti　5 privatum consilium auctoritate publica comprobemus. nec vero M. Antonium consulem post Lupercalia debuistis putare: quo enim ille die, populo Romano inspectante, nudus, unctus, ebrius est contionatus et id egit ut collegae diadema imponeret, eo die se non modo consulatu sed etiam libertate abdicavit. esset enim ipsi certe statim serviendum, si Cae-　10 sar ab eo regni insigne accipere voluisset. hunc igitur ego consulem, hunc civem Romanum, hunc liberum, hunc denique hominem putem qui foedo illo et flagitioso die et quid pati Caesare vivo posset et quid eo mortuo consequi ipse cuperet ostendit?

**13** Nec vero de virtute, constantia, gravitate provinciae Galliae taceri　15 potest. est enim ille flos Italiae, illud firmamentum imperi populi Romani, illud ornamentum dignitatis. tantus autem est consensus municipiorum coloniarumque provinciae Galliae ut omnes ad auctoritatem huius ordinis maiestatemque populi Romani defendendam conspirasse videantur.

Quam ob rem, tribuni plebis, quamquam vos nihil aliud nisi de praesi-　20 dio, ut senatum tuto consules Kalendis Ianuariis habere possint, rettulistis, tamen mihi videmini magno consilio atque optima mente potestatem nobis de tota re publica fecisse dicendi. cum autem tuto haberi senatum sine praesidio non posse iudicavistis, tum statuistis etiam intra muros Antoni scelus audaciamque versari.　25

**14** Quam ob rem omnia mea sententia complectar, vobis, ut intellego, non invitis: ut et praestantissimis ducibus a nobis detur auctoritas et fortissimis militibus spes ostendatur praemiorum et iudicetur non verbo, sed re non modo non consul sed etiam hostis Antonius. nam si ille consul, fustuarium meruerunt legiones quae consulem reliquerunt, sceleratus　30 Caesar, Brutus nefarius qui contra consulem privato consilio exercitus comparaverunt. si autem militibus exquirendi sunt honores novi propter eorum divinum atque immortale meritum, ducibus autem ne referri quidem potest gratia, quis est qui eum hostem non existimet quem qui armis persequuntur conservatores rei publicae iudicantur?　35

**12** 1–2 est *post* omnis *bcns, post* servitus *tv*: *post* misera *ponendum coni. Fedeli*　2 intolerabile est *ed. Romana*: -lis est *Vbnsv*: -le si *c*: -lis si *t*　5 p. c. nobis (n- *om. v*) *D*　8 contionatus est *cnstv*　9 die se] se *ante* abdicauit *D*　11 insigni *V*: -nia *Faërnus*　13 e caesare uno *V*: C. C- vivo *Halm*　**13** 21 possint *Faërnus*: possetint *V*: possent *D*　23 autem *scripsi*: enim *codd.*　haberi senatum *ς*: -ere sanatum *V*: senatum haberi *D*　24 tum] istum *c*: -ud *bnst*: illud *v*　**14** 32 sin *D*　33 referri] ferri *V¹t*　34 hostem non] non h- *cntv*　35 persequantur *V*　iudicantur (*cf.* 4.5 *init.*)] -centur *cnstvV²*

this race and name above all others to be cherished. **12** All slavery is miserable, but slavery to a vile, debauched effeminate, who is never sober even when he is terrified, is downright intolerable. In barring him from Gaul, and that by private initiative, Brutus judges that he is not consul, and he is entirely right. Accordingly, Members of the Senate, it is our duty to approve Decimus Brutus' initiative by public authority. Indeed, you ought not to have regarded Marcus Antonius as consul after the Feast of Lupercal. On the day when before the eyes of the Roman People he made a public speech naked, oiled, and drunk and tried to place a diadem on his colleague, on that day he not only abdicated the consulship but his personal freedom as well. For he himself would certainly have become a slave then and there if Caesar had chosen to accept the emblem of monarchy at his hands. Am I then to think of him as a consul, or as a Roman citizen, or as a free man, or even as a human being, when on that day of infamy and shame he showed what he was capable of enduring while Caesar lived and equally what he himself desired to encompass after Caesar's death?

**13** A word must also be said about the valor, resolution, and responsibility of the province of Hither Gaul—the flower of Italy, the bulwark of the empire of the Roman People, the ornament of its dignity. The municipalities and colonies of the province of Gaul are at one; they seem to have banded together in unanimous defense of the authority of this House and the majesty of the Roman People.

Therefore, Tribunes of the Plebs, although your reference is confined to the matter of a guard so that the consuls may hold a Senate in safety on the Kalends of January, I think you have shown great judgment and excellent intentions in thus giving us an opportunity to speak on public affairs in general. Moreover, your decision that a Senate cannot be held in safety without a guard also implies that M. Antonius' crime and audacity is at large even within the walls.

**14** Accordingly, I shall embrace it all in my motion, as I believe will not be disagreeable to you gentlemen, to provide that authority be given by us to the eminent commanders, hope of rewards held out to their brave troops, and Antonius judged, not in word but in fact, to be not only not a consul but a public enemy. For if he *is* a consul, the legions which deserted a consul have deserved to be beaten to death, Caesar is a criminal and Brutus a villain for having raised armies against a consul by private initiative. If, on the contrary, unprecedented honors are to be devised for the soldiers in recognition of their unforgettable, transcendent service, if their commanders are beyond our power to recompense, who but considers Antonius a public enemy, when those who attack him in arms are judged saviors of the Commonwealth?

**15** At quam contumeliosus in edictis, quam barbarus, quam rudis! primum in Caesarem maledicta congessit deprompta ex recordatione im-
pudicitiae et stuprorum suorum. quis enim hoc adulescente castior, quis
modestior, quod in iuventute habemus illustrius exemplum veteris sanc-
titatis? quis autem illo qui male dicit impurior? ignobilitatem obicit       5
C. Caesaris filio, cuius etiam natura pater, si vita suppeditasset, consul
factus esset. "Aricina mater." Trallianam aut Ephesiam putes dicere. videte quam despiciamur omnes qui sumus e municipiis, id est omnes
plane: quotus enim quisque nostrum non est? quod autem municipium
non contemnit is qui Aricinum tanto opere despicit, vetustate antiqu-    10
issimum, iure foederatum, propinquitate paene finitimum, splendore
municipum honestissimum? **16** hinc Voconiae, hinc Atiniae leges; hinc
multae sellae curules et patrum memoria et nostra; hinc equites Romani
lautissimi et plurimi. sed si Aricinam uxorem non probas, cur probas
Tusculanam? quamquam huius sanctissimae feminae atque optimae pa-    15
ter, M. At[t]ius Balbus, in primis honestus, praetorius fuit: tuae coniugis,
bonae feminae, locupletis quidem certe, Bambalio quidam pater, homo
nullo numero. nihil illo contemptius, qui propter haesitantiam linguae
stuporemque cordis cognomen ex contumelia traxerat. "at avus nobilis."
Tuditanus nempe ille, qui cum palla et cothurnis nummos populo de ros-    20
tris spargere solebat. vellem hanc contemptionem pecuniae suis reli-
quisset! habetis nobilitatem generis gloriosam. **17** qui autem evenit ut tibi
Iulia nata ignobilis videatur, cum tu eodem materno genere soleas gloriari? quae porro amentia est eum dicere aliquid de uxorum ignobilitate
cuius pater Numitoriam Fregellanam, proditoris filiam, habuerit uxorem,    25

**15** 2 ut maledicta *D*      4 in iuventute *D*: -ute *V*: -uti *coni. Halm*      5 qui male dicit *V*[1]:
maledico *bnstvV*[2]      6 naturalis *DV*[2]      9 quotus] notus *bcnstV*[2]: *om. v*      nostrum *om.*
*D*      10 non . . . Aricinum *om. V*[1]      12 municipium *D*      **16** atinitae *ex* -niaetae *V*:
anniae *b*: scantiniae *n*[1] (scat- *n*[2]): sanctin- *s*: santin- *t*: sancton- *v*      14 lautissimi plurimi
et honestissimi *D*      16 Atius *Ferrarius*: att- *codd.*      19 traxerat *Halm*: traxit traxerat
*in ras. V*: traxerit *D*      avus] a- huius *nsvV*[2]: h- *t*      20 ille ille *bst*      22 haberetis
*DV*[2]      uenit *V*[1]      **17** ut is *bcnt*: ut his *s*      23 Iulia nata[3] *Muretus*: iulia natus *V*: uigilia
n- *c*: aricina n- *bnst*: istus aricinatus *v*

**15** How insolent he waxes in his manifestos, what ill-breeding, what ignorance! First, he heaped abuse on Caesar, taken straight from the recollection of his own vicious, debauched past. There is no more pure and modest young man than Caesar, no more conspicuous example of old-time morality in this younger generation of ours, just as there is no fouler rake than his traducer. He taunts Gaius Caesar's son with humble birth, though even his natural father would have been elected consul had he lived.[3] "A mother[4] from Aricia": you would think he was saying "from Tralles" or "from Ephesus." Notice how all of us who come from the country towns are looked down upon—which is to say, just about all of us here, for how many of us do not? And if he has such contempt for Aricia, an immemorially ancient community, in status a Roman ally under treaty, so close as almost to adjoin the Roman boundaries, distinguished by the high standing of its members, what municipality does he not despise? **16** From Aricia came the Voconian[5] and Atinian[6] laws, many curule chairs[7] in our fathers' time and in our own, great numbers of very wealthy Roman knights. But if you don't approve of a wife from Aricia, why do you approve of one from Tusculum?[8] Particularly as the father of this blameless, excellent lady was Marcus Atius Balbus, a highly respected man of praetorian rank, whereas your wife, good lady that she is (rich,[9] at all events), is the daughter of a certain Bambalio,[10] a person of no consequence, in fact a contemptible being who got his opprobrious surname from his stammering tongue and dull wits. "Ah, but her grandfather was a nobleman!" You mean Tuditanus,[11] who used to throw coppers from the rostra among the crowd, dressed in a player's robe and buskins. I could wish that his family had inherited his contempt for money. Well, gentlemen, there is a noble family to boast of! **17** But how is it that Antonius thinks the daughter of a Julia a commoner when he constantly brags of coming from the same family on his mother's side?[12] What folly, again, this talk about low-born wives from a man whose father married a Numitoria of Fregellae, the daughter of a traitor,[13] and

---

3. C. Octavius was a candidate for the consulship when he died in 58.

4. Atia, Caesar's niece.

5. A law concerning wills, proposed by Q. Voconius Saxa in 169.

6. Three laws of this name are recorded, the last, concerning theft, passed ca. 150.

7. I.e. magistrates.

8. Fulvia's hometown.

9. Another gibe at Fulvia's rapacity.

10. Cf. 2.90.

11. Called a madman in *Acad.* 2.89; cf. Val. Max. 7.8.1. The Sempronii Tuditani were an old noble family.

12. Atia's mother was sister to the dictator Caesar, Antony's was sister to L. Julius Caesar (consul in 64), belonging to a different branch of the family.

13. The first wife of Antony's father, M. Antonius Creticus, was the daughter of Q. Numitorius

ipse ex libertini filia susceperit liberos? sed hoc clarissimi viri viderint,
L. Philippus qui habet Aricinam uxorem, C. Marcellus qui Aricinae filiam: quos certo scio dignitatis optimarum feminarum non paenitere.

    Idem etiam Q. Ciceronem, fratris mei filium, compellat edicto, nec
sentit amens commendationem esse compellationem suam. quid enim ac-     5
cidere huic adulescenti potuit optatius quam cognosci ab omnibus Caesaris consiliorum esse socium, Antoni furoris inimicum? **18** at etiam
gladiator ausus est scribere hunc de patris et patrui parricidio cogitasse. o
admirabilem impudentiam, audaciam, temeritatem, in eum adulescentem
hoc scribere audere quem ego et frater meus propter eius suavissimos at-  10
que optimos mores praestantissimumque ingenium certatim amamus omnibusque horis oculis, auribus, complexu tenemus! nam me isdem edictis
nescit laedat an laudet. cum idem supplicium minatur optimis civibus
quod ego de sceleratissimis ac pessimis sumpserim, laudare videtur,
quasi imitari velit; cum autem illam pulcherrimi facti memoriam refricat,  15
tum a sui similibus invidiam aliquam in me commoveri putat.

    **19** ⟨At⟩ cum tot edicta ⟨pro⟩posuisset, edixit ut adesset senatus frequens
a. d. VIII Kalendas Decembris. sed quid fecit ipse? eo die ipse non adfuit.
at quo modo edixit? haec sunt, ut opinor, verba in extremo: "si quis non
adfuerit, hunc existimare omnes poterunt et interitus mei et perditissimo-  20
rum consiliorum auctorem fuisse." quae sunt perdita consilia? an ea quae
pertinent ad libertatem populi Romani recuperandam? quorum consiliorum Caesari me auctorem et hortatorem et esse et fuisse fateor.
quamquam ille non eguit consilio cuiusquam; sed tamen currentem, ut
dicitur, incitavi. nam interitus quidem tui quis bonus non esset auctor,  25
cum in eo salus et vita optimi cuiusque, libertas populi Romani dignitas-
que consisteret? **20** sed cum tam atroci edicto nos concitavisset, cur ipse

---

5 commendationem] communem *nstv*    **18** 12 me isdem edictis] meis de me d- *b*: eis
de me d- *c*: in eis de me d- *ns*: in eisdem d- *v*    13 nescit *om. V*[1]    14 ac pessimis
*om. D*    15 pulcherrimi] -mam *nstv*    16 sui] suis *Vcnv*    **19** 17 at *addidi, verba* sed
quid fecit ipse (*ita V*: i- q- f-, *om.* sed *D*) *ante* eo die (*l.* 18) *posui*    proposuisset *Naugerius*: pos- *codd.*    18 a.d. *Lambinus*: ad *codd.*    ipse (*alt.*) *fort. omittendum*    20
hunc *om. V*[1]    omnes existimare *D*    22 peritnenat *V*[1]: -tineant *Halm*    23 caesaris
*DV*[2]    26 in *om. V*[1]    et libertas *D*

who himself acknowledged children by the daughter of a freedman![14] However, I leave this matter to two illustrious gentlemen, Lucius Philippus, who has a wife from Aricia,[15] and Gaius Marcellus, who is married to the daughter of a lady from Aricia,[16] and I am sure they are well satisfied with the social status of these excellent ladies.

He further takes my brother's son, Quintus Cicero, to task in a manifesto, not having the sense to perceive that such treatment coming from him is a commendation. I do not know what better the young man could hope for than to be generally recognized as associated in the counsels of Caesar and hostile to the madness of Antonius. **18** But this gladiator actually dared to allege that he had formed designs on the lives of his father and his uncle. Amazing impudence, audacity, recklessness, to dare write such stuff about a young man for whom my brother and I vie in affection, which his personal charm, fine character, and outstanding talents so well deserve, who is constantly in our sight, in our hearing, in our arms![17] In the same manifesto he mentions me, without knowing whether he is praising or attacking me. When he threatens loyal citizens with the punishment which I inflicted on criminals and traitors, he seems to be praising me, as though he wished to imitate me; but when he refurbishes the memory of that glorious act,[18] he thinks that he is stirring up some odium against me on the part of persons like himself.

**19** Having published all these manifestos, he published another, summoning a full Senate on the twenty-fourth of November. But what did he do himself? On the day appointed he himself was absent. The style of the document is noteworthy. These, I think, are its concluding words: "If any man fails to attend, all will be able to set him down as an instigator of my destruction and of the most desperate designs." What desperate designs? Does he refer to those which have to do with the recovery of the Roman People's freedom? To such designs I admit that I have instigated and encouraged Caesar, and still do. Not that he needed anybody's advice; all the same, I spurred a willing horse, as they say. As for your destruction, what honest man would not instigate it, when the status and lives of our best citizens and the freedom and dignity of the Roman People depend on it? **20** But having roused us with so grim a sum-

---

Pullus, who in 125 betrayed the town of Fregellae, which had revolted from Rome, to the besieging Roman army.

14. Cf. 2.3.

15. Atia married him after the death of her first husband.

16. Octavian's sister Octavia.

17. Actually Cicero's opinion of the young man, as frequently expressed in letters to Atticus, could hardly have been lower.

18. The execution of the Catilinarian conspirators in 63.

non adfuit? num putatis aliqua re tristi ac severa? vino atque epulis reten-
tus, si illae epulae potius quam popinae nominandae sunt, diem edicti
obire neglexit: in a. d. ɪv Kalendas Decembris distulit. adesse in Capitolio iussit; quod in templum ipse nescio qua per Gallorum cuniculum
ascendit. convenerunt corrogati et quidem ampli quidam homines sed im-     5
memores dignitatis suae. is enim erat dies, ea fama, is qui senatum vo-
carat ut turpe senatori esset nihil timere. ad eos tamen ipsos qui con-
venerant ne verbum quidem ausus est facere de Caesare, cum de eo
constituisset ad senatum referre: ⟨et⟩ scriptam attulerat consularis quidam
sententiam. **21** quid est aliud de eo referre non audere qui contra se con-     10
sulem exercitum duceret nisi se ipsum hostem iudicare? necesse erat
enim alterutrum esse hostem; nec poterat aliter de adversariis ducibus
iudicari. si igitur Caesar hostis, cur consul nihil refert ad senatum? sin
ille a senatu notandus non fuit, quid potest dicere quin, cum de illo tacue-
rit, se hostem confessus sit? quem in edictis Spartacum appellat, hunc in     15
senatu ne improbum quidem dicere audet.

At in rebus tristissimis quantos excitat risus! sententiolas edicti cuius-
dam memoriae mandavi quas videtur ille peracutas putare: ego autem qui
intellegeret quid dicere vellet adhuc neminem inveni. **22** "nulla contumelia est quam facit dignus." primum quid est dignus? nam etiam malo     20
multi digni, sicut ipse. an quam facit is qui cum dignitate est? quae autem
potest esse maior? quid est porro facere contumeliam? quis sic loquitur?
deinde: "nec timor quem denuntiat inimicus." quid ergo? ab amico timor
denuntiari solet? horum similia deinceps. nonne satius est mutum esse
quam quod nemo intellegat dicere? en cur magister eius ex oratore arator     25
factus [sit] possideat in agro publico campi Leontini duo milia iugerum
immunia, ut hominem stupidum magis etiam infatuet mercede publica!

**23** Sed haec leviora fortasse: illud quaero, cur tam mansuetus in senatu
fuerit, cum in edictis tam fuisset ferus. quid enim attinuerat L. Cassio

---

**20** 1 putati $V^1$: -astis $V^2$     2 si $V$: est *bct*: et *nsv*: est si *Faërnus*     illae] eae *c*: hee *b*: alea si
*n*: alea est si *sv*: aelea *t*     3 in] et *bcntv* $V^2$     ante diem] ad $V^1$     9 et *addidi* (*anne* autem
*post* scriptam?)     **21** 10–11 se ipsum hostem iudicare nisi (n- *om. bn*) *post* quid est aliud
*D*     12 alterum *D*     12–13 iudicari ducibus *V*     13 caesar] *c.* cae- *cnstv*     refert] referat (*numero minus bono*) *V*     15 hostem esse *D*     17 quantus *V*     **22** 21 digni multi
*D*     25 intellegitat $V^1$     26 sit *del. Faërnus*     publico p. r. *D*     27 stupidum] stul-
tum *D*     **23** 28 tam subito mansuetus $DV^2$     29 ferus fuisset *V*     enim] autem *bnsv*:
*om. t*     attinuerit (annu- *b*) *D*

mons, why did he not attend himself? Perhaps you think it was for some solemn, sober reason. Not at all, he was detained by wine and banqueting, unless I should rather call it a bistro blow-out. That was why he failed to appear on the day named in his notice, and postponed the meeting until the twenty-eighth of November. He ordered that it take place on the Capitol and himself made his way up to the temple through some Gauls' tunnel.[19] People who had been personally requested assembled, including some of quality, unmindful, however, of their dignity; for the day, the common report, and the convener were such that it was discreditable to a senator *not* to be afraid. However, even to those who did attend he did not dare to say a word about Caesar, although he had arranged to refer Caesar's conduct to the House; and a certain consular[20] had brought a draft motion. **21** Not to dare to bring up the conduct of a man who was leading an army against himself, the consul, what was that but to judge himself a public enemy? For one of the two had to be an enemy; no other judgment was possible on two opposing commanders. If Caesar was the enemy, why does the consul not refer to the Senate? But if Caesar was not to be censured by the Senate, what can he say except that by keeping silent about Caesar he admitted himself to be the enemy? He calls Caesar a Spartacus[21] in his manifestos, but in the Senate he dares not so much as call him disloyal.

And how he makes us laugh—on most serious matters! I have committed to memory some verbal gems from one of the manifestos, phrases which he seems to think extremely clever, though I have yet to find anyone who understood what he meant. **22** "An insult made by the worthy[22] is no insult." First, what is "worthy"? Many folk are worthy of a sound thrashing, as is Antonius himself. Or does he mean an insult made by someone who possesses worth? Can any insult be greater? And what is making an insult? Who talks like that? It goes on: "nor is a threat a threat when launched by an enemy." Come now: are threats usually launched by friends? And so on and so forth. Better be dumb, surely, than say what makes no sense to anybody. Now we see why his coach has turned from orator into farmer and occupies two thousand jugers of public land in the plain of Leontini tax-free, just to make a fool more fatuous still at the public expense.

**23** These are trivialities perhaps. But I should like to ask why he was so gentle in the Senate after the ferocities in his manifestos. What purpose did it

---

19. A tunnel through which the besieging Gauls entered the Capitol in 390 is mentioned in *Caec.* 88.

20. Probably Q. Fufius Calenus, Antony's principal sympathizer in the Senate.

21. Antony is so called by Cicero at 4.15 and 13.22.

22. Antony seems to have meant "worthy of insult." On this difficult passage see SB².

tribuno plebis, fortissimo et constantissimo civi, mortem denuntiare, si
in senatum venisset; D. Carfulenum, bene de re publica sentientem, senatu vi et minis mortis expellere; Ti. Cannutium, a quo erat honestis-
simis contionibus et saepe et iure vexatus, non templo solum verum etiam
aditu prohibere Capitoli? cui senatus consulto ne intercederent verebatur?      5
de supplicatione, credo, M. Lepidi, clarissimi viri, atque id erat periculum, de cuius honore extraordinario cotidie aliquid cogitabamus, ne
eius usitatus honos impediretur!

**24** Ac ne sine causa videretur edixisse ut senatus adesset, cum de re
publica relaturus fuisset, adlato nuntio de legione quarta mente concidit,      10
et fugere festinans senatus consultum de supplicatione per discessionem
fecit, cum id factum esset antea numquam. quae vero profectio postea,
quod iter paludati, quae vitatio oculorum, lucis, urbis, fori, quam misera
fuga, quam foeda, quam turpis!

Praeclara tamen senatus consulta illo ipso die vespertina, provinciarum      15
religiosa sortitio, divina vero opportunitas ut, quae cuique apta esset, ea
cuique obveniret. **25** praeclare igitur facitis, tribuni plebis, qui de praesidio consulum senatusque referatis, meritoque vestro maximas vobis gratias omnes et agere et habere debemus. qui enim metu et periculo carere
possumus in tanta hominum cupiditate et audacia? ille autem homo ad-      20
flictus et perditus quae de se exspectat iudicia graviora quam amicorum
suorum? familiarissimus eius, mihi homo coniunctus, L. Lentulus, et
P. Naso, omni carens cupiditate, nullam se habere provinciam, nullam
Antoni sortitionem fuisse iudicaverunt. quod idem fecit L. Philippus, vir
patre, avo maioribusque suis dignissimus; in eadem sententia fuit homo      25
summa integritate atque innocentia, C. Turranius; idem fecit Sp. Oppius;
ipsi etiam qui amicitiam M. Antoni veriti plus ei tribuerunt quam fortasse
vellent, M. Piso, necessarius meus, et vir et civis egregius, parique innocentia M. Vehilius, senatus auctoritati se obtemperaturos esse dixerunt.
**26** quid ego de L. Cinna loquar, cuius spectata multis magnisque rebus      30
singularis integritas minus admirabilem facit huius honestissimi facti
gloriam? qui omnino provinciam neglexit; quam item magno animo et
constanti C. Cestius repudiavit. qui sunt igitur reliqui quos sors divina

---

3 mortis *del. Cobet*      canutium *nstv*      4 contentionibus *D*      contentionibusque *post*
iure *add. V*      6 at quod erat *coni. Halm*      **24** 11 et fugere] eff- *D*      15 illo ipso] in
illo ipso *bnsv*: in ipso illo *t*      **25** 18 consulum (-silium *t*, -silio *v*) *D*: -lis *V*      19 metu
et periculo carere *Fedeli*: p- c- *V*: c- metu et p- *D*      23 nullam . . . provinciam *om.*
*V*[1]      24 vir *om. V*[1]      **26** m. anturranius (*om. v*) *D*      Sp.] p. (*om. v*) *D*      28 meus
et necessarius et *D*      29 M. Vehilius] uel *D*      **26** 32 C. Cestius *Ursinus*: c. es- *V*: c.
cesarius *b*: c. cesetius *cn*[2]: c. cessedius *n*[1]*stv*

serve to threaten our brave and resolute tribune of the plebs, Lucius Cassius, with death if he came to the Senate; or to drive Decimus Carfulenus, a loyal citizen, from the Senate with violence and threats to his life; or to bar Tiberius Cannutius, whose most commendable speeches have often and rightly harassed him, from approaching the Capitol, let alone entering the temple? Was he afraid of their vetoing a senatorial decree? What decree? That for the illustrious Marcus Lepidus' Thanksgiving, I suppose. Not much danger that a normal honor would be obstructed when every day we were thinking out some extraordinary honor for him!

**24** Antonius was about to lay the state of the Commonwealth before the House, so as not to appear to have summoned it for nothing, when the news arrived about the Fourth Legion. He lost his nerve and bolted, carrying the decree for the Thanksgiving by a floor vote, a quite unprecedented procedure. And then his departure from Rome! The route he took in his general's cloak, avoiding men's eyes, and the daylight, and the main streets, and the Forum! What a miserable, unseemly, disgraceful fashion of running away!

However, the Senate passed some very fine decrees that same day in the evening.[23] A scrupulous lottery of provinces took place, in which it fell out most providentially that every man got just what suited him best. **25** So, Tribunes of the Plebs, you do very well to refer the matter of a guard for the consuls and Senate to the House and you deserve the warmest thanks and gratitude of us all. For amid so much unscrupulous self-seeking how can we not be in fear and danger? As for that ruined and desperate individual, what harsher verdict upon himself does he expect than that of his friends? A special intimate of his, and a friend of mine, Lucius Lentulus, and Publius Naso, who is devoid of all selfish ambition, declared that they had no provinces and that Antonius' lottery was null and void. Lucius Philippus, a gentleman wholly worthy of his father, grandfather, and ancestors, did likewise. The same view was taken by Gaius Turranius, a man of stainless integrity and probity. Spurius Oppius did the same. Even my connection Marcus Piso, a good man and a good citizen, and the equally upright M. Vehilius, who out of consideration for their friendship with Antonius went further in his direction than perhaps they would have wished to do, declared that they would defer to the authority of the Senate. **26** What shall I say of Lucius Cinna, whose outstanding integrity, proved in many affairs of great consequence, makes his highly praised and honorable action on this occasion less surprising? He would have nothing to do with a province. And Gaius Cestius refused one in a similarly disinterested and resolute spirit. Who then are the others to whom the providentially guided lots

---

23. According to Varro (ap. Gell. 14.7.8), a senatorial decree passed between sunset and sunrise was invalid.

delectet? T. Annius, †M. Antonius†. o felicem utrumque! nihil enim ma-
luerunt. C. Antonius Macedoniam. hunc quoque felicem! hanc enim
habebat semper in ore provinciam. C. Calvisius Africam. nihil felicius!
modo enim ex Africa decesserat et quasi divinans se rediturum duos
legatos Uticae reliquerat. deinde M. Cusini Sicilia, Q. Cassi Hispania.    5
non habeo quid suspicer: duarum credo provinciarum sortis minus di-
vinas fuisse.

**27** O C. Caesar—adulescentem appello—quam tu salutem rei publicae attulisti, quam improvisam, quam repentinam! qui enim haec fugiens
fecit, quid faceret insequens? etenim in contione dixerat se custodem fore    10
urbis, seque usque ad Kalendas Maias ad urbem exercitum habiturum. o
praeclarum custodem ovium, ut aiunt, lupum! custosne urbis an direptor
et vexator esset Antonius? et quidem se introiturum in urbem dixit exi-
turumque cum vellet. quid illud? nonne audiente populo sedens pro aede
Castoris dixit, nisi qui vicisset, victurum neminem?    15

**28** Hodierno die primum, patres conscripti, longo intervallo in possessione libertatis pedem ponimus: cuius quidem ego quoad potui non modo
defensor sed etiam conservator fui. cum autem id facere non possem,
quievi, nec abiecte nec sine aliqua dignitate casum illum temporum et
dolorem tuli. hanc vero taeterrimam beluam quis ferre potest aut quo    20
modo? quid est in Antonio praeter libidinem, crudelitatem, petulantiam,
audaciam? ex his totus vitiis conglutinatus est. nihil apparet in eo in-
genuum, nihil moderatum, nihil pudens, nihil pudicum. **29** quapropter,
quoniam res in id discrimen adducta est utrum ille poenas rei publicae
luat an nos serviamus, aliquando, per deos immortalis, patres conscripti,    25
patrium animum virtutemque capiamus, ut aut libertatem propriam Romani generis et nominis recuperemus aut mortem servituti anteponamus!
multa quae in libera civitate ferenda non essent tulimus et perpessi sumus, alii spe forsitan recuperandae libertatis, alii vivendi nimia cupiditate: sed si illa tulimus quae nos necessitas ferre coegit, quae vis quaedam    30

1 T.] 1. *Vn²: om. t*    Annius] antonius *D*    m. (a. *s¹*) antonius *codd.*: M. Antoni vicinus
*Mommsen: provinciae nomen latere iure statuit Sumner, Phoenix 25 (1971) 265–67:*
M. Gallium *Clark perperam*    maluerunt]: metu- *bcnst*    3 semper habebat *D*    cal-
uissius *c*: celusius *V*    5 M. Cusini Sicilia] micus nisi illa (-am *b*) *bt*: micus in isio illa *c*: m.
iccius nisi illa (-am *ns*) *nsv*: M. Iccius Siciliam *Orelli*    **27** 10 fecit] fecerit *bcnst*    fore]
futurum *nstv*    11 seque usque *Muretus*: sequasque *V*: usque (*om. n*) *D*    13 dixit *om.*
*cnstv*    **28** 16 p(atres) c(onscripti) *om. V*    possessione *Ferrarius*: -nem *codd.* (*v.
Fe.: pro "K.-St. II" lege "K.-St. I"*)    19 quievi *Victorius*: qui fui (*om. b*) *D*: ui *V¹*: qui
*V²*    illorum *Lambinus, fort. recte* (*cf. Catil. 2.20* illorum temporum dolor)    20
potest *V Cus.*: posset *D*    22 totus (tot *c*) uitiis *Vc Cus.*: totus *bnstv*    **29** 26 ut *om.*
*D*    27 et generis et *V*    29 forsitan *om. D*

appeal? Titus Annius * * * A lucky combination! Exactly what they both wanted.[24] Gaius Antonius draws Macedonia. Another lucky man—he always had his eye on that province. Gaius Calvisius gets Africa. Nothing could be luckier. He had just sailed from Africa, and as though warned by a prophetic instinct that he would return he left two Legates behind him in Utica. Then we have Marcus Cusinius with Sicily and Quintus Cassius with Spain. Nothing suspicious there; I suppose Providence was less active in the draws for those two provinces.

**27** I think of the salvation which Gaius Caesar, the young man I mean, brought to the Commonwealth, how unexpected, how sudden. If Antonius did things like this as he ran away, what would he be doing if he were on our heels? He had told a meeting that he would be the guardian of Rome and would keep an army near Rome until the Kalends of May. A fine guardian—the proverbial wolf to guard the sheep! Would Antonius have been Rome's guardian or her plunderer and oppressor? He further said that he would enter the city and leave it when he chose.[25] To cap all, did he not say in the hearing of the people as he sat in front of the temple of Castor that none but victors would be left alive?

**28** Today for the first time, Members of the Senate, after a long interval we plant our feet on the soil of freedom, the freedom which, while I could, I not only defended but preserved. When I could play that role no longer, I held my peace and endured the disastrous and grievous times, not abjectly nor quite without dignity. But this hideous monster—who can endure him, or how? What is there in Antonius save lust, cruelty, insolence, audacity? He is wholly compact of these vices. No trace in him of gentlemanly feeling, moderation, self-respect, modesty. **29** Therefore, since the question now is whether he pays his penalty to the Commonwealth or we become slaves, in the Gods' name, Members of the Senate, let us at last take our fathers' heart and courage, resolving to regain the freedom that belongs to the Roman race and name or else to prefer death to slavery. Much that should be intolerable in a free community we steeled ourselves to tolerate, some of us maybe in the hope of regaining freedom, others from too much love of living. But if we bore what necessity and a force which seemed like destiny compelled us to bear (and yet

---

24. *M. Antonius* in the manuscripts is undoubtedly corrupt, but should not be replaced by *M. Gallius* (Clark). See the Apparatus Criticus.

25. As imperator, Antony could not legally cross the city boundary without special dispensation from the Senate.

paene fatalis—quae tamen ipsa non tulimus—etiamne huius impuri latronis feremus taeterrimum crudelissimumque dominatum? **30** quid hic
faciet, si poterit, iratus qui, cum suscensere nemini posset, omnibus
bonis fuerit inimicus? quid hic victor non audebit qui nullam adeptus victoriam tanta scelera post Caesaris interitum fecerit, refertam eius domum      5
exhauserit, hortos compilaverit, ad se ex eis omnia ornamenta trans-
tulerit, caedis et incendiorum causam quaesierit ex funere, duobus aut
tribus senatus consultis bene et e re publica factis reliquas res ad lucrum
praedamque revocaverit, vendiderit immunitates, civitates liberaverit,
provincias universas ex imperi populi Romani iure sustulerit, exsules re-    10
duxerit, falsas leges C. Caesaris nomine et falsa decreta in aes incidenda
et in Capitolio figenda curaverit, earumque rerum omnium domesticum
mercatum instituerit, populo Romano leges imposuerit, armis et praesidiis populum et magistratus foro excluserit, senatum stiparit armis, armatos in cella Concordiae, cum senatum haberet, incluserit, ad legiones     15
Brundisium cucurrerit, ex eis optime sentientis centuriones iugulaverit,
cum exercitu Romam sit ad interitum nostrum et ad †dispersionem† urbis
venire conatus? **31** atque is ab hoc impetu abstractus consilio et copiis
Caesaris, consensu veteranorum, virtute legionum, ne fortuna quidem
fractus minuit audaciam nec ruere demens nec furere desinit. in Galliam     20
mutilatum ducit exercitum; cum una legione et ea vacillante Lucium fratrem exspectat, quo neminem reperire potest sui similiorem. ille autem
ex myrmillone dux [ex gladiatore imperator] quas effecit strages,
ubicumque posuit vestigium! ⟨Fundit apothecas,⟩ caedit greges armen-
torum reliquique pecoris quodcumque nactus est; epulantur milites; ipse     25
autem se, ut fratrem imitetur, obruit vino; vastantur agri, diripiuntur vil-
lae, matres familiae, virgines, pueri ingenui abripiuntur, militibus tra-
duntur. haec eadem, quacumque exercitum duxit, fecit M. Antonius.

**32** His vos taeterrimis fratribus portas aperietis, hos umquam in urbem
recipietis? non tempore oblato, ducibus paratis, animis militum incitatis,    30
populo Romano conspirante, Italia tota ad libertatem recuperandam ex-
citata, deorum immortalium beneficio utemini? nullum erit tempus hoc

---

**30** 3 faciat *bcn*ˡ*sv*     potuerit *D*     5 eius domum] d- e- *nsv*: d- caesaris eius *ct*: d- c-
*b*     6 compilauerit] -arit *bcnst*     eis *Halm*: is *V*: his *D*     8 bene et e re p.] b- de re p.
*b*: e re p. b- *ns*: de re p. b- *t*     10 imperio *D*     13–14 praesides et populum *D*     14
armis (*cf.* 2.100, 13.18)] armatis *V*: *del. Madvig*     15 cellam *c* (*v. Fe.*)     17 disper-
sionem *Vtv*: disperditi- *bcns*: direpti- *Lambinus*: dispertiti- *R. Klotz* (*v. Fe.*)     **31** 18 atque
is] aut qualis *nstv*: at uel qualis qua ui *b*     21 uaccillante *V, Nonius 34*     23 ex . . .
imperator *seclusi*     effecit *R. Klotz*: -cerit *V*: et fecit *c*: f- *bnstv*     24 imperatori ubicumque *V*     uestigium *V Cus.*: -gia *D*: -um, quis vestrum ignorat? *Halm*     fundit
apothecas *add. Ernesti ex Serv. ad Ecl. 6.55*     fudit . . . cecidit *Serv.*     25 reliqui *nsv*
*Cus.*     27 familiae *V Cus.*: -ias *D*     28 M. *om. V Cus.*

we did *not* bear it), shall we bear the cruel and horrible despotism of this foul cutthroat? He was the enemy of all honest men when he had no grievance against anyone: **30** what will he do, given the power, now that he is angry? What lengths will he not go to as a victor when without gaining any victory he committed such heinous crimes after Caesar's death? He emptied Caesar's well-stocked house, plundered his suburban estate, transferred all its ornaments to his own; he sought to make the funeral a pretext for massacre and arson; having passed two or three good senatorial decrees in the public interest, in all else he thought only of profit and plunder, selling exemptions, granting freedom to communities, removing entire provinces from the imperial jurisdiction of the Roman People, bringing back exiles, having false laws and false orders in Gaius Caesar's name inscribed on bronze and posted up on the Capitol, setting up a mart for all these items in his house; he imposed laws on the Roman People, excluding people and magistrates from the Forum with armed soldiers; he surrounded the Senate with armed men, put armed men inside the sanctuary of Concord while holding a Senate; he hurried to Brundisium to the legions there, slaughtered their most loyal centurions, tried to return to Rome with an army to destroy us and sack the city. **31** When diverted from this headlong career by the initiative and forces of Gaius Caesar, the consensus of the veterans, and the valor of the legions, undismayed even by the change of fortune, he bates none of his audacity nor does he desist from his mad, furious plunge. He is leading his truncated army into Gaul, and with a single legion,[26] and that a wavering one, he waits for his brother Lucius, than whom he can find nobody more like himself. As for that myrmillo[27] turned general, what havoc he has made wherever he set his foot! He empties barns, slaughters herds of cattle and other animals, whatever comes his way. The soldiers feast, and he himself in imitation of his brother drowns himself in wine. Fields are laid waste, farmhouses ransacked, mothers of families and unmarried girls and boys of free birth torn away and handed over to the soldiery. Marcus Antonius has done just the same, wherever he has led an army.

**32** Will you open the gates to this hideous pair or ever admit them into Rome? Will you not rather use the proffered opportunity—the generals available, the spirit of the troops aroused, the Roman People united, all Italy stirred up to recover freedom, this heaven-sent boon? If we miss this moment, there

---

26. The Larks (Alaudae).
27. A sort of gladiator; see 5.20, 7.17.

amisso. a tergo, fronte, lateribus tenebitur, si in Galliam venerit. nec ille armis solum sed etiam decretis nostris urgendus est. magna vis est, magnum numen unum et idem sentientis senatus. videtisne refertum forum, populumque Romanum ad spem recuperandae libertatis erectum? qui longo intervallo cum frequentis hic videt nos, tum sperat etiam liberos convenisse. **33** hunc ego diem exspectans M. Antoni scelerata arma vitavi, tum cum ille in me absentem invehens non intellegebat quod ad tempus me et meas viris reservarem. si enim tum illi caedis a me initium quaerenti respondere voluissem, nunc rei publicae consulere non possem. hanc vero nactus facultatem, nullum tempus, patres conscripti, dimittam neque diurnum neque nocturnum quin de libertate populi Romani et dignitate vestra quod cogitandum sit cogitem, quod agendum atque faciendum, id non modo non recusem sed etiam appetam atque deposcam. hoc feci dum licuit; intermisi quoad non licuit. iam non solum licet sed etiam necesse est, nisi servire malumus quam ne serviamus armis animisque decernere. **34** di immortales nobis haec praesidia dederunt: urbi Caesarem, Brutum Galliae. si enim ille urbem opprimere potuisset, statim, si Galliam tenere, paulo post optimo cuique pereundum, reliquis serviendum. hanc igitur occasionem oblatam tenete, per deos immortalis, patres conscripti, et amplissimi orbis terrae consili principes vos esse aliquando recordamini! signum date populo Romano consilium vestrum non deesse rei publicae, quoniam ille virtutem suam non defuturam esse profitetur. nihil est quod moneam vos. nemo est tam stultus qui non intellegat, si indormierimus huic tempori, non modo crudelem superbamque dominationem nobis sed ignominiosam etiam et flagitiosam ferendam. **35** nostis insolentiam Antoni, nostis amicos, nostis totam domum. libidinosis, petulantibus, impuris, impudicis, aleatoribus, ebriis servire, ea summa miseria est summo dedecore coniuncta. quod si iam—quod di omen avertant!—fatum extremum rei publicae venit, quod gladiatores nobiles faciunt, ut honeste decumbant, faciamus nos, principes orbis terrarum gentiumque omnium, ut cum dignitate potius cadamus quam cum ignominia serviamus. **36** nihil est detestabilius dedecore, nihil foedius servitute. ad

5

10

15

20

25

30

**32** 1 fronte, lateribus *Garatoni*: f- alt- *V*[1] (a lat- *V*[2]): a f- a lat- *D*     tenetur *D*     2 nostris (ues- *b*) decretis *D*     est] et *V*     **33** 7 quod ad] ad q- *nstv*     8 initium a me *D*     11 et] de *nstv*: *om. bc*     13 id] idem *cnsv*: *om. t*     modo non] m- *bnstv*     appetam etiam *D*     14 feci semper dum *D*     14–15 necesse est etiam *D*     15 malumus] -uimus *bt*: malimus *V*     animis armisque *D, Nonius 285 (v. Fe.)*     **34** 17 opprimere urbem *V*     potuisset, esset *Sternkopf*     18 teneret *D*     pereundum erat *Halm*     esset seruiendum *n(?)sv*: erat s- *Schöll (iam n teste Clark)*     20 vos *om. D*     24 huic tempori] hoc tempore *nstv*     25 ferendam] -dem *V*: esse ferendam *bnstv*: f- e- *Muretus*     **35** 27 summa] sunt s- *nstv*     28 est *V Cus.*: *om. D*     **36** 32 et ad *V Cus.*: et *D*

will not come another. If Antonius enters Gaul, he will be caught in a trap—rear, front, and flanks. And he must be pressed not only with arms but with our decrees. Mighty is the force, mysterious the power of the Senate united in a single purpose. Do you see the crowd in the Forum, the Roman People excited by the prospect of liberty regained? After a long interval they see us meeting here in full numbers and they also hope we have met as free men. **33** In expectation of this day I avoided Marcus Antonius' criminal violence, when he assailed me in my absence;[28] little did he realize that I was reserving myself and my strength for a particular juncture. If I had elected to answer him then, just when he was looking for an excuse to start a massacre with me, I should be in no position to work for the Commonwealth now. But the opportunity has arrived. Members of the Senate, I shall employ every moment of the day and of the night in thinking, insofar as thought is required, of the freedom of the Roman People and of your dignity; as for deeds, I shall not recoil from action, where that is called for, in fact I shall seek and demand it. This I did while it was permitted; I ceased to do it temporarily, so long as it was not permitted. Now not only is it permitted, it is necessary, unless we prefer to be slaves rather than fight to determine with our courage and our weapons that slaves we shall not be. **34** The Immortal Gods have given us two bulwarks: Caesar for Rome, Brutus for Gaul. For if Antonius had been able to crush the city or to lay hold of Gaul, it would have meant death for our best men and slavery for the rest; immediate in the first case, a little later in the second. Therefore, Members of the Senate, in the name of Heaven, seize this proffered opportunity and at long last remember that you are leaders of the most august council in the world. Give a signal to the Roman People that your wisdom will not fail the Commonwealth, since the people declares that its courage will not be wanting. You do not need me to advise you. No man is so dull as not to realize that if we doze over this crisis we shall have to endure a despotism not only cruel and arrogant but ignominious and disgraceful. **35** You know Antonius' insolence, you know his friends and his whole retinue. To be slaves to libertines and bullies, foul profligates, gamblers, drunkards—that is the ultimate in misery joined with the ultimate in dishonor. If (may the Gods avert the omen!) the final episode in the history of the Commonwealth has arrived, let us behave like champion gladiators. They meet death honorably; let us, who stand foremost in the world and all its nations, see to it that we fall with dignity rather than serve with ignominy. **36** Nothing is more abominable than dis-

28. On 19 September.

decus et ad libertatem nati sumus: aut haec teneamus aut cum dignitate
moriamur. nimium diu teximus quid sentiremus; nunc iam apertum est.
omnes patefaciunt in utramque partem quid sentiant, quid velint. sunt
impii cives—pro caritate rei publicae nimium multi, sed contra multitudinem bene sentientium admodum pauci—quorum opprimendorum di　5
immortales incredibilem rei publicae potestatem et fortunam dederunt. ad
ea enim praesidia quae habemus iam accedent consules summa prudentia, virtute, concordia, multos mensis de populi Romani libertate com-
mentati atque meditati. his auctoribus et ducibus, dis iuvantibus, nobis
vigilantibus et multum in posterum providentibus, populo Romano con-　10
sentiente, erimus profecto liberi brevi tempore. iucundiorem autem faciet
libertatem servitutis recordatio.

**37** Quas ob res, quod tribuni plebis verba fecerunt uti senatus Kalendis
Ianuariis tuto haberi sententiaeque de summa re publica libere dici possint, de ea re ita censeo:　15

"Uti C. Pansa A. Hirtius, consules designati, dent operam uti senatus
Kalendis Ianuariis tuto haberi possit. quodque edictum D. Bruti, imperatoris, consulis designati, propositum sit, senatum existimare D. Brutum, imperatorem, consulem designatum, optime de re publica mereri,
cum senatus auctoritatem populique Romani libertatem imperiumque de-　20
fendat; **38** quodque provinciam Galliam citeriorem, optimorum et fortissimorum amicissimorumque rei publicae civium, exercitumque in senatus potestate retineat, id eum exercitumque eius, municipia, colonias
provinciae Galliae recte atque ordine exque re publica fecisse et facere.
senatum ad summam rem publicam pertinere arbitrari ab D. Bruto et　25
L. Planco imperatoribus, consulibus designatis itemque a ceteris qui provincias obtinent obtineri ex lege Iulia, quoad ex senatus consulto cuique
eorum successum sit, eosque dare operam ut eae provinciae eique exercitus in senati populique Romani potestate praesidioque rei publicae sint.
cumque opera, virtute, consilio C. Caesaris summoque consensu militum　30
veteranorum, qui eius auctoritatem secuti rei publicae praesidio sunt et
fuerunt, a gravissimis periculis populus Romanus defensus sit et hoc tem-

3 omnes iam *D*　　patefaciunt *Halm*: p- fecerunt *V*[1]: patefecerunt *DV*[2]　　sentiat quid
uelit *V*　　4 caritate] dignitate *expectarem; cf. 6.16, Sest. 1, Flacc. 94*　　sed *hoc loco
Lambinus, post* cives *V: om. D*　　pro multitudine *D*　　7 accedent] -dunt *bnstv*　　8 de
populi R(omani)] de r. p. *bt*: dei publicae *V*　　**37** 13 ut *D*　　Kalendis *om. V*　　16 ut
(*alt.*) *nstv*　　18 designati optime de re p. meriti (mereri *t*) *D ex l.* 19　　**38** 21–22 virorum *post* fortissimorum *bnstv, post* optimorum *c* (*cf. 4.6, 5.24*)　　22 amicorumque
*V*　　25 ab D. Bruto] Bd BR.IO *V*　　25–26 et ab l. *D*　　27 obtinere *V*　　Iulia] tullia
*D*　　28 eique (ii-)] que *V*: galliaeque *bnstv*: atque *Muretus*　　29 senatus *D*　　Romani
*om. V*　　rei p(ublicae)] populi r. *D*　　30 C. *om. v*　　militum consensu *V*　　32 a] et
a *stv*: et *n*

grace, nothing is uglier than servitude. We were born for honor and freedom; let us either retain them or die with dignity. Too long we have kept our feelings hidden. Now they are in the open. All are making plain on one side or the other what they feel and wish for. There are traitors: more than those who love the Commonwealth would wish, but quite few compared with the multitude of loyal-minded citizens. The Immortal Gods have given the Commonwealth unlooked-for power and good fortune by which to crush them. To the forces already at our disposal will shortly be added consuls, wise, courageous, like-minded, who for many months have been pondering deeply on the freedom of the Roman People. With their advice and leadership, with the Gods' help, with our vigilance and farsighted provision, and with the support of a united people, we shall without doubt be free in no long time. And freedom will be made sweeter by the memory of servitude.

**37** Accordingly, whereas the tribunes of the plebs have spoken to the intent that a Senate may be held in safety on the Kalends of January and that views on the state of the Commonwealth may be freely expressed, I propose as follows:

"That Gaius Pansa and Aulus Hirtius, Consuls-Elect, take measures to ensure that a Senate can be held in safety on the Kalends of January. Further that, whereas a manifesto has been issued by Decimus Brutus, Imperator and Consul-Elect, the Senate judges Decimus Brutus, Imperator and Consul-Elect, to deserve excellently well of the Commonwealth in that he defends the authority of the Senate and the liberty and empire of the Roman People; **38** and, whereas he retains the province of Hither Gaul, with its excellent, brave, and patriotic citizens, and his army under control of the Senate, the Senate judges that he and his army and the municipalities and colonies of the province of Gaul in so acting have acted and are acting rightly, properly, and in the public interest. That the Senate considers it of the highest public importance that Decimus Brutus and Lucius Plancus, Imperators and Consuls-Elect,[29] along with other holders of provinces, should continue to hold them under the Julian law until such time as a successor be appointed to each by decree of the Senate, and that they see to it that those provinces and those armies be at the disposition of the Senate and Roman People, ready to defend the Commonwealth. Further, since by the agency, courage, and judgment of Gaius Caesar and the united action of the veteran soldiers, who following his lead are and have been defending the Commonwealth, the Roman People has been protected from very grave dangers and is protected at this present time;

29. For 42, designated by Caesar.

pore defendatur; **39** cumque legio Martia Albae constiterit, in municipio
fidelissimo et fortissimo, seseque ad senatus auctoritatem populique Romani libertatem contulerit; et quod pari consilio eademque virtute legio
quarta usa, duce L. Egnatuleio quaestore, civi egregio, senatus auctoritatem populique Romani libertatem defendat ac defenderit, senatui mag-          5
nae curae esse ac fore ut pro tantis eorum in rem publicam meritis honores eis habeantur gratiaeque referantur. senatui placere uti C. Pansa
A. Hirtius, consules designati, cum magistratum inissent, si eis videretur, primo quoque tempore de his rebus ad hunc ordinem referrent, ita
uti e re publica fideque sua videretur."                                        10

**39** 3 et quod] eq- *V*: q- *bcntv*     4 duce . . . egregio *Orelli*: l. egn- que opti egregio mo *V*:
l. egnatio lecto duce ciui eg- *D*: L. Egn- duce, quaestore optimo, cive eg- *Muretus, alii
alia*     6 in rem p(ublicam) *om. D*     7 his *V*     uti] ut *ctn*²: utque *n*¹sv: *om. b*     8
videretur³] uidebitur *nsv*     9 referent *t*: -rant *nsv*     10 uti eis *Lutz*     videretur] -retur
(-rentur *t*) censuerunt *bct*: censuerint (-rit *v*) *nsv*

**39** and since the Martian Legion has stationed itself in Alba, a most loyal and brave township, and placed itself in support of the authority of the Senate and the liberty of the Roman People; and whereas the Fourth Legion, with equal judgment and the same courage, under the leadership of Quaestor Lucius Egnatuleius, an outstanding citizen, is defending and has defended the authority of the Senate and the liberty of the Roman People: that it is and will be of great concern to the Senate that in return for their eminent services to the Commonwealth, honors be accorded and recompense made to these same. That it pleases the Senate that Gaius Pansa and Aulus Hirtius, Consuls-Elect, if they see fit, should as soon as possible after taking office make reference to this House concerning these matters in whatever manner may appear consonant with the public interest and their own duty."

# IV

## INTRODUCTION

After the proceedings in the Senate on 20 December 44 Cicero went down to
the Forum and addressed a crowded assembly. His main theme, which he was
to reiterate, was that the decree passed in commendation of D. Brutus and
others for their actions against Antony made the latter "in fact, though not yet
in word," a public enemy (*hostis*). The speech was enthusiastically received,
the people shouting that once again Cicero had saved Rome.

**1** Frequentia vestrum incredibilis, Quirites, contioque tanta quantam meminisse non videor et alacritatem mihi summam defendendae rei publicae adfert et spem ⟨libertatis⟩ recuperandae. quamquam animus mihi quidem numquam defuit: tempora defuerunt, quae simul ac primum aliquid lucis ostendere visa sunt, princeps vestrae libertatis defendendae 5 fui. quod si id ante facere conatus essem, nunc facere non possem. hodierno enim die, Quirites, ne mediocrem rem actam arbitremini, fundamenta iacta sunt reliquarum actionum. nam est hostis a senatu nondum verbo appellatus, sed re iam iudicatus Antonius.

**2** Nunc vero multo sum erectior quod vos quoque illum hostem esse 10 tanto consensu tantoque clamore approbavistis. neque enim, Quirites, fieri potest ut non aut ei sint impii qui contra consulem exercitus comparaverunt aut ille hostis contra quem iure arma sumpta sunt. hanc igitur dubitationem, quamquam nulla erat, tamen ne qua posset esse senatus hodierno die sustulit. C. Caesar, qui rem publicam libertatemque vestram 15 suo studio, consilio, patrimonio denique tutatus est et tutatur, maximis senatus laudibus ornatus est. **3** laudo, laudo vos, Quirites, quod gratissimis animis prosequimini nomen clarissimi adulescentis vel pueri potius; sunt enim facta eius immortalitatis, nomen aetatis. multa memini, multa audivi, multa legi, Quirites: nihil ex omnium saeculorum memoria 20 tale cognovi: qui cum servitute premeremur, in dies malum cresceret, praesidi nihil haberemus, capitalem et pestiferum a Brundisio M. Antoni reditum timeremus, hoc insperatum omnibus consilium, incognitum certe ceperit, ut exercitum invictum ex paternis militibus conficeret Antonique furorem crudelissimis consiliis incitatum a pernicie rei publicae averteret. 25 **4** quis est enim qui hoc non intellegat, nisi Caesar exercitum paravisset, non sine exitio nostro futurum Antoni reditum fuisse? ita enim se recipiebat ardens odio vestri, cruentus sanguine civium Romanorum quos Suessae, quos Brundisi occiderat ut nihil nisi de pernicie populi Romani cogitaret. quod autem praesidium erat salutis libertatisque vestrae, si 30 C. Caesaris fortissimorum sui patris militum exercitus non fuisset? cuius

**1** 1 vestra *Ernesti* (*v. Fe.*)     Quirites *Poggius*: quam *V*: que *c*: *om. bnstv* (*vocabulum "Quirites" plerumque compendio scribunt; talia amplius non notabo*)     2–3 adfert rei p. defendendae *cnstv*: r. p. aff- def- *b*     3 libertatis recuperandae[3] *scripsi*: r- l- *D*: r- *V*     3–4 quidem mihi *D*     6 id *om. D*     **2** 10 ullum h- *v*: h- illum *bcnst*     11 Quirites *om. D*     12 aut *om. V*     **3** 17 quod *Vt Cus.*: cum *bcnsv*     19 memini] enim *V Cus.*     20 saeculorum memoria *V Cus.*: singulorum memoria (m- s- *t*) *D*     21 in *Vbc Cus.*: et in *stvn*[2]: et *n*[1]     22 a Brundisio *Pasoli*: a b- tum *V*: b- *D*     23–24 certe ceperit] ceteri rep(p)- *V Cus.*     24 paternis *V Cus.*: his p- *st*: hispanis *bv*: his paucis *n*: hispanis paucis *c*     conficeret *V Cus.*: conduc- *D*     25 consiliis *om. V Cus.*     **4** 28 Romanorum *om. D*     29 brundisio *V*     rei p. *D*     30 erat praesidium *D*     31 C. *om. Vt*     fortissimorum sui] -umque sui *c*: -um suique *nstv*

**1** Your extraordinary numbers, Men of Rome, the size of this assembly, larger than any I can remember, fills me with a lively eagerness to defend the Commonwealth and a lively hope of regaining freedom. True, my courage has never failed me; it was the times that failed. As soon as they seemed to show a glimmer of light, I took the lead in defending your freedom. Had I attempted to do this earlier, I should not be able to do it now. For today, Men of Rome, in case you think we have been transacting some business of minor importance, the groundwork has been laid for future operations. Antonius has been pronounced a public enemy by the Senate—in actuality, though not yet in words.

**2** Now it much emboldens me, this loud and unanimous agreement from you that he *is* a public enemy. And after all, Men of Rome, there is no way out of it: either those who have raised armies against a consul are traitors, or he against whom arms have rightfully been taken up is an enemy. This doubt, therefore, the Senate has today eliminated—not that any doubt existed, but in case there could be any. Gaius Caesar, who has protected and is protecting the Commonwealth and your freedom with his zeal, judgment, even his patrimony, has been honored by the Senate's highest commendations. **3** Bravo, Men of Rome, bravo! You are right to salute in heartfelt gratitude the name of an illustrious young man, or rather boy: for his deeds belong to immortality, the name is a matter of age.[1] I remember many things, Men of Rome, have been told of many, read of many; but the like of this I have never met with in the history of all ages. When we were under the yoke of slavery, with the evil gaining day by day and none to defend us, dreading the return of Marcus Antonius from Brundisium and the death and ruin it would bring, Caesar took a decision which none of us hoped for and certainly none of us knew of in advance: to raise from his father's soldiers an army which had never known defeat and turn Antonius' fury, and the cruel designs which inspired it, away from the destruction of the Commonwealth. **4** For who does not realize that if Caesar had not raised his army, Antonius' return would have entailed our destruction? He was coming back in a fever of hatred against you, stained with the blood of the Roman citizens he had killed in Suessa and Brundisium, his only thought the ruin of the Roman People. What was there to defend your lives and liberty if it had not been for Caesar's army of his father's brave

---

1. Cf. 13.24, 3.3. Octavian had come of age ("put on the manly gown") in October 49 and took strong exception to being called a boy. See my note on *Fam.* 11.7.2.

de laudibus et honoribus, qui ei pro divinis et immortalibus meritis divini immortalesque debentur, mihi senatus adsensus paulo ante decrevit ut primo quoque tempore referretur. **5** quo decreto quis non perspicit hostem esse Antonium iudicatum? quem enim possumus appellare eum contra quem qui exercitus ducunt, eis senatus arbitratur singularis exquirendos honores?

Quid? legio Martia, quae mihi videtur divinitus ab eo deo traxisse nomen a quo populum Romanum generatum accepimus, non ipsa suis decretis prius quam senatus hostem iudicavit Antonium? nam si ille non hostis, hos qui consulem reliquerunt hostis necesse est iudicemus. praeclare et loco, Quirites, reclamatione vestra factum pulcherrimum Martialium comprobavistis: qui se ad senatus auctoritatem, ad libertatem vestram, ad universam rem publicam contulerunt, hostem illum et latronem et parricidam patriae reliquerunt. **6** nec solum id animose et fortiter sed considerate etiam sapienterque fecerunt: Albae constiterunt, in urbe opportuna, munita, propinqua, fortissimorum virorum, fidelissimorum civium atque optimorum. huius [Martiae] legionis legio quarta imitata virtutem, duce L. Egnatuleio, quem senatus merito paulo ante laudavit, C. Caesaris exercitum persecuta est. quae exspectas, M. Antoni, iudicia graviora? Caesar fertur in caelum qui contra te exercitum comparavit; laudantur exquisitissimis verbis legiones quae te reliquerunt, quae a te arcessitae sunt, quae essent, si te consulem quam hostem maluisses, tuae: quarum legionum fortissimum verissimumque iudicium confirmat senatus, comprobat universus populus Romanus; nisi forte vos, Quirites, consulem, non hostem iudicatis Antonium. **7** sic arbitrabar, Quirites, vos iudicare ut ostenditis.

Quid? municipia, colonias, praefecturas num aliter iudicare censetis? omnes mortales una mente consentiunt omnia arma eorum qui haec salva velint contra illam pestem esse capienda. quid? D. Bruti iudicium, Quirites, quod ex hodierno eius edicto perspicere potuistis, num cui tandem contemnendum videtur? recte et vere negatis, Quirites. est enim quasi deorum immortalium beneficio et munere datum rei publicae Brutorum genus et nomen ad libertatem populi Romani vel constituendam vel recuperandam. **8** quid igitur D. Brutus de M. Antonio iudicavit? excludit

---

**5** 3 respicit *V*    4 appellare possumus *D*    8 nonne *D*    9 ille si *D*    10 hos *om.* *D*    11 et loco Quirites] eo loco quo *c*: eo loquo quo *b ex corr.*: et luculenta *nsv*: et iocose *t*    12 comprobastis *nstv*    **6** 16 fidelissimorum *om.* *V*[1]    17 Martiae *del. Manutius*    18 L. *om. D*    21 acersitae *nstv*    24 Quirites *om.* *V*    **7** 25 Quirites *om.* *sv*    27 quid] qui *bc*: *om. nstv*    31 recte uidetur *V*    negastis *nstv*    32–33 Brutorum . . . Romani *om. D*    33 vel recuperandam *scripsi*: uel ad r- *bc*: uel recipiendam *Vnstv*    **8** 34 excludit] -usit *bnsv*

soldiers? The Senate has just accepted my motion that reference be made to them at the earliest possible time concerning the commendations and honors due to him, godlike and immortal to match his godlike and immortal services. 5 Who fails to see that Antonius has been pronounced an enemy by this decree? What else can we call him, when the Senate decides that exceptional honors must be devised for those who lead armies against him?

And did not the Martian Legion, which derives its name providentially, so it seems to me, from the God whom tradition makes the progenitor of the Roman People, of its own accord and by its own decrees, in advance of the Senate, pronounce Antonius a public enemy? For if he is not an enemy, then we are bound to pronounce these soldiers, who abandoned a consul, to be enemies. Very plain! A most proper shout of protest, Men of Rome, approving the noble action of the Martians, who placed themselves behind the Senate's authority, your liberty, and the whole Commonwealth, abandoning an enemy, a bandit, a traitor to his country. 6 This they did not only with high courage but with circumspection and prudence, stationing themselves in Alba,[2] a city strategically placed, well fortified, close at hand, with a population of brave men, loyal, excellent citizens. Imitating their valor, the Fourth Legion, under the command of Lucius Egnatuleius, whom the Senate has just deservedly commended, followed Gaius Caesar's army. What harsher verdicts do you expect, Marcus Antonius? Caesar, who raised an army against you, is praised to the sky; the legions which abandoned you, which were summoned by you, which would have been your legions if you had preferred to be a consul instead of a public enemy, are commended in the most particular terms. The brave, true judgment of the legions is confirmed by the Senate and approved by the entire Roman People—unless you, Men of Rome, judge Marcus Antonius to be a consul, not a public enemy? 7 Yes, Men of Rome, I thought your judgment was as you now declare it.

Well, what of the municipalities, colonies, prefectures? Do you suppose *they* judge any differently? All living souls are united in the conviction that all the weapons of those who wish society to continue must be employed against that scourge. And what of Decimus Brutus' judgment, Men of Rome, which you could perceive from his manifesto today published? Do any of you think it of no account? You say no, Men of Rome, and right you are! The race and name of the Bruti has been given to the Commonwealth as though by grace and boon of the Immortal Gods whether for the establishment or for the recovery of the freedom of the Roman People. 8 So what was Decimus Brutus' judgment

2. Alba Fucens; see p. 107.

provincia; exercitu obsistit; Galliam totam hortatur ad bellum, ipsam
sua sponte suoque iudicio excitatam. si consul Antonius, Brutus hostis:
si conservator rei publicae Brutus, hostis Antonius. Num igitur utrum
horum sit dubitare possumus? atque ut vos una mente unaque voce dubitare vos negatis, sic modo decrevit senatus, D. Brutum optime de re      5
publica mereri, cum senatus auctoritatem populique Romani libertatem
imperiumque defenderet. a quo defenderet? nempe ab hoste: quae est
enim alia laudanda defensio? **9** deinceps laudatur provincia Gallia meritoque ornatur verbis amplissimis ab senatu quod resistat Antonio. quem si
consulem illa provincia putaret neque eum reciperet, magno scelere se    10
astringeret: omnes enim in consulis iure et imperio debent esse provinciae. negat hoc D. Brutus imperator, consul designatus, natus rei publicae civis; negat Gallia, negat cuncta Italia, negat senatus, negatis vos.
quis illum igitur consulem nisi latrones putant? quamquam ne ei quidem
ipsi, quod loquuntur, id sentiunt nec ab iudicio omnium mortalium, quam-  15
vis impii nefariique sint, sicut sunt, dissentire possunt. sed spes rapien-
di atque praedandi occaecat animos eorum quos non bonorum donatio,
non agrorum adsignatio, non illa infinita hasta satiavit; qui sibi urbem,
qui bona et fortunas civium ad praedam proposuerunt; qui, dum hic
sit quod rapiant, quod auferant, nihil sibi defuturum arbitrantur; qui-    20
bus M. Antonius—o di immortales, avertite et detestamini, quaeso, hoc
omen!—urbem se divisurum esse promisit. **10** ita vero, Quirites, ut pre-
camini eveniat atque huius amentiae poena in ipsum familiamque eius re-
c⟨c⟩idat! quod ita futurum esse confido. iam enim non solum homines sed
etiam deos immortalis ad rem publicam conservandam arbitror consen-     25
sisse. sive enim prodigiis atque portentis di immortales nobis futura
praedicunt, ita sunt aperte pronuntiata ut et illi poena et nobis libertas
appropinqu⟨are vid⟩eat⟨ur⟩; sive tantus consensus omnium sine impulsu
deorum esse non potuit, quid est quod de voluntate caelestium dubitare
possimus?                                                                 30

**11** Reliquum est, Quirites, ut vos in ista sententia quam prae vobis fertis
perseveretis. faciam igitur ut imperatores instructa acie solent, quamquam
paratissimos milites ad proeliandum vident, ut eos tamen adhortentur; sic

1 obsistit ς: obisistit V: obstitit D     4 atque ut] atqui *bnst*     7 defenderit *bis* D     **9** 9
ab] a (e *s*) D     10 neque] magnaeque V     11 in *om.* D     13 denegat cuncta V     vos,
Quirites *Buecheler*     14 igitur illum D     15 ab *Faërnus*: ad V: a D     16 sicut sunt
*om.* D     17 caecat D     donatio] dampn- *nstv*     18 pompei hasta D     19 posuerunt
V     hic *om.* D     20 sit] sic V     **10** 22 ei ut *c*     23 atque huius] quo h- *bnstv*: huius-
que *c*     23 reccidat *Zielinski*[3]: reci- D: praeci- V     27 praedicant (-ata *t*) D     denuntiata D     nobis libertas] l- n- *bnstv*     28 appropinquare videatur *scripsi*: appropinquet
*codd.*     **11** 33 uident ς: -eant *codd., numero minus bono*

on Marcus Antonius? He shuts him out of the province, he blocks his path with an army, he urges all Gaul to war, Gaul which is already aroused of her own accord and judgment. If Antonius is a consul, Brutus is an enemy; if Brutus is the savior of the Commonwealth, Antonius is an enemy. Can we hesitate between these two propositions? With one mind and voice you deny it; and so the Senate has decreed just now that Decimus Brutus deserves excellently well of the Commonwealth in defending the authority of the Senate and the freedom and empire of the Roman People. Defending from whom? Presumably from an enemy; what other defense calls for commendation? **9** Next the province of Gaul is commended and deservedly honored in the most ample terms by the Senate because it is resisting Antonius. If that province considered him to be a consul and refused him admittance, it would be guilty of a major crime; for all provinces ought to be under the jurisdiction and authority of a consul. Decimus Brutus, Imperator and Consul-Elect, a citizen born for the Commonwealth, denies it, Gaul denies it, all Italy denies it, the Senate denies it, you deny it. So who but brigands think him a consul? And even they do not believe what they say. Villainous traitors as they may be, as they are in fact, they cannot dissent from the judgment of all mankind. But the hope of loot and rapine makes them blind. The gift of goods, the allocation of lands, the limitless auctioning has not satisfied them. They have marked Rome and the goods and fortunes of its citizens for plunder. While there is something here for them to loot and rob, they reckon they will not go short of anything. And Marcus Antonius—I call upon the Immortal Gods to avert and abominate this omen—has promised to divide the city up among them. **10** May it so befall him, Men of Rome, as you pray, and may the retribution for this madness recoil upon himself and his family. I am confident it will be so. For it seems to me that not only men now but the Immortal Gods have united to save the Commonwealth. If they predict the future for us by prodigies and portents, these have been plainly enough set forth to show that retribution is coming to him and liberty to us. Or if such a universal consensus could not exist without an impulse from on high, how can we doubt the will of Heaven?

**11** It only remains, Men of Rome, that you stand fast in the sentiments you proclaim. So I shall do as generals are wont to do when the army is drawn up for battle: though they see that the soldiers are fully ready for the fray, they

ego vos ardentis et erectos ad libertatem recuperandam cohortabor. non est vobis, Quirites, cum eo hoste certamen cum quo aliqua pacis condicio esse possit. neque enim ille servitutem vestram, ut antea, sed iam iratus sanguinem concupiscit. nullus ei ludus videtur esse iucundior quam cruor, quam caedes, quam ante oculos trucidatio civium. **12** non est vobis     5
res, Quirites, cum scelerato homine ac nefario, sed cum immani taetraque belua quae, quoniam in foveam incidit, obruatur. si enim illim emerserit, nullius supplici crudelitas erit recusanda. sed tenetur, premitur, urgetur nunc eis copiis quas iam habemus, mox eis quas paucis diebus novi consules comparabunt. incumbite in causam, Quirites, ut facitis.     10
numquam maior consensus vester in ulla causa fuit; numquam tam vehementer cum senatu consociati fuistis. nec mirum: agitur enim non qua condicione victuri, sed victurine simus an cum supplicio ignominiaque perituri. **13** quamquam mortem quidem natura omnibus proposuit; crudelitatem mortis et dedecus virtus propulsare solet, quae propria est Ro     15
mani generis et seminis. hanc retinete, quaeso, Quirites, quam vobis tamquam hereditatem maiores vestri reliquerunt. [quamquam] alia omnia falsa, incerta sunt, caduca, mobilia: virtus est una altissimis defixa radicibus, quae numquam vi ulla labefactari potest, numquam demoveri loco. hac [virtute] maiores vestri primum universam Italiam devicerunt,     20
deinde Carthaginem exciderunt, Numantiam everterunt, potentissimos reges, bellicosissimas gentis in dicionem huius imperi redegerunt.

**14** Ac maioribus quidem vestris, Quirites, cum eo hoste res erat qui haberet rem publicam, curiam, aerarium, consensum et concordiam civium, rationem aliquam, si ita res tulisset, pacis et foederis: hic vester     25
hostis vestram rem publicam oppugnat, ipse habet nullam; senatum, id est orbis terrae consilium, delere gestit, ipse consilium publicum nullum habet; aerarium vestrum exhausit, suum non habet. nam concordiam civium qui habere potest, nullam cum habet civitatem? pacis vero quae potest esse cum eo ratio in quo est incredibilis crudelitas, fides nulla?     30
**15** est igitur, Quirites, populo Romano, victori omnium gentium, omne

---

1 non est non est *D*     2 cum quo] quocum *D*     4 concupiscit ς: -piuit *codd.*     **12** 6 quirites res *D*     7 illim] illinc *nsvt*[2]: illi ne *b*: illic *c*: illuc *t*[1]     9 iam *om.* *V*[1]     11 uester consensus maior *D*     **13** 14 omnibus natura *D*     16 seminis] nom- *Ernesti* (*v. Fe.*)     quaeso, Quirites *Naugerius*: quaeso *Vbc*: quirites quaeso *s*: quaeso q. r. *v*: quaeso qr. p. r. *n*: quaeso quaesoque *t*     17 quamquam *del. Madvig*     18 falsa *om. bns*: fluxa *P. R. Müller*: fallacia *coni. Halm*     sint *V*     19 ulla ui *D*     20 virtute *del. ed. Aldina*     **14** 29 cum habet] cum habeat *c*: qui habeat *nsv*: qui habet *t*

exhort them all the same. In the same way I shall urge you, eager and ready though you are, to the recovery of freedom. Men of Rome, you are not fighting an enemy with whom any terms of peace are possible. He does not, as formerly, desire to make slaves of you; he is angry now and thirsts for your blood. He knows no better sport than gore and carnage and the slaughter of fellow countrymen before his eyes. **12** You are not dealing, Men of Rome, with a felonious villain but with a cruel, hideous monster. He has fallen into a trap; let him be overwhelmed. For if he gets out of it, there is no torment so cruel but we must submit to it. But we have him fast, we are pushing and pressing him, now with the forces we already have, soon with others which the new consuls will raise in a few days time. Put your shoulders to the wheel, Men of Rome, as you are doing. You have never been more united in any cause, never so strongly linked with the Senate. Little wonder! It is not *how* we are going to live that is at stake, but whether we are to live or to perish in agony and shame. **13** Death is ordained by nature for all; but a cruel and dishonorable death is generally warded off by courage, and courage is the badge of the Roman race and breed. Cling fast to it, I beg you, Men of Rome, as a heritage bequeathed to you by your ancestors. All else is false and doubtful, ephemeral and changeful: only courage stands firmly fixed, its roots run deep, no violence can shake it or shift it from its place. With courage your ancestors conquered all Italy first, then razed Carthage, overthrew Numantia, brought the most powerful kings and the most warlike nations under the sway of this empire.

**14** Your ancestors, Men of Rome, had to deal with an enemy who possessed a Commonwealth, a Senate-house, a treasury, a consensus of like-minded citizens, one with whom a treaty of peace could be concluded if events took that turn. This enemy of yours is attacking your Commonwealth, but he himself has none. He is eager to destroy the Senate, the council of the world, but he himself has no public council. He has emptied your treasury but has none of his own. As for a united citizenry, how can he have that when no community calls him citizen? How can peace be made with an adversary whose cruelty taxes belief and whose good faith is nonexistent? **15** So, Men of

certamen cum percussore, cum latrone, cum Spartaco. nam quod se similem esse Catilinae gloriari solet, scelere par est illi, industria inferior. ille
cum exercitum nullum habuisset, repente conflavit: hic eum exercitum
quem accepit amisit. Ut igitur Catilinam diligentia mea, senatus auctoritate, vestro studio et virtute fregistis, sic Antoni nefarium latrocinium 5
vestra cum senatu concordia tanta quanta numquam fuit, felicitate et virtute exercituum ducumque vestrorum brevi tempore oppressum audietis.
**16** equidem quantum cura, labore, vigiliis, auctoritate, consilio eniti atque efficere potero, nihil praetermittam quod ad libertatem vestram pertinere arbitrabor; neque enim id pro vestris amplissimis in me beneficiis 10
sine scelere facere possum. hodierno autem die primum referente viro
fortissimo vobisque amicissimo, hoc M. Servilio, collegisque eius, or-
natissimis viris, optimis civibus, longo intervallo me auctore et principe
ad spem libertatis exarsimus.

**15** 1 cum percussore cum *Faërnus*: cum ded percursorem (dep- $V^2$) *V*: cum excursore cum
*D*    se] ei *V*[1]: d. bruto se *nsv*: *om. b*    1–2 similem . . . scelere] -lem re *D*    2 illi]
belli *D*    3 haberet *D*    7 ducumque vestrorum] ducum questrum ria *V*    **16** 8 cura]
cum *D*    niti *V*    12 m. hoc *D*

144

Rome, the whole conflict lies between the Roman People, the conqueror of all nations, and an assassin, a bandit, a Spartacus. He likes to boast of his resemblance to Catiline, but though he is Catiline's equal in criminality, he is his inferior in energy. Catiline, without an army, threw one together in a trice: Antonius took an army over and lost it. By my exertions, the Senate's authority, and your zeal and courage you broke Catiline. Even so you will soon be hearing that Antonius' villainous band of brigands has been crushed through your unprecedented cooperation with the Senate and the good fortune and valor of your armies and generals. **16** For my part, whatever I can effect by dint of care, toil, wakefulness, influence, and policy, I shall neglect nothing which shall seem to me to concern your freedom. I should be a criminal if I did, after the signal favors you have lavished upon me. And today, at the motion of Marcus Servilius here, a brave gentleman who loves you well, and his distinguished and patriotic colleagues, after a long interval, with me to prompt and lead, our hearts have kindled to the hope of liberty.

# V

## INTRODUCTION

On 1 January 43 the long-awaited meeting of the Senate took place in the temple of Jupiter on the Capitol. The new consuls spoke to Cicero's satisfaction. But the first consular called upon was Pansa's son-in-law, Q. Fufius Calenus, a man whom Cicero had never liked. He advised that an embassy be sent to Antony, now closely besieging D. Brutus in Mutina. Cicero spoke in opposition, proposing instead the declaration of a public emergency and active prosecution of the war. At the end of the debate, however, on 4 January, the Senate voted with Calenus: three senior consulars, Ser. Sulpicius Rufus, L. Marcius Philippus (Octavian's stepfather), and L. Piso, were commissioned to go to Antony with the Senate's instructions that he raise the siege and evacuate Cisalpine Gaul. Motions were also carried, mainly in accordance with proposals by Cicero, legitimizing the status of Octavian, who was now marching north against Antony, with the title of *pro praetore*, and honoring D. Brutus and the future triumvir M. Aemilius Lepidus, now governor of Narbonese Gaul and Hither Spain.

**1** Nihil umquam longius his Kalendis Ianuariis mihi visum est, patres conscripti: quod idem intellegebam per hos dies uni cuique vestrum videri. qui enim bellum cum re publica gerunt, hunc diem non exspectabant; nos autem, tum cum maxime consilio nostro subvenire communi saluti oporteret, in senatum non vocabamur. sed querelam praeteritorum     5
dierum sustulit oratio consulum, qui ita locuti sunt ut magis exoptatae Kalendae quam serae esse videantur.

Atque ut oratio consulum animum meum erexit spemque attulit non modo salutis conservandae verum etiam dignitatis pristinae recuperandae, sic me perturbasset eius sententia qui primus rogatus est, nisi vestrae     10
virtuti constantiaeque confiderem. **2** hic enim dies vobis, patres conscripti, illuxit, haec potestas data est ut quantum virtutis, quantum constantiae, quantum gravitatis in huius ordinis consilio esset, populo Romano declarare possetis. recordamini qui dies nudius tertius decimus fuerit, quantus consensus vestrum, quanta virtus, quanta constantia; quan-     15
tam sitis a populo Romano laudem, quantam gloriam, quantam gratiam consecuti. atque illo die, patres conscripti, ea constituistis ut vobis iam nihil sit integrum nisi aut honesta pax aut bellum necessarium.

**3** Pacem vult M. Antonius? arma deponat, roget, deprecetur. neminem aequiorem reperiet quam me, cui, dum se civibus impiis commendat, ini-     20
micus quam amicus esse maluit. nihil est profecto quod possit dari bellum gerenti; erit fortasse aliquid quod concedi possit roganti; legatos vero ad eum mittere de quo gravissimum et severissimum iudicium nudius tertius decimus feceritis, non iam levitatis est, sed, ut quod sentio dicam, dementiae. primum duces eos laudavistis qui contra illum bellum     25
privato consilio suscepissent; deinde milites veteranos qui, cum ab Antonio in colonias essent deducti, illius beneficio libertatem populi Romani anteposuerunt. **4** quid legio Martia? quid quarta? cur laudantur? si enim consulem suum reliquerunt, vituperandae sunt; si inimicum rei publicae, iure laudantur. atqui cum consules nondum haberetis, decrevistis ut et de     30
praemiis militum et de honoribus imperatorum primo quoque tempore referretur. placet eodem tempore praemia constituere eis qui contra Antonium arma ceperint et legatos ad Antonium mittere, ut iam pudendum sit honestiora decreta esse legionum quam senatus? si quidem legiones

**1** 1 his *om. D*     3 expectant *nstv*     4 nos] non *D*     5 non vocabamur *Manutius*: no uoc- *V*: conuoc- *bnsv*: uoc- *t*     6 exoptent *bnsv*     **2** 11 dies uobis *V Cus.*: u- d- (d- *om. v*) *D*     15 vester *Reid*     16 sitis a] sint a *bt*: sit ista *V Cus.*     quantam (*alt.*) *V Cus.*: *om. D*     17–18 iam nihil *V Cus.*: n- iam *b*: n- tam *nstv*     **3** 19 ponat *D*     20 aequiorem me (me ae- *v*) reperiet quanquam dum *nsv*: ae- rep- quam qui dum *t*     21 esse quam amicus *D*     dari possit *D*     23 et severissimum *om. D*     **4** 28 quid? legio Martia: quid? quarta *dist. vulg.*     laudatur *V*     30 ut et de] ut et *V*: ut de *Halm*     31 tempore] die *D*     34 legionum . . . quidem *om.* V¹

**1** Nothing has ever seemed to me longer in the coming, Members of the Senate, than these Kalends of January. During the past few days I saw that each one of you felt the same. Those who are making war upon the Commonwealth were not waiting for this day; while we, just when it was most incumbent on us to come to the aid of the common safety with our counsel, were not summoned to the Senate. But all complaint of days past has been set aside by the speech of the consuls. They have spoken in such a manner as to make the Kalends seem eagerly awaited rather than too long delayed.

But if the speech of the consuls raised my spirits and gave me hope not only of preserving safety but of recovering former dignity, that of the gentleman first called[1] would have perturbed me, but for my confidence in your courage and resolution. **2** Members of the Senate, the day has dawned, the opportunity is yours to show the Roman People how much courage, resolution, and responsibility lie in the deliberations of this House. Cast your minds back twelve days: what a day[2] that was, what unity, courage, and resolution you displayed! What praise and glory and gratitude you won from the Roman People! Your decisions that day, Members of the Senate, meant that you now have no choice except an honorable peace or a necessary war.

**3** Does Marcus Antonius want peace? Let him lay down his arms, make his petition, ask our pardon. Nobody will give him a fairer hearing than I, though in recommending himself to traitors he has preferred my enmity to my friendship. Obviously no concessions are possible while he is making war. If he petitions us, perhaps there will be something we can concede. But to send envoys to a man on whom twelve days ago you passed a judgment of the weightiest and sternest character is—not levity but, to speak my mind, stark lunacy. First you commended those commanders who had taken up arms against him on their private initiative, then the veteran soldiers who, after having been settled in colonies by Antonius, preferred the freedom of the Roman People to his benefaction. **4** What of the Martian Legion and the Fourth? Why are they commended? If it was their consul whom they abandoned, they are blameworthy; if it was an enemy of the Commonwealth, they are rightly commended. But when you did not yet have any consuls, you passed a decree providing that reference be made at the first opportunity concerning both rewards for the soldiers and honors for their commanders. Are you in favor of determining rewards for those who took up arms against Antonius and at the same time of sending envoys to Antonius? If so, we have cause to be ashamed: the decrees of the legions are more honorable than the decrees of the Senate. For the legions decreed to defend the Senate against

---

1. Q. Fufius Calenus; cf. 10.3.
2. 20 December 44.

decreverunt senatum defendere contra Antonium, senatus decernit legatos ad Antonium. utrum hoc est confirmare militum animos an debilitare
virtutem? **5** hoc dies duodecim profecerunt ut, quem nemo praeter Cotylam inventus sit qui defenderet, is habeat iam patronos etiam consularis?
qui utinam omnes ante me sententiam rogarentur—quamquam suspicor　　5
quid dicturi sint quidam eorum qui post me rogabuntur; facilius contra
dicerem si quid videretur.

Est enim opinio decreturum aliquem M. Antonio illam ultimam Galliam quam Plancus obtinet. quid est aliud omnia ad bellum civile hosti
arma largiri, primum nervos belli, pecuniam infinitam, qua nunc eget,　　10
deinde equitatum quantum velit? equitatum dico? dubitabit, credo, gentis
barbaras secum adducere. hoc qui non videt, excors, qui cum videt decernit, impius ⟨est⟩. **6** tu civem sceleratum et perditum Gallorum et Germa-
norum pecunia, peditatu, equitatu, copiis instrues? nullae istae excusa-
tiones sunt: "meus amicus est." sit patriae prius. "meus cognatus." an　　15
potest cognatio propior ulla esse quam patriae, in qua parentes etiam
continentur? "mihi pecuniam tribuit." cupio videre qui id audeat dicere.

Quid autem agatur cum aperuero, facile erit statuere quam sententiam
dicatis aut quam sequamini. agitur utrum M. Antonio facultas detur oppri-
mendae rei publicae, caedis faciendae bonorum, urbis dividendae, agro-　　20
rum suis latronibus condonandi, populi Romani servitute opprimendi, an
horum ei facere nihil liceat: dubitate quid agatis. "at non cadunt haec in
Antonium." **7** hoc ne Cotyla quidem dicere auderet. quid enim in eum
non cadit qui, cuius acta se defendere dicit, eius eas leges pervertit quas
maxime laudare poteramus? ille paludes siccare voluit; hic omnem Ita-　　25
liam moderato homini, L. Antonio, dividendam dedit. quid? hanc legem
populus Romanus accepit? quid? per auspicia ferri potuit? sed augur verecundus sine collegis de auspiciis ⟨silet⟩. quamquam illa auspicia non
egent interpretatione augurum; Iove enim tonante cum populo agi non
esse fas quis ignorat? tribuni plebis tulerunt de provinciis contra acta　　30

1 m. antonium *bnsv*　　**5** 3 Cotylam *Poggius*: cotyian cotyonem *V* (an *post* cotyian *add.*
*V*²): -ylonem *b*: -ylam eam (iam *n*²) *ns*: cotilone significat Curionem *t*: catyla meam *v*:
Cotylam tum *Ferrarius*: -am ante *Stangl*　　6 sunt *D*　　8 M. *om. Vb*　　9 hostilia
*nstv*　　13 est *add. Lambinus* (*ante* impius *Zielinski*)　　**6** 14 exercitu (-um *s*) pecunia
*D*　　instrueres *V*　　16 ulla propior *D*　　*Fort.* parentes et propinqui etiam　　17 at-
tribuit *D*　　qui id ⟨*ς*⟩] quid (qui *s*) *codd.*　　audiat *V*¹　　20 urbis diuidendae (-dundae),
agrorum *Halm*: u- eruendorum a- *V*² *in ras.*: eripiendorum (dir- *s*) u- a- *D*: u- diripiendae,
a- *Faërnus*: u- a- *Clark*: *alii alia*　　21 populi Romani *Manutius*: -lum -num *Vt*: rem p.
*bnsv, vulgari errore*　　22 at *Vb*²: an *D*　　**7** 23 Cotyla *ed. Rom.*: cotylo (coylo *v*) *D*:
catulo *V*　　enim autem *V*　　24 cuius] cum eius *D*　　27 sed] silet *Madvig, quod post*
auspiciis *addidi,*³ *ubi* agit *Wuilleumier, alii alia*　　29 augurum *om. V*

Antonius, whereas the Senate decrees envoys to Antonius. Is that fortifying the soldiers' morale or sapping their courage? **5** Have twelve days passed to such effect that a man who found nobody to defend him except Cotyla[3] now has consulars pleading his cause? I wish that all of them were called ahead of me (not that I do not have an inkling of what some of those who will follow me are going to say); it would be easier to speak in opposition, as might seem appropriate.

There is a notion that somebody will propose Outer Gaul, now governed by Plancus, for Marcus Antonius. That would simply be presenting the enemy with all the weapons required for civil war. First, the sinews of war, a limitless supply of money, of which he now stands in need. Then, cavalry, all he wants. I say "cavalry," but will he hesitate to bring up barbarous nations? Anyone who does not see this is a fool; anyone who does, and makes the proposal all the same, is a traitor. **6** Are you going to furnish an abandoned criminal with Gallic and German money, infantry, cavalry, resources generally? Your excuses are worthless. "He is my friend." Let him be a friend to his country first. "He is my relative." Can any relationship be closer than that of country, in which parents also are comprised? "He has given me money." Yes, I should like to see who has the courage to say that!

Let me make plain what is at issue; it will be easy then for you gentlemen to decide what to propose or support. The issue is whether Marcus Antonius should be given the means of crushing the Commonwealth, massacring honest men, plundering Rome, bestowing lands on his brigands, enslaving the Roman People; or whether none of this be placed within his power. Hesitate if you can. "Oh, but all this does not apply to Antonius." **7** Not even Cotyla would dare to say that. Anything applies to a man who subverts the laws of the very person whose acts he claims to be defending, those laws which we could most approve of. Caesar wanted to drain marshes:[4] Antonius gave all Italy over to that man of moderation, Lucius Antonius, to be parceled out. Did the Roman People accept this law? Could it be carried without violation of the auspices? But our modest augur says nothing about auspices without consulting his colleagues. Not that those auspices need augural interpretation. Everybody knows that it is contrary to religion to transact business with the people when Jupiter thunders. The tribunes of the plebs proposed a law concerning prov-

---

3. Or Cotylo? See *Two Studies*, 73.

4. According to Suetonius (*Iul.* 44.3), Plutarch (*Caes.* 58), and Dio (44.5.1) Caesar planned to drain the Pontine marshes.

C. Caesaris: ille biennium, hi sexennium. etiam hanc legem populus Romanus accepit? quid? promulgata fuit? quid? non ante lata quam scripta est? quid? non ante factum vidimus quam futurum quisquam est suspicatus? **8** ubi lex Caecilia et Didia, ubi promulgatio trinum nundinum, ubi poena recenti lege Iunia et Licinia? possuntne hae leges esse ratae  5
sine interitu legum reliquarum? eccui potestas in forum insinuandi fuit? quae porro illa tonitrua, quae tempestas! ut, si auspicia M. Antonium non moverent, sustinere tamen eum ac ferre posse tantam vim tempestatis, imbris, [ac] turbinum mirum videretur. quam legem igitur se augur dicit tulisse non modo tonante Iove sed prope caelesti clamore prohibente,  10
hanc dubitabit contra auspicia latam confiteri? **9** quid? quod cum eo collega tulit quem ipse fecit sua nuntiatione vitiosum, nihilne ad auspicia bonus augur pertinere arbitratus est? sed auspiciorum nos fortasse erimus interpretes qui sumus eius collegae: num ergo etiam armorum interpretes quaerimus? primum omnes fori aditus ita saepti ut, etiam si nemo  15
obstaret armatus, tamen nisi saeptis revulsis introiri in forum nullo modo posset; sic vero erant disposita praesidia ut quo modo hostium aditus urbe prohibentur castellis et operibus, ita ab ingressione fori populum tribunosque plebis propulsari videres.

**10** Quibus de causis eas leges quas M. Antonius tulisse dicitur omnis  20
censeo per vim et contra auspicia latas eisque legibus populum non teneri. si quam legem de actis Caesaris confirmandis deve dictatura in perpetuum tollenda deve coloniis in agros deducendis tulisse M. Antonius dicitur, easdem leges de integro ut populum teneant salvis auspiciis ferri placet. quamvis enim res bonas vitiose per vimque tulerit, tamen eae  25
leges non sunt habendae, omnisque audacia gladiatoris amentis auctoritate nostra repudianda est.

**11** Illa vero dissipatio pecuniae publicae ferenda nullo modo est per quam sestertium septiens miliens falsis perscriptionibus donationibusque avertit, ut portenti simile videatur tantam pecuniam populi Romani tam  30
brevi tempore perire potuisse. quid? illi immanes quaestus ferendine quos M. Antoni †tota† exhausit domus? decreta falsa vendebat, regna, civi-

1 C. *om. D*   biennii *D*   hi *Zumpt*: hic *V*: iste (ille *t*) *D*   sexennii *D*: quinquennium
*F. W. Schmidt*   num (non *b*) etiam *D*   3 quid *om. D*   uidemus *D*   **8** 5 poenae
*D*   haec *V*[1]   ratae esse *D*   6 introeundi *D*   7 ut] aut *D*   8 tamen eum ac
ferre] me non aff- *nstv*: me num auf- *b*   tempestatis *del. Madvig*   9 ac *del. Wesenberg*   **9** 11 eo *om. V*   13 arbitratus est pertinere *nstv*   16 introire *V*   17 urbe
*om. D*   18 ita *hoc loco n*[2], *ante* castellis *codd.*   **10** 21 eisque] sui- *D*   23 colonis
*Vb*[1]*tv*[1]   agros *Poggius*: agos *V*: agro *b*: agrum *nstv*   25 enim res] ergo leges *D*   eae]
ae *V*: he *b*: aeae *s*: a *t*: esse *v*   26 non *om. bnst*   **11** 29 sestertium *om. D*   30 uertit
*D*   31 potuisse K. *V*   32 tota] una *Ernesti*: tot una *coni. Halm*: tot *post* illi *Clark*

inces which ran contrary to the acts of Gaius Caesar. He fixed a two-year term,
they a six-year. Did the Roman People accept this law too? Was it promulgated? Was it not carried before it was drafted?[5] Did we not see an accomplished fact before anyone suspected it was coming? **8** What has become of the
Didian and Caecilian law, the three-market-day promulgation, the penalty
under the recent Junian and Licinian law?[6] Can these laws[7] be valid without
the dissolution of all the rest? Was anyone given a chance to sneak into the
Forum? And the thunder, the storm! If the auspices had no effect on Marcus
Antonius, it still seemed astonishing that he could manage to weather such a
fury of tempest and rain and hurricane. So will he balk to admit that a law
which he, an augur, says he carried not only while Jupiter was thundering but
almost with the heavens clamoring to forbid it, was carried in violation of the
auspices? **9** Add the fact that he carried it jointly with a colleague whose
election he had flawed by his own announcement. Did our adept augur not
think that relevant to the auspices? However, perhaps we who are his colleagues will interpret the auspices. Do we need interpreters for the weapons
too? All approaches to the Forum were barricaded, so that even if no armed
guard blocked entry, it was impossible to get in without tearing down the
barricades. But furthermore, posts were placed and the people and the tribunes
of the plebs might be seen being thrust back from the entrances to the Forum,
just as an approaching enemy is denied access to a town by works and
fortifications.

**10** For these reasons it is my judgment that the laws which Marcus Antonius
is said to have carried were all carried by violence and in contravention of the
auspices, and that the people is not bound by those laws. If Marcus Antonius is
said to have carried a law confirming Caesar's acts or abolishing the Dictatorship in perpetuity or founding colonies on lands, I think it proper that the same
laws be carried afresh with due observance of auspices so that they may bind
the people. For however good in themselves may be the measures he carried
improperly and by violence, they are not to be considered laws. The crazy
gladiator's insolence is to be repudiated in its entirety by our authority.

**11** Then there is the totally intolerable squandering of public money
through which he has embezzled seven hundred million sesterces in forged
assignments and donations.[8] It seems outside nature that so vast a sum belonging to the Roman People should vanish in so short a time. And can we tolerate
the monstrous profits that M. Antonius' house has engulfed? He sold false

---

5. Cf. 1.25.

6. The two laws, of 98 and 62, provided against the introduction of legislation without proper
notice.

7. Of Antony's.

8. I.e. to pay his debts Antony produced forged papers, supposedly Caesar's, making over the
money (cf. 2.93) to his creditors.

tates, immunitates in aes accepta pecunia iubebat incidi. haec se ex commentariis C. Caesaris, quorum ipse auctor erat, agere dicebat. calebant in
interiore aedium parte totius rei publicae nundinae; mulier sibi felicior
quam viris auctionem provinciarum regnorumque faciebat; restituebantur
exsules quasi lege sine lege; quae nisi auctoritate senatus rescinduntur,          5
quoniam ingressi in spem rei publicae recuperandae sumus, imago nulla
liberae civitatis relinquetur. **12** neque solum commentariis commenticiis
chirographisque venalibus innumerabilis pecunia congesta in illam domum est, cum, quae vendebat Antonius, ea se ex actis Caesaris agere diceret, sed senatus etiam consulta pecunia accepta falsa referebat, syn-       10
graphae obsignabantur, senatus consulta numquam facta ad aerarium
deferebantur. huius turpitudinis testes erant etiam exterae nationes. foe-
dera interea facta, regna data, populi provinciaeque liberatae, illarumque
rerum falsae tabulae gemente populo Romano toto Capitolio figebantur.
quibus rebus tanta pecunia una in domo coacervata est ut, si hoc genus   15
†pene in unum† redigatur, non sit pecunia rei publicae defutura.

  Legem etiam iudiciariam tulit, homo castus atque integer, iudiciorum
et iuris auctor; in quo nos fefellit. antesignanos et manipularis et Alaudas
iudices se constituisse dicebat: at ille legit aleatores, legit exsules, legit
Graecos. o consessum iudicum praeclarum! o dignitatem consili admi-  20
randam! **13** avet animus apud consilium illud pro reo dicere, ⟨sedentem
videre⟩ Cydam Cretensem, portentum insulae, hominem audacissimum
et perditissimum. sed facite non esse: num Latine scit? num est ex iudicum genere et forma? num, quod maximum est, leges nostras moresve
novit? num denique homines? est enim Creta vobis notior quam Roma   25
Cydae. dilectus autem et notatio iudicum etiam in nostris civibus haberi
solet; Gortynium vero iudicem quis novit aut quis nosse potuit? nam
Lysiaden Atheniensem plerique novimus; est enim Phaedri, philosophi
nobilis, filius; homo praeterea festivus, ut ei cum Curio consessore eodemque collusore facillime possit convenire. **14** quaero igitur, si Lysia-  30
des citatus iudex non responderit excuseturque Areopagites esse nec de-

2 C. *om.* D      calebant *om.* D      **12** 9 cum *om.* V      ex . . . diceret] ex caesare d-
D      11 tamquam D      12 referebantur D      13 illarumque *scripsi:* ipsa- V: ea- D      15
unam in domo V: unam in domum *coni. Garatoni*      16 pene V: *om.* D: pecuniae *Ursinus:*
rapinae *Kayser:* praedae *coni. Clark*      in unum *Vbnsv:* unus *t:* in aerarium *Orelli:*
in publicum *Ernesti*      17 is legem D      18 et Alaudas] Al- *Cobet:* ex Alaudis *coni.*
*Clark*      20 consensum *bnsv*      **13** 21 pauet D      illud consilium D      21–22 sed-
entem videre² *addidi:* (en *ante* cydam *etiam conieci*)      23 facite *Sternkopf:* faci V: fac ita
*bnt:* facetus *s:* faciat *v:* fac *Faërnus*      24 quod maximum est *om.* D      25 uobis creta
*bnsv*      27 cortynium *codd.*      29 homo] quo (o *t*) nemo D      m. curio D: M'. C- *Lam-*
*binus: fort.* Q. C- (*cf. Ascon. ed. Clark 93.19–23*)      30 eodem et collusore *bnv:* et c- eo- *t*

orders, caused kingdoms, grants of citizenship, exemptions to be inscribed on bronze in return for bribes. These things he claimed to do in execution of Gaius Caesar's memoranda, which were vouched for by himself.[9] A public market involving the whole Commonwealth went merrily ahead in the inner part of the dwelling. A lady who has brought more luck to herself than to her husbands[10] put up provinces and kingdoms for auction. Exiles were restored illegally under the pretense of law. If these proceedings are not rescinded by authority of the Senate, since we are now in hopes of reestablishing the Commonwealth, no semblance of a free community will be left. **12** And besides the money piled up beyond counting in that house from forged memoranda and holographs for sale—Antonius all the while claiming his transactions to be in execution of Caesar's acts—he even used to place on record false senatorial decrees in return for bribes. Bonds were sealed, senatorial decrees which the Senate never made were deposited in the Treasury. Even foreign nations were witnesses of this scandal. Meanwhile, treaties were made, kingdoms granted, freedom conferred on peoples and provinces, and lying placards of those proceedings posted up all over the Capitol amid the groans of the Roman People. So much money from these activities was heaped up in a single house that if this sort of plunder were called in to the Treasury the Commonwealth would not be short of funds in days to come.

He also carried a judiciary law; for he is a blameless, upright character, a supporter of law and law courts. But he took us in. He used to say that he had made jurors of elite fighters[11] and privates of the Larks. In fact he chose gamblers and exiles and Greeks. A fine assemblage of jurors! A wonderfully dignified court! **13** I cannot wait to speak for the defense before that tribunal and see Cydas of Crete in his place, the island monster,[12] a most unscrupulous and desperate character. But suppose he isn't that: does he know Latin? Is he of the type and cut for a juror? Most important, does he know our laws and customs? Does he know our folk? Crete is better known to you gentlemen than Rome is to Cydas. Even among our own countrymen jurymen are usually picked and designated. Who knows or could know a juryman from Gortyn? As for Lysiades of Athens, most of us know him, for he is the son of the eminent philosopher Phaedrus. Besides he is a cheerful person, who will have no difficulty in getting along with his fellow juror and fellow gamester, Manius Curius. **14** So let me put a question: suppose Lysiades is summoned for jury service and does not respond, if it were to be pleaded in excuse that he is a

9. Not "of which he was himself author"; cf. 1.16, 24, 2.100.
10. Cf. Philippic 2 n. 12.
11. *Antesignanos*; cf. Philippic 2 n. 67.
12. Probably an allusion to the Minotaur.

bere eodem tempore Romae et Athenis res iudicare, accipietne excusationem is qui quaestioni praeerit Graeculi iudicis, modo palliati, modo togati? an Atheniensium antiquissimas leges negleget? qui porro ille consessus, di boni! Cretensis iudex isque nequissimus. quem ad hunc reus adleget, quo modo accedat? dura natio est. at Athenienses misericordes. 5 puto ne Curium quidem esse crudelem, qui periculum fortunae cotidie facit. sunt item lecti iudices qui fortasse excusabuntur; habent enim legitimam excusationem, exsili causa solum vertisse nec esse postea restitutos. **15** hos ille demens iudices legisset, horum nomina ad aerarium detulisset, his magnam partem rei publicae credidisset, si ullam speciem 10 rei publicae ⟨relinquere⟩ cogitavisset?

Atque ego de notis iudicibus dixi: quos minus nostis nolui nominare: saltatores, citharistas, totum denique comissationis Antonianae chorum in tertiam decuriam iudicum scitote esse coniectum. em causam cur lex tam egregia tamque praeclara maximo imbri, tempestate, ventis, pro- 15 cellis, turbinibus, inter fulmina et tonitrua ferretur, ut eos iudices haberemus quos hospites habere nemo velit. scelerum magnitudo, conscientia maleficiorum, direptio eius pecuniae cuius ratio in aede Opis confecta est hanc tertiam decuriam excogitavit; nec ante turpes iudices quaesiti quam honestis iudicibus nocentium salus desperata est. **16** sed illud os, illam 20 impuritatem caeni fuisse ut hos iudices legere auderet quorum lectione duplex imprimeretur rei publicae dedecus: unum, quod tam turpes iudices essent; alterum, quod patefactum cognitumque esset quam multos in civitate turpis haberemus! hanc ergo et reliquas eius modi leges, etiam si sine vi salvis auspiciis essent rogatae, censerem tamen abrogandas: nunc vero 25 cur abrogandas censeam, quas iudico non rogatas?

---

**14** 4 quem] que *bt*: quem ad modum *V* (*vide interpretationem nostram*) 5 at *om*. *V* 6 cotidie *ante* periculum *D* 8 ex illa *nstv* **15** 11 relinquere³ *addidi* 14 collectum *nstv* em causam *V Cus*.: haec causa *D*: en causam *Lambinus* 16 feretur *V Cus*. 17 quos socios ad epulas hospites *D* **16** 21 fuisse] fecissent *D* 22 imprimeret (-tur *s*) *D* 23 cognitumque *om*. *D* 24 hanc ego *b* huius modi *D* 25 vi *om*. *V*

member of the Areopagus[13] and cannot properly try cases in Rome and Athens at the same time, will the president of the court accept the excuse of a little Greek juryman, who wears a mantle one day and a gown the next? Or will he make no account of the immemorially ancient laws of Athens? What an assemblage, ye Gods! A Cretan juror and an arrant rogue at that! Whom should a defendant send to him, how approach him?[14] They are a hard lot, the Cretans.[15] Well, but Athenians are merciful and I don't suppose even Curius, who tries his luck every day, is a cruel man.[16] There are also select jurors who perhaps *will* be excused; they have a legitimate excuse, that they have changed their country of residence by reason of banishment and have not subsequently been reinstated. **15** Would the madman have selected jurors such as these, given their names in to the Treasury, entrusted them with an important constituent of our Commonwealth, if he had intended to leave any semblance of a Commonwealth?

I have been speaking of jurors whom you have heard of. I have not thought proper to name persons whom you do not know, but take it from me that dancers, harpists, the whole Antonian troupe of carousers have been flung into the third panel of jurors. Here we have the reason why so excellent and admirable a law was put through in violent rain and tempest and wind and storm and hurricane amid thunder and lightning: it was to give us jurors whom nobody would want as guests.[17] This third panel was devised by crime on a large scale, by consciousness of wrongdoings, by the plunder of the money the account of which was kept in the temple of Ops. Disreputable jurors were in demand only when the guilty despaired of survival with respectable ones. **16** Oh, the effrontery of this sink of iniquity, to dare to select these jurors! Their choice put a double disgrace upon the Commonwealth, first because the jurors were such scoundrels and, second, because it thus stood revealed and ascertained how many scoundrels we had in our community. I should hold then that this law and others of a like character ought to be repealed even if they had been passed without violence and with due observance of auspices. As it is, however, why should I ask for the repeal of laws which in my judgment were never passed?

13. Ancient criminal court of Athens.

14. *Adleget* ("send as representative") cannot refer to the choice of an advocate; neither could a defendant properly approach a juror. This is sarcasm. These disreputable jurors would of course be open to bribery, which might be arranged through an emissary, like Staienus (*Cluent.* 68) or the slave used by Crassus in Clodius' trial (*Att.* 1.16.5), but in the particular case of Cydas defendants would be scared away by his rough exterior; not so with Lysiades and Curius.

15. Crete was famous for its pirates, second only to Cilicia.

16. He would be sympathetic to the bad luck of others.

17. *Hospites*, often used of foreigners to whom a Roman gave or from whom he received hospitality; a hit, therefore, at Cydas and Lysiades.

**17** An illa non gravissimis ignominiis monumentisque huius ordinis ad posteritatis memoriam sunt notanda, quod unus M. Antonius in hac urbe post conditam urbem palam secum habuerit armatos? quod neque reges nostri fecerunt neque ei qui regibus exactis regnum occupare voluerunt. Cinnam memini; vidi Sullam, modo Caesarem: hi enim tres post civita- 5 tem a L. Bruto liberatam plus potuerunt quam universa res publica. non possum adfirmare nullis telis eos stipatos fuisse; hoc dico: nec multis et occultis. **18** at hanc pestem agmen armatorum sequebatur; Crassicius, Mustela, Tiro, gladios ostentantes, sui similis greges ducebant per forum; certum agminis locum tenebant barbari sagittarii. cum autem erat ventum 10 ad aedem Concordiae, gradus complebantur, lecticae collocabantur, non quo ille scuta occulta esse vellet, sed ne familiares, si scuta ipsi ferrent, laborarent. illud vero taeterrimum non modo aspectu sed etiam auditu, in cella Concordiae collocari armatos, latrones, sicarios; de templo carcerem fieri; opertis valvis Concordiae, cum inter subsellia senatus versarentur 15 latrones, patres conscriptos sententias dicere. **19** huc nisi venirem [etiam] Kalendis Septembribus, fabros se missurum et domum meam distur- baturum esse dixit. magna res, credo, agebatur: de supplicatione refe- rebat. veni postridie: ipse non venit. locutus sum de re publica, minus equidem libere quam mea consuetudo, liberius tamen quam periculi mi- 20 nae postulabant. at ille homo vehemens et violentus, qui hanc consue- tudinem libere dicendi excluderet—fecerat enim hoc idem maxima cum laude L. Piso triginta diebus ante—inimicitias mihi denuntiavit; adesse in senatum iussit a. d. xiii Kalendas Octobris. ipse interea septemdecim dies de me in Tiburtino Scipionis declamitavit, sitim quaerens; haec enim 25 ei causa esse declamandi solet.

**20** Cum is dies quo me adesse iusserat venisset, tum vero agmine qua- drato in aedem Concordiae venit atque in me absentem orationem ex ore impurissimo evomuit. quo die, si per amicos mihi cupienti in senatum venire licuisset, caedis initium fecisset a me; sic enim statuerat; cum au- 30 tem semel gladium scelere imbuisset, nulla res ei finem caedendi nisi de- fetigatio et satietas attulisset. etenim aderat Lucius frater, gladiator Asia- ticus, qui myrmillo Mylasis depugnarat; sanguinem nostrum sitiebat,

**17** 1 ad *om. V*    3 post conditam urbem *hic om. D*    habuit *bntv*    armatos si post conditam urbem *D*    4 nostri *om. D*    **18** 8 at ς: ad *V*: *om. D*    crassicius *b²*: cla- nstv: cassinus *b¹*: cassius *V*    13 non modo . . . auditu *Schütz*: non m- auditus (-tu *Cus.*) sed etiam aspectu *V Cus.*: auditu non m- asp- *D*    14 de *V Cus.*: e *D*    16 patres con- scriptos *om. V¹*    **19** etiam *post* huc *D*: *del. Lutz*: *ante* fabros *Halm*    20 quam (*pr.*)] quod *V*    pericula *D*    23 ante me *D*    24 senatu *D*    a. d. ς: ad *D*: *om. V*    25 dies *b*: diebus *V*: dies ut digesto potius quam declamatio uideretur *nstv*    **20** 27 adesse] ad *V*    28 ex *V Cus.*: *om. D*

**17** Marcus Antonius is the only man since the foundation of Rome who has publicly kept armed men at his side. Is not that something to be censured by this House in the most severe and scathing terms as a record for posterity to remember? Our kings did not do this, neither did those who after the expulsion of the kings have tried to usurp the throne. I remember Cinna, I saw Sulla and latterly Caesar, the three who since Lucius Brutus liberated the community have possessed more power than the entire Commonwealth. I cannot say that no weapons surrounded them, but this I do say: there were not many, and they were hidden. **18** But this noxious creature was attended by an armed column. Crassicius, Mustela, Tiro, brandishing their swords, used to lead squads of fellows like themselves through the Forum. Barbarian archers[18] had their place in the column. When they reached the temple of Concord, the steps would be filled up, the litters set in place—not that he wanted the shields kept out of sight, but to spare his friends the trouble of carrying them. Most horrible of all, even to tell of, let alone to see, armed men, bandits, bravos, were stationed in the sanctuary of Concord. The temple was turned into a jail. The doors of Concord were closed, and senators delivered their speeches with bandits moving among the senatorial benches. **19** Antonius said that if I did not come here on the Kalends of September he would send workmen to wreck my house. The business in hand was of great importance, no doubt! Actually, he was consulting the House about a Thanksgiving. I came the day following; he himself did not attend. I spoke on the Commonwealth[19] with some freedom— my custom called for more, the threats of danger for less. Then this man of vehemence and violence, wishing to ban this habit of free speech (for Lucius Piso had done the same a month[20] previously, greatly to his credit), declared himself my enemy and demanded my presence in the Senate on the nineteenth of September. Meanwhile he spent seventeen days declaiming about me in Scipio's villa at Tibur, working up a thirst—his usual reason for declaiming.

**20** When the day on which he had commanded my presence arrived, he marched into the temple of Concord in battle array and vomited from his foul mouth a speech against me in my absence. If my friends had permitted me to come to the Senate that day as I wanted to do, he would have launched a massacre beginning with me; so he had determined. And when once he had dipped his blade in crime, nothing but weariness and satiety would have made him stop the slaughter. His brother Lucius was with him, the Asiatic gladiator, who once fought to the death as a myrmillo[21] at Mylasa. He was thirsting for

18. Ituraeans.

19. In the First Philippic.

20. Lit. "thirty days"; see my note on *Att.* 6.1.3 *tricesimo quoque die*. It was actually thirty-three days by inclusive reckoning.

21. See Philippic 3 n. 27. Cicero is fond of referring to this incident, which probably belonged to L. Antonius' quaestorship in Asia in 50–49.

suum in illa gladiatoria pugna multum profuderat. hic pecunias vestras
aestimabat; possessiones notabat et urbanas et rusticas; huius mendicitas
aviditate coniuncta in fortunas nostras imminebat; dividebat agros quibus
et quos volebat; nullus aditus erat privato, nulla aequitatis deprecatio.
tantum quisque habebat possessor quantum reliquerat divisor Antonius.    5
**21** quae quamquam, si leges irritas feceritis, rata esse non possunt, tamen
separatim suo nomine notanda censeo, iudicandumque nullos septem-
viros fuisse, nihil placere ratum esse quod ab eis actum diceretur.

  M. vero Antonium quis est qui civem possit iudicare potius quam taeterrimum et crudelissimum hostem, qui pro aede Castoris sedens au-   10
diente populo Romano dixerit nisi victorem victurum neminem? num
putatis, patres conscripti, dixisse eum minacius quam facturum fuisse?
quid vero quod in contione dicere ausus est, se, cum magistratu abisset,
ad urbem futurum cum exercitu, introiturum quotienscumque vellet? quid
erat aliud nisi denuntiare populo Romano servitutem? **22** quod autem eius   15
iter Brundisium, quae festinatio, quae spes, nisi ad urbem vel in urbem
potius exercitum maximum adduceret? qui autem dilectus centurionum,
quae effrenatio impotentis animi! cum eius promissis legiones fortissi-
mae reclamassent, domum ad se venire iussit centuriones quos bene sentire de re publica cognoverat eosque ante pedes suos uxorisque suae,   20
quam secum gravis imperator ad exercitum duxerat, iugulari coegit. quo
animo hunc futurum fuisse censetis in nos quos oderat, cum in eos quos
numquam viderat tam crudelis fuisset, et quam avidum in pecuniis locu-
pletium qui pauperum sanguinem concupisset? quorum ipsorum bona,
quantacumque erant, statim suis comitibus compotoribusque discripsit.   25

  **23** Atque ille furens infesta iam patriae signa a Brundisio inferebat,
cum C. Caesar deorum immortalium beneficio, divina animi, ingeni,
consili magnitudine, quamquam sua sponte eximiaque virtute, tamen ap-
probatione auctoritatis meae colonias patrias adiit, veteranos milites con-
vocavit, paucis diebus exercitum fecit, incitatos latronum impetus retar-   30
davit. postea vero quam legio Martia ducem praestantissimum vidit, nihil
egit aliud nisi ut aliquando liberi essemus; quam est imitata quarta legio.
quo ille nuntio audito cum senatum vocasset adhibuissetque consularem

1 in *om. nstv*      5 quisque . . . divisor] quisquerat diuisor *bnt*: quisque d- erat *s*: quisquis
e- d- *v*      **21** 8 quod] quod elegissent aut quod *D*      dicetur³ *Madvig*      11 non *V*      13
magistratus *V¹bntv*      14 futurum] uent- *nstv*      introiturum et exiturum *Cobet, coll.*
3.27      **22** 16 nisi ut ad *bnsv, fort. recte*      19 clamassent *V*      20 de re p. sentire
*D*      21 quo] quam *V¹*: quonam *Halm*      23 locupletum *bt*      25 discripsit *Buecheler*:
descripsit (-ibit *v*) *codd.*      **23** 26 a *om. D*      27 C. *om. D*      diuini *V Cus. nstv*      28
quamquam *V Cus.*: quam *D*      29 patrias *V Cus.*: -ris *D*      adit *V¹ Cus.*      30 confecit
*Lambinus*      latronis (laco- *t*) *D*      32 imitata est *numeri gratia coni. Clark*

our blood, having shed a good deal of his own in that gladiatorial combat. There he was, estimating your money, recording your properties in town and in the country, his pauper's greed threatening our possessions. He was assigning lands, which he pleased to whom he pleased. There was no access for any individual, no appeal on grounds of equity. Every landowner possessed just so much as allocator Antonius had left him. **21** These proceedings cannot be valid if you gentlemen invalidate the laws, but all the same they should in my judgment be separately and specifically branded, with a ruling that the Board of Seven had no legal existence and that it is the Senate's pleasure that no alleged action of that board be valid.

As for Marcus Antonius, who can consider him as a citizen and not as a most dire and savage public enemy? Sitting in front of the temple of Castor, in the hearing of the Roman People, he said that only victors would be left alive. Do you suppose, Members of the Senate, that he spoke more menacingly than he would have acted? And when he dared to say at a public meeting that after leaving office he would stay outside Rome with an army and enter as often as he pleased, what was that but pronouncing a doom of slavery upon the Roman People? **22** And then his journey to Brundisium: why the hurry, what did he have in view if he was not bringing up a great army close to Rome, or rather into Rome? And the picking out of the centurions, what an ungovernable outburst of fury! When the brave legions shouted their rejection of his promises, he ordered those centurions whom he had ascertained to be loyal to the Commonwealth to come to his house and had them slaughtered at his feet and those of his wife, whom this martinet of a general had brought with him to the army. What do you think his feelings would have been towards us whom he hated, when he had treated persons whom he had never seen with such cruelty? How greedily he would have dealt with the fortunes of the wealthy, this thirster after poor men's blood! And these same poor men's belongings, such as they were, he distributed on the spot among his companions and boozing partners.

**23** And now in his rage he was bringing hostile standards from Brundisium against his country, when Gaius Caesar intervened. By grace of the Immortal Gods and by godlike greatness of heart, mind, and judgment, of his own volition and noble impulse though not without approbation and encouragement from me,[22] he visited his father's colonies, called the veteran soldiers together, created an army in a matter of days, and put a brake on the rapid rush of the bandits. When the Martian Legion saw this peerless leader, it became their only purpose that we should at last be free. The Fourth Legion followed this example. Antonius had summoned the Senate and brought along a con-

---

22. This is contradicted in 4.3 and elsewhere.

qui sua sententia C. Caesarem hostem iudicaret, repente concidit. **24** post
autem neque sacrificiis sollemnibus factis neque votis nuncupatis non
profectus est, sed profugit paludatus. at quo? in provinciam firmissimo-
rum et fortissimorum civium qui illum, ne si ita quidem venisset ut nullum bellum inferret, ferre potuissent, impotentem, iracundum, con-  5
tumeliosum, superbum, semper poscentem, semper rapientem, semper
ebrium. at ille cuius ne pacatam quidem nequitiam quisquam ferre posset
bellum intulit provinciae Galliae; circumsedet Mutinam, firmissimam et
splendidissimam populi Romani coloniam; oppugnat D. Brutum, imperatorem, consulem designatum, civem non sibi, sed nobis et rei publicae  10
natum. **25** ergo Hannibal hostis, civis Antonius? quid ille fecit hostiliter
quod hic non aut fecerit aut faciat aut moliatur et cogitet? totum iter Antoniorum quid habuit nisi depopulationes, vastationes, caedis, rapinas?
quas non faciebat Hannibal, quia multa ad usum suum reservabat: at hi,
qui in horam viverent, non modo de fortunis et de bonis civium, sed ne de  15
utilitate quidem sua cogitaverunt.

Ad hunc, di boni, legatos mitti placet? norunt isti homines formam rei
publicae, iura belli, exempla maiorum, cogitant quid populi Romani
maiestas, quid senatus severitas postulet? legatos decernis? si ut de-
precere, contemnet; si ut imperes, non audiet; denique quamvis severa  20
legatis mandata dederimus, nomen ipsum legatorum hunc quem videmus
populi Romani restinguet ardorem, municipiorum atque Italiae franget
animos. ut omittam haec, quae magna sunt, certe ista legatio moram et
tarditatem adferet bello. **26** quamvis dicant quod quosdam audio dic-
turos, "legati proficiscantur: bellum nihilo minus paretur," tamen le-  25
gatorum nomen ipsum et animos hominum molliet et belli celeritatem
morabitur. minimis momentis, patres conscripti, maximae inclinationes
temporum fiunt, cum in omni casu rei publicae tum in bello et maxime
civili, quod opinione plerumque et fama gubernatur. nemo quaeret quibus
cum mandatis legatos miserimus: nomen ipsum legationis ultro missae  30
timoris esse signum videbitur.

sular[23] who was to propose that Gaius Caesar be named a public enemy, but on receipt of this news[24] he suddenly collapsed. **24** Afterwards, without making the customary sacrifices or taking vows, he did not set out, he ran away in his general's cloak. Where did he run? Into a province of very loyal and gallant citizens, who, even if he had come without any warlike intent, could not have put up with him—his ungovernable temper, his abusiveness, his arrogance, always demanding, always grabbing, always drunk. Yes, nobody could put up with such rascality, even in peaceful guise; but Antonius made war on the province of Gaul. He is besieging Mutina, one of the most loyal and distinguished of Roman colonies. He is attacking Decimus Brutus, Imperator, Consul-Elect, a citizen born not for himself but for us and the Commonwealth. **25** Was Hannibal an enemy and is Antonius a citizen? What hostile act did Hannibal commit which Antonius has not committed or is not committing or putting in hand and planning? Was not the entire march[25] of the two Antonii a series of acts of depopulation, devastation, massacre, and pillaging? Hannibal did not behave so because he reserved much for his own use, but these two, living from one hour to the next, had no thought for their own advantage, let alone for the fortunes and property of their countrymen.

And is this, in Heaven's name, the man to whom it pleases the Senate to send envoys? Do those fellows know the structure of the Commonwealth, the laws of war, the precedents set by our ancestors? Have they any thought for what the majesty of the Roman People and the gravity of the Senate require? You propose envoys?[26] If your purpose is to plead with him, he will despise you. If it is to give him orders, he will not listen. Finally, however stern a commission we give the envoys, their very name will quench the ardor of the Roman People, of which we see the evidence around us, will break the spirit of the townships and Italy. To leave aside these considerations, important as they are, such an embassy will at least put a drag upon the prosecution of the war. **26** People may say, as I hear some are going to say, "Let the envoys set out and let preparations for war go on just the same." For all that, the very name of envoys will soften men's minds and slow the pace of the war. Members of the Senate, situations are sometimes dramatically changed by very small impulses. It happens in all political crises, but especially in war, above all in civil war, which is apt to be ruled by public opinion and report. Nobody will ask what commission we have given the envoys to deliver. The very name of an embassy dispatched of our own motion will be taken as a sign of fear.

23. Cf. Philippic 3 n. 20.
24. Of the defection of the Fourth; cf. 3.24.
25. Cf. 3.31. Lucius had followed in Marcus' wake.
26. Addressing Calenus.

Recedat a Mutina, desinat oppugnare Brutum, decedat ex Gallia; non est verbis rogandus, cogendus est armis. **27** non enim ad Hannibalem mittimus ut a Sagunto recedat, ad quem miserat olim senatus P. Valerium Flaccum et Q. Baebium Tamphilum—qui, si Hannibal non pareret, Carthaginem ire iussi sunt: nostros quo iubemus ire, si non paruerit Antonius?—ad nostrum civem mittimus, ne imperatorem, ne coloniam populi Romani oppugnet. itane vero? hoc per legatos rogandum est? quid interest, per deos immortalis, utrum hanc urbem oppugnet an huius urbis propugnaculum, coloniam populi Romani praesidi causa collocatam? belli Punici secundi quod contra maiores nostros Hannibal gessit causa fuit Sagunti oppugnatio. recte ad eum legati missi: mittebantur ad Poenum, mittebantur pro Hannibalis hostibus, nostris sociis. quid simile tandem? nos ad civem mittimus ne imperatorem populi Romani, ne exercitum, ne coloniam circumsedeat, ne oppugnet, ne agros depopuletur, ne sit hostis. **28** age, si paruerit, hoc civi uti aut volumus aut possumus? ante diem XIII Kalendas Ianuarias decretis vestris eum concidistis; constituistis ut haec ad vos Kalendis Ianuariis referrentur quae referri videtis, de honoribus et praemiis bene de re publica meritorum et merentium: quorum principem iudicastis eum qui fuit, C. Caesarem, qui M. Antoni impetus nefarios ab urbe in Galliam avertit, deinde milites veteranos qui primi Caesarem secuti sunt, tum illas caelestis divinasque legiones, Martiam et quartam comproba⟨s⟩tis, quibus, cum consulem suum non modo reliquissent sed bello etiam persequerentur, honores et praemia spopondistis; eodemque die D. Bruti, praestantissimi civis, edicto adlato atque proposito factum eius collaudastis, quodque ille bellum privato consilio susceperat, id vos auctoritate publica comprobastis. **29** quid igitur illo die aliud egistis nisi ut hostem iudicaretis Antonium? his vestris decretis aut ille vos aequo animo aspicere poterit aut vos illum sine dolore summo videbitis? exclusit illum a re publica, distraxit, segregavit non solum scelus ipsius sed etiam, ut mihi videtur, fortuna quaedam rei publicae. qui si legatis paruerit Romamque redierit, num ⟨um⟩quam perditis civibus vexillum quo concurrant defuturum putatis?

5

10

15

20

25

30

2 est] et *V*[1]: est et *Cus. V*[2]    **27** 4 Flaccum] anfalcum (*vel* an f-) *D*    Tamphilum[3] *Sternkopf*: pa- *codd.*: Tampilum *Faërnus*    Karthaginem *V*    5 iussi sunt] iusserunt *V*[1]: iussi erant *Halm*    nostros legatos *bnsv*: l- *t*    iubebimus *ns*    6 ad . . . mittimus *om. D*    ne coloniam] coloniamque *D*    7 rogandus *D*    9 coloniam *V Cus.*: -mque *D*    13 mittemus *nstv*    **28** 15 ciue *D*    16 XIIII *nstv*    19 iudicauistis *D*    20 uertit *D*    deinde *D*: tum d- *V*: tum *Halm*    21 primum *V*    tum atque illas *V*: a- i- *Halm*    22 comprobastis *Faërnus*: -atis *V*: *om. D*    24 D. *om. D*    25 collaudastis ⌜: -atis *V*: -auistis *D*    26 comprobastis ⌜: -rouatis *V*: -robauistis *D*    **29** 27 ut *Vb*[2]: ut re *nst*: ut te *b*[1]: ut uere *v*    *num* decretis notatus?    28 animo aequo *bntv*    31 num umquam *Garatoni*: num q- *V*: num quando *D*

Let Antonius retire from Mutina, let him cease attacking Brutus, let him withdraw from Gaul. We should not request in words, we have to compel him by force of arms. **27** We are not sending to Hannibal to make him retire from Saguntum—Hannibal, to whom once upon a time the Senate sent Publius Valerius Flaccus and Quintus Baebius Tamphilus, instructing them to go on to Carthage if Hannibal refused compliance (where do we instruct our people to go if Antonius refuses?). We are sending to a fellow countryman, to ask him not to attack a Roman imperator and a Roman colony. Really? Is *that* something to be requested through envoys? What in Heaven's name is the difference between attacking Rome and attacking Rome's bulwark, a colony of the Roman People founded for their protection? The cause of the Second Punic War, waged by Hannibal against our ancestors, was the attack on Saguntum. It was right to send envoys to *him*. He was a Carthaginian; they were sent on behalf of Hannibal's enemies, our allies. Where is the similarity? We are sending to a fellow countryman to ask him not to blockade an imperator and an army and a colony of the Roman People, not to attack, not to devastate lands, not to be an enemy. **28** Now then, supposing he complies, do we wish or are we able to have him in our community? On December twentieth you cut him to pieces in your decrees. You determined that on the Kalends of January reference be made to the House (as you see, it is so made) concerning honors and rewards for those who have deserved and are deserving well of the Commonwealth, first among whom you judged to be (and first he was) Gaius Caesar, who turned Marcus Antonius' wicked onset away from Rome to Gaul; next you gave your approval to the veteran soldiers who were the first to follow Caesar and after them to those wonderful, God-inspired legions, the Martian and the Fourth, to whom you pledged honors and rewards after they had not only abandoned their consul but were actually making war on him. On the same day the manifesto of our great countryman Decimus Brutus arrived in Rome and was published; you praised what he had done and endorsed by public authority his action in taking up arms on his private initiative. **29** What, then, was your purpose that day but to declare Antonius a public enemy? After those decrees of yours will he be able to look at you calmly or will you see him without fierce indignation? His own crime and also, as it seems to me, a stroke of good fortune for the Commonwealth has shut him out, separated and segregated. If he obeys the envoys and returns to Rome, do you imagine that abandoned citizens will ever lack a banner to rally behind?

Sed hoc minus vereor: sunt alia quae magis timeam et cogitem. numquam parebit ille legatis. novi hominis insaniam, adrogantiam; novi perdita consilia amicorum, quibus ille est deditus. **30** Lucius quidem frater eius, utpote qui peregre depugnarit, familiam ducit. sit per se ipse sanus, quod numquam erit: per hos esse ei tamen non licebit. teretur interea tempus; belli apparatus refrigescent. unde est adhuc bellum tractum nisi ex retardatione et mora? ut primum post discessum latronis vel potius desperatam fugam libere senatus haberi potuit, semper flagitavi ut convocaremur. quo die primum convocati sumus, cum designati consules non adessent, ieci sententia mea maximo vestro consensu fundamenta rei publicae, serius omnino quam decuit—nec enim ante potui—sed tamen, si ex eo tempore dies nullus intermissus esset, bellum profecto nullum haberemus. **31** omne malum nascens facile opprimitur: inveteratum fit plerumque robustius. sed tum exspectabantur Kalendae Ianuariae, fortasse non recte. verum praeterita omittamus: etiamne hanc moram, dum proficiscantur legati, dum revertantur? quorum exspectatio dubitationem belli adfer⟨e⟩t. bello autem dubio quod potest studium esse dilectus?

Quam ob rem, patres conscripti, legatorum mentionem nullam censeo faciendam; rem administrandam arbitror sine ulla mora et confestim gerendam [censeo]; tumultum decerni, iustitium edici, saga sumi dico oportere, dilectum haberi sublatis vacationibus in urbe et in Italia praeter Galliam tota. **32** quae si erunt facta, opinio ipsa et fama nostrae severitatis obruet scelerati gladiatoris amentiam. sentiet ⟨s⟩ibi bellum cum re publica esse susceptum; experietur consentientis senatus nervos atque viris; nam nunc quidem partium contentionem esse dictitat. quarum partium? alteri victi sunt, alteri sunt e mediis C. Caesari⟨s⟩ partibus; nisi forte Caesaris partis a Pansa et Hirtio consulibus et a filio C. Caesaris oppugnari putamus. hoc vero bellum non ⟨est⟩ ex dissensione partium, sed ex nefaria spe perditissimorum civium ex[er]citatum, quibus bona

1 ob quae *bstv*      timeam et cogitem *om. D*      **30** 5 teretur *V Cus.*: fer- *nstv*: differ-
*b*      6 tractum *om. D*      8 libere *in ras.* $V^2$: tuto *coni. Halm*      10 consensu] c- adfuissem cum *V*      11 potui sed] -isset *b(?)nst*      **31** 15 moram adferemus $DV^2$      17 adferet *scripsi*: -rt *codd.*      18 mentionem] menti (-te $n^2$) *nst*: mentio quis non uidet quam alieno tempore nunc a uobis facta est *b*      *hinc incipit lacuna in D usque ad* 6.18 nullam      censeo *del. Lambinus*      22 tota *Muretus*: -am *V*      **32** 23 sentiet sibi bellum *Poggius*: -ienti bibellum (*ex* libellum $V^2$) *V*      24 senatus *Poggius*: in *V*      28 est *add. Gryphius*

This, however, is not my main apprehension. There are other dangers I fear more, have more in mind. He will never obey the envoys. I know his madness, his arrogance. I know the desperate counsels of the friends to whom he has surrendered himself. **30** His brother Lucius leads this troop of gladiators, with his experience of combat in foreign parts. Suppose Antonius is sane in himself, which he will never be: these people will not let him be so. Meanwhile, time will be wasted and military preparations will cool off. Is not the protraction of the war till now due solely to the way we have dragged our feet? From the moment when a free Senate could be held, after the departure of the bandit, or rather after his desperate flight, I continually demanded that we be convoked.[27] As soon as we were convoked, in the absence of the consuls-elect, I made a speech[28] in which I laid the foundations of the Commonwealth, with your full assent. It was later than it should have been, for I had no earlier opportunity; but if no day had been lost from that time forward, it is pretty clear that we should not have a war. **31** Every evil is easily nipped in the bud; with age it usually gets stronger. But then we were waiting for the Kalends of January. Perhaps that was a mistake, but let bygones be bygones. Is there now to be yet further delay, are we to wait for envoys to set out, for envoys to return? To wait for them will raise doubts about the war, and if the war is in doubt, how can a levy get an enthusiastic response?

Therefore, Members of the Senate, in my judgment no mention should be made of envoys. I think the business should be put in hand without any delay and prosecuted at once. I say that a state of tumult should be decreed, suspension of business proclaimed, military cloaks donned, and a levy held with no exemptions in Rome and in the whole of Italy, Gaul excepted. **32** If these measures are adopted, the mere opinion and report of our stringency will crush the madness of a felonious gladiator. He will realize that he has taken up arms against the Commonwealth, he will feel the sinews and strength of a united Senate. At present he talks of a conflict between parties. What parties? One group has been defeated;[29] the other comes from the midst of Gaius Caesar's party. Or do we suppose that the Caesarians are under attack from Consuls Pansa and Hirtius and from Gaius Caesar's son? No, no, this war is no party quarrel. It has been stirred up from the wicked hopes of desperate men, for

27. Antony left Rome on 28 November and Cicero did not return from the country until 9 December.

28. The Third Philippic.

29. The Pompeians. Cicero might have made himself clearer here. By "parties" Antony meant Pompeians and Caesarians. But Cicero slides into a dichotomy of the "loyalists" as Pompeians, who having been already vanquished could not contend as a party, and Caesarians like the consuls and Octavian (*alteri . . . alteri*). The Antonians, as enemies of the state, are ignored. An alternative interpretation which makes *victi* refer to the Antonians is evidently absurd.

fortunaeque nostrae notatae sunt et iam ad cuiusque optionem distribu-
tae. **33** legi epistulam Antoni quam ad quendam septemvirum, capitalem
hominem, collegam suum, miserat. "quid concupiscas tu videris: quod
concupiveris certe habebis." em ad quem legatos mittamus, cui bellum
moremur inferre: qui ne sorti quidem fortunas nostras destin⟨a⟩vit, sed       5
libidini cuiusque nos ita addixit ut ne sibi quidem quicquam integrum
quod non alicui promissum iam sit reliquerit. cum hoc, patres conscripti,
bello, ⟨bello⟩ inquam, decertandum est, idque confestim; legatorum tarditas repudianda est.

**34** Quapropter ne multa nobis cotidie decernenda sint, consulibus       10
totam rem publicam commendandam censeo eisque permittendum ut rem
publicam defendant provide⟨a⟩ntque ne quid res publica detrimenti ac-
cipiat, censeoque ut eis qui in exercitu M. Antoni sunt ne sit ea res fraudi,
si ante Kalendas Februarias ab eo discesserint.

Haec si censuerit⟨is⟩, patres conscripti, brevi tempore libertatem po-       15
puli Romani auctoritatemque vestram recuperabitis. si autem lenius age-
tis, tamen eadem, sed fortasse serius decernetis. de re publica quod ret-
⟨t⟩ulistis satis decrevisse videor.

**35** Altera res est de honoribus: de quibus deinceps intellego esse dicendum. sed qui ordo in sententiis rogandis servari solet, eundem tenebo in       20
viris fortibus honorandis. a Bruto igitur, consule designato, more maiorum capiamus exordium. cuius ut superiora omittam, quae sunt maxima
illa quidem sed adhuc hominum magis iudiciis quam publice laudata,
quibusnam verbis eius laudes huius ipsius temporis consequi possumus?
neque enim ullam mercedem tanta virtus praeter hanc laudis gloriaeque       25
desiderat, qua etiam si careat, tamen sit se ipsa contenta; quamquam in
memoria gratorum civium tamquam in luce posita laetatur. laus igitur
iudici testimonique nostri tribuenda Bruto est. **36** quam ob rem his verbis, patres conscripti, senatus consultum faciendum censeo:

"Cum D. Brutus, imperator, consul designatus, provinciam Galliam in       30
senatus populique Romani potestate teneat, cumque exercitum tantum
tam brevi tempore summo studio municipiorum coloniarumque provinciae

---

1 optionem *Manutius*: opinio- *V*    **33** 4 concupiveris *Poggius*: -isceris *V*    en *Lambinus*    8 bello *add. Naugerius*    **34** 13 exercitu M. *R. Klotz*: -tum *V*: -tu *Poggius*    16
uestram *V*²: bestiarum *V*¹    17 sero *Cobet*    quod *Faërnus*: quoad *V*: qua de *Lambinus*    **35** 26 quamquam] atque *Manutius*    27 laetatur¹ *scripsi*: -tentur *V*: -tetur *ed.
Romana*

whom our goods and fortunes have been marked down and already distributed to suit each individual's preference. **33** I have read a letter from Antonius to a member of the Board of Seven, a right dangerous character, his colleague: "*You* must make up your mind what you want; what you want you will certainly get." That is the man to whom we are sending envoys, against whom we delay to make war! He has not even put our fortunes into a lottery, but has given us over to every individual's cupidity, not even leaving something uncommitted for himself. Everything has already been promised to somebody. With this man, Members of the Senate, we must fight it out. It must be war, I repeat, war, and that right away. No drawn-out business of envoys!

**34** Therefore, to spare ourselves the necessity of many decrees day after day, I propose that the whole Commonwealth be committed to the consuls and that they be given full discretion to defend the Commonwealth and take measures to ensure that the Commonwealth suffer no harm.[30] I further propose that men now in the army of Marcus Antonius be subject to no penalty on that account provided that they leave him before the Kalends of February.

If you so order, Members of the Senate, you will ere long recover the liberty of the Roman People and your own authority. If, on the other hand, you take a milder course, you will nonetheless eventually pass the same decree, but perhaps too late. So far as your reference[31] to the House concerns the state of the Commonwealth, I think it is sufficiently covered by my motion.

**35** The other matter concerns honors. This must evidently be my next theme. Well, I shall observe the same order of precedence in honoring brave men as is customarily used in calling on senators to speak. Therefore, following traditional practice, let us begin with Consul-Elect Brutus. Even leaving aside his earlier achievements,[32] which, however great, have hitherto received general approval rather than any public acknowledgment, how can we find words to praise his conduct at this very time? And indeed such virtue asks for no reward save this of praise and glory, and even if that were not forthcoming, it would be content with itself; not but what it rejoices, placed in the memory of grateful countrymen as in a pool of light. So Brutus must be given the praise of our judgment and testimony. **36** Accordingly, Members of the Senate, I propose that a decree of the Senate be passed in the following terms:

"Whereas Decimus Brutus, Imperator, Consul-Elect, is holding the province of Gaul at the disposition of the Senate and People of Rome, and whereas he has enrolled and mustered so large an army in so short a time with the enthusiastic support of the municipalities and colonies of the province of Gaul,

---

30. The Ultimate Decree; cf. Philippic 2 n. 50.
31. Addressing the consuls.
32. Caesar's assassination.

Galliae, optime de re publica meritae merentisque, conscripserit, compararit, id eum recte et ordine exque re publica fecisse, idque D. Bruti praestantissimum meritum in rem publicam senatui populoque Romano gratum esse et fore: itaque senatum populumque Romanum existimare, D. Bruti imperatoris, consulis designati, opera, consilio, virtute incredibilique studio et consensu provinciae Galliae rei publicae difficillimo tempore esse subventum." 5

**37** Huic tanto merito Bruti, patres conscripti, tantoque in rem publicam beneficio quis est tantus honos qui non debeatur? nam si M. Antonio patuisset Gallia, si oppressis municipiis et coloni(i)s imparatis in illam 10 ultimam Galliam penetrare potuisset, quantus rei publicae terror impenderet! dubitaret, credo, homo amentissimus atque in omnibus consiliis praeceps et devius non solum cum exercitu suo sed etiam cum omni immanitate barbariae bellum inferre nobis, ut eius furorem ne Alpium quidem muro cohibere possemus. haec igitur habenda gratia est D. Bruto 15 qui illum, nondum interposita auctoritate vestra, suo consilio atque iudicio, non ut consulem recepit, sed ut hostem arcuit Gallia seque obsideri quam hanc urbem maluit. habeat ergo huius tanti facti tamque praeclari decreto nostro testimonium sempiternum; Galliaque, quae semper praesidet atque praesedit huic imperio libertatique communi, merito vereque 20 laudetur, quod se suasque viris non tradidit, sed opposuit Antonio.

**38** Atque etiam M. Lepido pro eius egregiis in rem publicam meritis decernendos honores quam amplissimos censeo. semper ille populum Romanum liberum voluit maximumque signum illo die dedit voluntatis et iudici sui, cum Antonio diadema Caesari imponente se avertit gemituque 25 et maestitia declaravit quantum haberet odium servitutis, quam populum Romanum liberum cuperet, quam illa quae tulerat temporum magis necessitate quam iudicio tulisset. quanta vero is moderatione usus sit in illo tempore civitatis quod post mortem Caesaris consecutum est, quis nostrum oblivisci potest? magna haec, sed ad maiora properat oratio. 30 **39** quid enim, o di immortales, admirabilius omnibus gentibus, quid optatius populo Romano accidere potuit quam, cum bellum civile maximum esset, cuius belli exitum omnes timeremus, sapientia et misericordia id potius exstingui quam armis et ferro rem in discrimen adduci? quod si eadem ratio Caesaris[i] fuisset in illo taetro miseroque bello, ut omittam 35 patrem, duos Cn. Pompei, summi et singularis viri, filios incolumis haberemus: quibus certe pietas fraudi esse non debuit. utinam omnis M. Le-

---

**37** 8 Bruti *Poggius*: p. c. bruti *V*    10 Gallia *Poggius*: gladia *V*    12 hominem amentissimum aque (adque *V²*) *V, corr. Poggius*    15 haec *Poggius*: hac *V*    18 facti tamque *Poggius*: facit tamquam *V*    **39** 32 cum *Poggius*: quim *V¹*: quod *V²*    33 et misericordia (*i.e.* et mīa) *Clark*: et iam *V*: *del. Lambinus*    34 adduci *Lambinus*: addecere *V*: adduc- *Poggius*: *anne* res . . . adduceretur?

a province which has deserved and is deserving excellently well of the Commonwealth: that he has acted rightly and properly and in the public interest; and that this outstanding service to the Commonwealth on the part of Decimus Brutus is and will be pleasing to the Senate and People of Rome; which same consider that by the act, policy, and courage of Decimus Brutus, Imperator, Consul-Elect, and the extraordinary zeal and unanimity of the province of Gaul, aid has been rendered to the Commonwealth at a most difficult time."

**37** For this sovereign service of Brutus, Members of the Senate, this benefaction conferred upon the Commonwealth, what honor could be too great? If Gaul had lain wide open to Marcus Antonius, if, after crushing its unprepared municipalities and colonies, he had been able to penetrate into that other, outer Gaul, what a cloud of terror would be hanging over the Commonwealth! Would he hesitate, this madman whose every move is an erratic plunge, to bring war upon us not only with his army but with all the savagery of a barbarous land? Even with the rampart of the Alps we should have been powerless to contain his fury. For this, then, we have Decimus Brutus to thank, who, without waiting for your authority, exercising his own initiative and judgment, did not admit Antonius as a consul but barred him from Gaul as an enemy and let himself, rather than this city, stand a siege. So let him by our decree have everlasting testimony to his great and noble action; and let Gaul, which protects and always has protected this empire and our common liberties, be deservedly and truly commended in that instead of surrendering herself and her strength to Antonius she placed them in his path.

**38** I further propose that honors the most ample be decreed to Marcus Lepidus for his outstanding services to the Commonwealth. Lepidus has ever wished the Roman People to be free. He gave an unmistakable indication of his desire and judgment that day when Antonius tried to place a diadem on Caesar's head. Lepidus turned away and declared by a groan and a sad countenance how much he hated slavery and desired the Roman People to be free, how wholly his tolerance of what he had tolerated had been due to the necessity of the times rather than his own choice. Which of us can forget Lepidus' moderation in the national crisis that followed Caesar's death? These are great merits, but my words hasten on to others greater still. **39** What event, in Heaven's name, could have created greater admiration among all nations and what could the Roman People more earnestly have desired to happen than the extinction of a great civil war, of which war we all dreaded the outcome, by wisdom and compassion instead of the arbitrament of the sword? If Caesar had taken the same course in that other hideous, miserable struggle, we should have the two sons of that greatest of Romans, Gnaeus Pompeius (to say nothing of their father) safe in our midst. Assuredly they ought not to have suffered for being good sons. If only Marcus Lepidus could have saved all

pidus servare potuisset! facturum fuisse declaravit in eo quod potuit, cum
Sex. Pompeium restituit civitati, maximum ornamentum rei publicae,
clarissimum monumentum clementiae suae. gravis illa fortuna populi Romani, grave fatum. Pompeio enim patre, quod imperi[o] populi Romani
lumen fuit, exstincto interfectus est patris simillimus filius. **40** sed omnia      5
mihi videntur deorum immortalium iudicio expiata Sex. Pompeio rei
publicae conservato. quam ob causam iustam atque magnam et quod periculosissimum civile bellum maximumque humanitate et sapientia sua
M. Lepidus ad pacem concordiamque convertit, senatus consultum his
verbis censeo perscribendum:                                                        10
    "Cum a M. Lepido imperatore, pontifice maximo, saepe numero res
⟨publica⟩ et bene et feliciter gesta sit, populusque Romanus intellexerit ei
dominatum regium maxime displicere, cumque eius opera, virtute, consilio singularique clementia et mansuetudine bellum acerbissimum civile
⟨s⟩it restinctum, **41** Sextusque Pompeius Cn. f. Magnus huius ordinis       15
auctoritate ab armis discesserit et a M. Lepido imperatore, pontifice
maximo, summa senatus populique Romani voluntate civitati restitutus
sit, senatum populumque Romanum pro maximis plurimisque in rem
publicam M. Lepidi meritis magnam spem in eius virtute, auctoritate, felicitate re⟨ponere⟩ oti, pacis, concordiae, libertatis, eiusque in rem pu-       20
blicam meritorum senatum populumque Romanum memorem fore, eique
statuam equestrem inauratam in rostris aut quo alio loco in foro vellet ex
huius ordinis sententia statui placere."
    Qui honos, patres conscripti, mihi maximus videtur, primum qu⟨i⟩a
iustus est; non enim solum datur propter spem temporum reliquorum sed       25
pro amplissimis meritis redditur; nec vero cuiquam possumus commemorare hunc honorem a senatu tributum iudicio senatus soluto et libero.
    **42** Venio ad C. Caesarem, patres conscripti; qui nisi fuisset, quis
nostrum esse potuisset? advolabat ad urbem a Brundisio homo impoten-
tissimus, ardens odio, animo hostili in omnis bonos cum exercitu An-       30
tonius. quid huius audaciae et sceleri poterat opponi? nondum ullos
duces habebamus, non copias; nullum erat consilium publicum, nulla libertas; dandae cervices erant crudelitati nefariae; fugam quaerebamus

---

4 imperi *ed. Romana*: -rio *V*     **40** 6 expiata *Faërnus*: -ieta *V¹*: et pietate *V²*     9 senatus
consultum *Poggius*: se *V*     12 publica *add. Poggius*     **41** 20 reponere *Poggius*: re
*V*     22 velit *Ernesti*     24 quia *Poggius*: qua *V*     **42** 30 Antonius *del. Cobet*

three! That he would have done so he made plain by doing what he could, in restoring Sextus Pompeius to the community, a shining ornament of the Commonwealth and a most notable memorial of his own clemency. Grievous was that stroke of fortune to the Roman People, a grievous destiny! In Pompeius the father the light of the Roman People's empire was put out; and then his son, who resembled him so closely,[33] was slain. **40** But by the judgment of the Gods, the preservation of Sextus Pompeius to the Commonwealth, has, as I see it, made amends for all. For this great and just reason and because Marcus Lepidus by his humanity and wisdom has transformed a very big and dangerous civil war into peace and concord I propose that a decree of the Senate be entered in the following terms:

"Whereas Marcus Lepidus, Imperator, Pontifex Maximus, has on many occasions well and successfully conducted the affairs of the Commonwealth, and the Roman People has perceived that monarchical rule is strongly repugnant to him; and whereas by his act, courage, policy, and notable clemency and gentle dealing a most bitter civil war has been extinguished, **41** and Sextus Pompeius Magnus, son of Gnaeus, has laid down his arms by the authority of this House and been restored to the community by Marcus Lepidus, Imperator, Pontifex Maximus, to the lively satisfaction of the Senate and People of Rome: that the Senate and People of Rome, conscious of Marcus Lepidus' great and numerous services to the Commonwealth, place high hope of peace, tranquility, concord, and liberty in his courage, authority, and good fortune; and that the Senate and People of Rome will be mindful of his services to the Commonwealth; and that it pleases the Senate that a gilt equestrian statue to him be placed by will of this House on the Rostra or in any other position in the Forum which he may choose."

Members of the Senate, I consider this a very great honor, first and foremost, because it is due. It is not accorded simply in the hope of things to come but rendered in recognition of very important services. Nor can we name any other person to whom this honor has been granted by the Senate acting freely and without constraint.

**42** Members of the Senate, I come to Gaius Caesar. Had it not been for him, what chance would there have been for any of us? Hastening up from Brundisium to Rome was a man of violent temper, burning with hatred, hostile to all honest men, with an army at his back: Antonius. What could we oppose to his audacity, his criminal intent? At that time we had no leaders, no forces. There was no public council, no freedom. We must needs submit our necks to

---

33. Cassius wrote of this young man to Cicero in January 45: "You know what a fool Gnaeus is, how he takes cruelty for courage, how he thinks we always made fun of him" (*Fam.* 15.19.4). Cicero had to be saved from his violence by Cato after Pharsalia (Plut. *Cic.* 39).

omnes, quae ipsa exitum non habebat. **43** quis tum nobis, quis populo
Romano obtulit hunc divinum adulescentem deus? qui, cum omnia ad
perniciem nostram pestifero illi civi paterent, subito praeter spem omnium exortus prius confecit exercitum quem furori M. Antoni opponeret
quam quisquam hoc eum cogitare suspicaretur. 5
Magni honores habiti Cn. Pompeio cum esset adulescens, et quidem
iure. subvenit enim rei publicae, sed aetate multo robustior et militum
ducem quaerentium studio par⟨a⟩tior et in alio genere belli. non enim omnibus Sullae causa grata: declarat multitudo proscriptorum, tot municipiorum maximae calamitates. **44** Caesar autem annis multis minor vete- 10
ranos cupientis iam requiescere armavit; eam complexus est causam quae
esset senatui, quae populo, quae cunctae Italiae, quae dis hominibusque
gratissima. et Pompeius ad L. Sullae maximum imperium victoremque
exercitum accessit: Caesar se ad neminem adiunxit, ipse princeps exercitus faciendi et praesidi comparandi fuit. ille [in] adversariorum partibus 15
agrum Picenum habuit inimicum: hic ex Antoni amicis sed amicioribus
libertati[s] contra Antonium confecit exercitum. illius opibus Sulla reg-
navit: huius praesidi⟨o⟩ Antoni dominatus oppressus est.
**45** Demus igitur imperium Caesari s⟨i⟩ne quo res militaris adminis-
trari, teneri exercitus, bellum geri non potest: sit pro praetore eo iure quo 20
qui optimo. qui honos quamquam est magnus illi aetati, tamen ad necessitatem rerum gerendarum, non solum ad dignitatem valet. itaque ⟨ne⟩ illa
quaeramus quae vix hodierno die consequemur. sed saepe spero fore
huius adulescenti⟨s⟩ [hortandi] honorandi et nobis et populo Romano potestatem; hoc autem tempore ita censeo decernendum: 25
**46** "Quod C. Caesar C. f. pontifex [pro praetore] summo rei publicae
tempore milites veteranos ad libertatem populi Romani cohortatus sit
eosque conscripserit, quodque legio Martia ⟨legio⟩que quarta summo
studio optimoque in rem publicam consensu C. Caesare duce et auctore
rem publicam, libertatem populi Romani defendant defe⟨nde⟩rint, et 30
quod C. Caesar [pro praetore] Galliae provinciae cum exercitu subsidio
profectus sit, equites, sagitt⟨ar⟩ios, elephantos in suam populique Romani potestatem redegerit, difficillimoque rei publicae tempore saluti
dignitatique populi Romani subvenerit, ob eas causas senatui placere

**43** 7 enim *ed. Romana*: etiam *V*   8 paratior *Poggius*: part- *V*: paratiore *Halm, fort.
recte*   **44** 12 hominibusque *Faërnus*: omnib- *V*   15 in *del. Ferrarius*   17 libertati
*ed. Romana*: -tis *V*   **45** 20 sit pro praetore *Ferrarius*: et pro pop. r. *V*   21 illi aetati
*Poggius*: illa ae- *V*: illa aetate *Graevius*   22 ne² *addidi*   24 honorandi *Halm*: hortandi
honorandi (-ique *V²*) *V*: ornandi honorandique *Ferrarius*: ornandi *coni. C. F. W. Müller*   **46** 26 pro pr⟨aetore⟩ *seclusi²*   28 legioque quarta *scripsi (cf. 5.53)*: q. quarta *V*:
quartaque *Poggius*: atque quarta *Halm*   30 defenderint, defendant *coni. Fedeli*   32
suam *Poggius*: suma *V*

the villain's cruelty. We all sought flight, but flight too offered no escape.
**43** What God then presented to us and to the Roman People this godlike young man? When every road to our destruction lay open to that bearer of bane, suddenly, to the surprise of all, *he* arose. He got together an army to oppose Marcus Antonius' madness before anyone suspected him of such a thought.

Great honors were accorded to Gnaeus Pompeius when he was a young man, and rightly so, for he came to the aid of the Commonwealth. But he was much stronger in years, had more to build on in the enthusiasm of soldiers looking for a leader, and it was a different sort of war. Sulla's cause was not universally favored: witness the multitude of the proscribed and the terrible disasters which befell so many townships. **44** Caesar, many years younger, armed veterans who now wanted peace and quiet; and he embraced a cause most highly favored by the Senate, the Roman People, all Italy, by Gods and men. Also Pompeius joined Lucius Sulla's mighty command and victorious army; Caesar attached himself to nobody, was himself the first to make an army, create a defense. Pompeius held the territory of Picenum, hostile to the opposing party; Caesar raised an army against Antonius from Antonius' friends— but better friends of freedom. With Pompeius' help Sulla reigned; by Caesar's intervention Antonius' despotism has been crushed.

**45** Therefore let us give Caesar that authority without which no military business can be conducted, no army held in being, no war waged: let him be propraetor in full status. It is a great honor at his age, but one relevant to the necessity of military operations, not just to prestige. So let us not ask for what we shall hardly obtain today—but I expect that both we and the Roman People will have many opportunities in times to come of distinguishing this young man. At present, however, I move a decree as follows:

**46** "Whereas Gaius Caesar, son of Gaius, Pontifex, at a grave crisis of the Commonwealth urged veteran soldiers to defend the freedom of the Roman People and enrolled them; and whereas the Martian Legion and the Fourth Legion with the greatest enthusiasm, in unanimous loyalty to the Commonwealth, under the leadership and at the instance of Gaius Caesar, are defending and have defended the Commonwealth and the freedom of the Roman People; and whereas Gaius Caesar has set out with his army to the assistance of the province of Gaul, has brought cavalry, archers, and elephants under his own control and that of the Roman People,[34] and at a most difficult crisis of the Commonwealth has come to the aid of the safety and dignity of the Roman People: for these reasons that it please the Senate that Gaius Caesar, son of

---

34. As foreign auxiliaries, presumably brought by Caesar from Africa.

C. Caesarem C. f. pontificem, pro praetore ⟨eo iure quo qui optimo et⟩
senatorem esse sententiamque loco praetorio dicere, eiusque rationem,
quemcumque magistratum petet, ita haberi ut haberi per leges liceret si
anno superiore quaestor fuisset."

**47** Quid est enim, patres conscripti, cur eum non quam primum am-    5
plissimos honores capere cupiamus? legibus enim annalibus cum gran-
diorem aetatem ad consulatum constituebant, adulescentiae temeritatem
verebantur: C. Caesar ineunte aetate docuit ab excellenti eximiaque virtute progressum aetatis exspectari non oportere. itaque maiores nostri
veteres illi admodum antiqui leges annalis non habebant, quas multis post    10
annis attulit ambitio, ut gradus essent petitionis inter aequalis. ita saepe
magna indoles virtutis, prius quam rei publicae prodesse potuisset, ex-
stincta est. **48** at vero apud antiquos Rulli, Decii, Corvini multique alii,
recentiore autem memoria superior Africanus, T. Flamini⟨n⟩us admodum
adulescentes consules facti tantas res gesserunt ut populi Romani impe-    15
rium auxerint, nomen ornarint. quid? Macedo Alexander, cum ab ineunte
aetate res maximas gerere coepisset, nonne tertio et tricesimo anno mortem obiit? quae est aetas nostris legibus decem annis minor quam consularis. ex quo iudicari potest virtu⟨ti⟩s esse quam aetatis cursum celerio-
rem. nam quod ei qui Caesari invident simulant se timere, ne verendum    20
quidem est ut tenere se possit, ut moderari, ne honoribus nostris elatus
intemperantius suis opibus utatur. **49** ea natura rerum est, patres conscripti, ut qui sensum verae gloriae ceperit quique se ab senatu, ab equitibus Romanis populoque Romano universo senserit civem c[l]arum haberi salutaremque rei publicae, nihil cum hac gloria comparandum putet.    25
utinam C. Caesari, pa⟨t⟩ri dico, contigisset adulescenti ut esset senatui
atque optimo cuique carissimus! quod cum consequi neglexisset, omnem
vim ingeni, quae summa fuit in illo, in populari levitate consumpsit. itaque cum respectum ad senatum et ad bonos non haberet, eam sibi viam
ipse patefecit ad opes suas amplificandas quam virtus liberi populi ferre    30
non posset.

    Eius autem fili longissime diversa ratio est: qui cum omnibus ⟨carus⟩
est, tum optimo cuique carissimus. in hoc spes libertatis posita est, ab
hoc accepta iam salus, huic summi honores et exquiruntur et parati sunt.

---

1 eo iure . . . et *addidi*[2]     2 praetorio *Naugerius*: populi r. *V*: pr. *Poggius*: quaestorio
*Nipperdey*     3 quemcumque magistratum *Faërnus*: quemcumquem ac *V*     appetet *V*[2]:
appeteret *Ernesti*: peteret *Schütz*     ut haberi per *Faërnus*: per ut h- *V*     **47** 11 esset
*Mommsen*     13 est *Faërnus*: sunt *V*     **48** Corvi *Pighius*     15–16 populus romanus
. . . auxerit *V Cus.*, *corr. Poggius*     19 uirtutis *V*[2]: uirtus *V*[1] *Cus.*     20 ne *Poggius*: non
*V*     **49** 24 carum *Ferrarius*: cla- *V*     30 populi *Poggius*: publici *V*     32 carus[3] *add.*
*Muretus*

Gaius, Pontifex, become propraetor in full status and a member of the Senate; that he be called upon to speak among the ex-praetors; and that for whatever magistracy he shall be a candidate, his candidature be accepted as it would legally be accepted if he had been quaestor in the year to this previous."

**47** For why, Members of the Senate, should we not wish him to gain the highest offices as soon as possible? When people fixed a later age for the consulship[35] by Annual Laws, they were afraid of the rashness of youth. But Gaius Caesar has shown in earliest youth that outstanding and exceptional abilities should not wait upon advancing years. And so our ancestors, that is our early ancestors, the men of old, did not have any Annual Laws. These laws came in at a much later period as a result of the struggle for offices, to create stages at which men of the same age should compete. The consequence often was that great natural abilities were snuffed out before they could be of service to the Commonwealth. **48** But in ancient times men like Rullus, Decius, Corvinus,[36] and many others and in more recent memory the elder Africanus and Titus Flamininus were elected consuls quite young and by their great achievements enlarged the empire of the Roman People and added luster to its name. Did not Alexander of Macedon begin his career of glorious achievement in earliest youth and die in his thirty-third year—an age ten years below the consular qualification under our laws? Hence we may conclude that ability outruns age. Persons jealous of Caesar pretend to dread that he may be unable to keep himself within the bounds of moderation, may be puffed up by our honors and use his power intemperately. Not even an apprehension on this account is justified. **49** It is a law of nature, Members of the Senate, that once a man has come to a perception of true glory and perceived that in the eyes of the Senate, the Roman Knights, and the entire Roman People he is a valued citizen and a benefit to the Commonwealth, he will think nothing comparable to this glory. I only wish it had been Gaius Caesar's fortune in early life (I am speaking of the elder Caesar) to be highly valued by the Senate and the best of our community. Neglecting to win that esteem, he squandered his powers of mind, which were of the highest order, in irresponsible demagogy. And so, paying no consideration to the Senate and the honest men, he opened a path to his own aggrandizement such as the spirit of a free people could not tolerate.

Far different is the course chosen by his son. He is valued by all, but particularly by the flower of the community. In him resides the hope of freedom. To him we already owe our lives. For him the highest honors are

35. Forty-two, under the *lex Villia annalis* of 180.
36. Actually (M. Valerius) Corvus, consul in 348; it was his son who took the name Corvinus.

**50** cuius igitur singularem prudentiam admiramur, eius stultitiam timemus? quid enim stultius quam inutilem potentiam, invidiosas opes, cupiditatem dominandi praecipitem et lubricam anteferre verae, gravi, soli-
dae gloriae? an hoc vidit puer: si aetate processerit, non videbit? "at est
quibusdam inimicus clarissimis atque optimis civibus." nullus iste timor      5
esse debet. omnis Caesar inimicitias rei publicae condonavit; hanc sibi
iudicem constituit, hanc moderatricem omnium ⟨consiliorum⟩ atque factorum. ita enim [ut enim] ad rem publicam accessit ut eam confirmaret,
non ut everteret. omnis habeo cognitos sensus adulescentis. nihil est illi
re publica carius, nihil vestra auctoritate gravius, nihil bonorum virorum     10
iudicio optatius, nihil vera gloria dulcius. **51** quam ob rem ab eo non
modo nihil timere sed maiora et meliora exspectare debetis, neque in eo
qui ad D. Brutum obsidione liberandum profectus sit timere ne memoria
maneat domestici doloris quae plus apud eum possit quam salus civitatis.
audeo etiam obligare fidem meam, patres conscripti, vobis populoque       15
Romano reique publicae; quod profecto, cum me nulla vis cogeret, facere
non auderem pertimesceremque in maxima re ⟨et⟩ periculosa opinionem
temeritatis. promitto, recipio, spondeo, patres conscripti, C. Caesarem
talem semper fore civem qualis hodie sit qualemque eum maxime velle
esse et optare debemus.                                                         20

　　**52** Quae cum ita sint, de Caesare satis hoc tempore dictum habebo. nec
vero de L. Egnatuleio, fortissimo et constantissimo civi amicissimoque
rei publicae, silendum arbitror; sed tribuendum testimonium virtutis
egregiae, quod is legionem quartam ad Caesarem adduxerit, quae praesidio consulibus, senatui populoque Romano reique publicae esset: ob eam       25
causam placere uti L. Egnatuleio triennio ante legitimum tempus magistratus petere, capere, gerere liceat. in quo, patres conscripti, non tantum
commodum tribuitur L. Egnatuleio quantus honos: in tali enim re satis
est nominari.

　　**53** De exercitu autem C. C⟨aes⟩aris ita censeo decernendum:               30
　　"Senatui placere militibus veteranis qui ⟨C.⟩ Caesaris pontificis, ⟨pro
praetore auctoritatem secuti libertatem populi Romani⟩ auctoritatemque
huius ordinis defenderint atque defendant i⟨ps⟩is liberisque eorum mili-

---

**50** 7 consiliorum *add. ante* omnium *Faërnus, hoc loco Halm*      8 ut enim *del. Poggius:*
animatus *coni. C. F. W. Müller*      **51** 15 audeo *Halm:* -ebo *in ras.* V      17 et periculosa[3]
(*anne* et maxime p-?) *scripsi:* periculosam V      19 sit] est *coni. Halm*      **52** 26 triennio
*Lambinus:* -ium V      magistratus *Poggius:* magna V      **53** 31 C. *addidi*      31–32
pro praetore[3] *add. Lambinus*      32 auctoritatem . . . populi Romani[3] *add. Garatoni (v.
Fe.)*      33 atque *del. Ernesti*      ipsis *coni. C. F. W. Müller:* iis V

being sought out and are in readiness. **50** We admire his exceptional good sense: do we fear his folly? For folly indeed it would be to prefer unprofitable power, invidious riches, the hazardous, treacherous desire for domination, to true, stable, solid glory. He has seen this while yet a lad: will he not see it once he has grown older? It may be alleged that he has a vendetta against certain excellent and illustrious citizens. There is nothing to fear on that score. Caesar has sacrificed all personal grudges to the Commonwealth, which he has made his arbiter and guide in all his decisions and actions. He has entered public life to strengthen the Commonwealth, not to overthrow it. I know the young man's mind inside out. He values nothing more than the Commonwealth, respects nothing more than your authority, desires nothing more than the good opinion of honest men, relishes nothing more than true glory. **51** So far from being in any way afraid of him, you should expect greater and better things of him. He has set out to liberate Decimus Brutus from siege. You should have no fear that the memory of a private grief may stay with him so as to outweigh the safety of the community. I even dare to pledge my word, Members of the Senate, to you and to the Roman People and to the Commonwealth—and that is something which unless I knew him thoroughly I obviously should not do, since no force compels me; I should be afraid of being thought rash in a great and dangerous business. I give you my promise, my guarantee, my pledge, Members of the Senate, that Gaius Caesar will always be such a citizen as he is today and such as we ought most to wish and pray for him to be.

**52** Accordingly, I shall take it that enough has been said about Caesar at this time. Nor do I think it fitting that Lucius Egnatuleius, a very brave, resolute, and patriotic citizen, receive no mention. His conspicuous merit in bringing over the Fourth Legion to Caesar for the protection of the consuls, the Senate and the People of Rome, and the Commonwealth, deserves a testimonial. For that reason I move that it please the Senate that Lucius Egnatuleius be permitted to stand for, take, and administer magistracies three years before the time by law prescribed. This proposal, Members of the Senate, is more to Lucius Egnatuleius' honor than to his practical advantage. In such a case to be named is enough.

**53** Now concerning Gaius Caesar's army I move the following decree:

"That it please the Senate that the veteran soldiers who, following the authority of Gaius Caesar, Pontifex, Propraetor,[37] have defended and are defending the freedom of the Roman People and the authority of this House, be granted exemption from military service for themselves and their children;

---

37. So below. The passage of the previous decree conferring the title is assumed.

tiae vacationem esse, utique C. Pansa A. Hirtius consules, alter ambove,
si eis videretur, cognoscerent qui ager eis coloniis esset quo milites veterani deducti essent qui contra legem Iuliam possideretur, ut is militibus
veteranis divideretur; de agro Campano separatim cognoscerent inirent-
que rationem de commodis militum veteranorum augendis, legionique    5
Martiae et legioni quartae et eis militibus qui de legione secunda, tri-
cesima quinta ad C. Pansam A. Hirtium consules venissent suaque nomina edidissent, quod eis auctoritas senatus populique Romani libertas
carissima sit et fuerit, vacationem militiae ipsis liberisque eorum esse
placere extra tumultum Gallicum Italicumque: easque legiones bello con-    10
fecto missas fieri placere; quantamque pecuniam militibus earum legionum in singulos C. Caesar pontifex, pro praetore pollicitus sit, tantam dari placere; utique C. Pansa A. Hirtius consules, alter ambove, si eis
videretur, rationem agri habe⟨re⟩nt qui sine iniuria privatorum dividi posset, eisque militibus, legioni Martiae et legioni quartae ita darent, adsig-    15
narent ut quibus militibus amplissime dati, adsignati essent."

Dixi ad ea omnia, consules, de quibus rettulistis: quae si erunt sine
mora matureque decreta, facilius apparabitis ea quae tempus et necessitas
flagitat. celeritate autem opus est: qua si essemus usi, bellum, ut saepe
dixi, nullum haberemus.    20

1–2 alter ambove (*ita Poggius*) si eis videretur *Ursinus*: aa. uesieo $V^1$: aa. designati $V^2$    12
singulos *Poggius*: -las *V*    pro praetore[3] $\varsigma$: populo romano *V*: *del. Poggius*    14 haberent
. . . posset *Schütz*: habent . . . possit *V*: -eant . . . possit *Poggius*    15 *anne* et legioni
Martiae?    16 quibus] *anne* qui (*sc.* agri)? (*cf.* 9.17)

further, that Gaius Pansa and Aulus Hirtius, either or both, if they see fit, make inquiry concerning land occupied in contravention of the Julian law[38] appertaining to those colonies in which veteran soldiers have been settled, with a view to the division of such land among the veteran soldiers; that they make separate inquiry concerning the Campanian land and investigate means of increasing the benefits of the veteran soldiers; and that it please the Senate that the Martian Legion, the Fourth Legion, and those soldiers of the Second and Thirty-fifth Legions who shall have presented themselves before Gaius Pansa and Aulus Hirtius, Consuls, and given in their names, in that they show and have shown their high regard for the authority of the Senate and People of Rome, be granted exemption from military service for themselves and their children, except in case of a Gallic or Italian tumult; and that it please the Senate that those legions be discharged at the end of the war; and that it please the Senate that money to the amount promised by Gaius Caesar, Pontifex, Propraetor, to the soldiers of those legions individually be given them; further, that Gaius Pansa and Aulus Hirtius, Consuls, either or both, if they see fit, take cognizance of land available for division without prejudice to individuals and do grant and assign such land to the said soldiers, that is, to the Martian Legion and the Fourth Legion, in terms no less liberal than any hitherto used in such grants and assignments."

Consuls, I have spoken to all those matters on which you have referred to the House. If the decrees are passed promptly and without delay, you will find it easier to make such preparations as the necessity of the situation urgently demands. But speed is essential. Had we used it, we should, as I have often said, have no war.

38. Caesar's agrarian law of 59.

# VI

## INTRODUCTION

Later in the day of 1 January 43 Cicero again addressed a public assembly in the Forum to give his account of the debate in the Senate. Though highly critical of the decision on the embassy, he made the best of his discomfiture: the embassy would certainly achieve nothing, and then all waverers would be convinced. With that in mind, he adds, he had pressed his view less strongly in the Senate than he might have done.

1 Audita vobis esse arbitror, Quirites, quae sint acta in senatu, quae fuerit cuiusque sententia. res enim ex Kalendis Ianuariis agitata paulo ante confecta est, minus quidem illa severe quam decuit, non tamen omnino dissolute. mora est adlata bello, non causa sublata. quam ob rem, quod quaesivit ex me P. Apuleius, homo et multis officiis mihi et summa     5
familiaritate coniunctus et vobis amicissimus, ita respondebo ut ea quibus non interfuistis nosse possitis.

Causa fortissimis optimisque consulibus Kalendis Ianuariis de re publica primum referendi fuit ex eo quod ⟨a. d.⟩ XIII Kalendas Ianuarias senatus me auctore decrevit. 2 eo die primum, Quirites, fundamenta sunt     10
iacta [sunt] rei publicae: fuit enim longo intervallo ita liber senatus ut vos aliquando liberi essetis. quo quidem tempore, etiam si ille dies vitae finem mihi adlaturus esset, satis magnum ceperam f⟨r⟩uctum, cum vos universi una mente atque voce iterum a me conservatam esse rem publicam conclamastis. hoc vestro iudicio tanto tamque praeclaro excitatus     15
ita Kalendis Ianuariis veni in senatum ut meminissem quam personam impositam a vobis sustinerem. itaque bellum nefarium illatum rei publicae cum viderem, nullam moram interponendam insequendi M. Antonium putavi, hominemque audacissimum, qui multis nefariis rebus ante commissis hoc tempore imperatorem populi Romani oppugnaret, colo-     20
niam vestram fidissimam fortissimamque obsideret, bello censui persequendum. tumultum esse decrevi; iustitium edici, saga sumi dixi placere, quo omnes acrius graviusque incumberent ad ulciscendas rei publicae iniurias, si omnia gravissimi belli insignia suscepta a senatu viderent. 3 itaque haec sententia, Quirites, sic per triduum valuit ut, quamquam discessio     25
facta non est, tamen praeter paucos [homines] omnes mihi adsensuri viderentur. hodierno autem die spe nescio qua ⟨pa⟩cis obiecta remissior senatus fuit. nam plures eam sententiam secuti sunt ut, quantum senatus auctoritas vesterque consensus apud Antonium valiturus esset, per legatos experiremur.     30

Intellego, Quirites, a vobis hanc sententiam repudiari, neque iniuria. ad quem enim legatos? ad eumne qui pecunia publica dissipata atque effusa per vim et contra auspicia impositis rei publicae legibus, fugata contione, obsesso senatu, ad opprimendam rem publicam Brundisio le-

**1** 3 illa quidem *coni. C. F. W. Müller*     9 a.d. *add. Orelli*     **2** 10–11 sunt iacta *Garatoni*: s- i- sunt *V*¹: i- s- *Poggius, V*²     13 fructum *Poggius*: fac- *V*¹: fuc- *V*²     18 Antoni *coni. C. F. W. Müller*     22 esse *del. Ernesti*     decerni *ed. Romana (v. Fe.)*     **3** 26 est *coni. Clark*: esset *V (sed* non est *add. V*¹ *post* dies)     homines *del. V*²     26–27 adsensuri uiderentur *V*²: -ri uiderem *V*¹: *anne* -ros uiderem?     27 dies non est (s non est *del. V*²) pene scio quaeis obiectarem *V, corr. Garatoni et Rau*     29 uestraeque *V*¹: -trumque *Halm*

**1** I think you have heard, Men of Rome, what has taken place in the Senate and the views expressed by the several speakers. The question which has been at issue since the Kalends of January has just been settled, in a fashion less stringent than befitted, but still not altogether lax. War has been delayed, but the ground for it has not been removed. So I will reply to the inquiry put to me by my good friend Publius Apuleius, to whom I am bound by many good offices and close friendship and who loves you well, so as to make you acquainted with proceedings at which you were not present.

On the Kalends of January our gallant and excellent consuls first made reference to the House concerning the Commonwealth, an action arising from the decrees passed by the Senate at my motion on the twentieth of December. **2** On that day, Men of Rome, for the first time the foundations of the Commonwealth were laid. For after a long interval the Senate was free, so free that at long last *you* were free. Even if that day were to have been the last of my life, it would have been fulfillment enough when with one heart and voice you all cried out that I had saved the Commonwealth a second time.[1] Aroused by so weighty and unambiguous a verdict, I entered the Senate on the Kalends of January mindful of the role for which you had cast me and which I was sustaining. Seeing that a wicked war had been launched against the Commonwealth, I considered that no delay should be allowed to hold up the pursuit of Marcus Antonius; I gave it as my judgment that war should be waged against this insolent man, who after many other acts of villainy was at this time attacking an imperator of the Roman People and laying siege to one of your bravest and most loyal colonies. I proposed a decree recognizing a state of tumult, ordering proclamation of a suspension of business and the donning of military cloaks, in order that every man should press to avenge the injuries of the Commonwealth more intensely and energetically when he saw the Senate authorizing all the outward signs of a major war. **3** This proposal of mine was strongly favored for a period of three days. Although no vote had been taken, all but a few seemed likely to support me. Today, however, the Senate's determination relaxed after some sort of hope for peace had been held out, and a majority backed another motion, namely to test through envoys how much the Senate's authority and your unanimous sentiment would count with Antonius.

I realize, Men of Rome, that you repudiate this proposal, and you are not wrong. To whom are we sending envoys? To the man who poured out public money like water, who foisted laws on the Commonwealth by violence and against the auspices, who put an assembly to flight and the Senate under siege? The man who after all this summoned legions from Brundisium to crush the

---

1. At the assembly to which Cicero addressed the Fourth Philippic.

giones arcessierit, ab eis relictus cum latronum manu in Galliam irruperit, Brutum oppugnet, Mutinam circumsedeat? quae vobis potest cum hoc gladiatore condicionis, aequitatis, legationis esse communitas? **4** quamquam, Quirites, non est illa legatio, sed denuntiatio belli, nisi paruerit: ita enim est decretum ut si legati ad Hannibalem mitterentur. mittuntur  5
enim qui nuntient ne oppugnet consulem designatum, ne Mutinam obsideat, ne provinciam depopuletur, ne dilectus habeat, sit in senatus populique Romani potestate. facile vero huic denuntiationi parebit, ut in patrum conscriptorum atque in vestra potestate sit qui in sua numquam fuerit! quid enim ille umquam arbitrio suo fecit? semper eo tractus est  10
quo libido rapuit, quo levitas, quo furor, quo vinolentia; semper eum duo dissimilia genera ⟨ten⟩uerunt, lenonum et latronum; ita domesticis stupris, forensibus parricidiis delectatur ut mulieri citius avarissimae paruerit quam senatui populoque Romano.

**5** Itaque, quod paulo ante feci in senatu, faciam apud vos. testificor,  15
denuntio, ante praedico nihil M. Antonium eorum quae sunt legatis mandata facturum; vastaturum agros, Mutinam obsessurum, dilectus qua possit habiturum. is est enim ille qui semper senatus iudicium et auctoritatem, semper voluntatem vestram potestatemque contempserit. an ille id faciat quod paulo ante decretum est, ut exercitum citra ⟨flu⟩men ⟨Rubi-  20
conem⟩, qui finis est Galliae, educeret, dum ne propius urbem Romam ducenta milia admoveret? huic denuntiationi ille pareat, ille se fluvio Rubicone ⟨ille⟩ ducentis milibus circumscriptum esse patiatur? **6** non is est Antonius; nam si esset, non commisisset ut ei senatus tamquam Hannibali initio belli Punici denuntiaret ne oppugnaret Saguntum. quod vero  25
ita avocatur a Mutina ut ab urbe tamquam pestifera flamma arceatur, quam habet ignominiam, quod iudicium senatus! quid quod a senatu dantur mandata legatis ut D. Brutum ⟨exercitum⟩que eius adeant eisque demonstrent summa in rem publicam merita beneficiaque eorum grata esse senatui populoque Romano eisque eam rem magnae laudi magnoque ho-  30
nori fore? passurumne censetis Antonium introire Mutinam legatos, exire inde tuto? numquam patietur, mihi credite. novi vi[n]olentiam, novi impudentiam, novi audaciam. **7** nec vero de illo sicut de homine aliquo debemus, sed ut de importunissima belua cogitare.

Quae cum ita sint, non omnino dissolutum est quod decrevit senatus:  35

1 accerserit (-sierit *Poggius*) *V* (*cf.* 4.6)    **4** 4 denuntiatione *V²*: -tiatio *V¹*    6 denunt-
*Pluygers*    7 populique *Poggius*: atque populi *V*    10 est *Halm*: et *V*: *om. Cus.*    11
uiolentia *codd. Ferrarii*    12 genera tenuerunt *Poggius*: generauerunt (te *supra lin. add.*
*V²*) *V*    13 post delectatur *aliqua excidisse suspicor*    **5** 20 flumen rubicem *V²*: men
*V*    21 propius *Poggius*: plus *V*    22 flumine *Poggius*: fluuione *V*: fluuio ⟨*    23 ille
*om. V in ras., add. Schöll*: et *Faërnus*    **6** 28 exercitumque *Hasebroek*: que *V*: militesque
*Poggius*    32 uiolentiam *Naugerius*: uino- *V*

Commonwealth and, when they abandoned him, burst into Gaul with a band of cutthroats and is now attacking Brutus, besieging Mutina? What can there be between you and this gladiator in the way of terms or fair play or an embassy? **4** And yet, Men of Rome, that is no embassy; it is a declaration of war if he does not obey. The decree reads as though envoys were being dispatched to Hannibal. They are sent to order him not to attack a consul-elect, not to besiege Mutina, not to lay waste the province, not to levy troops, and to be at the disposition of the Senate and People of Rome. Oh, doubtless he will find it an easy matter to obey such a message and to be at the Senate's disposition and yours—a man who was never at his own! What did he ever do of his own choice? Always he has been dragged in the wake of lust, frivolity, madness, inebriety. Always two quite different sets of people have had him in their grip—pimps and robbers. Such pleasure does he take in private debauchery and public murders that[2] he preferred to obey a rapacious female rather than the Senate and People of Rome.

**5** And so I shall do before you what I have just done in the Senate. I testify, I warn, I predict that Marcus Antonius will not carry out a single item in the envoys' commission: he *will* ravage the country, he *will* besiege Mutina, he *will* levy troops where he can. For he is a man who has always flouted the judgment and authority of the Senate, as he has your will and power. Or will *he* do what has just been decreed—that he must withdraw his army south of the river Rubicon, the boundary of Gaul, provided that he does not bring it within less than two hundred miles of the city of Rome? Is *he* one to obey such an order, to let himself be circumscribed by the river Rubicon and a two-hundred-mile limit? **6** No, not Antonius. If he were, he would never have so acted as to receive such a warning, like Hannibal at the beginning of the Punic War, warned by the Senate not to attack Saguntum. He is ordered off from Mutina but at the same time barred from Rome like a destructive conflagration. What a disgrace, what a judgment by the Senate that implies! The envoys are also commissioned by the Senate to proceed to Decimus Brutus and his men and make clear to them that their fine services and benefactions to the Commonwealth are appreciated by the Senate and People of Rome and that their conduct will be to their great credit and honor. Do you suppose Antonius will allow the envoys to enter Mutina or to leave the place in safety? He never will, take my word. I know his violence, his shamelessness, his audacity. **7** And truly we should not think of him as a human being, but as a savage, monstrous beast.

All this considered, what the Senate decreed is not altogether flabby. The

---

2. The logical connection between the *ita* and the *ut* clauses leaves something to be desired; hence my suspicion of a lacuna in the text.

habet atrocitatis aliquid legatio: utinam nihil haberet morae! nam cum
plerisque in rebus gerendis tarditas et procrastinatio odiosa est, tum hoc
bellum indiget celeritatis. succurrendum est D. Bruto, omnes undique
copiae colligendae; horam eximere unam in tali cive liberando sine scelere non possumus. **8** an ille non potuit, si Antonium consulem, si Gal-   5
liam Antoni provinciam iudicasset, legiones Antonio et provinciam
tradere, domum redire, triumphare, primus in hoc ordine, quoad magistratum iniret, sententiam dicere? quid negoti fuit? **9** sed cum se Brutum
esse meminisset vestraeque libertati natum, non otio suo, quid egit aliud
nisi ut paene corpore suo Gallia prohiberet Antonium?                       10

Ad hunc utrum legatos an legiones ire oportebat? sed praeterita omittamus: properent legati, quod video esse facturos; vos saga parate. est
enim ita decretum ut, si ille auctoritati senatus non paruisset, ad saga
iretur. ibitur; non parebit: nos amissos tot dies rei ge⟨re⟩ndae queremur.

Non metuo, Quirites, ne, cum audierit Antonius, me hoc et in senatu   15
et in contione confirmasse, numquam illum futurum in senatus potestate,
refellendi mei causa, ut ego nihil vidisse videar, vertat se et senatui pareat. numquam faciet; non invidebit huic meae gloriae; malet me sapien-
tem a vobis quam se modestum existimari. **10** quid? ipse si velit, num
etiam Lucium fratrem passurum arbitramur? nuper quidem dicitur ad   20
Tibur, ut opinor, cum ei labare M. Antonius videretur, mortem fratri esse
minitatus. etiamne ab hoc myrmillone Asiatico senatus mandata, legatorum verba audientur? nec enim secerni a fratre poterit, tanta praesertim
auctoritate. nam hic inter illos ⟨Laelius, ille⟩ Africanus est: pluris habetur
quam L. Trebellius, pluris quam T. Plancus, quam †tum exiluerit† adu-   25
lescens nobilis. Plancum quidem, qui omnibus sententiis maximo vestro
plausu condemnatus nescio quo modo se coniecit in turbam atque ita
maestus redi⟨i⟩t ut retractus, non reversus videretur, sic contemnit tamquam si illi aqua et igni interdictum sit: aliquando negat ei locum esse

**7** 2 plerisque *Poggius*: -rique *V*: *fort.* plerumque     4 horam eximere *Budaeus* (*cf.* 6.19):
h- exhibere *V*: moram exh- *Ursinus, alii alia*     unam *Lutz*: nullam *V*: ullam *Ursinus*     **9** 13 senatus *V²*: -tu *V¹*: -ti *coni. Halm*     **10** 24 Laelius, ille *addidi³*     25 *post*
plancius (*sic*) *legitur in V* uidete quan, *tum ex* 6.5 decertum (*i.e.* decretum) est . . . pareat     quam Extitius *Faërnus* (*cf. Two Studies, 36–37*): quantum exsiluerit *Sternkopf,
inepte*

embassy carries a certain amount of bite. I only wish it carried no delay. In warfare tardiness and procrastination is generally an infliction, and certainly this war calls for speed. We have to come to Decimus Brutus' aid; forces must be assembled from every quarter. The waste of a single hour in the liberation of such a fellow countryman is criminal. **8** If he had thought of Antonius as consul and of Gaul as Antonius' province, could he not have handed over the legions and the province to Antonius and returned home, celebrated a Triumph, spoken first in this House until he came into office?[3] Where was the difficulty? **9** But no, he remembered that he is a Brutus, born for your freedom, not his own comfort. And so what else did he do but block Antonius' entry into Gaul almost with his own body?

Which should we have sent to this man, envoys or legions? But let bygones be bygones. Let the envoys make haste, as I see they will. You, on your side, get your military cloaks ready. For it is so decreed: if he does not obey the authority of the Senate, it is military cloaks for us. It will be. He will not obey. But we shall be sorry to have lost so many days which might have been actively employed.

Men of Rome, I am not afraid that when Antonius hears I have asserted in the Senate and in an assembly that he will never be at the disposition of the Senate, he will turn around and obey the Senate in order to give me the lie and prove me blind. He will never do that. He will not begrudge me this credit. He will rather you think me shrewd than him well-conducted. **10** And even if he himself were willing, can we suppose that brother Lucius would allow it? Not long ago, near Tibur I think, Lucius is said to have threatened his brother's life, when he thought Marcus Antonius was wavering. Will he too, this myrmillo from Asia, listen to the Senate's commission, the words of the envoys? There is no chance of separating him from his brother, especially as he is so highly thought of. For in that company he is like Laelius to Africanus. He stands higher than Lucius Trebellius or Titus Plancus or *,[4] that young nobleman. Plancus, who was found guilty by a unanimous verdict, to loud applause from you, and who somehow or other threw himself into the crowd[5] and came back so down in the mouth that he looked as though he had been hauled back, not returned of his own accord—Plancus he[6] despises, as though he were an outlaw.[7] Sometimes he remarks that a man who set the Senate-

---

3. His right as consul-elect, the other consul-elect, L. Plancus, being in Gaul.

4. The reference in the corrupt manuscript text is almost certainly to the *clarissimus adulescens* of 13.28; *nobilis* is doubtless ironical.

5. Exiles whom Caesar allowed to return.

6. "He," I think, means Mark Antony, not Lucius, though Cicero has failed to make that clear.

7. Lit. "banned from fire and water," i.e. still in exile.

oportere in curia qui incenderit curiam. **11** nam Trebellium valde iam diligit: oderat tum, cum ille tabulis novis adversabatur; iam fert in oculis, postea quam ipsum Trebellium vidit sine tabulis novis salvum esse non posse. audisse enim vos arbitror, Quirites, quod etiam videre potuistis, cotidie sponsores et creditores L. Trebelli convenire. o Fides!—hoc enim       5
opinor Trebellium sumpsisse cognomen—quae potest esse maior fides quam fraudare creditores, domo profugere, propter aes alienum ire ad arma? ubi plausus ille in triumpho est, saepe ludis, ubi aedilitas delata summo studio bonorum? quis est qui hunc non casu existimet recte fecisse, nequitia sceleste?       10

**12** Sed redeo ad amores deliciasque vestras, L. Antonium, qui vos omnis in fidem suam recepit. negatis? num quisnam est vestrum qui tribum non habeat? certe nemo. atqui illum quinque et triginta tribus patronum adoptarunt. rursus reclamatis? aspicite illam a sinistra equestrem statuam inauratam, in qua quid inscriptum est? "quinque et triginta tribus       15
patrono." populi Romani igitur est patronus L. Antonius. malam quidem illi pestem! clamori enim vestro adsentior. non modo hic latro, quem clientem habere nemo velit, sed quis umquam tantis opibus, tantis rebus gestis fuit qui se populi Romani victoris dominique omnium gentium patronum dicere auderet? **13** in foro L. Antoni statuam videmus, sicut illam       20
Q. Tremuli, qui Hernicos devicit, ante Castoris. o impudentiam incredibilem! tantumne sibi sumpsit, quia Mylasis myrmillo Thraecem iugulavit, familiarem suum? quonam modo istum ferre possemus, si in hoc foro spectantibus vobis depugnasset? sed haec una statua. altera ⟨ab⟩ equitibus Romanis equo publico: qui item ascribunt, "patrono." quem umquam iste       25
ordo patronum adoptavit? si quemquam, debuit me. sed me omitto; quem censorem, quem imperatorem? agrum eis divisit. o sordidos qui acceperunt, improbum qui dedit! **14** statuerunt etiam tribuni militares qui in exercitu Caesaris bis fuerunt. quis est iste ordo? multi fuerunt multis in

**11** 5 Fide *Pluygers*      hoc] hinc *Poggius*      8 est] et *Sternkopf*      10 sceleste *Nipperdey*: est scelere *V*: scelerate *R. Klotz*      **13** 21 Tremuli *Beroaldus*: -melli *V*      24 ab *add. ed. Cratandrina*      27 acceperint *Ernesti*      28 dedit *Zielinski*: derrit *V*: dederit *Poggius*      **14** 29 bis *Garatoni*: duobus *V*: iterum *Orelli*

house on fire has no business to sit there. **11** For Trebellius he has a great regard nowadays. He used to hate him, when Trebellius was opposing the clean slate;[8] but now Trebellius is the apple of his eye, now that he has seen that Trebellius himself cannot survive without the clean slate. For I think you have heard, Men of Rome—you could have actually seen it—that Lucius Trebellius' sureties and creditors are meeting every day. Faith!—I think Trebellius has taken that word as his surname—what better *faith* than to defraud one's creditors, flee from home, join an army under pressure of debt? Where now is that applause at the Triumph,[9] and often at the games, where is that aedileship conferred with the enthusiastic support of the honest men? Can anybody doubt that his good behavior was due to chance, his criminality to a worthless character?

**12** But I return to your[10] favorite, your darling Lucius Antonius, who has taken you all under his wing. Oh, you say not? Is there any of you who doesn't have a tribe? Certainly not. Well, the thirty-five tribes chose him as their patron. More protest? Look at that gilt equestrian statue to the left. What does the inscription say? "The thirty-five tribes to their patron." So: Lucius Antonius is patron of the Roman People. To the devil with him!—I agree with your shouts. Who ever had so great a position, such a record of achievement as to dare to call himself the patron of the Roman People, conqueror and lord of all nations?—let alone this brigand whom nobody would want to have as a client. **13** We see a statue of Lucius Antonius in the Forum, like that of Quintus Tremulus who conquered the Hernicans in front of the temple of Castor. Unbelievable effrontery! Did he assume so much because as a myrmillo he killed his Thracian[11] (a friend of his own) at Mylasa? He would be quite insufferable if he had fought his bout in this Forum before your eyes! But this is only one statue. There is another from the Roman knights with public horses:[12] they too inscribe it "to our patron." Whom did this order ever adopt as patron? If anybody, it ought to have been myself![13] But forget me: what censor, what imperator? He divided land among them. A sordid business on the part of the recipients, an outrageous one on the part of the giver! **14** Yet another was put up by those who were twice military tribunes in Caesar's army.

8. Lit. "new tablets," i.e. cancellation of debts; cf. 10.22, 11.15.

9. Caesar's in 46. The applause must have come from men of property (*boni*) whose interests he had defended against Dolabella in 47.

10. Addressing the people.

11. I.e. a differently equipped gladiator, the standard opponent of a myrmillo.

12. Knights officially recognized as such by the censors. In general use the term "knight" was more widely applied, to any citizen possessing wealth above a certain figure.

13. The "Advice to a Candidate" addressed to Cicero by his brother in 64 (if genuine) says that he was supported by almost the entire order of knights (*Comm. petit.* 3).

legionibus per tot annos. eis quoque divisit Semurium. campus Martius restabat, nisi prius cum fratre fugisset. sed haec agrorum adsignatio paulo ante, Quirites, L. Caesaris, clarissimi viri et praestantissimi senatoris, sententia dissoluta est: huic enim adsensi septemvirum acta sustulimus. iacent beneficia Nuculae; friget patronus Antonius. nam possessores animo aequiore discedent: nullam impensam fecerant; nondum instruxerant, partim quia non confidebant, partim quia non habebant. 15 sed illa statua palmaris de qua, si meliora tempora essent, non possem sine risu dicere: "L. Antonio a Iano Medio patrono." itane? iam Ianus Medius in L. Antoni clientela est? quis umquam in illo Iano inventus est qui L. Antonio mille nummum ferret expensum? sed nimis multa de nugis: ad causam bellumque redeamus; quamquam non alienum fuit personas quasdam a vobis recognosci, ut quibuscum bellum gereretur possetis taciti cogitare.

Ego autem vos hortor, Quirites, ut, etiam si melius aliud fuit, tamen legatorum reditum [legatorum] exspectetis animo aequo. celeritas detracta de causa est; boni tamen aliquid accessit ad causam. 16 cum enim legati renuntiarint quod certe renuntiabunt, non in vestra potestate, non in senatus esse Antonium, quis erit tam improbus civis qui illum civem habendum putet? nunc enim sunt pauci illi quidem, sed tamen plures quam re publica dignum est, qui ita loquantur: "ne legatos quidem exspectabimus?" istam certe vocem simulationemque clementiae extorquebit istis res ipsa [publica]. quo etiam, ut confitear vobis, Quirites, minus hodierno die contendi, minus laboravi, ut mihi senatus adsentiens tumultum decerneret, saga sumi iuberet. malui viginti diebus post sententiam meam laudari ab omnibus quam a paucis hodie vituperari. 17 quapropter, Quirites, exspectate legatorum reditum et paucorum dierum molestiam devorate. qui cum redierint, si pacem adferent, cupidum me, si bellum, providum iudicatote.

An ego non provideam meis civibus, non dies noctesque de vestra libertate, de rei publicae salute cogitem? quid enim non debeo vobis, Quirites, quem vos ⟨a s⟩e ortum hominibus nobilissimis omnibus honoribus praetulistis? an ingratus sum? quis minus? qui partis honoribus eosdem in foro gessi labores quos petendis. rudis in re publica? quis ex⟨er⟩citatior?

5

10

15

20

25

30

**15** 9 itane? iam *Halm*: ita in eam *V*: itane *Gell. 1.16.5*     10 L. *V*², *Gell.*: *om. V*¹     est *V*², *Gell.*: sit *V*¹     quis *V*², *Gell.*: qui *V*¹, *Macrob. Sat. 1.5.5*     16 legatorum *del. Poggius*     17 ad causam] *num omittendum?*     **16** 23 publica *del. Muretus*     **17** 31–32 Quirites quem vos *Poggius*: quos plus quam *V*     32 a se *Poggius*: e *V*     33 partis *V*²: parus *V*¹

What category is this? There were many in many legions during all those years. For them too he divided the Semurian land. The Field of Mars remained—but he decamped with his brother before he got that far. However, this allocation of lands, Men of Rome, has just been annulled on the motion of that illustrious gentleman and outstanding senator Lucius Caesar. Following his motion we canceled the acts of the Board of Seven. Nucula's favors are at a discount. Patron Antonius is out of date. As for the occupiers, they will leave without too much distress. They had not been put to any expense. They had not yet equipped their holdings, some from lack of confidence, others from lack of money. **15** But then there is the statue that takes the prize—if the times were better, I could not help laughing as I say the words: "To Lucius Antonius, our patron, from the Exchange."[14] Really? Is the Exchange now numbered among Lucius Antonius' clientele? Who was ever found in that Exchange to lend Lucius Antonius a thousand sesterces? But I have dwelt too long on trifles. Let us get back to our cause and our war. All the same, it was not amiss that you should pass certain personages in review, so that in your own minds you could think about the kind of people we are fighting.

Now I urge you, Men of Rome, to wait calmly for the return of the envoys, even though a different course would have been better. Our cause has lost something in speed, but it has gained something too. **16** When the envoys report, as report they surely will, that Antonius is *not* at your disposition, nor at the Senate's, who will be so bad a citizen as to think that *he* should be considered one? At present there are some, few to be sure but more than befits the Commonwealth, who say: "Are we not even going to wait for the envoys?" The event itself will wrench that slogan, that pretense of clemency, away from them. For that reason, Men of Rome, to be frank with you, I put up less of a fight today, was less concerned that the Senate should adopt my motion to decree a tumult and order the wearing of military cloaks. I thought it better that my motion be praised by everyone in twenty days' time than blamed by a few today. **17** Therefore, Men of Rome, wait for the return of the envoys. Swallow a few days' inconvenience. When they do return, if they bring peace, count me as prejudiced; if war, as provident.

*Should* I not look ahead for my fellow countrymen? *Should* I not be thinking day and night about your freedom and the safety of the Commonwealth? What ought I not to do for you,[15] Men of Rome? You preferred me to all offices, a man whose family starts with himself, before the noblest in the land. Am I ungrateful? None less so. When I had won my honors, I went on working in the Forum just as when I was seeking them. Am I a novice in public affairs?

---

14. Janus Medius, an archway leading into the Forum where bankers carried on their business.
15. Not "what do I not owe to you?"

qui viginti iam ⟨an⟩nos bellum geram cum impiis civibus. **18** quam ob
rem, Quirites, consilio quantum potero, labore plus paene quam potero,
excubabo, vigilaboque pro vobis. etenim quis est civis, praesertim hoc
gradu quo me vos esse voluistis, tam oblitus benefici vestri, tam immemor patriae, tam inimicus dignitati suae quem non excitet, non inflammet    5
tantus vester iste consensus? multas magnasque habui consul contiones,
multis interfui: nullam umquam vidi tantam quanta nunc vestrum est.
unum sentitis omnes, unum studetis, M. Antoni conatus avertere a re
publica, furorem exstinguere, opprimere audaciam. idem volunt omnes
ordines; eodem incumbunt municipia, coloniae, cuncta Italia. itaque se-    10
natum bene sua sponte firmum firmiorem vestra auctoritate fecistis.

   **19** Venit tempus, Quirites, serius omnino quam dignum populo Romano fuit, sed tamen ita maturum ut differri iam hora non possit. fuit
aliquis fatalis casus, ut ita dicam, quem tulimus, quoquo modo ferendus
fuit: nunc si quis erit, erit voluntarius. populum Romanum servire fas    15
non est, quem di immortales omnibus gentibus imperare voluerunt. res in
extremum est adducta discrimen; de libertate decernitur. aut vincatis
oportet, Quirites, quod profecto et pietate vestra et tanta concordia con-
sequemini, aut quidvis potius quam serviatis. aliae nationes servitutem
pati possunt, populi Romani est propria libertas.    20

**18** 7 umquam] *hic rursus inc. D*    uestra *nstv*    8 conatus *Poggius*: -ur *V*: -um *D*    **19**
12 Quirites *om. D*    12–13 populo Romano fuit sed] re p. fuisset *D*    16 gentibus *om.*
*D*    18 consequamini *V*    20 est *V*²: es *V*¹: res est *D*

Who has more experience? For twenty years I have been waging war against traitors. **18** Therefore, Men of Rome, I shall keep watch and ward for you. I shall advise to the best of my power, and labor almost beyond my power. After all, is any citizen, especially of the rank to which you have been pleased to call me, so forgetful of your favor, so unmindful of his country, so inimical to his own standing, as not to be aroused and fired by your amazing unanimity? As consul I held many great assemblies, I have taken part in many more; never have I seen one so large as yours today. You all have one sentiment, one desire: to turn Marcus Antonius' attempts away from the Commonwealth, to quench his fury, crush his audacity. All classes want the same. The municipalities, the colonies, all Italy are throwing their weight the same way. The Senate is commendably firm of its own volition, but you have made it firmer by your backing.

**19** The time has come, Men of Rome, later than befitted the Roman People it is true, but not too late—only it cannot be deferred another hour. What may be called a fate-ordained misfortune befell us. We endured it as best we could. If anything of the kind happens now, it will be of our own choice. The Immortal Gods willed that the Roman People rule over all nations; it is against their law that the Roman People should be slaves. The ultimate crisis is upon us. The stake is freedom. Either you must be victorious, Men of Rome, as you surely will be in virtue of your patriotism and united will, or—anything but slavery! Other races can endure servitude, but the birthright of the Roman People is freedom.

# VII

## INTRODUCTION

Shortly after the meetings of 1–4 January 43 the Senate passed a decree instructing the consuls, either one or both, to go to the war at Mutina. The lot fell to Hirtius. Recruiting and arming was in progress throughout Italy, though damped down, as Cicero claimed (7.1, 14), by news of the embassy to Antony. Meanwhile Antony's sympathizers in Rome were using the interval to make propaganda on his behalf (7.1–4). Cicero took advantage of a routine meeting of the Senate, probably in the third week of January, to reinforce his own message. Peace with Antony would be dishonorable, dangerous—and impossible.

**1** Parvis de rebus sed fortasse necessariis consulimur, patres conscripti. de Appia via et de Moneta consul, de Lupercis tribunus plebis refert. quarum rerum etsi facilis explicatio videtur, tamen animus aberrat a sententia suspensus curis maioribus. adducta est enim, patres conscripti, res in maximum periculum et in extremum paene discrimen. non  5
sine causa legatorum istam missionem semper timui, numquam probavi: quorum reditus quid sit adlaturus ignoro; exspectatio quidem quantum adferat languoris animis quis non videt? non enim se tenent ei qui senatum dolent ad auctoritatis pristinae spem revirescere, coniunctum huic ordini populum Romanum, conspirantem Italiam, paratos exercitus, ex-  10
peditos duces. **2** iam nunc fingunt responsa Antoni eaque defendunt. alii postulare illum ut omnes exercitus dimittantur: scilicet legatos ad eum misimus, non ut pareret et dicto audiens esset huic ordini, sed ut condiciones ferret, leges imponeret, reserare nos exteris gentibus Italiam iuberet, se praesertim incolumi a quo maius periculum quam ab ullis na-  15
tionibus extimescendum est. **3** alii remittere eum nobis Galliam citeriorem, illam ultimam postulare: praeclare, ex qua non legiones solum sed etiam nationes ad urbem conetur adducere. alii nihil eum iam nisi modeste: postulare Macedoniam, ⟨quam⟩ suam vocat omnino, quoniam Gaius frater est inde revocatus. sed quae provincia est ex qua illa fax ex-  20
citare non possit incendium?

Itaque idem quasi providi cives et senatores diligentes bellicum me cecinisse dicunt, suscipiunt pacis patrocinium. nonne sic disputant? irritatum Antonium non oportuit: nequam est homo ille atque confidens; multi praeterea improbi, quos quidem a se primum numerare possunt qui  25
haec loquuntur; eos cavendos esse denuntiant. utrum igitur in nefariis civibus ulciscendi, cum possis, an pertimescendi diligentior cautio est? **4** atque haec ei loquuntur qui quondam propter levitatem populares habebantur. ex quo intellegi potest animo illos abhorruisse semper ab optimo civitatis statu, ⟨casu⟩ non voluntate fuisse popularis. qui enim evenit ut,  30
qui in rebus improbis populares fuerint, idem in re una maxime populari, quod eadem salutaris rei publicae sit, improbos se quam populares esse malint? me quidem semper, uti scitis, adversarium multitudinis temeritati

**1** 2 pl. *om. V*[1]    4 a curis *Nonius 386*    6 istam *om. V*    9 spem reuiuiscere (r- s- *b*) *D*    **2** 14 leges imponeret *om. D*    **3** 19 modesti *D*    quam *add. Gruter, quo non recepto post* postulare *vel post* Macedoniam *dist. vulgo*    20 Gaius *om. V*    inde *om. V*    21 posset *D*    22 providi cives et] prouendicius esset *vel sim. D*    23 pacis *Ursinus* (*cf.* 12.6): patris *Vtv*: partis *bns*    nonne *V*[2] *in ras.*: qui (*om. t*) *D, fort. recte*    23–24 irritatum . . . nequam est *om. V*[1]    irritatum *Halm*: -tatu *V*[2]: -tari *D*    27 ulciscendis *nstv*: -dum *b*    pertimescendis *nstvV*[2]    **4** 28 habebantur] appellabantur *D*    30 casu[3] *addidi*    conuenit (u- *t*) *D*    33 aduersatum *D*

**1** Members of the Senate, we are being consulted about minor matters, though necessary perhaps. The consul refers to us concerning the Appian Way and the Mint, the tribune of the plebs concerning the Luperci. The arrangement of these items seems to offer no difficulty, but the mind strays from the motion before us, held in suspense by larger anxieties. For the time of maximum danger has arrived, well-nigh the ultimate crisis. It was not for nothing that I feared that mission of envoys, never approved of it. What their return will bring I know not, but the slackening of men's spirits which the waiting brings is plain to everyone. Those who are sorry to see the Senate reinvigorated in the hope of regaining its old authority, sorry to see the Roman People leagued with this House, Italy in unison, the armies prepared, the generals ready—such persons are letting themselves go. **2** They are already inventing Antonius' answer and defending it. Some say he is demanding that all armies be dismissed. I suppose we sent envoys to him, not for him to obey and bow to the will of this House, but to have him state terms, impose conditions, order us to open Italy to foreign races—and that while he himself, from whom there is worse to fear than from any tribes, keeps his position intact. **3** Others say he is letting us have Hither Gaul and demanding the other, outer Gaul. Splendid! From there he will set about bringing up not merely legions but tribes against Rome. Others say he is now asking nothing but what is reasonable: he wants Macedonia, which he calls absolutely his own seeing that his brother Gaius has been recalled from it. But where is the province from which such a firebrand cannot start a conflagration?

And so these same people, posing as provident citizens and conscientious senators, say that I am a warmonger and set themselves up as advocates of peace. Doesn't their line of argument go like this? Antonius should not have been provoked. He is a bold, bad man. And there are many wicked folk besides (those who talk this way may as well begin the list with their own names); they warn us to beware of these. Well, when you are dealing with villains, which is the safest precaution, to punish them when you can or to be frightened of them? **4** Those who talk in this vein are the politicians who for their irresponsibility used to be called "people's men."[1] Hence we can see that all along they disliked the constitution at its best, and that they were "people's men" by chance, not inclination. How else does it happen that the same folk who were "people's men" in bad causes, prefer to be disloyal rather than "popular" in the most popular cause that ever was, because it is also for the good of the Commonwealth? As you know, I have always opposed the caprices

---

1. Cf. Philippic 1 n. 32.

haec fecit praeclarissima causa popularem. **5** et quidem dicuntur vel potius se ipsi dicunt consularis: quo nomine dignus est nemo, nisi qui tanti honoris onus potest sustinere. faveas tu hosti, ille litteras ad te mittat de sua spe rerum secundarum, eas tu laetus proferas, recites, describendas etiam des improbis civibus, eorum augeas animos, bonorum spem virtutemque debilites; et te consularem aut senatorem, denique civem putes? accipiet in optimam partem C. Pansa, fortissimus consul atque optimus; etenim dicam animo amicissimo: hunc ipsum, mihi hominem familiarissimum, nisi talis consul esset ut omnis vigilias, curas, cogitationes in rei publicae salute defigeret, consulem non putarem. **6** quamquam nos ab ineunte illius aetate usus, consuetudo, studiorum etiam honestissimorum societas similitudoque devinxit, eiusdemque cura incredibilis in asperrimis belli civilis periculis perspecta docuit non modo salutis sed etiam dignitatis meae fuisse fautorem, tamen eundem, ut dixi, nisi talis consul esset, negare esse consulem auderem: idem non modo consulem esse dico sed memoria mea praestantissimum atque optimum consulem, non quin pari virtute et voluntate alii fuerint, sed tantam causam non habuerunt in qua et voluntatem suam et virtutem declararent. **7** huius magnitudini animi, gravitati, sapientiae tempestas est oblata formidolosissimi temporis. tum autem illustratur consulatus, cum gubernat rem publicam, si non optabili, at necessario tempore. magis autem necessarium, patres conscripti, nullum tempus umquam fuit.

Itaque ego ille qui semper pacis auctor fui cuique pax, praesertim civilis, quamquam omnibus bonis, tamen in primis fuit optabilis—omne enim curriculum industriae nostrae in foro, in curia, in amicorum periculis propulsandis elaboratum est; hinc honores amplissimos, hinc mediocris opes, hinc dignitatem si quam habemus consecuti sumus— **8** ego igitur pacis, ut ita dicam, alumnus, qui quantuscumque sum (nihil enim mihi adrogo) sine pace civili certe non fuissem—periculose dico: quem ad modum accepturi, patres conscripti, sitis, horreo, sed pro mea perpetua cupiditate vestrae dignitatis retinendae et augendae quaeso oroque vos, patres conscripti, ut primo, etsi erit vel acerbum auditu vel incredibile a M. Cicerone esse dictum, accipiatis sine offensione quod di-

1 fecit aduersatum *V*     **5** 2 se] idem (id *b*) *D*     non quo *V*[1]     3 onus *Cobet*: nomen *codd.*     hosti . . . mittat] hostiliter sat tibi ille mittat *nstv*     6 aut denique *DV*[2]     7 in *om. D*     10 configeret *D*     **6** 11–16 illius h. m (= hic minus, *lacunae signum*) pagate memoria mea *V*[1] (*de V*[2] *v. Fe.*), *sed quae desunt in* 7.11 *inter* quod *et* erat bellum *reponit*     11 aetate illius *nstV*[2]     12 devinxit] coniunxit *D*: -iungit *V*[2]     curam incredibilem *DV*[2]     13 perspecta docuit] perspexi *DV*[2]     14 fuisse factorem (*corr. Ursinus*) *V*[1]: *om. DV*[2]: eum esse fautorem *C. F. W. Müller*     16 sed etiam *DV*[2]     quin] quia non *D*     17 alii non *V*[1]     18 et uirtutem (-te *t*) et uoluntatem (-te *t*) suam (sua *t*) *D*     **7** 20 gubernauit *V*: -abit *R. Klotz*     24 mihi tamen *D*     **8** 28 igitur] itaque *D*     32 si erit (fie- *n*) *D*

of the crowd, but this splendid cause has made a "people's man" of me. **5** And these gentry are called consulars, or rather that is what they call themselves. Nobody deserves that name unless he can support the burden of so great an honor. Are you,[2] sir, to back the enemy? Is he to send you letters about his hopes of success? Are you to produce them blithely, read them aloud, even give them to disloyal citizens to copy, hearten such, sap the hope and courage of honest men? And then are you to regard yourself as a consular, or a senator, or even a Roman? Our brave and excellent consul Gaius Pansa will take what I am about to say in good part, for I speak in the friendliest spirit: even him, my intimate friend, I should not consider a consul if he were not a consul who concentrates all his watching and worrying and thinking upon the safety of the Commonwealth. **6** From his earliest youth we have been linked by friendly intercourse and, furthermore, by our similarity and association in honorable pursuits. In the most alarming situations during the Civil War the sedulous concern I saw on his part showed that he was anxious not only for my safety but for my dignity. And yet, all this notwithstanding, I repeat that I should make bold to declare him no consul if he were not the consul he is. At the same time I declare that he *is* a consul; not only that, but the best, most outstanding consul I can remember. I do not say that others were not possessed of equal ability and goodwill, but they had no such great cause in which to demonstrate both their goodwill and their ability. **7** Pansa's high-mindedness, responsibility, and wisdom have been challenged by a political storm, a terrifying crisis. Now a consulship comes into the limelight when it guides the Commonwealth, at a crucial, if undesired, juncture. Members of the Senate, no juncture has ever been more crucial than the present.

I have always been an advocate of peace. All good men desire peace, especially peace between fellow countrymen, but I have desired it more than most. My round of activity has always been worked out in the Forum, in the Senate-house, in protecting friends in danger. That is how I have won the highest honors, moderate wealth, and any prestige I may enjoy. **8** Well, then: I, who might call peace my foster mother, who, whatever I am (I make no claims for myself), certainly should not have been what I am without peace in the community—these are dangerous words, Members of the Senate, and I tremble to think how you are going to receive them; but I beg and beseech you, Members of the Senate, bearing in mind my unflagging zeal for the maintenance and enhancement of your prestige, first of all to receive what I am about to say without offense and not to repudiate it until I have explained its meaning, even though the words grate upon your ears and you can scarcely believe they are Marcus Cicero's—I, the life-long encomiast and advocate of

---

2. Addressing Calenus; cf. 12.1.

xero, neve id prius quam quale sit explicaro repudietis—ego ille, dicam saepius, pacis semper laudator, semper auctor, pacem cum M. Antonio esse nolo. magna spe ingredior in reliquam orationem, patres conscripti, quoniam periculosissimum locum silentio sum praetervectus.

**9** Cur igitur pacem nolo? quia turpis est, quia periculosa, quia esse non　5 potest. quae tria dum explico, peto a vobis, patres conscripti, ut eadem benignitate qua soletis mea verba audiatis.

Quid est inconstantia, levitate, mobilitate cum singulis hominibus, tum vero universo senatui turpius? quid porro inconstantius quam quem modo hostem non verbo sed re multis decretis iudicaritis, cum hoc subito pacem　10 velle coniungi? **10** nisi vero, cum C. Caesari meritos illi quidem honores et debitos, sed tamen singularis et immortalis decrevistis, unam ob causam quod contra M. Antonium exercitum comparavisset, non hostem tum Antonium iudicavistis, nec tum hostis est a vobis iudicatus Antonius cum laudati auctoritate vestra veterani milites qui C. Caesarem secuti es-　15 sent, nec tum hostem Antonium iudicastis cum fortissimis legionibus, quod illum qui consul appellabatur, cum esset hostis, reliquissent, vacationes, pecunias, agros spopondistis. **11** quid? cum Brutum omine quodam illius generis et nominis natum ad rem publicam liberandam exercitumque eius pro libertate populi Romani bellum gerentem cum Antonio　20 provinciamque fidelissimam atque optimam, Galliam, laudibus amplissimis adfecistis, tum non hostem iudicastis Antonium? quid? cum decrevistis ut consules, alter ambove, ad bellum proficiscerentur, quod erat bellum, si hostis Antonius non erat? **12** ad id igitur profectus est vir fortissimus, meus collega et familiaris, A. Hirtius consul. at qua imbecilli-　25 tate, qua macie! sed animi viris corporis infirmitas non retardavit. aequum, credo, putavit vitam quam populi Romani votis retinuisset pro libertate populi Romani in discrimen adducere. **13** quid? cum dilectus haberi tota Italia iussistis, cum vacationes omnis sustulistis, tum ille hostis non est iudicatus? armorum officinas in urbe videtis; milites cum　30 gladiis sequuntur consulem; praesidio sunt specie consuli, re et veritate nobis; omnes sine ulla recusatione, summo etiam cum studio nomina dant, parent auctoritati vestrae: non est iudicatus hostis Antonius?

---

1 explicaro *Vb*²: -auero *D*　　2 M. *om. V*　　**9** 8 mobilitate leuitate *D*　　9 vero] uero inconstanti *V*¹　　10 iudicaritis *V*²: -aretis *V*¹: -auistis *bnsv*: -abitis *t*　　**10** 11 merito *V*　　quidem illi *D*　　14 tum *Halm*: cum *V*¹ (*del. V*²): *om. D*　　iudicatus est *nstv*　　15 C. *om. D*　　16 iudicauistis *bnst*　　**11** 18 homine *V*: -em *nsv*: non enim *t*　　quondam *nsV*²: quoddam *t*: quendam *v*　　19 istius *V*　　21 Galliam *del. Baiter*　　23 ad bellum .R. (= require) *V*　　*post* quod *verba* te usus . . . dico sed *habet V; cf. ad 7.6*　　**12** 24 ad id³ *scripsi*: quid *Vb*: quo *nstv*　　27 pertinuisset *V*　　**13** 30 me (*del. n*²) milites *D*　　32–33 nomina dant] -inandi (-da *t*) *D*

peace, I say it again, am against peace with Marcus Antonius. Members of the Senate, I enter upon the rest of my speech in good hope, now that I have passed the danger point without a sound of protest.

**9** Why, then, am I against peace? Because it is dishonorable, because it is dangerous, because it is impossible. While I explain these three points, Members of the Senate, may I request you to listen to my words with your customary benevolence?

Is anything more dishonorable to individuals and especially to the entire Senate than inconsistency, irresponsibility, fickleness? And could anything be more inconsistent than suddenly to want peace made with a man whom in many recent decrees you have declared a public enemy, not in word but in substance? **10** Or did you not declare Antonius an enemy when you conferred extraordinary, unforgettable honors (not but that they were his right and due) upon Gaius Caesar for the sole reason that he had raised an army against Marcus Antonius? Did you not declare Antonius an enemy when the veteran soldiers who had followed Gaius Caesar were commended by your authority? Did you not declare Antonius an enemy when you promised exemptions, money, and lands to the gallant legions because they had abandoned an enemy who was called a consul? **11** When in the most ample terms you commended Brutus, whose family and name presaged him born to liberate the Commonwealth, and his army, as they waged war against Antonius for the freedom of the Roman People, and the loyal and faithful province of Gaul, did you not then declare Antonius an enemy? When you decreed that the consuls, either or both, should set forth to war, where was the war if Antonius was not an enemy? **12** To that war, therefore, our gallant consul Aulus Hirtius, my colleague[3] and friend, set out. How frail he was, how emaciated! But bodily infirmity did not retard the strength of his spirit. I imagine he thought it only fair to hazard on behalf of the Roman People a life saved by the Roman People's prayers. **13** When you ordered levies of troops to be held throughout Italy and canceled all exemptions, was Antonius not declared an enemy then? You see arms factories in Rome. Soldiers follow the consul sword in hand, outwardly for his protection, in truth and reality for ours. Everyone is enlisting, without any excuses, in fact with the greatest enthusiasm, obeying your authority. Has not Antonius been declared an enemy?

---

3. As augur.

**14** At legatos misimus. heu, me miserum! cur senatum cogor, quem
laudavi semper, reprehendere? quid? vos censetis, patres conscripti,
legatorum missionem populo Romano vos probavisse? non intellegitis,
non auditis meam sententiam flagitari? cui cum pridie frequentes essetis
adsensi, postridie ad spem estis inanem pacis devoluti. quam turpe porro    5
legiones ad senatum legatos mittere, senatum ad Antonium! quamquam
illa legatio non est, denuntiatio est paratum illi exitium, nisi paruerit huic
ordini. quid refert? tamen opinio est gravis. missos enim legatos omnes
vident; decreti nostri non omnes verba noverunt. retinenda est igitur nobis
constantia, gravitas, perseverantia; repetenda vetus illa severitas, si qui-    10
dem auctoritas senatus decus, honestatem, laudem dignitatemque desiderat, quibus rebus hic ordo caruit nimium diu. sed erat tunc excusatio
oppressis, misera illa quidem, sed tamen iusta: nunc nulla est. liberati
regio dominatu videbamur: multo postea gravius urgebamur armis domesticis. ea ipsa depulimus nos quidem: extorquenda sunt. quod si non    15
possumus facere—dicam quod dignum est et senatore et Romano homine—moriamur.

**15** Quanta enim illa erit rei publicae turpitudo, quantum dedecus,
quanta labes, dicere in hoc ordine sententiam M. Antonium consulari
loco! cuius ut omittam innumerabilia scelera urbani consulatus, in quo    20
pecuniam publicam maximam dissipavit, exsules sine lege restituit, vectigalia divendidit, provincias de populi Romani imperio sustulit, regna
addixit pecunia, leges civitati per vim imposuit, armis aut obsedit aut exclusit senatum: ut haec, inquam, omittam, ne hoc quidem cogitatis, eum
qui Mutinam, coloniam populi Romani firmissimam, oppugnarit, impe-    25
ratorem populi Romani, consulem designatum, obsederit, depopulatus
agros sit, hunc in eum ordinem recipi a quo totiens ob has ipsas causas
hostis iudicatus sit quam foedum flagitiosumque sit?

**16** Satis multa de turpitudine. dicam deinceps, ut proposui, de periculo: quod etsi minus est fugiendum quam turpitudo, tamen offendit ani-    30
mos maioris partis hominum magis.

Poteritis igitur exploratam habere pacem, cum in civitate Antonium
videbitis vel potius Antonios? nisi forte contemnitis Lucium: ego ne
Gaium quidem. sed, ut video, dominabitur Lucius. est enim patronus

---

**14** 3 vos *om. D*      probisse $V^1$: -basse $V^2$      4 audistis $V^1$      cui] qui $DV^2$      5 revoluti
*Ernesti*      porro est *b*: est p- *nstvV²*      7 est (*alt.*)] sit *Vb*      7–8 nisi . . . quid *om.*
*V*      8 fert *V*      grauis *Pluygers*: grui $V^1$: grauior $DV^2$      9 uestri *D*      11 dignita-
temque *V Cus.*: -atem *D*      12 rebus *om. D*      tum *bnst*      14 tum regio *D*      multo
. . . urgebamur *om. D*      15 nos] nunc *D*      ui extorquenda *D*      **15** 18 erit illa *D*
*Cus.*      23 aut (*pr.*) *om. D*      25–26 firmissimam . . . Romani *om. D*      27 hunc]
nunc *coni. Clark, fort. recte*      **16** 30 etsi] si *D*      32 ciuitatem *V*: -e M. *coni.*
*Halm*      33 uideatis *D*      33–34 ne Gaium] egnatium *vel sim. D*      34 est] sed *V*

**14** Ah, but we have sent envoys. This is a sad moment for me. Why am I forced to find fault with the Senate, which I have always praised? Do you, Members of the Senate, really think you have won the Roman People's approval for the envoys' mission? Don't you understand, don't you hear that they are crying out for *my* motion, the motion which you flocked to support one day only to tumble over the next because of an empty hope of peace? How dishonorable that legions should send envoys to the Senate[4] and the Senate send envoys to Antonius! True, it is not an embassy, it is a warning that he must expect to be destroyed if he does not obey this House. Never mind; the effect on public opinion is serious all the same. Everyone sees that envoys have been dispatched, but not everyone knows the wording of our decree. Therefore we must hold to our resolution, responsibility, and determination. We must get back to the old strict standards—if the authority of the Senate needs seemliness, respectability, credit, and dignity, things this House has too long been without. *Then*,[5] however, there was some excuse, held down as we were; a sorry excuse, but a fair one. There is none now. It looked as though we had been freed from the rule of a monarch. Later we were pressed far harder by weapons in our midst. Those too we thrust off; now we must wrench them away. If we cannot do that—I speak as befits a Senator and a Roman—let us die.

**15** For what a dishonor to the Commonwealth, what a disgrace, what a blot it will be if Marcus Antonius speaks in this House as a consular! To say nothing of the countless misdeeds of his consulship in Rome, during which he dissipated a vast sum of public money, brought back exiles without a law, sold off state revenues, removed provinces from the empire of the Roman People, foisted laws on the community by violence, beleaguered or excluded the Senate with armed men—to say nothing, I repeat, of all this, do you not even consider how foul a scandal it will be that the man who has laid siege to Mutina, one of the most staunch of Roman colonies, and blockaded a Roman imperator and consul-elect, and devastated the territory should be readmitted to this House, which has repeatedly declared him an enemy for these very reasons?

**16** So much for dishonor. Next, as I proposed, I shall speak of danger. That is less to be avoided than dishonor, but the majority of people dislike it more.

Well, then, can you have any assurance of peace seeing Antonius, or rather the three of them, in the community? Perhaps you don't take Lucius seriously? I take even Gaius seriously. But, as I see it, Lucius will rule the roost. He is

4. Nothing is known of these envoys.
5. Under Caesar.

quinque et triginta tribuum, quarum sua lege qua cum C. Caesare magistratus partitus est suffragium sustulit, patronus centuriarum equitum Romanorum quas item sine suffragio esse voluit, patronus eorum qui tribuni
militares fuerunt, patronus Iani Medii. **17** quis huius potentiam poterit
sustinere? praesertim cum eosdem in agros etiam deduxerit. quis um-        5
quam omnis tribus, quis equites Romanos, quis tribunos militaris, ⟨quis
Ianum Medium habuit clientis⟩? Gracchorum potentiam maiorem fuisse
arbitramini quam huius gladiatoris futura sit? quem gladiatorem non ita
appellavi ut interdum etiam M. Antonius gladiator appellari solet, sed ut
appellant qui plane et Latine loquuntur. myrmillo in Asia depugnavit.     10
cum ornasset Thraecidicis comitem et familiarem suum, illum miserum
fugientem iugulavit, luculentam tamen ipse plagam accepit, ut declarat
cicatrix. **18** qui familiarem iugularit, quid is occasione data faciet inimico? et qui illud animi causa fecerit, hunc praedae causa quid facturum
putatis? non rursus improbos decuriabit, non sollicitabit rursus agrarios,  15
non queretur expulsos? M. vero Antonius non is erit ad quem omni motu
concursus fiat civium perditorum? ut nemo sit alius nisi ei qui una sunt et
ei qui hic ei nunc aperte favent, parumne erunt multi, praesertim cum
bonorum praesidia discesserint, illi parati sint ad nutum futuri? ego vero
metuo, si hoc tempore consilio lapsi erimus, ne illi brevi tempore nimis    20
multi nobis esse videantur.

    **19** Nec ego pacem nolo, sed pacis nomine bellum involutum refor-
mido. qua re si pace frui volumus, bellum gerendum est; si bellum omittimus, pace numquam fruemur. est autem vestri consili, patres conscripti, in posterum quam longissime providere. idcirco in hac custodia et  25
tamquam specula collocati sumus uti vacuum metu populum Romanum
nostra vigilia et prospicientia redderemus. turpe est summo consilio orbis
terrae, praesertim in re tam perspicua, consilium intellegi defuisse. **20** eos
consules habemus, eam populi Romani alacritatem, eum consensum Italiae, eos duces, eos exercitus, ut nullam calamitatem res publica accipere  30
possit sine culpa senatus. equidem non deero: monebo, praedicam, de-

1 magistratum *V*: -tuum comitia (*vel* nominationem) *coni. Halm*     2 Romanorum *om.*
*nstv*    3 idem *D*    **17** 6–7 quis (*ult.*) . . . clientis *addidi*     8 futura est *Halm*     10
ei qui *D*    **18** 13 iugularat *D*    is *Faërnus*: si *V*: hic *D*     14 fecerit . . . causa *om.*
*D*    16 qu(a)eret *bnsv*: quaeret urbe *Muretus*: conquiret *Busche*     M. *om. V*¹     17
fiat] fit *bv*: sit *ns*: sit at *t*     17–18 ii . . . et ii *V*: illi . . . et hi *D*     19 praesidiis (-ii *s*)
cesserint *D*     20 consilii *V*: -iis *coni. Halm*     **19** 22 nouolutum *V*: nouo (*ex* noluo)
latum *Cus.*: obvol- *Muretus, fort. recte*     23 omittimus *V*¹ *Cus.*: -temus *DV*²     24
uestri *V*¹ *Cus.*: ueteris *DV*²     25 custodia et *V*²: -iet *V*¹: -ia *D Cus.*     26 specula *V*
*Cus.*: in s- *D*     uti vacuum *Garatoni*: ut tua quom *V*: ut tutum ab omni *Cus.*: ut uacuum
*bnsv*: utacum *t*     27 prospicientia *Vb Cus.*: -enda *t*: prouidentia *nsv*     28 intelligendi
*nstv*    **20** 31 praedicabo (-co *t*) *D*

patron of the thirty-five tribes, whose votes he took away by the law in which he shared out the magistracies with Gaius Caesar.[6] He is patron of the centuries of Roman knights, whom he likewise chose to disenfranchise, patron of the ex–military tribunes, patron of the Exchange. **17** Who will be able to stand up to his power, especially when he has settled those same on lands? Who ever had all the tribes, the Roman knights, the military tribunes, the Exchange for clients? Do you imagine the Gracchi had greater power than this gladiator will have? And I do not call him a gladiator as Marcus Antonius too is sometimes called a gladiator, but speaking plain Latin. He fought a bout in Asia as a myrmillo. He got up one of his staff, a personal friend, as a Thracian, slaughtered the poor devil as he tried to get away, but took a swingeing cut himself; he still has the scar to show it. **18** He slaughtered a familiar friend: what will he do to an enemy, given the chance? He did that for fun; what do you think he will do for loot? Will he not be impaneling rascals yet again, stirring up the land-hungry, protesting against evictions? As for Marcus Antonius, whenever there is trouble, he will be the rallying point for desperate elements, will he not? Even if these include only the people he has with him and those who are now openly supporting him here, won't there be enough of them, especially as the forces protecting honest citizens will have gone away, while *they* will be ready to move at a nod? For my part I am afraid that if we make a mistake now, we shall soon find there are only too many of them.

**19** I am not against peace, but I dread war camouflaged as peace. Therefore, if we wish to enjoy peace, we must wage war. If we fail to wage war, peace we shall never enjoy. It is for you in your wisdom, Members of the Senate, to look ahead as far as you can. We have been given this charge, placed as it were on a watchtower, in order that by our vigilance and foresight we might make the Roman People void of fear. It is a dishonor if the supreme council of the world is seen to lack wisdom, especially in so plain a case as this. **20** Such are our consuls, such is the ready spirit of the Roman People, such is the unanimous sentiment of Italy, such are our generals and armies, that no calamity can befall the Commonwealth save by the fault of the Senate. As for me, I shall not fail. I shall warn, I shall foretell, I shall give notice, I

---

6. As tribune in 44 he put through a law authorizing Caesar to appoint half the magistrates, consuls excluded (Suet. *Iul.* 41).

nuntiabo, testabor semper deos hominesque quid sentiam, nec solum
fidem meam, quod fortasse videatur satis esse, sed in principe civi non
est satis: curam, consilium vigilantiamque praestabo.

**21** Dixi de periculo: docebo ne coagmentari quidem posse pacem; de
tribus enim quae proposui hoc extremum est.      5

Quae potest pax esse M. Antonio primum cum senatu? quo ore vos ille
poterit, quibus vicissim vos illum oculis intueri? quis vestrum illum,
quem ille vestrum non oderit? age, vos ille solum et vos illum? quid? ei
qui Mutinam circumsedent, qui in Gallia dilectus habent, qui in vestras
fortunas imminent amici umquam vobis erunt aut vos illis? an equites Ro-   10
manos amplectetur? occulta enim fuit eorum voluntas iudiciumque de
Antonio. qui frequentissimi in gradibus Concordiae steterunt, qui nos ad
libertatem recuperandam excitaverunt, arma, saga, bellum flagitaverunt,
me una cum populo Romano in contionem vocaverunt, hi Antonium dili-
gent et cum his pacem servabit Antonius? **22** nam quid ego de universo   15
populo Romano dicam? qui pleno ac referto foro bis me una mente atque
voce in contionem vocavit declaravitque maximam libertatis recuperandae cupiditatem. ita, quod erat optabile antea ut populum Romanum
comitem haberemus, nunc habemus ducem. quae est igitur spes, qui Mutinam circumsedent, imperatorem populi Romani exercitumque oppug-   20
nant, eis pacem cum populo Romano esse posse? **23** an cum municipiis
pax erit quorum tanta studia cognoscuntur in decretis faciendis, militibus
dandis, pecuniis pollicendis, ut in singulis oppidis curiam populi Romani
non desideretis? laudandi sunt ex huius ordinis sententia Firmani, qui
principes pecuniae pollicendae fuerunt; respondendum honorifice est   25
Marrucinis, qui ignominia notandos censuerunt eos si qui militiam sub-
terfugissent. haec iam tota Italia fiunt. magna pax Antonio cum eis, his
item cum illo. quae potest esse maior discordia? in discordia autem pax
civilis esse nullo pacto potest. **24** ut omittam multitudinem, L. Visidio,
equiti Romano, homini in primis ornato atque honesto civique semper   30
egregio, cuius ego excubias et custodias mei capitis cognovi in consulatu
meo, qui vicinos suos non cohortatus est solum ut milites fierent sed
etiam facultatibus suis sublevavit: huic, inquam, tali viro, quem nos senatus consulto collaudare debemus, poteritne esse pacatus Antonius? quid

1 et testabor *D*     2 uidetur *D*     ciue *D*     **21** 4 coamentari *V*     6 esse pax *D*     6
*et* 8 vos ille] i- uos *D*     12 m. antonio *D*     steterunt] sed er- *V*     13 arma saga]
armato *V*: -ti *coni. Halm*     15 et *om. D*     **22** 18 itaque quod *D*: itaque *Nipper-*
*dey*     20–21 oppugnant, iis *Faërnus*: -gnatis *V*[1]: -gnantis *V*[2]: -gnantes *D*     21 esse
posse] se habere possunt *ns*: h- p- *btv*     **23** 24 desideres *bt*: -ret *nsv*     26 si *om.*
*D*     27 fient *V*     **24** 29 nisidio *bt*: Nas- *Ferrarius*     34 collaudare debemus] col-
laudaremus *nstv*

shall continually call Gods and men to witness my sentiments. You may count not only on my good faith, which might perhaps seem enough to promise but in a leader of the community is *not* enough; you may count on my care and counsel and vigilance.

**21** I have spoken of the danger. I shall show that it is not even possible to patch up peace—the last of my three propositions.

What peace can exist between Marcus Antonius and, first, the Senate? How will he endure the sight of you, how will you in your turn stand the sight of him? Which of you will not hate him? Which of you will he not hate? But will the hatred be confined to him and you? What of the men who are besieging Mutina, levying troops in Gaul, reaching for your possessions? Will they ever be your friends or you theirs? Will he grasp the hands of the Roman knights? Their sentiments and judgment concerning Marcus Antonius were hardly a secret. They thronged the steps of the temple of Concord, spurred us on to the recovery of freedom, demanded arms, military cloaks, war, joined the Roman People in summoning me to an assembly: will they love Antonius and will Antonius keep peace with them? **22** As for the entire Roman People, what need I say? Twice they packed the Forum full to summon me to their assembly with one heart and voice, declaring their passionate desire to regain their freedom.[7] Formerly, we could only pray to have the Roman People at our side: now we have them to lead us. So what hope exists that the men who are besieging Mutina and attacking a Roman imperator and army can be at peace with the Roman People? **23** Or will they be at peace with the municipalities, who have shown such zeal in passing decrees, providing soldiers, and promising subsidies that you can find a Senate of the Roman People in every town? The men of Firmum, who were the first to promise a subsidy, should be commended by a resolution of this House. The Marrucini, who decreed that dodgers of military service should be publicly disgraced, deserve an honorific acknowledgment. Such things are now happening throughout Italy. A fine peace Marcus Antonius will have with them and they with him! What strife can be sharper? And peace in the community cannot possibly exist amid strife. **24** To say nothing of the multitude, take Lucius Visidius, Roman knight, an eminently substantial and respectable person, always a model citizen; I remember how he kept watch and ward over my life when I was consul. He has urged his neighbors to enlist and even helped them out of his own pocket. I say again: can Antonius be at peace with such a man as this, a man whom we ought to commend in a senatorial decree? Or with Gaius Caesar, who banned him

---

7. When Cicero delivered the Fourth and Sixth Philippics.

C. Caesari qui illum urbe, quid D. Bruto qui Gallia prohibuit? **25** iam vero ipsi se placabit et leniet provinciae Galliae, a qua exclusus et repudiatus est? omnia videbitis, patres conscripti, nisi prospicitis, plena odiorum, plena discordiarum, ex quibus oriuntur bella civilia. nolite igitur id velle quod fieri non potest, et cavete, per deos immortalis, patres　5 conscripti, ne spe praesentis pacis perpetuam pacem amittatis.

**26** Quorsum haec omnis spectat oratio? quid enim legati egerint nondum scimus. at vero excitati, erecti, parati, armati animis iam esse debemus, ne blanda aut supplici oratione aut aequitatis simulatione fallamur. omnia fecerit oportet quae interdicta et denuntiata sunt, prius quam　10 aliquid postulet: Brutum exercitumque eius oppugnare, urbis et agros provinciae Galliae populari destiterit; ad Brutum adeundi legatis potestatem fecerit; exercitum citra flumen Rubiconem eduxerit, nec propius urbem milia passuum ducenta admoverit; fuerit in senatus et in populi Romani potestate. haec si fecerit, erit integra potestas nobis deliberandi;　15 si senatui non paruerit, non illi senatus, sed ille populo Romano bellum indixerit. **27** sed vos moneo, patres conscripti: libertas agitur populi Romani, quae est commendata vobis; vita et fortunae optimi cuiusque, quo cupiditatem infinitam cum immani crudelitate iam pridem intendit Antonius; auctoritas vestra, quam nullam habebitis, nisi nunc tenueritis. tae-　20 tram et pestiferam beluam ne inclusam et constrictam dimittatis cavete.

Te ipsum, Pansa, moneo—quamquam non eges consilio, quo vales plurimum, tamen etiam summi gubernatores in magnis tempestatibus a vectoribus admoneri solent—hunc tantum tuum apparatum tamque praeclarum ne ad nihilum rec⟨c⟩idere patiare. tempus habes tale quale nemo　25 habuit umquam. hac gravitate senatus, hoc studio equestris ordinis, hoc ardore populi Romani potes in perpetuum rem publicam metu et periculo liberare.

Quibus de rebus refers, P. Servilio adsentior.

---

1 C. *om.* D　　**25** 2 ipsi *scripsi*: ipse *codd.*　　a] ei D　　expulsus V (*cf.* 4.8)　　4 plena discordiarum *om.* V[1]　　6 amittatis D Cus.: m- V　　**26** 8 excitati erecti] er- citati (inc- *b*) D　　iam] tamen *Muretus*　　14 fuerit et in V　　15 erit *om.* V　　16 si *om.* V　　**27** 20 tenueritis *Faërnus*: tenume- V: retinue- D　　21 et (*alt.*) *om.* V　　22 moneo pansa D　　24 praeclarum *om.* V　　25 reccidere *Zielinski* (*cf. ad* 4.10): reci- *codd.*　　29 quibus . . . adsentior *om.* nsv　　de rebus *om. bt*: adsentior *om. t*

from Rome, or Decimus Brutus, who banned him from Gaul? **25** As for the province of Gaul itself, which has repudiated and excluded him, will he appease and soothe his wrath? Unless you take care, Members of the Senate, you will see a society riddled with hatreds and feuds, and such are the seeds of civil wars. So do not hanker after the impossible and in Heaven's name, Members of the Senate, beware of losing a lasting peace in the hope of peace tomorrow.

**26** Where is it all leading, this speech of mine? We don't yet know how the envoys have fared. But in spirit we should already be aroused, erect, ready, armed, lest we be taken in by some soothing, deprecatory words or pretense of fair play. He must do all that has been expressly enjoined[8] before he asks any concession: give up attacking Brutus and his army and ravaging the territory of the province of Gaul; allow the envoys access to Brutus; withdraw his army south of the Rubicon and not bring it within two hundred miles of Rome; be at the disposition of the Senate and People of Rome. If he does all this, then we shall be free to deliberate. If he does not obey the Senate, he will have declared war upon the Roman People, not the Senate upon him. **27** But I warn you, Members of the Senate: the freedom of the Roman People, consigned to your charge, is at stake, as are the lives and possessions of every leading patriot, long menaced by Antonius' insatiable greed combined with savage cruelty, as is your authority, which you will totally lose unless you hold it firmly now: this evil, destructive monster is fast in the toils; be sure you don't let him loose.

Pansa, let me say to you personally—not that a man of your sagacity needs counsel, but even the best of helmsmen are often advised by passengers in a hurricane—do not let all the fine preparations you have made fall away to nothing. You have an opportunity the like of which no man has ever had. With the support of a determined Senate, an enthusiastic order of knights, and an ardent Roman People you can forever free the Commonwealth from fear and danger.

On the business before us, I agree with Publius Servilius.

8. On the meaning of *interdicta* see SB[2]

# VIII

## INTRODUCTION

Ser. Sulpicius died in the performance of his mission. His two colleagues, Piso and Philippus, returned to Rome about the end of January 43, with counterproposals from Antony, which, in Cicero's opinion, they should have known better than to transmit (8.28). Also from Antony's camp came the ex-aedile L. Varius Cotyla, who was admitted to the Senate (of which he was, of course, a member) when it met on 2 February to consider the situation. A motion by Antony's uncle, L. Caesar, calling for the declaration of a "tumult," was put to the vote. Cicero had proposed that the word should be "war," but the consul Pansa and the majority of the Senate supported Caesar. A proposal to send a second embassy was rejected.

The Eighth Philippic, delivered in the Senate on 4 February, comments on the previous day's proceedings. A large section of it consists of an expostulation addressed to Calenus (8.11–19) and then to the other consulars (8.20–22), whose lack of fighting spirit was all too evident.

**1** Confusius hesterno die est acta res, C. Pansa, quam postulabat institutum consulatus tui. parum mihi visus es eos quibus cedere non soles sustinere. nam cum senatus ea virtus fuisset quae solet, et cum re viderent omnes esse bellum quidamque id verbum removendum arbitrarentur, tua voluntas in discessione fuit ad lenitatem propensior. victa est igitur prop- 5
ter verbi asperitatem te auctore nostra sententia: vicit L. Caesaris, amplissimi viri, qui verbi atrocitate dempta oratione fuit quam sententia lenior. quamquam is quidem, ante quam sententiam diceret, propinquitatem excusavit. idem fecerat me consule in sororis viro quod hoc tempore in sororis filio fecit, ut et luctu sororis moveretur et saluti populi 10
Romani provideret. **2** atque ipse tamen Caesar praecepit vobis quodam modo, patres conscripti, ne sibi adsentiremini, cum ita dixit, aliam se sententiam dicturum fuisse eamque se ac re publica dignam, nisi propinquitate impediretur. ergo ille avunculus: num etiam vos avunculi qui illi estis adsensi? 15

At in quo fuit controversia? belli nomen ponendum quidam in sententia non putabant: tumultum appellare malebant, ignari non modo rerum sed etiam verborum: potest enim esse bellum ut tumultus non sit, tumultus autem esse sine bello non potest. **3** quid est enim aliud tumultus nisi perturbatio tanta ut maior timor oriatur? unde etiam nomen ductum est tu- 20
multus. itaque maiores nostri tumultum Italicum quod erat domesticus, tumultum Gallicum quod erat Italiae finitimus, praeterea nullum nominabant. gravius autem tumultum esse quam bellum hinc intellegi potest quod bello [Italico] vacationes valent, tumultu non valent. ita fit, quem ad modum dixi, ut bellum sine tumultu possit, tumultus sine bello esse non 25
possit. **4** etenim cum inter bellum et pacem medium nihil sit, necesse est tumultum, si belli non sit, pacis esse: quo quid absurdius dici aut existimari potest?

Sed nimis multa de verbo: rem potius videamus, patres conscripti, quam quidem intellego verbo fieri interdum deteriorem solere. nolumus 30
hoc bellum videri. quam igitur municipiis et coloniis ad excludendum

---

**1** 3 ut cum *nstv*    6 verbi *om. nstv*    L.] c. *V*    8 is] si *V*    10 filio . . . sororis] f-
ne in nepotem *bnsv*: *om. t*    10–11 populi Romani] rei p. *D*    **2** 12–13 se sententiam
*coni. Halm*: sent- se *D*: sent- *V* (se *post* fuisse *Baiter*)    16 in sententia quidam (-dem *v*)
*D*    18–19 ut . . . esse *Isid. Orig. 18.1.7* (autem *om. Garatoni*): ut tumultus esse *V*[1]:
sine tumultu tumultus (ut tumultus *V*[2]) esse (e- *post* bello *b*) *DV*[2]    **3** 19 enim est *tv*,
*Quint. 7.3.25* (*om. 3.8.5*)    22 nullum tumultum nominabant *D*    23 hic *V*    potest]
licet *D* (hinc . . . potest *om. Isid.*)    24 quod] nam *Isid.*    bello *Faërnus*: in b- *Isid.*: b-
italico *V*: b- gallico *D*    24 in tumultu *Isid.*    **4** 30 nolimus *V*

**1** Our proceedings yesterday, Gaius Pansa, lacked something of the clarity which our normal practice under your consulship called for. It seemed to me that you did not take a firm enough stand against persons to whom you do not generally give way. The Senate showed its usual courage, everyone saw that war exists in fact, but there were some who wanted the *word* removed; and in the vote you inclined to the milder course. So because of the harshness of the word, my motion was defeated with your approval, and that of our distinguished fellow member Lucius Caesar won the day. In this motion the offensive word was withdrawn, but the mildness lay in the language rather than the substance. To be sure, its author pleaded the excuse of a family relationship before he put it forward. When I was consul, he acted in the case of his brother-in-law[1] as he has acted now in that of his nephew: he was both affected by his sister's sorrow and attentive to the welfare of the Roman People. **2** And yet, Members of the Senate, Caesar himself after a fashion advised you not to follow him, when he said that he would have proposed a different motion, one worthy of himself and the Commonwealth, had he been free of family ties. Very good, Caesar is Antonius' uncle. What about you gentlemen who supported Caesar? Are you Antonius' uncles too?

But let us examine the point at issue. Certain persons thought that the name of war ought not to be in the motion. They preferred to call it "tumult," showing their ignorance not only of facts but of words. For while a war can exist without a tumult, a tumult cannot exist without a war. **3** For what else is a tumult but a commotion so serious that *fear* beyond the ordinary arises from it—that being the origin of the word "tumult."[2] Accordingly, our ancestors spoke of an "Italian tumult" (because it took place within our borders) and a "Gallic tumult" (because it was next door to Italy), and of no other tumult whatsoever. And that a tumult is something more serious than a war can be inferred from the fact that exemptions are valid in a war but not in a tumult.[3] Hence, as I have just observed, war can exist without tumult, but not tumult without war. **4** After all, there is no halfway house between war and peace. If "tumult" does not come under the heading of war, it must come under the heading of peace—than which nothing more incongruous can well be said or thought.

But I have dwelt too long upon a word. Let us rather look at substance, Members of the Senate—which indeed I have noticed is sometimes apt to be made worse by a word. We do not want this to be seen as a war. Then what authority do we give to the municipalities and colonies to refuse Antonius

1. Cf. Philippic 2 n. 14.
2. Actually *tumultus* is connected etymologically with *tumere* ("to swell"), not *timere*.
3. Cf. 5.53.

Antonium auctoritatem damus? quam ut milites fiant sine vi, sine multa, studio, voluntate? quam ut pecunias in rem publicam polliceantur? si enim belli nomen tolletur, municipiorum studia tollentur; consensus populi Romani, qui iam descendit in causam, si nos languescimus, debilitetur necesse est. 5

**5** Sed quid plura? D. Brutus oppugnatur: non est bellum. Mutina obsidetur: ne hoc quidem bellum est. Gallia vastatur: quae pax potest esse certior? illud vero quis potest bellum esse dicere quo consulem, fortissimum virum, cum exercitu misimus? qui, cum esset infirmus ex gravi diuturnoque morbo, nullam sibi putavit excusationem esse oportere, cum 10 ad rei publicae praesidium vocaretur. C. quidem Caesar non exspectavit vestra decreta, praesertim cum illud esset aetatis: bellum contra Antonium sua sponte suscepit. decernendi enim tempus nondum erat: bellum autem gerendi tempus si praetermisisset, videbat re publica oppressa nihil posse decerni. **6** ergo illi nunc et eorum exercitus in pace versantur. 15 non est hostis is cuius praesidium Claterna deiecit Hirtius; non est hostis qui consuli armatus obsistit, designatum consulem oppugnat, nec illa hostilia verba nec bellica quae paulo ante ex collegae litteris Pansa recitavit: "deieci praesidium; Claterna potitus sum; fugati equites; proelium commissum; occisi aliquot." quae pax potest esse maior? dilectus 20 tota Italia decreti sublatis vacationibus; saga cras sumentur; consul se cum praesidio descensurum esse dixit. **7** utrum hoc bellum non est, an est tantum bellum quantum numquam fuit?

Ceteris enim bellis maximeque civilibus contentionem rei publicae causa faciebat. Sulla cum Sulpicio de iure legum quas per vim [con. 25 Sulla] latas esse dicebat; Cinna cum Octavio de novorum civium suffragiis; rursus cum Mario et Carbone Sulla ne dominarentur indigni et ut clarissimorum hominum crudelissimam puniretur necem. horum omnium bellorum causae ex rei publicae contentione natae sunt. de proximo bello civili non libet dicere: ignoro causam, detestor exitum. **8** hoc bellum 30 quintum civile geritur—atque omnia in nostram aetatem inciderunt—primum non modo non in dissensione et discordia civium sed in maxima consensione incredibilique concordia. omnes idem volunt, idem defen-

---

1 fiant] sint *D*    1–2 multa studio] tumultu s- et *D*    3 tolletur ς: -leitur *V*: -litur *D*    tolluntur *D*    **5** 6 Mutina] mutine dominaretur seturna *V*    7 potest pax *D*    **8** quo consulem *Garatoni*: consulem *V*: quo *D*    9 ex] et *V*    11 C. *om. V*    12 esset illud *t*: e- illius *bnsv*    13 erat] uenerat *bntv*: noue- *s*    belli *D*    **6** 17 obsistit] obsidet *t*: -det qui *b*: *om. nsv*    22 esse *om. D*    **7** an est *C. F. W. Müller*: an etiam *D*: e- *V*: an est iam *Lutz*    25 contendebat (*vel* -dit) *ante* Sulla *add. Sternkopf, fort. recte*    26 latas *Fedeli*: con. sulla latas *V*[1] (con. *del. V*[2]): latas (-ta *t*) sulla *D*: consul Sulla latas *Halm*    28 poenirentur *V*: puniret *bvn*[2]    **8** 32 non modo in *nstv*

admission? Or to enlist, without the use of force or fines, from spontaneous enthusiasm? Or to promise subsidies in aid of the Commonwealth? If the name of war is removed, the enthusiasm of the municipalities will go with it. The united impulse of the Roman People, which has now joined the struggle, must inevitably be weakened if *we* falter.

5 But why waste words? Decimus Brutus is under attack, but it is not a war! Mutina under siege, but that is no war either! Gaul is being laid waste: can any peace be more assured? Who can say it is a war to which we have dispatched a very gallant consul at the head of an army? Ill as he was of a serious, long-standing ailment, he thought there should be no excuse for him when summoned to defend the Commonwealth. Gaius Caesar did not wait for your decrees, young though he was; he went to war with Antonius of his own accord. The time for decrees had not yet arrived, but he saw that if he let the time for military action pass, the Commonwealth would be crushed and nothing could be decreed. 6 Well, they and their armies are now at peace. It is no enemy whose garrison was thrown out of Claterna by Hirtius, no enemy who is in armed opposition to a consul, attacking a consul-elect. Those were not hostile or warlike words which Pansa has just read out from his colleague's dispatch: "Threw out the garrison. Took possession of Claterna. Cavalry routed. Battle joined. Some killed."[4] How profoundly peaceful it all sounds! Levies have been decreed throughout Italy, exemptions canceled. Military cloaks will be donned tomorrow. The consul has stated that he will appear in public with an armed escort. 7 Is this not war? Or is it not the greatest war that ever was?

In other wars, and particularly civil wars, the conflict had a political basis. Sulla fought Sulpicius[5] about the validity of laws which according to him had been passed by violence. Cinna fought Octavius about voting rights for the new citizens.[6] Sulla again fought Marius[7] and Carbo to put an end to the rule of the unworthy and to avenge the cruel deaths of illustrious men. All these wars had their origin in a political dispute. As for the last civil war,[8] I would rather not speak of it. I do not know its cause and I abominate its outcome. 8 We are now fighting a fifth civil war (they all occurred in my lifetime), and for the first time there is no division or discord in the community, but on the contrary the most complete unity, an extraordinary consensus. All have one

4. No doubt Cicero is summarizing what Hirtius wrote.
5. In 88. Most important was Sulpicius' attempt to transfer the command in the war against Mithridates of Pontus from Sulla to Marius.
6. The Italian allies granted citizenship during the Social War in 90–89. The *bellum Octavianum* in 87 left Marius and Cinna in control of Italy.
7. Son of the great Marius. The war of 83–82 ended in Sulla's victory and dictatorship.
8. Between Caesar and Pompey.

dunt, idem sentiunt. cum omnis dico, eos excipio quos nemo civitate dignos putat.

Quae est igitur in medio belli causa posita? nos deorum immortalium templa, nos muros, nos domicilia sedesque populi Romani, aras, focos, sepulcra maiorum; nos leges, iudicia, libertatem, coniuges, liberos, patriam defendimus: contra M. Antonius id molitur, id pugnat ut haec omnia perturbet, evertat, praedam rei publicae causam belli putet, fortunas nostras partim dissipet partim dispertiat parricidis. **9** in hac tam dispari ratione belli miserrimum illud est quod ille latronibus suis pollicetur primum domos—urbem enim divisurum se confirmat—deinde omnibus portis quo velint deducturum. omnes Cafones, omnes Saxae ceteraeque pestes quae sequuntur Antonium aedis sibi optimas, hortos, Tusculana, Albana definiunt. atque etiam homines agrestes, si homines illi ac non pecudes potius, inani spe ad Aquas usque et Puteolos pervehuntur. ergo habet Antonius quod suis polliceatur. quid nos? num quid tale habemus? di meliora! id enim ipsum agimus ne quis posthac quicquam eius modi possit polliceri. invitus dico, sed dicendum est: hasta Caesaris, patres conscripti, multis improbis et spem adfert et audaciam. viderunt enim ex mendicis fieri repente divites; itaque semper hastam videre cupiunt ei qui nostris bonis imminent; quibus omnia pollicetur Antonius. **10** quid nos? nostris exercitibus quid pollicemur? multo meliora atque maiora; scelerum enim promissio et eis qui exspectant perniciosa est et eis qui promittunt. nos libertatem nostris militibus, leges, iura, iudicia, imperium orbis terrae, dignitatem, pacem, otium pollicemur. Antoni igitur promissa cruenta, taetra, scelerata, dis hominibusque invisa, nec diuturna neque salutaria: nostra contra honesta, integra, gloriosa, plena laetitiae, plena pietatis.

**11** Hic mihi etiam Q. Fufius, vir fortis ac strenuus, amicus meus, pacis commoda commemorat. quasi vero, si laudanda pax esset, ego id aeque commode facere non possem. semel enim pacem defendi? non semper otio studui? quod cum omnibus bonis utile est, tum praecipue mihi. quem enim cursum industria mea tenere potuisset sine forensibus causis, sine legibus, sine iudiciis? quae esse non possunt civili pace sublata. **12** sed quaeso, Calene, quid tu? servitutem pacem vocas? maiores quidem nostri

3 nos deorum *V Cus.*: d- *D*: d- nos *n²*     **9** 10 diuisurum se ç: -rum es *V*: se diuisurum *D*: se d- esse *Faërnus*     13 homines agrestes si *om. V*     13–14 illi ac (an *V*) non pecudes potius *V, Faërnus*: sunt illi (i- s- *v*) potius quam (q- p- *b*: q- p- quam *n¹s*) pecudes *D*     14 et Puteolos] et puteolas *ns*: puteolanas *btv*     provehuntur *ed. Romana*     16 di] det *nstv*     ne] p. ne *V*     18–19 viderunt . . . mendicis] sui enim ex me didicerunt *D*     **10** 20–21 quid nos? nostris] *ita distinxi*: quid? nos n- *vel* quid nos n- *alii*     22 et his . . . et his *D*     23 iura leges *D*     **11** 29 id aeque] idem *nsv*: id *t*     31 est] esset *V*

desire, one cause, one sentiment. When I say "all," I mean all but those whom nobody thinks worthy to be citizens.

What is the reason for this war, what is each side fighting for? *We* are defending the temples of the Immortal Gods, the city walls, the dwelling-houses of the Roman People, the altars and hearths, the tombs of our ancestors; we are defending our laws, our courts of law, our freedom, our wives and children and fatherland. Marcus Antonius on the contrary is purposing and fighting for the violent overthrow of everything I have just mentioned. He wants to regard the plunder of the Commonwealth as his reason for war, to squander our possessions or parcel them out among traitors. **9** Thus differently do the two sides conceive of the war. The most deplorable part of it is the promises he is making to his cutthroats. First our town houses, for he assures them that he will divide up the city; then that he will take them out of all the city gates and settle them where they will. Cafo, Saxa, and their kind, all the evil creatures in Antonius' train, are earmarking the best houses, suburban estates, villas at Tusculum and Alba. These yokels, or should I rather call them cattle, even let their idle hopes carry them as far as the Waters[9] and Puteoli. Well, Antonius has something to promise his followers. What about us? Do we have anything of the sort? Heaven forfend! Our purpose is precisely to make sure that nobody can promise anything of this kind in the future. I say it with reluctance, but say it I must: Caesar's lance,[10] Members of the Senate, brings hope and daring to many a rascal. They saw beggars suddenly become rich; and so those who menace our property, to whom Antonius is promising the earth, are always eager to see such a lance. **10** What about us? What do *we* promise our armies? Far better and greater rewards. The promise of crimes spells ruin both for him who expects and for him who promises. We promise our fighting men freedom, justice, laws, law courts, the empire of the world, dignity, peace at home and abroad. Antonius' promises are bloody, sinister, criminal, hateful to Gods and men; they will not last, bring no good. Ours are honorable, fair, glorious, full of joy and patriotism.

**11** But here is my gallant and energetic friend Quintus Fufius actually reminding me of the blessings of peace—as though, if this were the time to sing the praises of peace, I could not do it as well as himself. How many times have I defended peace? Have I not always favored it? Peace is good for all honest men, but particularly good for me. Where would my activity have found scope without cases in the Forum, laws, law courts? These cannot exist if internal peace is taken away. **12** But let me ask you something, Calenus: do you call slavery peace? Our ancestors took up arms not only for freedom but

9. I.e. Baiae.
10. See Philippic 2 n. 62.

non modo ut liberi essent sed etiam ut imperarent arma capiebant: tu
arma abicienda censes ut serviamus? quae causa iustior est belli gerendi
quam servitutis depulsio? in qua etiam si non sit molestus dominus,
tamen est miserrimum posse, si velit. immo aliae causae iustae, haec necessaria est. nisi forte ad te hoc non putas pertinere quod te socium fore     5
speras dominationis Antoni. in quo bis laberis: primum quod tuas rationes communibus interponis; deinde quod quicquam stabile aut iucundum in regno putas. non, si tibi antea profuit, semper proderit. **13** quin
etiam de illo homine queri solebas: quid te facturum de belua putas?

Atque ais eum te esse qui semper pacem optaris, semper omnis civis     10
volueris salvos. honesta oratio, sed ita si bonos et utilis et e re publica
civis: sin eos qui natura cives sunt, voluntate hostes, salvos velis, quid
tandem intersit inter te et illos? pater tuus quidem, quo utebar sene auctore adulescens, homo severus et prudens, primas omnium civium P. Na-
sicae, qui Ti. Gracchum interfecit, dare solebat: eius virtute, consilio,     15
magnitudine animi liberatam rem publicam arbitrabatur. **14** quid? nos a
patribus num aliter accepimus? ergo is tibi civis, si temporibus illis
fuisses, non probaretur, quia non omnis salvos esse voluisset.

"Quod L. Opimius consul verba fecit de re publica, de ea re ita censuerunt uti L. Opimius consul rem publicam defenderet." senatus haec     20
verbis, Opimius armis. num igitur eum, si tum esses, temerarium civem
aut crudelem putares, aut Q. Metellum, cuius quattuor filii consulares,
P. Lentulum, principem senatus, compluris alios summos viros qui cum
Opimio consule armati ⟨C.⟩ Gracchum in Aventinum persecuti sunt? quo
in proelio Lentulus grave volnus accepit, interfectus est Gracchus et     25
M. Fulvius consularis, eiusque duo adulescentuli filii. illi igitur viri vi-
tuperandi: non enim omnis civis salvos esse voluerunt.

**15** Ad propiora veniamus. C. Mario L. Valerio consulibus senatus rem
publicam defendendam dedit: L. Saturninus tribunus plebis, C. Glaucia
praetor est interfectus. omnes illo die Scauri, Metelli, Claudii, Catuli,     30
Scaevolae, Crassi arma sumpserunt. num aut consules illos aut claris-

**12** 4 esse posse *Pluygers*      alia causa iusta (-ta ac *nsv*) *D*      5 est *om. D*      6 laberis
*V*²: lib- *V*¹: falleris *D*      7 anteponis *D*      7–8 in regno aut iucundum *bnv*      **13** 9 etiam
enim *V*: etiam, memini *Faërnus, haud absurde*      10 atque ais] at qui es *bnsv*: atque
aes *t*      11 honesta] omne ista *V*      et e] et *nsv*: *om. bt*      13 interest *D*      pater
tuus quidem] quid p- tandem tuus *b*: quid p- dein t- *nsv*: qui p- dem t- *t*      auctore
*om. D*      **14** 17 civis *post* omnis *transp. Schwartz* (8.15 qui omnis salvos vis *confert
Fe.*)      20 L. *om. D*      23 senatus *Ferrarius*: -torem (-tores *s*) *codd.*      cum] cum l.
*D*      24 C. *addidi*      26 consularis *Ferrarius*: -res *codd.*      **15** 28 Valerio *om. V*      30
praetor *s*²: p(opuli) r(omani) *codd.*      31 aut consules] autem *D*

for empire. Do you think we should throw our arms away in order to be slaves? Is there any better reason for waging war than to ward off slavery? In slavery, even if the master is not oppressive, the sorry thing is that he can be if he wishes. No, other reasons are good, but this reason is compelling. Or do you think perhaps that this does not concern you because you expect to be a partner in Antonius' despotism? You make two mistakes there. Your first mistake is in mixing up your personal interests with the interests of the community; your second mistake is in thinking that anything can be stable or agreeable in a tyranny. It may have worked to your advantage once, but it will not therefore work to your advantage always. **13** After all, you were apt to grumble when the master was a human being; what will you do when he's a monster?

You describe yourself as one who has always prayed for peace, always wanted all citizens to survive. That is an honorable sentiment, but only if you mean good citizens, men of use and benefit to the Commonwealth. But should you want the survival of people who are citizens by birth but public enemies by choice, where would be the difference between you and them? Your father was a strict man and a wise one. When I was young and he was old, I used to ask his advice. Among all Romans he used to give the place of honor to Publius Nasica, who killed Tiberius Gracchus, holding that Nasica's courage, judgment, and unselfishness had brought freedom to the Commonwealth. **14** Have we not heard the same from *our* fathers? Well, if you had been alive in those days, you would not have approved of Nasica as a citizen because he had not wanted all citizens to survive.

"Whereas Consul Lucius Opimius spoke concerning the Commonwealth, the Senate resolved that Consul Lucius Opimius defend the Commonwealth."[11] Such were the Senate's words; Opimius responded with weapons. Would you have deemed him rash or cruel, if you had lived then? Or Quintus Metellus, who had four consular sons, or Publius Lentulus, leader of the Senate, or a number of other eminent men who chased Gaius Gracchus to the Aventine with weapons in their hands along with Consul Opimius? Lentulus was seriously wounded in the affray, Gracchus was killed, as was the consular Marcus Fulvius and his two young sons. So: those men were much to blame, for they did not wish all citizens to survive.

**15** Let us come to events closer to our own time. The Senate committed the defense of the Commonwealth to Consuls Gaius Marius and Lucius Valerius.[12] Tribune of the Plebs Lucius Saturninus and Praetor Gaius Glaucia were killed. That day all the Scauri, Metelli, Claudii, Catuli, Scaevolae, and Crassi took up arms. Do you think those consuls or those illustrious men were blameworthy? I

---

11. The first instance of the Senate's Ultimate Decree, in 121; cf. Philippic 2 n. 50, 5 n. 30.
12. In 100.

simos viros vituperandos putas? ego Catilinam perire volui. num tu qui
omnis salvos vis Catilinam salvum esse voluisti? hoc interest, Calene, inter meam sententiam et tuam. ego nolo quemquam civem committere ut
morte multandus sit; tu, etiam si commiserit, conservandum putas. in
corpore si quid eius modi est quod reliquo corpori noceat, id uri secari- 5
que patimur, ut membrum aliquod potius quam totum corpus intereat. sic
in rei publicae corpore, ut totum salvum sit, quicquid est pestiferum am-
putetur. **16** dura vox! multo illa durior: "salvi sint improbi, scelerati, impii; deleantur innocentes, honesti, boni, tota res publica!"

Uno in homine, Q. Fufi, fateor te vidisse plus quam me. ego P. Clo- 10
dium arbitrabar perniciosum civem, sceleratum, libidinosum, impium,
audacem, facinerosum, tu contra sanctum, temperantem, innocentem,
modestum, retinendum civem et optandum. in hoc uno te plurimum vidisse, me multum errasse concedo.

Nam quod me tecum iracunde agere dixisti solere, non est ita. vehe- 15
menter me agere fateor, iracunde nego. omnino irasci amicis non temere
soleo, ne si merentur quidem. **17** itaque sine verborum contumelia a te
dissentire possum, sine animi summo dolore non possum. parva est enim
mihi tecum aut parva de re dissensio? ego huic faveo, tu illi? immo vero
ego D. Bruto faveo, tu M. Antonio: ego conservari coloniam populi Ro- 20
mani cupio, tu expugnari studes. an hoc negare potes, qui omnis moras
interponas quibus infirmetur Brutus, melior fiat Antonius?

Quo usque enim dices pacem velle te? res geritur; conductae vineae
sunt; pugnatur acerrime. qui intercurrerent, misimus tris principes civitatis. hos contempsit, reiecit, repudiavit Antonius: tu tamen permanes con- 25
stantissimus defensor Antoni. **18** et quidem, quo melior senator videatur,
negat se illi amicum esse debere: cum suo magno esset beneficio, venisse
eum contra se. vide⟨te⟩ quanta caritas sit patriae: cum homini sit iratus,
tamen rei publicae causa defendit Antonium.

31–1 clarissimos hos viros *Mommsen*    3 civem] quem *V*    4–5 ut in corpore *Cobet*
5 id uri] aduri *Cus. V*²: uri *D*    6 membrum *V Cus.*: -ra *t*: -rorum *bnsv*    **16** 14 me *om.*
*nstv*    15 quod *om. D*    **17** 19 huic] huic uel illi (uelliti *t*, uel illi *del. n*²) uidelicet
*D*    20 conseruare *D*    22 interponis *D*    melior³] firmior *vel* valentior *coniece-*
*ram*    23 dicis *D*    conductae *suspectum: varia coniecerunt, velut* comminus copiae,
actae vineae *Sternkopf*    vineae *ed. Veneta*: liniae *V*: lineae *D*    **18** 26 equidem
*D*    27 se illi] ei i- *V*: se ei *coni. Clark*    esset] esse *D*    28 eum] reum *D*    videte
*Manutius*: uide *codd.*

wanted Catiline destroyed. Did you, who want everyone to survive, wish for Catiline's survival? The difference between my view and yours, Calenus, is this: I wish that no citizen act in such a way that he has to be punished with death, you think a citizen should be preserved even if he does so act. If something in the body is causing harm to the rest, we allow it to be cauterized or cut so that this or that member may perish rather than the whole body. Likewise in the body politic: let whatever is noxious be amputated so that the whole may be saved. **16** A hard saying? I will give you a far harder one: "Let the rascals, the criminals, the traitors be saved; let the innocent, the respectable, the honest, the entire Commonwealth be wiped out."

I do admit, Quintus Fufius, that in one case your perception was better than mine. I used to think Publius Clodius a pernicious citizen, criminal, lustful, unpatriotic, insolent, villainous. You on the contrary regarded him as blameless, moderate, innocent, and unassuming, a valuable and desirable member of the community. In this one instance I acknowledge your keen perspicacity and my own grave error.[13]

You have said that I am apt to take an angry tone with you. That is not so. I admit to vehemence, but anger I deny. In general it is not my habit to be easily angry with my friends, even if they deserve it. **17** I can differ from you without using offensive expressions, though not without heartfelt distress. For is it a minor disagreement I have with you, is it about a trifle, a matter of my backing X and your backing Y? No, it is a matter of my backing Decimus Brutus and your backing Marcus Antonius; of my being anxious to see a Roman colony saved, your wanting it taken by storm. Can you deny as much, when you are putting up all manner of delays to make Brutus weaker and Antonius stronger?

How much longer will you say you want peace? War is in progress. Siege-works[14] have been assembled. There is bitter fighting. We sent three of our leading men to intervene. Antonius has rejected their mission with utter contempt. And yet you still remain Antonius' most resolute defender. **18** And what is more, to make himself appear a more conscientious senator, he[15] says he has no call to be Antonius' friend, seeing that Antonius appeared against him in court though owing him a great favor. Behold the power of patriotism! He has a personal grievance, but for the Commonwealth's sake he defends Antonius!

13. Ponderous irony. As tribune in 61 Calenus had protected Clodius in his trial for sacrilege (*Att.* 1.14.5), and after Clodius' murder in 52 he was active in the Senate against Milo (Asconius, ed. Clark, 44.21).

14. *Vineae* ("penthouses") is usually read for *lineae*, but the meaning of *conductae* is doubtful; we expect *aguntur*, "are being moved up."

15. Still Calenus. Such switches from second to third person or vice versa are common in these speeches.

Ego te, cum in Massiliensis tam es acerbus, Q. Fufi, non animo aequo audio. quo usque enim Massiliam oppugnabis? ne triumphus quidem finem fecit belli, per quem lata est urbs ea sine qua numquam ex Transalpinis gentibus maiores nostri triumpharunt? quo quidem tempore populus Romanus ingemuit: quamquam proprios dolores suarum rerum omnes 　5 habebant, tamen huius civitatis fidelissimae miserias nemo erat civis qui a se alienas arbitraretur. **19** Caesar ipse, qui illis fuerat iratissimus, tamen propter singularem eius civitatis gravitatem et fidem cotidie aliquid iracundiae remittebat: te nulla sua calamitate civitas satiare tam fidelis potest? rursus iam me irasci fortasse dices. ego autem sine iracundia dico 　10 omnia nec tamen sine dolore animi: neminem illi civitati inimicum esse arbitror qui amicus huic sit civitati. excogitare quae tua ratio sit, Calene, non possum. antea deterrere te ne popularis esses non poteramus: exorare nunc ut sis popularis non possumus.

Satis multa cum Fufio ac sine odio omnia, nihil sine dolore. credo autem, qui generi querelam moderate ferat, aequo animo laturum amici. 　15 **20** venio ad reliquos consularis, quorum nemo est—iure hoc meo dico—quin mecum habeat aliquam coniunctionem gratiae, alii maximam, alii mediocrem, nemo nullam. quam hesternus dies nobis, consularibus dico, turpis illuxit! iterum legatos? quid si ille faceret indutias? ante os oculos-　20 que legatorum tormentis Mutinam verberavit; opus ostendebat munitionemque legatis; ne punctum quidem temporis, cum legati adessent, oppugnatio respiravit. ad hunc legatos? cur? an ut eorum reditu vehementius pertimescatis? **21** equidem cum ante legatos decerni non censuissem, hoc me tamen consolabar, [quod] cum illi ab Antonio contempti et reiecti 　25 revertissent renuntiavissentque senatui non modo illum de Gallia non discessisse, uti censuissemus, sed ne a Mutina quidem recessisse, potestatem sibi D. Bruti conveniendi non fuisse, fore ut omnes inflammati odio, excitati dolore, armis, equis, viris D. Bruto subveniremus. nos etiam languidiores postea facti sumus quam M. Antoni non solum audaciam et 　30 scelus sed etiam insolentiam superbiamque perspeximus. **22** utinam

---

1 es] sis *D*　　Q. *om. D*　　3 facit *V*: faciet *Pluygers*　　sublata *D*　　4 triumphauerunt *Vv*　　6–7 civis qui a se] quis quas *V*¹ (se *add. V*²)　　**19** 8 de iracundia *Cobet*　　9 te nulla sua] nulla *D*　　11 ut omnia *D*　　animi. *om. D*　　12 sit huic *D*　　13 antea] ate antea *V*: ante *coni. Clark*　　exorare *post* popularis *D*　　16 aequo . . . amici] aequoniam o (*corr. V*²) laturum *V*: aequo animo amici lat- *coni. Halm*　　**20** 17 uenio nunc ad *D*　　18 quin *tvV*²: quia *V*¹: qui non *bns*　　20 quid si *C. F. W. Müller*: qui si *V*: quod si *bt*: quid *nsv*: quasi *Clark*　　os] hos *V*: c̄s *nsv*: eos *t*　　**21** 24 antea cum *D*　　25 quod *del. Lambinus*　　relicti *nstv*　　26 renuntiavissentque] dixiss- *bsv*: que *t*　　de] e *D*　　27 ut *D*　　28 foret *Halm*: sperabam fore *C. F. W. Müller*　　29 uiribus *D*　　30 facti sumus postea *D*　　M. *Faërnus*: marus *V*: *om. D*

I find it hard to listen with patience, Quintus Fufius, to your bitter language against the Massilians. How long are you going to attack Massilia? Did not even the Triumph[16] bring the war to an end, the Triumph in which that city was borne,[17] that city without which our ancestors never triumphed over the races beyond the Alps? The Roman People groaned thereat. Though everyone had personal griefs peculiar to himself, there was not a citizen but felt the sufferings of this most faithful of communities as his own. **19** Caesar himself, furious as he had been with them, abated something of his anger every day in face of the extraordinary loyalty and sense of responsibility shown by that community. Can so loyal a community not content you with any measure of calamity? Perhaps you will say that I am now getting angry again. No, all I say is said without anger, though not without distress of mind. I do not think any man who is an enemy of that community is a friend of this one. Calenus, I cannot make you out. Time was when we could not deter you from being a "people's man"; now we cannot beg you into being one.

I have dealt long enough with Fufius—all without anger, nothing without distress. And I believe that he will not take a friend's remonstrance amiss, seeing that he is patient under his son-in-law's.[18] **20** I come now to the other consulars. I am entitled to say that there is no one among them who does not have some personal tie with me; very close in some cases, not so close in others, but in every case something. What a day of dishonor yesterday was for us, I mean for us consulars! Send envoys once again? It is not even as though he had been observing a truce. He pounded Mutina with his artillery before the envoys' very eyes. He showed the envoys his works and fortifications. There was not a moment's respite in the assault while the envoys were present. Envoys to him? Why? To make you more frightened than ever when they get back? **21** I opposed authorizing an embassy before, but I had one consolation: I reckoned that when they returned from Antonius despised and rejected, when they reported to the Senate that not merely had he failed to evacuate Gaul as we had decreed, but he had not even withdrawn from Mutina, and that they had not been permitted to meet Decimus Brutus, the result would be that all of us, aflame with hatred, spurred by indignation, would go with might and main[19] to Decimus Brutus' assistance. But we have become even more languid than ever, now that we have seen the insolence and arrogance of Marcus Antonius as well as his unscrupulous audacity. **22** If only Lucius Caesar were well and

16. Caesar's in 46.
17. In effigy.
18. The consul Pansa.
19. Lit. "with weapons, horse, and foot"; cf. Liv. 5.37.5. *Equis viris* or *viris equisque* is standard for using every means at one's disposal.

L. Caesar valeret, Ser. Sulpicius viveret! multo melius haec causa ageretur a tribus quam nunc agitur ab uno.

Dolenter hoc dicam potius quam contumeliose: deserti, deserti, inquam, sumus, patres conscripti, a principibus. sed—saepe iam dixi—omnes in tanto periculo qui recte et fortiter sentient erunt consulares. animum nobis adferre legati debuerunt: timorem attulerunt—quamquam mihi quidem nullum—quamvis de illo ad quem missi sunt bene existiment; a quo etiam mandata acceperunt. **23** pro di immortales! ubi est ille mos virtusque maiorum? C. Popilius apud maiores nostros cum ad Antiochum regem legatus missus esset et verbis senatus nuntiasset ut ab Alexandria discederet, quam obsidebat, cum tempus ille differret, virgula stantem circumscripsit dixitque se renuntiaturum senatui, nisi prius sibi respondisset quid facturus esset quam ex illa circumscriptione exisset. praeclare! senatus enim faciem secum attulerat auctoritatemque [r.p.]; cui qui non paret, non ab eo mandata accipienda sunt, sed ipse est potius repudiandus. **24** an ego ab eo mandata acciperem qui senatus mandata contemneret? aut ei cum senatu quicquam commune iudicarem qui imperatorem populi Romani senatu prohibente obsideret? at quae mandata! qua adrogantia, quo stupore, quo spiritu! cur autem ea legatis nostris dabat, cum ad nos Cotylam mitteret, ornamentum atque arcem amicorum suorum, hominem aedilicium, si vero tum fuit aedilis cum eum iussu Antoni in convivio servi publici loris ceciderunt?

**25** At quam modesta mandata! ferrei sumus, patres conscripti, qui quicquam huic negemus. "utramque provinciam" inquit "remitto: exercitum depono: privatus esse non recuso." haec sunt enim verba. redire ad se videtur. "omnia obliviscor, in gratiam redeo." sed quid adiungit? "si legionibus meis sex, si equitibus, si cohorti praetoriae praemia agrumque dederitis." eis etiam praemia postulat quibus ut ignoscatur si postulet, impudentissimus iudicetur. addit praeterea ut, quos ipse cum Dolabella dederit agros, teneant ei quibus dati sint. **26** hic est Campanus ager et Leontinus, quae duo maiores nostri annonae perfugia ducebant. cavet mimis, aleatoribus, lenonibus: Cafoni etiam et Saxae cavet, quos centuriones pugnacis et lacertosos inter mimorum et mimarum greges col-

5

10

15

20

25

30

**22** 3 deserti inquam *om. D* 4 saepiam *V* (*corr. Poggius*): iam saepe *D*: ut s- iam *Orelli* 7 mihi quidem amissi sunt *V*[1] nullum umquam timorem *D* **23** 10 denuntiasset *s* 12 se] se non ante (-ea *b*) *D* 13 exisset] excessit *bn*[1]*tv*: -essisset *sn*[2] 14 r(e) p(ublica) *del. Sternkopf*: rei publicae *Kayser*: populi Romani *Lambinus* 15 cui] cui is *b*: ciuis *nst*: cuius *v* potius] totus *D* **24** 19 stupore] tumore *Mommsen* 22 servi publici loris] seruitores *D* **25** 25 non] nunc *V*[1] 27 sex] et *D* (*del. n*[2]) praemia[3] *Ernesti*: praedam (-da *v*) *codd.*: -dia *Clark* 29 ut *om. D* 30 sunt *nstv* **26** 32 memisi (mim- *V*[2]) *V*: mimis et *D*

Servius Sulpicius were alive! This cause would be much better pleaded by three than, as now, by one.

I say it in sorrow rather than with any wish to affront: we are deserted, yes, Members of the Senate, I repeat, deserted by our leading men. But (I have often said it) in so dangerous a situation all right-minded and courageous senators shall be consulars. The envoys ought to have heartened us. Instead, they alarmed us (to be sure, I must except myself), although they think well of the person to whom they were sent. They even accepted a message from him. **23** In Heaven's name, what has happened to the customs and the spirit of our ancestors? In those days[20] Gaius Popilius was sent as envoy to King Antiochus. In the name of the Senate he warned the king to retire from Alexandria, which city he was besieging. Antiochus temporized. Whereupon Popilius drew a line round him with a cane where he stood, and said he would report back to the Senate unless the king gave him an answer as to his intentions before he left that circle. Admirable! He carried with him the semblance and authority of the Senate. If any man does not obey that, no messages should be accepted from such; rather, *he* should be repudiated. **24** Should I have accepted a message from one who was defying the Senate's message? Should I have thought that a man who was besieging a Roman imperator against the Senate's orders had anything in common with the Senate? And what a message! The arrogance, the insensate haughtiness of it! And why give it to our envoys when he was sending Cotyla to us, his friends' ornament and strong refuge, an ex-aedile—if indeed he *was* an aedile when public slaves beat him with leather straps at a dinner party on Antonius' orders.

**25** But what a modest message it is! We must have hearts of stone, Members of the Senate, to refuse this man anything. "I resign both provinces,"[21] he says. "I lay down my army. I am willing to become a private citizen." These are his words. You would think he was coming to his senses. "I forget all that has happened, am ready for a reconciliation." Ah, but what comes next? "If you will give bounties and land to my six legions, my cavalry, and my praetorian cohort." He actually demands bounties for these men; he would be considered grossly impudent if he asked for their pardon. On top of that, he demands that lands granted by himself and Dolabella remain with the grantees. **26** This means the Campanian and Leontine territories, looked upon by our ancestors as the ultimate reserves of the corn supply. He is safeguarding the actors, the gamblers, the pimps. He also safeguards Cafo and Saxa, those pugnacious, brawny centurions whom he settled among the droves of comedi-

20. In 168.
21. Cisalpine Gaul and Macedonia.

locavit. Postulat praeterea ut [chirographorum et commentariorum] sua
collegaeque sui decreta maneant. quid laborat ut habeat quod quisque
mercatus est, si quod accepit habet qui vendidit? et ne tangantur rationes
ad Opis: id est, ne septiens miliens recuperetur. ne fraudi sit septemviris
quod egissent. Nucula hoc, credo, admonuit; verebatur fortasse ne amit-　5
teret tantas clientelas. caveri etiam vult eis qui secum sint quicquid contra
leges commiserint. Mustelae et Tironi prospicit: de se nihil laborat.
**27** quid enim commisit umquam? num aut pecuniam publicam attigit aut
hominem occidit aut secum habuit armatos? sed quid est quod de eis la-
boret? postulat enim ne sua iudiciaria lex abrogetur. quo impetrato quid　10
est quod metuat? an ne suorum aliquis a Cyda, Lysiade, Curio condem-
netur? neque tamen nos urget mandatis pluribus; remittit aliquantum et
relaxat. "Galliam" inquit "togatam remitto, comatam postulo"—otiosus
videlicet esse non vult—"cum sex legionibus" inquit "eisque suppletis
ex D. Bruti exercitu," non modo ex dilectu suo, tam diuque ut obtineat　15
dum M. Brutus C. Cassius consules prove consulibus provincias obtine-
bunt. huius comitiis Gaius frater—eius est enim annus—iam repulsam
tulit. **28** "ipse autem ut quinquennium" inquit "obtineam." at istud vetat
lex Caesaris, et tu acta Caesaris defendis.

Haec tu mandata, L. Piso, et tu, L. Philippe, principes civitatis, non　20
dico animo ferre verum auribus accipere potuistis? sed, ut suspicor, terror
erat quidam: nec vos ut legati apud illum fuistis nec ut consulares, nec
vos vestram nec rei publicae dignitatem tenere potuistis. et tamen nescio
quo pacto sapientia quadam, credo, quod ego non possem, non nimis
irati revertistis. vobis M. Antonius nihil tribuit, clarissimis viris, legatis　25
populi Romani: nos quid non legato M. Antoni Cotylae concessimus? cui

---

1 *del. Schelle*: chirographorum *iam del. Mommsen auctore Halm*　　sua *ante* et *loc.*
*V*　　3 habeat *D*　　ne tangantur] nega- *V*　　4 ne (*pr.*)] ne sestertium *D*　　5 hoc *om.*
*D*　　admonuit] *anne* adm- *vel potius* L. fr.*?*[3]　　**27** 8 attingit *V*　　13 togatam] totam
*D*　　14 non vult[3] *scripsi*: mauolt *V*: mauolo *t*: malo *bnsv*　　15 obtineam *Cobet*　　17
enim] enim iam *V*: *num* enim etiam[2]*?*　　annus] a- ut *V*　　**28** 18 ipse autem ut] aut (ut *s*)
*D*　　obtineant *nsv*: -at *t*　　vetat] tua et *nsv*: tue et ad *t*: et *b*　　19 et . . . Caesaris *om.*
*D*　　defendit *D*　　20 L. (*pr.*) *om. V*　　24–25 nimis irati] miserati *nstv*　　26 quid]
qui *V*　　M. *om. D*

ans and comediennes. He further demands that his and his colleague's orders remain valid. Why is he concerned that every buyer keep what he bought, so long as the seller keeps his price? Further, that the accounts in the temple of Ops be left as they are: that is to say, that the seven hundred million not be recovered. That no penalty attach to the Board of Seven on account of their actions: I take this to be Nucula's suggestion; perhaps he was afraid of losing such important clienteles.[22] Also Antonius wants an indemnity for those who are with him to cover any breach of law they have committed; **27** he is looking after Mustela and Tiro[23]—no concern on his own account! After all, what law did *he* ever break? Did he lay hands on public funds or kill somebody or have armed men about him? But why should he worry about them, since he demands that his judiciary law not be repealed? If he gets that, what has he to fear?—that one of his associates be found guilty by Cydas and Lysiades and Curius? However, he does not press us with further demands, but yields a little, relaxes. "I resign Cisalpine Gaul," he says.[24] "I ask for Outer Gaul"— apparently he does not want to be unemployed—"with six legions," says he; these to be brought up to strength out of Decimus Brutus' army, not just from his own levy; and he demands tenure as long as Marcus Brutus and Gaius Cassius hold provinces as consuls or proconsuls. In *his* elections his brother Gaius (for it is his year too) has already been defeated.[25] **28** "Provided," he says, "that I myself have tenure for five years." But your demand is forbidden under Caesar's law[26] and you are defending Caesar's acts.

Was this a message to which you, Lucius Piso, and you, Lucius Philippus, leaders of the community, could listen—I don't say listen with acquiescence, but simply listen? But I suspect there was some intimidation. You did not stand in his presence as envoys or as consulars, you could not protect your own dignity or that of the Commonwealth. And yet, somehow or other, by some sort of philosophy[27] as I imagine (I could not have risen to it myself), you were not too angry when you came back. Marcus Antonius did you no courtesies, illustrious figures as you were, envoys of the Roman People. What courtesies have we not extended to Marcus Antonius' envoy Cotyla? The gates of this

---

22. Is Cicero implying that a model of propriety like Nucula could have nothing personally to fear, only the loss of clients if the assignments of land were rescinded? Or is he anticipating the point he makes below, that Antony's judiciary law would shield his followers?

23. Cf. 5.18.

24. Lit. "Gowned Gaul," *Gallia togata*; Outer Gaul (*ultima Gallia*, Transalpine Gaul beyond the old Roman province of Narbonensis) is "Long-haired Gaul," *Gallia comata*.

25. Gaius Antonius, like M. Brutus and Cassius, had been praetor in 44 and so could stand for the consulship in 42. On what Antony really meant see SB².

26. Limiting the tenure of consular provinces to two years.

27. Perhaps an allusion to Piso's well-known Epicureanism.

portas huius urbis patere ius non erat, huic hoc templum patuit, huic
aditus in senatum fuit, hic hesterno die sententias vestras in codicillos et
omnia verba referebat, huic se etiam summis honoribus usi contra suam
dignitatem venditabant.

**29** O di immortales! quam magnum est personam in re publica tueri　　5
principis! quae non animis solum debet sed etiam oculis servire civium.
domum recipere legatum hostium, in cubiculum admittere, etiam se-
ducere hominis est nihil de dignitate, nimium de periculo cogitantis.
quod autem est periculum? nam si maxime in discrimen venitur, aut libertas parata victori est aut mors proposita victo: quorum alterum optabile　　10
est, alterum effugere nemo potest. turpis autem fuga mortis omni est
morte peior.

**30** Nam illud quidem non adducor ut credam, esse quosdam qui invi-
deant alicui, ⟨qui ei⟩us constantiam, qui laborem, qui perpetuam in re
publica adiuvanda voluntatem et senatui et populo Romano probari mo-　　15
leste ferant. omnes id quidem facere debebamus, eaque erat non modo
apud maiores nostros sed etiam nuper summa laus consularium vigilare
[cogitare], adesse animo, semper aliquid pro re publica aut cogitare aut
facere aut dicere. **31** ego, patres conscripti, Q. Scaevolam augurem memoria teneo bello Marsico, cum esset summa senectute et perdita valetu-　　20
dine, cotidie simul atque luceret facere omnibus conveniendi potestatem
sui: nec eum quisquam illo bello vidit in lecto, senexque et debilis primus
veniebat in curiam. huius industriam maxime equidem vellem ut imita-
rentur ei quos oportebat; secundo autem loco ne alterius labori inviderent.

**32** Etenim, patres conscripti, cum in spem libertatis sexennio post　　25
sumus ingressi diutiusque servitutem perpessi quam captivi servi frugi et
diligentes solent, quas vigilias, quas sollicitudines, quos labores liberandi
populi Romani causa recusare debemus? equidem, patres conscripti,
quamquam hoc honore usi togati solent esse cum est in sagis civitas,
statui tamen a vobis ceterisque civibus in tanta atrocitate temporis tanta-　　30

---

1 erat] fuit *D*　　1–2 huic . . . fuit *del. Pluygers*　　3 usi *cod. Ferrarii:* i *Vt*: hii *b*: sed *s*[1]:
si *n*[1] (*eras. n*[2]) *s*[2]: hic *v*　　3–4 dignitatem suam *D*　　**29** 6 animis] armis *D*　　8 reducere *D*　　9 est] et *V*　　maxime *Faërnus:* -mum *codd.*　　uenietur (-iet *v*) *D*　　10
parta *D*　　exposita *D*　　victo] uicit *V*: victis *coni. Halm*　　**30** 14 alicui . . . constantiam *scripsi:* -uius constantiae *codd.*　　laborem, qui *scripsi:* -ri eius *V*: -ri eius qui
eius *bstv:* -ribus qui eius *n:* -ri, qui *Clark*　　15 et senatui et populo *Halm:* et a senatui (-u
*D*) et (et a *D*) populi (-lo *D*) *codd.*　　16 debemus *btv:* debeamus *ns*　　18 cogitare *del.*
*Faërnus*　　aut cogitare *om. D*　　**31** 19 p(atres) c(onscripti) *om. D*　　21 conueniendũi
*V*　　21–22 potestatem sui *Halm:* potest autem sui *V:* sui potestatem *D*　　22 neque
*D*　　et *om. V*　　23 quidem *V*　　**32** 25 cum] quoniam *Orelli*　　post *om. D*　　26
simus *nstv*　　diutiusque] *anne* diutius?　　servi *om. D* (*cf. Dig. 49.15.12.16* in captivo
servo; *Liv. 32.26.6* captiva aliquot . . . mancipia)

city ought not to have been open to him; but this temple was open, he was admitted into the Senate, he took down your speeches yesterday in his note-books every word, persons who had filled the highest offices made themselves agreeable to him to the detriment of their own dignity.

**29** Immortal Gods, how hard it is to sustain the role of a leader in the Commonwealth! That role demands concern not only about what the public thinks but about what it sees. To receive an enemy envoy into one's house, to admit him to one's bedroom, even draw him aside—that is the conduct of a man who thinks nothing of dignity and too much of danger. But what is the danger? However critical the situation, the outcome will be either freedom if we win or death if we lose. The first we pray for, the second no man can escape. Worse than any death is a dishonorable flight from death.

**30** For I cannot bring myself to believe that there are certain folk who are jealous of somebody,[28] who are ill pleased that his resolution, hard work, and unflagging will to aid the Commonwealth meet with approval from both the Senate and the People of Rome. That is how we should all behave. Quite recently as well as in the good old days the highest glory of a consular was to be watchful and alert, always thinking or doing or saying something for the public good. **31** Members of the Senate, I recall Quintus Scaevola the augur in the Marsic War.[29] He was very old and broken in health, but every day as soon as it grew light he would give admittance to everyone. Nobody during that war ever saw him in bed. Old and feeble as he was, he was the first to arrive at the Senate-house. I could have wished that those whom it behooved were follow-ing his conscientious example; or at least that they were not jealous of some-one else's toil.

**32** Indeed, Members of the Senate, now that after six years[30] we have begun to entertain the hope of liberty, after enduring servitude longer than enslaved prisoners of war[31] are wont to do if they are well behaved and conscientious, we must decline no vigils, no anxieties, no labors in the cause of the freedom of the Roman People. For my part, although persons of consular rank by custom retain their gowns when the community at large is in military cloaks, I decided that in so dire a situation, with the Commonwealth in such a state of

---

28. I.e. Cicero himself.

29. I.e. the Social War of 91–88. The Marsi in central Italy took a leading part in the revolt of the Italian allies against Rome.

30. Reckoned from the outbreak of war in January 49.

31. They were normally enslaved.

que perturbatione rei publicae non differre vestitu. non enim ita gerimus nos hoc bello consulares ut aequo animo populus Romanus visurus sit nostri honoris insignia, cum partim e nobis ita timidi sint ut omnem populi Romani beneficiorum memoriam abiecerint, partim ita a re publica aversi ut se hosti favere prae se ferant, legatos nostros ab Antonio despec-　5 tos et irrisos facile patiantur, legatum Antoni sublevatum velint. hunc enim reditu ad Antonium prohiberi negabant oportere et in eodem excipiendo sententiam meam corrigebant. quibus geram morem. redeat ad imperatorem suum Varius, sed ea lege ne umquam Romam revertatur. ceteris autem, si errorem suum deposuerint et cum re publica in gratiam　10 redierint, veniam et impunitatem dandam puto.

**33** Quas ob res ita censeo:

"Eorum qui cum M. Antonio sunt, qui ab armis discesserint et aut ad C. Pansam consulem aut ad A. Hirtium consulem aut ad D. Brutum imperatorem, consulem designatum, aut ad C. Caesarem pro praetore ante　15 Idus Martias proximas adierint, eis fraudi ne sit quod cum M. Antonio fuerint. si quis eorum qui cum M. Antonio sunt fecerit quod honore praemiove dignum esse videatur, uti C. Pansa A. Hirtius consules, alter ambove, si eis videbitur, de eius honore praemiove primo quoque die ad senatum referant. si quis post hoc senatus consultum ad Antonium pro-　20 fectus esset praeter L. Varium, senatum existimaturum eum contra rem publicam fecisse."

3 e *om. D*　　　timidi . . . omnem] -dis in tuto ne *b*: -dis induto est nem *t*: -dis in tuto est ne ii (hi) *nsv*　　5 ut] ut huic *nstv*　　6 et inrisos esse *b*: esse et i- *nstv*　　huic *D*　　7 reditum *D*　　prohibere *D*　　10 cum . . . gratiam] in r. p. gr- *nstv*　　**33** 13 et aut ad (ad *om. sv*) *D*: ita quia ad *V*: atque ad *Christ*　　14 consulem (*pr.*) *scripsi*: consul *V*: *om. D*　　ad *om. nstv*　　A. *om. V*　　consulem *scripsi*: -es *D*: *om. V*　　16 proximas¹ *scripsi*: primas *D*: *om. V*　　17 si quis . . . fecerit *om. D*　　quod] quo *bnsv*　　19 primo quoque die *om. V*　　21 esset] fuerit *D*

turmoil, I would not dress differently from you and the rest of the community. We consulars are not conducting ourselves so nobly in this war that the Roman People is likely to view the outward signs of our rank with complacency. Some of us are so fainthearted that they have cast away all recollection of the Roman People's favors, others so unpatriotic that they openly admit to supporting the enemy, are quite happy to see our envoys despised and ridiculed by Antonius, want to ease matters for Antonius' envoy. They said he should not be prevented from rejoining Antonius and wished to correct my motion by making an exception of him. I shall humor them. Let Varius go back to his imperator, but on condition that he never return to Rome. As for the rest, if they put their error aside and are reconciled with the Commonwealth, I am for granting them pardon and immunity.

33 Therefore I propose as follows:

"That of the persons now with Marcus Antonius those who shall leave his army and join either Gaius Pansa, Consul, or Aulus Hirtius, Consul, or Decimus Brutus, Imperator and Consul-Elect, or Gaius Caesar, Propraetor, before the Ides of March next, shall suffer no penalty because they were with Marcus Antonius. If any of those now with Marcus Antonius shall perform any action deemed worthy of honor or reward,[32] that Gaius Pansa and Aulus Hirtius, Consuls, either or both, if they see fit, shall refer to the Senate concerning honor or reward for that person on the first day possible. If any person shall join Marcus Antonius after this decree, Lucius Varius excepted, that the Senate shall deem him to have acted against the Commonwealth."

32. An attempt on Antony's life seems to be in mind.

# IX

## INTRODUCTION

Early in February 43 the Senate discussed the honors to be paid to Ser. Sulpicius Rufus, who had died in discharge of his mission just as he was about to meet Antony at Mutina, thus ending a distinguished career as statesman, orator, and jurist. As consul in 51 he had striven for peace; but when war broke out, after some wavering he joined Pompey in Greece. After Pharsalia Caesar pardoned him and made him governor of Achaia in 46. Cicero's friendship with Sulpicius went back to their early days. Letters between them survive, including a famous letter of condolence on the death of Cicero's daughter (*Fam.* 4.5). In correspondence with Atticus, however, Cicero was apt to take a patronizing or sarcastic tone about his old friend, whom "he always tended to regard as something of an old woman." Ever a man of peace and moderation, Sulpicius' line in the current crisis may not have been as hard as Cicero liked to represent.

**1** Vellem di immortales fecissent, patres conscripti, ut vivo potius Ser. Sulpicio gratias ageremus quam honores mortuo quaereremus. nec vero dubito quin, si ille vir legationem renuntiare potuisset, reditus eius et vobis gratus fuerit et rei publicae salutaris futurus, non quo L. Philippo et L. Pisoni aut studium aut cura defuerit in tanto officio tantoque munere,   5 sed cum Ser. Sulpicius aetate illis anteiret, sapientia omnibus, subito ereptus e causa totam legationem orbam et debilitatam reliquit.

**2** Quod si cuiquam iustus honos habitus est in morte legato, in nullo iustior quam in Ser. Sulpicio reperietur. ceteri qui in legatione mortem obierunt ad incertum vitae periculum sine ullo mortis metu profecti sunt:   10 Ser. Sulpicius cum aliqua perveniendi ad M. Antonium spe profectus est, nulla revertendi. qui cum ita adfectus esset ut, si ad gravem valetudinem labor accessisset, sibi ipse diffideret, non recusavit quo minus vel extremo spiritu, si quam opem rei publicae ferre posset, experiretur. itaque non illum vis hiemis, non nives, non longitudo itineris, non asperitas   15 viarum, non morbus ingravescens retardavit, cumque iam ad congressum colloquiumque eius pervenisset ad quem erat missus, in ipsa cura ac meditatione obeundi sui muneris excessit e vita.

**3** Ut igitur alia, sic hoc, C. Pansa, praeclare, quod et nos ad honorandum Ser. Sulpicium cohortatus es et ipse multa copiose de illius laude   20 dixisti. quibus a te dictis nihil praeter sententiam dicerem, nisi P. Servilio, clarissimo viro, respondendum putarem, qui hunc honorem statuae nemini tribuendum censuit nisi ei qui ferro esset in legatione interfectus. ego autem, patres conscripti, sic interpretor sensisse maiores nostros ut causam mortis censuerint, non genus esse quaerendum. etenim cui lega-   25 tio ipsa morti fuisset, eius monumentum exstare voluerunt, ut in bellis periculosis obirent homines legationis munus audacius. non igitur exempla maiorum quaerenda, sed consilium est eorum a quo ipsa exempla nata sunt explicandum.

**4** Lars Tolumnius, rex Veientium, quattuor legatos populi Romani   30 Fidenis interemit, quorum statuae steterunt usque ad meam memoriam in rostris. iustus honos; eis enim maiores nostri qui ob rem publicam mor-

---

**1** 2 mortuo honores *D*     6 illis . . . omnibus *D*, *Aurusian.* 7 : *454 Keil*: illos anteeire sapientia omnis *V* (anteiret *et* omnibus *V²*)    **2** 9 quam . . . reperietur *om. V¹*: quam . . . Sulpicio *del. C. F. W. Müller*    13 in extremo *D*    15 asperitatis *V*: -tes *coni. Halm*    16 viarum . . . cumque] uiarumque *V¹* (*medd. omissis;* non . . . retardavit *add. V²*)    **3** 19 C. *om. D*     quod et *V²*: quodenset *V¹*: quod *D*    20 es] est *Vstv*     illius] ipsius *V*    21 P. *om. V*    22 clarissimo viro *Mommsen*: cui *V¹*: c. u. *V²*: cum *t*: *om. bnsv*    23 ei] ei p. *V*: *om. nstv*    24 patres conscripti sic *om. V¹* (.ps. *add. V²*)    26 morti] -is causa *ς*     ut in *om. V*    28 a *om. D*    **4** 31 meam] nostram *D*     in rostris (*l.* 32) *ante* steterunt *D*    32 eis *om. V*

**1** I would the Immortal Gods had so willed it, Members of the Senate, that we should thank Servius Sulpicius in life rather than seek ways of honoring him in death. Neither do I doubt that if that great man could have reported on his mission, his return would have been both welcome to you and beneficial to the Commonwealth. I do not imply that Lucius Philippus and Lucius Piso lacked either zeal or diligence in so important a duty and charge, but the sudden loss of Servius Sulpicius, who surpassed them in age and all of us in wisdom, left the whole embassy bereft and enfeebled.

**2** Now if ever an honor was properly accorded to an envoy in death, no case will be found more deserving than that of Servius Sulpicius. Others who met their deaths on an embassy set out in face of an uncertain risk to life but without any fear of death. Servius Sulpicius set out with some hope of reaching Marcus Antonius, but none of returning. He was in such poor health that he himself hardly hoped to survive if exertion should be added to grave illness. Yet he did not decline to try with his last breath whether he could render a service to the Commonwealth. Not winter's violence, nor snow, nor the length of the journey, nor the roughness of the roads, nor his worsening sickness retarded him. And when finally he reached the point of meeting and speaking with the person to whom he had been sent,[1] just as he was pondering and preparing to execute his charge, he departed this life.

**3** In this as in other respects, Gaius Pansa, you have done excellently well in that you both urged us to honor Servius Sulpicius and yourself eulogized him at abundant length. After what you have said, I should do no more than signify my assent, were it not that I feel some answer should be given to our illustrious fellow member Publius Servilius, who has given it as his opinion that this honor of a statue ought to be conferred only on an envoy killed by the sword in the course of his mission. Now I, Members of the Senate, interpret our ancestors' intention to have been that the cause of death be examined, not the manner of it. They wanted there to be a monument to an envoy whose actual mission had cost him his life, so that in dangerous wars such missions should be the more boldly discharged. So we should not just look for historical precedents, but make plain the design out of which those very precedents arose.

**4** Lars Tolumnius, King of Veii, killed four envoys of the Roman People at Fidenae,[2] and within my own recollection their statues stood on the Rostra. Rightly so. To those who had met their deaths in the service of the Common-

---

1. They did not actually meet; see 9.15.
2. In 437.

te:n obierant pro brevi vita diuturnam memoriam reddiderunt. Cn. Octavi, clari viri et magni, qui primus in eam familiam quae postea viris fortissimis floruit attulit consulatum, statuam videmus in rostris. nemo tum novitati invidebat; nemo virtutem non honorabat. at ea fuit legatio Octavi in qua periculi suspicio non subesset. nam cum esset missus a se- 5
natu ad animos regum perspiciendos liberorumque populorum, maxime-que, ut nepotem regis Antiochi, eius qui cum maioribus nostris bellum gesserat, classis habere, elephantos alere prohiberet, Laudiceae in gymnasio a quodam Leptine est interfectus. 5 reddita est ei tum a maioribus statua pro vita quae multos per annos progeniem eius honestaret, nunc ad 10
tantae familiae memoriam sola resta[re]t.

Atqui et huic et Tullo Cluilio et L. Roscio et Sp. Antio et C. Fulcinio, qui a Veientium rege caesi sunt, non sanguis qui est profusus in morte, sed ipsa mors ob rem publicam obita honori fuit. itaque, patres conscripti, si Ser. Sulpicio casus mortem attulisset, dolerem equidem tanto 15
rei publicae vulnere, mortem vero eius non monumento, sed luctu publico esse ornandam putarem. nunc autem quis dubitat quin ei vitam abstulerit ipsa legatio? secum enim ille mortem extulit quam, si nobiscum remansisset, sua cura, optimi fili fidelissimaeque coniugis diligentia vitare potuisset. 6 at ille cum videret, si vestrae auctoritati non paruisset, 20
dissimilem se futurum sui, sin paruisset, munus sibi illud pro re publica susceptum vitae finem fore, maluit in maximo rei publicae discrimine emori quam minus quam potuisset videri rei publicae profuisse. multis illi in urbibus iter qua faciebat reficiendi se et curandi potestas fuit. aderat et hospitum invitatio liberalis pro dignitate summi viri et eorum hortatio 25
qui una erant missi ad requiescendum et vitae suae consulendum. at ille properans, festinans, mandata vestra conficere cupiens, in hac constantia morbo adversante perseveravit. 7 cuius cum adventu maxime perturbatus esset Antonius, quod ea quae sibi iussu vestro denuntiarentur auctoritate erant et sententia Ser. Sulpici constituta, declaravit quam odisset senatum 30
cum auctorem senatus exstinctum laete atque insolenter tulit. non igitur magis Leptines Octavium nec Veientium rex eos quos modo nominavi quam Ser. Sulpicium occidit Antonius: is enim profecto mortem attulit

2 et magni uiri *D*    4 et ea *Kraffert*    6 respiciendos *V*    7 antiochi regis *D*    **5** 11 restat *Ernesti*: -aret *codd.*    12 atque *D*    Cluilio *Garatoni*: cluuio *codd.*: Cloelio *Ursinus*    14 habita *Vbnsv*    15 dolerem *n²*: dolorem *codd.*    quidem *V*    16 monu(-i-)mentis et *stv*: -is sed *bn*    17 ornandam] ora- *n¹*: decora- *b*: honora- *sn²*    19 fidelissimae (-a *t*) *D*    **6** 21 pro re p(ublica)] p. r. *D*    22 fore] allaturum *D*    24 recipiendi *V²* *in ras.*    se] sui *coni.* *C. F. W. Müller*    25 et (*pr.*) *om. V*    27 festinansque *bnst*    **7** 32 octauium leptines *D*

wealth our ancestors gave long-lasting memory in return for brief life. We see on the Rostra the statue of the great and famous Gnaeus Octavius, who first brought the consulship into a family which later could be proud of its brave men.[3] Nobody in those days begrudged newcomers; everybody respected worth. But Octavius' mission[4] was one in which lay no suspicion of danger. He was sent by the Senate to observe the dispositions of monarchs and free states, and more particularly to forbid the grandson of that King Antiochus who went to war with our ancestors to maintain fleets and keep elephants. At Laodicea he was assassinated by one Leptines in a public hall. 5 In return for his life a statue was then granted him by our ancestors, which was to honor his descendants for many years and is now the sole memorial of so great a family.

Both in Octavius' case and in that of the victims of the king of Veii, namely Tullus Cluilius, Lucius Roscius, Spurius Antius, and Gaius Fulcinius, it was not the blood they shed as they died which brought them the honor but the death itself, incurred in the service of the Commonwealth. So, Members of the Senate, if Servius Sulpicius' death had been an accident, however much I grieved at so heavy a public loss, I should think it appropriately honored by public mourning, not by a monument. But as matters stand, is it not clear to all that it was the embassy itself that took his life? He carried his death out with him, a death which, had he remained with us, he might have avoided by his own care and the diligence of an excellent son and a very devoted wife. 6 But when he saw that he would be unlike himself if he did not obey your authority, whereas if he did obey it that charge undertaken for the sake of the Commonwealth would be the end of his life, he preferred at a public crisis of the utmost gravity to die outright rather than appear to have done less for the Commonwealth than he might have done. In many towns through which he passed he had opportunity for refreshment and treatment. There were invitations from friends, liberal as befitted the dignity of one so eminent, and encouragement from his fellow envoys to rest and take thought for his life. But hastening, hurrying, eager to discharge your commission, he held to his resolve in the face of his sickness. 7 His arrival threw Antonius into consternation, for the commands presented to him on your orders had been drawn up with the authority and vote of Servius Sulpicius. He made plain his hatred of the Senate by his insolent delight at the passing of the Senate's counselor. Therefore I say, Leptines did not kill Octavius, nor the king of Veii those whose names I have just mentioned, more certainly than Antonius killed Servius Sulpicius. For

3. Though Octavian was related only very remotely, if at all, to the noble Octavii, Cicero's special attention to the latter in this speech was probably a compliment to him; cf. 9.5 and *Two Studies*, 94–95. *Fortissimis* will have been suggested by Cinna's opponent, the consul of 87, and by M. Octavius, who had fought and died on the republican side in the last civil war.

4. In 163.

qui causa mortis fuit. quocirca etiam ad posteritatis memoriam pertinere arbitror exstare quod fuerit de hoc bello iudicium senatus. erit enim statua ipsa testis bellum tam grave fuisse ut legati interitus honoris memoriam consecutus sit.

**8** Quod si excusationem Ser. Sulpici, patres conscripti, legationis obeundae recordari volueritis, nulla dubitatio relinquetur quin honore mortui quam vivo iniuriam fecimus sarciamus. vos enim, patres conscripti—grave dictu est sed dicendum tamen—vos, inquam, Ser. Sulpicium vita privastis: quem cum videretis re magis morbum quam oratione excusantem, non vos quidem crudeles fuistis—quid enim minus in hunc ordinem convenit?—sed cum speraretis nihil esse quod non illius auctoritate et sapientia effici posset, vehementius excusationi obstitistis atque eum qui semper vestrum consensum gravissimum iudicavisset de sententia deiecistis. **9** ut vero Pansae consulis accessit cohortatio gravior quam aures Ser. Sulpici ferre didicissent, tum vero denique filium meque seduxit atque ita locutus est ut auctoritatem vestram vitae suae se diceret anteferre. cuius nos virtutem admirati non ausi sumus adversari voluntati. movebatur singulari pietate filius; non multum eius perturbationi meus dolor concedebat: sed uterque nostrum cedere cogebatur magnitudini animi orationisque gravitati, cum quidem ille maxima laude et gratulatione omnium vestrum pollicitus est se quod velletis esse facturum, neque eius sententiae periculum vitaturum cuius ipse auctor fuisset: quem exsequi mandata vestra properantem mane postridie prosecuti sumus. qui quidem discedens mecum ita locutus est ut eius oratio omen fati videretur.

**10** Reddite igitur, patres conscripti, ei vitam cui ademistis. vita enim mortuorum in memoria est posita vivorum. perficite ut is quem vos inscii ad mortem misistis immortalitatem habeat a vobis. cui si statuam in rostris decreto vestro statueritis, nulla eius legationem posteritatis obscurabit oblivio.

Nam reliqua Ser. Sulpici vita multis erit praeclarisque monumentis ad omnem memoriam commendata. semper illius gravitatem, constantiam, fidem, praestantem in re publica tuenda curam atque prudentiam omnium mortalium fama celebrabit. nec vero silebitur admirabilis quaedam et incredibilis ac paene divina eius in legibus interpretandis, aequitate expli-

**8** 6 honorem *nstvb²*    7 mortuo *nstvb²*    arceamus *V*    8 dictum *Vsv*    9 priuauistis *bntv*    re] se *DV²*    morbo *bnsv*    10 crudeles quidem *V*    12 vehementius eius *Lambinus*    **9** 15 vero denique *om. D*    filium meque] pi- (triumphum *b*) equitem (-e *v*) *D*    17 eius uoluntati *ns*: u- eius *V²*    **10** 25 ei uitam *nsv²V²*: si u- *V¹*: ciu- *t*: uitam ei *bv¹*    26–27 ad mortem inscii *D*    27 a *om. V¹n¹tv¹*    28 decretis uestris *V*    obscurabit *Faërnus*: -auit *V*: inobscurabit *D*    32 praestantiam *D*    34 ac] et *D*

obviously he who was the cause of death is responsible for it. Accordingly, I think it also relevant to the way in which posterity will remember these events that the judgment of the Senate concerning this war should stand recorded. The statue itself will bear witness that the war was so formidable that the death of an envoy received an honorable memorial.

**8** If you will remember, Members of the Senate, Servius Sulpicius' excuse for not undertaking the mission, no doubt will remain about our obligation to repair the injury we did him in life by honoring him in death. For you, Members of the Senate—it is a hard thing to say, but it has to be said—yes, *you* took Servius Sulpicius' life. Seeing him offer the excuse of illness, not in words so much as in actuality, I will not say you were cruel (that would be altogether unlike this House), but in your hope that nothing was beyond his authority and wisdom to accomplish you strenuously opposed his excuse and made him change his mind; for in his judgment your united will always weighed most heavily. **9** But then, when Consul Pansa added an exhortation in terms more pressing than Servius Sulpicius' ears had learned to tolerate, then he drew his son and myself aside and said in effect that he put your authority before his own life. We admired his courage; we did not venture to oppose his will. His son, the most affectionate of sons, was deeply moved. My sorrow almost matched his distress. But we were both forced to yield to the nobility of the man's spirit and the authority of his words when to enthusiastic applause and expressions of gratitude[5] from all of you he promised to do as you wished and not to shun the dangers of a proposal which he himself had sponsored. Early the following day we saw him off, in his haste to execute your commission. And as he said good-bye, he spoke to me in words which seemed an omen of his doom.

**10** Therefore, Members of the Senate, restore life to him from whom you took it away. The life of the dead is in the memory of the living. Unknowingly you sent him to his death; let him gain immortality at your hands. If by your decree you set up his statue in the Rostra, no forgetfulness of generations to come shall dim the memory of his mission.

The rest of Servius Sulpicius' life will be handed down to everlasting recollection by many shining memorials. His gravity, steadfastness, honor, exceptional diligence, and wisdom in guarding the Commonwealth will ever be on the lips of all mankind. Nor will posterity have nothing to say about his amazing, unbelievable, almost superhuman expertise in the interpretation of

---

5. For this meaning of *gratulatio*, which suits the context better than "congratulations," see my note on *Fam.* 11.18.3.

canda scientia. omnes ex omni aetate qui in hac civitate intellegentiam
iuris habuerunt si unum in locum conferantur, cum Ser. Sulpicio non sint
comparandi. nec enim ille magis iuris consultus quam iustitiae fuit. **11** ita
ea quae proficiscebantur a legibus et ab iure civili semper ad facilitatem
aequitatemque referebat, neque instituere litium actiones malebat quam　5
controversias tollere.

Ergo hoc statuae monumento non eget; habet alia maiora. haec enim
statua mortis honestae testis erit, illa memoria vitae gloriosae, ut hoc
magis monumentum grati senatus quam clari viri futurum sit. **12** multum
etiam valuisse ad patris honorem pietas fili videbitur; qui quamquam　10
adflictus luctu non adest, tamen sic animati esse debetis ut si ille adesset.
est autem ita adfectus ut nemo umquam unici fili mortem magis doluerit
quam ille maeret patris. et quidem etiam ad famam Ser. Sulpici fili
arbitror pertinere ut videatur honorem debitum patri praestitisse. quamquam nullum monumentum clarius Ser. Sulpicius relinquere potuit quam　15
effigiem morum suorum, virtutis, constantiae, pietatis, ingeni filium,
cuius luctus aut hoc honore vestro aut nullo solacio levari potest.

**13** Mihi autem recordanti Ser. Sulpici multos in nostra familiaritate
sermones gratior illi videtur, si qui est sensus in morte, aenea statua futura et ea pedestris quam inaurata equestris, qualis L. Sullae primum　20
statu⟨t⟩a est. mirifice enim Servius maiorum continentiam diligebat,
huius saeculi insolentiam vituperabat. ut igitur si ipsum consulam quid
velit, sic pedestrem ex aere statuam tamquam ex eius auctoritate et voluntate decerno: quae quidem magnum civium dolorem et desiderium honore monumenti minuet et leniet.　25

**14** Atque hanc meam sententiam, patres conscripti, P. Servili sententia
comprobari necesse est: qui sepulcrum publice decernendum Ser. Sulpicio
censuit, statuam non censuit. nam si mors legati sine caede atque ferro
nullum honorem desiderat, cur decernit honorem sepulturae, qui maximus haberi potest mortuo? sin id tribuit Ser. Sulpicio, quod non est　30
datum Cn. Octavio, cur quod illi datum est huic dandum esse non censet?
maiores quidem nostri statuas multis decreverunt, sepulcra paucis. sed
statuae intereunt tempestate, vi, vetustate, sepulcrorum autem sanctitas
in ipso solo est, quod nulla vi moveri neque deleri potest, atque, ut cetera

2 iuris *om. D*　　3 neque enim *bnsv*: n- *t*　　**11** 3–4 ita ea] itaque *D*　　4 a iure *stvb²*:
aure *b¹*: iure *n*　　5 constituere *D*　　9 magis] maius *Vbt*　　gratiae *bns*: -ia *tvV²*　　**12**
13 quidem] eq- *D*　　16 morum] maio- *D*　　**13** 20 et ea] et *b*: aere *nstv*　　prima
*D*　　21 statuta *Graevius*: -ua *codd.*　　magnifice *D*　　ser. sulpicius *nstv*　　**14** 26 P.
*om. V*　　27 probari *D*　　29 *post* sepulturae *fort.* publicae *addendum*　　33 tempestate
uetustate *V¹n²* (uel *post* temp- *add. V²*)

our laws and the unfolding of equity. If all who at any period have had understanding of jurisprudence in this community were brought together in one place, they could not be compared with Servius Sulpicius. For he was an expert in justice no less than in jurisprudence. **11** To the conclusions emerging from statutes and civil law he would always bring flexibility and a sense of fair play. He was not fonder of setting up the forms of litigation than of clearing away disputes.

Therefore he needs no statue to keep his memory green; he has other and greater monuments. As distinct from those memorials of a glorious life, this statue will testify to an honorable death. It will commemorate a grateful Senate rather than an illustrious man. **12** Moreover the devotion of the son will appear to have counted for much in the honor paid to the father. Although he is too heavily stricken with grief to be here today, you should feel in your hearts as if he were present. Such is his distress that no man ever grieved more for the death of an only son than he mourns the death of his father. Indeed I think it concerns the reputation of Servius Sulpicius junior that he should appear to have brought his father the honor his father deserved. To be sure, Servius Sulpicius could have left no finer memorial than a son in his own likeness—the likeness of his character, courage, steadfastness, piety, and intellect—whose grief can be comforted by this honor of your conferring, or not at all.

**13** As I recall my many conversations with Servius Sulpicius in the course of our friendship, I have the feeling that if consciousness exists after death, he will prefer a statue of bronze, and on foot, to a gilt equestrian statue such as was first erected for Lucius Sulla. Servius had an extraordinary love for old-world restraint and used to inveigh against the extravagances of the present epoch. It is therefore by his authority and will as it were, as though he were here for me to ask his wishes, that I propose a bronze statue on foot. Our countrymen's deep grief and sense of loss will be abated and eased by the honor of this monument.

**14** And this motion of mine, Members of the Senate, must necessarily be endorsed by Publius Servilius' motion. He proposed that Servius Sulpicius be voted a public sepulcher, but was against a statue. If the death of an envoy without bloodshed and weapons calls for no honor, why does he propose the honor of public burial, the greatest that can be conferred upon a dead man? But if he grants Servius Sulpicius something not given to Gnaeus Octavius, why is he opposed to giving the former what *was* given to the latter? Our ancestors decreed statues for many, but sepulchers only for a few. But statues perish by weather or violence or time, whereas the sanctity of sepulchers is inherent in the soil, which no force can move or obliterate. Other things are destroyed by

exstinguuntur, sic sepulcra sanctiora fiunt vetustate. **15** augeatur igitur
isto honore etiam is vir cui nullus honos tribui non debitus potest; grati
simus in eius morte decoranda cui nullam iam aliam gratiam referre
possumus. notetur etiam M. Antoni nefarium bellum gerentis scelerata
audacia. his enim honoribus habitis Ser. Sulpicio repudiatae reiectaeque　　5
legationis ab Antonio manebit testificatio sempiterna.

Quas ob res ita censeo:

"Cum Ser. Sulpicius Q. f. Lemonia Rufus difficillimo rei publicae
tempore, gravi periculosoque morbo adfectus, auctoritatem senatus, salutem rei publicae vitae suae praeposuerit contraque vim gravitatemque　10
morbi contenderit, ut in castra M. Antoni quo senatus eum miserat per-
veniret, isque, cum iam prope castra venisset, vi morbi oppressus vitam
amiserit maximo rei publicae tempore, eiusque mors consentanea vitae
fuerit sanctissime honestissimeque actae, in qua saepe magno usui rei
publicae Ser. Sulpicius et privatus et in magistratibus fuerit: **16** cum talis　15
vir ob rem publicam in legatione mortem obierit, senatui placere Ser.
Sulpicio statuam pedestrem aeneam in rostris ex huius ordinis sententia
statui, circumque eam statuam locum ludis gladiatoribusque liberos
posterosque eius quoquo versus pedes quinque habere, eamque causam in
basi inscribi quod is ob rem publicam mortem obierit; utique C. Pansa A.　20
Hirtius consules, alter ambove, si eis videatur, quaestoribus urb⟨an⟩is
imperent ut eam basim statuamque faciendam et in rostris statuendam
locent, quantique locaverint, tantam pecuniam redemptori attribuendam
solvendamque curent.

"Cumque antea senatus auctoritatem suam in virorum fortium funeribus　25
ornamentisque ostenderit, placere eum quam amplissime supremo suo
die efferri. **17** et cum Ser. Sulpicius Q. f. Lemonia Rufus ita de re publica
meritus sit ut eis ornamentis decorari debeat, senatum censere atque e
re publica existimare aedilis curulis edictum quod de funeribus habeant

---

**15** 1 igitur *om. V*　　2 etiam honore *D*　　2–3 grati simus *ed. Romana:* -issimus
*codd.*　　9 salutemque *D*　　12 isque] ipse *V*　　13 in maximo rei p. munere *D*　　15–
16 Ser. Sulpicius . . . ob rem publicam *om. D*　　**16** 18 gladiatoribus ludisque *D*　　19
quoque *V*[1]: quaque *nsvb*[2]: quaqua *V*[2]　　20 quod . . . obierit *huc transp. Clark, post*
habere *habent codd., del. Manutius:* quodque is . . . obierit, eam causam *Scaliger*　　21
uidebitur *D*　　urbanis *Ferrarius:* urbis *V:* -i *D*　　22 in rostris] in hortis *nsv:* in horis *t:*
*om. b*　　23 redemptores *D*　　23–24 soluendam attribuendamque *D*　　25 suam]
quam *t: om. bnsv*　　26 eos *Cobet, quo recepto* auctoritatem suam (*l.* 25) *vix est ut reti-*
*neas*　　**17** 29 aestimare *V*

the lapse of time, but sepulchers only grow more sacred. **15** Therefore let this great man, on whom no honor can be conferred beyond his deserving, be glorified by this honor also. Let us show ourselves grateful in distinguishing the death of one to whom we can now make no other return. Also let the criminal audacity of Marcus Antonius as he wages a wicked war be branded. For in these honors paid to Servius Sulpicius there will remain for all time a testimony to Antonius' repudiation and rejection of the mission.

For which reasons I make the following motion:

"Whereas Servius Sulpicius Rufus, son of Quintus, of the tribe Lemonia, in a situation of great difficulty for the Commonwealth, being afflicted by a severe and dangerous malady, did set the authority of the Senate and the welfare of the Commonwealth before his own life and did contend against the strength and severity of his sickness in order to reach the camp of Marcus Antonius, whither the Senate had sent him, and whereas, having almost arrived at the said camp, overborne by the strength of his sickness he lost his life at a juncture most serious for the Commonwealth; and whereas his death was in harmony with a most upright and honorable life, in the course of which Servius Sulpicius was often of great service to the Commonwealth both as a private citizen and in public offices; **16** since such a man has met his death while an envoy in the service of the Commonwealth: that it please the Senate that a statue, on foot and of bronze, be erected to Servius Sulpicius on the Rostra by resolution of this House; further that at games and gladiator shows his children and descendants be entitled to a space ten feet square[6] around the said statue; further that the pedestal record as the reason for its erection that he met his death in the service of the Commonwealth; further that Gaius Pansa and Aulus Hirtius, Consuls, either or both, if they see fit, direct the city quaestors to make a contract for the construction and placement on the Rostra of the said pedestal and statue and see to it that the sum agreed be allocated and paid to the contractor.

"And whereas in the past the Senate has shown its authority in dignifying the funerals of brave men, that it please the Senate that on the day of his funeral he be borne to burial with all possible ceremony. **17** And whereas Servius Sulpicius, son of Quintus, of the tribe Lemonia, has deserved of the Commonwealth to be honored by the said distinctions, that the Senate resolve and deem it in the public interest that the curule aediles suspend their standing order

---

6. *Quoquo versus pedes quinque*, lit. "five feet in any direction," generally understood to mean five feet square. But this would hardly leave room for the spectators. I take "five feet" to be the shortest distance from the center of the square (the statue) to its periphery, giving an area of ten feet square. Some support for this view can be found in Festus (Paulus), ed. Lindsay, p. 45, *Cybium dictum quia eius medium aeque patet in omnes partes, quod genus a geometricis κύβος dicitur.*

Ser. Sulpici Q. f. Lemonia Rufi funeri remittere; utique locum sepulcro in campo Esquilino C. Pansa consul, seu quo in loco videbitur, pedes triginta quoquo versus adsignet quo Ser. Sulpicius inferatur; quod sepulcrum ipsius, liberorum posterorumque eius esset, uti quod optimo iure publice sepulcrum datum esset." 5

1 funeri remittere *Faërnus*: funerreim- $V^1$ (-rre- $V^2$ *in ras.*): funere (-ri *ns*) m- *D*     2 uidebitur $V^2$: -ebatur $V^1$: -etur *D*     4 posterorum *btv*     sit *bntv*     5 sepulchrum publice *D*     est *bnst*

concerning funerals[7] insofar as concerns the funeral of Servius Sulpicius, son of Quintus, of the tribe Lemonia; further that Gaius Pansa, Consul, assign a space sixty feet square for a sepulcher in the Campus Esquilinus, or wherever shall be thought fitting, whereto Servius Sulpicius shall be conveyed, which sepulcher shall belong to him and his children and descendants with the full legal title appertaining to a sepulcher by public grant."

7. Limiting expenditure.

# X

## INTRODUCTION

The province of Macedonia, originally assigned by Caesar to M. Brutus, had been transferred to C. Antonius under Antony's direction at the meeting of the Senate on 28 November 44. Antony's assignments were rescinded by the Senate on 20 December. The incumbent proconsul, Q. Hortensius, remained in charge until January 43 (?), when C. Antonius landed at Dyrrachium with one legion. Meanwhile M. Brutus, who had arrived in Athens the previous autumn, was raising troops and money; Hortensius recognized him as his successor, and P. Vatinius, governor of Illyricum, cooperated. After a defeat and the defection of most of his force to Brutus, C. Antonius shut himself up in Apollonia. Shortly after 4 February a dispatch from Brutus to the Senate arrived announcing these events. Pansa convened the Senate to hear it. Speaking first as usual, Fufius Calenus moved that Brutus be required to give up his army and the provinces. In the Tenth Philippic Cicero counterproposed that Brutus' actions be approved and his authority recognized, and the Senate so ordered.

**1** Maximas tibi, Pansa, gratias omnes et habere et agere debemus qui, cum hodierno die senatum te habiturum non arbitraremur, ut M. Bruti, praestantissimi civis, litteras accepisti, ne minimam quidem moram interposuisti quin quam primum maximo gaudio et gratulatione frueremur. cum factum tuum gratum omnibus debet esse, tum vero oratio qua   5 recitatis litteris usus es. declarasti enim verum esse id quod ego semper sensi, neminem alterius qui suae confideret virtuti invidere.

**2** Itaque mihi qui plurimis officiis sum cum Bruto et maxima familiaritate coniunctus minus multa de illo dicenda sunt. quas enim ipse mihi partis sumpseram, eas praecepit oratio tua. sed mihi, patres conscripti,   10 necessitatem attulit paulo plura dicendi sententia eius qui rogatus est ante me; a quo ita saepe dissentio ut iam verear ne, id quod fieri minime debet, minuere amicitiam nostram videatur perpetua dissensio.

**3** Quae est enim ista tua ratio, Calene, quae mens, ut numquam post Kalendas Ianuarias idem senseris quod is qui te sententiam primum   15 rogat, numquam tam frequens senatus fuerit ut unus aliquis sententiam tuam secutus sit? cur semper tui dissimilis defendis? cur cum te et vita et fortuna tua ad otium, ad dignitatem invitet, ea probas, ea decernis, ea sentis quae sint inimica et otio communi et dignitati tuae?

Nam ut superiora omittam, hoc certe quod mihi maximam admira-   20 tionem movet non tacebo. **4** quod est tibi cum Brutis bellum? cur eos quos omnes paene venerari debemus solus oppugnas? alterum circumsederi non moleste fers, alterum tua sententia spolias eis copiis quas ipse suo labore et periculo ad rei publicae, non ad suum praesidium per se nullo adiuvante confecit. qui est iste tuus sensus, quae cogitatio, Brutos   25 ut non probes, Antonios probes; quos omnes carissimos habent, tu oderis, quos acerbissime ceteri oderunt, tu constantissime diligas? amplissimae tibi fortunae sunt, summus honoris gradus, filius, ut et audio et spero, natus ad laudem, cui cum rei publicae causa faveo, tum etiam tua. **5** quaero igitur, eum Brutine similem malis an Antoni; ac permitto ut de   30 tribus Antoniis eligas quem velis. "di meliora!" inquies. cur igitur non eis faves, eos laudas quorum similem tuum filium esse vis? simul enim et rei publicae consules et propones illi exempla ad imitandum.

---

**1** 4 maxime *V Cus.*     6 semper *om. D*     **2** 9–10 ipse mihi partis] sententias ipse *b*: -as mihi ipse *nst*: -am ipse mihi *v*     **3** 14 oratio *D*     ut] sui *t*: qui *bnsv*     15 censueris *Muretus* (*cf. Att. 7.1.4* aliter sensero?)     primum] prius *V*     16 ut *Naugerius*: cum *codd.*: quo *Faërnus*     18 et ad dignitatem *D*     19 sunt *D Cus.*     20 me maxima admiratione *D*     **4** 22 circumsedere *V*: -derit *b*: -derint *ntv*     23 non *om. bntv*     feres *V*[1]: ferres *V*[2]     25 perfecit *V*: *om. b*[1]     qui *V Cus.*: quis *bnst*: quos *v*     29 cum] quamquam *D*     **5** 30 eumne bruti *V*     32 et *om. nstv*     33 consulis et proponis *D*

**1** All of us, Gaius Pansa, ought to thank you most warmly and sincerely. We were not expecting you to hold a Senate today, but after receiving the letter of our distinguished fellow citizen Marcus Brutus you did not let even the slightest of intervals delay our enjoyment of so great a cause for happiness and congratulation. All should welcome your action, and also your speech after the letter had been read. You proved something I have always observed, that a man who is confident of his own worth is never jealous of another's.

**2** And so there is no need for me to say very much about Brutus, to whom I am attached by a great many good offices and the closest friendship. The role for which I had cast myself has been forestalled by your speech. But the motion of the gentleman who was called before me, Members of the Senate, has placed me under the necessity of saying a little more than I otherwise would. I disagree with him so often that I am beginning to fear that continual disagreement may seem to be detracting from our friendship, which would be a great pity.

**3** Calenus, what are you about? What is your thinking? How is it that ever since the Kalends of January you have never once been of the same mind as the gentleman who calls you first?[1] And that there have never been so many senators present as to provide you with a single supporter? Why are you forever defending persons unlike yourself? Your career and fortune invite you to tranquility and dignity. Yet all that you approve, propose, and advocate is contrary both to general tranquility and your individual dignity.

**4** Leaving previous matters aside, this at least I will mention—it surprises me most of all. What is this war you have on with the Bruti? Why do you alone attack men whom all of us ought, I might almost say, to worship? One of them is under siege, and you are not sorry for it. The other by your motion you rob of the forces which he has raised by his own efforts at his own risk, without assistance from any quarter, not for his own protection but for that of the Commonwealth. By what sentiment or process of thought do you disapprove of the Bruti and approve of the Antonii, hating those whom everyone else holds dearest, whereas those whom everyone else most bitterly hates, you steadfastly favor? You are a man of the amplest fortune and the highest official rank. You have a son, as I hear and hope, born for distinction. I wish him well for the public's sake and for yours. **5** Let me ask you then: would you rather he turned out like a Brutus or like an Antonius (and you are free to take your pick among the three Antonii)? "Heaven forbid!" you say. Then why do you not support and applaud those whom you wish your son to resemble? Thus you will serve the public interest and at the same time set before him models for his imitation.

---

1. His father-in-law, Pansa.

Hoc vero, Q. Fufi, cupio sine offensione nostrae amicitiae sic tecum ut
a te dissentiens senator queri: ita enim dixisti et quidem de scripto—nam
te inopia verbi lapsum putarem—litteras Bruti recte et ordine scriptas
videri. quid est aliud librarium Bruti laudare, non Brutum? **6** usum in re
publica, Calene, magnum iam habere et debes et potes. quando ita de-          5
cerni vidisti aut quo senatus consulto huius generis—sunt enim innumerabilia—bene scriptas litteras decretum a senatu? quod verbum tibi non
excidit, ut saepe fit, fortuito: scriptum, meditatum, cogitatum attulisti.

Hanc tibi consuetudinem plerisque in rebus bonis obtrectandi si qui
detraxerit, quid tibi quod sibi quisque velit non relinquetur? quam ob rem    10
collige te placaque animum istum aliquando et mitiga: audi viros bonos,
quibus multis uteris; loquere cum sapientissimo homine, genero tuo,
saepius quam ipse tecum: tum denique amplissimi honoris nomen obtinebis. an vero hoc pro nihilo putas, in quo equidem pro amicitia tuam
vicem dolere soleo, efferri hoc foras et ad populi Romani auris pervenire,    15
ei qui primus sententiam dixerit neminem adsensum? quod etiam hodie
futurum arbitror.

Legiones abducis a Bruto. quas? nempe eas quas ille a C. Antoni
scelere avertit et ad rem publicam sua auctoritate traduxit. rursus igitur
vis nudatum illum atque solum a re publica relegatum videre. **7** vos au-       20
tem, patres conscripti, si M. Brutum deserueritis et prodideritis, quem
tandem civem umquam ornabitis, cui favebitis? nisi forte eos qui diadema imposuerint conservandos, eos qui regnum omnino sustulerint de-
serendos putatis. ac de hac quidem divina atque immortali laude Bruti
silebo quae gratissima memoria omnium civium inclusa nondum publica     25
auctoritate testata est: tantamne patientiam, di boni, tantam moderationem, tantam in iniuria tranquillitatem et modestiam! qui cum praetor
urbanus esset, urbe caruit, ius non dixit, cum omne ius rei publicae re-
cuperavisset, cumque concursu cotidiano bonorum omnium qui admirabilis ad eum fieri solebat praesidioque Italiae cunctae saeptus posset      30
esse, absens iudicio bonorum defensus esse maluit quam praesens manu;
qui ne Apollinaris quidem ludos pro sua populique Romani dignitate

---

1 cupio] copiosius *D*      2 nam] ne *Clark*      3 putarem nisi tuam in dicendo facultatem (familiarita- *v*) nossem *bnsvV²*      4 aliud] a- quam *bnsvV²*      **6** 6 quo] quod *D*      8
fit] set *V¹*: seit *V²*: sit *bv*: solet *coni. Halm*      fortuito] -tu *bnsv*: fortitudo *t*      9 bonos
*nst*: honos *v*      11 istum *om. D*      12 uteris multum *D*      13 *"fort.* honoris amplissimi *(clausulae gratia)" Clark; num voluit* nomen obtinebis hon- amp- *vel* nom- hon- obt-
amp-*?*      14 equidem] q- *V*      tua *bn¹tv*      18 a C. Antonii *Muretus:* a catonis *V:* ab
antonii *D*      20 videre *Cobet:* -ri *codd.*      **7** 22 cui favebitis *om. V*      23 regnum om-
nino³ *scripsi:* regni nomen *V, Nonius 404:* regis n- *D*      27 in iure *bstv*      28 urbanus *D:*
urbis *V*

On one point, Quintus Fufius, I wish to remonstrate with you, without offense to our friendship, as one senator disagreeing with another. You said, speaking from a written draft (otherwise I should suppose you made a slip because you were at a loss for a word), that Brutus' letter appeared "rightly and properly written."[2] That, surely, is to praise Brutus' secretary, not Brutus. **6** By this time, Calenus, you should have and perhaps do have a large experience of public affairs. When did you see a decree in this form? In what senatorial decree of this nature (and there are countless such) did you see it determined by the Senate that a letter was well written? You did not let the phrase fall by chance, as often happens; you brought it with you, written down, prepared, pondered.

If someone rids you of this habit of constantly running down honest folk, will you not be left with all a man could desire? So take stock. Is it not time to calm this mood of yours, soften it? Listen to honest men, of whom you have many among your acquaintance. Speak with your son-in-law, who is a very wise man, more often than with yourself. *Then* you will fully possess the title of our highest office. Does it matter nothing to you (for my part, as a friend of yours it often distresses me on your account) that it is bruited abroad, comes to the ears of the Roman People, that nobody supported the senator who spoke first? And I fancy today will be no exception.

You take legions from Brutus. Which legions? Presumably those which *he* diverted from the criminal enterprise of Gaius Antonius and brought over to the Commonwealth by his own authority. So you want Brutus to appear once again as a man banished from the Commonwealth, naked and alone. **7** But you, Members of the Senate, if you desert and betray Marcus Brutus, what citizen will you ever foster and favor? Or are you of the opinion that those who laid a crown upon a head are to be preserved while those who abolished monarchy altogether are to be forsaken? However, I shall not speak of this divine, immortal glory of Brutus, enshrined as it is in the grateful memory of all our countrymen, though as yet unrecognized by public authority. But what patience, gracious Heavens, what moderation, what quiet self-effacement under injustice! Though he was city praetor, he stayed away from Rome. He did not administer the law, he who had given all law back to the Commonwealth. He might have been fenced around by the daily rally of all honest men—it was remarkable how they used to cluster to his side—and the protection of all Italy, but he preferred to be defended by the approval of honest men in his absence rather than by their strong arms in his presence. He did not even celebrate the Apollinarian games in person, though they were produced in a

---

2. Cicero chooses to take this as referring to style, or even handwriting. Calenus, of course, meant it to refer to content.

apparatos praesens fecit, ne quam viam patefaceret sceleratissimorum hominum audaciae. **8** quamquam qui umquam aut ludi aut dies laetiores fuerunt quam cum in singulis versibus populus Romanus maximo clamore et plausu Bruti memoriam prosequebatur? corpus aberat liberatoris, libertatis memoria aderat: in qua Bruti imago cerni videbatur. 5

At hunc eis ipsis ludorum diebus videbam in insu[gu]la c⟨l⟩arissimi adulescentis, ⟨M.⟩ Luculli, propinqui sui, nihil nisi de pace et concordia civium cogitantem. eundem vidi postea Veliae, cedentem Italia ne qua oreretur belli civilis causa propter se. o spectaculum illud non modo hominibus sed undis ipsis et litoribus luctuosum! cedere e patria serva- 10 torem eius, manere in patria perditores! Cassi classis paucis post diebus consequebatur, ut me puderet, patres conscripti, in eam urbem redire ex qua ill⟨i⟩ abirent. **9** sed quo consilio redierim initio audistis, po⟨s⟩t estis experti.

Exspectatum igitur tempus a Bruto est. nam quoad vos omnia pati 15 vidit, usus est ipse incredibili patientia: postea quam vos ad libertatem sensit erectos, praesidia vestrae libertati paravit. at cui pesti quantaeque restitit! si enim C. Antonius quod animo intenderat perficere potuisset, ut potuisset nisi eius sceleri virtus M. Bruti obstitisset, Macedoniam, Illyri- cum, Graeciam perdidissemus; esset vel receptaculum pulso Antonio vel 20 agger oppugnandae Italiae Graecia: quae quidem nunc M. Bruti imperio, auctoritate, copiis non instructa solum sed etiam ornata tendit dexteram Italiae suumque ei praesidium pollicetur. quod qui ab illo abducit exerci- tum, et respectum pulcherrimum et praesidium firmissimum adimit rei publicae. 25

**10** Equidem cupio haec quam primum Antonium audire, ut intellegat non D. Brutum, quem vallo circumsedeat, sed se ipsum obsideri. tria tenet oppida to⟨to⟩ in orbe terrarum; habet inimicissimam Galliam; eos etiam quibus confidebat alienissimos, Transpadanos; Italia omnis infesta

---

**8** 2 aut dies $V^2n^2$: aut audies $V^1$: aut *b*: auidiis (-dius *s*) $n^1stv$    3 uersibus festa est (10.10) *medd. omissis D*    6 iis *Muretus*: his *V*    insula] insugula $V^1$: insulula *Garatoni*: Neside domi *Reid*: *anne* Neside[3]?    7 M.[2] *addidi*: Cn. *Clark, imperite*    **9** 18–19 ut potuisset *scripsi* (*cf. Planc. 92* ut oportuisset): aut p- *V*: p- autem *Poggius*: aut potius *Muretus*: at potuisset *Clark*    23 quod (*v. Fe.*)] quare *Faërnus*: quod si *Busche*: *del. Clark*    **10** 26 M. Antonium *coni. Halm*    intellegat *Poggius*: -as *V*

style befitting his own and the Roman People's dignity, for fear of giving a loophole to the audacity of reckless criminals. **8** And yet, were any games, any days ever more joyous than when the Roman People thundered its applause for the memory of Brutus as verse followed verse?[3] The liberator was absent in the flesh, but the memory of liberation was there, and in that memory, as though plain to the eye, was the likeness of Brutus.

During that very period of the festival I was seeing Brutus on the island owned by his relative, that very distinguished young man Marcus Lucullus. His thoughts were all of peace and civil concord. Later I saw him at Velia as he was leaving Italy for fear that some occasion of civil war might arise on his account. Indeed a sight for men, aye, for the very waves and beaches, to mourn for! The savior of his country was leaving her; her betrayers were remaining in her midst. Cassius' flotilla was following a few days later. I felt ashamed, Members of the Senate, to be returning to the city from which they were departing. **9** But you were told my purpose in returning at the outset,[4] and later you have seen it in execution.

So Brutus bided his time. As long as he saw you putting up with every outrage, he himself showed unbelievable patience. But when he perceived that you were ready to fight for freedom, he prepared means to protect your freedom. And what a deadly threat he opposed! For if Gaius Antonius had succeeded in accomplishing what he intended—as he would have succeeded if the valor of Marcus Brutus had not foiled his criminal attempt—we should have lost Macedonia, Illyricum, and Greece. Greece would have become a refuge for Antonius[5] if beaten, or a rampart from which to launch an attack on Italy; the same Greece which now, equipped more than adequately with Marcus Brutus' military authority, prestige, and forces, holds out her hand to Italy and promises her protection. Whoever withdraws Brutus' army from Brutus deprives the Commonwealth of a splendid refuge at need and a powerful bulwark.

**10** For my part, I want Antonius to hear of these developments as soon as may be, to let him understand that he himself, and not Decimus Brutus, whom he is surrounding with his palisade, is under siege. He holds three towns[6] in the whole world. Gaul is bitterly hostile to him. Even the Transpadanes, on whom he relied,[7] are thoroughly estranged. All Italy is against him. Foreign

---

3. Cf. 1.36, and n. 46 there. Some of the verses in the play (Accius' *Tereus*) would have admitted of a topical application; cf. *Sest.* 118ff., *Att.* 2.19.3.

4. In the First Philippic, though the purpose as given there is not the one implied here.

5. Marcus.

6. Bononia (Bologna), Regium Lepidi (Reggio Emilia), and Parma; cf. *Fam.* 12.5.2.

7. Because they owed their Roman citizenship to Caesar; cf. 12.10.

est; exterae nationes a prima ora Graeciae usque ad Aegyptum optimorum
et fortissimorum civium imperiis et praesidiis tenentur. erat ei spes una in
C. Antonio, qui duorum fratrum aetatibus medius interiectus viti⟨i⟩s cum
utroque certabat. is tamquam extruderetur a senatu in Macedoniam et
non contra prohiberetur proficisci, ita cucurrit. **11** quae tempestas, di im-    5
mortales, quae flamma, quae vastitas, quae pestis Graeciae, nisi incredibilis ac divina virtus furentis hominis conatum atque audaciam compres-
sisset! quae celeritas illa Bruti, quae cura, quae virtus! etsi ne C. quidem
Antoni celeritas contemnenda est, quam nisi in via caducae hereditates
retardassent, volasse eum, non iter fecisse diceres. alios ad negotium    10
publicum ire cum cupimus, vix solemus extrudere: hunc retinentes elusi
sumus. at quid ei cum Apollonia, quid cum Dyrrachio, quid cum Illyrico,
quid cum P. Vatini imperatoris exercitu? succedebat, ut ipse dicebat,
Hortensio. certi fines Macedoniae, certa condicio, certus, si modo erat
ullus, exercitus: cum Illyrico vero et cum Vatini legionibus quid erat    15
Antonio? "at ne Bruto quidem": **12** id enim fortasse quispiam improbus
dixerit. omnes legiones, omnes copiae quae ubique sunt rei publicae sunt:
nec enim eae legiones quae M. Antonium reliquerunt Antoni potius quam
rei publicae fuisse dicentur. omne enim et exercitus et imperi ius amittit
is qui eo imperio et exercitu rem publicam oppugnat. quod si ipsa res    20
publica iudicaret aut si omne ius decretis eius statueretur, Antonione an
Bruto legiones populi Romani adiudicaret? alter advolarat subito ad di-
reptionem pestemque sociorum ut, quacumque iret, omnia vastaret, di-
riperet, auferret, exercitu populi Romani contra ipsum populum Romanum uteretur; alter eam legem sibi statuerat, ut, quocumque venisset,    25
lux venisse quaedam et spes salutis videretur. denique alter ad everten-
dam rem publicam praesidia quaerebat, alter ad conservandam. nec vero
nos hoc magis videbamus quam ipsi milites a quibus tanta in iudicando
prudentia non erat postulanda.

1 a prima ora *Poggius*: a primo ore *V*: a (ad *b*) primori *bns*: ad primum *t*      graecia *D*    2
ei spes una] eis pecunia *V*: ei spes unica *coni. Halm*    3 C.] m *bnv*: *om. st*      vitiis *om.*
*D*    4 is] s *t*: *om. bns*    **11** 6 flammae *V*      gr(a)eci(a)e fuisset *D*    7 uirtus caes.
*V*    8 ne C. *Muretus*: nec *V*: ne illa *D*    9 quem *D*    11–12 elusi sumus¹ *scripsi*:
exclusimus *D*: extruinus *V*: extrusimus *Muretus*    14–15 certus . . . ullus] certissimo
(-mus *s*) modo erat illius *D*    16 at] ac *bnsv*: an *t*    **12** 17 omnes copiae quae ubi *om.*
*V*¹      rei p(ublicae)] populi r. *D*    18 neque enim hee (hae *t*) *D*    19 dicuntur *bnsv*:
dixerunt *t*      omnes *V*¹*ns*      et (*pr.*) *om. D*    23 quocunque *V*: quocum *t*    25 sibi
legem *D*

nations, from the west coast of Greece as far as Egypt, are held by the military authority and forces of excellent, brave citizens. His only hope was in Gaius Antonius, inserted midway in years between his two brethren and in vices the rival of both, who hurried off to Macedonia as though the Senate were thrusting him forth[8] and not, on the contrary, forbidding him to go. **11** There was a storm, great Heavens, a ravaging conflagration, the destruction of Greece, but for the amazing, superhuman courage which quelled the madman's reckless enterprise. How speedily Brutus acted, how circumspectly, how boldly! Not that Gaius Antonius is to be despised so far as speed goes; if he had not been held up by some inheritances falling on the road,[9] he might he said to have flown rather than traveled. When we want people to go on a public business, we usually have difficulty in thrusting them out;[10] but *he* gave us the slip as we tried to hold him back. But what had he to do with Apollonia or Dyrrachium or Illyricum or Imperator Publius Vatinius' army?[11] He was succeeding Hortensius,[12] as he said himself. Macedonia has fixed boundaries, fixed terms, a fixed army—if there was any army. What business had Antonius with Illyricum and the legions of Vatinius? "Or Brutus either?" **12** some rascal may say. All legions, all forces, wherever they are, belong to the Commonwealth. The legions which abandoned Marcus Antonius will not be said to have belonged to Antonius rather than to the Commonwealth. For whoever uses military authority and an army to attack the Commonwealth forfeits all right to that army and to that authority. If the Commonwealth itself were judge or if everyone's rights were determined by its decisions, would it adjudge the legions of the Roman People to Antonius[13] or to Brutus? The former had rushed up all of a sudden to plunder and plague our allies,[14] ravaging, pillaging, robbing wherever he went, using an army of the Roman People against the Roman People itself; the latter had made it his rule that wherever he came a light, a hope of deliverance would seem to shine. In a word, the former was looking for military forces in order to overthrow the Commonwealth, the latter to preserve it. We did not see this more clearly than the troops themselves saw it, from whom we had no right to expect such wise discrimination.

---

8. Cf. n. 10 below.

9. *Caduca* was the legal term for an unclaimed inheritance. C. Antonius is here accused of seizing upon such on his way to Macedonia. But we are surely meant to think of Atalanta, who lost her race because she stopped to pick up the golden apples thrown by her competitor.

10. Cicero also uses the verb *extrudere* in connection with his legate C. Pomptinus in 51, who was slow in setting out for Cilicia (*Att.* 5.1.5).

11. In Illyricum. Vatinius handed it over to Brutus (10.13).

12. The orator's son, governor of Macedonia since 44.

13. Gaius.

14. *Socii*, a term often used euphemistically of the provincials subject to Rome.

**13** Cum septem cohortibus esse Apolloniae scribit Antonium, qui iam aut captus est—quod di duint!—aut certe homo verecundus in Macedoniam non accedit ne contra senatus consultum fecisse videatur. dilectus habitus in Macedonia est summo Q. Hortensi studio et industria; cuius animum egregium dignumque ipso et maioribus eius ex Bruti 5 litteris perspicere potuistis. legio quam L. Piso ducebat, legatus Antoni, Ciceroni se filio meo tradidit. equitatus qui in Syriam ducebatur bipertito alter eum quaestorem a quo ducebatur reliquit in Thessalia seseque ad Brutum contulit, alterum in Macedonia Cn. Domitius, adulescens summa virtute, gravitate, constantia, a legato Syriaco abduxit. P. autem Vatinius, 10 qui et antea iure laudatus a vobis et hoc tempore merito laudandus est, aperuit Dyrrachi portas Bruto et exercitum tradidit. **14** tenet igitur res publica Macedoniam, tenet Illyricum, tuetur Graeciam: nostrae sunt legiones, nostra levis armatura, noster equitatus, maximeque noster est Brutus semperque noster, cum sua excellentissima virtute rei publicae 15 natus tum fato quodam paterni maternique generis et nominis.

Ab hoc igitur viro quisquam bellum timet qui, ante quam nos id coacti suscepimus, in pace iacere quam in bello vigere maluit? quamquam ille quidem numquam iacuit neque hoc cadere verbum in tantam virtutis praestantiam potest. erat enim in desiderio civitatis, in ore, in sermone 20 omnium. tantum autem aberat a bello ut, cum cupiditate libertatis Italia arderet, defuerit civium studiis potius quam eos in armorum discrimen adduceret. itaque illi ipsi si qui sunt qui tarditatem Bruti reprehendant tamen idem moderationem patientiamque mirantur.

**15** Sed iam video quae loquantur; neque enim id occulte faciunt. timere 25 se dicunt quo modo ferant veterani exercitum Brutum habere. quasi vero quicquam intersit inter A. Hirti, C. Pansae, D. Bruti, C. Caesaris et hunc exercitum M. Bruti. nam si quattuor exercitus ei de quibus dixi propterea laudantur quod pro populi Romani libertate arma ceperunt, quid est cur hic M. Bruti exercitus non in eadem causa reponatur? at enim veteranis 30 suspectum nomen est M. Bruti. magisne quam Decimi? equidem non arbitror. etsi est enim Brutorum commune factum et laudis societas

---

**13** 1 esse] isse *nsv*: *om. t*    apolloniam *nst*: -io *bv*    2 di duint *Halm*: dicit *V*[1]: di dent *bnsvV*[2]: didicit *t*    3 senatus consultum] se *D*    4 Q. *om. V*    5 et ipso (ipsi *v*) et *D*    8 alter eum quaestorem] alterum *D*    10 gravitate *om. D*    Syriaco *del. Pluygers*    11 et (*pr.*)] est *D*    **14** 14 nostra equitatus *V*: nostri e- *n's*    17 viro *om. D*    19 nec *D*    23 *anne* illi ipsi, si qui sunt, qui . . . reprehendunt?    **15** 30 ponatur *V*[1], *numero minus bono*

**13** Brutus writes that Antonius is in Apollonia with seven cohorts. By now he has been taken prisoner—Heaven grant it!—or at all events he is modestly keeping away from Macedonia for fear of seeming to act contrary to the Senate's decree. A levy has been held in Macedonia, most zealously and energetically directed by Quintus Hortensius, whose fine spirit, worthy of himself and his ancestors, you could perceive from Brutus' letter. The legion commanded by Antonius' legate, Lucius Piso, surrendered to my son.[15] Of a force of cavalry which was being marched to Syria in two sections, one section left the quaestor in command and joined Brutus in Thessaly; the other was withdrawn from the Syrian legate[16] by Gnaeus Domitius, a young man of the highest courage, responsibility, and resolution. And Publius Vatinius, whom you have rightly commended in the past and who deserves your commendation now, opened the gates of Dyrrachium to Brutus and handed over his army. **14** Thus the Commonwealth holds Macedonia and Illyricum and protects Greece. The legions are ours, so are the light-armed units and the cavalry, and most of all Brutus is ours, always ours, born for the Commonwealth in virtue of his own outstanding qualities and of his name and family, his father's and his mother's, as fate ordained.[17]

Does anyone fear war from this man, who, before we took up arms under compulsion, preferred obscurity in peace to celebrity[18] in war? Not that he was ever obscure. That word cannot apply to such superiority of worth. The community longed for him, his name was on every tongue, the general theme of conversation. But war was so far from his mind that when Italy was aflame with desire for freedom, he disappointed his countrymen's hopes rather than lead them into armed conflict. Even those who censure Brutus' tardiness, if any such there be, admire his moderation and patience.

**15** But I see what they are saying—they make no secret of it. They profess to be afraid of how the veterans will take it that Brutus has an army. As though there were a difference between the armies of Aulus Hirtius, Gaius Pansa, Decimus Brutus, and Gaius Caesar and this army of Marcus Brutus! If the four armies I have mentioned are commended for taking up arms in defense of the freedom of the Roman People, why should this army of Marcus Brutus not be placed in the same category? Ah, but Marcus Brutus' name is suspect to the veterans. More than Decimus'? I think not. The Bruti share their deed, they

---

15. The younger M. Tullius Cicero, who had left his studies in Athens to serve under Brutus.

16. I.e. legate to Dolabella, governor of Syria. According to Plutarch (*Brut.* 25.1) the name of either the quaestor or the legate (probably the latter) was Cinna—perhaps L. Cornelius Cinna who became consul suffect in 32.

17. Cf. Philippic 2 n. 26.

18. For the sense of *vigere* (something like "riding high") see my note on *Q. fr.* 3.5.8.

aequa, Decimo tamen iratiores erant ei qui id factum dolebant quo minus
ab eo rem illam dicebant fieri debuisse. quid ergo agunt nunc tot exercitus
nisi ut obsidione Brutus liberetur? qui autem hos exercitus ducunt? ei,
credo, qui C. Caesaris [res] acta[s] everti, qui causam veteranorum prodi
volunt. **16** si ipse viveret C. Caesar, acrius, credo, acta sua defenderet       5
quam vir fortissimus defendit Hirtius, aut amicior causae quisquam
inveniri potest quam filius! at horum alter nondum ex longinquitate
gravissimi morbi recreatus quicquid habuit virium, id in eorum libertatem defendendam contulit quorum votis iudicavit se a morte revocatum;
alter virtutis robore firmior quam aetatis cum istis ipsis veteranis ad       10
D. Brutum liberandum est profectus. ergo illi certissimi idemque acer-
rimi Caesaris actorum patroni pro D. Bruti salute bellum gerunt, quos
veterani sequuntur; de libertate enim populi Romani, non de suis commodis armis decernendum vident. **17** quid est igitur cur eis qui D. Brutum
omnibus opibus conservatum velint M. Bruti sit suspectus exercitus?       15

An vero, si quid esset quod a M. Bruto timendum videretur, Pansa
id non videret, aut, si videret, non laboraret? quis aut sapientior ad
coniecturam rerum futurarum aut ad propulsandum metum diligentior?
atqui huius animum erga M. Brutum studiumque vidistis. praecepit
oratione sua quid decernere nos de M. Bruto, quid sentire oporteret,       20
tantumque afuit ut periculosum rei publicae M. Bruti putaret exercitum
ut in eo firmissimum rei publicae praesidium et gravissimum poneret.
scilicet hoc Pansa aut non videt—hebeti enim ingenio est—aut neglegit:
quae enim Caesar egit, ea rata esse non curat: de quibus confirmandis et
sanciendis legem comitiis centuriatis ex auctoritate nostra laturus est.       25

Desinant igitur aut ei qui non timent simulare se timere et prospicere
rei publicae, aut ei qui omnia verentur nimium esse timidi, ne illorum
simulatio, horum obsit ignavia. **18** quae, malum, est ista ratio semper optimis causis veteranorum nomen opponere? quorum etiam si amplecterer
virtutem, ut facio, tamen, si essent adrogantes, non possem ferre fasti-       30
dium. at nos conantis servitutis vincla rumpere impediet si quis veteranos
nolle dixerit? non sunt enim, credo, innumerabiles qui pro communi
libertate arma capiant! nemo est praeter veteranos milites vir qui ad

---

1 eo *ante* tamen *add. Naugerius, ante* iratiores *C. F. W. Müller, fort. recte, sed* v.
*Fe.*       bruto ratiores (-ones *v*) hii qui *bv*: brutorum actiones ii qui *nst*       2 eo rem *V²*:
eorum *V¹*: illo rem *D*       decuisse *D*       nunc agant (agunt *v*) *D*       4 C. *om. D*       acta
*Pluygers*: res actas *codd.*       **16** 5 C. *om. bstv*       11 recertissimi *V*       **17** 17 aut (*alt.*)]
autem *bnsV²*: aut non *t*: illo aut *Cus.*       ad] aut ad *V¹*: aut *Cus.*       19 atquin *V*       20 de
M. Bruto *Faërnus*: dē b- *V*: b- *D*       21 afuit *Halm*: abf- *D*: f- *V*       M. *om. V*       26 et]
set *V*: sed *bnsv*       27 ei *DV²*: hic arte *V¹*: hi cauti *coni. Halm*       28 emulatio *V*       **18** 31
at] an *V²*       32 id nolle *D*       33 vir *om. D*

are equal partners in glory, but all the same those who lamented what was done were more angry with Decimus because they said it was particularly unfitting for him to be involved.[19] Well, what are all these armies trying to achieve at the present time except Brutus' liberation from siege? And who are commanding these armies? Persons, I suppose, who want to see Gaius Caesar's acts overthrown and the cause of the veterans betrayed! **16** Am I to believe that if Gaius Caesar himself were alive he would defend his own acts more vigorously than our gallant Hirtius defends them? Or that a better friend to Caesar's cause can be found than his son? And yet the former, who had not yet recovered from a lengthy and very serious illness, devoted all the strength he had to defending the freedom of those whose prayers, as he believed, had called him back from death. As for the latter, stronger in courage than in years he set out to liberate Decimus Brutus with those very veterans. And so those most committed and vigorous champions of Caesar's acts are waging war to save Decimus Brutus, and the veterans are following them. For they see that it is the freedom of the Roman People, not their own benefits, that has to be decided by arms. **17** Why should those who want Decimus Brutus saved by every means be suspicious of Marcus Brutus' army?

If there were anything which might seem to give us cause to fear Brutus, would not Pansa see it? Or, seeing it, would he not be concerned? Is there a man wiser in forecasting the future or more sedulous in warding off a threat? And yet you see his sentiments towards Brutus, how warmly he regards him. In his speech he told us what we should resolve and what we should feel about Marcus Brutus. Far from thinking Marcus Brutus' army a danger to the Commonwealth, he saw in it the Commonwealth's strongest and weightiest support. Well, I suppose Pansa either doesn't see it (he is such a dull fellow!) or disregards it. After all, he cares nothing for the validity of Caesar's acts—he is about to bring a law confirming and ratifying them before the Centuriate Assembly on our authority.[20]

Well then, let those who are not afraid stop pretending to be afraid and to be looking out for the Commonwealth, or let those who fear shadows put aside their excessive timidity, lest harm come of the hypocrisy of the former and the cowardice of the latter. **18** For pity's sake, where is the sense in perpetually thrusting the name of the veterans in the way of every excellent cause? Even if I loved their courage, which I do, I could not submit to their haughtiness if they turned arrogant. Are we going to be stopped in our effort to break the bonds of slavery if somebody tells us that the veterans don't like it? Are not countless numbers taking up arms for the common freedom? Is there no man

19. Because of his close friendship with Caesar.
20. Cf. 13.31.

servitutem propulsandam ingenuo dolore excitetur! potest [igitur] stare
res publica freta veteranis sine magno subsidio iuventutis! quos quidem
vos libertatis adiutores complecti debetis: servitutis auctores sequi non
debetis. **19** postremo—erumpat enim aliquando vera et me digna vox—si
veteranorum nutu mentes huius ordinis gubernantur omniaque ad eorum    5
voluntatem nostra dicta facta referuntur, optanda mors est, quae civibus
Romanis semper fuit servitute potior. omnis est misera servitus; sed fuerit
quaedam necessaria: ecquodnam principium ponetis libertatis capessen-
dae? an, cum illum necessarium et fatalem paene casum non tulerimus,
hunc feremus voluntarium?    10

    Tota Italia desiderio libertatis exarsit; servire diutius non potest civitas;
serius populo Romano hunc vestitum atque arma dedimus quam ab eo
flagitati sumus. **20** magna quidem nos spe et prope explorata libertatis
causam suscepimus; sed ut concedam incertos exitus esse belli Martemque
communem, tamen pro libertate vitae periculo decertandum est. non    15
enim in spiritu vita est, sed ea nulla est omnino servienti. omnes nationes
servitutem ferre possunt, nostra civitas non potest, nec ullam aliam ob
causam nisi quod illae laborem doloremque fugiunt, quibus ut careant
omnia perpeti possunt, nos ita a maioribus instituti atque imbuti sumus ut
omnia consilia atque facta ad dignitatem et ad virtutem referremus. ita    20
praeclara est recuperatio libertatis ut ne mors quidem sit in repetenda
libertate fugienda. quod si immortalitas consequeretur praesentis periculi
fugam, tamen eo magis [ea] fugienda videretur quo diuturnior servitus
esset. cum vero dies et noctes omnia nos undique fata circumstent, non
est viri minimeque Romani dubitare eum spiritum quem naturae debeat    25
patriae reddere.

    **21** Concurritur undique ad commune incendium restinguendum; vete-
rani qui⟨dem⟩ primi Caesaris auctoritatem secuti conatum Antoni reppu-
lerunt; post eiusdem furorem Martia legio fregit, quarta adflixit. sic a suis
legionibus condemnatus irrupit in Galliam, quam sibi armis animisque    30
infestam inimicamque cognovit. hunc A. Hirti, C. Caesaris exercitus
insecuti sunt; post Pansae dilectus urbem totamque Italiam erexit; unus
omnium est hostis.

1 igitur *seclusi*    2 sine veteranis, freta *Pluygers*    **19** 5 gubernabuntur (-bantur *s*)
*DV*²    6 factaque *D*    referentur *D*    8 et quenam *V*: ecquandone *coni. Halm*    po-
netis³ *scripsi*: putatis (-astis *b*) *codd.*: alii alia    **20** 13 magnam nos quidem spem et
prope exploratam *D*    17 nec nullam *V*: nullam *Faërnus*    20 ad dignitatem et ad
uirtutem *V Cus.*: ad u- et d- *D*    referremus *V*¹ *Cus.*: referamus *DV*²    22 libertate
fugienda *om. V*¹    23 ea *seclusi*    25 minimeque Romani] nominisque R. *bsv*: nominis
romanique *t*    **21** 28 quidem *Faërnus*: qui *V*: que *D*: *del. Cobet*    29 legio . . . suis
*om. V*¹

except the veteran soldiers who is spurred by generous indignation to resist slavery? Can the Commonwealth simply rely for survival on the veterans without a large measure of help from our young men? You ought to welcome the veterans as aiders of freedom, but not follow them as supporters of slavery. **19** Lastly (let the word break out at last, a true word worthy of its speaker), if the views of this House are governed by a nod from the veterans and all we say and do is subject to their wishes, then better death, which Romans have ever preferred to slavery. Slavery of any kind is miserable. But let us grant that a sort of slavery was unavoidable: will you ever set a point from which to start exercising your liberties? We rebelled against a necessary, almost fate-given tribulation: shall we endure this voluntary one?

All Italy is burning with desire to be free. The community can be slaves no longer. We gave the Roman People this dress and these arms only after they had cried out for them. **20** We have taken up the cause of freedom in high hope, almost in the assurance of triumph. But let me admit that the issues of war are uncertain and that Mars takes both sides:[21] even so, we must fight for freedom at peril of life. Life is not a matter of breathing. A slave does not live at all. Other nations can endure slavery, our community cannot, and the reason is simply this: they shrink from labor and pain and are ready to put up with anything in order to avoid them, whereas we have been thoroughly schooled by our ancestors to make dignity and valor our touchstones in every decision and act. So splendid is the recovery of freedom that even death is nothing to be shunned in the struggle to regain it. If we could live forever by shunning present danger, slavery would seem all the more repulsive for lasting longer. But death in all its forms is all around us by day and by night, and it is not the part of a man, least of all of a Roman, to balk at yielding up to his country the breath he owes to nature.

**21** From all quarters they are rushing to stamp out the general conflagration. The veterans were the first to beat back Antonius' attempt, following Caesar's lead. Then the Martian Legion broke his fury, and the Fourth dashed it to the ground. Thus condemned by his own legions, he burst into Gaul, which he has found to be his mortal foe in arms and spirit. Hither the armies of Aulus Hirtius and Gaius Caesar pursued him. Then Pansa's levy raised Rome and all Italy. All have a single enemy.

---

21. *Mars communis* is proverbial, from the Homeric ξυνὸς Ἐννάλιος (*Il.* 18.309).

Quamquam habet secum Lucium fratrem, carissimum populo Romano civem, cuius desiderium ferre diutius civitas non potest. **22** quid illa taetrius belua, quid immanius? qui ob eam causam natus videtur ne omnium mortalium turpissimus esset M. Antonius. est una Trebellius, qui iam cum tabulis novis redi⟨i⟩t in gratiam, ⟨est⟩ T. Plancus et ceteri   5
pares, qui id pugnant, id agunt ut contra rem publicam restituti esse videantur. et sollicitant homines imperitos Saxa et Cafo, ipsi rustici atque agrestes, qui hanc rem publicam nec viderunt umquam nec videre constitutam volunt, qui non Caesaris, sed Antoni acta defendunt, quos avertit agri Campani infinita possessio; cuius eos non pudere demiror, cum   10
videant se mimos et mimas habere vicinos.

**23** Ad has pestis opprimendas cur moleste feramus quod M. Bruti accessit exercitus? immoderati, credo, hominis et turbulenti! videte ne nimium paene patientis. etsi in illius viri consiliis atque factis nihil nec nimium nec parum umquam fuit. omnis voluntas M. Bruti, patres   15
conscripti, omnis cogitatio, tota mens auctoritatem senatus, libertatem populi Romani intuetur: haec habet proposita, haec tueri vult. temptavit quid patientia perficere posset: nihil cum proficeret, vi contra vim experiendum putavit. cui quidem, patres conscripti, vos idem hoc tempore tribuere debetis quod a. d. XIII Kalendas Ianuarias D. Bruto C. Caesari   20
me auctore tribuistis: quorum privatum de re publica consilium et factum auctoritate vestra est comprobatum atque laudatum. **24** quod idem in M. Bruto facere debetis, a quo insperatum et repentinum rei publicae praesidium legionum, equitatus, auxiliorum magnae et firmae copiae comparatae sunt. adiungendus est Q. Hortensius qui, cum Macedoniam   25
obtineret, adiutorem se Bruto ad comparandum exercitum fidissimum et constantissimum praebuit. nam de M. Apuleio separatim censeo referendum, cui testis est per litteras M. Brutus, eum principem fuisse ad conatum exercitus comparandi.

**25** Quae cum ita sint, quod C. Pansa consul verba fecit de litteris quae   30
a Q. Caepione Bruto pro consule adlatae et in hoc ordine recitatae sunt, de ea re ita censeo:

"Cum Q. Caepionis Bruti pro consule opera, consilio, industria,

---

1 L.] *om.* V¹    2 ferre ciuitas diutius *btv*: c- f- d- *ns*    **22** 3 qui] quid si *D*    uideatur
V¹    4 M. *om. D*    5 rediit *b*²: redit *codd.*    est *addidi*    T. *om.* V    et *om.*
*D*    7 Saxa et Cafo *Muretus*: saxas et cafones *V*: saxa capho *s*: saxa (saxi *t*) captant *bntv*:
Saxae et Cafones *Naugerius*    10 miror *D*    **23** 12 cur] est cur *bn¹s*: est curam *t*    13
videte ne] -et -en *V*¹: uide ne *D*    14 paene tientes *V*¹: patientis *t*    16 senatum libertatem
*om.* V¹    18 prospiceret *V*: perfi- *bt*    vi] ut *t*: *om. bnsv*    19–20 tribuere hoc tempore debetis *bnsv*: tr- de- hoc te- *t*    20 et c. *D*    **24** 27 censebo *D*    28 M. *om.*
*bntv*    **25** 31 huic ordini *D*

True, he has his brother Lucius with him, the favorite of the Roman People. The community cannot bear to be without him much longer. **22** A hideous, monstrous beast, who seems to have been created solely in order that Marcus Antonius should not be the foulest of humankind! Trebellius is there; he has made up his differences with the "clean slate."[22] Titus Plancus is there and others of his kind, whose one aim and endeavor is to let their restoration be seen as an act against the Commonwealth. And Saxa and Cafo work upon ignorant men, being themselves country boors, who never saw nor wish to see this Commonwealth properly established, who defend Antonius' acts, not Caesar's, who are seduced by the occupation of unlimited areas of Campania—I wonder they are not ashamed of it when they see they have actors and actresses for neighbors.

**23** Why should it worry us that Marcus Brutus' army has come to join in crushing these vermin? An intemperate fellow, no doubt, a troublemaker! Ask yourselves whether he is not almost too patient. And yet, in that great man's decisions and acts nothing was ever too much or too little. Marcus Brutus' every wish, Members of the Senate, his every thought, his whole mind is focused upon the authority of the Senate and the freedom of the Roman People. These are his goals, these he wishes to protect. He tried what patience could effect; when it effected nothing, he thought it time to try force against force. To Brutus, Members of the Senate, you ought at this time to pay the same tribute as on my proposal you paid to Decimus Brutus and Gaius Caesar on the twentieth of December, when their private initiative and action concerning the Commonwealth was approved and commended by your authority. **24** You should do the same in the case of Marcus Brutus, who has raised numerous and strong forces—legions, cavalry, auxiliaries—as a sudden and unexpected defense of the Commonwealth. With him should be associated Quintus Hortensius, who as governor of Macedonia proved Brutus' loyal and steadfast helper in raising an army. As for Marcus Apuleius, I consider there should be a separate reference to the House with regard to him. Marcus Brutus' letter bears witness that he took the lead in the endeavor to raise an army.

**25** In view of these facts, inasmuch as Gaius Pansa, Consul, has spoken of the letter from Quintus Caepio Brutus,[23] Proconsul, which has been brought and read out in this House, concerning that matter I propose as follows:

"Whereas through the agency, policy, energy, and courage of Quintus Cae-

22. See Philippic 6 n. 8.
23. After his adoption by his uncle Q. Servilius Caepio in or before 59, Brutus' name was formally Q. (Servilius) Caepio Brutus; cf. *Two Studies*, 86, 129ff. In general usage he remained M. Brutus.

virtute difficillimo rei publicae tempore provincia Macedonia et Illyricum et cuncta Graecia et legiones, auxilia, equitatus, in consulum, senatus populique Romani potestate sint, id Q. Caepionem Brutum pro consule bene et e re publica pro sua maiorumque suorum dignitate consuetudineque rei publicae bene gerendae fecisse; eam rem senatui populoque Romano gratam esse et fore; **26** utique Q. Caepio Brutus pro consule provinciam Macedoniam, Illyricum cunctamque Graeciam tueatur, defendat, custodiat incolumemque conservet, eique exercitui quem ipse constituit, comparavit praesit, pecuniamque ad rem militarem, si qua opus sit, quae publica sit et exigi possit, exigat, utatur, pecuniasque a quibus videatur ad rem militarem mutuas sumat, frumentumque imperet, operamque det ut cum suis copiis quam proxime Italiam sit; cumque ex litteris Q. Caepionis Bruti pro consule intellectum sit, Q. Hortensi pro consule opera et virtute vehementer rem publicam adiutam omniaque eius consilia cum consiliis Q. Caepionis Bruti pro consule coniuncta fuisse, eamque rem magno usui rei publicae fuisse, Q. Hortensium pro consule recte et ordine exque re publica fecisse, senatuique placere Q. Hortensium pro consule cum quaestore prove quaestore et legatis suis provinciam Macedoniam obtinere quoad ei ex senatus consulto successum sit."

5

10

15

2 auxilia *scripsi* (*cf.* 10.24, 14): exercitus *codd.*     3 Brutum *om. V*     4 et e] et *bn¹s*: de *t*     5 eamque *D*     **26** 7 totamque *D*     9 praestitit *V*     pecuniaque *sn²*     10 exigat utatur *Clark*: u- e- (e- *del. n²*, exigatque *v*) *codd.*     11 frumentumque imperet *Halm*: i- f- *V*: frumentum i- *D*     17 Q. *om. V*     18 cum quaestore prove quaestore *Mommsen*: cum quaestoribus proue quaestores *V*: cum q. caepione procos. *bnsv*: cumque proue q. *t*

pio Brutus, Proconsul, in a situation of great difficulty for the Commonwealth, the province of Macedonia and Illyricum and all Greece together with legions, auxiliaries, and cavalry are at the disposition of the consuls, Senate, and People of Rome: that Quintus Caepio Brutus, Proconsul, has acted well and in the public interest, in accordance with his own and his ancestors' dignity and their habit of good service to the Commonwealth in public office; and that his action is and will be pleasing to the Senate and People of Rome; **26** further that Quintus Caepio Brutus, Proconsul, shall protect, defend, guard, and keep safe the province of Macedonia, Illyricum, and all Greece; that he command the army which he himself has established and raised; that if money be required for military purposes, he levy and use such public money as can be levied and borrow monies for military purposes from whom he may see fit; that he requisition grain; and that he see to it that he with his forces be as close to Italy as possible. And whereas it is perceived from the letter of Quintus Caepio Brutus, Proconsul, that through the agency and courage of Quintus Hortensius, Proconsul, the Commonwealth has been powerfully assisted and that all his counsels have been conjoined with the counsels of Quintus Caepio Brutus, Proconsul, wherefrom the Commonwealth has derived great benefit: that Quintus Hortensius, Proconsul, has acted rightly and properly and in the public interest; and that it please the Senate that Quintus Hortensius, Proconsul, with his quaestor or proquaestor and legates, hold the province of Macedonia until a successor be appointed by decree of the Senate."

# XI

## INTRODUCTION

In April 44 the consul Dolabella had been assigned Syria as his future province. In the latter part of February 43 the news reached Rome that on his way there he had entered the province of Asia with a body of troops and treacherously seized the city of Smyrna and the person of the Roman governor, C. Trebonius, formerly one of Caesar's chief followers, now one of his assassins. Dolabella had him savagely tortured and put to death. The Senate's response was to declare Dolabella a public enemy on Calenus' motion. The next day it deliberated on how to deal with the resulting situation. Cicero's speech discusses and condemns two proposals: the first, from L. Caesar, that P. Servilius should be given an extraordinary command to cope with Dolabella; the second, from Calenus, that the consuls, Hirtius and Pansa, should draw lots for Asia and Syria and leave for the East after finishing operations against Antony. Cicero for his part proposed that C. Cassius, who was already rumored to be in Syria, should be recognized as its governor with wide extraneous powers for the conduct of the war. This would have passed easily, so Cicero wrote to Cassius (*Fam.* 12.7.1), but for opposition from Pansa. As it was, Calenus' motion was carried. But it made no difference. Cassius "was his own Senate." The armies of the East placed themselves or were placed by their generals under his command, and Dolabella, besieged in the town of Laodicea, committed suicide rather than fall into his hands.

**1** Magno in dolore, patres conscripti, vel maerore potius, quem ex crudeli et miserabili morte C. Treboni, optimi civis moderatissimique hominis, accepimus, inest tamen aliquid quod rei publicae profuturum putem. perspeximus enim quanta in eis qui contra patriam scelerata arma ceperunt inesset immanitas. nam duo haec capita nata sunt post homines 5 natos taeterrima et spurcissima, Dolabella et Antonius: quorum alter effecit quod optarat, de altero patefactum est quid cogitaret. L. Cinna crudelis, C. Marius in iracundia perseverans, L. Sulla vehemens; neque ullius horum in ulciscendo acerbitas progressa ultra mortem est; quae tamen poena in civis nimis crudelis putabatur. **2** ecce tibi geminum in 10 scelere par, invisitatum, inauditum, ferum, barbarum. itaque quorum summum quondam inter ipsos odium bellumque meministis, eosdem postea singulari inter se consensu et amore devinxit improbissimae naturae et turpissimae vitae similitudo. ergo id quod fecit Dolabella in quo potuit multis idem minatur Antonius. sed ille cum procul esset a consu- 15 libus exercitibusque nostris neque dum senatum cum populo Romano conspirasse sensisset, fretus Antoni copiis ea scelera suscepit quae Romae iam suscepta arbitrabatur a socio furoris sui. **3** quid ergo hunc aliud moliri, quid optare censetis aut quam omnino causam esse belli? omnis, qui libere de re publica sensimus, qui dignas nobis sententias diximus, 20 qui populum Romanum liberum esse voluimus, statuit ille quidem non inimicos, sed hostis: maiora tamen in nos quam in hostem supplicia meditatur: mortem naturae poenam putat esse, iracundiae tormenta atque cruciatum. qualis igitur hostis habendus est is a quo victore, si cruciatus absit, mors in benefici parte numeretur? 25

Quam ob rem, patres conscripti, quamquam hortatore non egetis— ipsi enim vestra sponte exarsistis ad libertatis recuperandae cupiditatem—tamen eo maiore animo studioque libertatem defendite quo maiora proposita victis supplicia servitutis videtis. **4** in Galliam invasit Antonius, in Asiam Dolabella, in alienam uterque provinciam. alteri se Brutus 30 obiecit impetumque furentis atque omnia divexare ac diripere cupientis vitae suae periculo colligavit, progressu arcuit, a reditu refrenavit, obsideri se passus ex utraque parte constrinxit Antonium. alter in Asiam irrupit. cur? si ut in Syriam, ⟨cur terra? sin ut Zmyrnam,⟩ patebat via et certa neque longa: quid opus fuit cum legione? praemisso Marso nescio 35

---

**1** 2 et] ac *V*    4 quanta] quam *V*[1]    7 optabat *D*    **2** 11 inusitatum *Vbnsv*    12 quoddam *Vb*[1]: *om. t*    13 improbissimae *V Cus.*: impuris- *D*    14 similitudine *V*    id *del. Lambinus*    15 abesset *D*    17 conspirare *Ernesti*    **3** 19 omnis *om. D*    21 r. p. liberam *D*    uolumus *bntvs*[2]    23 poenam *del. Faërnus*: debitam *expectares*    iracundiam *nstv*    **4** 32 a progressu *DV*[2]    34 cursim ut *bnsV*[2]: c- uti *v*: c-*t*    cur terra . . . Zmyrnam[2] *addidi*    petebat *D*    35 sin ut ad Trebonium *post* longa *Lambinus*: sin ut Zmyrnam *post* longa *Sternkopf*    mario *D*

**1** In our great sorrow, Members of the Senate, our lamentation rather, at the cruel and pitiable death of Gaius Trebonius, a fine citizen and the gentlest of men, there is nonetheless an element which I believe will prove beneficial to the Commonwealth. We have now seen what depths of savagery lie in the hearts of those who have criminally taken up arms against their country. In Dolabella and Antonius we have the two foulest and filthiest beings ever born since the birth of mankind. The former has done what he longed to do, the latter's intentions have been revealed. Lucius Cinna was a cruel man, Gaius Marius' anger was stubborn, Lucius Sulla's violent; but none of these carried his lust for vengeance further than death;[1] and even that was thought too cruel a punishment to be inflicted on fellow countrymen. **2** And now, behold! A pair of twins in crime, unprecedented, unheard of, bestial, barbarous! You remember the bitter hatred, the war which once existed between them; later the likeness of two outrageous natures and two vile lives knit them together in a remarkable relationship of harmonious affection. And so what Dolabella has done to the victim in his power, Antonius threatens to do to many. Dolabella was far from our consuls and armies, nor had he yet realized that the Senate had become one with the Roman People; relying on Antonius' forces, he perpetrated crimes which he supposed had already been committed in Rome by his partner in madness. **3** What else then do you suppose Antonius is working for and dreaming of? What in fact is the cause of the war? All of us who felt politically like free men, who spoke worthily of ourselves, who wished the Roman People to be free, all these he set down as enemies, not merely private but public; though he plans worse fates for us than are inflicted upon such. He considers that death is the satisfaction we pay to nature, whereas anger demands the pains of torture. What sort of enemy, then, must we think a man from whom, if he wins, death without torture will be reckoned a favor?

Accordingly, Members of the Senate, although you need no one to urge you—for your hearts have kindled spontaneously to the desire of regaining liberty—still, defend liberty with all the greater spirit and enthusiasm as you see worse penalties of slavery in store for the defeated. **4** Antonius broke into Gaul, Dolabella into Asia, each into a province which did not belong to him. Brutus blocked the former, tying down at the risk of his own life the onslaught of a madman eager for universal plunder and pillage. Barring his advance, curbing his retreat, allowing himself to be put under siege, he has Antonius fast either way he turns. The other broke into Asia. Why? If he was making for Syria, why by land? If for Smyrna, a safe road of no great length lay open before him: what need to take a legion? He sent in advance a villainous, needy

---

1. Cicero forgets or ignores the gruesome death of his own relative, Marius Gratidianus, a victim of Sulla.

quo Octavio, scelerato latrone atque egenti, qui popularetur agros, vexaret urbis, non ad spem constituendae rei familiaris, quam tenere eum posse negant qui norunt—mihi enim hic senator ignotus est—sed ad praesentem pastum mendicitatis suae, consecutus est Dolabella. **5** nulla suspicione belli—quis enim id putaret?—secutae collocutiones fami- 5 liarissimae cum Trebonio complexusque summae benevolentiae falsi indices exstiterunt in amore simulato; dexterae, quae fidei testes esse sole[ba]nt, sunt perfidia et scelere violatae: nocturnus introitus Zmyrnam quasi in hostium urbem, quae est fidissimorum antiquissimorumque sociorum; oppressus Trebonius, si ut ab eo qui aperte hostis esset, incau- 10 tus; si ut ab eo qui civis etiam tum speciem haberet, miser.

Ex quo nimirum documentum nos capere Fortuna voluit quid esset victis extimescendum. consularem hominem consulari imperio provinciam Asiam obtinentem Samiario exsuli tradidit: interficere captum statim noluit, ne nimis, credo, in victoria liberalis videretur. cum verbo- 15 rum contumeliis optimum virum incesto ore lacerasset, tum verberibus ac tormentis quaestionem habuit pecuniae publicae, idque per biduum. post cervicibus fractis caput abscidit, idque adfixum gestari iussit in pilo; reliquum corpus tractum atque laniatum abiecit in mare.

**6** Cum hoc hoste bellandum est [a] cuius taeterrima crudelitate omnis 20 barbaria superata est. quid loquar de caede civium Romanorum, de direptione fanorum? quis est qui pro rerum atrocitate deplorare tantas calamitates queat? et nunc tota Asia vagatur, volitat ut rex; nos alio bello distineri putat: quasi vero non idem unumque bellum sit contra hoc iugum impiorum nefarium. 25

Imaginem M. Antoni crudelitatis in Dolabella cernitis: ex hac illa efficta est; ab hoc Dolabellae scelerum praecepta sunt tradita. num leniorem quam in Asia Dolabella fuit in Italia, si liceat, fore putatis Antonium? mihi quidem et ille pervenisse videtur quoad progredi potuerit feri hominis amentia, neque Antonius ullius supplici adhibendi, si potestatem 30 habeat, ullam esse partem relicturus.

**7** Ponite igitur ante oculos, patres conscripti, miseram illam quidem et flebilem speciem, sed ad incitandos nostros animos necessariam:

**5** 6 complexus *Clark, qui etiam* complexus quoque *coni.* 8 solent *coni. C. F. W. Müller:* solebant *codd.* perfidia sunt *D* 9 fidelissimorum *D* 10 si ut] sicut *D* erat esset *V* 14 Asiam *del. Schelle* exul *V:* nescio cui *Mommsen* 18 fractis *om.* *D* adfixum *V, Arusian. 7:454 Keil:* f- *D* 19 atque laniatum *om. V*[1] **6** 20 a *del.* *Poggius* 24 unum idemque *D* 25 impium *nstv* 26 M. *om. D* ex hac *scripsi:* ex hoc *V:* ab hoc *D* efficta *Ursinus:* effecta *codd.* 31 esse *Ursinus:* es *V*[1]: est *DV*[2] **7** 33 nostros animos *V, Serv. ad Aen. 2.407:* a- n- (uestros *sv*) *D*

bandit, a fellow called Octavius Marsus, to ravage the countryside and harass the towns, not in the hope of making his fortune, which those who know him (I myself have no acquaintance with this senator) say he would be incapable of keeping anyway, but to feed his beggar's appetite for the time being. Dolabella followed. **5** There being no suspicion of war—who would have thought of such a thing?—very friendly conversations with Trebonius ensued. There were embraces in feigned affection, lying evidence of the heartiest goodwill. Right hands, the accustomed pledges of good faith, were violated in perfidy and crime. There was an entry into Smyrna by night, as though it were a city of enemies, not of very loyal and ancient allies. Trebonius was taken by surprise. He was careless if we think of his assailant as an open enemy; but if we think of him as still bearing the semblance of a fellow countryman, Trebonius is to be pitied.

It looks as if Fortune wished us to take his fate as an example of what the defeated have to fear. Dolabella handed him over, a man of consular rank holding the province of Asia by consular authority, to one Samiarius, an exile. He did not choose to kill his prisoner out of hand; that would have looked too much like generosity in victory. First he lacerated his noble victim with insults from his unclean mouth, then interrogated him concerning public money under lashes and torments for two days together. After which he broke his neck, cut off his head, and ordered it to be stuck on a pike and carried about. The rest of the body, dragged and torn, was flung into the sea.

**6** This is the enemy, surpassing all barbarian races in abominable cruelty, whom we have to fight. How am I to speak of the slaughter of Roman citizens and the plundering of temples? Who could find words to deplore such calamities as befits their atrocious character? And now he is footloose over all Asia, moving around like a king. He thinks our attention is held by another war, as though it were not one and the same war against this nefarious brace of miscreants.

In Dolabella you see mirrored the cruelty of Marcus Antonius. The one is modeled on the other. It is from Antonius that Dolabella learned his lessons in crime. Do you suppose that Antonius will be more lenient in Italy, given the chance, than Dolabella was in Asia? To me Dolabella seems to have gone as far as the madness of a savage could go, while Antonius, if he should have the power, seems sure to exploit every variety of physical cruelty to the full.

**7** Picture the scene, Members of the Senate, grievous and lamentable indeed, but needful to stir our spirits: the onslaught by night upon the most

nocturnum impetum in urbem Asiae clarissimam, irruptionem armatorum in Treboni domum, cum miser ille prius latronum gladios videret
quam quae res esset audisset; furentis introitum Dolabellae, vocem impu-
ram atque os illud infame, vincla, verbera, eculeum, tortorem carni-
ficemque Samiarium: quae tulisse illum fortiter et patienter ferunt. magna　5
laus meoque iudicio omnium maxima. est enim sapientis, quicquid homini accidere possit, id praemeditari ferendum modice esse, si evenerit.
maioris omnino est consili providere ne quid tale accidat, animi non
minoris fortiter ferre [si evenerit].

**8** Ac Dolabella quidem tam fuit immemor humanitatis—quamquam　10
eius numquam particeps fu[er]it—ut suam insatiabilem crudelitatem
exercuerit non solum in vivo, sed etiam in mortuo, atque in eius corpore
lacerando atque vexando, cum animum satiare non posset, oculos pav⟨er⟩it
suos. o multo miserior Dolabella quam ille quem tu miserrimum esse
voluisti! "dolores Trebonius pertulit magnos." multi ex morbi gravitate　15
maiores, quos tamen non miseros, sed laboriosos solemus dicere. "longus
fuit dolor." bidui, at compluribus annorum saepe multorum. nec vero
graviora sunt carnificum cruciamenta quam interdum tormenta morbo-
rum. **9** alia sunt, alia, inquam, o perditissimi homines et amentissimi,
multo miseriora. nam quo maior vis est animi quam corporis, hoc sunt　20
graviora ea quae concipiuntur animo quam illa quae corpore. miserior
igitur qui suscipit in se scelus quam is qui alterius facinus subire cogi-
tur. cruciatus est a Dolabella Trebonius: et quidem a Carthaginiensibus
Regulus. qua re cum crudelissimi Poeni iudicati sint in hoste, quid in cive
de Dolabella iudicandum est? an vero hoc conferendum est aut dubi-　25
tandum uter miserior sit, isne cuius mortem senatus populusque Romanus
ulcisci cupit, an is qui cunctis senatus sententiis hostis est iudicatus? nam
ceteris quidem vitae partibus quis est qui possit sine Treboni maxima
contumelia conferre vitam Treboni cum Dolabellae? alterius consilium,
ingenium, humanitatem, innocentiam, magnitudinem animi in patria　30
liberanda quis ignorat? alteri a puero pro deliciis crudelitas fuit; deinde ea
libidinum turpitudo ut in hoc sit semper ipse laetatus, quod ea faceret
quae sibi obici ne ab inimico quidem possent verecundo. **10** et hic, di
immortales, aliquando fuit meus. occulta enim erant vitia non inquirenti.

---

4 carnificem tortoremque *D*　　7 si evenerit *del. Ernesti, refragante numero*　　8 animi]
-mo *V*¹: sed animi *D*　　9 si evenerit *del. Clark*　　**8** 11 fuit *cod.* Barbadorii: fuerit
*codd.*　　12 exacuerit *bnsv*: exuerit *t*　　13 paverit *Ferrarius*: pauit *codd.*　　18 carnificum tormenta (t- c- *b*) quam interdum cruciamenta *D*　　**9** 21 in corpore *D*　　22 suscepit *V*　　is qui] si ui *V*: si qui *P. R. Müller*　　23 Karthaginiensibus *V*　　24 in qua re
*D*　　25 de *om. D*　　est (*pr.*) *om. V*　　aut] an *D*　　26 sit *om. bnst*　　isne] nonne
*V*　　27 ulcisci cupit *Ferrarius*: ulcis cupitur *V*: ulciscitur *D*　　cuncti senatus sententia
*stv*: cuncti sent- sena- *bn*　　31 alterius *D*　　a puero *om. D*　　deliciis] dilectis *D*

famous city in Asia; armed men bursting into Trebonius' house, while he, poor wretch, saw the swords of the brigands before he heard what was going on; the entry of the raging Dolabella, his foul voice, his infamous mouth, the chains, the lashes, the rack, the torturer and executioner Samiarius. They say Trebonius bore it all bravely and patiently. That does him much honor, the highest a man can win in my opinion. For a wise man ought to prepare himself in advance for all that can happen to a human being, resolving to bear each thing calmly if it comes his way. To make sure that nothing happens such as happened to Trebonius does indeed imply a greater measure of prudence, but to bear it with fortitude calls for a measure of courage no less.

**8** So completely did Dolabella forget all human feeling (not that he ever had any) that he exercised his insatiable cruelty not only on the living but on the dead, and fed his eyes, since he could not satisfy his soul, by mangling and savaging his victim's body. Ah, Dolabella, how vastly greater is your misery than that of him whom you wished to be most miserable! Trebonius suffered terribly, no doubt, but many endure worse sufferings from severe sickness; we do not, however, call them miserable, but sorely tried. His pain was long drawn out, yes, for two days; for some, such pain lasts for many years. The tortures inflicted by executioners are no worse than are sometimes the torments of disease. **9** There are other miseries, yes, you lost souls, you madmen, other miseries I say, far worse than these. In proportion as the mind's power is greater than the body's, so mental pain is worse than physical pain. Therefore he who takes a crime upon his conscience is more miserable than he who falls victim to the misdeed of another. Trebonius was tortured by Dolabella; and so was Regulus[2] by the Carthaginians. They are held to have treated an enemy with great cruelty; what is to be thought of the way Dolabella treated a fellow countryman? Is there any comparison, or can we doubt which of the two is the more miserable, the man whose death the Senate and People of Rome are eager to avenge or the man who has been declared a public enemy by a unanimous vote of the Senate? As for the rest of their lives, who could compare Trebonius' life to Dolabella's without grossly insulting the former? Everyone knows his wisdom, intellect, humanity, integrity, and the magnanimity[3] he showed in liberating his country. Dolabella delighted in cruelty from a boy. His morals are so depraved that he has always piqued himself on committing acts which even an enemy could not in decency bring up against him.[4] **10** And this man, Immortal Gods, was once a member of my family![5] Yes, for his vices were

2. Roman general, taken prisoner in the First Punic War and tortured to death.

3. *Magnitudo animi* implies subordination of personal interest or feeling to a higher cause. Trebonius showed it by joining the plot against Caesar, to whom he owed his advancement.

4. Similarly of Antony in 2.47.

5. Married to Cicero's daughter Tullia.

neque nunc fortasse alienus ab eo essem, nisi ille bonis, nisi moenibus patriae, nisi huic urbi, nisi dis penatibus, nisi aris et focis omnium nostrum, nisi denique naturae et humanitati inventus esset inimicus.

A quo admoniti diligentius et vigilantius caveamus Antonium. etenim Dolabella non ita multos secum habuit notos atque insignis latrones: at 5 videtis quos et quam multos habeat Antonius. primum Lucium fratrem: quam facem, di immortales, quod facinus, quod scelus, quem gurgitem, quam voraginem! quid eum non sorbere animo, quid non haurire cogitatione, cuius sanguinem non bibere censetis, in cuius possessiones atque fortunas non impudentissimos oculos spe et mente defigere? **11** quid 10 Censorinum? qui se verbo praetorem esse urbanum cupere dicebat, re certe noluit. quid Bestiam? qui consulatum in Bruti locum se petere profitetur. atque hoc quidem detestabile omen avertat Iuppiter! quam absurdum autem, qui praetor fieri non potuerit, petere eum consulatum! nisi forte damnationem pro praetura putat. alter Caesar Vopiscus ille 15 summo ingenio, summa potentia, qui ex aedilitate consulatum petit, solvatur legibus: quamquam leges eum non tenent propter eximiam, credo, dignitatem! at hic me defendente quinquiens absolutus est: sexta palma urbana etiam in gladiatore difficilis. sed haec iudicum culpa, non mea est. ego defendi fide optima: illi debuerunt clarissimum et prae- 20 stantissimum senatorem in civitate retinere. qui tamen nunc nihil aliud agere videtur nisi ut intellegamus illos quorum res iudicatas irritas fecimus bene et e re publica iudicavisse. **12** neque hoc in hoc uno est: sunt alii in isdem castris honeste condemnati, turpiter restituti. quod horum consilium qui omnibus bonis hostes sunt nisi crudelissimum putatis fore? 25 accedit Saxa nescio quis, quem nobis Caesar ex ultima Celtiberia tribunum plebis dedit, castrorum antea metator, nunc, ut sperat, urbis: a qua cum sit alienus, suo capiti salvis nobis ominetur. cum hoc veteranus Cafo, quo neminem veterani peius oderunt. his quasi praeter dotem quam in civilibus malis acceperant agrum Campanum est largitus Antonius, 30

**10** 1 bonis *V Cus.*: uobis *D*: nobis *Halm*     6 Lucium *om. D*     9 cuius . . . in *om.* *V*[1]     **11** 12 se *post* qui *D*     15 damnationem pro praetura *varie corrumpunt D*     Vopiscus ille] uobiscum homo *D*     16 consulatum petit] ad c- *D*     17 teneant *V*     propter eximiam *om. D*     23 e *om.* *V*[1]     **12** 27 ut] ui *D*     28 dominetur *nstvb*[2]

276

concealed and I did not inquire. Even now perhaps I should be on amicable terms with him if he had not been found an enemy to honest men, to his country's walls, to this city, to its Household Gods, to the altars and hearths of us all, in fact to nature and humanity.

Warned by him, let us guard ourselves against Antonius with greater care and vigilance. After all, Dolabella did not have very many notorious, eminent cutthroats with him, but you see whom Antonius has and how many they are. First, brother Lucius: what a firebrand, great Heavens, what an outrage, what a villainy, what a cesspool, what a chasm! What, do you suppose, is he not mentally sucking dry, engulfing in imagination, whose blood is he not drinking, on whose property and fortunes does he not fix his shameless eyes in hopeful fantasy? 11 Then there is Censorinus, who used to say that he wanted to be city praetor but in fact certainly had no such desire.[6] Then there is Bestia, who announces his candidature for the consulship in place of Brutus. May Jupiter avert so abominable an omen! And how incongruous that a man who failed to become praetor should stand for consul!—or perhaps he counts a conviction as a praetorship. Well, let him be granted legal dispensation, this second Caesar Vopiscus, this marvel of intellect and influence, who stands for the consulship as an ex-aedile[7]—not that I imagine the laws apply to so extraordinarily eminent a personage. I defended him five times and each time he was acquitted. Even a gladiator finds it hard to win a sixth Roman palm.[8] However, this is the jury's fault, not mine. I defended him in all good faith; they ought to have kept so illustrious and outstanding a senator in the community. However, he now seems to be solely out to prove to us that the jurors whose verdicts we have annulled gave them properly and to the public benefit. 12 Bestia is no isolated case. Others in the same camp were honorably convicted and disgracefully rehabilitated.[9] Do you suppose these enemies of all honest men have any but the cruelest intentions? To these add one Saxa, whom Caesar brought from the wilds of Celtiberia and gave us for a tribune of the plebs, formerly a marker-out of camps, now, as he hopes, of this city. He is a stranger to Rome, so may the omen be on his own head, and we unharmed. Associated with him is the veteran Cafo, than whom no man is more cordially hated by the veterans. On this pair, over and above, so to speak,[10] the dowry they had received in the civil troubles, Antonius bestowed Campanian land, to

6. He *was* praetor, though not city praetor (*praetor urbanus*) in 43, but left the city (*urbs*) to join Antony.

7. As C. Julius Caesar Vopiscus tried to do in 88.

8. I.e. victory in games held in Rome.

9. I.e. their convictions were honorable to the juries, their conduct after restoration disgraceful to themselves and those who brought them back.

10. Despite the word order I take *quasi* with *dotem*.

ut haberent reliquorum nutriculas praediorum. quibus utinam contenti
essent! ferremus, etsi tolerabile non erat, sed quidvis patiendum fuit ut hoc
taeterrimum bellum non haberemus. **13** quid? illa castrorum M. Antoni
lumina, nonne ante oculos proponitis? primum duos collegas Antoniorum
et Dolabellae, Nuculam et Lentonem, Italiae divisores lege ea quam      5
senatus per vim latam iudicavit; quorum alter commentatus est mimos,
alter egit tragoediam. quid dicam de Apulo Domitio? cuius modo bona
proscripta vidi. tanta procuratorum est neglegentia. at hic nuper sororis
filio infudit venenum, non dedit. sed non possunt non prodige vivere qui
nostra bona sperant, cum effundant sua. vidi etiam P. Deci auctionem,     10
clarissimi viri, qui maiorum exempla persequens pro alieno se aere
devovit. emptor tamen in ea auctione inventus est nemo. hominem ri-
diculum qui se †exercere† aere alieno putet posse, cum vendat aliena!
**14** nam quid ego de Trebellio dicam? quem ultae videntur Furiae
debitorum; vindicis enim novarum tabularum novam tabulam vidimus.     15
quid de T. Planco? quem praestantissimus civis, Aquila, Pollentia expulit
et quidem crure fracto: quod utinam illi ante accidisset, ne huc redire
potuisset! lumen et decus illius exercitus paene praeterii, T. Annium
Cimbrum, Lysidici filium, Lysidicum ipsum Graeco verbo, quoniam
omnia iura dissolvit, nisi forte iure Germanum Cimber occidit. cum hanc   20
et huius generis copiam tantam habeat Antonius, quod scelus omittet,
cum Dolabella tantis se obstrinxerit parricidiis nequaquam pari latronum
manu et copia?

**15** Quapropter, ut invitus saepe dissensi a Q. Fufio, ita sum eius sententiae libenter adsensus: ex quo iudicare debetis me non cum homine so-   25
lere, sed cum causa dissidere. itaque non adsentior solum sed etiam gratias

2 essent] esse possent *D*      **13** 3 M. *om. D*      4 antonii *bnsv*      6 quorum . . . est *om.*
*V*      7 bona modo *D*      8 uidimus *D*      9 infulsit³ *conieci olim*      10 effundunt
*D*      uide *D* (uidi *s*)      11 clari³ *V*      maiorum suorum *D*      13 exercere] exire *D*:
exserere *Halm*: emergere ex *C. F. W. Müller*: expedire (-iri *mallem*) *Cobet: alii alia*      **14**
14 quem ultae *Ubaldinus*: q- ute *V*: quam multae *D*      15 vindicis³ *Ferrarius*: -cem is *V*:
-ces *D*: -cem *Poggius*      uidemus *V*      16 T. *Zumpt*: l. *V*: *om. D*      quae *V*: qui
*nstvb²*      civis] cuius *V*: ciues ciuis *nsv*: ciuis ciui *t*: ciues *b²*      19 ipsum] -um in
*nstv*      Graeco verbo *del. Manutius, fort. recte (sed v. Fe.)*      21 eius *D*      **15** 24 Q.
*om. V*

give suck, as it were, to the rest of their estates. A pity they were not content with them! We should have put up with that, intolerable though it was; anything was worth bearing as the price of avoiding this dreadful war. **13** Well then, are you not picturing to yourselves the other luminaries of Marcus Antonius' camp? First, those two colleagues[11] of the Antonii and Dolabella, Nucula and Lento, the parcelers-out of Italy under a law which the Senate has declared to have been passed by violence. One of them has written mimes, the other acted in a tragedy. What am I to say of Domitius the Apulian?[12] I noticed that his goods were put up for sale the other day. His agents must be very careless! Recently he gave his nephew poison, or rather poured it down his throat.[13] After all, they can't help living extravagantly, hoping as they do for our property while they squander their own. I also saw Publius Decius' auction, that illustrious gentleman who, following in the footsteps of his ancestors,[14] has offered himself up for—debt. Nobody, however, was heard bidding at that sale. A funny fellow, Decius! He thinks he can get himself out of debt by selling other people's belongings. **14** What am I to say of Trebellius? The Furies of the debtors seem to have wreaked their vengeance; no "clean slate" for him, so they've cleaned him out.[15] Or Titus Plancus? Our distinguished fellow countryman Aquila drove him out of Pollentia with a broken leg; a pity that did not happen to him sooner, to stop him coming back here![16] I almost left out the pride and glory of that army, Titus Annius Cimber, Lysidicus' son, and a Lysidicus[17] himself since he has dissolved all laws—or perhaps it was legal for a Cimbrian to kill a German![18] With this crew and so many more of the same breed, what crime will Antonius not commit, when Dolabella with so much inferior a band of ruffians to call upon has made himself guilty of such heinous murders?

**15** Therefore, having often reluctantly disagreed with Quintus Fufius, I gladly assented to his motion, from which you are to conclude that the differences I am apt to have with him are not personal but abstract. So I not only

11. On the agrarian Board of Seven.

12. Apulus may be a cognomen. Nothing is known of him.

13. See Textual Appendix.

14. P. Decius Mus and his son are supposed to have "devoted" themselves for their armies in battle in 340 and 295 respectively. As for the grandson in 279 see T. R. S. Broughton, *Magistrates of the Roman Republic* (New York, 1951) 1:192, 193 n. 1.

15. See Philippic 6 n. 8. Lit. "We have seen the new tablet (i.e. auctioneer's catalogue) of the punisher of new tablets" (i.e. cancellations of debts, which Trebellius opposed in 47). On the reading see Textual Appendix.

16. To Rome from exile.

17. Λυσίδικος = dissolver of laws.

18. Cimber is supposed to have killed his brother. Thus *Germanum* is a pun, meaning both "German" and "brother." The Cimbri were a German tribe.

ago Fufio: dixit enim severam, gravem, re publica dignam sententiam: iudicavit hostem Dolabellam; bona censuit publice possidenda. quo cum addi nihil potuisset—quid enim atrocius potuit, quid severius decernere?—dixit tamen, si quis eorum qui post se rogati essent graviorem sententiam dixisset, in eam se iturum. quam severitatem quis potest non 5 laudare?

**16** Nunc, quoniam hostis est iudicatus Dolabella, bello est persequendus. neque enim quiescit; habet legionem, habet fugitivos, habet sceleratam impiorum manum; est ipse confidens, impotens, gladiatorio generi mortis addictus. quam ob rem, quoniam Dolabella hesterno die 10 hoste decreto bellum gerendum est, imperator est deligendus. duae dictae sunt sententiae, quarum neutram probo: alteram, quia semper, nisi cum est necesse, periculosam arbitror; alteram, quia alienam his temporibus existimo.

**17** Nam extraordinarium imperium populare atque ventosum est, mi- 15 nime nostrae gravitatis, minime huius ordinis. bello Antiochino magno et gravi, cum L. Scipioni provincia Asia obvenisset, parumque in eo putaretur esse animi, parum roboris, senatusque ad collegam eius, C. Laelium, illius Sapientis patrem, negotium deferret, surrexit P. Africanus, frater maior L. Scipionis, et illam ignominiam a familia deprecatus est, dixitque 20 et in fratre suo summam virtutem esse summumque consilium neque se ei legatum, id aetatis eisque rebus gestis, defuturum. quod cum ab eo esset dictum, nihil est de Scipionis provincia commutatum; nec plus extraordinarium imperium ad id bellum quaesitum quam duobus antea maximis Punicis bellis quae a consulibus aut a dictatoribus gesta et confecta sunt, 25 quam Pyrrhi, quam Philippi, quam post Achaico bello, quam Punico tertio; ad quod populus Romanus ita sibi ipse delegit idoneum ducem, P. Scipionem, ut eum tamen bellum gerere consulem vellet. **18** cum Aristonico bellum gerendum fuit P. Licinio L. Valerio consulibus. rogatus est populus quem id bellum gerere placeret. Crassus consul, pontifex 30 maximus, Flacco collegae, flamini Martiali, multam dixit, si a sacris

---

1 gravem, re publica dignam] grecauem re publicam *V*      3 posset (-sit *b*) *D*      decernere] degenere *V*¹: decen- *V*²      **16** 7 num *D*      8 quiescet *D*      10 quoniam cum *bnsv*      **17** 15 semper imperium *D*      16 antiochi *bnsv*      17 provincia Asia *Faërnus*: pc. ia *V*: p. f. asia *D*      18 C. *om. V*      19 illius *Ernesti*: huius *codd.*      20 a familia] familia *t*: -liae *bnsv*      est *om. V*      21 *post* summam uir *in V sequitur* 12.12–23 sumus iudicare . . . corpo, *tum* 13.1–10 a principio . . . acerbam, *tum* 11.17–22 -tutem . . . uirum (*reliqua perierunt*)      25 et confecta] it conta *t*: ita (aut *b*) consummata *bns*      26–27 quam Punico tertio *om. D*      27 ad quod] at quo domitii *V*¹      **18** 29 P. Licinio L. Valerio *Poggius*: p. licioni p. (p. *om. V*¹) ualerio *V*: l. ualerio p. scipione *D*      30 est] *et t*: *om. bnsv*

assent to Fufius but thank him for a stern, impressive speech, worthy of the Commonwealth. He has declared Dolabella a public enemy and proposed the confiscation of his property. And though this motion admitted of nothing further—what harsher, sterner proposal could he have made?—he added that if any subsequent speaker made a more drastic proposal he would support it. No one can fail to applaud such severity.

**16** Now, since Dolabella has been declared a public enemy, he must be pursued with war. He is not lying low. He has a legion, runaway slaves, and a criminal band of traitors. He himself is confident, unbridled, marked out for a gladiator's death. Accordingly, since after yesterday's declaration of Dolabella as a public enemy war must be waged, we have to choose a commander. Two proposals are before us, neither of which has my approval. I disapprove of one because I think it is always dangerous except when it is necessary; of the other because I consider it inappropriate to the present situation.

**17** An extraordinary command smacks of "popular" politics, of truckling to the public whim; it does not at all suit the grave traditions of this House. In the war against Antiochus, a serious war on a large scale, the province[19] of Asia fell to Lucius Scipio, who was considered to lack spirit and strength for the job. The Senate therefore was about to give it to his colleague, Gaius Laelius, father of Laelius the Wise, when Lucius Scipio's elder brother, Publius Africanus, rose and asked the House not to put such a slight upon the family. His brother, he said, was a man of first-rate capacity and judgment; and he himself, for all his seniority and past record, would not refuse to accompany him as legate. After that speech Scipio's province was left unchanged. No extraordinary command was required for that war any more than in the two great Punic Wars earlier on, which were waged and brought to their conclusions by consuls or dictators, or the wars of Pyrrhus[20] and Philip,[21] or the subsequent Achaian War or the third Punic War. True, the Roman People chose the right[22] general for itself, Publius Scipio, but it had him conduct the war as consul. **18** In the consulship of Publius Licinius and Lucius Valerius[23] there was a war to wage with Aristonicus.[24] The people was asked whom they wished to conduct it. The consul Crassus, who was Pontifex Maximus, imposed a fine on his colleague Flaccus, who was Priest of Mars, if he should leave his religious

19. *Provincia* originally meant the sphere of action assigned to a magistrate. The incident happened in 190.

20. 281–275.

21. The First and Second Macedonian Wars (214–205 and 200–197).

22. For *idoneus* = "capable," especially of generals, see *TLL* 7:1.230.39.

23. Crassus and Flaccus in 131.

24. Claimant to the kingdom of Pergamum, which his natural father, Attalus III, had bequeathed to Rome.

discessisset: quam multam populus remisit; pontifici tamen flaminem
parere iussit. sed ne tum quidem populus Romanus ad privatum detulit
bellum, quamquam erat Africanus qui anno ante de Numantinis tri-
umpharat; qui, cum longe omnis belli gloria et virtute superaret, duas
tamen tribus solas tulit. ita populus Romanus consuli potius Crasso quam     5
privato Africano bellum gerendum dedit. de Cn. Pompei imperiis, summi
viri atque omnium principis, tribuni plebis turbulenti tulerunt. nam Ser-
torianum bellum a senatu privato datum est quia consules recusabant,
cum L. Philippus pro consulibus eum se mittere dixit, non pro consule.

**19** Quae igitur haec comitia, aut quam ambitionem constantissimus et    10
gravissimus civis, L. Caesar, in senatum introduxit? clarissimo viro
atque innocentissimo decrevit imperium, privato tamen: in quo maximum nobis onus imposuit. adsensus ero, ambitionem induxero in curiam;
negaro, videbor suffragio meo, tamquam comitiis, honorem homini
amicissimo denegavisse. quod si comitia placet in senatu haberi, peta-    15
mus, ambiamus, tabella modo detur nobis, sicut populo data est. cur
committis, Caesar, ut aut praestantissimus vir, si tibi non sit adsensum,
repulsam tulisse videatur aut unus quisque nostrum praeteritus, si, cum
pari dignitate simus, eodem honore digni non putemur? **20** at enim—nam
id exaudio—C. Caesari adulescentulo imperium extraordinarium mea    20
sententia dedi. ille enim mihi praesidium extraordinarium dederat: cum
dico mihi, senatui dico populoque Romano. a quo praesidium res publica, ne cogitatum quidem, tantum haberet ut sine eo salva esse non
posset, huic extraordinarium imperium non darem? aut exercitus adi-
mendus aut imperium dandum fuit. quae est enim ratio aut qui potest fieri    25
ut sine imperio teneatur exercitus? non igitur, quod ereptum non est,
id existimandum est datum. eripuissetis C. Caesari, patres conscripti,

1 populus *D*: -li romani *V*¹: -lus romanus *V*²     3 triumphauerat *bstv*     5 solas *om.*
*D*     ita] et *V*     6 *post* dedit *ex* 11.20–21 sed de . . . designatus *add. V*     9 se
eum (secum *v*) *D*     **19** 13 maximum *post* imposuit *collocandum coni. Clark, numeri
gratia*     assensero *DV*²     14 negaro] -auero *nsv*: -are *V*     15 habere *D*     17 committis *Faërnus*: comitiis *codd.*     adsensus *nstv*     19 sumus *D*     **20** 20 adolescenti
(-cens *t*) *D*     22 res p. praesidium (p. *om. v*) *D*     27 est] esse *nstv*

duties. The Roman People remitted the fine, but ordered the priest to obey the pontifex. But even on that occasion the people did not appoint a private individual, though Africanus was available, who had celebrated his Triumph over Numantia the previous year. He stood far above all his contemporaries in military renown and ability, but he only carried two tribes. So the Roman People gave the conduct of the war to the consul Crassus in preference to the private citizen Africanus. As for the commands of Gnaeus Pompeius, a great man, indeed the first of men, the legislation was put through by troublemaking tribunes of the plebs,[25] except that the war against Sertorius was assigned to him as a private citizen by the Senate because the consuls declined,[26] whereupon Lucius Philippus said he was sending him, not as proconsul, but instead of the consuls.[27]

**19** And now we have a gentleman of unimpeachable consistency and responsibility, Lucius Caesar, making the Senate into a hustings where candidates compete for office. He has proposed to give the command to a person[28] of the highest distinction and integrity, who is, however, a private citizen, thereby putting us in a very awkward position. Suppose I support the motion: I shall be bringing electioneering into the Senate-house. Suppose I say no: it will look as though I have refused an honor to a close friend by my vote, as in an election. Well, if elections are to be held in the Senate, let us present ourselves as candidates, let us canvass, but let us be given a ballot as are the people. Why put us in such a dilemma, Caesar? If your motion fails, it will appear that a most eminent personage has been rejected; or else each one of us will seem to have been passed over, if we are not deemed worthy of the same honor as an equal in rank. **20** I think I hear a murmur that I proposed a motion giving an extraordinary command to young Gaius Caesar. Well, he had given me extraordinary protection—when I say "me," I mean the Senate and People of Rome. Was I not to give an extraordinary command to one from whom the Commonwealth had received undreamed-of succor, failing which it could not have survived? The choice lay between taking his army away or granting him military authority. For by what rationale can an army be held without such authority? How can it be done? So we must not regard as granted what was merely not snatched away. Yes, Members of the Senate, you would have snatched military authority away from Gaius Caesar if you had not granted it.

25. By A. Gabinius in 67 (command against piracy) and C. Manilius in 66 (eastern command). Cicero "forgets" that he supported the latter bill in his extant speech *De imperio Cn. Pompei.*
26. In 77.
27. *Pro consulibus.* The witticism does not alter the fact that the Senate did appoint a private citizen.
28. P. Servilius; see 11.25.

imperium nisi dedissetis. milites veterani qui illius auctoritatem, imperium, nomen secuti pro re publica arma ceperant volebant sibi ab illo
imperari; legio Martia et legio quarta ita se contulerant ad auctoritatem
senatus et rei publicae dignitatem ut deposcerent imperatorem et ducem
C. Caesarem. imperium C. Caesari belli necessitas, fascis senatus dedit. 5
otioso vero et nihil agenti privato, obsecro te, L. Caesar—cum peri-
tissimo homine mihi res est—quando imperium senatus dedit?

Sed de hoc quidem hactenus, ne refragari homini amicissimo ac de me
optime merito videar. etsi quis potest refragari non modo non petenti
verum etiam recusanti? **21** illa vero, patres conscripti, aliena consulum 10
dignitate, aliena temporum gravitate sententia est, ut consules Dolabellae
persequendi causa Asiam et Syriam sortiantur. dicam cur inutile rei
publicae, sed prius quam turpe consulibus sit videte.

Cum consul designatus obsideatur, cum in eo liberando salus sit posita
rei publicae, cum a populo Romano pestiferi cives parricidaeque de- 15
sciverint, cumque id bellum geramus quo bello de dignitate, de libertate,
de vita decernamus, si in potestatem quis Antoni venerit, proposita sint
tormenta atque cruciatus, cumque harum rerum omnium decertatio consulibus optimis et fortissimis commissa et commendata sit, Asiae et
Syriae mentio fiet, ut aut suspicioni crimen aut invidiae materiam dedisse 20
videamur? **22** at vero ita decernunt ut "liberato Bruto": id enim restabat
ut relicto, deserto, prodito. ego vero mentionem omnino provinciarum
factam dico alienissimo tempore. quamvis enim intentus animus tuus sit,
C. Pansa, sicut est, ad virum fortissimum et omnium clarissimum liberandum, tamen rerum natura coget te necessario referre animum ali- 25
quando ad Dolabellam persequendum et partem aliquam in Asiam et
Syriam derivare curae et cogitationis tuae. si autem fieri posset, vel pluris te animos habere vellem quos omnis ad Mutinam intenderes. quod
quoniam fieri non potest, isto t⟨e⟩ animo quem habes praestantissimum
atque optimum nihil volumus nisi de Bruto cogitare. **23** facis tu id quidem 30
et eo maxime incumbis, intellego; duas tamen res, magnas praesertim,
non modo agere uno tempore sed ne cogitando quidem explicare quisquam
potest. incitare et inflammare tuum istuc praestantissimum studium, non
ad aliam ulla ex parte curam transferre debemus. adde istuc sermones

---

3 Martia et legio *om. D*    contulerat *D*    4 et rei p(ublicae)] reique p. *bt*: p. q. r. *n*: r. p.
p. q. r. *s*: p. r. *v*    5 C. . . . C. *om. D*    6 et *om. D*    **21** 13 consulibus *om. D*    14
cum in eo] in eoque *bns*: in eo *t*: cumque *v*    16 de (*alt.*) *om. D*    **22** 24 ad virum] *hic
deficit V* (*v. ad* 11.17)    fortissimum uirum *D*    25 coget *bt*: cogit *nsv, vulg.*: cogat²
conieceram    29 isto te *Halm*: istoc (isto *n²*) *D*    **23** 31 intellego *om. nsv*    34 ullam
*bn¹st*

The veteran soldiers who, following his authority, command, and name, had taken up arms for the Commonwealth wished to be commanded by him. The Martian and Fourth legions had given their support to the authority of the Senate and the dignity of the Commonwealth, but at the same time they demanded Gaius Caesar as their general and leader. The necessity of war gave Gaius Caesar his command, the Senate only gave him the rods.[29] But when, I beg you, Lucius Caesar (I am dealing with a man very well versed in these matters), did the Senate give a command to a private individual living at his ease and leisure?

But enough on this subject. I would not wish to seem to be opposing the appointment of a close friend to whom I owe a great deal—and yet, who can oppose a man who is not seeking the assignment, indeed is actually refusing it? **21** Let me come to the other motion, Members of the Senate, which ill accords with the dignity of the consuls or the gravity of the situation, namely that the consuls draw lots for Asia and Syria with a view to pursuing Dolabella. I shall explain why this is not to the public advantage, but first just see how discreditable it would be to the consuls.

A consul-elect is under siege and the survival of the Commonwealth depends on his release. Pernicious citizens, traitors, have defected from the Roman People. We are fighting a war for dignity, liberty, and life, and whoever falls into Antonius' power has to expect the agonies of torture. The conflict to determine these matters has been committed and commended to our brave, excellent consuls. In these circumstances, is there to be talk of Asia and Syria, letting us seem to have given a handle to suspicion or a cause for jealousy? **22** Ah, but the motion says "when Brutus has been relieved." To be sure it might have said "abandoned, forsaken, betrayed!" But I maintain that the very mention of provinces comes at a most inappropriate moment. Although your mind, Gaius Pansa, may be intent on relieving that most gallant and illustrious gentleman, as indeed it is, yet in the nature of things you would necessarily be forced at times to put your thoughts to pursuing Dolabella and divert some part of your attention and consideration to Asia and Syria. But if it were possible, I should wish you had more than one mind so that you could fix them all on Mutina. Since that is not possible, we want you to use that excellent, outstanding mind you have for thinking of nothing except Brutus. **23** That is what you are doing, that is the object of your strenuous effort, I know it. All the same, no one can do two things, especially two important things, at once or even work them out in his mind. We should be spurring and firing your admirable zeal to that purpose, not transferring any part of it to another preoccupation.

---

29. *Fasces*, emblem of magisterial power.

hominum, adde suspiciones, adde invidiam. imitare me, quem tu semper
laudasti: qui instructam ornatamque a senatu provinciam deposui ut
incendium patriae omissa ⟨alia⟩ omni cogitatione restinguerem. nemo erit
praeter unum me, quicum profecto, si quid interesse tua putasses, pro
summa familiaritate nostra communicasses, qui credat te invito pro-       5
vinciam tibi esse decretam. hanc, quaeso, pro tua singulari sapientia
reprime famam atque effice ne id quod non curas cupere videare. 24 quod
quidem eo vehementius tibi laborandum est quia in eandem cadere suspicionem collega, vir clarissimus, non potest. nihil horum scit, nihil suspi-
catur; bellum gerit, in acie stat, de sanguine et de spiritu decertat; ante   10
provinciam sibi decretam audiet quam potuerit tempus ei rei datum sus-
picari. vereor ne exercitus quoque nostri, qui non dilectus necessitate,
sed voluntariis studiis se ad rem publicam contulerunt, tardentur animis,
si quicquam aliud a nobis nisi de instanti bello cogitatum putabunt.

    Quod si provinciae consulibus expetendae videntur, sicut saepe ⟨a⟩   15
multis clarissimis viris expetitae sunt, reddite prius nobis Brutum, lumen
et decus civitatis; qui ita conservandus est ut id signum quod de caelo
delapsum Vestae custodiis continetur; quo salvo salvi sumus futuri. tunc
vel in caelum vos, si fieri potuerit, umeris nostris tollemus; provincias
certe dignissimas vobis deligemus; nunc quod agitur agamus. agitur au-   20
tem liberine vivamus an mortem obeamus, quae certe servituti antepo-
nenda est.

    25 quid si etiam tarditatem adfert ista sententia ad Dolabellam perse-
quendum? quando enim veniet consul? an id exspectamus quoad ne
vestigium quidem Asiae civitatum atque urbium relinquatur? at mittent   25
aliquem de suo numero. valde mihi probari potest, qui paulo ante clarissimo viro privato imperium extra ordinem non dedi! at hominem
dignum mittent. num P. Servilio digniorem? at eum quidem civitas non
habet. quod ergo ipse nemini putavi dandum, ne a senatu quidem, id ego
unius iudicio delatum comprobem?                                          30

---

3 alia *add. Halm in app.*   **24** 15 a³ *add. Halm*   17 id] illud *Ernesti*   de *om.*
*bnst*   18 tunc *Ferrarius*: hunc *D*   19 vos *hic Nonius 407, ante* umeris *b, post* si *v*: *om.*
*nst*   potuerit *cod. Regius 15 A. XIV* (*cf. Cluent. 10, Sest. 60, Planc. 48*): poterit *D* (*cf.*
*3.30, Har. resp. 11*): de *Nonio v. Lindsay*   **25** 24 quoad ne *Christ*: quo ante *t*: quo nec *b*:
quo ne *sv*: quo *n*   26 suo] suorum *Cobet, fort. recte*   *fort.* valde hoc mihi   29
putavi *Madvig*: -at *D*

And besides, consider the talk, the suspicion, the jealousy. Follow my example—you have always commended me. I resigned a province[30] already furnished and equipped by the Senate in order to put aside every thought but that of extinguishing the country's conflagration. Except for myself (for if you had thought your interests were in any way involved, you would surely have communicated with such a very close friend as I am), nobody will believe that you have been assigned a province against your wish. Like the wise man you are, check such talk, I beg you; do not let yourself appear to be coveting an appointment for which you care nothing. **24** You should be the more anxious not to let that happen because your illustrious colleague cannot fall under the same suspicion. He knows nothing and suspects nothing of all this. He is fighting a war, standing in the battle line, risking his blood and breath. He will hear that a province has been assigned to him before he can suspect that any time has been given to the matter. I fear that our armies too, who have come to the aid of the Commonwealth in voluntary enthusiasm, not under the compulsion of a levy, may lose something of their ardor if they think we have anything under consideration except the present war.

But if it be right for you consuls to look for provinces, as many illustrious men have done before you, first give us back Brutus, the pride and glory of the community, who must be treasured like the image[31] which fell from the sky and is guarded in the temple of Vesta, whose safety is our safety.[32] Then we shall carry you to heaven on our shoulders if we can. At least, we shall choose you provinces entirely worthy of yourselves. But now, let us attend to the business in hand. And that is to determine whether we are to live free or die, which latter is certainly preferable to slavery.

**25** Moreover, does not this motion actually hold up the pursuit of Dolabella? When will the consul arrive? Are we waiting until the communities and cities of Asia are wiped out of existence? Perhaps I shall be told that they will send one of their staff.[33] Am I expected to approve of that, when just now I opposed an extraordinary command for a most illustrious person who is a private citizen? They will send a man worthy of the charge, perhaps? Worthier than Publius Servilius? Our community contains nobody of that description. I was against the command being given to anybody even by the Senate: am I to approve of an appointment made by a single individual?

---

30. Cisalpine Gaul in 63.
31. The Trojan Palladium.
32. Cf. Ovid *Fasti* 6.427 *aetheriam servate deam, servabitis urbem.*
33. Generally understood as "one of their own sort," i.e. a consular. But how would that be possible? A quaestor or legate might be sent out in advance. Such a person would not technically be *privatus*, but he would be a mere subordinate with no proper title to such a responsibility.

**26** Expedito nobis homine et parato, patres conscripti, opus est et eo qui imperium legitimum habeat, qui praeterea auctoritatem, nomen, exercitum, perspectum animum in re publica liberanda. quis igitur is est? aut M. Brutus aut C. Cassius aut uterque. decernerem plane, sicut multa, "consules, alter ambove," ni Brutum colligassemus in Graecia et eius   5 auxilium ad Italiam vergere quam ad Asiam maluissemus; non ut ex [ea] acie respectum haberemus, sed ut ipsa acies subsidium haberet etiam transmarinum. praeterea, patres conscripti, M. Brutum retinet etiam nunc C. Antonius, qui tenet Apolloniam, magnam urbem et gravem, tenet, opinor, Byllidem, tenet Amantiam, instat Epiro, urget Oricum,   10 habet aliquot cohortis, habet equitatum. hinc si Brutus erit traductus ad aliud bellum, Graeciam certe amiserimus. est autem etiam de Brundisio atque illa ora Italiae providendum. quamquam miror tam diu morari Antonium; solet enim ipse accipere manicas nec diutius obsidionis metum sustinere. quod si confecerit Brutus et intellexerit plus se rei publicae pro-   15 futurum si Dolabellam persequatur quam si in Graecia maneat, aget ipse per sese, ut adhuc quoque fecit, neque in tot incendiis quibus confestim succurrendum est exspectabit senatum. **27** nam et Brutus et Cassius multis iam in rebus ipse sibi senatus fuit. necesse est enim in tanta conversione et concursatione perturbatarum rerum temporibus potius   20 parere quam moribus. nec enim nunc primum aut Brutus aut Cassius salutem libertatemque patriae legem sanctissimam et morem optimum iudicabit. itaque si ad nos nihil referretur de Dolabella persequendo, tamen ego pro decreto putarem cum essent tali virtute, auctoritate, nobilitate summi viri, quorum alterius iam nobis notus esset exercitus, alterius   25 auditus. num igitur Brutus exspectavit decreta nostra, cum studia nosset? neque enim est in provinciam suam Cretam profectus: in Macedoniam alienam advolavit; omnia sua putavit quae vos vestra esse velitis; legiones conscripsit novas, excepit veteres; equitatum ad se abduxit Dolabellae atque eum nondum tanto parricidio oblitum hostem sua sententia iudi-   30 cavit. nam ni ita esset, quo iure equitatum a consule abduceret? **28** quid? C. Cassius, pari magnitudine animi et consili praeditus, nonne eo ex Italia consilio profectus est ut prohiberet Syria Dolabellam? qua lege, quo

---

**26** 5 consulibus *t*     alterum *bsv*     ambove *Orelli*: -osue *D*     in consulibus, alterum ambosve *Halm*     6 auxilium] vexillum *Jeep*     6–7 ex acie *Rau*: ex ea a- *D*: eo ex a- *Ferrarius*     7 ea ipsa *Clark*     15 quod] quem *coni. Halm*     **27** 20 concursatione *bns*: -rsione *t*: conuersione *v*     perturbatarum *scripsi*: -tionum *D*     conversione et perturbatione omnium rerum *Ferrarius*     23 iudicabit *scripsi*: -auit *D*     24 tali *Faërnus*: tales *D*     28 velitis vestra esse *Schöll*

**26** What we need, Members of the Senate, is a man whose hands are free and ready, who possesses legal military authority, and besides that, prestige, a name, an army, and a spirit proved in the liberation of the Commonwealth. His name? Either Marcus Brutus or Gaius Cassius or both. In fact I should propose, as is so often done in the case of consuls, "one or both," if we had not tied Brutus down in Greece and preferred that the aid he offers be turned towards Italy rather than Asia—not for us to look to over our shoulders from the battle line but so that the battle line itself should have backing overseas. Furthermore, Members of the Senate, Marcus Brutus is still detained by Gaius Antonius, who holds the large and important city of Apollonia. I imagine he also holds Byllis and Amantia, threatens Epirus, presses upon Oricum, has some cohorts and cavalry. If Brutus is drawn away from this theater to another war, we shall certainly have lost Greece. We also have to look to Brundisium and the adjacent coast of Italy. By the way, I am surprised that Antonius is taking so long—he usually puts on the handcuffs voluntarily, doesn't stand the perils of beleaguerment for any length of time![34] However, if Brutus finishes his business and comes to the conclusion that he will better serve the Commonwealth by following Dolabella than by remaining in Greece, he will act of his own initiative, as he has done hitherto, and not wait for the Senate when there are so many trouble spots calling for immediate attention. **27** For both Brutus and Cassius have already been their own Senate on a number of occasions. In such an upheaval, such a confluence of confused events, we have to look to situations, not standard procedures. This will not be the first time for either Brutus or Cassius to see the most sacred law and the best possible procedure in the safety and freedom of their country. So if nothing were referred to us concerning the pursuit of Dolabella, I should still take it as the equivalent of a decree that there are great men, men of such ability, prestige, and birth, whose armies are already known to us in the one case and heard tell of in the other. So did Brutus wait for our decrees when he knew our wishes? Instead of going to Crete, his own province, he hastened to somebody else's, Macedonia. He considered as his everything which you would like to be yours. He raised new legions, took over old ones. He drew away Dolabella's cavalry to himself and by his personal decision judged him a public enemy, though not yet stained with so foul a murder. For were it otherwise, what right had he to draw cavalry away from a consul? **28** And did not Gaius Cassius, Brutus' equal in patriotism and judgment, set out from Italy with the design of keeping Dolabella out of Syria? Under what law, by what right? By the right

---

34. A glancing reference to C. Antonius' youthful morals; like his brothers, he will have been "easy." See 14.9 and SB².

iure? eo quod Iuppiter ipse sanxit, ut omnia quae rei publicae salutaria
essent legitima et iusta haberentur. est enim lex nihil aliud nisi recta et[iam]
a numine deorum tracta ratio, imperans honesta, prohibens contraria.
huic igitur legi paruit Cassius, cum est in Syriam profectus, alienam
provinciam, si homines legibus scriptis uterentur, eis vero oppressis suam          5
lege naturae.

**29** Sed ut ea vestra quoque auctoritate firmetur, ⟨ita⟩ censeo:

"Cum P. Dolabella quique eius crudelissimi et taeterrimi facinoris
ministri, socii, adiutores fuerunt hostes populi Romani a senatu iudicati
sint, cumque senatus P. Dolabellam bello persequendum censuerit, ut is          10
qui omnia deorum hominumque iura novo, inaudito, inexpiabili scelere
polluerit nefarioque se patriae parricidio obstrinxerit poenas dis hominibusque meritas debitasque persolvat, **30** senatui placere C. Cassium pro
consule provinciam Syriam obtinere, ut qui optimo iure eam provinciam
obtinuerit, eum a Q. Marcio Crispo pro consule, L. Staio Murco pro          15
consule, A. Al⟨l⟩ieno legato exercitus accipere, eosque ei tradere, cumque
eis copiis et si quas praeterea paraverit bello P. Dolabellam terra marique
persequi. eius belli gerendi causa quibus ei videatur navis, nautas, pecuniam ceteraque quae ad id bellum gerendum pertineant, ut imperandi in
Syria, Asia, Bithynia, Ponto ius potestatemque habeat, utique, quam-          20
cumque in provinciam eius belli gerendi causa advenerit, ibi maius imperium C. Cassi pro consule sit quam eius erit qui eam provinciam tum ob-
tinebit cum C. Cassius pro consule in eam provinciam venerit; **31** regem
Deiotarum patrem et regem Deiotarum filium, si, ut multis bellis saepe
numero imperium populi Romani iuverint, item C. Cassium pro consule          25
copiis suis opibusque iuvissent, senatui populoque Romano gratum esse
facturos. itemque si ceteri reges, tetrarchae dynastaeque fecissent, senatum populumque Romanum eorum offici non immemorem futurum.
utique C. Pansa A. Hirtius consules, alter ambove, si eis videretur, re
publica recuperata de provinciis consularibus, praetoriis, ad hunc ordi-          30
nem primo quoque tempore ⟨re⟩ferant. interea provinciae ab eis a quibus
obtinentur obtineantur quoad cuique ex senatus consulto successum sit."

**32** Hoc senatus consulto ardentem inflammabitis et armatum armabitis
Cassium; nec enim animum eius potestis ignorare nec copias. animus is

**28** 2 et *Poggius*: etiam *D*     5 suam *ed. Romana*: sua *D*     **29** 7 ea . . . firmetur
*Ferrarius*: ex . . . f- *D*: ea . . . firmentur *Bake*: ea lex . . . firmetur *coni. C. F. W.*
*Müller*     ita *addidi*     10 sint *Poggius*: sunt *D*     **30** 15 Staio *Sternkopf*: stato *b*: statu
*st*: -um *v*: statilio *n*: Statio *Ferrarius*     16 A. Allieno *Ferrarius* (*item infra*): ab alieno *vel*
*sim. D*     exercitum *btv*     19 ceteraque quae *n²*: -raque (-raque omnia quae *b*) *D*: -ra
quae *s²*     **31** 29 utque *nsv*     31 referant *Naugerius*: f- *D*     a *om. nstv*     **32** 34–1 is
est] ipse *ns*: ipsius est *coni. Clark*

which Jupiter himself established, that all things beneficial to the Common-wealth be held lawful and proper. Law is nothing but a code of right conduct derived from the will of the Gods, ordaining what is good and forbidding its opposite. This law Cassius obeyed when he went to Syria; another man's province, if people were following written laws, but such laws having been overthrown, his by the law of nature.

**29** But in order that this law may be strengthened by your authority, I move as follows:

"Whereas Publius Dolabella along with the instruments, partners, and abet-tors of his cruel and abominable act has been declared an enemy of the Roman People by the Senate, and whereas the Senate has determined that Publius Dolabella shall be pursued with war, to the end that he who has defiled all the laws of Gods and men by a novel, unheard-of, inexpiable crime and made himself guilty of a criminal assault upon his country may pay a due and proper penalty to Gods and men: **30** that it please the Senate that Gaius Cassius, Proconsul, shall hold the province of Syria as governor in full status; and that he take over their armies from Quintus Marcius Crispus, Proconsul, Lucius Staius Murcus, Proconsul, and Aulus Allienus, Legate, and that they hand the said armies over to him, and that with these forces and any which he may raise in addition he pursue Publius Dolabella by land and sea; that for the purpose of waging the war aforesaid he have the right and power to requisition ships, crews, money, and all else pertaining to the prosecution of the war aforesaid from whomsoever he may see fit in Syria, Asia, Bithynia, and Pontus; and that whatever province he enter in order to prosecute the war aforesaid, the au-thority of Gaius Cassius, Proconsul, shall supersede that of the governor of that province at the time when Gaius Cassius, Proconsul, shall enter it; **31** that if King Deiotarus the father and King Deiotarus the son, as in many wars they have often aided the empire of the Roman People, shall likewise aid Gaius Cassius, Proconsul, with their forces and resources, their action shall be pleasing to the Senate and People of Rome; and that if other kings, tetrarchs, and dynasts do likewise, the Senate and People of Rome will not be unmindful of their service; and that Gaius Pansa and Aulus Hirtius, Consuls, one or both, if they see fit, shall make reference to this House concerning the consular and praetorian provinces as soon as possible after the Commonwealth has been reestablished; and that in the meantime the provinces shall remain under their present governors until such time as a successor to each be appointed by decree of the Senate."

**32** By this decree you will put fire into Cassius' heart, which is already aflame, and arms into his hands, which already grasp them. For neither his spirit nor his forces can be unknown to you. His spirit is as you see, his forces

est quem videtis; copiae quas audistis, ⟨primum legiones quas ducunt
Q. Marcius et L. Staius⟩, fortes et constantes viri, qui ne vivo quidem
Trebonio Dolabellae latrocinium in Syriam penetrare sivissent. Al⟨l⟩ie-
nus, familiaris et necessarius meus, post interitum Treboni profecto ne
dici quidem se legatum Dolabellae volet. est Q. Caecili Bassi, privati      5
illius quidem, sed fortis et praeclari viri, robustus et victor exercitus,
**33** Deiotari regis et patris et fili et magnus et nostro more institutus
exercitus. summa in filio spes, summa ingeni indoles, summa virtus.
quid de patre dicam? cuius benevolentia in populum Romanum est ipsius
aequalis aetati; qui non solum socius imperatorum nostrorum fuit in      10
bellis verum etiam dux copiarum suarum. quae de illo viro Sulla, quae
Murena, quae Servilius, quae Lucullus, quam ornate, quam honorifice,
quam graviter saepe in senatu praedicaverunt! **34** quid de Cn. Pompeio
loquar? qui unum Deiotarum in toto orbe terrarum ex animo amicum
vereque benevolum, unum fidelem populo Romano iudicavit. fuimus      15
imperatores ego et M. Bibulus in propinquis finitimisque provinciis: ab
eodem rege adiuti sumus et equitatu et pedestribus copiis. secutum est
hoc acerbissimum et calamitosissimum civile bellum in quo quid faciendum Deiotaro, quid omnino rectius fuerit dicere non est necesse, praesertim cum contra ac Deiotarus sensit victoria belli iudicarit. quo in bello      20
si fuit error, communis ei fuit cum senatu; sin recta sententia, ne victa
quidem causa vituperanda est. ad has copias accedent alii reges, etiam
dilectus accedent. **35** neque vero classes deerunt: tanti Tyrii Cassium faciunt, tantum eius in Syria nomen atque Phoenice est. paratum habet imperatorem C. Cassium, patres conscripti, res publica contra Dolabellam nec      25
paratum solum sed peritum atque fortem. magnas ille res gessit ante
Bibuli, summi viri, adventum, cum Parthorum nobilissimos duces maximas copias fudit Syriamque immani Parthorum impetu liberavit. maximam eius et singularem laudem praetermitto; cuius enim praedicatio
nondum omnibus grata est, hanc memoriae potius quam vocis testimonio      30
conservemus.

**36** Animadverti, patres conscripti, exaudivi etiam nimium a me Brutum, nimium Cassium ornari, Cassio vero sententia mea dominatum et
principatum dari. quos ego orno? nempe eos qui ipsi sunt ornamenta rei

---

1 vidistis *Ferrarius*      1–2 primum . . . Staius *addidi, praeeunte Madvig* (primum legiones Q. Marci, deinde L. Stati)      4 profecto ne *Christ*: -tione *t*: -tus ne *bnsv*      6 *post*
exercitus *plene interpungunt vulg. Fort.* est Deiotari      **33** 8 summa (*ult.*) *ς*: -aque
*D*      9 dicam de patre *ns*      **35** 24 tantum *Ferrarius*: tanti *D*      27–28 cum Pacori no-
bilissimi ducis magnas copias *codd. Ursini*      **36** 32 exaudivi *Pluygers*: -di rui *t*: -ditu *b*:
exornari *nsv*: exaudire videor *Busche*: et audio videri *Madvig*      33 nimium Cassium] c- *t*:
*del. Halm*

as you have heard. First, the legions commanded by Quintus Marcius and Lucius Staius, men of courage and resolution, who would not have allowed Dolabella's bandits to gain entrance into Syria even while Trebonius was alive. Allienus, my good friend and connection,[35] will surely not wish even to be called Dolabella's legate after Trebonius' death. There is the stout and victorious army of Quintus Caecilius Bassus; he holds no office, but he is a fine, gallant man. **33** There is the army of the two kings, Deiotarus father and son, large and trained in Roman fashion. The son is a man of the highest promise, mental capacity, and courage. What shall I say of his father? His goodwill to the Roman People is lifelong; he was not only the ally of our generals in their wars but led his troops in person. Think of all the eloquent, flattering, impressive tributes often paid to that monarch in the Senate by Sulla, Murena, Servilius,[36] Lucullus. **34** As for Gnaeus Pompeius, he declared that Rome had one sincere friend, one true and faithful well-wisher in the whole world: Deiotarus. Marcus Bibulus and I commanded armies in provinces near to, in fact adjoining one another;[37] we were aided by this same king with both horse and foot. Then came this cruel, disastrous civil war. What Deiotarus should have done, what was in general the more proper course, does not have to be said, especially as victory in the war went contrary to Deiotarus' sentiments. If in that war he made a mistake, the Senate shared it; but if his was the right decision, it should not be blamed, even though the cause was defeated.[38] To these forces will accrue other kings and also levies. **35** Nor will navies be lacking. Cassius is a hero to the Tyrians, a mighty name in Syria and Phoenicia. Yes, Members of the Senate, in Gaius Cassius the Commonwealth has a general ready to fight Dolabella, and not only ready but experienced and brave. He won a great victory before the arrival of the eminent Bibulus, routing celebrated Parthian commanders and a mighty force, delivering Syria from a massive Parthian invasion.[39] His greatest, unique glory I pass by.[40] Since its celebration is not yet agreeable to everyone, let us preserve it by the testimony of memory rather than of words.

**36** I have noticed, Members of the Senate, I have even heard it murmured, that I honor Brutus overmuch and Cassius overmuch, while my motion gives Cassius a position of dominance and primacy. Whom do I honor? Why, men who are themselves an honor to the Commonwealth. Have I not always

35. He had been one of Q. Cicero's legates when he was proconsul of Asia in 61–58.
36. The elder Isauricus.
37. Cilicia and Syria in 51–50.
38. I take *ne victa quidem causa* as ablative absolute.
39. In 51.
40. Caesar's assassination.

publicae. quid? D. Brutum nonne omnibus sententiis semper ornavi?
num igitur reprehenditis? an Antonios potius ornarem, non modo suarum
familiarum sed [p.] Romani nominis probra atque dedecora? an Censorinum ornem in bello hostem, in pace sectorem? an cetera ex eodem
latrocinio naufragia colligam? ego vero istos oti, concordiae, legum,          5
iudiciorum, libertatis inimicos tantum abest ut ornem ut effici non possit
quin eos tam oderim quam rem publicam diligo.

**37** "Vide," inquit "ne veteranos offendas": hoc enim vel maxime
exaudio. ego autem veteranos tueri debeo, sed eos quibus sanitas est;
certe timere non debeo. eos vero veteranos qui pro re publica arma       10
ceperunt secutique sunt C. Caesaris auctoritatem beneficiorum ⟨memores⟩
paternorum, hodieque rem publicam defendunt vitae suae periculo, non
tueri solum sed etiam commodis augere debeo. qui autem quiescunt, ut
septima, ut octava legio, in magna gloria et laude ponendos puto. comites
vero Antoni, qui, postquam beneficia Caesaris comederunt, consulem    15
designatum obsident, huic urbi ferro ignique minitantur, Saxae se et
Cafoni tradiderunt ad facinus praedamque natis, num quis est qui tuendos
putet? ergo aut boni sunt, quos etiam ornare, aut quieti, quos conservare
debemus, aut impii, quorum contra furorem bellum et iusta arma cepimus. **38** quorum igitur veteranorum animos ne offendamus veremur?   20
eorumne qui D. Brutum obsidione cupiunt liberare? quibus cum Bruti
salus cara sit, qui possunt Cassi nomen odisse? an eorum qui utrisque
armis vacant? non vereor ne acerbus c⟨u⟩ivis quisquam istorum sit qui otio
delectantur. tertio vero generi, non militum veteranorum sed importu-
nissimorum hostium, cupio quam acerbissimum dolorem inurere.          25

Quamquam, patres conscripti, quousque sententias dicemus veteranorum arbitratu? quod eorum tantum fastidium est, quae tanta adrogantia ut
ad arbitrium illorum imperatores etiam deligamus? **39** ego autem—dicendum est enim, patres conscripti, quod sentio—non tam veteranos me-
tuendos nobis arbitror quam quid tirones milites, flos Italiae, quid novae   30
legiones ad liberandam patriam paratissimae, quid cuncta Italia de vestra
gravitate sentiat. nihil enim semper floret; aetas succedit aetati. diu

---

3 Romani *Ferrarius*: p. R. *D*      4 ornarem *Halm*      **37** 9 sed eos quibus $n^2$: sed iis q-
$n^1sv$: quod iis quod quibus *t*: est quod iis quos quibus *b*      11 Caesaris³ *scripsi*: -rem
*D*      auctoritatem] -ate *sv*: auctore *b*¹: -orem *nb*²      memores *addidi*      12 vitae suae
periculo *Halm*: uideo e p- *t*: magno (cum m- *s*) p- *bnsv*      **38** 23 cuivis³ *Sternkopf*: ciuis
*D*      **39** 30 intuendos *Poggius*      uobis *nsv*

honored Decimus Brutus in every speech I have made in this House? Do you censure me for that? Or should I rather honor the Antonii, a reproach and disgrace not only to their families[41] but to the Roman name? Or should I honor Censorinus, an enemy in war, a profiteer[42] in peace? Or shall I assemble the rest of the wreckage from the same robber band? No, far from honoring these foes of peace, concord, laws, law courts, and liberty, there is no way that I shall not hate them as much as I love the Commonwealth.

**37** "Mind you don't offend the veterans," he[43] says. Yes, this in particular I hear murmured. Now I have a duty to look after the veterans, but only those of sound mind; I certainly have no duty to be afraid of them. The veterans who took up arms for the Commonwealth and followed Gaius Caesar's lead mindful of his father's benefits, and are today risking their lives in defense of the Commonwealth—these I am bound not only to defend but to add to their emoluments. Those who remain passive, like the Seventh and Eighth legions, I consider deserving of great praise and glory.[44] But the men with Antonius, who after squandering Caesar's benefits are besieging a consul-elect and threatening this city with sword and fire, who have handed themselves over to Saxa and Cafo, those born malefactors and plunderers—does anyone think *they* should be looked after? So then, we have three groups: the loyal men, whom we ought actually to favor, the peaceful men, whom we should preserve, and the traitors, against whose madness we have taken up arms in a just war. **38** To which veterans, then, do we fear to give umbrage? Those who are anxious to free Decimus Brutus from siege? How can they hate the name of Cassius when they hold Brutus' life dear? Or those who stand neutral? I am not afraid that any of these peace-loving folk will be bitter against anybody. As for the third category, not veteran soldiers but savage enemies, the more painfully their feelings are scarified, the better I shall be pleased.

After all, Members of the Senate, how much longer shall we frame our motions at the discretion of the veterans? What presumption, what arrogance, to expect us even to choose commanders at their pleasure! **39** For my part (I have to speak as I feel, Members of the Senate), I don't think we should be so much apprehensive of the veterans as of how the recruits, the flower of Italy, and the new legions who stand fully ready to liberate our country, and the whole of Italy are going to judge of your steadfastness. Nothing blooms forever. Generation succeeds generation. Caesar's legions flourished for a

---

41. The Antonii and the Julii.
42. *Sectorem*, a buyer of confiscated property.
43. An imaginary critic.
44. There seems to be some irony here, in keeping with *non vereor . . . delectentur* below.

legiones Caesaris viguerunt; nunc vigent Pansae, vigent Hirti, vigent
Caesaris fili, vigent Planci; vincunt numero, vincunt aetatibus; nimirum etiam auctoritate vincunt. id enim bellum gerunt quod ab omnibus
gentibus comprobatur. itaque his praemia promissa sunt, illis persoluta.
fruantur illi suis, persolvantur his quae spopondimus. id enim deos    5
immortalis spero aequissimum iudicare.

    **40** Quae cum ita sint, eam quam dixi sententiam vobis, patres con-
scripti, censeo comprobandam.

---

5 illi suis *Gryphius*: i- sues *t*: illis uel *ns*: his uel *v*: illis *b*

long while; now it is the turn of Pansa's legions, and Hirtius', and young Caesar's, and Plancus'. They have the advantage in number and youth, and also, one might add, in respect; for they are fighting a war which all nations approve. And so they have been promised rewards, whereas the others have already received them. Let the latter enjoy their own, and let the former be paid in full what we have pledged. That I trust is fairest in the judgment of the Immortal Gods.

**40** In view of which, Members of the Senate, I conceive that my motion deserves your approval.

# XII

## INTRODUCTION

About the beginning of March 43 the consulars Calenus and Piso were spreading reports that Antony was now ready to come to terms. The Senate was sufficiently impressed to authorize another embassy to Mutina, consisting of five consulars: Calenus, Piso, L. Caesar, Servilius—and Cicero. At a second meeting, however, Servilius announced his withdrawal, and Cicero followed with the Twelfth Philippic.

It is a curious episode. Cicero claimed a few weeks later (14.5) that from 1 January onwards he had never voted in favor of sending envoys to Antony. The opening of the Twelfth Philippic seems to imply the contrary. At any rate he had not opposed it on this occasion, and by his own admission (12.2–3) he had shared the delusion that Antony had become amenable. He had even allowed himself to be included in the mission (12.6).

After his vigorous condemnation of the first embassy and his insistence on the impossibility of any compromise, his own explanation, that his mental vision had been blurred by his concern for D. Brutus' safety (12.3), is hardly adequate. And the speech itself ends with a singular reservation. After denouncing the proposal and arguing that his own participation would be improper and personally dangerous, he promises to participate if he safely can, to think the matter over and decide in the best interests of the Commonwealth. Evidently something was going on behind the scenes, a final effort to avert full-scale conflict. But a few weeks later, probably on 20 March, Pansa left with an army of recruits for Mutina, where his approach set the stage for the bloody battles of April.

**1** Etsi minime decere videtur, patres conscripti, falli, decipi, errare eum cui vos maximis saepe de rebus adsentiamini, consolor me tamen quoniam vobiscum pariter et una cum sapientissimo consule erravi. nam cum duo consulares spem honestae pacis nobis attulissent, quod erant familiares M. Antoni, quod domestici, nosse aliquod eius vulnus quod 5 nobis ignotum esset videbantur. apud alterum uxor, liberi; alter cotidie litteras mittere, accipere, aperte favere Antonio. **2** hi subito hortari ad pacem, quod iam diu non fecissent, non sine causa videbantur. accessit consul hortator. at qui consul? si prudentiam quaerimus, qui minime falli posset; si virtutem, qui nullam pacem probaret nisi cum cedente atque 10 victo; si magnitudinem animi, qui praeferret mortem servituti. vos autem, patres conscripti, non tam immemores vestrorum gravissimorum decretorum videbamini quam spe adlata deditionis, quam amici pacem appellare mallent, de imponendis, non accipiendis legibus cogitare. auxerat autem meam quidem spem, credo item vestram, quod domum 15 Antoni adflictam maestitia audiebam, lamentari uxorem. hic etiam fautores Antoni, quorum in vultu habitant oculi mei, tristiores videbam. **3** quod si non ita est, cur a Pisone et Caleno potissimum, cur hoc tempore, cur tam improviso, cur tam repente pacis est facta mentio? negat Piso scire se, negat audisse quicquam; negat Calenus rem ullam novam adla- 20 tam esse. atque id nunc negant, postea quam nos pacificatoria legatione implicatos putant. quid ergo opus est novo consilio, si in re nihil omnino novi est?

Decepti, decepti, inquam, sumus, patres conscripti. Antoni est acta causa ab amicis eius, non publica. quod videbam equidem, sed quasi per 25 caliginem; praestrinxerat aciem animi D. Bruti salus. quod si in bello dari vicarii solerent, libenter me ut D. Brutus emitteretur pro illo includi paterer. **4** atque hac voce Q. Fufi capti sumus: "ne si a Mutina quidem recesserit, audiemus Antonium, ne si in senatus quidem potestate futurum se dixerit?" durum videbatur; itaque fracti sumus, cessimus. re- 30 cedit igitur a Mutina? "nescio." paret senatui? "credo," inquit Calenus "sed ita ut teneat dignitatem." valde hercules vobis laborandum est, patres conscripti, ut vestram dignitatem amittatis, quae maxima est, Antoni, quae neque est ulla neque esse potest, retineatis, ut eam per vos reciperet quam per se perdidit. 35

**1** 2 assentiebamini *t*      7 Antonio *del. voluit Schöll*      **2** 10 cum cedente *Jeep*: concedente (-ti *b*) *bt*: ced- *n*¹*sv*: ced- hoste *n*²      12 tam] iam *bstv*      13 oblata *Ursinus*      14 appellare mallent *n*²: -rem (-rent *b*) alieni *D*      **3** 24 decepti *semel nst* (*cf.* 8.22)      26 praestrinxerant *t*: perstrinxerat *bv*      **4** 28 atqui *Naugerius*      29 potestatem *bnst*

**1** Members of the Senate, it seems by no means fitting that one to whose views on matters of the highest importance you frequently give your assent, should be deceived, misled, in error. I console myself, however, with the fact that I erred in common with yourselves and in the company of a very sapient consul. Two consulars[1] brought us hope of peace with honor. As familiar friends of Marcus Antonius and part of his domestic circle, we supposed they knew of some reverse that had befallen him of which we were ignorant. His wife and children are staying with one of these gentlemen, the other is in daily correspondence with Antonius and openly supports him. **2** There must be a reason, we thought, for their suddenly urging us to make peace, something they had not done for a long while. The consul added his encouragement. What sort of a consul? Is he a man of prudence? Why yes, the last person to make a mistake. Of courage? He would approve of no peace except with a yielding and defeated adversary. Of lofty spirit? One who would prefer death to slavery. As for you, Members of the Senate, it was not as though you had forgotten your weighty decrees but rather were thinking of laying down terms, not accepting them, having been given reason to hope for a surrender which Antonius' friends preferred to call a peace. My hopes rose, as I expect did yours, when I was told that gloom reigned in Antonius' house and that his wife was in tears. Here too I saw his backers, whose faces I keep under constant observation, looking glum. **3** If this is not the case, why the mention of peace by Piso and Calenus of all people, why at this time, why so unexpectedly and suddenly? Piso says he knows nothing, has heard nothing. Calenus says that nothing new has come his way. They say this now, after they think we have entangled ourselves in a peacemaking embassy. Well, where is the need for a new policy if there is nothing whatever new in the facts?

We have been misled, Members of the Senate, I say again, misled. Antonius' friends have pleaded *his* cause, not that of the Commonwealth. I saw it, but I saw it through a fog; my vision was blurred by my anxiety for Decimus Brutus. If substitutes were customary in war, I would gladly let myself be shut in to secure Decimus Brutus' release. **4** Moreover, we were taken in by Quintus Fufius' words: "Shall we not listen to Antonius even if he withdraws from Mutina, even if he promises to be at the Senate's disposition?" It seemed hard. So we softened and gave in. Well, has he withdrawn from Mutina? "I don't know." Is he obedient to the Senate? "I believe so," says Calenus, "but with the proviso that he maintain his dignity." Of course, of course, Members of the Senate, you must make every effort to lose your own dignity, which is great, and keep intact Antonius' dignity, which does not and cannot exist; having destroyed it by his own doing, let him get it back by yours!

---

1. Piso and Calenus.

Si iacens vobiscum aliquid ageret, audirem fortasse; quamquam—sed hoc malo dicere, audirem: stanti resistendum est aut concedenda una cum dignitate libertas. **5** at non est integrum: constituta legatio est. quid autem non integrum est sapienti quod restitui potest? cuiusvis hominis est errare; nullius nisi insipientis perseverare in errore. posteriores enim 5 cogitationes, ut aiunt, sapientiores solent esse. discussa est illa caligo quam paulo ante dixi; diluxit, patet, videmus omnia, neque per nos solum, sed admonemur a nostris. attendistis paulo ante praestantissimi viri quae esset oratio. "maestam" inquit "domum offendi, coniugem, liberos. admirabantur boni viri, accusabant amici quod spe pacis lega- 10 tionem suscepissem." nec mirum, P. Servili: tuis enim ⟨se⟩verissimis gravissimisque sententiis omni est non dico dignitate sed etiam spe sa- lutis spoliatus Antonius. **6** ad eum ire te legatum quis non miraretur? de me experior: cuius idem consilium quod tuum sentio quam reprehenda- tur. nos reprehendimur soli? quid? vir fortissimus Pansa sine causa paulo 15 ante tam accurate locutus est tam diu? quid egit nisi uti falsam proditionis a se suspicionem depelleret? unde autem ista suspicio est? ex pacis pa- trocinio repentino quod subito suscepit eodem captus errore quo nos.

**7** Quod si est erratum, patres conscripti, spe falsa atque fallaci, re- deamus in viam. optimus est portus paenitenti mutatio consili. quid enim 20 potest, per deos immortalis, rei publicae prodesse nostra legatio? pro- desse dico? quid si etiam obfutura est? obfutura? quid si iam nocuit atque obfuit? an vos acerrimam illam et fortissimam populi Romani libertatis recuperandae cupiditatem non imminutam ac debilitatam putatis lega- tione pacis audita? quid municipia censetis? quid colonias? quid cunctam 25 Italiam? futuram eodem studio quo contra commune incendium exarserat? an non putamus fore ut eos paeniteat professos esse et prae se tulisse odium in Antonium qui pecunias polliciti sunt, qui arma, qui se totos et animis et corporibus in salutem rei publicae contulerunt? quem ad modum nostrum hoc consilium Capua probabit, quae temporibus his 30 Roma altera est? illa impios civis iudicavit, eiecit, exclusit. illi, inquam, urbi fortissime ⟨constringere⟩ conanti e manibus est ereptus Antonius. **8** quid? legionum nostrarum nervos nonne his consiliis incidimus? quis est enim qui ad bellum inflammato animo futurus sit spe pacis oblata? ipsa illa Martia caelestis et divina legio hoc nuntio languescet et mollietur 35 atque illud pulcherrimum nomen [Martium] amittet: excident gladii, flu-

---

**5** 5 in errore perseuerare *tv*     11 severissimis *Gulielmius*: uer- *D* (*cf. Dom. 68*)     **6** 13 miretur *s, fort. recte*     **7** 24 debilitatam] delibatam *bns¹t*     26 exarserit *t*     31 illi illi *bv*     32 fortissima *Boyancé*     constringere conanti *scripsi auctore Koch* (conanti cons-)     **8** 36 Martium *del. Manutius*

If he had something to say to you on his knees, perhaps I should listen, even though—but I prefer to say, I should listen. As he stands upright we must resist him or surrender freedom along with dignity. **5** I shall be told that the choice is no longer open; the delegation has been appointed. To a man of sense everything is open that can be corrected. Anyone can make a mistake, but only a fool persists in error. Second thoughts, they say, are usually wiser. The fog of which I spoke just now is dispersed. Light has broken through, all is plain, we see everything, and not only with our own eyes; our families and friends warn us. You heard what a very distinguished gentleman said a little while ago: "I found my house in mourning," he says, "as were my wife and children. Honest men were astonished, and my friends upbraided me for accepting the mission in the hope of peace." No wonder, Publius Servilius! It was your most just and weighty speeches that deprived Antonius of all hope of survival, let alone dignity. **6** Who would not be surprised to see you go to him as envoy? I speak from my own experience. I took the same view as you, and I see how strongly it is censured. Nor are we two the only targets for criticism. Was it for nothing that our gallant Pansa spoke in such detail and at such length just now? What was his purpose except to rebut a false suspicion of treachery? And what has caused that suspicion? It was his sudden advocacy of peace, which he launched on the spur of the moment, deceived by the same error as ourselves.

**7** Well, Members of the Senate, we have been led astray by a false, delusive hope. Let us get back to our path. The best recourse in dissatisfaction is a change of policy. For what good, in Heaven's name, can our mission do the Commonwealth? I say "what good?"—but supposing it does the opposite? Supposing it already has done the opposite, done harm? Do you imagine that the Roman People's ardent, courageous desire to recover its freedom has not been diminished and enfeebled by the news of a peace mission? How do you think the municipalities will react, and the colonies, and the whole of Italy? Will the enthusiasm which flamed up to fight the common peril be the same? Must we not expect that those who have promised subsidies and arms, who have committed themselves unreservedly body and soul to the survival of the Commonwealth, will regret having professed and declared their hatred of Antonius? How will Capua, which is a second Rome these days, approve this step of ours? She judged the traitors, threw them[2] out, kept them out. Yes, Antonius was barely snatched from that city's hands as she bravely tried to hold him. **8** What of our legions? Have we not hamstrung them by this policy? What heart will burn for war once the hope of peace has been held out? Even the Martian, that wonderful legion of supermen, will droop at the news and soften and lose its splendid name; the swords will fall, the shields will drop

---

2. The new colonists brought in by Antony; cf. 2.100.

ent arma de manibus. senatum enim secuta non arbitrabitur se graviore odio debere esse in Antonium quam senatum. pudet huius legionis, pudet quartae, quae pari virtute nostram auctoritatem probans non ut consulem et imperatorem suum, sed ut hostem et oppugnatorem patriae reliquit Antonium; pudet optimi exercitus qui coniunctus est ex duobus, qui iam   5
lustratus, qui profectus ad Mutinam est; qui si pacis, id est timoris nostri, nomen audierit, ut non referat pedem, insistet certe. quid enim revocante et receptui canente senatu properet dimicare? **9** quid autem hoc iniustius quam nos inscientibus eis qui bellum gerunt de pace decernere, nec solum inscientibus sed etiam invitis? an vos A. Hirtium, praeclarissimum   10
consulem, C. Caesarem, deorum beneficio natum ad haec tempora, quorum epistulas spem victoriae declarantis in manu teneo, pacem velle censetis? vincere illi expetunt pacisque dulcissimum et pulcherrimum nomen non pactione, sed victoria concupiverunt. quid? Galliam quo tandem animo hanc rem audituram putatis? illa enim huius belli pro-   15
pulsandi, administrandi, sustinendi principatum tenet. Gallia D. Bruti nutum ipsum, ne dicam imperium, secuta armis, viris, pecunia belli prin-cipia firmavit; eadem crudelitati M. Antoni suum totum corpus obiecit; exhauritur, vastatur, uritur: omnis aequo animo belli patitur iniurias, dum modo repellat periculum servitutis. **10** et ut omittam reliquas partis   20
Galliae—nam sunt omnes pares—Patavini alios excluserunt, alios eiece-runt missos ab Antonio, pecunia, militibus, et, quod maxime deerat, armis nostros duces adiuverunt. fecerunt idem reliqui, qui quondam in eadem causa erant et propter multorum annorum iniurias alienati a senatu putabantur: quos minime mirum est communicata cum eis re publica   25
fidelis ⟨esse⟩, qui etiam expertes eius fidem suam semper praestiterunt. his igitur omnibus victoriam sperantibus pacis nomen adferemus, id est desperationem victoriae?

    **11** Quid si ne potest quidem ulla esse pax? quae enim est condicio pacis in qua ei cum quo pacem facias nihil concedi potest? multis rebus ⟨nefariis   30
ante commissis⟩ a nobis est invitatus ad pacem Antonius: bellum tamen

---

7 sistet *Gulielmius*      quis *s*      **9** 9 scientibus *stv*: scientius *n*[1]: ins- *n*[2]      11 et C.
*Muretus*      19 iniurias *Ferrarius*: -am *D*      **10** 26 esse *add. Poggius*      **11** 29 ne] non
*nstv*      30–31 nefariis ante commissis[3] *addidi*      est *om. tv*

from their hands. They followed the Senate, and will not feel it right to hate Antonius more than the Senate hates him. I am ashamed to think of this legion, and the Fourth too, which approving our authority with equal courage abandoned Antonius, not as their consul and imperator but as an enemy and assailant of their country. I am ashamed to think of that excellent army, made up of two armies,[3] which has already been reviewed and has set out for Mutina. If they hear the name of peace, that is, of our fear, they will halt, if not turn around. Why should they hasten to battle, when the Senate calls them back, sounding the signal for retreat? **9** And what can be more improper than for us to decide upon peace without the knowledge of those who are fighting the war—and not only without their knowledge but against their will? Or do you imagine that Aulus Hirtius, our splendid consul, or Gaius Caesar, born by the grace of the Gods to match these times, whose letters declaring their hope of victory I hold in my hand—do you imagine they want peace? They are out to win. They have set their hearts on peace, that sweetest and most beautiful of words, through victory, not bargaining. Again, how do you think Gaul will feel about this news? She plays the leading role in repelling, conducting, and sustaining this war. Gaul strengthened its beginnings with arms, men, and money, following Decimus Brutus' simple nod—I won't say his orders. Gaul put her whole body in the way of Marcus Antonius' cruelty; she is being drained, ravaged, burned. She calmly endures all the injuries of war, if only she can thrust back the danger of slavery. **10** To say nothing of the other parts of Gaul (they are all equal), the people of Patavium kept out some of Antonius' men and threw out others, while helping our commanders with money, troops, and what they needed most, weapons. The rest did likewise, though formerly they were in the same cause as Antonius and were believed to be alienated from the Senate because of the wrongs of many years.[4] But it is not at all surprising that having always shown their loyalty when they were outside the Commonwealth they should be faithful now that they have been given a share in it. All of them hope for victory. Shall we offer them the name of peace, which means despair of victory?

**11** What if no peace is even possible? How can peace terms be negotiated when those terms cannot include any concession to the party with whom you are making peace? After committing many acts of villainy Marcus Antonius was invited by us to make peace, but he preferred war. Envoys were dis-

---

3. Octavian's and Hirtius'. Hirtius as consul was in command. He had previously stayed outside Gaul, perhaps at Claterna (cf. 8.6).

4. Before the Civil War Caesar's efforts to get full citizenship for the Gauls north of the Po had been thwarted by his opponents in the Senate. Cicero here takes no account of the fact that those south of the river had been given this in 89.

maluit. missi legati repugnante me, sed tamen missi; delata mandata:
non paruit. denuntiatum est ne Brutum obsideret, a Mutina discederet:
oppugnavit etiam vehementius. et ad eum legatos de pace mittemus qui
pacis nuntios repudiavit? verecundioremne coram putamus in postulando
fore quam fuerit tum cum misit mandata ad senatum? atqui tum ea      5
petebat quae videbantur improba omnino sed tamen aliquo modo posse
concedi; nondum erat vestris tam gravibus tamque multis iudiciis igno-
miniisque concisus: nunc ea petit quae dare nullo modo possumus, nisi
prius volumus bello nos victos confiteri. **12** senatus consulta falsa delata
ab eo iudicavimus: num ea vera possumus iudicare? leges statuimus     10
per vim et contra auspicia latas eisque nec populum nec plebem teneri:
num eas restitui posse censetis? sestertium septiens miliens avertisse
Antonium pecuniae publicae iudicavistis: num fraude poterit carere pecu-
latus? immunitates ab eo, civitates, sacerdotia, regna venierunt: num
figentur rursus eae tabulae quas vos decretis vestris refixistis?      15

   Quod si ea quae decrevimus obruere, num etiam memoriam rerum delere possumus? quando enim obliviscetur ulla posteritas cuius scelere in
hac vestitus foeditate fuerimus? ut centurionum legionis Martiae Brundisi
profusus sanguis eluatur, num elui praedicatio crudelitatis potest? ut
media praeteream, quae vetustas tollet operum circum Mutinam taetra   20
monumenta, sceleris indicia latrocinique vestigia?

   **13** Huic igitur importuno atque impuro parricidae quid habemus, per
deos immortalis, quod remittamus? an Galliam ultimam et exercitum?
quid est aliud non pacem facere, sed differre bellum, nec solum pro-
pagare bellum sed concedere etiam victoriam? an ille non vicerit, si    25
quacumque condicione in hanc urbem cum suis venerit? armis nunc
omnia tenemus; auctoritate valemus plurimum; absunt tot perditi cives,
nefarium secuti ducem; tamen eorum ora sermonesque qui in urbe ex eo
numero relicti sunt ferre non possumus. quid censetis, cum tot uno
tempore irruperint, nos arma posuerimus, illi non deposuerint, nonne   30
nos nostris consiliis victos in perpetuum fore? **14** ponite ante oculos
M. Antonium consularem; sperantem consulatum Lucium adiungite;
supplete ceteros neque nostri ordinis solum honores et imperia medi-

---

7 grauissimis (-mus *v*) *nstvb*²     8 conscisus *v*     **12** 10 -sumus iudicare] *hinc rursus in-cipit V* (*v. ad* 11.17)     14 ciuitatibus *V*     16 obruere uolumus *DV*²     19 eleuatur *V*¹: eluitur *n*¹*stv*     elui] aeui *t*: eius *bnsv*     20 circa *D*     21 munimenta *D*     **13** 24 quam non *nsv*     25 si *om. bnst*     26 suis armis uenerit *D*     28 sermones *D*     31 nos *om. V*

patched—I opposed it, but they were dispatched. A message was delivered: he disobeyed. He was warned not to besiege Brutus, to withdraw from Mutina: he attacked with even greater vigor than before. Shall we send peace envoys to a man who rebuffed the messengers of peace? Do we suppose he will be more modest in his demands face to face than he was when he sent his message to the Senate? All the same, his demands at that time appeared exorbitant to be sure, but in some sort within the limits of possible concession. He had not yet been mauled by so many condemnatory judgments and disgraces on your part. Now he is asking what we cannot possibly grant unless we first choose to acknowledge ourselves defeated in the war. **12** We have declared that he entered false decrees of the Senate: can we declare them genuine? We have determined that laws were passed by violence and contrary to auspices and that neither people nor plebs[5] are bound by them: do you think they can be restored? You have declared that Antonius embezzled seven hundred million of public money: can peculation carry no penalty? He sold exemptions, citizenships, priesthoods, kingdoms: shall those placards, which you took down by your decrees, be replaced?

Suppose, however, we can bury our decrees, can we wipe out the memory of events? When will any future generations forget whose crime it was that made us put on this repellent dress?[6] The blood of the centurions of the Martian Legion shed at Brundisium may be washed away, but can the recital of that atrocity be washed away? To pass by all that happened in between, what lapse of years will remove the works around Mutina, those sinister memorials, the evidence of crime, the traces of banditry?

**13** What concession do we have to make, in Heaven's name, to this savage, foul traitor? Outer Gaul and an army? That would not be making peace but simply deferring the war, and not only prolonging the war but conceding victory. For will he not have won if he comes back to this city with his followers on any terms? At present our arms are in full control; our authority has enormous weight; many desperate characters are elsewhere, following their wicked leader: and yet the countenances and talk of those of their number who are left in Rome are more than we can tolerate. How do you think it will be when so many of them burst in at once, when we have laid aside our arms and they have not laid down theirs? Shall we not have been defeated once and for all through our own devices? **14** Picture Marcus Antonius, the consular. Add Lucius, aspirant to the consulship. Throw in the rest, not all of them members of this House, whose minds are on offices and awards. Don't despise even a

5. *Populus* = the whole citizen body, *plebs* = the same with patricians excluded. The latter could legislate for the whole people.
6. The military cloak (*sagum*).

tantis: nolite ne Tirones quidem Numisios et Mustelas Seios contemnere.
cum eis facta pax non erit pax, sed pactio servitutis. L. Pisonis, amplissimi
viri, praeclara vox a te non solum in hoc ordine, Pansa, sed etiam in
contione iure laudata est. excessurum se ex Italia dixit, deos penatis et
sedes patrias relicturum, si—quod di omen avertant!—rem publicam      5
oppressisset Antonius. **15** quaero igitur a te, L. Piso, nonne oppressam
rem publicam putes, si tot tam impii, tam audaces, tam facinerosi recepti
sint? quos nondum tantis parricidiis contaminatos vix ferebamus, hos
nunc omni scelere coopertos tolerabilis censes civitati fore? aut isto tuo,
mihi crede, consilio erit utendum, ut cedamus, abeamus, vitam inopem      10
et vagam persequamur, aut cervices latronibus dandae atque in patria
cadendum est. ubi sunt, C. Pansa, illae cohortationes pulcherrimae tuae
quibus a te excitatus senatus, inflammatus populus Romanus non solum
audivit sed etiam didicit nihil esse homini Romano foedius servitute?
**16** idcircone saga sumpsimus, arma cepimus, iuventutem omnem ex tota      15
Italia excussimus, ut exercitu florentissimo et maximo ⟨confecto⟩ legati
ad pacem mitterentur? si accipiendam, cur non rogamur? si postulandam,
quid timemus?

　　In hac ego legatione sim aut ad id consilium admiscear in quo ne si
dissensero quidem a ceteris sciturus populus Romanus sit? ita fiet ut, si      20
quid remissum aut concessum sit, meo semper periculo peccet Antonius,
cum ei peccandi potestas a me concessa videatur. **17** quod si habenda cum
M. Antoni latrocinio pacis ratio fuit, mea tamen persona ad istam pacem
conciliandam minime fuit deligenda. ego numquam legatos mittendos
censui; ego ante reditum legatorum ausus sum dicere, pacem ipsam si      25
adferrent, quoniam sub nomine pacis bellum lateret, repudiandam; ego
princeps ⟨sumendorum⟩ sagorum; ego semper illum appellavi hostem,
cum alii adversarium, semper hoc bellum, cum alii tumultum. nec haec
in senatu solum: eadem ad populum semper egi; neque solum in ipsum
sed in eius socios facinorum et ministros, et praesentis et eos qui una      30
sunt, in totam denique M. Antoni domum sum semper invectus. **18** itaque
ut alacres et laeti spe pacis oblata inter se impii cives, quasi vicissent,
gratulabantur, sic me iniquum eierabant, de me querebantur. diffide-
bant etiam Servilio: meminerant eius sententiis confixum Antonium.

**14** 1 numisios et $V^2n^2$: -oste $V^1$: *varia D*　　5 avertant] auerterit *V*: -terent *bv*: aurtent *t*:
averterint *Faërnus*　　**15** 6 L. *om. bnst*　　12 est *om. D*　　**16** 16 excussimus *V*, *Nonius
299*: exciuimus *D*　　ut] ut de *bns*: et de *v*: et *t*　　confecto *addidi*　　ut legati *tv*　　17
si . . . rogamur *post* in quo ne (*l.* 19) *D*　　rogamus $V^1$　　19 admiscear *Poggius*: -aris *D*:
admis *V*　　19–20 in quo . . . a *om. V*　　20 sciturus *Poggius*: sicit- *V*: si it- *bstv*: fut-
*n*　　**17** 23 M. *om. D*　　25 legatorum reditum *D*　　26 r. p. repudiandam *D*　　27 su-
mendorum$^3$ *addidi*　　hostem appellavi *D*　　28 cum (*pr.*)] dum *V*　　30 et (*pr.*) *om.*
*bnsv*　　et (*ult.*) *om. V*　　**18** 33 inimicum *D*

Tiro Numisius or a Mustela Seius. Peace made with them will be no peace, but a pact of slavery. Not only in this House but in a public meeting, Pansa, you rightly praised a fine saying of our distinguished fellow member Lucius Piso. He declared that he would leave Italy, abandon his Household Gods and his ancestral home, if (may the Gods avert the omen!) Antonius crushed the Commonwealth. **15** Then I ask you, Lucius Piso, would you not regard the Commonwealth as crushed if so many such bold, villainous traitors were taken back? We had all we could do to put up with them before they had polluted themselves with such atrocities. Do you think the community can tolerate them now that they are steeped in every crime? Believe me, we shall either have to follow your plan, leave, retire, lead the life of needy wanderers, or yield our necks to the robbers' knives and fall in our fatherland. Where now, Gaius Pansa, are those noble exhortations of yours with which you roused the Senate and fired the people, as they not only heard but learned that to a Roman no fate is more horrible than slavery? **16** Did we put on military cloaks, take up arms, drum up all our young men from all over Italy, in order that after we had raised a great army in the finest fettle envoys should be sent to treat for peace? If to accept a peace, why are we not asked? If to demand it, what are we afraid of?[7]

Am *I* to be a member of this delegation, added to a body in which even if I dissent from the rest, the Roman People will not know it? The consequence will be that if there should be any relaxation or concession, I shall be answerable in the future for Antonius' wrongdoings, since it will appear that the power to do wrong was conceded to him by me. **17** But supposing peace with Marcus Antonius' banditry was something to be considered, I was the last person who should have been chosen to negotiate such a peace. I was never in favor of sending envoys. Before the envoys returned, I made bold to say that even if they brought peace itself, it should be rejected, since under the name of peace war would lurk. I took the lead in the putting on of military cloaks. I ever called Antonius an enemy when others called him an adversary; I ever called this a war, when others called it a tumult. And this I did not in the Senate only; I always used the same language before the people. And I have all along inveighed not only against Antonius but against the partners and ministers of his crimes, both those present and those who are with him, in fact against his entire circle. **18** So the traitors among us who were so brisk and cheerful when the hope of peace was held out, congratulating each other as though they had triumphed, were for rejecting me as biased, were protesting at my inclusion. Neither did they trust Servilius, remembering how Antony had been transfixed

---

7. If Antony is offering peace, why has he not asked us to send a mission? If we are in a position to demand it on our own terms, what have we to fear (why send a mission at all)?

L. Caesarem fortem quidem illum et constantem senatorem, avunculum tamen, Calenum procuratorem, Pisonem familiarem, te ipsum, Pansa, vehementissimum et fortissimum consulem, factum iam putant leniorem; non quo ita sit aut esse possit, sed mentio a te facta pacis suspicionem multis attulit immutatae voluntatis. inter has personas me interiectum 5 amici Antoni moleste ferunt: quibus gerendus mos est, quoniam semel liberales esse coepimus. **19** proficiscantur legati optimis ominibus, sed ei proficiscantur in quibus non offendatur Antonius.

Quod si de Antonio non laboratis, mihi certe, patres conscripti, consulere debetis. parcite oculis saltem meis et aliquam veniam iusto dolori 10 date. quo enim aspectu videre potero—omitto hostem patriae, ex quo mihi odium in illum commune vobiscum est—sed quo modo aspiciam mihi uni crudelissimum hostem, ut declarant eius de me acerbissimae contiones? adeone me ferreum putatis ut cum eo congredi aut illum aspicere possim qui nuper, cum in contione donaret eos qui ei de parricidis 15 audacissimi videbantur, mea bona donare se dixit Petusio Urbinati, qui ex naufragio luculenti patrimoni ad haec Antoniana saxa proiectus est? **20** an L. Antonium aspicere potero, cuius ego crudelitatem effugere non potuissem, nisi me moenibus et portis et studio municipi mei defendissem? atque idem hic myrmillo Asiaticus, latro Italiae, collega Lentonis et 20 Nuculae, cum Aquilae primi pili nummos aureos daret, de meis bonis se dare dixit: si enim de suis dixisset, ne Aquilam quidem ipsum crediturum putavit. non ferent, inquam, oculi Saxam, Cafonem, non duo praetores, non tribunos plebis [non] duo designatos [tribunos], non Bestiam, non Trebellium, non T. Plancum. non possum animo aequo videre tot tam 25 importunos, tam sceleratos hostis; nec id fit fastidio meo, sed caritate rei publicae.

**21** Sed vincam animum mihique imperabo: dolorem iustissimum, si non potuero frangere, occultabo. quid? vitae censetisne, patres conscripti, habendam mihi aliquam esse rationem? quae mihi quidem minime cara 30 est, praesertim cum Dolabella fecerit ut optanda mors esset, modo sine cruciatu atque tormentis; vobis tamen et populo Romano vilis meus spiritus esse non debet. is enim sum, nisi me forte fallo, qui vigiliis, curis, sententiis, periculis etiam, quae plurima adii propter acerbissimum omnium in me odium impiorum, perfecerim ut non obstarem rei publi- 35

---

1 illum quidem *Muretus* 2 tamen *om. V* **19** 11 mitto *bnsv* 12 sed] et *V*[1]: set *V*[2]: *om. D* 16 de meis bonis *D* (*cf. l.* 21) Petusio *C. F. W. Müller* (*cf.* 13.3): petissio *V*: pitisio *b*: pisidio *t*: praes- *nsv* **20** 21 primipilo *Manutius* 22 ipsum credituram *V*: -am -am *nstv* 23–24 duos . . . duos *bnsv* 24 non tr. pl. *codd.*: *del. Garatoni* non *et* tribunos[2] *seclusi* 25 T. *om. D* **21** 33 sum] est *bnsv*: *om. t* 34 etiam perfecerit (prof- *s*) *bnsv* (*cf. l.* 35) adii *om. D* 35 perfecerim] per me f- *t*: pertulerim (-int *v*) *bnsv* obstarent *bnsv*

by his speeches. Lucius Caesar, they recognized, was a brave, resolute senator; but he was Antonius' uncle. Calenus was his agent, Piso his close friend. As for yourself, Pansa,[8] our most energetic and valiant consul, they believe you have softened; not that this is true or could be, but your introduction of the topic of peace made many suspect a shift of attitude. The friends of Antonius take it ill that I should be thrust among these personages. We ought to humor them, now that we have started to be liberal. 19 Let the envoys set out with the best of omens, but only those who will not offend Antonius.

But if you are not worried about Antonius' feelings, Members of the Senate, you ought at least to have some regard for mine. Spare my eyes at any rate and make some allowance for a legitimate indignation. How shall I look when I see him? That he is the enemy of our country I put aside, since you have as much cause as I to hate him on that account; but how shall I look at so cruel an enemy to me individually, as his savage harangues about me declare? Do you think I am of such iron mold that I can meet with or look at a man who the other day, when announcing largesses at a public meeting to the boldest-seeming among his traitor band, said that he was granting my property to Petusius of Urbinum, a fellow who was flung from the wreck of a fine patrimony onto these Antonian rocks? 20 Or shall I be able to look at Lucius Antonius, whose cruelty I escaped only under the protection of the walls and gates and goodwill of my native town?[9] When this same Asiatic myrmillo, robber of Italy, colleague of Lento and Nucula, gave some gold pieces to Chief Centurion Aquila, he said that he was giving them out of my property; if he had said they came out of his own, he thought that even Aquila would not believe him. My eyes, I say, will not bear the sight of Saxa and Cafo, of the two praetors, of the two tribunes-elect of the plebs, of Bestia, of Trebellius, of Titus Plancus. I cannot calmly behold so many savage, ruffianly enemies. That is not because I am squeamish, but because I love the Commonwealth.

21 But I shall conquer my feelings and force myself along. If I cannot overcome my most legitimate indignation, I shall hide it. Very well, but do you not think, Members of the Senate, that I ought to have some regard for my life? Indeed I set little store by it, especially now that thanks to Dolabella death is a thing to wish for provided it be not accompanied by the pains of torture. But by you and by the Roman People my life should not be lightly accounted. For if I do not deceive myself, I am one whose vigils, anxieties, speeches in this House, even risks, of which I have encountered a great many because of the bitter hatred all traitors feel for me, have enabled me—let me avoid any

8. Pansa was not one of the envoys; cf. 13.36 *consularis quinque*.
9. On this obscure reference see my note on *Fam.* 9.24.1.

cae, ne quid adrogantius videar dicere. **22** quod cum ita sit, nihilne mihi
de periculo meo cogitandum putatis? hic cum essem in urbe ac domi,
tamen multa saepe temptata sunt, ubi me non solum amicorum fidelitas
sed etiam universae civitatis oculi custodiunt: quid censetis, cum iter
ingressus ero, longum praesertim, nullasne insidias extimescendas?          5

Tres viae sunt ad Mutinam—quo festinat animus ut quam primum
illud pignus libertatis populi Romani, D. Brutum, aspicere possim; cuius
in complexu libenter extremum vitae spiritum ediderim, cum omnes
actiones horum mensum, omnes sententiae meae pervenerint ad eum
qui mihi fuit propositus exitum. tres ergo, ut dixi, viae: a supero mari   10
Flaminia, ab infero Aurelia, media Cassia. **23** nunc, quaeso, attendite
num aberret a coniectura suspicio periculi mei. Etruriam discriminat
Cassia. scimusne igitur, Pansa, quibus in locis nunc sit Lentonis Caesenni
septemviralis auctoritas? nobiscum nec animo certe est nec corpore. si
autem aut domi est aut non longe a domo, certe in Etruria est, id est in   15
via. quis igitur mihi praestat Lentonem uno capite esse contentum? dic
mihi praeterea, Pansa, Ventidius ubi sit, cui fui semper amicus ante quam
ille rei publicae bonisque omnibus tam aperte est factus inimicus. possum
Cassiam vitare, ⟨tenere⟩ Flaminiam: quid si Anconam, ut dicitur, Ventidius
venerit? poterone Ariminum tuto accedere? restat Aurelia. hic quidem    20
etiam praesidia habeo; possessiones enim sunt P. Clodi. tota familia
occurret; hospitio invitabit propter familiaritatem notissimam.

**24** Hisce ego me viis committam, qui Terminalibus nuper in subur-
b⟨an⟩um, ut eodem die reverterer, ire non sum ausus? domesticis me
parietibus vix tueor sine amicorum custodiis. itaque in urbe maneo, si    25
licebit, manebo. haec mea sedes est, haec vigilia, haec custodia, hoc
praesidium stativum. teneant alii castra, gerant res bellicas, oderint
hostem; nam hoc caput est: nos, ut dicimus semperque fecimus, urbem et
res urbanas vobiscum pariter tuebimur.

Neque vero recuso munus hoc: quamquam populum Romanum video    30
pro me recusare. nemo me minus timidus, nemo tamen cautior. res
declarat. vicesimus annus est cum omnes scelerati me unum petunt.
itaque ipsi, ne dicam mihi, rei publicae poenas dederunt: me salvum

---

**22** 5 pertimescendas *D*     9 horum mensum *V²*: h- mensunusum *V¹*: honorum *D*: horum
mensium *R. Klotz*     omnium *V*     ad eum] ad eum exitum *s*     10 exitum *Manutius*:
-us *codd.*     **23** 12 a *del. Madvig* (*v. Fe.*)     14 *in litt.* corpo *deficit V usque ad orationis
finem* (*v. ad* 11.17)     19 uitare et *t*     tenere *add. Poggius, sequi ante* quid si *addendum
coni. Clark*     21 habebo *b*     **24** 23 uiis me *v*     suburbanum *scripsi*: -bium *D*     25
*Anne* tuear³?     maneo *om.* ς     si] sisi *t*: si sic *ns*: et si *Sternkopf*: ac si *Schöll*     27
gerant res *Orelli*: regna res (tres *t*) *D*     oderint³] fuderint *Faërnus, alii alia*     28 di-
dicimus *Gruter*: diximus *Ernesti*: facimus *R. Klotz, fort. recte*     31 tamen *Halm*: tam *t*:
*om. bnsv*

touch of arrogance—to be of no disservice to the Commonwealth. **22** That being so, do you think I ought not to take any thought for the risks I should run? Even here, as I live in Rome in my home, many attempts have been made, where I am guarded by the loyalty of friends and the eyes of the whole community. How do you suppose it will be when I have set out on a journey, and a long one? Will there be no fear of an ambush?

There are three roads to Mutina, the town to which I am hastening in spirit so that I may see that pledge of the Roman People's freedom, Decimus Brutus, as soon as may be. In his embrace I would gladly breathe my last, when all that I have been doing and saying these past months has reached the end I had in view. Well, as I have said, there are three roads: the Flaminian along the east coast, the Aurelian along the west coast, and the Cassian in the middle. **23** Now let me ask for your attention: consider whether my suspicion of personal danger is beside the mark. The Cassian way divides Etruria. Do we know, Pansa, the present whereabouts of that pillar of the Board of Seven, Lento Caesennius? He certainly is not with us, either in body or spirit. If he is at home or not far away, he is certainly in Etruria; that is, on the road. Who guarantees me that Lento is content with one life?[10] Tell me, furthermore, Pansa, where is Ventidius? I was always his friend before he became so open an enemy to the Commonwealth and to all honest men. Well, I can avoid the Cassian way and follow the Flaminian. What if Ventidius comes to Ancona, as it is said he will? Shall I be able to approach Ariminum safely? That leaves the Aurelian way. Now here I even have protection. These are the lands of Publius Clodius. The whole establishment will turn out to meet me and offer hospitality because of our notorious friendship.

**24** Shall I then trust myself to those roads, when recently at the Festival of Terminus[11] I did not dare to go to a house near Rome[12] and return the same day? I should be hard put to it to protect myself with the walls of my house but for my friends' keeping guard. So I stay in Rome; if I am permitted, I shall continue to do so. This is my dwelling, this my watch and ward, this my standing guard. Let others keep camp, wage war, hate the enemy (that is the main point!): I, as I say and as I have always done, shall attend to Rome and its affairs along with you gentlemen.

At the same time, I am not refusing this commission, though I perceive that the Roman People is refusing it for me. No man is less timid than I, but no man is more cautious. The facts declare it. For twenty years past, all the villains have attacked me and me only. Well, they themselves paid their penalties, I will not say to me but to the Commonwealth; while the Commonwealth has up

---

10. He had killed Pompey's elder son in 45.
11. 23 February.
12. The Tusculan villa?

adhuc res publica conservavit sibi. timide hoc dicam—scio enim quidvis
homini accidere posse—verum tamen: ⟨numquam imprudens oppressus
sum⟩. semel circumsessus ⟨col⟩lectis valentissimorum hominum viribus
cecidi sciens ut honestissime possem exsurgere.

**25** Possumne igitur satis videri cautus, satis providus, si me huic itineri    5
tam infesto tamque periculoso commisero? gloriam in morte debent
ei qui in re publica versantur, non culpae reprehensionem et stultitiae
vituperationem relinquere. quis bonus non luget mortem Treboni? quis
non dolet interitum talis et civis et viri? at sunt qui dicant, dure illi
quidem, sed tamen dicunt, minus dolendum quod ab homine impuro    10
nefarioque non caverit. etenim qui multorum custodem se profiteatur,
eum sapientes sui primum capitis aiunt custodem esse oportere. cum
saeptus sis legibus et iudiciorum metu, non sunt omnia timenda neque ad
omnis insidias praesidia quaerenda. quis enim audeat luci, quis in militari
via, quis bene comitatum, quis illustrem aggredi? **26** haec neque hoc    15
tempore neque in me valent. non modo enim poenam non extimescet qui
mihi vim attulerit sed etiam gloriam sperabit a latronum gregibus et
praemia. haec ego in urbe provideo: facilis est circumspectus unde exeam,
quo progrediar, quid ad dexteram, quid ad sinistram sit. num idem in
Appennini tramitibus facere potero? in quibus etiam si non erunt in-    20
sidiae, quae facillime esse poterunt, animus tamen erit sollicitus, ut nihil
possit de officiis legationis attendere. sed effugi insidias, perrupi Ap-
penninum: nempe in Antoni congressum colloquiumque veniendum est.
quinam locus capietur? si extra castra, ceteri viderint: ego me vix tuto
futurum puto. novi hominis furorem, novi effrenatam violentiam. cuius    25
acerbitas morum immanitasque naturae ne vino quidem permixta tem-
perari solet, hic ira dementiaque inflammatus adhibito fratre Lucio,
taeterrima belua, numquam profecto a me sacrilegas manus atque impias
abstinebit.

**27** Memini colloquia et cum acerrimis hostibus et cum gravissime    30
dissidentibus civibus. Cn. Pompeius Sex. f. consul me praesente, cum
essem tiro in eius exercitu, cum P. Vettio Scatone, duce Marsorum, inter
bina castra collocutus est: quo quidem memini Sex. Pompeium, fratrem
consulis, ad colloquium ipsum Roma venire, doctum virum atque sa-

---

2–3 numquam . . . sum[3] *addidi*    3 circumcisses *t*: -msaeptus *Faërnus*: -mclusus *coni.*
*Halm*    collectis *Busche*: le- *D*    **25** 9 at sunt *n*[2]: ads- *vel* ass- *D*    14 luci] duce *s*[1]:
luce *n*[2]: *om. t*    **26** 16 extimescet *Naugerius*: -cit *D*    18 prouideo ς: -ero *b*: praeuideo
*nstv*    24 me vix tuto (*sc.* extra castra) *C. F. W. Müller*: mortem acutum *b*: m- actutum
(actuum *n*[1]) *svn*: me ui ac toto *t*: me vix tutum *Halm*: me vix in tuto *Hauschild*    **27** 31
dissentientibus *bnv*    33 quo] quod *ns*    tempore *post* quidem *add. Ernesti,* die *add.*
*Clark, alteruter fort. recte*

to this time preserved me for its service. I shall say this with hesitation, for I know that anything can happen to mortal man, but anyhow: I was never taken unawares, though on one occasion,[13] surrounded by the massed strength of some very powerful people, I fell, deliberately, to rise again in triumph.

25 Can I then appear reasonably cautious and prudent if I trust myself to this journey so fraught with menace and peril? Those who take part in public affairs should leave a legacy of glory when they die, not of censure for shortcoming and blame for folly. What honest man does not mourn the death of Trebonius? Who does not grieve for the destruction of such a man and such a citizen? And yet there are those who say (harshly, indeed, but they say it) that our grief should be diminished by the fact that he was not on his guard against a villainous traitor. Wise men say that a man who sets himself up as the guardian of many should first of all guard his own life. When one is protected by laws and the fear of the courts, there is no need to be afraid of everything or to seek defenses against all manner of plots. Who would dare to attack a well-known public figure traveling well-attended by daylight on a military highway? 26 Such considerations do not apply at this time or in my case. Anyone who employs violence against me will have no fear of punishment; on the contrary he will hope for glory and reward from the robber bands. In Rome I take precautions. It is easy to look around, to the rear and to the front, right and left. Shall I be able to do the same on the Apennine paths? Even if there is no ambush, which there very easily may be, my mind will be distracted and unable to attend to the duties of the mission. But imagine I have escaped an attack, forced my way through the Apennines: I must then presumably meet and talk with Antonius. What venue will be chosen? If outside the camps, let others look after themselves: *I* scarcely think I shall be safe. I know the man's fury, I know his unbridled violence. His savage ways and natural cruelty are seldom tempered even when mingled with wine. Ablaze with wrath and madness, with that horrible beast his brother Lucius at his elbow, he will surely never keep his impious, sacrilegious[14] hands off my person.

27 I remember parleys both with Rome's bitterest enemies and with fellow countrymen at daggers drawn. Consul Gnaeus Pompeius, son of Sextus, conferred with Publius Vettius Scato, the Marsian leader, between their two camps in my presence, when I was a recruit in the former's army.[15] I remember that Sextus Pompeius, the consul's brother, a man of learning and good sense,

13. His exile.
14. Sacrilegious, not because Cicero was an augur, but because he would be the Senate's ambassador.
15. In 89.

pientem. quem cum Scato salutasset, "quem te appellem?" inquit. at ille
"voluntate hospitem, necessitate hostem." erat in illo colloquio aequitas;
nullus timor, nulla suberat suspicio, mediocre etiam odium. non enim ut
eriperent nobis socii civitatem, sed ut in eam reciperentur petebant. Sulla
cum Scipione inter Cales et Teanum, cum alter nobilitatis florem, alter   5
belli socios adhibuisset, de auctoritate senatus, de suffragiis populi,
de iure civitatis leges inter se ⟨et⟩ condiciones contulerunt. non tenuit
omnino colloquium illud fidem: a vi tamen periculoque afuit. possu-
musne igitur in Antoni latrocinio aeque esse tuti? non possumus; aut, si
ceteri possunt, me posse diffido.   10

**28** Quod si non extra castra congrediemur, quae ad colloquium castra
sumentur? in nostra ille numquam veniet; multo minus nos in illius.
reliquum est ut et accipiantur et remittantur postulata per litteras. ergo
erimus in castris, meaque ad omnia postulata una sententia; quam cum
hic vobis audientibus dixero, isse [et] redisse me putatote: legationem   15
confecero. omnia ad senatum mea sententia reiciam, quaecumque postu-
labit Antonius. neque enim licet aliter neque permissum est nobis ab hoc
ordine, ut bellis confectis decem legatis permitti solet more maiorum,
neque ulla omnino a senatu mandata accepimus. quae cum agam in
consilio non ⟨n⟩ullis, ut arbitror, repugnantibus, nonne metuendum est ne   20
imperita militum multitudo per me pacem distineri putet? **29** facite hoc
meum consilium legiones novas non improbare; nam Martiam et quartam
nihil cogitantis praeter dignitatem et decus comprobaturas esse certo scio.
quid veteranos? non veremur—nam timeri se ne ipsi quidem volunt—
quonam modo accipiant severitatem meam? multa enim falsa de me   25
audierunt, multa ad eos improbi detulerunt; quorum commoda, ut vos
optimi testes estis, semper ego sententia, auctoritate, oratione firmavi:
sed credunt improbis, credunt turbulentis, credunt suis. sunt autem fortes
illi quidem, sed propter memoriam rerum quas gesserunt pro populi
Romani libertate et salute rei publicae nimis feroces et ad suam vim   30
omnia nostra consilia revocantes. **30** horum ego cogitationem non vereor;
impetum pertimesco.

Haec quoque tanta pericula si effugero, satisne tutum reditum putatis
fore? cum enim et vestram auctoritatem meo more defendero et meam

4 petebat *t*    7 et de iure *bns*    leges *Ferrarius*: legis *D*    et *add. Garatoni*    9 tuti
*b*: uti *t*: ut hi *v*: sic *ns*[1]: si hic *s*[2]    **28** 14 mea quidem *Halm*    15 isse redisse me *Clark*
(*v. Fe.*): i- et redi- me *bnsv*: i- me et redi- *t*    16 confecero] -fero *nstv*    20 non nullis
*Poggius*: nu- *btv*: non u- *ns*: multis *Pluygers*    **29** 23 cogitantis *Madvig*: -tatis *t*: -tetis
*bnsv*    certo *Orelli* (*cf. quae scripsi ad Fam. 5.2.7*): -te *D*    25 sed quonam modo acci-
pient (-piam *v*) *bnsv*    26 improbi detulerunt *Poggius*: improuide tu- *D*    **30** 34 meo
more ς: more meo *b*: meo (et meo *nsv*) me more *nstv*

came down from Rome to take part. Scato greeted him, saying, "What am I to call you?" The other replied: "Friend by inclination, enemy by necessity." There was fair play at that parley; no covert fear, no suspicion. Even the hostility was not extreme. Our allies, after all, were not seeking to take our citizenship away from us but to be admitted to a part in it. Sulla and Scipio met between Cales and Teanum,[16] one with the flower of the nobility at his side, the other with his wartime allies, to discuss terms and conditions relating to the authority of the Senate, the votes of the people, and the right of citizenship. Faith was not kept at that conference, it is true,[17] but there was no violence or danger. Can we be equally safe amidst Antonius' brigand band? We cannot; or if others can, I do not believe I can.

**28** But if we do not meet outside the camps, which camp will be chosen for the parley? He will never come to ours; much less we to his. There remains the possibility of receiving and returning demands by letter. Well then, we shall be in camp, and I shall have only one opinion in reply to all demands. When I tell you who are listening to me here what it is, you may suppose that I have gone and come back: I shall have discharged the mission. I shall be for referring all Antonius' demands to the Senate, whatever their nature. That is the only permissible course. We have not received discretion from this House such as is given by traditional custom to delegations of ten after the conclusion of a war, nor have we received any mandates whatsoever from the Senate. When I take this line in council, probably against some opposition, is there not a danger that the mass of uninstructed soldiery may think I am obstructing a peace? **29** Suppose the new legions do not disapprove of this advice of mine—for I am sure that the Martian and Fourth, who have no thought but of honor and glory, will approve of it—what of the veterans? Have we no apprehensions (they themselves do not wish to be *feared*) as to how they will take my hard line? They have heard many untruths about me. Rascals have told them many tales, though as you are best able to witness, I have always voted and advised and spoken in support of their benefits. But they believe the rascals and troublemakers, they believe their own. They are brave men, but the memory of what they have done for the freedom of the Roman People and the survival of the Commonwealth makes them overbearing and inclined to regard their force as arbiter in all our decisions. **30** I am not afraid of their considered views, but I dread their impetuosity.

If I escape these grave dangers also, do you think my return will be sufficiently safe? When I have defended your authority in my usual way and kept

16. In 83.

17. Sulla took advantage of the truce to win over Scipio's army. Scipio himself was taken prisoner, but his life was spared. I take *omnino* concessively; otherwise: "faith was not altogether kept. . . ."

fidem rei publicae constantiamque praestitero, tum erunt mihi non ei
solum qui me oderunt sed illi etiam qui invident extimescendi.

Custodiatur igitur vita mea rei publicae eaque, quoad vel dignitas vel
natura patietur, patriae reservetur; mors aut[em] necessitatem habeat fati
aut, si ante oppetenda est, oppetatur cum gloria.                              5

Haec cum ita sint, etsi hanc legationem res publica, ut levissime
dicam, non desiderat, tamen si tuto licebit ire, proficiscar. omnino, patres
conscripti, totum huiusce rei consilium non periculo meo, sed utilitate rei
publicae metiar. de qua mihi quoniam liberum est spatium, multum etiam
atque etiam considerandum puto idque potissimum faciendum quod        10
maxime interesse rei publicae iudicaro.

3 mea rei publicae eaque] r. p. eaque *b*: r. p. mea *t*: mea rei p- causa eaque *Fritsch*: mea,
patres conscripti, (p- c-., mea *iam Halm*) eaque (atque *Halm*) *Sternkopf*        4 aut *Faërnus*:
autem *D*        8 meo periculo *t*

my faith resolutely with the Commonwealth, I shall have to fear not only those who hate me but those who are jealous of me.

Therefore let my life be safeguarded for the Commonwealth and reserved for my country, so long as honor and nature allow. Let my death come by natural necessity,[18] or, if I must meet it sooner, let me meet it gloriously.

In these circumstances, although the Commonwealth, to say the least, does not need this embassy, nevertheless I shall go if I can safely do so. In general, Members of the Senate, in this whole question I shall make advantage to the Commonwealth my criterion, not personal risk. Since I have plenty of time, I conceive that I must give much further consideration to the matter and do whatever I shall judge to be in the best interest of the Commonwealth.

18. Lit. "by necessity of fate"; cf. Philippic 1 n. 18.

# XIII

## INTRODUCTION

On 20 March 43 the city praetor, M. Cornutus, convened the Senate to consider letters received from the two governors of Transalpine Gaul, Lepidus and Plancus, advocating peace. A motion proposed by Servilius, apparently politely rejecting their interference, was supported by Cicero. His speech makes no mention of Plancus' letter, of which we know only from Cicero's contemporary letter to the writer (*Fam.* 10.6.1; see my note ad loc.). The most plausible explanation is that references were removed by Cicero before the speech was published.

As we have it, the Thirteenth Philippic is in two parts: a reiteration of the unthinkability of compromise, mainly directed to Lepidus, whose intentions Cicero rightly mistrusted (13.1–21), and a sentence-by-sentence commentary on a letter recently addressed by Antony to Hirtius and Octavian—no doubt an open letter.

**1** A principio huius belli, patres conscripti, quod cum impiis civibus
consceleratisque suscepimus, timui ne condicio insidiosa pacis libertatis
recuperandae studia restingueret. dulce enim etiam nomen est pacis, res
vero ipsa cum iucunda tum salutaris. nam nec privatos focos nec publicas
leges videtur nec libertatis iura cara habere quem discordiae, quem　　5
caedes civium, quem bellum civile delectat, eumque ex numero hominum eiciendum, ex finibus humanae naturae exterminandum puto. itaque
sive Sulla sive Marius sive uterque sive Octavius sive Cinna sive iterum
Sulla sive alter Marius et Carbo sive qui alius civile bellum optavit, eum
detestabilem civem rei publicae natum iudico. **2** nam quid ego de proximo　　10
dicam cuius acta defendimus, a[u]ctorem ipsum iure caesum fatemur?
nihil igitur hoc cive, nihil hoc homine taetrius, si aut civis aut homo
habendus est, qui civile bellum concupiscit.

Sed hoc primum videndum est, patres conscripti, cum omnibusne pax
esse possit an sit aliquod bellum inexpiabile, in quo pactio pacis lex　　15
sit servitutis. pacem cum Scipione Sulla sive faciebat sive simulabat, non
erat desperandum, si convenisset, fore aliquem tolerabilem statum civitatis. Cinna si concordiam cum Octavio confirmare voluisset, ⟨aliqua⟩
[hominum] in re publica sanitas remanere potuisset. proximo bello si
aliquid de summa gravitate Pompeius, multum de cupiditate Caesar re-　　20
misisset, et pacem stabilem et aliquam rem publicam nobis habere
licuisset.

Hoc vero quid est? cum Antoniis pax potest esse? cum Censorino,
Ventidio, Trebellio, Bestia, Nucula, Munatio, Lentone, Saxa? exempli
causa paucos nominavi: genus infinitum immanitatemque ipsi cernitis　　25
reliquorum. **3** addite illa naufragia Caesaris amicorum, Barbas Cassios,
Barbatios Polliones; addite Antoni collusores et sodalis, Eutrapelum,
Melam, Pontium, Caelium, Crassicium, Tironem, Mustelam, Petusium:
comitatum relinquo, duces nomino. huc accedunt Alaudae ceterique

**1** 4 cum] tum *V*: tamen *b*　　9 quis *DV²*　　**2** 11 actorem ς: auc- *V*: cum auc- *bns*:
cum auctoritatem *tv*　　15 expiabile *D*　　16 sive simulabat *om. D*　　18 aliqua³ *ad-*
*didi*　　19 hominum . . . potuisset *om. V¹*　　hominum] omnino *Faërnus*　　20 di-
misisset *D*　　26 reliquorum (*i.e.* relicuorum)] belli quorum *D*　　**3** 27 Barbatios, Polliones *edd., corr. Syme* (*v. Two Studies, 18*)　　27–28 *fort.* Eutrapelum, Lenticulam (*v.*
*ibid., 47*)　　28 Pontium *om. V*　　coelium³ *V*　　petusium (*cf.* 12.19)] pestutum *t*: pedi-
tum *bnsv*　　29 relinquo nomino duces *b*: reliquo nomine (-no *v²*) d- *v*: reliquos omitto d- *nst*

1 From the outset of this war, Members of the Senate, which we have undertaken against traitors and criminals, I have been afraid that an insidious proposal of peace might quell enthusiasm for the recovery of freedom. Even the name of peace is sweet, the reality beneficial as well as agreeable. A man who delights in strife and the slaughter of his countrymen and civil war surely loves neither private hearth nor public law nor the rights of liberty.[1] Such a man I would exclude from membership in the human race, banish beyond the confines of human nature. Whoever desired civil war, be it Sulla or Marius or both, be it Octavius or Cinna, be it Sulla again or the other Marius and Carbo,[2] or anyone else, I hold him a citizen born to the Commonwealth accursed 2 I need not speak of the latest example,[3] whose acts we defend while admitting that their author was justly put to death. There is no fouler thing than that citizen, that man, if he is to be deemed a citizen or a man, who desires a civil war.

But one point has to be considered at the outset, Members of the Senate: is peace with all men possible, or is there such a thing as an inexpiable war, in which a pact of peace is a prescription for slavery? When Sulla tried, or pretended to try, to make peace with Scipio,[4] it was not unreasonable to hope that if they came to terms a tolerable state of the community would emerge. If Cinna had chosen to come to an agreement with Octavius,[5] the Commonwealth might have retained some degree of health. In the last war, if Pompeius had been a little less stiffly steadfast and Caesar a great deal less greedy, we could have had a stable peace and some sort of Commonwealth.

But what of the present? Can there be peace with the Antonii? Or with Censorinus, Ventidius, Trebellius, Bestia, Nucula, Munatius, Lento, Saxa? I have named a few as examples; you see for yourself the endless number and the savagery of the rest. 3 Add the flotsam of Caesar's friends, a Barba Cassius, a Barbatius Pollio.[6] Add Antonius' gambling partners and cronies, Eutrapelus, Mela,[7] Pontius, Coelius, Crassicius, Tiro, Mustela, Petusius: I name only the captains; the rank and file I leave. After these come the Larks and the rest of the veterans, the seedbed of jurymen of the third panel, who,

---

1. Cicero seems to be recalling Nestor's words in the *Iliad* (9.63–64): "a clanless, lawless, hearthless man is he that loveth strife among his own folk."

2. Cf. 8.7, 14.23.

3. Caesar.

4. Cf. 12.27.

5. Not simply "if Cinna had been willing to establish harmony with Octavius," but apparently a reference to actual negotiations mentioned in Appian (*B.C.* 1.69–70).

6. See R. Syme, *Historia* 4 (1955) 57 ( = *Roman Papers* [Oxford, 1979] 276–77.)

7. Nobody of this name is mentioned elsewhere among Antony's following. Perhaps read *Eutrapelum* ⟨*Lenticu*⟩*lam*, as proposed in *Two Studies*, 47.

veterani, seminarium iudicum decuriae tertiae, qui suis rebus exhaustis, beneficiis Caesaris devoratis, fortunas nostras concupiverunt.

**4** O fidam dexteram Antoni qua ille plurimos civis trucidavit, o ratum religiosumque foedus quod cum Antoniis fecerimus! hoc si Marcus violare conabitur, Luci eum sanctitas a scelere revocabit. illis locus si in hac urbe 5 fuerit, ipsi urbi locus non erit. ora vobis eorum ponite ante oculos et maxime Antoniorum, incessum, aspectum, vultum, spiritum, latera tegentis alios, alios praegredientis amicos. quem vini anhelitum, quas contumelias fore censetis minasque verborum! nisi forte eos pax ipsa leniet maximeque, cum in hunc ordinem venerint, salutabunt benigne, 10 comiter appellabunt unum quemque nostrum. **5** non recordamini, per deos immortalis, quas in eos sententias dixeritis? acta M. Antoni rescidistis; leges refixistis; per vim et contra auspicia latas decrevistis; totius Italiae dilectus excitavistis; collegam et scelerum socium omnium hostem iudicavistis. cum hoc quae pax potest esse? hostis si esset externus, 15 id ipsum vix talibus factis, sed posset aliquo modo. maria, montes, regionum magnitudines interessent; odisses eum quem non videres. hi in oculis haerebunt et, cum licebit, in faucibus; quibus enim saeptis tam immanis beluas continebimus?

At incertus exitus belli. est omnino fortium virorum, quales vos esse 20 debetis, virtutem praestare—tantum enim possunt—fortunae culpam non extimescere. **6** sed quoniam ab hoc ordine non fortitudo solum verum etiam sapientia postulatur—quamquam vix videntur haec posse seiungi, seiungamus tamen—fortitudo dimicare iubet, iustum odium incendit, ad confligendum impellit, vocat ad periculum: quid sapientia? cautioribus 25 utitur consiliis, in posterum providet, est omni ratione tectior. quid igitur censet? parendum est enim atque id optimum iudicandum quod sit sapientissime constitutum. si hoc praecipit ne quid vita existimem antiquius, ne decernam capitis periculo, fugiam omne discrimen, quaeram ex ea: "etiamne, si erit, cum id fecero, serviendum?" si adnuerit, ne ego 30 sapientiam istam, quamvis sit erudita, non audiam. sin responderit: "tu vero ita vitam corpusque servato, ita fortunas, ita rem familiarem, ut haec libertate posteriora ducas itaque his uti velis, si libera re publica

---

**4** 4 cum antoniis] cum antonianis *t*: cum his *v*: cum *ns*  m. antonius *nv*: ant- *st*  6 urbi ipsi *D*  uobis ponite eorum (e- u- p- *v*) ante oculos (p.c. *post* eorum *ns, post* oculos *v*) *bnsv*: eorum p.c. ponite uobis ante oculos *t*  5 11–12 per deos . . . eos *om.* *V*[1]: quas in eos *V*[2]  12 M. *om. D*  14 dilectum excitastis *D*  socium scelerum *btv*: sc- *ns*  15 iudicastis *D*  si esset externus hostis *D*  16 tamen id *D*  21 uirtute *D*  **6** 26 rectior *b*: prote- *nsvV*[2]  27 censes *V*  sit] est *coni. Halm*  00 ne] non *D*  30 si erit] fue- *nstv*  31 erudita non] eruditam *tv*: -ta *bns*  32 servato *om. V, unde* tu vero tuere *coni. Halm*, tuere (*pro* tu vero) *Madvig*  33 posteriora libertate *D*

after running through their own property and devouring Caesar's bounties, have cast covetous eyes on our possessions.

**4** Trusty indeed is Antonius' right hand, the hand which has slaughtered so many of our countrymen! Binding and sacred will be the treaty we make with the Antonii! Should Marcus try to break it, the virtuous Lucius will call him back from such a crime. If there is to be a place for these people in Rome, there will be no place for Rome. Picture to yourselves their faces, above all those of the Antonii, their gait, appearance, expression, air of consequence; and their friends, some walking by their side, others in front. Imagine the reek of wine, the abusive, threatening language. Or will the very fact of peace mollify them? In particular, when they come into this House, will they have a friendly greeting, a pleasant word for each of us? **5** Don't you remember, in Heaven's name, the votes you cast against them? You rescinded Marcus Antonius' acts, tore down his laws, decreed that they were passed by violence and contrary to auspices, you raised levies all over Italy, you declared his colleague, the partner in all his crimes, a public enemy. What peace can there be with him? If he were a foreign enemy, it would indeed be difficult after such doings, but it would be possible somehow or other. There would be seas, mountains, wide tracts of country to separate us. One would hate him without seeing him. But these fellows will be right before our eyes and, when they get the chance, at our throats. For how shall we find cages for such monstrous beasts?

We are told that the issue of the war is uncertain. It is for brave men, such as you should be, to do their best (they can do no more) and not to fear what is Fortune's fault. **6** But since not only courage but wisdom too is demanded from this House (the two seem hardly separable, but let us separate them all the same), well, courage commands us to fight, kindles just hatred in our hearts, urges us to conflict, summons us to danger. And what does wisdom do? Her counsels are more cautious, she looks ahead, she is altogether more guarded. What, then, is her advice? For it must be obeyed; the wisest decision is to be judged the best. If she tells me to deem nothing more important than life, not to risk my skin in battle, shun all danger, I shall ask her a question: "Even if, having done all this, I am to be a slave?" If she nods assent, then I for one shall refuse to listen to that wisdom, whatever her learning. But perhaps she may reply: "No. Preserve your life and body, your fortunes and property, but only as valuing them less than freedom and as desiring to enjoy them only

possis, nec pro his libertatem, sed pro libertate haec proicias tamquam
pignora inuriae ⟨oblata⟩," tum sapientiae vocem audire videar eique uti
deo paream. **7** itaque si receptis illis esse possumus liberi, vincamus
odium pacemque patiamur; sin otium incolumibus eis esse nullum potest,
laetemur decertandi oblatam esse fortunam. aut enim interfectis illis    5
fruemur victrice re publica aut oppressi—quod omen avertat Iuppiter!—
si non spiritu, at virtutis laude vivemus.

    At enim nos M. Lepidus, imperator iterum, pontifex maximus, optime
proximo civili bello de re publica meritus, ad pacem adhortatur. nullius
apud me, patres conscripti, auctoritas maior est quam M. Lepidi vel    10
propter ipsius virtutem vel propter familiae dignitatem. accedunt eodem
multa privata magna eius in me merita, mea quaedam officia in illum.
maximum vero eius beneficium numero quod hoc animo in rem publicam est, quae mihi vita mea semper fuit carior. **8** nam cum Magnum
Pompeium, clarissimum adulescentem, praestantissimi viri filium, aucto-    15
ritate adduxit ad pacem remque publicam sine armis maximo civilis belli
periculo liberavit, tum me eius beneficio plus quam pro virili parte
obligatum putavi. itaque et honores ei decrevi quos potui amplissimos, in
quibus mihi vos estis adsensi, nec umquam de illo et sperare optime et
loqui destiti. magnis et multis pignoribus M. Lepidum res publica illi-    20
gatum tenet. summa nobilitas est, omnes honores, amplissimum sa-
cerdotium, plurima urbis ornamenta, ipsius, fratris maiorumque monumenta; probatissima uxor, optatissimi liberi, res familiaris cum ampla
tum casta a cruore civili. nemo ab eo civis violatus, multi eius beneficio
et misericordia liberati. talis igitur vir et civis opinione labi potest,    25
voluntate a re publica dissidere nullo pacto potest.

    **9** Pacem vult M. Lepidus. praeclare, si talem potest efficere qualem
nuper effecit, qua pace Cn. Pompei filium res publica aspiciet suoque
sinu complexuque recipiet, neque solum illum, sed cum illo se ipsam sibi

---

2 oblata¹ *addidi* (*an* obiecta?)      ut *D*     **7** 3 possumus esse *D*     4 sin otium] sin ius
*nsv*: si uis *bt*     5 interfectis illis *del. Faërnus*     **8** M. Lepidus *om. Vbntv*     imperator
*om. s*     12 ac magna *Schöll, fort. recte*     ac mea *DV*²     officia *om. D*     **8** 16
pacem] urbem *D*     sine *om. V*     18 putavi *coni. Halm*: putet *V*¹: puto *DV*²     ei et
honores *D*     in *om. V*     20 obligatum *D*     21 honores *V Cus.*: -r ei *t*: -r est *s*: -r ei
(eius *n*) est *bnv*     24 eius *om. D*     **9** 27 M. *om. Vbv*     28 efficit *Vt*

326

if you can do so in a free Commonwealth. Do not sacrifice liberty to these things but them to liberty, regarding them as hostages exposed to ill-usage." Then I should think I heard the voice of wisdom and obey as I should obey a God. 7 Therefore, if we can take those people back and still be free, let us conquer our hatred and suffer peace. If, on the other hand, there can be no quiet in the community if they are part of it, let us rejoice that we are given the opportunity to fight it out. Either they will be killed and we shall enjoy the victorious Commonwealth or, if overwhelmed (may Jupiter avert the omen!), we shall live, if not with breath, yet with the glory of valor.

But I shall be told that Marcus Lepidus, Imperator for the second time, Pontifex Maximus, who has deserved excellently of the Commonwealth in the most recent civil war,[8] urges us to peace. No man's authority, Members of the Senate, stands higher with me than that of Marcus Lepidus by reason of his own worth and the dignity of his family. Added to these considerations are his great private services to me and certain good offices of mine to him. But I count it as his greatest benefaction that he feels as he does toward the Commonwealth, which has ever been more dear to me than my own life. 8 For when the weight of his prestige induced young Magnus Pompeius, the illustrious son of so eminent a father, to accept peace and so delivered the Commonwealth without a sword drawn from a very grave threat of civil war, I conceived myself under more than my individual share of obligation[9] for the benefit. Accordingly I proposed for him the most ample honors I could, in respect to which you gave me your assent; nor have I ever ceased both to hope and to speak of him in the highest terms. The Commonwealth holds Marcus Lepidus bound by many great pledges. His birth is of the highest, he has passed through the gamut of offices, he holds a most distinguished priesthood, and many adornments[10] of our city commemorate him, and his brother,[11] and their ancestors; his wife is greatly respected, his children are all that could be desired, his wealth is ample and untainted by civil bloodshed. No fellow countryman has been harmed by him, many have been rescued by his kindness and compassion. Such a man and such a citizen can make an error of judgment, but in his sympathies he cannot by any manner of means be at variance with the Commonwealth.

9 Marcus Lepidus wants peace. Admirable, if he can make such a peace as he made recently, whereby the Commonwealth will see and take into her arms the son of Gnaeus Pompeius, and not him alone: she will deem that along with

---

8. Cf. 5.39–41.
9. Perhaps alluding to the personal ties between Cicero and the elder Pompey.
10. Such as the Basilica Aemilia.
11. L. Aemilius Paullus, consul in 50.

restitutam putabit. haec causa fuit cur decerneretis statuam in rostris cum inscriptione praeclara, cur absenti triumphum. quamquam enim magnas res bellicas gesserat et triumpho dignas, non erat tamen ei tribuendum quod nec L. Aemilio nec Aemiliano Scipioni nec superiori Africano nec Mario nec Pompeio, qui maiora bella gesserunt; sed quod sine ⟨caede 5 atque fe⟩rro bellum civile confecerat, cum primum licuit, honores in eum maximos contulistis. **10** existimasne igitur, M. Lepide, qualem Pompeium res publica habitura sit civem, talis futuros in re publica Antonios? in altero pudor, gravitas, moderatio, integritas; in illis—et cum hos compello, praetereo animo ex grege latrocini neminem—libidines, scelera, ad omne 10 facinus immanis audacia.

Deinde vos obsecro, patres conscripti, quis hoc vestrum non videt quod Fortuna ipsa quae dicitur caeca vidit? salvis enim actis Caesaris, quae concordiae causa defendimus, Pompeio sua domus patebit, eamque non minoris quam emit Antonius redimet; redimet, inquam, Cn. Pompei 15 domum filius. o rem acerbam! sed haec satis diu multumque defleta sunt. decrevistis tantam pecuniam Pompeio quantam ex bonis patriis in praedae dissipatione inimicus victor redegisset. **11** sed hanc mihi dispensationem pro paterna necessitudine et coniunctione deposco: redimet hortos, aedis, urbana quaedam quae possidet Antonius. nam argentum, vestem, su- 20 pellectilem, vinum amittet aequo animo, quae ille helluo dissipavit. Albanum, Formianum a Dolabella recuperabit; etiam ab Antonio Tuscu-lanum; eique qui nunc Mutinam oppugnant, D. Brutum obsident, de Falerno Anseres depellentur. sunt alii plures fortasse, sed ⟨e⟩ mea memoria dilabuntur. ego etiam eos dico qui hostium numero non sunt Pompeianas 25 possessiones quanti emerint filio reddituros. **12** satis inconsiderati fuit, ne dicam audacis, rem ullam ex illis attingere; retinere vero quis poterit clarissimo domino restituto? an is non reddet qui domini patrimonium circumplexus quasi thesaurum draco, Pompei servus, libertus Caesaris,

---

1 putauit *nstvb²V²*    cur ei *Lambinus*    3 tamen *om. V*    ei *anne* eo?    5–6 sine caede atque ferro *scripsi*³: silentio *codd.*: sapientia *Pluygers*: sedendo *Sydow*    6 cum *om. D*    **10** 8 in re p(ublica) *om. D*    12 obsecro uos *D*    uidet *D*    16 *post* acer-bam *iterum deficit V* (*v. ad* 11.17)    **11** 18 sed *del. Manutius*    22 firmianum *bv*: -manum *n*: -minum *s*    23–24 ex agro Falerno *Serv. ad Ecl. 9.36*    24 depellantur *n¹st, Serv.*    sed e mea *coni. Clark*: sed mea *ns*: de mea *b*: mea *tv*: sed de mea *Naugerius*: sed ex mea *Wesenberg*    25 elabuntur *coni. Clark*    **12** 29 thesaurum *om. t*

him she has been restored to herself. This was the reason why you voted him a statue on the Rostra with a splendid inscription and a Triumph in absentia. He had indeed achieved important military successes worthy of a Triumph, but that did not warrant our granting to him what was not granted to Lucius Aemilius[12] or to Aemilianus Scipio or to the elder Africanus or to Marius or to Pompeius, who conducted greater wars. But because he had brought a civil war to a bloodless conclusion, you conferred the greatest honors upon him at the first opportunity. **10** Well, Marcus Lepidus, do you expect the Antonii to make citizens in the Commonwealth such as the Commonwealth will have in Pompcius? In him is modesty, responsibility, moderation, integrity; in them— and when I name them, I mentally include every member of that robber gang—lusts, crimes, monstrous audacity stopping at nothing.

Next, I beg you, Members of the Senate: which of you does not see what Fortune herself has seen,[13] who is said to be blind? With no violation of Caesar's acts, which we defend for concord's sake, Pompeius' house will be open to him, and he will repurchase it for not less than Antonius paid for it. I repeat, Gnaeus Pompeius' house will be repurchased by his son. A bitter thought! But enough tears, and for long enough, have been shed over these things. You voted Pompeius a sum of money equal to that which his victorious enemy[14] had realized from his father's property in the dispersal of the plunder. **11** But I claim for myself the management of this matter in virtue of my friendship and close association with his father. He will repurchase the suburban estates, the house, and certain urban properties now occupied by Antonius. As for the plate, fabrics, furniture, and wine which that wastrel squandered, he will take their loss philosophically. He will recover the villas at Alba and Formiae from Dolabella and the villa at Tusculum, again, from Antonius. The Ansers,[15] who are now attacking Mutina and blockading Decimus Brutus, will be ousted from the Falernian property. There are others beside, perhaps, but they escape my memory. I also declare that those who are not in the number of our enemies will restore Pompeius' possessions to his son at the price they paid for them. **12** It was inconsiderate enough, not to say audacious, to touch any one of those items; who will have the effrontery to hold on to such after the restoration of its illustrious owner? There is a former slave of Pompeius[16] and freedman of Caesar's who has taken possession of lands in Lucania, coiled round his master's property like a dragon: will he not give it

---

12. Paullus, victor of the Third Macedonian War (168) and father of Scipio Aemilianus.

13. See 13.12 fin.

14. Caesar.

15. Presumably brothers. One of them may have been the poet Anser mentioned by Ovid, *Trist.* 2.435; cf. Servius on Virg. *Ecl.* 9.36.

16. Name unknown.

agri Lucani possessiones occupavit? itaque illud bis miliens, quod adulescenti, patres conscripti, spopondistis, ita discribetur ut videatur a
vobis Cn. Pompei filius in patrimonio suo collocatus.

Haec senatus: reliqua populus Romanus in ea familia quam vidit .
amplissimam persequetur, in primis paternum auguratus locum, in quem　5
ego eum, ut quod a patre accepi filio reddam, mea nominatione cooptabo.
utrum igitur augurem Iuppiter Optimus Maximus cuius interpretes in-
ternuntiique constituti sumus, utrum populus Romanus libentius sanciet,
Pompeiumne an Antonium? mihi quidem numine deorum immortalium
videtur hoc Fortuna voluisse, ut actis Caesaris firmis ac ratis Cn. Pompei　10
filius posset et dignitatem et fortunas patrias recuperare.

**13** Ac ne illud quidem silentio, patres conscripti, praetereundum puto
quod clarissimi viri legati, L. Paul⟨l⟩us, Q. Thermus, C. Fannius, quorum
habetis cognitam voluntatem in rem publicam eamque perpetuam atque
constantem, nuntiant se Pompei conveniendi causa devertisse Massiliam　15
eumque cognovisse paratissimo animo ut cum suis copiis iret ad Mutinam, ni vereretur ne veteranorum animos offenderet. est vero eius patris
filius qui sapienter faciebat non minus multa quam fortiter. itaque intellegitis et animum ei praesto fuisse nec consilium defuisse.

Atque etiam hoc M. Lepido providendum est, ne quid adrogantius　20
quam eius mores ferunt facere videatur. **14** si enim nos exercitu terret,
non meminit illum exercitum senatus populique Romani atque universae
rei publicae esse, non suum. at uti potest pro suo. quid tum? omniane
bonis viris quae facere possunt facienda sunt? etiamne si turpia, si perniciosa erunt, si facere omnino non licebit? quid autem turpius aut foedius　25
aut quod minus deceat quam contra senatum, contra civis, contra patriam exercitum ducere? quid vero magis vituperandum quam id facere
quod non liceat? licet autem nemini contra patriam ducere exercitum,
si quidem licere id dicimus quod legibus, quod more maiorum institu-
tisque conceditur. neque enim, quod quisque potest, id ei licet, nec, si　30
non obstatur, propterea etiam permittitur. tibi enim exercitum, Lepide,
tamquam maioribus tuis patria pro se dedit. hoc tu arcebis hostem, finis

1 itaque *scripsi*: atque *codd.*　　bis³ *nescio quis*: septiens *codd.*　　5 in quem *b²*: in que *t*:
in quo *nsv*: *om. b¹*　　7 i. o. m. *D*　　8 sumus nos *Madvig* (*mallem* nos sumus)　　9 an
*om. bns*　　**14** 23 uti] ubi *n¹stvb²*　　28 licet] -eat *n¹stv*　　32 tam quam *Halm*

back? Thus that two hundred million[17] which you have promised the young man, Members of the Senate, will be so disposed that Gnaeus Pompeius' son will be seen established in his patrimony by you.

So far the Senate. The Roman People will attend to the rest in the case of the most illustrious family it has ever seen:[18] first and foremost, his father's place in the College of Augurs, into which I shall co-opt him by my nomination, thus returning to the son what I received from the father.[19] So which of these two will Jupiter Best and Greatest, of whom we have been constituted interpreters and intermediaries, which of them will the Roman People more willingly ratify as augur, Pompeius or Antonius? For my part, I think it is by the will of the Immortal Gods that Fortune has chosen to allow the son of Gnaeus Pompeius to recover his father's dignity and possessions while Caesar's acts remain firmly established.

**13** There is another point, Members of the Senate, which I think should not be passed over in silence. Our illustrious envoys, Lucius Paullus, Quintus Thermus, and Gaius Fannius, whose unflagging, steadfast patriotism you know well, report that they stopped at Massilia[20] in order to meet Pompeius and found him perfectly ready to go to Mutina with his forces were he not afraid of offending the veterans. Truly he is the son of his father, whose acts of wisdom were no less numerous than his acts of valor. So you see that his courage was ready and his discretion did not fail him.

Moreover, Marcus Lepidus should guard against the appearance of behaving with an arrogance out of character. **14** If he seeks to intimidate us with his army, he forgets that that army belongs to the Senate and the People of Rome and the entire Commonwealth, not to him. Ah, but he can use it as though it did belong to him. What then? Are honest men to do all things that lie in their power, even things dishonorable and destructive, even things quite unpermissible? What can be more dishonorable and ugly and unseemly than to lead an army against the Senate and one's fellow countrymen and one's country? And what is more blameworthy than to do the impermissible? Now to no one is it permitted to lead an army against his country, if by "permitted" we mean what is allowed by laws and by the customs and institutions of our ancestors. It is not permissible for a man to do everything he is able to do; and if he is not opposed, it does not follow that he is allowed. To you, Lepidus, your country has given an army, just as she did to your ancestors, for her own benefit. With it you will ward off the enemy and extend the boundaries of empire. You will

17. See Textual Appendix.

18. Or "a family which it once saw in its greatness."

19. Cicero was nominated by Pompey and Hortensius in 53 or 52.

20. *Devertisse*, "turned aside," must imply that these envoys had another destination. Perhaps they were going to Lepidus.

imperi propagabis: senatui populoque Romano parebis, si quam ad aliam
rem te forte traduxerit.

**15** Haec si cogitas, es M. Lepidus, pontifex maximus, M. Lepidi, pontificis maximi, pronepos; sin hominibus tantum licere iudicas quantum
possunt, vide ne alienis exemplis eisque recentibus uti quam et antiquis et     5
domesticis malle videare. quod si auctoritatem interponis sine armis,
magis equidem laudo, sed vide ne hoc ipsum non sit necesse. quamquam
enim est tanta in te auctoritas quanta debet in homine nobilissimo, tamen
senatus se ipse non contemnit, nec vero fuit umquam gravior, constantior,
fortior. incensi omnes rapimur ad libertatem recuperandam. non potest     10
ullius auctoritate tantus senatus populique Romani ardor exstingui. odimus, irati pugnamus; extorqueri ⟨e⟩ manibus arma non possunt; receptui
signum aut revocationem a bello audire non possumus; speramus optima,
pati vel difficillima malumus quam servire. **16** Caesar confecit invictum
exercitum; duo fortissimi consules adsunt cum copiis; L. Planci, consulis     15
designati, varia et magna auxilia non desunt; in D. Bruti salute certatur;
unus furiosus gladiator cum taeterrimorum latronum manu contra patriam, contra deos penatis, contra aras et focos, contra quattuor consules
gerit bellum. huic cedamus, huius condiciones audiamus, cum hoc pacem fieri posse credamus?     20

At periculum est ne opprimamur. non metuo ne is qui suis amplissimis
fortunis nisi bonis salvis frui non potest prodat salutem suam. bonos civis
primum natura efficit, adiuvat deinde Fortuna. omnibus enim bonis expe-
dit salvam esse rem publicam, sed in eis qui fortunati sunt magis id
apparet. **17** quis fortunatior Lepido, ut ante dixi, quis eodem sanior? vidit     25
eius maestitiam atque lacrimas populus Romanus Lupercalibus; vidit
quam abiectus, quam confectus esset, cum Caesari diadema imponens
Antonius servum se illius quam collegam esse malebat. qui si reliquis
flagitiis et sceleribus abstinere potuisset, tamen unum ob hoc factum
dignum illum omni poena putarem. nam si ipse servire poterat, nobis     30
dominum cur imponebat? et si eius pueritia pertulerat libidines eorum qui

**15** 10 fortior *om. stv*     12 e *add. Halm*     **16** 14 confecit *Poggius*: -ficit *D*     22 bonis]
nobis *bnst*     **17** 25 vidit *om. t*     28–29 se *post* si *add. t, ante* abstinere *bsv*

obey the Senate and People of Rome if they happen to transfer you to some other duty.

**15** If you think on these lines, you are Marcus Lepidus, Pontifex Maximus, great-grandson of Marcus Lepidus, Pontifex Maximus. But if you judge that people are permitted to do anything they have the power to do, consider lest you seem to be preferring to follow alien and recent precedents rather than ancient and domestic ones.[21] If, however, you are bringing into play the respect in which you are held without any implication of armed force, the more credit to you, say I; but consider whether even this much is unnecessary. You enjoy all the respect that is due to your exalted birth; but the Senate does not undervalue itself, nor indeed was it ever more dignified, resolute, and courageous. Our fiery enthusiasm for the recovery of liberty sweeps us onward, nor can the passionate ardor of the Senate and People of Rome be quelled by respect for any man. We hate, we fight angry.[22] Our arms cannot be wrenched out of our hands. We cannot hear a signal for retreat, a recall from battle. We hope for the best, but would rather suffer any extremity than be slaves. **16** Caesar has raised an army which has never known defeat. Two very valiant consuls and the forces they command are with him. Large auxiliary forces of various kinds under Consul-Elect Lucius Plancus are not wanting. The struggle is for the life of Decimus Brutus. A single frantic gladiator with a band of horrible brigands makes war upon our country and her Household Gods, her altars and hearths, against four consuls.[23] Shall we yield to him? Shall we listen to his terms? Shall we believe it possible to make peace with him?

It may be urged that there is a danger of our being overwhelmed. I am not afraid that one who cannot enjoy his own ample fortunes if honest men go under may betray his own welfare. Nature makes good citizens in the first place; then Fortune aids. For while the well-being of the Commonwealth is to the advantage of all honest men, that is more obviously the case with the fortunate among them. **17** Nobody is more fortunate than Lepidus, as I have already said, and nobody is of sounder mind. The Roman People saw his distress, his tears, at the Lupercalia, saw how cast down, how crushed he was when Antonius tried to put the diadem on Caesar and preferred the status of Caesar's slave to that of Caesar's colleague. Even if Antonius had been able to hold back from his other infamies and crimes, I should count him deserving of every punishment because of this one act. If he found slavery bearable for himself, why foist a master on *us*? If in his boyhood days he endured the lusts

---

21. Cicero ignores the fact that Lepidus' father, consul in 78, died leading a rebellion against the government.

22. An adaptation of a line of Lucilius quoted in *Tusc.* 4.48, *odi hominem, iratus pugno* . . . .

23. The two consuls-elect, D. Brutus and Plancus, are included.

erant in eum tyranni, etiamne in nostros liberos dominum et tyrannum
compararet? itaque illo interfecto qualem in nos eum esse voluit, talis
ipse in ceteros exstitit.

**18** Qua enim ⟨in⟩ barbaria quisquam tam taeter, tam crudelis tyrannus
quam in hac urbe armis barbarorum stipatus Antonius? Caesare domi-   5
nante veniebamus in senatum, si non libere, at tamen tuto. hoc archi-
pirata—quid enim dicam tyranno?—haec subsellia ab Ituraeis occupa-
bantur. prorupit subito Brundisium ut inde agmine quadrato ad urbem
accederet; lautissimum oppidum nunc municip[i]um honestissimorum,
quondam colonorum, Suessam fortissimorum militum sanguine implevit;   10
Brundisi in sinu non modo avarissimae sed etiam crudelissimae uxoris
delectos Martiae legionis centuriones trucidavit. inde se quo furore, quo
ardore ad urbem, id est ad caedem optimi cuiusque rapiebat!

Quo tempore di ipsi immortales praesidium improvisum nec opinanti-
bus nobis obtulerunt. **19** Caesaris enim incredibilis ac divina virtus latronis   15
impetus crudelis ac furibundos retardavit: quem tum ille demens laedere
se putabat edictis, ignorans quaecumque falso diceret in sanctissimum
adulescentem, ea vere rec⟨c⟩idere in memoriam pueritiae suae. ingressus
urbem est quo comitatu vel potius agmine, cum dextra sinistra, gemente
populo Romano, minaretur dominis, notaret domos, divisurum se urbem   20
palam suis polliceretur! rediit ad milites; ibi pestifera illa Tiburi contio.
inde ad urbem cursus; senatus in Capitolium; parata de circumscribendo
adulescente sententia consularis, cum repente—nam Martiam legionem
Albae consedisse sciebat—adfertur ei de quarta nuntius. quo perculsus
abiecit consilium referendi ad senatum de Caesare: egressus est non viis,   25
sed tramitibus paludatus. eoque ipso die innumerabilia senatus consulta
fecit, quae quidem omnia ⟨paene⟩ citius delata quam scripta sunt. **20** ex
eo non iter, sed cursus et fuga in Galliam. Caesarem sequi arbitrabatur
cum legione Martia, cum quarta, cum veteranis, quorum ille nomen prae
metu ferre non poterat, eique in Galliam penetranti D. se Brutus obiecit,   30
qui se totius belli fluctibus circumiri quam illum aut regredi aut progredi
maluit Mutinamque illi exsultanti tamquam frenos furoris iniecit. quam
cum operibus munitionibusque saepsisset nec eum coloniae florentissimae dignitas neque consulis designati maiestas a parricidio deterreret,

2 compararet *scripsi*: -arabat *D*: -arare debebat *Pluygers*     **18** 4 in *ς*: *om. D*     9 municipum *Manutius*: -pium *D*     **19** 16 tum] tu *t*: tamen *b, fort. recte*     17 diceret] ind- *v*:
in eum d- *bt*: ed- *Pluygers*: intenderet *R. Klotz*     18 reccidere *scripsi* (*cf. ad* 4.10): re-
cidere *b*: -ret *v*: -rent *nst*     21 ibi] ubi *st*     Tibure *Muretus*     23 nam] iam *Faër-*
*nus*     26–27 eoque . . . scripta sunt *post* polliceretur (*l.* 21) *transp. Clark* (*v. Fe.*)     27
paene[3] *addidi*     deleta *bn*: perfecta perlata *s*     *fort.* perscripta     **20** 30 se D. *coni.*
*Clark, coll.* 4.16

of his tyrants, was he also to produce a master and tyrant for our children? And so, when Caesar was killed, he became to the rest of the community what he wanted Caesar to be to us.

**18** In what barbarous land was there ever so grim and cruel a tyrant as was Antonius in Rome, surrounded by armed barbarians? Under Caesar's despotism we used to come to the Senate in safety, if not in freedom. With this pirate chief ("tyrant" is too good for him) these benches were occupied by Ituraeans. Suddenly he burst forth to Brundisium intending to march from there on Rome in battle array. He made Suessa, a very thriving town, once of colonists, now of most respectable burghers, run with the blood of brave soldiers. At Brundisium, in the lap of his wife, a woman as cruel as she is greedy, he slaughtered picked centurions of the Martian Legion. From there in what a blaze of fury he hurried back to Rome, which is to say to the slaughter of the best of her citizens!

Then it was that the Immortal Gods themselves brought us a totally unforeseen protection. **19** Caesar's amazing, superhuman courage checked the brigand's ferocious, furious onslaught. Antonius in his delirium thought to damage him with manifestos, unaware that all his slanders of a young man of irreproachable character recoiled as truths upon the memory of his own early life. When he entered Rome, his entourage was more like a regiment on the march. To right and to left, while the Roman People groaned, he threatened householders, noted down houses, openly promised his men that he would parcel out the city among them. He returned to his troops. There at Tibur he made that pernicious speech. Back to Rome posthaste. Senate called to the Capitol. A consular motion to clip the young man's wings was in readiness, when suddenly (he already knew that the Martian Legion had stationed itself at Alba) he gets the news about the Fourth. Shocked thereat, he gave up his intention of putting the matter of Caesar before the Senate. He left Rome in general's uniform,[24] not using the highroads but bypaths. And that very day[25] he made countless senatorial decrees, all of which were deposited almost before they were put in writing. **20** Next, not a march, but a headlong flight to Gaul. He thought Caesar was in pursuit with the Martian Legion and the Fourth and the veterans, whose name made him shake in his boots. As he pushed into Gaul, Decimus Brutus blocked his path, voluntarily letting himself be surrounded by the billows of the whole war rather than let Antonius go forward or backward, and using Mutina to curb his fury like a bridle on a rampant horse. Antonius surrounded the town with works and fortifications; neither the dignity of a flourishing colony nor the majesty of a consul-elect deterred him from his

24. Wearing the *paludamentum*, the (usually) scarlet cloak worn by commanding generals.
25. 28 November. Antony left Rome before daybreak (3.24).

tum me—testor et vos et populum Romanum et omnis deos qui huic urbi praesident—invito et repugnante legati missi tres consulares ad latronum et gladiatorum ducem. **21** quis tam barbarus umquam, tam immanis, tam ferus? non audivit, non respondit; neque eos solum praesentis sed multo magis nos a quibus illi erant missi sprevit et pro nihilo putavit. postea 5 quod scelus, quod facinus parricida non edidit? circumsedet colonos nostros, exercitum populi Romani, imperatorem, consulem designatum; agros divexat civium optimorum; hostis taeterrimus omnibus bonis cruces ac tormenta minitatur. cum hoc, M. Lepide, pax esse quae potest? cuius ne supplicio quidem ullo satiari videtur posse res publica. 10

**22** Quod si quis adhuc dubitare potuit quin nulla societas huic ordini populoque Romano cum illa importunissima belua posset esse, desinet profecto dubitare his cognitis litteris quas mihi missas ab Hirtio consule modo accepi. eas dum recito dumque de singulis sententiis breviter disputo, velim, patres conscripti, ut adhuc fecistis, me attente audiatis. 15

"Antonius Hirtio et Caesari." neque se imperatorem neque Hirtium consulem nec pro praetore Caesarem. satis hoc quidem scite: deponere alienum nomen ipse maluit quam illis suum reddere.

"Cognita morte C. Treboni non plus gavisus sum quam dolui." videte quid se gavisum, quid doluisse dicat: facilius de pace deliberabitis. 20

"Dedisse poenas sceleratum cineri atque ossibus clarissimi viri et apparuisse numen deorum intra finem anni vertentis aut iam soluto supplicio parricidi aut impendente laetandum est." o Spartace! quem enim te potius appellem, cuius propter nefanda scelera tolerabilis videtur fuisse Catilina? laetandum esse ausus es scribere Trebonium dedisse poenas? 25 sceleratum Trebonium? quo scelere, nisi quod te Idibus Martiis a debita tibi peste seduxit? **23** age, hoc laetaris: videamus quid moleste feras.

"⟨A senatu⟩ iudicatum hostem populi Romani Dolabellam eo quod sicarium occiderit et videri cariorem populo Romano filium scurrae quam C. Caesarem, patriae parentem, ingemiscendum est." quid ingemiscis? 30 hostem Dolabellam? quid? te non intellegis dilectu tota Italia habito, consulibus missis, Caesare ornato, sagis denique sumptis hostem iudicatum? quid est autem, scelerate, quod gemas hostem Dolabellam iudicatum a

2–3 latronum et *Halm*: -nes m *bt*: -nes (-nem *n²*) m. antonii (-ium *n²*) *n¹sv*    **21** 10 r(es) p(ublica)] populus romanus *nv*    **22** 12 desinet³ *n²*: -inat *bv*: -ignat *n¹st*    17 pro praetore *Orelli*: pro p.r. *b*: p.r.p.r. *n¹st*: praetorem pr *v*: p.r. *n²*    scire *b*: scito *t*    23 parricidae *vn²*, *fort. recte*: -diae *n¹s*: -da *t*    24 uidetur fuisse *cod. Regius 15 A. XIV, prob. Clark numeri causa*: f- u- *D*    25 es] est *t*: om. *b*    **23** 28 a senatu (*i.e.* a s.) *add. C. F. W. Müller*    hostem p(opuli) R(omani) *idem*: hoc tempore *stv*: hoc t- hostem *bn*    29 p(opulo) R(omano) *Poggius*: r.p. *D*    31 qui te *bstv*

work of treason. At that point, against my will (I call you gentlemen and the Roman People and all the presiding deities of Rome to witness), against my opposition, three consular envoys were sent to this leader of bandits and gladiators. **21** Was there ever such a barbarian, such a monster, such a beast? He did not listen, he did not reply. He treated not only them in their presence, but much more us who sent them, with total contempt. Thereafter what crime and villainy has the traitor not perpetrated? He invests our colonists and a Roman army and its imperator, a consul-elect. He ravages the lands of loyal citizens. As a ferocious enemy, he threatens all honest men with crucifixion and torments. What peace can there be with him, Marcus Lepidus? Why, no punishment for him seems harsh enough to satisfy the Commonwealth.

**22** If anyone could still doubt the impossibility of any sort of fellowship between this House and the Roman People on the one hand and that savage monster on the other, I imagine his doubts will cease when he learns of the letter which has just come into my hands, sent by Consul Hirtius. While I read it aloud and briefly comment on it sentence by sentence, may I request you, Members of the Senate, to give me your close attention, as you have done so far?

"Antonius to Hirtius and Caesar." He does not call himself imperator nor Hirtius consul nor Caesar propraetor. Neat enough, that. Rather than give them their proper titles he chose to drop one which is not rightfully his.

"When I learned of Gaius Trebonius' death, my joy was no greater than my distress." Mark well what he says gave him joy and what gave him distress. It will be the easier for you to deliberate about peace.

"It is matter for gladness that a criminal has paid his penalty to the ashes and bones of an illustrious man, and that before the year is out the will of the Gods has been shown by the punishment of parricide, inflicted or impending." Spartacus! What better name to call you by? Your abominable crimes make Catiline look tolerable in retrospect. Did you dare to write that it is a matter for gladness that Trebonius has paid his penalty? That Trebonius was a criminal? What was his crime, except to draw you away on the Ides of March from the destruction you deserved? **23** Well, this gladdens your heart: let us see what you take hard.

"But it is matter for lamentation that Dolabella has been declared an enemy of the Roman People by the Senate because he put an assassin to death, and that the son of a buffoon should seem dearer to the Commonwealth than Gaius Caesar, the father of the fatherland." What are you lamenting? That Dolabella has been declared a public enemy? With a levy held all over Italy, the consuls dispatched, Caesar honored, and finally military cloaks put on, don't you understand that *you* have been declared a public enemy? And why, you felon, should you lament that Dolabella has been declared an enemy by the Senate?

senatu? quem tu ordinem omnino esse nullum putas, sed eam tibi causam
belli gerendi proponis ut senatum funditus deleas, reliqui boni et locuple-
tes omnes summum ordinem subsequantur. at scurrae filium appellat.
quasi vero ignotus nobis fuerit splendidus eques Romanus, Treboni pater.
is autem humilitatem despicere audet cuiusquam qui ex Fadia sustulerit     5
liberos?

**24** "Acerbissimum vero est te, A. Hirti, ornatum [esse] beneficiis Caesaris et talem ab eo relictum qualem ipse miraris—" equidem negare non
possum a Caesare Hirtium ornatum, sed illa ornamenta in virtute et industria posita lucent. tu vero qui te ab eodem Caesare ornatum negare    10
non potes, quid esses, si tibi ille non tam multa tribuisset? ecquo te tua
virtus provexisset, ecquo †genus†? in lustris, popinis, alea, vino tempus
aetatis omne consumpsisses, ut faciebas, cum in gremiis mimarum mentum mentemque deponeres.

"—et te, o puer—" puerum appellat quem non modo virum sed etiam     15
fortissimum virum sensit et sentiet. est istuc quidem nomen aetatis, sed
ab eo minime usurpandum qui suam amentiam huic puero praebet ad
gloriam.

**25** "—qui omnia nomini debes—" debet vero solvitque praeclare. si
enim ille patriae parens, ut tu appellas—ego quid sentiam videro—cur     20
non hic parens verior a quo certe vitam habemus e tuis facinerosissimis
manibus ereptam?

"—id agere ut iure damnatus sit Dolabella—" turpem vero actionem,
qua defenditur amplissimi auctoritas ordinis contra crudelissimi gladiatoris amentiam!                                                          25

"—et ut venefica haec liberetur obsidione—" veneficam audes appellare eum virum qui tuis veneficiis remedia invenit? quem ita obsides,
nove Hannibal aut si quis acutior imperator fuit, ut te ipse obsideas neque
te istinc, si cupias, possis explicare. recesseris: undique omnes insequen-
tur; manseris: haerebis. nimirum recte veneficam appellas a quo tibi prae-  30
sentem pestem vides comparatum.

**26** "—ut quam potentissimus sit Cassius atque Brutus." putes Censorinum dicere aut Ventidium aut etiam ipsos Antonios. cur autem nolint

---

5 cuiusque *bntv*    Fadia *Ferrarius*: ea die *D*    **24** 7 uero est *ς*: u- esse *t*: est u-
*bnsv*    esse *del. Gryphius*    9 in industria *s*    12 genus] ingenium *Ursinus*: industria *Pluygers*: genus vitae *Schelle*    13–14 mentum mentemque *st, Arusian. 7:466
Keil*: mentem mentumque *bnv*    17 huic puero³ *scripsi*: p- h- *bv*: h- *ns*: pueri *t*: -ro
*Clark*    **25** 19 eius (ei *v*) nomini *nvb²*    debes] debet *bn¹sv*    23 damnatus] demi-
nutus *Clark*    **26** 33 nolint *Manutius*: -im *D*: -it *n²*

You think this House of no account whatsoever. You propose to yourself as your reason for making war that you are going to wipe out the Senate utterly and that all other honest and substantial citizens are to go the same way as the leading echelon. Then he calls Trebonius "the son of a buffoon"—as though we had never heard of that distinguished Roman knight, Trebonius' father. And does the father of Fadia's children dare to despise anybody's lowly social origins?[26]

**24** "But the cruelest cut of all is that you, Aulus Hirtius, favored as you were by Caesar's benefactions, left by him in a position which surprises yourself—" I cannot deny that Hirtius was favored by Caesar, but such favors shine when they are bestowed on worth and diligence. You, on the contrary, who cannot deny that you were favored by the same Caesar, where would you be if he had not done so much for you? Would your worth or your intellect have advanced you? You would have spent your entire life in brothels, cookshops, gaming, drinking, as you used to do when you laid your mind and your mouth[27] in the lap of actresses.

"—and you, boy—" "Boy," he calls him; but he has found him and will find him a man, and a very brave man too. That name does indeed go with his age,[28] but it comes very ill from one who makes this boy glorious through his own madness.

**25** "—who owe everything to your name—" Yes, he owes, and splendidly he pays. If Caesar was father of the fatherland, as you call him (never mind what I think), does not that title apply more truly to this young man, to whom we assuredly owe the life which he snatched from your villainous hands?

"—should be making out that Dolabella was justly condemned—" Indeed a disgraceful line of action, by which the authority of this august body is defended against the madness of a ruthless gladiator!

"—and trying to get this viper[29] liberated from the siege—" You dare call "viper" the man who found the antidote to your venoms? Yes, you latter-day Hannibal (or any cleverer general, if there was one), you are besieging him and in doing so you are besieging yourself, nor could you extricate yourself from your present situation if you wished. If you retire, they will all be after you from every side; if you stay put, you will be stuck in a trap. I suppose you are entitled to call "viper" the contriver of the destruction you see staring you in the face.

**26** "—in order to give maximum power to Cassius and Brutus." You would think he was talking about Censorinus or Ventidius or even the Antonii them-

26. Cf. 2.3.
27. Lit. "chin." Cicero is fond of jingles like *mentum mentemque*.
28. Cf. 4.3.
29. Lit. "she-poisoner," the feminine gender aggravating the insult.

potentis esse non modo optimos et nobilissimos viros sed secum etiam in
rei publicae defensione coniunctos?
  "Nimirum eodem modo haec aspicitis ut priora." quae tandem? "castra Pompei senatum appellatis." an vero tua castra potius senatum ap-
pellaremus? in quibus tu es videlicet consularis cuius totus consulatus est　5
ex omni monumentorum memoria evulsus; duo praetores sine causa dif-
fisi se aliquid habituros—nos enim Caesaris beneficia defendimus; praetorii Philadelphus Annius et innocens Gallius; aedilicii, corycus laterum
et vocis meae, Bestia, et fidei patronus, fraudator creditorum, Trebellius,
et homo diruptus dirutusque Caelius, columenque amicorum Antoni,　10
Cotyla Varius, quem Antonius deliciarum causa loris in convivio caedi
iubebat a s⟨er⟩vis publicis; septemvirales Lento, Nucula, tum deliciae atque amores populi Romani, L. Antonius; tribuni plebis duo designati,
primum Tullus Hostilius, qui suo iure in porta nomen inscripsit qua, cum
prodere imperatorem suum non potuisset, reliquit; alter est designatus In-　15
steius nescio qui fortis, ut aiunt, latro; quem tamen temperantem fuisse
ferunt Pisauri balneatorem. 27 sequuntur alii tribunicii, T. Plancus in primis: qui ⟨ni⟩si senatum dilexisset, numquam curiam incendisset. quo
scelere damnatus in eam urbem redi⟨i⟩t armis, ex qua excesserat legibus.
sed hoc ei commune cum pluribus sui similibus. illud tamen ⟨non⟩ verum　20
in hoc Planco quod proverbi loco dici solet, perire eum non posse, nisi ei
crura fracta essent. fracta sunt et vivit. hoc tamen, ut alia multa, Aquilae
referatur acceptum. est etiam ibi Decius, ab illis, ut opinor, Muribus Deciis; itaque Caesaris munera erosit: Deciorum quidem multo intervallo

4 appellabatis *ed. Cratandrina*　　6 auulsus *b ex corr., v*: uu- *ns*: revu- *Poggius*　　10
diruptus dirutusque] -ptus diuitique *bn¹tv*: dirutus diuiciisque *n²*: diruptus dirutusque Q.
*Poggius, fort. recte*: dirutus aere Q. *Reid*　　11 quem *ed. Ascensiana a. 1529*: que *t*: que
quem *b*: quos *nsv*　　12 servis *Ferrarius*: suis (sui *t*) *D*　　publicis *t*: -ce *bnsv*　　13 tribuni plebis² (*i.e.* tr. pl.) *scripsi*: tribunicii *D*: -uni *Faërnus*　　14 qua *Rau*: qui *D*　　15
potuit *s*: posset *v*　　Insteius *Gruter*: insicieius *vel* insieius *D*　　**27** 17 alii] *anne* ali-
qui?　　18 nisi³ *scripsi*: si *D*　　19 rediit *Poggius*: redit *D*　　ex qua] unde *s*　　20 sui
similibus *Zielinski*: dissimillimis *D*: sui simillimis *Halm*　　non verum *Zumpt*: u- *D*:
mirum *R. Klotz*　　21 in hoc Planco quod *Clark*: q- in hoc pl- *D*　　23 feratur *v*: fertur
*ns*　　Deciis *del. Bardili*　　24 munera erosit³ *scripsi*: -ra rosit *b*: numerose (muner- *v*)
sit (sed *n*) *nstv*: munera arrosit *Clark, numeri gratia*

selves. Why should they not wish men of the highest merit and birth, joined moreover with themselves in the defense of the Commonwealth, to be powerful?

"I suppose you look at all this as you do at earlier events." What events, pray? "You call Pompeius' camp[30] 'the Senate.' " Well, were we rather to call *your* camp "the Senate"? You are the consular in it, to be sure—whose entire consulate has been struck off every form of record. There are two praetors,[31] who fear they will be left with nothing (without any grounds, since we are defending Caesar's benefactions). Ex-praetors next: Philadelphus[32] Annius and Gallius the Innocent.[33] Ex-aediles: Bestia, the punching-bag on which I exercised my voice and lungs;[34] Trebellius, patron of credit and defrauder of creditors; Caelius, a ruptured wreck of a man; and the mainstay of Antonius' friends, Cotyla Varius, whom Antonius used to have flogged by public slaves at dinner, just for fun. Members of the Board of Seven: Lento, Nucula, and then the Roman People's darling and delight, Lucius Antonius. Two tribunes of the plebs designate, first Tullus Hostilius, who inscribed his name, as he had a right to do, on the gate by which he deserted his imperator, not having succeeded in betraying him;[35] the other designate is one Insteius, said to be a stout bandit, though they say that when he was a baths-attendant in Pisaurum he was a good mixer.[36] **27** Others, ex-tribunes, follow, headed by Titus Plancus, who would never have set fire to the Senate-house[37] if he had not had a great regard for the Senate. Convicted of that crime, he returned by force of arms to the city from which he had departed by force of law. That, however, he has in common with many others of the same stamp as himself. But in the case of this Plancus the old saying "he can't die unless his legs are broken"[38] has proved false: they *were* broken, and he is alive. But let this, like many other things, go down to Aquila's credit. Decius too is there, a scion, I believe, of the Mures Decii,[39] which accounts for his gnawing up Caesar's gifts. The

---

30. In 49–48. We do not know what Antony refers to, presumably some joint utterance of Hirtius and Octavian.

31. Censorinus and Ventidius, mentioned above.

32. Philadelphus ("brother-loving") is Cicero's nickname for T. Annius Cimber, alleged to have murdered his brother (11.14).

33. A reference to some notorious crime?

34. Cicero had defended him six times (11.11).

35. Nothing is known of this.

36. A play on two senses of *temperans*: "mixing" (as hot and cold water) and "temperate." Insteius may be the "bathman" of *Att.* 14.5.1 (see my note there).

37. In the rioting after Clodius' murder.

38. Slaves had their legs broken before they were put to death, so the saying is equivalent to "born to be hanged." For Plancus' broken leg see 11.14.

39. See 11.13. This Decius may or may not have claimed descent from the Decii Mures (*mus* = "mouse" or "rat").

per hunc praeclarum virum memoria renovata est. Saxam vero Decidium praeterire qui possum, hominem deductum ex ultimis gentibus ut eum tribunum plebis videremus quem civem numquam videramus? **28** est quidem alter Saserna: sed omnes tamen tantam habent similitudinem inter se ut in eorum praenominibus errem. nec vero †Extitius†, Philadelphi 5 frater, quaestor, praetermittendus est, ne, si de clarissimo adulescente siluero, invidisse videar Antonio. est etiam Asinius quidam senator voluntarius, lectus ipse a se. apertam curiam vidit post Caesaris mortem: mutavit calceos; pater conscriptus repente factus est. non novi Sex. Albisium, sed tamen neminem tam maledicum offendi qui illum negaret 10 dignum Antoni senatu. arbitror me aliquos praeterisse; de eis tamen qui occurrebant tacere non potui.

Hoc igitur fretus senatu Pompeianum senatum despicit, in quo decem fuimus consulares: qui si omnes viverent, bellum omnino hoc non fuisset; auctoritati cessisset audacia. **29** sed quantum praesidi fuerit in ceteris, 15 hinc intellegi potest, quod ego unus relictus ex multis contudi et fregi adiuvantibus vobis exsultantis praedonis audaciam. quod si non Fortuna nobis modo eripuisset Ser. Sulpicium eiusque collegam ante, ⟨M.⟩ Marcellum—quos civis, quos viros!—si duo consules, amicissimos patriae, simul ex Italia eiectos, si L. Afranium, summum ducem, si P. Lentulum, 20 civem cum in ceteris rebus tum in salute mea singularem, si ⟨M.⟩ Bibulum, cuius est in rem publicam semper merito laudata constantia, si L. Domitium, praestantissimum civem, si Appium Claudium, pari nobilitate et voluntate praeditum, si P. Scipionem, clarissimum virum maiorumque suorum simillimum, res publica tenere potuisset, certe eis con- 25 sularibus non esset Pompeianus despiciendus senatus. \* \* \* **30** utrum igitur aequius, utrum melius rei publicae fuit, Cn. Pompeium an sectorem Cn. Pompei vivere Antonium? qui vero praetorii! quorum princeps

**28** 4 quidam *b*: ibidem *Madvig*      tamen *del. Rau*      5 Extitius *cruce notavi* (*v. ad* 6.10): Sex. Titius *Münzer*      9 Albisium *Syme; sed nomen dubium; v. Two Studies,* 6: albesium *bt*: albedium *nsv*      **29** 16 ex] e *bnsv*      17–18 si non (non *del. n*[2]) fortuna nobis modo non eripuisset *bn*[1]*s*: si f- non e- nobis modo *v*      18 M. *add. Naugerius*      20 Italia] *posthac deficit n*      21 M. *add. R. Klotz*      26 despiciendus pompeianus *b*      **30** *ante* utrum *aliqua de Cn. Pompeio ipso excidisse videntur*[3]      28 antonius *t*: *del. Jordan*

memory of the Decii has been revived after a long interval through this noble personality. And how can I pass over Saxa Decidius, fetched from far-off lands[40] for us to behold as a tribune of the plebs, though we had never seen him as a citizen? **28** One of the Sasernae is there, but they are all so much of a muchness that I get their first names muddled. Nor must we leave out Philadelphus'[41] brother, * the quaestor; if I say nothing about this illustrious young man, it might be thought I was jealous of Antonius. There is also a certain Asinius, a volunteer senator, chosen by himself. He saw the Senate-house open after Caesar's death. He changed his boots[42] and, hey, presto! became a member. I don't know Sextus Albisius,[43] but I have never met anyone scurrilous enough to deny that he deserves a place in Antonius' Senate. I think I have left a few out, but I had to mention those who came to mind.

Relying then upon this Senate, he despises the Pompeian Senate, which included ten of us consulars. If they were all alive, this war would never have taken place; audacity would have yielded to authority. **29** How much the others would have contributed to our protection may be inferred from the fact that I, the sole survivor out of many, have with your help crushed and broken the audacity of this ramping pirate. If Fortune had not snatched Servius Sulpicius away from us a little while ago and his colleague Marcus Marcellus earlier on (what men they were, what Romans!), if the Commonwealth could have kept the two consuls,[44] great patriots both, who were driven out of Italy at the same time, and Lucius Afranius, that fine commander, and Publius Lentulus, an outstanding citizen in general and particularly in the matter of my restoration, and Marcus Bibulus, whose steadfast loyalty to the Commonwealth has always been deservedly praised, and that fine Roman Lucius Domitius, and Appius Claudius, whose patriotism matched his lofty birth, and the illustrious Publius Scipio, the image of his ancestors—with those consulars assuredly the Pompeian Senate would not have been contemptible.[45] * * * **30** Which then was fairer and better for the Commonwealth: that Gnaeus Pompeius be alive or Antonius, who bought up Gnaeus Pompeius' property? And then the ex-praetors! First among them was Marcus Cato, who also stood

---

40. Celtiberia in north central Spain (11.12).

41. A joke of Cicero's with reference to T. Annius Cimber (see n. 32 above). The name of the brother (or cousin) mentioned here is probably corrupt in the manuscripts; see Philippic 6 n. 4 and *Two Studies*, 36–37.

42. Senators wore special boots with an ivory crescent at the toe.

43. Spelling uncertain; see *Two Studies*, 6.

44. Of 49, L. Cornelius Lentulus Crus and C. Claudius Marcellus. Cicero's real opinion of them and the consulars (except perhaps for P. Lentulus Spinther) was very much less flattering than he pretends.

45. Something about Pompey seems to have dropped out of the text.

M. Cato idemque omnium gentium virtute princeps. quid reliquos clarissimos viros commemorem? nostis omnis. magis vereor ne longum me
in enumerando quam ne ingratum in praetereundo putetis. qui aedilicii,
qui tribunicii, qui quaestorii! quid multa? talis senatorum et dignitas et
multitudo fuit ut magna excusatione opus eis sit qui in illa castra non        5
venerunt.

Nunc reliqua attendite. "victum Ciceronem ducem habuistis." eo libentius "ducem" audio quod certe ille dicit invitus; nam de victo nihil
laboro. fatum enim meum est sine re publica nec vinci posse nec vincere.

"Macedoniam munitis exercitibus." et quidem fratri tuo qui a vobis      10
nihil degenerat extorsimus.

"Africam commisistis Varo bis capto." hic cum Gaio fratre putat se
litigare.

"In Syriam Cassium misistis." non igitur sentis huic causae orbem terrae patere, te extra munitiones tuas vestigium ubi imprimas non habere?     15

**31** "Cascam tribunatum gerere passi estis." quid ergo? ut Marullum, ut
Caesetium a re publica removeremus eum per quem ut neque idem hoc
posthac neque multa eius modi accidere possent consecuti sumus?

"Vectigalia Iulianis Lupercis ademistis." Lupercorum mentionem facere audet neque illius diei memoriam perhorrescit quo ausus est obrutus     20
vino, unguentis oblitus, nudus gementem populum Romanum ad servitutem cohortari?

"Veteranorum colonias, deductas lege senatus consulto sustulistis."
nos sustulimus an contra lege comitiis centuriatis lata sanximus? vide ne
tu veteranos, eos tamen qui erant perditi, perdideris in eumque locum de-     25
duxeris ex quo ipsi iam sentiunt se numquam exituros.

1 uirtute *s*²: uir uite *b*¹*sv*: uir iute *t*      1–2 uiros clarissimos *b*      10 et quidem] eq-
*stv*      12 se putat *coni. Clark, numeri causa*      15 patere *Lambinus*: parere *s*: fauere *b*:
om. *tv*      **31** 17 moueremus *b*¹: moremus *t*      idem hoc] idem *b*: hoc est *t*: hoc idem
*Halm*      19 Iulianis *Ferrarius coll. Dion. 44.6.2*: -ni *t*: -na *bsv*      23 lege et *btv*      24
lege *Ferrarius*: legem *D*      lata *t*: latam *b*: latas *sv*      25 eos tamen *Madvig*: t- eos *D*: set
[*sic*] t- eos *idem Madvig*: etiam eos *Clark*

first in virtue among all mankind. Why should I remind you of the other illustrious figures? You know them all. I am more afraid of your thinking me tedious in the enumeration than of appearing ungrateful in the omission. Remember the ex-aediles, the ex-tribunes of the plebs, the ex-quaestors! In a word, the rank and number of the senators were such that any who did not join that camp stand in sore need of excuse.

Now listen to the rest. "You have taken the loser Cicero for your leader." I am the more gratified to hear the word "leader" because he certainly uses it against his will. As for "loser," that does not worry me. It is my ineluctable destiny to lose and to win only along with the Commonwealth.

"You fortify Macedonia with armies."[46] Yes, and we have wrenched it away from your brother, who does no discredit to the two of you.

"You consigned Africa to Varus,[47] a prisoner twice over." He thinks he's having an argument with his brother Gaius.[48]

"You sent Cassius to Syria." So don't you see that the whole world lies open to our cause, whereas you have nowhere to set your foot outside your fortifications?

**31** "You allowed Casca to hold the Tribunate." And why not? Were we to remove him from public life like Marullus and Caesetius,[49] when we have him to thank that this and many similar proceedings cannot occur in future?

"You took their revenues away from the Julian Luperci." Does he dare make mention of the Luperci?[50] Does he not shudder at the memory of that day when soaked in wine, smeared with aromatics, and naked he dared to urge a groaning Roman People into slavery?

"You have abolished by a senatorial decree colonies of veterans legally established." Did we abolish them, or did we on the contrary legalize them by a bill passed in the Centuriate Assembly?[51] You had best consider whether *you* have not ruined the veterans (those, it is true, who were ruined already)[52] and brought them into a situation from which they themselves now realize there is no way out.

---

46. Antony writes as though Hirtius and Octavian were responsible for the actions of the Senate, which would not have been in a position to act without their support.

47. Sex. Quinctilius Varus, who was taken prisoner at Corfinium in 49 and presumably again in Africa.

48. C. Antonius was captured by the Pompeian admiral M. Octavius in 49. News of his surrender to Brutus at Apollonia would by now have reached Rome.

49. Tribunes in 44, arbitrarily dismissed from office by Caesar.

50. Caesar had added a third college of Luperci to the two previously existing and given it his name. I have adopted Ferrarius' conjecture *Iulianis*.

51. Apparently refers to the rescinding of Antony's agrarian law; see 10.17.

52. I.e. those who had remained loyal to Antony.

**32** "Massiliensibus iure belli adempta reddituros vos pollicemini." nihil disputo de iure belli—magis facilis disputatio est quam necessaria—
illud tamen animadvertite, patres conscripti, quam sit huic rei publicae
natus hostis Antonius, qui tanto opere eam civitatem oderit quam scit
huic rei publicae semper fuisse amicissimam.                                                5

"Neminem Pompeianum qui vivat teneri lege Hirtia dictitatis." quis,
quaeso, iam legis Hirtiae mentionem facit? cuius non minus arbitror
latorem ipsum quam eos de quibus lata est paenitere. omnino mea quidem sententia legem illam appellare fas non est; et, ut sit lex, non debemus illam Hirti legem putare.                                                            10

"Apuleiana pecunia Brutum subornastis." quid? si omnibus suis copiis
excellentem virum res publica armasset, quem tandem bonum paeniteret?
nec enim sine pecunia exercitum alere nec sine exercitu fratrem tuum
capere potuisset.

**33** "Securi percussos Petr⟨ae⟩um et Menedemum, civitate donatos et      15
hospites Caesaris, laudastis." non lauda⟨vi⟩mus quod ne audivimus quidem. valde enim nobis in tanta perturbatione rei publicae de duobus nequissimis Graeculis cogitandum fuit!

"Theopompum, nudum, †non† expulsum a Trebonio, confugere Ale-
xandream neglexistis." magnum crimen senatus! de Theopompo, summo   20
homine, neglEximus, qui ubi terrarum sit, quid agat, vivat denique an
mortuus sit, quis aut scit aut curat?

"Ser. Galbam eodem pugione succinctum in castris videtis." nihil tibi
de Galba respondeo, fortissimo et constantissimo civi: coram aderit;
praesens et ipse et ille quem insimulas pugio respondebit.                      25

"Milites aut meos aut veteranos contraxistis tamquam ad exitium
eorum qui Caesarem occiderant: et eosdem nec opinantis ad quaestoris
sui aut imperatoris aut commilitonum suorum pericula impulistis." scilicet verba dedimus, decepimus: ignorabat legio Martia, quarta, nesciebant veterani quid ageretur; non illi senatus auctoritatem, non liberta-   30
tem populi sequebantur: Caesaris mortem ulcisci volebant, quam omnes
fatalem fuisse arbitrabantur; te videlicet salvum, beatum, florentem

**32** 3 quam ς: q. *t*: qui *b*: quis *sv*      6 tenere *bsv*      dictitatis *Orelli*: digni- *bt*: dignitates
*sv*      6–7 quis quaeso *codd.* *Ursini*: quis (qui *sv*) quasi *D*      11 subornatis *Manu-*
*tius*      **33** 15 Petraeum *Haupt*: petrum *D*      16 laudavimus *Lambinus*: -damus *bsv*:
-demus *t*      19 non] domo *Busche*: vi *Clark*: del. ς      26 exitum *bv*      29 dedimus
verba *tv*      nesciebant ς: nec sc- *btv*: ignorabant *s*      30 non . . . non ς: non (num *s*)
. . . an *D*: non . . . aut *Ferrarius*

**32** "You promise to restore to the Massilians what was taken away from them by right of war." I will not debate about right of war (that would be more easy than needful), but please observe, Members of the Senate, what a born enemy is Antonius to this Commonwealth. How intensely he hates a community which he knows has always been its devoted friend!

"You are saying that no Pompeian now living is subject to the Hirtian law." Who, pray, talks about the Hirtian law[53] any more? I daresay its sponsor disapproves of it no less than do those against whom it was passed. In my opinion, it is a sin to call it a law at all; and if it be a law, we ought not to think of it as Hirtius' law.

"You furnished Brutus with Apuleius' money." If the Commonwealth had armed that excellent personage with all its resources, what honest man would be sorry? He could not have maintained an army without money or taken your brother prisoner without an army.

**33** "You applauded the beheading of Petraeus and Menedemus, hosts of Caesar who had been granted Roman citizenship." We did not applaud something we had never even heard of. I suppose we have nothing more important to think about in this national upheaval than a couple of rascally little Greeks![54]

"Theopompus[55] was stripped bare and expelled by Trebonius. He fled to Alexandria. You did nothing." Here indeed the Senate[56] has a lot to answer for! We did nothing about the great Theopompus! And where in the world he is, what he is doing, whether he is alive or dead in fact, who either knows or cares?

"You see in your camp Servius Galba wearing that same dagger."[57] I make you no answer about my most gallant and resolute fellow countryman Galba. He will be present in person. He himself and the dagger with which you reproach him will reply on the spot.

"You have mustered soldiers of mine or veterans as though to destroy Caesar's killers, and you have surprised them into endangering their quaestor or imperator or their comrades." Oh, yes indeed, we hoodwinked them, we took them in! The Martian Legion and the Fourth were ignorant of what was going on; the veterans did not know! They were not supporting the authority of the Senate and the liberty of the People, they were out to avenge Caesar's death—which they all considered to have been fate-ordained. As for you, of

53. This law penalizing supporters of Pompey may have been carried by Hirtius as tribune, perhaps in 48.

54. Both were men of considerable standing; see index. It appears that Brutus had them executed.

55. Possibly Theopompus of Cnidus, a writer on myth and an influential friend of Caesar.

56. See n. 46 above.

57. With which he had stabbed Caesar.

esse cupiebant. **34** o miser cum re, tum hoc ipso quod non sentis quam miser sis!

Sed maximum crimen audite: "denique quid non aut probastis aut fecistis quod faciat, si reviviscat—" quis? credo enim, adferet aliquod scelerati hominis exemplum! "—Cn. Pompeius ipse—" o nos turpis, si 5 quidem Cn. Pompeium imitati sumus! "—aut filius eius, si modo possit?" poterit, mihi crede: nam paucis diebus et in domum et in hortos paternos immigrabit.

"Postremo negatis pacem fieri posse, nisi aut emisero Brutum aut frumento iuvero." alii istuc negant: ego vero, ne si ista quidem feceris, um- 10 quam tecum pacem huic civitati futuram puto.

"Quid? hoc placetne veteranis istis? quibus adhuc omnia integra sunt." nihil vidi tam integrum quam ut oppugnare imperatorem incipiant quem tanto studio consensuque ostenderint ⟨quam oderint⟩.

**35** "Quos iam vos adsentationibus et venenatis muneribus venistis de- 15 pravatum." an corrupti sunt quibus persuasum sit foedissimum hostem iustissimo bello persequi?

"At militibus inclusis opem fertis. nihil moror eos salvos esse et ire quo libet, si tantum modo patiuntur perire eum qui meruit." quam benigne! ⟨ei⟩ denique usi liberalitate Antoni milites imperatorem reliquerint 20 et se ad hostem metu perterriti contulerint per quos si non stetisset, non Dolabella prius imperatori suo quam Antonius etiam collegae parentasset.

**36** "Concordiae factam esse mentionem scribitis in senatu et legatos esse consularis quinque. difficile est credere eos qui me praecipitem egerint, aequissimas condiciones ferentem et tamen ex his aliquid remit- 25 tere cogitantem, putare aliquid moderate aut humane esse facturos. vix etiam veri simile est, qui iudicaverint hostem Dolabellam ob rectissimum facinus, eosdem nobis parcere posse idem sentientibus." parumne videtur omnium facinorum sibi cum Dolabella societatem initam confiteri? nonne cernitis ex uno fonte omnia scelera manare? ipse denique fatetur, hoc 30 quidem satis acute, non posse eos qui hostem Dolabellam iudicaverint ob rectissimum facinus—ita enim videtur Antonio—sibi parcere idem sen-

---

**34** 3 probauistis *bs*     4 que faciat *b*: quid f- *tvs²*     6 imitaturi *bsv*     modo *t*: domo *b*: domi *sv*     14 ostenderint quam oderint *Lehmann*: ostenderint *t*: offend- *bsv*: oderint *Clark*     **35** 15 quos iam *Clark*: quoniam *btv*: quem *s*: quamquam eos *Madvig*     depravatum *Madvig*: -ti *bsv*: om. *t*: -turi *Clark*     16 an] itane *Madvig*     sit] est *b²*     19 libet si] iubetis si *bv*: iubetis *t*     20 ei denique *scripsi*: d- *D*: itaque *Ferrarius*: ea denique *coni. Clark*     20–21 reliquerint . . . contulerint² *scripsi*: -runt . . . -runt *D*     **36** 24 credere *del. Madvig*     eos] cos *s*: consules *v*: esse cons. *t*: eosque *Sternkopf*     26 putare *D, Prisc. 3:70 Keil*: del. *Manutius*: hos p- *Schöll*

course they wanted you safe and happy and flourishing! **34** What a miserable creature you are, not only in actuality but from the very fact that you don't realize *how* miserable!

But hear the heaviest charge of all: "To sum up, what have you not approved or done which, if he came back to life, would not be done by—" By whom? No doubt he will produce some stock villain! "—Gnaeus Pompeius himself—" We are disgraced indeed if we have made Gnaeus Pompeius our model! "—or his son, if he but had the power?" Oh, he'll have it, take my word. In a few days' time he will be moving into his father's house and suburban estates.

"Finally, you say peace cannot be made unless I let Brutus go or assist him with grain." Others say that. For my part, I do not think this community will ever have peace with you, even if you do that.

"Well, does this please your veterans? As yet they are quite free to choose." Nothing could be more free than their choice to start attacking a commander for whom they have shown their hatred with such zeal and unanimity.

**35** "You have now come to deprave them with flatteries and poisoned gifts." Are they corrupted because they are determined to pursue a foul enemy in a most legitimate war?

"You say you are bringing help to the beleaguered troops. I don't care if they go in safety wherever they please, so long as they let perish the individual who has deserved it." How kind! In a word, by Antonius' generous permission the soldiers will desert their commander and betake themselves in terror to the enemy, those soldiers but for whom Dolabella would not have made a grave-offering to his dead commander before Antonius had made one to his colleague.[58]

**36** "You say that the subject of reconciliation has been brought up in the Senate and that five consulars[59] have been appointed as envoys. It is difficult to believe that those who drove me headlong when I was offering very fair terms and was even thinking of making further concessions will do anything moderate and reasonable. Also it is scarcely probable that the same people who declared Dolabella an enemy because of an eminently proper action can spare us who share his sentiments." Is that not a clear admission that he has entered into partnership with Dolabella for all manner of villainies? Don't you see that all the crimes flow from a single source? He himself finally admits (quite clever of him, I must say) that those who declared Dolabella a public enemy because of an eminently proper action (for so it seems to Antonius) cannot spare Antonius himself, sharing Dolabella's sentiments as he does.

---

58. I.e. Antony would have massacred the Senate as an offering to Caesar's *manes* before Dolabella killed Trebonius.
59. Cf. 12.18.

tienti. **37** quid huic facias qui hoc litteris memoriaeque mandarit, ita sibi
convenisse cum Dolabella ut ille Trebonium et, si posset, etiam Brutum,
Cassium, discruciatos necaret, eadem ipse inhiberet supplicia nobis? o
conservandus civis cum tam pio iustoque foedere! is etiam queritur condiciones suas repudiatas, aequas quidem et verecundas, ut haberet Gal- 5
liam ultimam, aptissimam ad bellum renovandum instruendumque provinciam; ut Alaudae in tertia decuria iudicarent, id est ut perfugium
scelerum esset cum turpissimis rei publicae sordibus; ut acta sua rata essent, cuius nullum remanet consulatus vestigium. cavebat etiam L. Antonio, qui fuerat aequissimus agri privati et publici decempedator, 10
Nucula et Lentone collega.

**38** "Quam ob rem vos potius animadvertite utrum sit elegantius et partibus utilius Treboni mortem persequi an Caesaris, et utrum sit aequius
concurrere nos quo facilius reviviscat Pompeianorum causa totiens iugulata an consentire ne ludibrio simus inimicis." si esset iugulata, num- 15
quam exsurgeret: quod tibi tuisque contingat. "utrum" inquit "elegantius." atqui hoc bello de elegantia quaeritur! "et partibus utilius."
**39** partes, furiose, dicuntur in foro, in curia. bellum contra patriam
nefarium suscepisti; oppugnas Mutinam, circumsedes consulem designatum; bellum contra te duo consules gerunt cumque eis pro praetore 20
Caesar; cuncta contra te Italia armata est. istas tu partis potius quam a
populo Romano defectionem vocas? potiusne Treboni mortem quam Caesaris persequimur? Treboni satis persecuti sumus hoste iudicato Dolabella; Caesaris mors facillime defenditur oblivione et silentio. sed videte
quid moliatur: cum mortem Caesaris ulciscendam putat, mortem pro- 25
ponit non eis solum qui illam rem gesserunt sed eis etiam si qui non moleste tulerunt.

**40** "Quibus, utri nostrum ceciderint, lucro futurum est, quod spectaculum adhuc ipsa Fortuna vitavit, ne videret unius corporis duas acies
lanista Cicerone dimicantis: qui usque eo felix est ut isdem ornamentis 30
deceperit vos quibus deceptum Caesarem gloriatus est." pergit in me
maledicta, quasi vero ei pulcherrime priora processerint: quem ego inus-
tum verissimis maledictorum notis tradam hominum memoriae sempiternae. ego lanista? et quidem non insipiens: deteriores enim iugulari

**37** 3 eadem ipse *Garatoni*: eademque *D*      o *om. bsv*      6 instruendamque *stv*      8
cum] quam *Clark, alii alia*: *del. Garatoni*      9 remanet uestigium consulatus *t*: c- r- u-
*v*      **38** 16 resurgeret *v*[1]      17 et partibus] partibusque *b*[1]*t*: et partibus que (quid *s*[2]) *s*[1]:
et p- quae *v*      **39** 22 potiusne] -us *stv*: *del. Ferrarius*      quam] an *idem*      23 persequi *idem, fort. recte*      **40** 29 membra[3] *post* corporis *cave ne desideres*      31 in mea
*bsv*      32 iacere *vel* iactare *post* maledicta *add. Halm*, dicere *Clark*      34 equidem *sv*

**37** What are we to do with a man who puts in writing, for the record, that he agreed with Dolabella that Dolabella should kill Trebonius and, if he could, Brutus and Cassius, first putting them to the torture, while he himself should inflict the same cruelties upon us? Indeed a citizen to be preserved along with so righteous and just a compact! He even complains that his terms were rejected, fair and modest as they were: namely, that he have Outer Gaul, a province ideally suited for resuming the war and supplying its requirements; that the Larks be jurors in the third panel, which is to say that there be a refuge for crime at the cost of disgraceful indignity to the Commonwealth; and that his acts be valid, although not a trace of his consulship remains. He also provided for Lucius Antonius, who had been a most equitable surveyor of public and private land, with Nucula and Lento for colleagues.

**38** "Therefore I ask you gentlemen to observe which is in better taste and more expedient for the party, to avenge Trebonius' death or Caesar's; and which is fairer, for us to clash so as to facilitate the revival of the Pompeians' cause, so often slaughtered, or to work together, so as not to be a laughing-stock to our enemies." If the cause had been slaughtered, it would never rise again, which is what I wish for you and your followers. "Which is in better taste?" says he. To be sure, *taste* is what this war is all about! "And more expedient for the party." **39** We speak of "party," you lunatic, in the Forum and the Senate-house. You commenced a wicked war on your country. You are attacking Mutina, besieging a consul-elect. Two consuls are waging war against you, and Propraetor Caesar with them. All Italy is in arms against you. Do you call your following a "party" rather than a defection from the Roman People? Do we avenge Trebonius' death rather than Caesar's? We avenged Trebonius' death sufficiently when Dolabella was declared a public enemy; Caesar's is most easily vindicated[60] with silent oblivion. But notice what he is at. Holding that Caesar's death calls for vengeance, he proposes death not only for those who did the deed but also for any whom it did not displease.

**40** "Whichever of us go down, it will be a windfall for them.[61] Thus far Fortune herself has avoided the spectacle, not caring to see two battle lines from one corps,[62] fighting each other with Cicero as trainer. He is lucky enough to have deceived you with the same compliments with which he boasted of deceiving Caesar." He goes on flinging insults at me as though his previous efforts in that line had been a brilliant success; and I shall hand him down to everlasting memory branded with the marks of insults which are true to the letter. So I am a gladiator-trainer? Yes, and I know my job. I want to see

---

60. Not "defended." In juristic language *defendere* = *ulcisci*, especially of legal action.
61. Anti-Caesarians like Cicero.
62. Lit. "body" (*corpus*), apparently used by Antony to mean a school of gladiators.

351

cupio, meliores vincere. utri ceciderint, scribit lucro nobis futurum. **41** o
praeclarum lucrum, cum te victore—quod di omen avertant!—beata
mors eorum futura sit qui e vita excesserint sine tormentis. a me deceptos
ait isdem ornamentis Hirtium et Caesarem. quod, quaeso, adhuc a me est
tributum Hirtio ornamentum? nam Caesari plura et maiora debentur. de-   5
ceptum autem patrem Caesarem a me dicere audes? tu, tu, inquam, illum occidisti Lupercalibus: cuius, homo ingratissime, flamonium cur
reliquisti?

Sed iam videte magni et clari viri admirabilem gravitatem atque constantiam: **42** "mihi quidem constat nec meam contumeliam nec meorum   10
ferre, nec deserere partis quas Pompeius odivit nec veteranos sedibus suis
moveri pati nec singulos ad cruciatum trahi nec fallere fidem quam dedi
Dolabellae—" omitto alia: fidem Dolabellae, sanctissimi viri, deserere
homo pius non potest. quam fidem? an optimi cuiusque caedis, urbis et
Italiae partitionis, vastandarum diripiendarumque provinciarum? nam   15
quid erat aliud quod inter Antonium et Dolabellam, impurissimos parricidas, foedere et fide sanciretur?

**43** "—nec Lepidi societatem violare, piissimi hominis—" tibi cum
Lepido societas aut cum ullo, non dicam bono civi, sicut ille est, sed
homine sano? id agis ut Lepidum aut impium aut insanum existimari   20
velis. nihil agis—quamquam adfirmare de altero difficile est—de Lepido
praesertim, quem ego metuam numquam; bene sperabo, dum licebit. re-
vocare te a furore Lepidus voluit, non adiutor esse dementiae. tu porro ne
pios quidem, sed piissimos quaeris et, quod verbum omnino nullum in
lingua Latina est, id propter tuam divinam pietatem novum inducis.   25

**44** "—nec Plancum prodere participem consiliorum." Plancum participem? cuius memorabilis ac divina virtus lucem adfert rei publicae—
nisi forte eum subsidio tibi venire arbitraris cum fortissimis legionibus,
maximo equitatu peditatu Gallorum—quique, nisi ante eius adventum rei
publicae poenas dederis, ille huius belli feret principatum. quamquam   30
enim prima praesidia utiliora rei publicae sunt, tamen extrema sunt
gratiora.

**45** Sed iam se colligit et ad extremum incipit philosophari: "si me rec-
tis sensibus euntem di immortales, ut spero, adiuverint, vivam libenter.

---

**41** 2 cum *A. Augustinus*: quo *btv*: quo lucro *s*      4 quaeso *Poggius*: quasi *D*      6 patrem
Caesarem a me] c- a me *t*: p- a me c- *s*: p- a me *Clark*      7 flamminia *b¹s*: -iam *v*: -ium *b²*
(*v. Fe.*)      **42** 10 meam quidem *st*      11 poneius uidi *t*: sponte adivi *coni. Clark*      15
partitionis *Ferrarius*: -nes *D*      vastandarum] suas (suis *s²*) dan- *s¹v*      **43** 18 nec] ne
*btv*      uiolarent *sv*      23 te a furore *Poggius*: a te furorem *t*: a te fure (-em *v*) *sv*: furorem
a te *b*      **44** 29 peditatu] -tuque *ed. Romana*: *del. Madvig*      30 ille] ipse *Clark*: *del.*
*Gryphius* (*v. Fe.*)

the bad ones killed off and the good ones win. Whichever go down, he writes that it will be a windfall for us. **41** A fine windfall, when if *you* win (may the Gods avert the omen!), happy will be the death of those who quit their lives without torture. He says that Hirtius and Caesar have been deceived by me "with the same compliments." What compliment, pray, have I bestowed on Hirtius up till now? As for Caesar, he deserves more and greater. But do you dare to say that the elder Caesar was deceived by me? You, yes, *you* killed him at the Lupercalia. And why have you abandoned his priesthood, ingrate?

Now observe the high seriousness and resolution of a great and famous man: **42** "As for me, I am determined to brook no insult to myself or my friends, and not to desert the party which Pompeius hated, nor yet to allow the veterans to be evicted from their homes and dragged off to torture one by one, nor yet to break my word to Dolabella—" The rest I leave: as a man of honor he cannot prove false to his word given to that pattern of integrity, Dolabella. Word on what? The massacre of our best, the parceling out of Rome and Italy, the plunder and devastation of the provinces? What else was there to be guaranteed by pact and pledge between those two foul traitors, Antonius and Dolabella?

**43** "—nor yet to violate my alliance with Lepidus, the honorablest of men—" You an ally of Lepidus or any other—I won't say good citizen, as he is, but sane man? You are out to have Lepidus thought either a traitor or a madman. You are wasting your time (though it is difficult to be positive about another person), especially in Lepidus' case. I shall never fear him and I shall hope well of him as long as I can.[63] Lepidus wished to recall you from your frenzy, not to be your abettor in folly. And then you look not merely for honorable men but for "honorablest," importing a new word which does not exist in the Latin language to gratify your marvelous sense of honor![64]

**44** "—nor yet to betray Plancus, the partner of my counsels." Plancus your partner? Plancus, whose memorable, marvelous manliness is a beacon of hope to the Commonwealth (perhaps you think he is coming to help you with his brave legions and his host of Gallic horse and foot!) and who will take the leading role in this war, unless you pay your penalty to the Commonwealth before he arrives. The help that comes first is of greater use to the Commonwealth, but the help that comes last earns more gratitude.

**45** But now he takes stock and in conclusion begins to philosophize: "If the Immortal Gods help me as I go my way in rectitude of purpose, which I trust they will, I shall live in good cheer. But if a different fate awaits me, I joyfully

63. A clear intimation of mistrust, like the parenthesis in the previous sentence.

64. The second-century grammarian Caper quoted *piissimus* from Cicero's own letters according to later testimony (Cic. *ep. frag.* 17.3 ed. Watt). It is found in many post-Augustan writers.

sin autem me aliud fatum manet, praecipio gaudia suppliciorum vestrorum. namque si victi Pompeiani tam insolentes sunt, victores quales
futuri sint vos potius experiemini." Praecipias licet gaudia: non enim tibi
cum Pompeianis, sed cum universa re publica bellum est. omnes te di
homines, summi medii infimi, cives peregrini, viri mulieres, liberi servi    5
oderunt. sensimus hoc nuper falso nuntio; vero prope diem sentiemus.
quae si tecum ipse recolueris, aequiore animo et maiore consolatione
moriere.

    **46** "Denique summa iudici mei spectat huc ut meorum iniurias ferre
possim, si aut oblivisci velint ipsi fecisse aut ulcisci parati sunt una no-    10
biscum Caesaris mortem." hac Antoni sententia cognita dubitaturumne
A. Hirtium aut C. Pansam consules putatis quin ad Antonium transeant,
Brutum obsideant, Mutinam expugnare cupiant? quid de Pansa et Hirtio
loquor? Caesar, singulari pietate adulescens, poteritne se tenere quin
D. Bruti sanguine poenas patrias persequatur? itaque fecerunt ut his lit-    15
teris lectis ad munitiones propius accederent. quo maior adulescens Caesar, maioreque deorum immortalium beneficio rei publicae natus est, qui
nulla specie paterni nominis nec pietate abductus umquam est et intellegit
maximam pietatem conservatione patriae contineri. **47** quod si partium
certamen esset, quarum omnino nomen exstinctum est, Antoniusne po-    20
tius et Ventidius partis Caesaris defenderent quam primum Caesar, adulescens summa pietate et memoria parentis sui, deinde Pansa et Hirtius,
qui quasi cornua duo tenuerunt Caesaris tum cum illae vere partes voca-
bantur? hae vero quae sunt partes, cum alteris senatus auctoritas, populi
Romani libertas, rei publicae salus proposita sit, alteris caedes bonorum,    25
urbis Italiaeque partitio?

    Veniamus aliquando ad clausulam. "legatos venire non credo." bene
me novit; veniat qui velit, proposito praesertim exemplo Dolabellae.
sanctiore erunt, credo, iure legati quam duo consules contra quos arma
fert, quam Caesar cuius patris flamen est, quam consul designatus quem    30
oppugnat, quam Mutina quam obsidet, quam patria cui igni ferroque
minitatur!

    **48** "Cum venerint, quae postulant cognoscam." quin tu abis in malam
pestem malumque cruciatum? ad te quisquam veniat nisi Ventidi similis?
oriens incendium qui restinguerent summos viros misimus; repudiasti:    35

---

**45** 1 nostrorum *stv*     2 sunt insolentes *b*     7 recolis *sv*: coleris *t*     **46** 10 sint *v*     14
loquor *Poggius*: -uar *D*     18 et *om. s*: sed *coni. Halm*     **47** 28 veniat qui velit (*anne* qui
velit, veniat?) *scripsi* (*cf. Verr. 2.4.142, Cael. 43*): uelim quo (quod *s*) uenias *bs*: bellum
quod ueniat *v*: quod uenias *t*: reliqui veniant *Clark*     29 sanctiores *tvb*²     **48** 33 cum
*fort. delendum*     cum vero venerint *Lehmann*     postulent *vb*²

anticipate what you will suffer. For if the Pompeians are so insolent in defeat, what they will be like in victory you will find out rather than I." Joyfully anticipate you may! You are not at war with Pompeians but with the entire Commonwealth. All Gods and men, from the highest to the lowest, citizens and foreigners, men and women, freemen and slaves, all hate you. This was proved to us the other day by a false report,[65] and will soon be by a true one. If you think this over quietly, you will die with an easier mind and better consolation.

**46** "Finally, the sum of my judgment is to this effect: I could forget the injuries done to me by my friends, if they on their side would forget that they have done them or are ready to make common cause with us in avenging Caesar's death." When they learn this sentiment of Antonius', do you suppose Consuls Aulus Hirtius and Gaius Pansa will hesitate to go over to him and besiege Brutus and try to take Mutina by storm? Why do I speak of Hirtius and Pansa? Caesar is a young man with a remarkable sense of family duty; will he be able to restrain himself from seeking vengeance for his father with Decimus Brutus' blood? And so, after reading this letter they—proceeded to move in closer to the siegeworks. So much the greater is young Caesar, so much the greater the gift of the Immortal Gods who gave him to the Commonwealth. For he has never been led astray by the show of his father's name or by filial duty, and he understands that the highest duty of a son lies in the preservation of the fatherland. **47** But if this were a struggle of parties, the very name of which is extinct, would Antonius and Ventidius be standing up for Caesar's party rather than, in the first place, Caesar, a young man with the highest sense of family duty and devoted to his father's memory, and, in the second place, Pansa and Hirtius, who captained Caesar's two wings, as it were, when that party was truly so called? But what parties are these, when the aim on the one side is the authority of the Senate, the freedom of the Roman People, and the survival of the Commonwealth; on the other, the massacre of honest men, the parceling out of Rome and Italy?

Let us at length come to the finale: "I do not believe the envoys are coming." He knows me well. Let him go who chooses, especially with Dolabella's example before his eyes. Envoys, no doubt, will bear a more sacred character than the two consuls, against whom Antonius is in arms, or Caesar, of whose father he is priest, or the consul-elect, whom he is attacking, or Mutina, which he is besieging, or Rome, which he is threatening with fire and sword.

**48** "When they come, I shall learn their demands." To the devil with you! To the rack with you! Would anyone come to you except a fellow like Ventidius? We sent persons of the highest quality to put out the rising flame: you rebuffed

---

65. Of Antony's death, presumably.

nunc in tantam flammam tamque inveteratam mittamus, cum locum tibi reliquum non modo ad pacem sed ne ad deditionem quidem feceris?

Hanc ego epistulam, patres conscripti, non quo illum dignum putarem, recitavi, sed ut confessionibus ipsius omnia patefacta eius parricidia videretis. **49** cum hoc pacem M. Lepidus, vir ornatissimus omnibus et vir- 5 tutis et fortunae bonis, si haec audiret, aut vellet ⟨aut⟩ denique fieri posse arbitraretur? "prius undis flamma," ut ait poeta nescio quis, prius denique omnia quam aut cum Antoniis res publica aut cum re publica Antonii redeant in gratiam. monstra quaedam ista et portenta sunt et prodigia rei publicae. moveri sedibus huic urbi melius est atque in alias, si fieri pos- 10 sit, terras demigrare, unde Antoniorum "nec facta nec nomen audiat," quam illos, Caesaris virtute eiectos, Bruti retentos, intra haec moenia videre. optatissimum est vincere; secundum est nullum casum pro dignitate et libertate patriae non ferendum putare. quod reliquum est, non est tertium, sed postremum omnium, maximam turpitudinem suscipere vitae 15 cupiditate.

**50** Quae cum ita sint, de mandatis litterisque M. Lepidi, viri clarissimi, Servilio adsentior, et hoc amplius censeo:

"Magnum Pompeium, Gnaei filium, pro patris maiorumque suorum animo studioque in rem publicam suaque pristina virtute, industria, vo- 20 luntate fecisse quod suam eorumque quos secum haberet operam senatui populoque Romano pollicitus esset, eamque rem senatui populoque Romano gratam acceptamque esse, eique honori dignitatique eam rem fore."

Hoc vel coniungi cum hoc senatus consulto licet vel seiungi potest se- 25 paratimque perscribi, ut proprio senatus consulto Pompeius collaudatus esse videatur.

**1** cum nullum locum *Halm*     2 relictum *stvb*²     **49** 6 audiret *scripsi* (*cf. quae scripsi ad Fam. 11.25.1*): uideret denique *bsv*: d- *t*: uideret, audiret d- *Madvig*: legeret, suaderet, d- *C. F. W. Müller*: uideret *Clark*     vellet aut denique *Schöll*: u- aut ς: u- *D*     7 undis flamma *cod. P. Laeti*: undas flammam *D*     9 sunt et] sunt *b*¹     et prodigia *del. Halm*     10 in *om. s* (*etiam* alias), *tv, ante* terras *hab. cod. Graevii*

them. Should we send now, to a fire that has spread so wide and taken such hold, now that you have left yourself no room for capitulation, let alone peace?

I have read out this letter, Members of the Senate, not that I thought him worthy, but to let you see all his treasons laid bare by his own confessions. **49** Would Marcus Lepidus, so richly endowed with all the blessings of nature and fortune, wish peace with this man or think it possible if he saw this letter? "Sooner fire with water," as some poet[66] or other has it, sooner anything in fact, than the Commonwealth will be reconciled with the Antonii or the Antonii with the Commonwealth. They are a kind of monsters, portents, prodigies of the Commonwealth. It were better for this city to be moved from her foundations and to migrate to other lands, if that were possible, where she would "hear neither deeds nor name"[67] of the Antonii, than to see them, who were thrown out by Caesar's prowess and held back by Brutus', once more inside her walls. Best of all is victory, but second-best is to think no misfortune insupportable if it be for our country's freedom. That leaves no third-best, only the worst of all, to plumb the lowest depth of dishonor out of craving for life.

**50** In these circumstances, concerning the illustrious Marcus Lepidus' message and letter, I agree with Servilius, and I further propose as follows:

"That Magnus Pompeius, son of Gnaeus, acted worthily of the spirit and patriotic zeal of his father and ancestors and of his own former prowess, diligence, and goodwill in that he promised his services and those of his companions to the Senate and People of Rome; and that his action is welcome and pleasing to the Senate and People of Rome and will redound to his honor and dignity."

This can either be conjoined with the decree of the Senate now under discussion or separated and drafted independently, so that Pompeius may be seen to have been commended by a decree of the Senate special to himself.

---

66. Unknown. A verb "will mingle" is understood; cf. Dio 55.13.1.
67. Fragment of an unknown play, several times quoted in Cicero's letters.

# XIV

## INTRODUCTION

Flashpoint at Mutina was reached on 15 April 43. At Forum Gallorum some miles up the Aemilian way to the east, Pansa's forces marching to join the republican armies were ambushed by Antony; but the ensuing series of engagements ended in the latter's defeat at the hands of Hirtius, who had already sent the Martian Legion to join Pansa and now hurried up from Mutina to his colleague's support. Pansa received a wound from which he died a few days later. An eyewitness account by Servius Galba, in command of the Martian Legion, survives in Cicero's correspondence (*Fam.* 10.30).

The news arrived in Rome on 20 April, making the greater sensation because it followed on an earlier false report of an Antonian victory, which had caused temporary panic. A crowd escorted Cicero in triumph to the Capitol to offer thanks, and back to his house. Next day the city praetor Cornutus summoned the Senate to hear dispatches from the three commanders. Servilius proposed a Thanksgiving and resumption of civilian dress for the day only. The second proposal was briefly attacked by Cicero in the Fourteenth Philippic. He went on to deal with a false rumor which had been spread about himself, and ended with a eulogy of the three republican commanders and their troops, concluding with his formal motion.

A week later came news of a second victory, this time apparently decisive. But Hirtius was among the dead, and with the disappearance of both consuls the war took a new turn. Antony was able to escape westwards to join Lepidus in Gaul, only tardily pursued by D. Brutus. Caesar's veterans at Mutina, contrary to the Senate's directions, put themselves under Octavian's orders, making him the military master of Italy.

From then on history moved with unrelenting logic. Caesar's heir joined Caesar's two principal lieutenants in a Triumvirate which ended the Roman Republic. Cicero paid the loser's price, murdered at his Formian villa on 7 December 43, in his sixty-fourth year.

**1** Si, ut ex litteris quae recitatae sunt, patres conscripti, sceleratissimorum hostium exercitum caesum fusumque cognovi, sic, id quod et
omnes maxime optamus ⟨et⟩ ex ea victoria quae parta est consecutum arbitramur, D. Brutum egressum iam Mutina esse cognossem, propter
cuius periculum ad saga issemus, propter eiusdem salutem redeundum ad　5
pristinum vestitum sine ulla dubitatione censerem. ante vero quam sit ea
res quam avidissime civitas exspectat adlata, laetitia frui satis est maximae praeclarissimaeque pugnae; reditum ad vestitum confectae victoriae
reservate. confectio autem huius belli est D. Bruti salus.

**2** Quae autem est ista sententia ut in hodiernum diem vestitus mutetur,　10
deinde cras sagati prodeamus? nos vero cum semel ad eum quem cupimus optamusque vestitum redierimus, id agamus ut eum in perpetuum
retineamus. nam hoc quidem cum turpe est, tum ne dis quidem immortalibus gratum, ab eorum aris, ad quas togati adierimus, ad saga sumenda
discedere. **3** atque animadverto, patres conscripti, quosdam huic favere　15
sententiae quorum ea mens idque consilium est ut, cum videant gloriosis-
simum illum D. Bruto futurum diem quo die propter eius salutem ⟨ad ves-
titum⟩ redierimus, hunc ei fructum eripere cupiant, ne memoriae posteri-
tatique prodatur propter unius civis periculum populum Romanum ad
saga isse, propter eiusdem salutem redisse ad togas. tollite hanc: nullam　20
tam pravae sententiae causam reperietis.

Vos vero, patres conscripti, conservate auctoritatem vestram, manete
in sententia, tenete vestra memoria quod saepe ostendistis, huius totius
belli in unius viri fortissimi et maximi vita positum esse discrimen. **4** ad
D. Brutum liberandum legati missi principes civitatis qui illi hosti ac par-　25
ricidae denuntiarent ut a Mutina discederet; eiusdem D. Bruti conservandi gratia consul sortitu ad bellum profectus A. Hirtius, cuius im-
becillitatem valetudinis animi virtus et spes victoriae confirmavit; Caesar
cum exercitu per se comparato cum prius his pestibus rem publicam libe-
rasset, ne quid postea sceleris oreretur, profectus est ad eundem Brutum　30
liberandum vicitque dolorem aliquem domesticum patriae caritate. **5** quid
C. Pansa egit aliud dilectibus habendis, pecuniis comparandis, senatus
consultis faciendis gravissimis in Antonium, nobis cohortandis, populo
Romano ad causam libertatis vocando, nisi ut D. Brutus liberaretur? a
quo populus Romanus frequens ita salutem D. Bruti una voce depoposcit　35

---

**1** 1 si ut *cod. Harl. 2682*: sicut *bstv*　　2 fusum caesumque *Nonius 312* (*v. Fe.*)　　3 et
*add. Naugerius*　　4 esse si *sv*　　cognovissem *stv*　　7 laetitia frui *b* (quam . . . satis
est *om. t*): -ae risus (rursus *s¹*) *vs*　　9 reseruare (ser- *t*) *bst*　　**3** 17–18 ad vestitum *add.*
*Orelli*　　**4** 29 cum prius his *scripsi praeeuntibus C. F. W. Müller* (cum prius) *et Clark*
(cum primum his): cum (eum *v*) primis *D*: compressis *coni. Halm, alii alia*　　30 oreretur
*Halm*: orir- *D*　　**5** 32 pecunia comparanda *b*: -ae -dis *v*

**1** Members of the Senate, the dispatches which have been read out have told me that an army of felonious enemies has been cut to pieces and routed. If those dispatches had also told me that Decimus Brutus is already out of Mutina, the consummation which we all most pray for and which we believe to be the consequence of the victory gained by our forces, then I should have no hesitation in moving a return to normal dress on account of his deliverance, since it was on account of his peril that we put on our military cloaks. But until the news which the community is so impatiently awaiting arrives, it is enough to enjoy the happy knowledge of a great and glorious battle. Reserve a return to normal dress for final victory. And final victory in this war means Decimus Brutus' rescue.

**2** As for the proposal that we change our dress for today only and reappear tomorrow in military cloaks, I wonder what it means. No, when once we have returned to the dress we want and pray for, let us make sure we keep it forever. Having approached the altars of the Immortal Gods in gowns, to leave them and put on our military cloaks again would be unseemly, nor would it be pleasing to the Gods themselves. **3** I notice, Members of the Senate, that certain persons favor this proposal, and I perceive their purpose and plan. They see that the day we return to normal dress on account of Decimus Brutus' deliverance will be a most glorious day for him. Therefore they wish to deprive him of this gratification and not let it be handed down for posterity to remember that the Roman People put on military cloaks because of one citizen's peril and went back into gowns because of the same citizen's rescue. Take away this reason and you will find no reason at all for so misguided a proposal.

But do you, Members of the Senate, maintain your authority, stand by your opinion, keep fixedly in mind what you have often made plain: that the decision in this entire war turns on the life of one very great and gallant man. **4** To liberate Decimus Brutus, leaders of the community were sent as envoys to order that enemy and traitor to withdraw from Mutina. To save the same Decimus Brutus, Consul Aulus Hirtius, after drawing lots, set out to war, his bodily infirmity strengthened by a courageous spirit and the prospect of victory. Caesar, as soon as he had liberated the Commonwealth from these evil creatures, set out with the army he raised by himself to liberate the same Brutus and stop the commission of further crimes, thus overcoming a private grief by the love he bears his country. **5** What was Gaius Pansa's object in holding levies, raising funds, passing damning decrees against Antonius, exhorting us, summoning the Roman People to the cause of liberty, unless it was Decimus Brutus' liberation? From him the Roman People in their thousands with one voice demanded Decimus Brutus' deliverance, putting it not

ut eam non solum commodis suis sed etiam necessitati victus anteferret. quod sperare nos quidem debemus, patres conscripti, aut inibi esse aut iam esse confectum: ⟨s⟩ed spei fructum rei convenit et evento reservari, ne aut deorum immortalium beneficium festinatione praeripuisse aut vim Fortunae stultitia contempsisse videamur. 5

**6** Sed quoniam significatio vestra satis declarat quid hac de re sentiatis, ad litteras veniam quae sunt a consulibus et a pro praetore missae, si pauca ante quae ad ipsas litteras pertineant dixero. imbuti gladii sunt, patres conscripti, legionum exercituumque nostrorum vel madefacti potius duobus duorum consulum, tertio Caesaris proelio. si hostium fuit ille 10 sanguis, summa militum pietas: nefarium scelus, si civium. quo usque igitur is qui omnis hostis scelere superavit nomine hostis carebit? nisi mucrones etiam nostrorum militum tremere vultis dubitantis utrum in cive an in hoste figantur. **7** supplicationem decernitis: hostem non appellatis. gratae vero nostrae dis immortalibus gratulationes erunt, gratae 15 victimae, cum interfecta sit civium multitudo! "de improbis" inquit "et audacibus." nam sic eos appellat clarissimus vir: quae sunt urbanarum maledicta litium, non in[i]ustae belli internecivi notae. Testamenta, credo, subiciunt aut eiciunt vicinos aut adulescentulos circumscribunt: his enim vitiis adfectos et talibus malos ⟨aut⟩ audacis appellare consue- 20 tudo solet. **8** bellum inexpiabile infert quattuor consulibus unus omnium latronum taeterrimus; gerit idem bellum cum senatu populoque Romano; omnibus—quamquam ruit ipse suis cladibus—pestem, vastitatem, cruciatum, tormenta denuntiat: Dolabellae ferum et immane facinus quod nulla barbaria posset agnoscere, id suo consilio factum esse testatur; 25 quaeque esset facturus in hac urbe, nisi eum hic ipse Iuppiter ab hoc templo atque moenibus reppulisset, declaravit in Parmensium calamitate, quos optimos viros honestissimosque homines, maxime cum auctoritate huius ordinis populique Romani dignitate coniunctos, crudelissimis exemplis interemit propudium illud et portentum, L. Antonius, insigne 30 odium omnium hominum vel, si etiam di oderunt quos oportet, deorum. **9** refugit animus, patres conscripti, eaque dicere ⟨re⟩formidat quae L. Antonius in Parmensium liberis et coniugibus effecerit. quas enim tur-

---

3 sed *Manutius*: et *D*    uento *t*: euentui *sv*    **6** 6 nostra satis *b*: s- uestra *t*    7 consulibus *Ferrarius*: -ule *D*    a p. r. *st*: praetore p. r. *v*    **8** *anne* pertinent? 10 duobus duorum] duorum *sv*: duobus *Ferrarius*    11 si *om. bsv*    13 dubitantes *b*: -itatis *sv*    **7** 14 decernis . . . appellas *b*    18 inustae belli internecini (-ivi *Halm*) notae *Ferrarius*: in iusta euelli inter necti nota *s*: iniusta euelli internecuno te *tv*: iniuste belli interiectionis *b*    20 aut *add. Halm*: et *Poggius*    **8** 26 hinc *sv*    30 proludium *stv*    31 deorum *om. sv*    **9** 32 reformidat *Naugerius*: fo- *D*

only before their own benefits but before the very necessity of nourishment.[1] We must hope, Members of the Senate, that it is on the point of achievement or already achieved. But the enjoyment of that for which we hope should be reserved for the actual event. We must not appear to have grasped too hastily at the gift of the Immortal Gods or like fools to have despised the power of Fortune.

**6** But since the intimation you give sufficiently declares your views on this matter, I shall come to the dispatches of the consuls and the propraetor; but first a few words relevant to the dispatches themselves. The swords of our legions and armies have been dipped, Members of the Senate, or rather steeped in blood in two battles fought by the two consuls and a third fought by Caesar. If that blood was the blood of enemies, its shedding by our soldiers was the highest patriotism, but an abominable crime if it was the blood of fellow citizens. How long then shall this man, who has outdone all enemies in crime, go without the name of enemy? Do you wish the very blades of our soldiers to waver, uncertain whether they are plunged into an enemy or a fellow citizen? **7** You decree a Thanksgiving, but you do not use the word "enemy." Pleasing indeed will be our thanks to the Immortal Gods, pleasing our sacrificial offerings for the slaughter of a multitude of—fellow citizens! "Wicked and unscrupulous citizens"—that is what the illustrious proposer[2] calls them: terms of abuse appropriate to a city lawsuit, not brands of deadly warfare. They forge wills, no doubt, or turn out their neighbors, or defraud young men! Walkers in these and similar evil ways are customarily called "bad" or "unscrupulous." **8** War, inexpiable war, is being waged upon four consuls by the most savage brigand under the sun. He also wages war against the Senate and People of Rome. He threatens us all (though he himself is collapsing under the weight of his disasters) with destruction, devastation, and the pains of torture. He testifies that Dolabella's brutal and monstrous act, which no race of barbarians could acknowledge, was carried out on his advice. What he would have done in this city, had not Jupiter here[3] himself thrust him back from this temple and these walls, he made plain in the ruin of Parma. Its inhabitants, very loyal and respectable folk, closely attached to the authority of this House and the dignity of the Roman People, were slaughtered in the cruelest ways by that vile monster Lucius Antonius, the conspicuous target of all men's hatred, of all Gods' too, if the Gods hate whom they ought. **9** My mind recoils, Members of the Senate, and shudders to speak of what Lucius Antonius did to the wives and children of the people of Parma. The Antonii delight in having brought

---

1. Presumably an allusion to some incident involving Rome's corn supply.
2. Servilius.
3. Pointing to the statue of the god.

pitudines Antonii libenter cum dedecore subierunt, easdem per vim lae-
tantur aliis se intulisse. sed vis calamitosa est quam illis obtulerunt: libido
flagitiosa qua Antoniorum oblita est vita. est igitur quisquam qui ⟨hos⟩
hostis appellare non audeat quorum scelere crudelitatem Carthaginien-
sium victam esse fateatur? qua enim in urbe tam immanis Hannibal capta   5
quam in Parma surrepta Antonius? nisi forte huius coloniae et ceterarum
in quas eodem est animo non est hostis putandus. **10** si vero coloniarum et
municipiorum sine ulla dubitatione hostis est, quid tandem huius censetis
urbis quam ille ad explendas egestates latrocini sui concupivit, quam iam
peritus metator et callidus decempeda sua Saxa diviserat? recordamini,   10
per deos immortalis, patres conscripti, quid hoc biduo timuerimus a domesticis hostibus [id est qui intra moenia hostes sunt] rumoribus im-
probissimis dissipatis. quis liberos, quis coniugem aspicere poterat sine
fletu? quis domum, quis tecta, quis larem familiarem? aut foedissimam
mortem omnes aut miserabilem fugam cogitabant. haec a quibus time-   15
bantur, eos hostis appellare dubitamus? gravius si quis attulerit nomen,
libenter adsentiar: hoc vulgari contentus vix sum, leviore non utar.

   **11** Itaque cum supplicationes iustissimas ex eis litteris quae recitatae
sunt decernere debeamus, Serviliusque decreverit, augebo omnino numerum dierum, praesertim cum non uni, sed tribus ducibus sint decer-   20
nendae. sed hoc primum faciam ut imperatores appellem eos quorum virtute, consilio, felicitate maximis periculis servitutis atque interitus liberati sumus. etenim cui viginti his annis supplicatio decreta est ut non
imperator appellaretur aut minimis rebus gestis aut plerumque nullis?
quam ob rem aut supplicatio ab eo qui ante dixit decernenda non fuit aut   25
usitatus honos pervulgatusque tribuendus eis quibus etiam novi singula-
resque debentur. **12** an si quis Hispanorum aut Gallorum aut Thraecum
mille aut duo milia occidisset, illum hac consuetudine quae increbruit imperatorem appellaret senatus: tot legionibus caesis, tanta multitudine hostium interfecta—[dico] ita, inquam, hostium, quamvis hoc isti hostes do-   30
mestici nolint—clarissimis ducibus supplicationum honorem tribuemus,
imperatorium nomen adimemus? quanto enim honore, laetitia, gratulatione in hoc templum ingredi debent illi ipsi huius urbis liberatores, cum
hesterno die propter eorum res gestas me ovantem et prope triumphantem
populus Romanus in Capitolium domo tulerit, domum inde reduxerit!   35

2 intulerunt *bsv*    3 hos *addidi*    **10** 9 expiandas *tv*    12 id est . . . sunt *del. Fer-*
*rarius*    **11** 21 imperatores *hic Poggius, post* sumus (*l.* 23) *b*: *om. stv*    **12** 27 an] at
*stv*    28 illum *cod. CCLII Collegii Novi Oxon.*: unum *stv*: *om. b*: eum *Muretus*    30 ita
inquam *Manutius*: dico ita in- *btv*: dico in- *s*: hostium dico? ita in- *Ursinus*    31 supplicationem honorum *s*: -nem bonorum *tv*

upon others by violence the degradations to which they cheerfully submitted with infamy. But it is calamitous violence they made those people suffer; it is scandalous lust that stains the lives of the Antonii. Is there anyone who scruples to call enemies men whose crimes he will admit put the cruelty of the Carthaginians into the shade? What city taken by force did Hannibal treat so savagely as Antonius treated Parma, which he took by stealth? Perhaps he is not to be reckoned an enemy of this colony and of others toward which he is similarly disposed! 10 But if without any doubt he is an enemy of the colonies and municipalities, what is he in your judgment to this city, on which he has set greedy eyes as a means of satisfying his hungry gang and which Saxa, that skilled and crafty surveyor, had already marked out with his ten-foot rule? In the name of Heaven, Members of the Senate, remember our alarm this past two days, the product of wicked rumors spread by enemies within the gates. Who could look dry-eyed at his wife and children, or at his house or roof or Household God? All had a horrible death or a wretched flight in their thoughts. Do we hesitate to call enemies those at whose hands we feared such calamities? If anybody produces a harsher name, I will gladly agree to it. This ordinary word barely contents me. A milder one I will not use.

11 Therefore, pursuant to the dispatches which have been read, we ought to decree Thanksgivings most justly due, and since Servilius has so decreed, I shall increase the number of days, to be sure, especially as they are to be decreed not to one commander but three. First, however, I shall proceed to salute as imperators those by whose courage, judgment, and good fortune we have been preserved from the gravest perils of slavery and destruction. After all, who in twenty years past has been decreed a Thanksgiving and not been saluted as imperator, though his military achievements were minimal or often nonexistent? Accordingly, either the Thanksgiving should not have been proposed by the previous speaker, or a regular, customary honor should be accorded to those who deserve honors unprecedented and extraordinary. 12 If somebody had killed one or two thousand Spaniards or Gauls or Thracians, the Senate would salute him as imperator, following what has now become normal practice: and after the cutting to pieces of so many legions and the slaughter of such a multitude of enemies (I repeat, enemies, however much our enemies within the gates may dislike the word), shall we accord the honor of Thanksgivings to our illustrious commanders and take away the title of imperator? For with what honor, rejoicing, and congratulation should Rome's liberators enter this shrine in person, when yesterday on account of their achievements the Roman People bore me from my house to the Capitol and back again in an

**13** is enim demum est mea quidem sententia iustus triumphus ac verus,
cum bene de re publica meritis testimonium a consensu civitatis datur.
nam sive in communi gaudio populi Romani uni gratulabantur, magnum
iudicium, sive uni gratias agebant, eo maius, sive utrumque, nihil mag-
nificentius cogitari potest.　　　　　　　　　　　　　　　　　　　5
"Tu igitur ipse de te?" dixerit quispiam. equidem invitus, sed iniuriae
dolor facit me praeter consuetudinem gloriosum. nonne satis est ab hominibus virtutis ignaris gratiam bene merentibus non referri? etiam in eos
qui omnis suas curas in rei publicae salute defigunt, [impetus] crimen ⟨et⟩
invidia quaeretur? **14** scitis enim per hos dies creberrimum fuisse ser- 10
monem, me Parilibus, qui dies hodie est, cum fascibus descensurum. in
aliquem credo hoc gladiatorem aut latronem aut Catilinam esse collatum,
non in eum qui ne quid tale in re publica fieri posset effecerit. an [ut] ego,
qui Catilinam haec molientem sustulerim, everterim, adflixerim, ipse ex-
stiterim repente Catilina? quibus auspiciis istos fascis augur acciperem, 15
quatenus haberem, cui traderem? quemquamne fuisse tam sceleratum qui
hoc fingeret, tam furiosum qui crederet?
　　Unde igitur ista suspicio vel potius unde iste sermo? **15** cum, ut scitis,
hoc triduo vel quadriduo tristis a Mutina fama manaret, inflati laetitia
atque insolentia impii cives unum se in locum, ad illam curiam furiis po- 20
tius suis quam rei publicae infelicem congregabant. ibi cum consilia ini-
rent de caede nostra partirenturque inter se qui Capitolium, qui rostra,
qui urbis portas occuparent, ad me concursum futurum civitatis putabant.
quod ut cum invidia mea fieret et cum vitae etiam periculo, famam istam
fascium dissipaverunt; fascis ipsi ad me delaturi fuerunt. quod cum esset 25
quasi mea voluntate factum, tum in me impetus conductorum hominum
quasi in tyrannum parabatur; ex quo caedes esset vestrum omnium con-

**13** 2 a *del. Cobet*　　3 uni *om. s*　　5 excogitari *tv*　　6 et quidem *stv*　　9 impetus *bt*:
in peius *sv*: *del. Faërnus, Clark*　　9–10 et invidia *Clark*: inu- *bsv*: *om. t*: invidiaque *Faërnus*　　10 queretur *t*: quereretur *sv*　　**14** 11 Parilibus] per idus quintiles *bsv*　　in *om.*
*sv*　　12 collatum *Halm*: consultatum *b*: -sulatum *t*: -sultum *s*: -sulum *v*: conflatum *Busche*　　13 an *Faërnus*: an ut *D*: an vero *Clark*　　14 exsisterem *Manutius*　　16 quemquamne ς: quaequamne *s*: quamquam nec *tv*: quaequam *b*　　17 furiosum] fuit *t*: fatuum
*coni. Halm*　　18 vel] uel susum *b*¹: uel fusum *t*　　**15** 20 curiam furiis *Madvig*: furiam
uiribus *b*: cur- iuris *t*: cur- uiribus *sv*: cur- partibus *R. Klotz*　　22 rostra *Faërnus*: hostia
(os- *s*) *D*

Ovation, almost a Triumph! **13** For to my mind the true, genuine Triumph is when those who have deserved well of the Commonwealth receive the tributes of a united community. If in the shared joy of the Roman People they were congratulating an individual, that was a great mark of esteem; if they were thanking an individual, all the greater; if both, no more splendid compliment can be conceived of.

Self-applause? It is against my will, to be sure, but a sense of injury makes me vainglorious, contrary to my habit. Is it not enough that persons ignorant of the meaning of true worth make no return to the deserving? Must those who devote all their care to the preservation of the Commonwealth be targets for backbiting and envy? **14** You know that during the past few days there was a vast amount of talk that on Shepherds' Day,[4] that is today, I would come down to the Forum with rods.[5] One might suppose that such a rumor was concocted against a gladiator or a brigand or a Catiline, not against a man who has made sure that nothing of that kind can happen in the Commonwealth. Was it likely that I, who hoisted[6] and overthrew and dashed down Catiline when he made such an attempt, should suddenly reveal myself a Catiline? With what auspices should I, an augur, have accepted those rods, how long was I going to keep them, to whom should I have handed them over? It is hard to believe that anyone could be such a blackguard as to invent this tale or such a lunatic as to believe it.

So what is the origin of this suspicion, or rather this talk? **15** As you know, three or four days ago a sinister report from Mutina was circulating. Puffed up with joy and insolence, our traitors gathered together in that senate-house of theirs,[7] a place of ill omen for their own mad designs rather than for the Commonwealth. There they plotted our massacre and assigned functions among themselves—who would seize the Capitol, who the Rostra, who the city gates. They thought it likely that the community would rally to me, so in order to bring me into odium or even peril of my life if that should happen, they spread this rumor about the rods. They were going to offer me the rods themselves, and when it was done as though with my blessing, an attack upon me by a hired gang was planned, as if upon a despot. A massacre of the whole

---

4. Parilia or Palilia (Feast of Pales, the shepherds' god) on 21 April.

5. *Fasces*, symbol of magisterial power (*imperium*). Cicero would in effect be proclaiming a dictatorship.

6. *Sustulerim* could mean "removed." But I think the three verbs refer to successive stages in the overturning of a statue.

7. As generally supposed, the Curia Pompeii, where Caesar was assassinated. But how should the plotters meet in such a place? Cicero is speaking figuratively, referring to a private meeting place, perhaps Calenus' house. *Infelicem* may mean no more than "unlucky," i.e. likely to prove so, but probably alludes to something specific in the history of the locality.

secuta. quae res ⟨non⟩ patefecit, patres conscripti, sed suo tempore totius huius sceleris fons aperietur. **16** itaque P. Apuleius, tribunus plebis, meorum omnium consiliorum periculorumque iam inde a consulatu meo testis, conscius, adiutor, dolorem ferre non potuit doloris mei: contionem habuit maximam populo Romano unum atque idem sentiente. in qua contione cum me pro summa nostra coniunctione et familiaritate liberare suspicione fascium vellet, una voce cuncta contio declaravit nihil esse a me umquam de re publica nisi optime cogitatum. post hanc habitam contionem duabus tribusve horis optatissimi nuntii et litterae venerunt: ut idem dies non modo iniquissima me invidia liberarit sed etiam celeberrima populi Romani gratulatione auxerit.

**17** Haec interposui, patres conscripti, non tam ut pro me dicerem— male enim mecum ageretur si parum vobis essem sine defensione purgatus—quam ut quosdam nimis ieiuno animo et angusto monerem, id quod semper ipse fecissem, uti excellentium civium virtutem imitatione dignam, non invidia putarent. magnus est in re publica campus, ut sapienter dicere M. Crassus solebat, multis apertus cursus ad laudem. utinam quidem illi principes viverent qui me post meum consulatum, cum eis ipse cederem, principem non inviti videbant! hoc vero tempore in tanta inopia constantium et fortium consularium quo me dolore adfici creditis, cum alios male sentire, alios nihil omnino curare videam, alios parum constanter in suscepta causa permanere sententiamque suam non semper utilitate rei publicae, sed tum spe tum timore moderari? **18** quod si quis de contentione principatus laborat, quae nulla esse debet, stultissime facit, si vitiis cum virtute contendit; ut enim cursu cursus, sic in viris fortibus virtus virtute superatur. tu, si ego de re publica optime sentiam, ut me vincas, ipse pessime senties? aut, si ad me bonorum concursum fieri videbis, ad te improbos invitabis? nollem, primum rei publicae causa, deinde etiam dignitatis tuae. sed si principatus ageretur, quem numquam expetivi, quid tandem mihi esset optatius? ego enim malis sententiis vinci non possum, bonis forsitan possim et libenter.

5

10

15

20

25

30

1 quae] quod *coni. Clark*     non³ *addidi*     totiusque *tv*     **16** 10 liberarit *Manutius*: -aret *D*     **17** 12 dicerem *Naugerius*: dixerim *D*     17 dicere M. *Clark*: dicerem *t*: -re *bsv*: -re L. *coni. Halm*     23 tum spe tum *Halm* (cum spe tum *Naugerius*): tum spectum *t*: conspecto *bsv*     **18** 27 aut] nam *t*: num *coni. Clark, inutiliter*     bonorum ad me *t*     28 nolim *Ernesti*     30 esset *om. t*

Senate would have been the next stage. These plans, Members of the Senate, were not revealed in operation, but when the time is ripe the source[8] of all this villainy will be disclosed. **16** And so, Tribune of the Plebs Publius Apuleius, who has been witness, confidant, and helper in all my counsels and dangers from my consulship onwards, could not bear the distress he felt for my distress. He held a great assembly, at which the Roman People was completely of one mind. When he there tried to exonerate me from the suspicion about the rods, as our close attachment and friendship made appropriate, the whole meeting declared with one voice that I had never had any but the most loyal thoughts concerning the Commonwealth. Two or three hours after the meeting came the news and dispatches we were praying for. Thus the same day not only relieved me of a most unjust odium but exalted me by the congratulations[9] of the Roman People in vast numbers.

**17** I have put in these remarks, Members of the Senate, not so much in self-justification (I should be in a bad way if I needed any defense to clear myself with you) as by way of warning certain mean and petty-minded persons that they should regard the merit of outstanding citizens as deserving imitation, not envy, as I have always done. Public life is a broad field, in Marcus Crassus'[10] wise words, and the path to glory is open to many. I only wish those leaders of the community were still alive who after my consulship saw me in a position of leadership not unwillingly, though I myself gave them prior place. But today, when we are so badly off for brave and resolute consulars, what distress do you think I feel when I see some disloyal, others totally indifferent, others not persevering resolutely enough in the cause they have embraced and not always regulating their views by the public advantage but sometimes by hope and sometimes by fear! **18** If, however, anybody is concerned about rivalry for leadership, which ought not to exist, he is very foolish if he competes with merit by means of demerit. As speed is overcome by speed, so, when brave men are rivals, merit is overcome by merit. If I am a good patriot, will you[11] be a bad one in order to get the better of me? If you see honest men rally to me, will you invite rascals to join you? I wish it were not so, first for the sake of the Commonwealth, and also, secondly, for the sake of your reputation. But if leadership, which I have never sought, were the issue, what would suit me better? I cannot be bested by bad proposals, but perhaps I could by good ones—and gladly.

---

8. Calenus?

9. Or perhaps better, "thanks."

10. A praenomen is needed to distinguish the orator L. Crassus from the triumvir M. Crassus. The choice is uncertain, but *t*'s reading favors the latter.

11. Addressing Calenus.

**19** Haec populum Romanum videre, animadvertere, iudicare quidam moleste ferunt. poteratne fieri ut non proinde homines ⟨de⟩ quoque ut quisque mereretur iudicarent? ut enim de universo senatu populus Romanus verissime iudicat nullis rei publicae temporibus hunc ordinem firmiorem aut fortiorem fuisse, sic de uno quoque nostrum et maxime qui   5 hoc loco sententias dicimus sciscitantur omnes, avent audire quid quisque senserit, ita de quoque ut quemque meritum arbitrantur existimant. **20** memoria tenent me ante diem xiii[i] Kalendas Ianuarias principem revocandae libertatis fuisse; me ex Kalendis Ianuariis ad hanc horam invigilasse rei publicae; meam domum measque auris dies noctesque omnium prae-   10 ceptis monitisque patuisse; meis litteris, meis nuntiis, meis cohortationibus omnis qui ubique essent ad patriae praesidium excitatos; meis sententiis a Kalendis Ianuariis numquam legatos ad Antonium, semper illum hostem, semper hoc bellum, ut ego, qui omni tempore verae pacis auctor fuissem, huic essem nomini pestiferae pacis inimicus; **21** idem Venti-   15 dium, cum alii praetorem, ego semper hostem. has in sententias meas si consules [designati] discessionem facere voluissent, omnibus istis latronibus auctoritate ipsa senatus iam pridem de manibus arma cecidissent.

Sed quod tum non licuit, patres conscripti, id hoc tempore non solum licet verum etiam necesse est, eos qui re sunt hostes verbis notari, senten-   20 tiis nostris hostis iudicari. **22** antea cum hostem ac bellum nominassem, semel et saepius sententiam meam de numero sententiarum sustulerunt: quod in hac causa fieri iam non potest. ex litteris enim C. Pansae A. Hirti consulum, C. Caesaris pro praetore, de honore dis immortalibus habendo sententias dicimus. supplicationem modo qui decrevit, idem imprudens   25 hostis iudicavit; numquam enim in civili bello supplicatio decreta est. decretam dico? ne victoris quidem litteris postulata est. **23** civile bellum consul Sulla gessit, legionibus in urbem adductis quos voluit expulit, quos potuit occidit: supplicationis mentio nulla. grave bellum Octavianum insecutum est: supplicatio nulla victori. Cinnae victoriam imperator   30 ultus est Sulla: nulla supplicatio decreta a senatu. ad te ipsum, P. Servili, num misit ullas collega litteras de illa calamitosissima pugna Pharsalia? num te de supplicatione voluit referre? profecto noluit. at misit postea de

**19** 2 perinde *bsv*    de *add. Ferrarius*    7 de quoque] diu q- *s*: de uno q- *v*    **20** 8 xiii *Budaeus*: xiiii *D*    10 et noctes *bs*: n- *v*    **21** 15 r. (= require) uentidium *tv*: P. Ve-*Ferrarius*    16 cum alii praetorem *Garatoni*: cum alii p. r. t. r. uolusenum *b*: cum aliis tr. pl. uol- *t*: cum aliis tr. pl. uoluisse unum *s*: cum alii tr. pl. uoluissent num *v*    17 consules *Manutius*: gg. *t*: coss. designati *bsv*    20 verbis notari *del. Pluygers*    **22** 21 ac] aut *bsv*    23 fieri iam (*cf. Rosc. Am. 150* id quod fieri profecto non potest)] iam f- *t*: f-*s*    25 diximus *sv*    **23** 30 supplicatio cinnae nulla *btv*    uictoris *bsv*    31–32 seruili, num] -ilium *stv*    32–33 Pharsalia? num *Halm* (-ica? num *iam Orelli*): parsalie num *bs*: pars alienum *tv*

**19** Some folk are annoyed because the Roman People sees and notices and judges what goes on. Was it not inevitable that the public judge each of us according to his deserts? The Roman People judges very truly of the Senate as a whole that never in its history has this House shown itself braver and more resolute. In the same way everyone asks questions about each individual among us and especially about those who speak in the first rank.[12] They are eager to hear what line each of us has taken, and they estimate each of us as they think he has deserved. **20** They remember that on the twentieth of December I led the recovery of freedom; that from the Kalends of January up to this hour I have watched over the Commonwealth; that my house and my ears have been open day and night to the advice and warnings of all; that my letters, my messages, my encouragements roused all and sundry, wherever they might be, to come to the aid of our country; that in this House ever since the Kalends of January I have never countenanced embassies to Antonius,[13] but always called him an enemy and this conflict a war, so that I, who have at all times striven for true peace, was hostile to this name of a pernicious peace; **21** that I likewise always called Ventidius an enemy when others called him a praetor. If the consuls had chosen to call a vote on these proposals of mine, the authority of the Senate would of itself long ago have caused the weapons to drop from all those brigands' hands.

But what could not be done then, Members of the Senate, not only can but must be done now. Those who are enemies in fact must be branded such in words, declared enemies by our votes. **22** Previously when I used the terms "enemy" and "war," they repeatedly removed my motion from the list; that is impossible in the present case. Pursuant to dispatches from Consuls Gaius Pansa and Aulus Hirtius and Propraetor Gaius Caesar we are delivering our views on an honor to be paid to the Immortal Gods. The gentleman who just proposed a Thanksgiving has in so doing and unbeknown to himself declared them enemies; for no Thanksgiving has ever been voted in a civil war. I say "voted," but none has ever been asked for in the victor's dispatch. **23** Sulla as consul fought a civil war; he marched his legions into Rome, banished whom he chose, killed whom he could: no mention of a Thanksgiving. A major war, the war of Octavius, came next: no Thanksgiving voted to the victor. Sulla as imperator avenged Cinna's victory: no Thanksgiving voted by the Senate. You yourself, Publius Servilius—did your colleague[14] send you any dispatch concerning the disastrous battle of Pharsalia or want you to refer to the Senate concerning a Thanksgiving? Of course not. But he sent one subsequently

---

12. Lit. "in this position," i.e. as consulars. Senators did not sit in any fixed order.
13. Not literally true; see Philippic 12.
14. Caesar and Servilius were consuls in 48.

Alexandria, de Pharnace: Pharsaliae vero pugnae ne triumphum quidem
egit. eos enim civis pugna illa sustulerat quibus non modo vivis sed etiam
victoribus incolumis et florens civitas esse posset. **24** quod idem con-
tigerat superioribus bellis civilibus. nam mihi consuli supplicatio nullis
armis sumptis non ob caedem hostium, sed ob conservationem civium    5
novo et inaudito genere decreta est. quam ob rem aut supplicatio re publica pulcherrime gesta postulantibus nostris imperatoribus deneganda
est, quod praeter A. Gabinium contigit nemini, aut supplicatione decernenda hostis eos de quibus decernitis iudicetis necesse est.

Quod ergo ille re, id ego etiam verbo, cum imperatores eos appello:   10
hoc ipso nomine et eos qui iam devicti sunt et eos qui supersunt hostis
iudico [cum victores appello imperatores]. **25** quo modo enim potius
Pansam appellem, etsi habet honoris nomen amplissimi; quo Hirtium? est
ille quidem consul, sed alterum nomen benefici populi Romani est, alterum virtutis atque victoriae. quid? Caesarem, deorum beneficio rei pu-   15
blicae procreatum, dubitemne appellare imperatorem? qui primus Antoni
immanem et foedam crudelitatem non solum a iugulis nostris sed etiam a
membris et visceribus avertit.

Unius autem diei quot et quantae virtutes, di immortales, fuerunt!
**26** princeps enim omnium Pansa proeli faciendi et cum Antonio con-   20
fligendi fuit; dignus imperator legione Martia, digna legio imperatore.
cuius si acerrimum impetum cohibere Pansa potuisset, uno proelio confecta res esset. sed cum libertatis avida legio effrenatius in aciem hostium
irrupisset ipseque in primis Pansa pugnaret, duobus periculosis vul-
neribus acceptis sublatus e proelio rei publicae vitam reservavit. ego vero   25
hunc non solum imperatorem sed etiam clarissimum imperatorem iudico,
qui, cum aut morte aut victoria se satis facturum rei publicae spopon-
disset, alterum fecit, alterius di immortales omen avertant!

**27** Quid dicam de Hirtio? qui re audita e castris duas legiones eduxit
incredibili studio atque virtute, quartam illam quae relicto Antonio se   30
olim cum Martia legione coniunxit, et septimam quae constituta ex veteranis docuit hoc proelio militibus eis qui Caesaris beneficia servassent
senatus populique Romani carum nomen esse. his viginti cohortibus,

**24** 5 sumptis *om. t*    6–7 ob res r. p. pulcherrime gestas *b*: ob r. p. pul- ges- (ges- *om. s*)
*sv*    8 A.] ea *b*: *om. sv*    12 cum . . . imperatores *del. Ferrarius*    **25** 18 avertit]
*posthac deficit t*    19 quot] quae *s*    **27** 32 hoc] illo *codd. Ferrarii*

concerning Alexandria and another concerning Pharnaces.[15] For the battle of
Pharsalia he did not celebrate a Triumph either. For if the citizens whom that
battle took away had lived, or even if they had been victorious, the community
could have survived and prospered. **24** That was likewise the case in previous
civil wars. As for the Thanksgiving voted to me as consul,[16] there had been no
resort to arms and the vote was not on account of the slaughter of enemies but
of the preservation of citizens, a proceeding altogether without precedent.
Therefore, you must either refuse a Thanksgiving to our commanders for their
splendid successes when they are asking for it, something that has never
happened to anybody except Aulus Gabinius,[17] or by decreeing a Thanksgiving you necessarily declare enemies those to whom your decree refers.

Therefore, when I salute our commanders as imperators, I am saying in
words what Servilius is saying in fact. By this very title I declare enemies both
those already finally vanquished and those who remain. **25** How better should
I address Pansa, though he bears the title of our highest office of state? Or
Hirtius? He is consul, to be sure, but that title came as the gift of the Roman
People, this is the meed of valor and victory. What of Caesar, him who was
engendered for the Commonwealth by the favor of the Gods? Should I hesitate
to salute him as imperator—Caesar, who was the first to turn Antonius' foul,
monstrous cruelty aside from our throats, nay, from our limbs and vitals?

Immortal Gods, how many and how great were the deeds of valor which a
single day brought forth! **26** Pansa was first among them all to join battle and
clash with Antonius: a commander worthy of the Martian Legion, as the legion
is worthy of its commander. And if Pansa had been able to check their
passionate onslaught, the issue would have been settled in a single engagement. But in their eagerness for freedom the legion broke too impetuously into
the enemy's lines. Pansa himself, fighting among the foremost, received two
dangerous wounds and was removed from the field to reserve his life for the
Commonwealth. I declare him not only imperator but a most illustrious imperator. He had pledged himself to do his duty to the Commonwealth by either
death or victory. He has achieved the one. As for the other, may the Immortal
Gods avert the omen!

**27** What shall I say of Hirtius? When the report reached him, he led two
legions out of camp with remarkable zeal and energy: the Fourth, which earlier
on had abandoned Antonius and joined the Martian Legion, and the Seventh,
made up of veterans, who showed in this battle that those soldiers who had
kept Caesar's bounties hold dear the name of the Senate and People of Rome.

15. His victories in Egypt and Pontus in 47.
16. On 3 December 63.
17. In 56; see my note on *Q. fr.* 2.7(6).1.

nullo equitatu, Hirtius ipse aquilam quartae legionis cum inferret, qua
nullius pulchriorem speciem imperatoris accepimus, cum tribus Antoni
legionibus equitatuque conflixit, hostisque nefarios, huic Iovi⟨s Optimi⟩
Maximi ceterisque deorum immortalium templis, urbis tectis, libertati
populi Romani, nostrae vitae sanguinique imminentis prostravit, fudit,　　5
occidit, ut cum admodum paucis, nocte tectus, metu perterritus, princeps
latronum duxque fugerit. o solem ipsum beatissimum qui, ante quam se
abderet, stratis cadaveribus parricidarum cum paucis fugientem vidit
Antonium!

　　**28** An vero quisquam dubitabit appellare Caesarem imperatorem?　　10
aetas eius certe ab hac sententia neminem deterrebit, quando quidem virtute superavit aetatem. ac mihi semper eo maiora beneficia C. Caesaris
visa sunt quo minus erant ab aetate illa postulanda: cui cum imperium
dabamus, eodem tempore etiam spem eius nominis deferebamus; quod
cum es⟨se⟩t consecutus, auctoritatem decreti nostri rebus gestis suis com-　　15
probavit. hic ergo adulescens maximi animi, ut verissime scribit Hirtius,
castra multarum legionum paucis cohortibus tutatus est secundumque
proelium fecit. ita trium imperatorum virtute, consilio, felicitate uno die
locis pluribus res publica est conservata. **29** decerno igitur eorum trium
nomine quinquaginta dierum supplicationes: causas, ut honorificentis-　　20
simis verbis consequi potuero, complectar ipsa sententia.

　　Est autem fidei pietatisque nostrae declarare fortissimis militibus quam
memores simus quamque grati. quam ob rem promissa nostra atque ea
quae legionibus bello confecto tributuros nos spopondimus hodierno senatu consulto renovanda censeo; aequum est enim militum, talium prae-　　25
sertim, honorem coniungi. **30** atque utinam, patres conscripti, protinus
omnibus solvere nobis praemia liceret! quamquam nos ea quae promisimus studiose cumulata reddemus. sed id quidem restat, ut spero, victoribus, quibus senatus fides praestabitur: quam quoniam difficillimo rei
publicae tempore secuti sunt, eos numquam oportebit consili sui paeni-　　30
tere. sed facile est bene agere cum eis a quibus etiam tacentibus flagitari
videmur: illud admirabilius et maius maximeque proprium senatus sapientis est, grata eorum virtutem memoria prosequi qui pro patria vitam
profuderunt. **31** quorum de honore utinam mihi plura in mentem venirent!
duo certe non praeteribo quae maxime occurrunt: quorum alterum per-　　35

---

3–4 Iovis Optimi Maximi *Muretus*: ioui marti *v*: ioui m. *s*: ioui *b*　　　**28** 14 etiam *Fer-*
*rarius*: et *D*　　　15 esset *coni. Halm*: est *D*　　　**29** 23 simus *ed. Romana*: sumus *D*　　　**30**
26 protinus[3] *scripsi*: ciuibus *D*: *del. Pluygers*　　　28 cumulata *P. Laetus*: quam multa *b*:
quamquam m- *v*: cumulata . . . praestabitur *om. s*: atque cumulate *Halm*　　　29 quam
quoniam *Orelli*: quamquam *b*[1]: quamquam id *svb*[2]: quam cum *Naugerius*　　　33 grata
eorum *idem*: gr̄e horum *b*: gratiarum *s*

374

With these twenty cohorts and no cavalry, Hirtius himself bore forward the eagle of the Fourth Legion. History has no finer picture of an imperator to show. He clashed with the three legions and cavalry of Antonius. Those wicked enemies, who were threatening this temple of Jupiter Best and Greatest and the other temples of the Immortal Gods, the roofs of Rome, the liberty of the Roman People, and our lives and lifeblood, them he laid low, routed them, slew them. The chief and leader of the bandits fled in a panic under cover of darkness with a very few companions. Happiest of days! That sun, before his setting, saw Antonius and a few others in flight over a field strewn with the carcasses of traitors.

**28** Or will anyone hesitate to salute Caesar as imperator? Assuredly his age will deter no one from so doing, since he has surpassed his age with his valor. I have always rated what we owe to Gaius Caesar all the higher the less it was to be expected from one of his years. When we were giving him military command, we were at the same time holding out to him the prospect of that title. Having obtained it,[18] he confirmed the authority of our decree by his own exploits. This young man of the highest spirit, as Hirtius most truly writes, defended a camp of many legions with a few cohorts and fought a successful engagement. Thus by the courage, judgment, and good fortune of three imperators in the course of a single day and in different areas the Commonwealth was preserved. **29** Therefore I move a Thanksgiving of fifty days in the name of the three. The grounds I shall embrace in my motion, in the most laudatory terms I can command.

Further, in good faith and gratitude, we should declare to our brave soldiers how mindful we are, and how sensible, of what we owe them. Therefore I propose that our promises and all we pledged ourselves to do for the legions after the conclusion of hostilities be renewed in today's senatorial decree. It is only fair that the soldiers, especially such soldiers as these, be honored along with their commanders. **30** I only wish, Members of the Senate, that it were possible for us to pay their rewards to all of them straightaway; not but that we shall zealously discharge the promises we have made, and with interest. But that awaits the victors, I hope. The Senate's word to them will be kept. Since they trusted that word in a very grave crisis of the Commonwealth, they must never regret their decision. But it is easy to deal fairly with men who seem to demand it even though they do not open their mouths. What is a more admirable and a greater thing, and one peculiarly fitting for a wise Senate, is to accompany with grateful memory the valor of those who have laid down their lives for their country. **31** I only wish I could think of more ways to do them honor. At least I shall not omit the two ways which most readily occur to me.

---

18. The command (*imperium*), not the title.

tinet ad virorum fortissimorum gloriam sempiternam, alterum ad lenien-
dum maerorem et luctum proximorum.

Placet igitur mihi, patres conscripti, legionis Martiae militibus et eis
qui una pugnantes occiderint monumentum fieri quam amplissimum.

Magna atque incredibilia sunt in rem publicam huius merita legionis.  5
haec se prima latrocinio abrupit Antoni; haec tenuit Albam; haec se ad
Caesarem contulit; hanc imitata quarta legio parem virtutis gloriam con-
secuta est. quarta victrix desiderat neminem: ex Martia non nulli in ipsa
victoria conciderunt. o fortunata mors quae naturae debita pro patria est
potissimum reddita! **32** vos vero patriae natos iudico; quorum etiam no-  10
men a Marte est, ut idem deus urbem hanc gentibus, vos huic urbi ge-
nuisse videatur. in fuga foeda mors est; in victoria gloriosa. etenim Mars
ipse ex acie fortissimum quemque pignerari solet. illi igitur impii quos
cecidistis etiam ad inferos poenas parricidi luent; vos vero qui extremum
spiritum in victoria effudistis piorum estis sedem et locum consecuti.  15
brevis a natura vita nobis data est; at memoria bene redditae vitae sempiterna. quae si non esset longior quam haec vita, quis esset tam amens
qui maximis laboribus et periculis ad summam laudem gloriamque
contenderet?

**33** Actum igitur praeclare vobiscum, fortissimi, dum vixistis, nunc  20
vero etiam sanctissimi milites, quod vestra virtus neque oblivione eorum
qui nunc sunt nec reticentia posterorum sepulta esse poterit, cum vobis
immortale monumentum suis paene manibus senatus populusque Romanus exstruxerit. multi saepe exercitus Punicis, Gallicis, Italicis bellis
clari et magni fuerunt, nec tamen ullis tale genus honoris tributum est.  25
atque utinam maiora possemus, quando quidem a vobis maxima accepimus! vos ab urbe furentem Antonium avertistis; vos redire molientem
reppulistis. erit igitur exstructa moles opere magnifico incisaeque litterae,
divinae virtutis testes sempiternae, numquamque de vobis eorum qui aut
videbunt vestrum monumentum aut audient gratissimus sermo conti-  30
cescet. ita pro mortali condicione vitae immortalitatem estis consecuti.

**34** Sed quoniam, patres conscripti, gloriae munus optimis et fortissimis civibus monumenti honore persolvitur, consolemur eorum proximos,
quibus optima est haec quidem consolatio: parentibus, quod tanta rei
publicae praesidia genuerunt; liberis, quod habebunt domestica exempla  35
virtutis; coniugibus, quod eis viris carebunt, quos laudare quam lugere
praestabit; fratribus, quod in se ut corporum, sic virtutis similitudinem

---

**31** 4 occiderunt *s*    9 est] sit *coni. Halm*    **32** 14 occidistis ς    16 uobis *bv*    sem-
piterna] perpetua *s*    **33** 22 insepulta *sv*    **34** 37 uirtutum *sv*

One of them relates to the everlasting glory of these heroes, the other to alleviating the grief and lamentation of their families.

I therefore think proper, Members of the Senate, that a monument on the most splendid scale be erected to the soldiers of the Martian Legion and to those who fell fighting at their side.

Great and extraordinary are the services of this legion to the Commonwealth. This legion was the first to sever itself from Antonius' brigand company; this held Alba; this joined Caesar. Following its example the Fourth Legion won equal glory for its manly conduct. The conquering Fourth has not lost a man. Of the Martian, some fell in the hour of victory. Death, our debt to nature, is fortunate indeed when it is paid for country's sake. **32** But you I declare were born for your country, you whose very name is from Mars, so that the same God may be said to have given birth to this city for the world and to you for this city. Death in flight is shameful, in victory glorious. Mars himself often takes the bravest in the battle line for his own. Those traitors you killed will pay for their crime even in the world below; whereas you who breathed your last in victory have attained to the dwelling place of pious souls. Brief is the life granted us by nature, but the memory of a life nobly sacrificed is eternal. If it lasted no longer than this present life, who would be mad enough to strive after highest praise and glory at the cost of most grievous toils and perils?

**33** Well therefore has it gone with you, soldiers most gallant while you lived, and now also most revered. Your valor can never be buried in the oblivion of the living or the silence of posterity, for the Senate and People of Rome will raise for you, I might almost say with their own hands, an immortal memorial. Many armies were great and famous in the Punic, Gallic, and Italian wars, but to none was paid an honor of this kind. Would that we could do more, since from you we have received so much! You turned Antonius in his fury away from Rome. You repelled him as he was getting ready to return. Therefore a magnificent structure will be raised with an inscription which will bear eternal witness to your godlike valor; and the tongues of them that shall see or hear of your monument shall never cease to talk of you in profound gratitude. Thus in return for mortal life you have won immortality.

**34** But since, Members of the Senate, their due gift of glory is paid to our loyal and gallant countrymen by the honor of a monument, let us try to console their kinsfolk. The best consolation is this: to their parents, that they gave birth to such bulwarks of the Commonwealth; to their children, that they will have examples of courage in their own families; to their wives, that the husbands they have lost will be better praised than mourned; to their brothers, that they will be confident of resembling them in valor as well as in bodily appearance.

esse confident. atque utinam his omnibus abstergere fletum sententiis nostris consultisque possemus, vel aliqua talis eis adhiberi publice posset oratio qua deponerent maerorem atque luctum gauderentque potius, cum multa et varia impenderent hominibus genera mortis, id genus quod esset pulcherrimum suis obtigisse eosque nec inhumatos esse nec desertos, 5 quod tamen ipsum pro patria non miserandum putatur, nec dispersis bustis humili sepultura crematos, sed contectos publicis operibus atque muneribus eaque exstructione quae sit ad memoriam aeternitatis ara Virtutis. **35** quam ob rem maximum quidem solacium ⟨erit⟩ propinquorum eodem monumento declarari et virtutem suorum et populi Romani pieta- 10 tem et senatus fidem et crudelissimi memoriam belli: in quo nisi tanta militum virtus exstitisset, parricidio M. Antoni nomen populi Romani occidisset.

Atque etiam censeo, patres conscripti, quae praemia militibus promisimus nos re publica recuperata tributuros, ea vivis victoribusque cumu- 15 late, cum tempus venerit, persolvenda; qui autem ex eis quibus illa promissa sunt pro patria occiderunt, eorum parentibus, liberis, coniugibus, fratribus eadem tribuenda censeo.

**36** Sed ut ⟨omnia⟩ aliquando sententia complectar, ita censeo:

"Cum C. Pansa consul, imperator, initium cum hostibus confligendi 20 fecerit, quo proelio legio Martia admirabili incredibilique virtute libertatem populi Romani defenderit, quod idem legiones tironum fecerint; ipseque C. Pansa consul, imperator, cum inter media hostium tela versaretur, vulnera acceperit, cumque A. Hirtius consul, imperator, proelio audito, re cognita, fortissimo praestantissimoque animo exercitum castris 25 eduxerit impetumque in M. Antonium exercitumque hostium fecerit eiusque copias occidione occiderit, suo exercitu ita incolumi ut ne unum quidem militem desiderarit, **37** cumque C. Caesar ⟨pro praetore⟩, imperator, consilio diligentiaque sua castra feliciter defenderit copiasque hostium quae ad castra accesserant profligarit, occiderit: ob eas res senatum 30 existimare et iudicare eorum trium imperatorum virtute, imperio, consilio, gravitate, constantia, magnitudine animi, felicitate populum Romanum foedissima crudelissimaque servitute liberatum; cumque rem publicam, urbem, templa deorum immortalium, bona fortunasque omnium liberosque conservarint dimicatione et periculo vitae suae, uti ob 35

1–2 sententiis nostris atque consultis fletum *b*    3 oratio] consolatio *coni. Burman*    **35** 9 maximum quidem ς: q- m- *D*    erit *add. Poggius*    erit illud quidem max- sol- *coni. Halm, fort. recte*    10 et (*alt.*) . . . pietatem] et etatem *sv*    11–12 militum nisi tanta *b*    **36** 19 omnia *addidi* (*cf.* 14.29, 3.14 *init.*)    sententiam ς    24–25 proelio audito *del. Pluygers*: re cognita *delere voluit C. F. W. Müller*    praesentissimo *vellem*    27 occisione *sv*    **37** 28 pro pr. *add. P. Laetus*    29 feliciter ς: -icia *D*

Would that we could wipe away the tears of all of these by our motions and decrees, or that a public oration could be made to them such as might persuade them to lay aside lamentation and mourning and rather rejoice that among the various forms of death which hang over men's heads, the fairest of all should have befallen their kinsfolk; and that those they loved are not unburied and forsaken, though even that is accounted no pitiable fate if it is for country's sake, nor yet burnt with humble obsequies and placed in scattered graves; no, they will lie beneath a public work publicly presented, a structure which to all eternity shall be an altar of Valor. **35** Therefore it will be the relatives' greatest consolation that by the same monument is declared the valor of their kin, the gratitude of the Roman People, the good faith of the Senate, and the memory of a most brutal war, a war in which, but for the signal valor of our soldiers, the name of the Roman People would have perished by Marcus Antonius' treason.

I further move, Members of the Senate, that the rewards which we promised to bestow upon the soldiers after the Commonwealth had been regained are to be paid to them, living and victorious, with interest when the time comes. To the parents, children, wives, and brothers of those to whom these promises were made and who have died for their country I move that the same be paid.

**36** Let me then finally embrace all this in a motion. I move as follows:

"Forasmuch as Gaius Pansa, Consul and Imperator, did commence battle with the enemy, in which battle the Martian Legion defended the freedom of the Roman People with wonderful and incredible valor, as did also the legions newly recruited; and forasmuch as Gaius Pansa, Consul and Imperator, did himself receive wounds in the thick of combat; and forasmuch as Aulus Hirtius, Consul and Imperator, on report of the engagement and cognizance of the situation, did with exceptional gallantry lead out his army from camp and attack Marcus Antonius and his army and cut them to pieces without the loss of a single man from his own ranks; **37** and forasmuch as Gaius Caesar, Propraetor and Imperator, by skillful and prudent generalship did successfully defend his camp, putting to rout and slaughter such enemy forces as approached the position: therefore that this House judge and pronounce that by the courage, ordinance, skill, steadfastness, resolution, devotion, and fortune of the three said commanders the Roman People has been freed from most cruel and degrading servitude. And forasmuch, further, as in combat and hazard of their lives they have preserved the Commonwealth, the city of Rome, the temples of the Immortal Gods, and the property, estate, and children of us all; in honor of the said courageous and successful actions that Gaius

eas res bene, fortiter feliciterque gestas C. Pansa A. Hirtius consules, imperatores, alter ambove, aut si aberunt, M. Cornutus, praetor urbanus,
supplicationes per dies quinquaginta ad omnia pulvinaria constituat:
**38** cumque virtus legionum digna clarissimis imperatoribus exstiterit,
senatum, quae sit antea pollicitus legionibus exercitibusque nostris, ea     5
summo studio re publica recuperata persoluturum; cumque legio Martia
princeps cum hostibus conflixerit, atque ita cum maiore numero hostium
contenderit ut plurimos caederent, caderent non nulli, cumque sine ulla
retractatione pro patria vitam profuderint; cumque simili virtute reliquarum legionum milites pro salute et libertate populi Romani mortem    10
oppetiverint, senatui placere ut C. Pansa A. Hirtius consules, imperatores, alter ambove, si eis videatur, eis qui sanguinem pro vita, libertate,
fortunis populi Romani, pro urbe, templis deorum immortalium profudis-
sent monumentum quam amplissimum locandum faciendumque ⟨curent:
quaestoresque⟩ urbanos ad eam rem pecuniam dare, attribuere, solvere    15
iubeant, ut testetur ad memoriam posteritatis sempiternam scelus crude-
lissimorum hostium militumque divinam virtutem; utique, quae praemia
senatus militibus ante constituit, ea solvantur eorum qui hoc bello pro patria occiderunt parentibus, liberis, coniugibus, fratribus, eisque tribuan-
tur quae militibus ipsis tribui oporteret, si vivi vicissent qui morte    20
vicerunt."

**38** 6 persoluturum *Manutius*: sol- *b*: resol- *sv*     cumque *ed. Romana*: quod *D*     8 ut
*Ferrarius*: cum *D*: ut cum *Halm*     caderent nonnulli ς: cadere nonnullos *bv*: caederent
nulli *s*     14–15 curent *add. Ferrarius*     15 quaestoresque urbanos *A. Augustinus et
Garatoni*: urbem *D*     16 testetur *Madvig*: exstet *D*     ad scelus *sv*     17 diuina uirtus
*b*     19 fratribus, eisque *Ferrarius*: fratribus hisque (eaque *s²*) fratribus *s¹v*: fr- *b*     20
vivi vicissent *Ernesti*: illi uici- (uixi- *s²*) *D*

Pansa and Aulus Hirtius, Consuls and Imperators, either one or both, or in their absence Marcus Cornutus, City Praetor, institute a public Thanksgiving, for the period of fifty days in every place of worship.[19] **38** And forasmuch, further, as the legions have shown valor worthy of their illustrious commanders: that the Senate on the restoration of public order shall discharge with all zeal the promises previously made to our legions and armies. And forasmuch as the Martian Legion took the lead in engaging the enemy, and, fighting against odds, lost certain of their own number while inflicting heavy losses on their adversaries, sacrificing their lives for their country with no backward thought; and forasmuch as soldiers of the remaining legions died no less gallantly for the safety and liberty of the Roman People: that it please this House that Gaius Pansa and Aulus Hirtius, Consuls and Imperators, either one or both, if they see fit, make provision and contract for the erection of a monument on the grandest scale to those who have shed their blood for the life, liberty, and estate of the Roman People, for the City of Rome, and for the temples of the Immortal Gods; and that they direct the City Quaestors to give, assign, and pay monies for the said monument, to the end that it bear eternal testimony before posterity both to the wickedness of our savage foes and to the noble valor of our own men. Further, that the gratuities which this House has previously authorized to the soldiers of the Republic be paid to the parents, children, wives, or brothers of those who died for their country in this war; and that these receive what the men themselves should have received, had they lived victorious who for victory died."

---

19. Lit. "at every *pulvinar*" (cf. Philippic 2 n. 103), placed outside the various temples.

.

# TEXTUAL APPENDIX

1.11 *minus frequentes.* A rather disconcerting sequence. Both the first two rhetorical questions linked by *an* constitute excuses for Cicero's absence from the meeting: he was not the only absentee; attendance was not particularly thin (so he was not needed). But on the face of it they go opposite ways. *Magis* for *minus* would make the second question reinforce the first.

1.14 *consularis.* Fedeli, reading *consulari*, cites Clark, *CR* 14 (1900) 403, who took it as ablative, "worthy of a consul." Any ordinary reader would take it as a dative, agreeing with *Pisoni*, which makes sense, but not the sense required. And Cicero's point is not that none of the consulars said anything worthy of a consul, but that none of them said anything at all in Piso's support. Taken as Clark understood it, *consulari* would inevitably be applied also to *vultu*, which is slightly comic.

1.15 *fecistis adhuc.* Either order is Ciceronian; cf. 13.22 *ut adhuc fecistis, me attente audiatis, Verr.* 2.4.102 *diligenter, sicut adhuc fecistis, attendite, Verr.* 2.5.42 *quaeso, ut fecistis adhuc, diligenter attendite.* The rhythm decides.

1.20 *legis index,* which Ker translates "the meaning of the law," can only be the preliminary description of content. To show that Cicero is speaking metaphorically a supplement (*prope dicam*) is required.

1.30 The words added in *V* are usually held to be genuine on the strength of *Fam.* 9.14.8 *liberasti igitur et urbem periculo et civitatem metu.* If so, *incendio* should be changed to *incendiorum*; cf. 3.30 *caedis et incendiorum* and many other examples of this combination in Merguet's index to Cicero's orations.

1.35 *tutus.* Infinitely the best of many substitutes proposed for *unctus* (six others in Fedeli); it insinuates the threat of assassination made more distinct in 1.37–38. Perhaps the corruption arose from an inversion of adjoining letters: *nectutus—necuctus (necūctus).*

2.2 *quid ⟨enim⟩? Cf. Verr.* 2.4.52 *quid enim putatis?* Or perhaps *quid ⟨enim aliud⟩?* (homoeoteleuton *-uid . . . -iud*); cf. 2.53 *quid enim aliud ille dicebat?* and 2.77 *quid enim aliud dicam?* Cicero is not asking "what am I to think of Antony's conduct?"— having just said what he thought—but "what else am I to think . . . ?" He goes on to moot other conceivable interpretations in order to reject them and comes back to his own: *illud profecto est,* "no, that must be it."

2.18 *an verebare . . . disciplina?* If the text is sound, Cicero seems to be saying sarcastically that Antony's reminder of his upbringing was perhaps meant to offer an explanation of his depravity: people might not be able to believe that he would have turned out such a monster simply by nature without the assistance of training. This would be clearer if he had written *ne putaremus te non potuisse* and left out *nisi . . . accessisset.* But since Antony was what he was, what else could people believe? The addition of *non* before *potuisse* would help logically: was it because he was afraid people might fail to realize that education as well as nature was needed to produce such a creature?

2.27 *quid duo Servilii?* W. S. Watt, *CP* 78 (1983) 227, defending *quid? duos Servilios*, cites several Ciceronian passages where *et* followed by the demonstrative pronoun is equivalent to *etiam*. None of them helps the paradosis, because in none of them does the pronoun refer back resumptively to a noun earlier in the sentence, as *hos* has to be referred back to *duos Servilios*. After so short a parenthesis this seems to me very hard to accept. With my emendation the passages do become parallel.

2.35 *ut tu dicebas quidem.* I am inclined to regard these words as an interpolation. It is difficult to take them with Denniston as referring to the period in 46 when Antony and Caesar were at loggerheads. Cicero would have made his meaning clearer.

2.45 *recordare* sqq. A difficult passage; see SB[1], where I proposed *peterentur* (it should have been *peteretur*), reading *ut se* (so editors) and supposing that the money would be demanded from Curio junior by Antony's creditors. But *te mihi commendabat* before and *desiderium tui* after support *te*. The problem is, how Curio senior could sue Antony in such circumstances. The fact that Curio junior was in his father's *potestas* (2.46 *patrio iure et potestate*) may be relevant somehow. The following note has been kindly supplied by my former colleague Bruce W. Frier:

> Personal security in all its forms involves the giving of a stipulation. The stipulation of a *filiusfamilias* is entirely valid at classical law, and there is no reason to believe that this was not also true in the late Republic. For classical law, cf. Gaius, (2 *Verb. Obl.*) D. 45.1.141.2; and also Gaius, *Inst.* 3.104. Hence the pertinent actions are granted only against the *filiusfamilias*: Gaius, (3 *Ed. Prov.*) D. 44.7.39; *et al.* The problem, of course, is that even if the *filius* is condemned, the judgement may not be realizable so long as the *paterfamilias* remains alive. There are, however, various ways in which the debt may be enforceable even earlier. (1) The *actio de peculio et de in rem verso*, for up to the amount in the son's *peculium*, and beyond that for anything applied to the uses of the *pater*; for an example having to do with *fideiussum*, see Ulpian, (29 *Ed.*) D. 15.3.10 pr. (2) The *actio quod iussu*, if the obligation was undertaken on the father's order to a third party; for an example concerning *fideiussum*, see Julian, (17 *Dig.*) D. 39.5.2. pr. It is not certain that this action was available in the late Republic. Beyond that, the obligation is regarded as a natural one, so that if the money is paid it cannot be recovered.

In his article referred to above (at 2.27) Watt contends that *peteret* may naturally apply to an attempt by Curio junior to "touch" his father for money, citing Plaut. *Curc.* 68. Merguet's index to Cicero's orations (3:576) provides seventeen examples of *pecuniam petere*, none of them referring to a private petition and all but one (*Sest.* 66) referring to a legal claim. The same holds for similar expressions (Merguet s.v. *petere*), as *petere aurum, fundos, multam, nomen, possessionem,* or where the object is, as here, a specified sum of money. So I still maintain that "*petere* in such a context means 'demand'; it would not be used of a plea *ad misericordiam* from son to father."

2.49 *observatus.* Defended by Watt. I am not entirely convinced, but he is right in claiming that this is to be regarded as the paradosis. The antiquity of the conjecture *adiutus* was recognized in my note (SB[1]). Fedeli ascribes it to Halm.

2.56 *sed ⟨id egit⟩*. Dio (45.47.4) and Mommsen, *Röm. Strafrecht*, 861 n. 4, drew from this passage the conclusion that Lenticula's conviction for gambling carried the penalty of exile. Actually it proves the contrary. In exile Lenticula could not have been Antony's gambling partner. *Restituit* refers to the removal of other disabilities consequent on the conviction, as in *Sull.* 63 *ut restitueretur Sulla.*

Why, then, had Antony rehabilitated Lenticula? He did not have to do that in order to go on gambling with him. "No, but his object was . . . ." Without *id egit* or the like the sentence halts; *non quo* would be needed instead of *quasi vero.*

2.58 *lenonibus*. Cf. 6.4, 8.26. *Leonibus* has virtually no authority and was probably suggested by the story in Pliny and Plutarch that Antony used lions to draw his carriage in 48–47. See my note on *Att.* 10.13.1.

2.64 *infelix*. Hardly to be rejected for the colorless *hostis*, which looks like an attempt at reconstruction after *infelix* had fallen out. For the dative cf. 14.15 *curiam furiis potius suis quam rei publicae infelicem.*

2.71 *⟨iam⟩*. Needed to show that the reference is to the African campaign. As Cicero goes on to say, Antony *had* been active in the war down to Pharsalia.

2.71 *tantis ⟨et⟩ talibus*. *Planc.* 29 *de his tot viris talibus* and *Lig.* 36 *his tot talibus viris* do not bear out *tantis talibus* since *tantus* is not a numerical adjective like *tot* (cf. 12.20 *tot tam importunos, tam sceleratos hostis*).

2.84 *ubi . . . id est*. *Id est* betrays a gloss, but *ubi campus Leontinus appareat* hardly comes from a marginal note on *ubi rhetoris sit tanta merces*. Rather it was the other way round. When the gloss *id est, ubi . . . merces* had found its way into the text, *id est* was transferred to mend the syntax.

2.88 *ingress⟨ur⟩a*. What are *eis rebus*? Not the matter of the auspices, to which Cicero does not recur in this Philippic, but Antony's conduct in the period following Caesar's death. Therefore a future tense seems required.

2.91 *propter proximum dictatorem*. These words confuse a statement which their absence leaves clear and complete in *D*. Their intrusion will derive from 1.4 *non modo regno . . . sed etiam regni timore sublato . . . cum dictatoris nomen . . . propter perpetuae dictaturae recentem memoriam sustulisset*. Attempts to reconstruct from *V* have miscarried (see Fedeli).

2.104 *receptaculum*. The balance of the sentence seems to me to require the addition. *Deversorium* fits with *libidinum* (cf. *Rosc. Am.* 134 *officina nequitiae et deversorium flagitiorum omnium*, Sen. *Epist.* 51.3 *deversorium vitiorum*, et sim.), but ill with *studiorum*; studies need a home, with library, not a mere place of call. Note also Liv. 7.20.7, *Caere, sacrarium populi Romani, deversorium sacerdotum ac receptaculum Romanorum sacrorum.*

3.17 *nata*. Fedeli has now put *nata* (see SB[2]) in the text; cf. *Gnomon* 55 (1983) 544–45.

3.39 The historic tenses *inissent, videretur, referrent, videretur* call for notice. Such are found elsewhere along with primaries, depending, as here, on *senatui placere ut* vel sim.: 5.21 *diceretur*, 5.41 *vellet*, 5.53 passim, 9.17 *datum esset*, 11.31 *iuvissent, fecissent, videretur*. Is this to be explained as due to confusion between decrees as proposed and the form they would take when passed, with the routine conclusion *censuere* (cf. *Fam.* 8.8.5–8)?

4.1 *libertatis recuperandae.* I keep these words from *D*, inverting them for a better rhythm; cf. 3.32 *populum . . . Romanum ad spem recuperandae libertatis erectum*, 3.29 *spe . . . recuperandae libertatis*, and Merguet's index to the speeches, 3:49. *Recuperare rem publicam* is no less common a phrase, but it is a little odd to speak first of defending the Republic and then of restoring it.

4.10 *rec⟨c⟩idat.* From the examples of the word in Merguet considered from the standpoint of rhythm it is clear that this is the right spelling.

4.10 *appropinqua⟨re appare⟩at.* The supplement is logically required. A clear omen of a coming event does not make the event approach but shows that it is coming.

5.7 *silet.* Better at the end than substituted for *sed* (Madvig), which has a function. Even if *decernit* or the like could be understood from *de auspiciis*, sense forbids it, as sense forbids all the other suggested supplements. There would have been nothing presumptuous or irregular in an augur's making a judgment about auspices or even announcing them without his colleagues. That much is clear from the story of Tiberius Gracchus in *Nat. Deor.* 2.10–11. On the contrary, Cicero sarcastically implies that Antony was too conscious of his own lack of proficiency to make a pronouncement without colleagues to support him.

Professor Badian has suggested to me that *silet* dropped out before *sine*. If it is restored in that position, *de auspiciis* trails hopelessly; but, as he also points out, these words could be a gloss and would be better away, wherever we put *silet*.

5.15 ⟨*relinquere*⟩. Cf. 5.11 *imago nulla liberae civitatis relinquetur*, *Leg. agr.* 2.88 *si . . . imaginem rei publicae nullam reliquissent*, and H. Kasten's translation (*Cicero, Staatsreden*, vol. 3 [Berlin, 1970]) here: "wenn er auch nur einen Schein von einem Staate hätte bestehen lassen wollen."

5.21 *diceretur.* Rhythm supports the text against *dicetur*, which is needless anyway; see above on 3.39.

5.27 *Tamphilus.* Spelled Tampilus by recent editors, as on two coins dated by Crawford to 137 (no. 236). But coins are not always to be imitated in such matters: cf. Egatuleius (Crawford no. 33, dated to 97), and Pilipus (Crawford no. 259, dated to 129). Moreover, "aspiration of *tenues* was hardly ever shown at the time of this moneyer, and never on coins. The first instance of it on a coin is . . . in 119" (E. Badian, *Klio* 66 [1984] 294).

5.49 Despite Vahlen, *Opusc. Acad.*, 2:402, *carus* is a necessary supplement because *omnibus* includes *optimo cuique*.

5.51 *et periculosa.* Cf. *Rab. perd.* 4 *rem nullam maiorem, magis periculosam.* The danger lay in the undertaking itself, not in people's opinion of it.

5.53 Professor Badian points out that Octavian would properly be called *pro praetore* in the second decree on the assumption that the first had already been passed.

6.10 ⟨*Laelius, ille*⟩. Lucius was not number one in Mark Antony's camp, but number two. Cf. the end of Cicero's letter to Pompey (*Fam.* 5.7.3) *ut tibi multo maiori quam Africanus fuit me non multo minorem quam Laelium . . . adiunctum esse patiare.* The explanation in the Budé edition that L. Antonius stands to Marcus as Scipio Africanus the elder to his unimpressive brother Asiaticus does not suit *inter illos*; Cicero was thinking of the "Scipionic circle." Also he would not have gone so far, and by "Africanus" normally means the younger.

7.4 *casu*. Easily lost after *statu*; cf. *Catil.* 3.29 *ut ea virtute non casu gesta esse videantur* and 6.11 fin.

7.12 *ad id*. Cf. 14.4 *ad bellum profectus A. Hirtius.* The question "why then did Hirtius set out (if Antony was not an enemy)?" is otiose, because it is already contained in the previous question, "why did you decree that the consuls or one of them set out to the war?" Hirtius merely acted in accordance with the decree.

8.17 *melior*. My conjecture *firmior* (SB[1]) could be improved paleographically to *valentior*, but perhaps it is unnecessary. Livy (7.12.11) can say *hostem, quem tempus deteriorem in dies faceret*, meaning "in worse shape." Cicero to be sure has nothing analogous.

8.25 *praemia*. Cf. 3.7 *eorumque commoda, honores, praemia*, 5.4 *praemia constituere eis qui contra Antonium arma ceperint*; and elsewhere. *Praedia* is not used in this sort of context and would be synonymous with *agrum*; cf. 11.12 *agrum Campanum est largitus Antonius ut haberent reliquorum nutriculas praediorum.*

8.26 *ne fraudi sit septemviris quod egissent*. Nucula hoc, credo, admonuit; *verebatur fortasse ne amitteret tantas clientelas*. Cf. 6.14 *iacent beneficia Nuculae; friget patronus Antonius*. But *tantas clientelas* rather points to L. Antonius, whose "patronage" of the thirty-five tribes and various other bodies is mocked at length in 6.12–15 (cf. esp. 6.15 *iam Ianus Medius in L. Antoni clientela est?*) and again in 7.16. Perhaps *vel potius l. fr.* has fallen out before *verebatur*.

8.27 *non vult*. Governing Gallia Comata could hardly be considered a sinecure. Cicero sarcastically explains that Antony could not bear to have nothing to do.

10.7 *regnum omnino*. The tyrannicides had not abolished the *name* of monarchy, for the name was just what Caesar did *not* have. The corruption is ancient, already in Nonius (see apparatus criticus).

10.8 If my suggestion *in Neside* is right, *insu(gu)la* is a gloss and *Neside* = "Nesis estate," like *Misenum* in 2.48 (see n. 46 ad loc.).

10.19 *ponetis*. Cf. *Orat.* fr. VII.51 (Schoell) *ponam principium iustissimae libertatis* and *Att.* 10.18.2 *male posuimus initia.*

11.13 *infudit*. As distinguished from *dedit* this would not imply extra quantity, nor was the amount of the dose significant. With poison, enough is enough. Cicero seems to be suggesting that Domitius forced the poison down his victim's throat; cf. *Dig.* 29.5.1.19 *si venenum per vim infusum sit*, [Quint.] *Decl. mai.* ed. Håkanson,

p. 349.20 *quid restat quam ut recusantis ora diducas, ut infundas per oppositas manus?* By itself, however, *infundere (venenum)* is normally equivalent to *dare* (cf. *TLL* 5:1.1503.57), so possibly some word like *recusanti* has fallen out. I once thought of *infulsit*.

11.13 *clarissimi. D* should be followed here. The sarcasm demands the superlative, Cicero's standard way of referring to particularly distinguished senators. He does not so use *vir clarus*.

11.14 *vindicis.* The vulgate *vindicem*, taken as "avenger," will not do. In Cicero, and as far as I know in classical Latin, *vindex* means either "defender" (champion) or "punisher."

11.24 ⟨*a*⟩ *multis.* For the omission of the preposition Fedeli refers to *TLL* 5:2.1692.41 s.v. *expeto*: "transitive (in struct. pass. acced. dat. auctoris passim, rarius *ab*)." This seems to be untrue, except in the gerundive construction. It is certainly not true of Cicero: see J. S. Reid on *Arch.* 22.

11.37 ⟨*memores*⟩. *Auctor* does not mean "guarantor" and *auctoritatem secuti* is standard in this context; cf. 3.38, 10.21, 11.20.

11.38 *cuivis.* Besides its closeness to the manuscript reading this conjecture makes far better sense than other attempts, of which Fedeli cites five. These pacifically minded soldiers would hold no grudge against Cassius or anybody else. There is a note of sarcasm here as in the words *in magna gloria et laude ponendos puto* (neutrality was not really glorious in Cicero's eyes).

12.11 ⟨*nefariis ante commissis*⟩. Cf. 6.2 *multis nefariis rebus ante commissis.* With *multis rebus est invitatus* we have to ask "what things?" *Rebus* cannot mean "occasions," and if it could, the statement would still be false.

12.17 ⟨*sumendorum*⟩. The gerundive construction with *princeps* is common in these speeches; cf. 4.1, 5.44, 7.23, 10.24, 14.20, 26. Cicero says *belli princeps* (fitting in with a string of parallel genitives) in 2.71 and *principem malefici* in *Cluent.* 106, but *princeps sagorum* is surely too much.

12.24 *tueor.* If the indicative is right, there is an ellipsis: "I have trouble . . . , (or would have) without the protection of my friends." See my note on *Att.* 11.5.4 *deest.*

12.24 *oderint.* If this is right, Cicero is thinking of soldiers actually in contact with the enemy. They should fight angry (cf. 13.15 *odimus, irati pugnamus*). Clark conjectured and read *occiderint.* But then why not *occidant?*

12.24 ⟨*numquam . . . sum*⟩. The words *timide . . . posse*, which cannot apply to *semel . . . exsurgere*, call for such a supplement. For the punctuation after *verum tamen* (sc. *dicam*), cf. *Att.* 13.2, 14.8.2.

13.2 *aliqua . . . potuisset.* The words in *DV²* are probably conjectural, since Cicero would not have written *hominum*, but if *aliqua* were substituted for this they would serve as well as any other supplement. Cf. *aliquem tolerabilem status civitatis* in the previous sentence and *aliquam rem publicam* in the following.

13.3 *Caelium.* Or *Coelium?* We cannot be sure. See *Two Studies*, 21: "'Similarly the Antonian Q. Caelius (*Phil.* XIII.3; 26) is presumably a Coelius' (Syme, *JRS* 53 [1963]

55 n. 4). His praenomen so indicates." Unfortunately, the praenomen Quintus, with which he is usually credited, rests only on the uncertain text of 13.26.

13.9 *si⟨ne caede atque fe⟩rro.* Cf. 13.8 *remque publicam sine armis maximo civilis belli periculo liberavit;* also 9.14 *sine caede atque ferro* and *Caec.* 93 *ad ferrum, ad arma, ad caedem. Sine ferro* (cf. *Planc.* 86 *quos ego . . . sine ferro viceram*) and *sine sanguine* (*Rosc. Am.* 146 al.) are equivalent possibilities.

13.12 *bis.* I.e. II for VII; cf. App. *B.C.* 3.11. *Septiens* may be a reminiscence of the seven hundred million mentioned in 2.93 and elsewhere.

13.19 *quae . . . scripta sunt.* Without *paene,* this could only mean that the decrees were never passed; cf. 1.25 *illae enim* (sc. *leges) sine ulla promulgatione latae sunt ante quam scriptae,* 5.7 *quid? promulgata fuit? quid? non ante lata quam scripta est?* Perhaps read *perscripta,* the usual term for drawing up the text of a decree after it had been voted and prior to depositing it.

13.22 *desinet.* According to King (see p. 15), "the imperative suits better with the imperious tone of Cicero's criticism." It does not suit with *profecto.*

13.24 *huic puero.* Clark, *CR* 14 (1900) 409, reading *puero,* explains that *puero* was corrupted in *t* and expelled by *huic* from *n,* while *b* combines the variants. But *huic* is better in than out, and I would rather suppose that the variants arose from its omission and subsequent addition above *puero.*

13.27 ⟨*ni*⟩*si.* With *si* this thrust is pointless. Who ever suggested that T. Plancus loved the Senate? His incendiarism showed how much he hated it. Cicero gives this idea a paradoxical turn by saying the opposite of what he means.

13.27 *erosit.* The meaning must be that Decius devoured Caesar's bounties, not just nibbled at them (*rosit,* or *arrosit*).

13.30 The missing words will have run something like *quid de Cn. Pompeio loquar? quod imperi populi Romani decus ac lumen fuit* (cf. 2.54).

13.40 If the writer were Cicero, I should be tempted to add *membra* after *corporis,* but with Antony almost any oddity is possible. He seems to be using *corpus* for *ludus gladiatorius:* see *Thes.* 4:1021.40.

14.15 ⟨*non*⟩ *patefecit.* The event did not reveal the conspiracy; but, says Cicero, we shall get to the bottom of it eventually.

14.29 *protinus.* I.e. *ptinus. Civibus* is evidently wrong and a word meaning "straightaway" is essential.

# INDEX OF PROPER NAMES

# INDEX OF PROPER NAMES